Financial Planning Applications

This publication has been underwritten by the AXA Foundation, the philanthropic arm of AXA Financial.

Huebner School Series

Walt J. Woerheide, Editor

Huebner School Series

Financial Planning Applications
Eighteenth Edition

Thomas P. Langdon
and William J. Ruckstuhl

The American College/*Bryn Mawr, Pennsylvania*

———

This publication is designed to provide accurate and authoritative information about the subject covered. While every precaution has been taken in the preparation of this material, the authors and The American College assume no liability for damages resulting from the use of the information contained in this publication. The American College is not engaged in rendering legal, accounting, or other professional advice. If legal or other expert advice is required, the services of an appropriate professional should be sought.

The information in this text is current as of April 2002 but may be subject to change pending new tax legislation.

Library of Congress Control Number 2002105357
ISBN 1-57996-056-1

Printed in the United States of America

To my parents
who taught me the value of careful planning

T.P.L.

Contents

Acknowledgments

Gary K. Stone, PhD, CLU, executive vice president at The American College, for his support and encouragement

Gwenda L. Cannon, JD, a former faculty member of The American College, for her creation of several cases that are used in this course and that have survived multiple revisions and continuous changes in the financial and tax environments

Current and former American College faculty members who have had authorship roles in this text, especially James F. Ivers III, JD, LLM, ChFC; David A. Littell, JD; and Jeffrey B. Kelvin, JD, LLM, CLU, ChFC

Maria Marlowe, manuscript editor at The American College, for her editing of the manuscript

Patricia G. Berenson for her able production assistance in typing the manuscript

Lillian G. Pedrick, instructional designer at The American College, for her indispensable assistance in operating ExecPlan

Joseph L. Brennan of media services at The American College for his design of the cover and excellent graphics

We would also like to acknowledge the input of the numerous colleagues, students, and friends whose helpful suggestions have been incorporated into this text.

Thomas P. Langdon
William J. Ruckstuhl

The computer illustrations contained in this book were generated by ExecPlan, a financial planning software system. We wish to thank ExecPlan, Inc., Princeton, New Jersey, for providing us with continuous cooperation and assistance in the use of version 4.13c of their system to enhance and illustrate various elements of the cases.

About the Authors

Thomas P. Langdon, JD, LLM, CLU, ChFC, CFP, CFA, is associate professor of taxation at The American College. His primary responsibility is course development in business succession planning and wealth transfer tax planning. Prior to joining the faculty of The American College he was an asset/liability manager for the Travelers Asset Management and Pension Services Division for 7 years. He is a frequent presenter at financial planning, tax, and estate planning seminars and has published numerous articles on these topics. He earned his JD at Western New England College School of Law and a Master of Law in Taxation (LLM) at Villanova University School of Law.

William J. Ruckstuhl, MBA, CLU, ChFC, is a former professor of finance at The American College. His primary responsibility is course development in accounting, investments, and financial planning. He earned his BA degree from Grove City College and his MBA from the Wharton School of the University of Pennsylvania. Coauthor of books on economic policy and personal financial planning, he has also presented papers at professional meetings. His previous faculty positions include the University of Maine and Villanova University.

Financial Planning Applications

Introduction

Although comprehensive financial planning has become a popular practice in recent years, it is not for everyone. While studying the case materials in this text, you may discover that you have no real interest in changing your existing business in order to do comprehensive financial planning. One of the reasons for providing financial planning education is to help individuals determine the appropriate nature and scope of their practice. If the discipline of comprehensive financial planning does not appeal to you, it is much better to be aware of that fact before time and money are spent in redirecting your career.

You may wish to broaden your practice to include some additional types of planning but not engage in comprehensive financial planning. In that event, the cases in this text should be helpful in identifying tax, investment, or insurance problems that require additional advice from a tax attorney, accountant, or other adviser.

If you do wish to expand your business to include a comprehensive financial planning practice, these case studies represent some very typical family and business problems and objectives that arise in actual practice and suggest the tax, insurance, and investment recommendations that are appropriate for solving those problems or achieving those objectives.

The purpose of this text is not to convince you to become a comprehensive financial planner. Many individuals have achieved a high degree of professional success and personal satisfaction by being traditional advisers such as attorneys, accountants, life underwriters, investment advisers, or registered representatives. Expertise in most of these areas is needed on virtually every financial planning team. However, if you choose to remain in your individual discipline, it is still important that you understand what a comprehensive financial planner does and how he or she approaches problem solving. In this way advisers can become aware of what will be asked of them if they work with a financial planner. Experience indicates that when comprehensive financial planning is properly presented, most advisers understand and appreciate its utility even if they choose not to pursue it themselves.

OVERVIEW OF TEXT DESIGN

This text has been designed to provide those interested in comprehensive financial planning with the opportunity to simulate, to the fullest possible extent, real-world experience by working with hypothetical yet realistic client cases. It is intended to provide practice in integrating tax, insurance, and investment planning strategies into comprehensive plans for dealing with the financial problems or objectives of individuals and/or businesses.

Chapter 1 is introductory in nature. It reviews the comprehensive financial planning process and contains a brief discussion of the components of this process: tax planning, insurance, and investments.

Chapter 2 presents comprehensive data about a client. After becoming familiar with the objectives, needs, facts, and other considerations, both personal and business-related, the planner prepares preliminary and working outlines for the development of the client's financial plan. Chapter 2 provides the facts to be used in developing outlines and organizing suggested solutions for financial plans. It also provides a practical exercise in the preparation of outlines for a financial plan. This format is utilized throughout the remainder of the book.

Chapter 2 also includes information on developing a financial plan for the hypothetical client for whom the data was presented and the working outline prepared.

In this and all subsequent cases the solution should

- Identify and incorporate the client's objectives.
- Identify and briefly describe the technical requirements and characteristics of various planning techniques that can be used to achieve each client objective.
  - The strengths and weaknesses of each technique, as applied to a particular client's situation, should be explored.
  - This determination is generally based on how well the technique's requirements and characteristics meet the client's objectives.
- Indicate the techniques and/or products that best achieve the client's overall objectives or solve the client's problems, and give the reasons for your recommendations.

The format proposed in chapter 2 is followed by the development of these planning solutions in the remaining chapters: tax planning issues should be addressed first, followed by insurance planning, and finally, investment planning.

Chapters 3 through 9 each contain a detailed case narrative providing information about a hypothetical client and family. Each requires the development of both a working outline and a financial planning solution based on the client's problems and objectives.

Following each case narrative are suggested working outlines and suggested financial planning solutions. It is strongly recommended that you first prepare the working outline listing client objectives and possible techniques for achieving those objectives prior to consulting the suggested solution. This outline should then be compared with the suggested working outline. This comparison should give you confidence that you are proceeding satisfactorily toward compiling a list of available techniques for preparing a financial planning solution. On the other hand, if there are additional techniques that should be considered before attempting to prepare a plan solution, the suggested working outline can be used as a reminder of these additional alternatives. It is also possible that you may have listed techniques that for various reasons may not be included in the suggested working outline.

Before consulting the suggested financial planning solution, formulate a plan solution, including recommendations, and then compare that plan with the suggested solution in the text. Solutions in the text contain detailed descriptions of tax, insurance, and investment planning techniques that are designed to be a review of the substantive issues encountered in using the particular technique. This amount of detail is in excess of what is typically included in a financial plan presented to a client. It is provided as a review of important concepts for the planner.

You should, however, have sufficient command of the subject to present a well-reasoned recommendation. If you do not have the required level of knowledge, the relevant portion of the case solution can be reviewed. The detailed technical information in case solutions is intended to be utilized in the same way that it would be used in an actual financial plan, that is, to provide the client with decision-making information.

UTILIZING COMPUTER-PRODUCED NUMERICAL ILLUSTRATIONS

Computer-produced numerical illustrations have been included for the purpose of demonstrating the relative effect of particular recommendations on the client's income tax, balance sheet, cash-flow, and estate tax situations—that is, the effect a recommendation will have assuming all other assumptions are valid and remain constant. Computer projections are helpful in the actual practice of financial planning to illustrate the results of various planning recommendations.

Numerical projections, especially those that involve a time period extending far into the future, are particularly problematic because so many assumptions must be made to ascertain the results, and a change in any assumption will alter those results. Two fundamental problems in using projections should be considered here:

- What assumptions should be used?
- Over how long a time period should projections be run?

In the first instance it is usually better to use a set of assumptions with which the client is comfortable as opposed to assumptions imposed by the planner. Even if the planner is absolutely correct in every assumption, it is unlikely that the client will remain a client long enough to discover that fact. In the event that the planner believes the client's assumptions are outlandish, another set of projections based on more conservative (or more liberal) assumptions can be included in the plan to demonstrate the results under such different hypothetical circumstances.

Numerical results should be projected into the future no longer than absolutely necessary. Unless there are compelling reasons to project farther ahead, projections of 4 to 5 years in the initial plan are usually adequate. Projections for the current tax year and the one immediately following are generally sufficient for an annual update of the plan, because these time periods allow problem areas to be pinpointed in time to do some long-range planning and still provide for reasonable accuracy.

The computer-produced illustrations in this text are provided by ExecPlan, a financial planning software system. You are not expected to duplicate them but are encouraged to use them solely for comparative purposes when evaluating various recommendations.

QUESTIONS OF LOCAL LAW

Despite the fact that the Internal Revenue Code controls all matters of federal taxation, many federal tax results are determined indirectly by local law. For example, if funds are used to discharge the legal support obligations of a taxpayer, those payments will be taxable income to the taxpayer regardless of who pays them. This is a matter of federal tax law. The determination of what constitutes a legal obligation of support, on the other hand, is generally determined under the law of the various states. To provide a complete case solution, it is necessary to give the clients a state of domicile in order to apply the local law of a particular state to these issues. The hypothetical clients whose cases appear in this text are generally domiciled in the state of Georgia. In the areas in which reference is made to a point of Georgia law, that reference should alert a planner to check that point under the law of his or her own or the client's state. Obviously a difference in local law may necessitate a different planning result.

For example, Georgia has an estate tax equal to the federal state death tax credit, and it has no inheritance tax. Therefore there is no actual advantage in avoiding probate in Georgia unless a corporate executor is being utilized, as corporate fiduciaries often base fees on the amount of assets they must deal with. In contrast, if the client is domiciled in a state that imposes an inheritance tax only on probate property, especially if there is no exemption for property transferred to a surviving spouse, the recommendation for the form of ownership in which a client owns certain property (such as a principal residence) may be altered.

If a state imposes an estate tax, it is the legal responsibility of the estate itself to pay the tax. In contrast, if the state imposes an inheritance tax, the responsibility for paying the tax rests with the beneficiary who receives property from the estate.

All of the cases in this text are set in Georgia with the exception of the Kelley case (chapter 8), which is set in Pennsylvania. Georgia has an estate tax, while Pennsylvania has an inheritance tax. After a "family allowance" of $5,000 is deducted from the taxable estate, Pennsylvania imposes a flat tax rate of 6 percent on estate assets that pass to the decedent's lineal descendants or a flat tax rate of 15 percent on estate assets that pass to anyone else. Under Pennsylvania law, property passing to a spouse is not subject to tax.

A CONCLUDING COMMENT

In financial planning there is rarely one single answer to a particular problem that will work for every client; there are always several possible alternatives. The ultimate recommendation will depend on the financial planner's professional judgment, which is based on personal knowledge of and experience with the client and the client's family. While the importance of this professional judgment makes financial planning an art rather than a science (and therefore more difficult to teach and to learn), it also makes financial planning a very personal and creative experience for both the planner and the client.

Utilizing the Financial Planning Process: Principles and Strategies

Chapter Outline

The world of financial services has become so complex that many people have difficulty coping with it. Most fortunate and capable individuals can deal with the requirements of their occupations and the demands of their families. Many, however, cannot successfully sift through and understand the vast quantity of information on the various legal and financial concepts that affect their daily lives. Even if there were some way to deal with the enormous amount of information, it is often impossible to distinguish fact from opinion without being an expert in a given field.

The result is that the majority of people have become less confident that they can make well-informed decisions about their personal and business affairs and have become increasingly dependent on advice from technical experts in various financial services areas. If these experts were consistent in their philosophies or levels of expertise, advice could at least be compared on an apples-to-apples basis. Philosophies and levels of expertise vary so widely, however, that the realistic evaluation of advice often requires significant expertise in itself. This implies that tier upon tier of technical knowledge is required to evaluate and solve a particular problem.

Too many times this type of problem solving becomes so impersonal that the aspirations and preferences of the client and family are barely, if at all, considered in the suggested solution. In these circumstances the client may react with apprehension because the planner has not truly understood and applied the client's total financial and personal situation. Comprehensive financial planning is a client-oriented process of problem solving that attempts to discover what a problem means to a client or family before exploring potential solutions. It is a method of problem solving that educates the client, encouraging informed decision making about his or her own life.

Many clients express the feeling that they are unable to evaluate advice from particular advisers or to evaluate the performance of the advisers in a particular technical specialty. These clients look for a problem solver who will not only evaluate potential solutions within the adviser's primary discipline but also evaluate and coordinate the approaches of advisers from other disciplines. A properly qualified financial planner who can prepare a comprehensive financial plan can function well in this capacity.

The comprehensive financial planner must possess many skills. Sensitivity to a client and an understanding of human behavior and human needs in addition to technical expertise in one or more of the financial services areas such as law, accounting, insurance, investments, and banking are required. Comprehensive financial planning is not an easy discipline. The knowledge and information demands placed on the comprehensive financial planner are enormous. Financial planning is an especially challenging occupation because emerging disciplines (financial planning being one of them) lack the tried-and-true guidelines on procedural, ethical, and other matters that are already present in established disciplines. During the past decade, however, the financial planning profession has successfully taken many steps to establish itself.

The amount of information necessary to do comprehensive financial planning is vast. No one person can be expected to master such diverse subject areas as tax laws, securities laws, probate and local property laws, life insurance, property and casualty insurance, and investment planning. Since it is better to be a master of one trade than a superficial dabbler in many, planning is best accomplished by utilizing a team of experts under the coordinated control of a comprehensive financial planner. The team approach allows for the use of appropriate expertise when necessary within the overall context of the client's personal and business situation.

The team approach to financial planning is an approach to problem solving that is designed to deal with many of the failures of traditional problem-solving methods. Traditional problem solving has too often resulted in advice that is both isolated and fragmented. This does not occur because of the failure of traditional advisers but because of the traditional methods of approaching and solving problems. If we look closely at the traditional problem-solving process, it becomes apparent that problems and potential problems are usually presented to advisers in an isolated manner; that is, each is examined for the specific purpose of finding a solution.

Prevention has not been widely regarded by the public as the province of traditional planning methods. Too often problems are presented to advisers only after they have become troublesome. If a client is attempting to deal with a particularly troublesome problem, that problem tends to demand the client's total attention, becoming disproportionately important. When advice is sought on such a problem, most of the client's interest and energy are centered on an immediate or speedy solution. Traditional advisers have naturally attempted to accommodate the client's wishes in this regard and often focus almost exclusively on the problem at hand. Advice of this sort is bound to be problematic, as this traditional problem-solving method does not allow for full consideration of the impact of such advice on a client's total personal and financial situation. As long as clients allow problems to ripen into troublesome issues, they will continue to demand the isolated-solution approach to problem solving.

If problems can be anticipated before they become crises, preventive solutions to potential problems can be substituted for crisis-intervention methods. Comprehensive financial planning, the process that has been devised to meet this need for preventive solutions to potential problems, involves the gathering of sufficient data to produce a total overview of the client's financial, legal, and personal situation. This overview enables the financial planner to establish realistic and attainable personal and business financial goals with the client after a careful analysis has been made of the client's total personal and financial situation. The comprehensive financial planning process also involves restructuring of the client's current financial situation to allow for maximum tax advantage and to eliminate, to the greatest possible extent, the legal and tax problems contained therein. Comprehensive financial planning is both a preventive and a remedial system of problem solving.

The financial planning process is further differentiated from traditional problem solving by the utilization of a team of experts so that the advice of individual subject matter experts can be considered in conjunction with all other advice. This approach has not been prevalent in traditional problem solving methods due to the necessity for single-discipline expertise directed at specific, isolated problems. Indeed, good advice in one area of a client's life may produce significant adverse effects in another area unless the planning effects on the client's total legal, financial, and personal situation are considered together. Traditional problem solving has provided no effective mechanism for dealing with this problem. In fact, traditional problem solving does not purport to be comprehensive problem solving. Generally traditional planning methods are not even comprehensive with respect to one's total legal affairs or one's total business affairs. Traditional problem-solving methods generally contain no mechanism for integrating prevention or solutions of technical problems with personal planning. This has been left to the individual practitioner and is more honored in the breach than in the practice.

The net result of traditional problem-solving methods is that traditional advice is often impersonal, inconclusive, and possibly even contradictory to other valid advice. The client is often confused when faced with the prospect of coordinating good advice on diverse subjects from several sources. Clients seek an adviser (or advisers) who understands the technical depth and the personal components of their problems, who will evaluate both technical detail and personal planning considerations, and who will present a cohesive, coordinated, well-developed, well-researched, and well-documented plan. This person is the comprehensive financial planner working with a qualified team of expert advisers. It is only the commitment of the financial services industry to *comprehensive* financial planning that will produce these results. Without such a commitment, financial planning will be prone to the errors and problems faced by traditional problem-solving methods.

THE FINANCIAL PLANNING PROCESS

The financial planning process usually begins when a financial planner introduces prospective clients to the concept of comprehensive financial planning. This introduction may take place in a one-to-one interview, but more often it takes place in a group presentation. Unless prospective clients become acquainted with the services that comprehensive financial planning can provide for them, there is typically a reluctance on their part to commit to pay for those services. In fact, until a potential client has met with the financial planner, submitted data for analysis, and learned what specific areas will be addressed in the financial plan (and the estimated potential savings it can generate), resistance to planning fees is likely to continue.

The best way to find financial planning clients is to employ a screening approach that determines which prospective clients are genuinely interested in financial planning, which clients have sufficient assets to make it worthwhile, and which clients are in occupations or businesses with which the particular financial planning firm can deal. Most financial planning firms choose a segment of the market and concentrate their efforts on a particular group or class of clients. For example, many financial planning firms specialize in planning for the self-employed professional, while other firms rarely, if ever, accept such clients and concentrate instead on closely held business owners, middle or upper management personnel, or other groups.

If the prospective client has a genuine interest in obtaining the services of a financial planning firm, the next step in the process is to have the client submit appropriate documentation to the financial planning firm for preliminary analysis prior to an in-depth meeting between the client and the planner. This documentation will vary from client to client but should include such items as wills, trusts, income tax returns for 3 to 5 years, business agreements, and financial statements. Once the financial planning firm has received this information, a financial planner can review it and ascertain the more obvious trouble spots. Based on this preliminary review, a tentative list of planning techniques can be made, and a rough estimate of the money the client can save in income tax, estate taxes, or state and local taxes can be determined.

The next meeting should be an in-depth meeting with the client and spouse and any other advisers the clients choose to have attend. The attendance of advisers should be considered carefully. It should be made clear to the client that all advisers are welcome, while at the same time reminding the client and spouse that they must feel free to discuss very personal matters (including their assessment of their advisers and the advisers' performance, as well as family problems about which the various advisers may know nothing). Once these issues are brought to the attention of the client, the client will make the decision about whether to include advisers. It may be helpful to give the client the option of inviting one or more advisers to attend a portion of the meeting, reserving some time for the client, the spouse, and the financial planner to spend privately.

This data-gathering session with the client is one of the most important steps in the financial planning process. It is in this interview that the financial planner will begin to establish credibility and rapport with the client. It is more than a session to gather omitted or additional data or to clarify misleading or confusing quantitative information, although it serves those purposes as well. It is a time for learning as much as possible about the client and the client's spouse and family. This means that the financial planner must not only listen carefully to what the client and spouse have to say during the session but must also watch their body language and pay careful attention to subjects they seem uncomfortable with or try to avoid entirely. These subtle signals may convey to the financial planner important information about the client's personality and relationships with others. These factors can significantly affect the financial plan.

Data-gathering sessions are usually intense and can be very fatiguing to the client who may be dealing with difficult and painful subjects, and to the financial planner whose total concentration must be on the client. During these sessions important subjective data should be carefully noted. Many planning decisions are based on subjective information rather than on hard data.

The initial data-gathering session should be a counseling session in the truest sense of the word. The financial planner should attempt to suspend any inherent biases and to put himself or herself in the position of the client, to see the world and the client's problems through the client's eyes. This does not mean that the financial planner will or should always agree with a client's point of view. The planner must, however, see the problem from the client's viewpoint in order to understand precisely what the problem means to the client. It is not the task of the financial planner to rearrange the client's affairs to meet the planner's goals, objectives, or values. It *is* the planner's task to plan for the client's goals and objectives based on the client's perception of his or her problems and according to the client's value system, provided, however, that no impropriety or illegality is involved.

For example, it may be exceedingly difficult for a financial planner to understand why her client, Tom Jones, who enjoys a substantial income and pays extremely high income taxes, keeps a total of $200,000 in accounts at 20 different banks. These accounts do not earn the highest return, and the interest on them is taxable. When Tom is asked about this amount in a nonjudgmental way, the planner may be able to establish that Tom's grandparents lost most of their savings during the Great Depression or that Tom's parents suffered some losses resulting from the bank and savings and loan crisis in the 1980s–1990s. This $200,000 of insured deposits (scattered across several banks) is the ultimate fallback fund. Because Tom's grandparents, parents, or Tom himself experienced serious financial insecurity in the past, it may in fact be nonproductive to suggest to him that those funds be invested in some other way. The planner should realize that these funds meet an important need in Tom's life, which has very little to do with the amount of income they produce or the amount of tax liability that the income generates. To Tom, these funds are a safety blanket, and ensure that he will never again be without financial resources. The financial planner must understand human responses of this type. Failure to do so will result in an uncomfortable, perhaps disgruntled, client, despite the fact that the advice offered to the client is accurate and otherwise well considered.

The data-gathering session should be an in-depth opportunity for the financial planner and the client to begin their personal relationship. It should leave the client with a feeling of confidence and trust, since it will sometimes be necessary for the financial planner to probe sensitive personal areas of the client's life and to ask painful questions. Well-considered and truthful answers to sensitive inquiries will be forthcoming only in an atmosphere of trust. In order to create an atmosphere of trust it is helpful to preface the session by explaining a few ground rules to the client. These ground rules should at least include comments on protecting the client's confidentiality, the necessity for full disclosure of facts and feelings, and the specific tasks the planner will perform for the client. In this situation it is beneficial to be especially candid about the fact that the planner is not sitting in judgment of the client's attitudes, values, or the previous management of personal or business affairs. In order to make appropriate decisions about planning recommendations, the planner should strive to understand the client and the client's present situation and to ascertain what basic motivations are at work in the client's life. Honesty and a down-to-earth attitude are important.

It is also important to note that a strong positive relationship between the client and the planner usually results in a better plan for the client and more self-satisfaction for the planner. It is axiomatic that satisfied clients are an excellent source of future business.

If the planner encounters a client with whom there is a personality conflict or with whom the communication or rapport so necessary for the development of a satisfactory financial plan cannot be established, it is often counterproductive to pursue the relationship, as neither the planner nor the client is likely to be happy with the end product. If there is another available planner in the firm, it is often a good idea to assign him or her to the client as soon as the difficulties become apparent. In this way the client has a better chance of having a satisfactory relationship with the firm.

A formal agreement to proceed with the financial planning process is often entered into between the client and the financial planner after the first data-gathering interview. It is rare that prior to this in-depth discussion either the client or the financial planner has sufficient information about the other to make the required commitment to the financial planning relationship. When the formal agreement for planning is entered into, an appropriate channel of communication for follow-up questions or additional information must be established. Many times communication will be directly with the client. In other cases, particularly when a business ownership is involved, others may be able to facilitate the gathering of additional data as necessary without taking the client's time. However this is to be handled, such channels must be established because the need to clarify a point or to obtain other information is virtually inevitable.

Once the client and the financial planner agree to the scope of the relationship, the financial planner takes charge of the client's data and begins the process of producing the financial plan. By this time the financial planner usually has some idea of which areas of the client's situation will need significant work, and the expertise besides his or her own that will be necessary to develop the client's financial plan. At this point an intense analysis of the client's data must be completed. It is often helpful to organize the client file into related or logically coherent pieces to aid in this analysis and to create an outline of the planning process. Many approaches can be used in this organization and outline, but basic divisions or headings, such as lifetime and death planning or personal and business planning, are good starting points.

Once a thorough analysis is completed, the client's objectives are relatively easy to test for consistency. For example, suppose a client expresses the desire to treat his children equally when he dies, but the client's will leaves his closely held business interest to his daughter. If both items of information are noted under the death planning section of the file, it is apparent that there is a possible conflict, since the client may be leaving a disproportionately large portion of the potential estate to his daughter. The planner must clarify whether the client meant that he or she wanted the children treated *equally* (all to inherit exactly the same) or *equitably* (all to be treated fairly and to inherit roughly the same value of assets). This is a subtle but important distinction. If the estate is large enough, it may be possible for the client's children to inherit equitably while preserving the business interest for the daughter. However, if the bulk of the estate is tied up in the family business, the planner may have to plan for a partial disposition of the business interest that will provide an equitable inheritance for the other children while leaving the daughter with control of the business.

Planning recommendations should be consistent with both the client's lifetime objectives and the client's wishes for postmortem disposition of property. There is nothing intrinsically contradictory in lifetime and postmortem planning, although the client's wishes concerning these planning alternatives may expose some inherent conflicts. One of the tasks of financial planning is to expose those inherent conflicts so the client can make informed decisions to eliminate or minimize them. Prior to the emergence of comprehensive financial planning as a discipline, lifetime transactions were not considered in view of postmortem objectives, and the results were often shocking.

After analyzing and organizing the data and noting any conflicting information or objectives, the financial planner summarizes the client's objectives that are to be addressed in the financial plan. This becomes the foundation on which the plan is built. In addition to specific objectives that the client may have voiced, the planner may have been able to determine additional objectives from the subjective information obtained from the client. However, these objectives should be confirmed with the client to assure that they are in fact the client's—and not the financial planner's—objectives.

The first issue to be considered generally involves tax planning. In this section of the plan the client's current assets, family status, and objectives are analyzed as they relate to the effective utilization of the tax laws. The planner should question whether every transaction the client is engaged in, every asset held, and every stated client objective functions in the most tax-advantageous manner. If not, is there the possibility of renegotiating the transaction, repositioning or retitling the asset, or redirecting the mechanism for achieving the client's objectives in a more tax-efficient manner?

At this stage of the planning process it is very helpful to review the various objectives listed under the outline headings and to expand that preliminary outline for the client's plan to include the various tax techniques that may be used to accomplish those objectives. It is too early to be definitive about which of these techniques will be implemented, so all viable alternatives should be noted at this point.

After all the tax planning techniques that are available for successfully attaining the client's objectives have been noted, it may become apparent that some of the available techniques or strategies will not fit this particular client. The financial planner may discard them as potential solutions but must use good judgment about whether to explain such methods in the plan and why they do not seem best suited for the client. One rule of thumb in such situations is that if the client has expressed a particular interest in a strategy or technique, the planner cannot ignore it even if it appears inappropriate given the client's situation. The technique or strategy must be explained sufficiently to allow the client to feel that his or her concerns have been acknowledged and that the relevant information has been given due consideration.

This does not imply, however, that the financial planner must rubber-stamp the client's choice of techniques and strategies. On the contrary, the financial planner, aided by other members of the financial planning team, should independently and objectively explore the various techniques and strategies available to accomplish each client objective and then recommend the one(s) that in his or her professional judgment is (are) best suited to this client's overall situation. This is not a task that is accomplished immediately. Many times members of the financial planning team will need to research various issues to ascertain the available techniques and to understand how they operate and what constraints, if any, are applicable to their use. The choice of the best tax planning technique for the client cannot be made until both the client's situation and the available techniques are fully understood by the planner after consultation with appropriate team members.

When all tax planning considerations have been reviewed, the same process is repeated with insurance planning. Various insurance planning techniques and products are evaluated in light of the client's objectives. Each proposed insurance strategy or product is checked in the context of tax planning strategies to assure that all recommendations are compatible.

The final planning recommendations are investment recommendations, including new acquisitions as well as adjustments in the client's current portfolio. Again recommendations in this area are carefully coordinated with the tax and insurance planning recommendations and with the client's objectives.

Whenever one of the primary areas (tax planning, insurance planning, and investment planning) in the financial planning process is outside the financial planner's area of primary expertise, the assistance of a technical expert in that area must be sought. For example, a financial planner with a primary background in law will need to enlist an insurance specialist to analyze the client's insurance needs and to compare them to the client's present coverage. As additional problems are uncovered, additional experts will be added to the team, and each member will provide analysis and information, including recommendations, related to his or her area of technical expertise. The primary planner (the planner in charge of the client's case) must coordinate and organize input from these other technical experts into a comprehensive plan after making sure that the recommendations will not adversely affect each other or the client's particular situation.

Once all information about various techniques and strategies has been reviewed in light of the client's circumstances and objectives, definitive recommendations that meet the client's objectives can be formulated. It is often helpful from an organizational viewpoint to divide the final plan into business and personal planning sections and to further divide each section into tax, insurance, and investment planning. Under each of these sections lifetime planning and planning for dispositions at death can be considered. It is also helpful to further organize the plan into subsections, each of which deals with a particular objective. Thus the objective of funding for children's education could discuss various techniques and their related tax impacts—for example, outright gifts, Sec. 2503(c) trusts, gifts made under the Uniform Gifts (or Transfers) to Minors Act, Education IRAs, and Sec. 529 plans. In this way the plan outline is not only utilized as an organizational tool by the financial planner, it also remains as the framework for the plan itself.

In developing the formal plan document for presentation to the client, planners will differ in the amount of documentation and background information that they deliver with the plan. Some may choose to list only the recommendation of choice for a particular objective. While this may be an economical way to develop plans, it is unlikely to meet the client's need to make an informed decision about his or her own life and affairs. If several alternative techniques are available (as is usually the case), the better approach is to discuss each of them in the plan. The planner should include in the discussion the strengths and weaknesses of each technique and the reasons such a strategy or technique is either well suited or poorly suited to this particular client.

At the end of the discussion the planner will want to state the recommendation of choice for achieving a particular objective and to indicate any additional reasons why the planner's recommendation should be adopted by the client. The planner should include in any planning recommendation citations of authority or data (tax code sections, case names and citations, numbers, assumptions, and so on) that were drawn upon in formulating, explaining, or illustrating that recommendation. This information is particularly helpful to the client's other advisers when they review the financial plan because it allows them to follow the logic of the work product without spending unnecessary time in research. Too often the client's other advisers will have little confidence in an undocumented plan because they cannot afford to do an exhaustive research project on the particular subject in an effort to validate the planner's solution. If the figures or citations of authority are available to them, it is much easier for them to validate the planner's recommendation if they wish to do so. It is also much harder for them to dismiss the plan as trivial or superficial. A well-documented plan is a work product that the client's attorney, accountant, or other adviser can use as a reliable blueprint in preparing documents or proposals in the implementation stage of the planning process.

After the plan has been prepared in this fashion, the planner and the client meet for a second extended session to go over the recommendations. In this meeting the client is not asked to merely rubber-stamp the planner's recommendations, but is asked instead to make decisions about alternative techniques and strategies after considering all the information the financial planner has provided. The planner's recommendations are simply part of that information. Although these recommendations should carry considerable weight, they are not binding on the client. While the financial planner may have based the recommendations on his or her best professional judgment and may believe strongly in their validity, the planner must not expect the client to accept any recommendation on faith. A financial planner who falls into that type of thinking is acting as a traditional problem solver and is asking the client to make a decision based on what the client believes the *planner* knows about the subject matter, not what the client knows. In other words, the client is put back in the position of having to evaluate the expert in order to evaluate the advice. While that is always true to some extent, part of the purpose of the financial planning process is to educate clients about legal, investment, insurance, and tax matters in order to allow them to function as informed decision makers, thereby giving them more control over these important decisions.

This is the humanizing aspect of financial planning. When the process is well executed, clients become participants in making decisions about their lives and their families while receiving appropriate advice and support from the financial planner and the financial planning team. The best decisions are those made by the person or persons involved after reviewing sufficient information to make an informed selection from several known alternatives. The planner must learn to function within this framework, learning to accept and even to encourage clients' questioning of planning recommendations.

By its very nature comprehensive financial planning is intended to be an ongoing relationship between the financial planner, the client, and the client's family. The facts are constantly changing. While financial planners attempt to deliver plans that are current and up-to-date, this is not always possible. Continuous additions and changes in data and the need for updating the plan are simply a part of the process. Consequently the last stage in the financial planning process is the monitoring and updating of the client's plan at regular intervals. Changes in the client's circumstances must also be recorded and dealt with during the plan's preparation and implementation.

Many times making a particular strategy work for a client is a good deal like having a suit tailored. If the measurements were taken several weeks ago, circumstances may have occurred in the meantime that will affect the final fit. At the final presentation of a comprehensive financial plan, it may be necessary to change the recommendations entirely based on new facts or circumstances facing the client. On the other hand a slight modification—a tuck here or there—may be sufficient to adapt the existing recommendation to the new situation.

Once the client has received an explanation of the viable alternatives and the planner's recommendations for achieving each of his or her objectives and has discussed them with the planner, the client may immediately make decisions on some recommendations, ask for additional clarification on other recommendations, and reserve others for future consideration. This is a typical and appropriate response. If there are serious matters that require immediate attention, it is appropriate to list those items for the client on a proposed priority list. The planner should remind the client that the plan must be implemented to be effective, and should suggest a plan for implementing all or a part of the plan while the client and the planner are together.

Once the implementation part of the plan has been agreed to, the client is likely to take all or part of the financial plan to other advisers for actual implementation. It is often a good idea to prepare an additional copy of the plan for the client to give to his or her attorney, accountant, life insurance agent, or investment adviser. If the client's existing advisers can review the planning recommendations from the plan itself rather than depending on the client to explain the planning concepts, the chances for misunderstanding are diminished. In addition, a well-prepared, well-documented plan often reduces the amount of possible resistance from the client's existing advisers and promotes its quick implementation.

The financial planner should arrange to review documents or proposals in draft form with the client's advisers to ensure that the planning recommendations have been correctly embodied. Draft copies should always be reviewed since it is easier to change them than the final work product. Furthermore, if there is a misunderstanding about a recommendation, it is better to discover and correct it as quickly as possible.

Implementation can be accomplished in a relatively short time for a decisive, well-organized client, or it can stretch out for months for clients with large holdings who have many documents and agreements to execute. The planner can often facilitate the implementation by keeping in touch with the client's advisers and checking on the progress of various projects if they seem to be lagging. The implementation portion of the plan is completed when all the necessary documents and agreements have been signed and all necessary products are purchased and titled correctly. Note, however, that it would be a violation of securities laws for the client to be led to the conclusion that implementation must be accomplished by the same planner who provided the advice.

The final stage of the comprehensive financial planning process is the ongoing monitoring and updating of the client's plan to take into account both new developments and changes in financial or family circumstances. As already noted, changes are inevitable, and the failure to update the plan to take these changes into account results in a plan that is no longer suited to the client's needs and is potentially disadvantageous to his or her interests. In fact, failure to keep the plan adjusted for changes in the client's personal or business affairs for more than a year or two will often necessitate a new data-gathering interview and the development of an entirely new plan.

Clients who appreciate the benefits of comprehensive financial planning and the necessity of keeping the plan updated to take account of current information are very reliable in notifying their financial planner of major changes in their situation. Other clients may be less forthcoming with up-to-date information.

In either case the planner should arrange a personal meeting with a client at least annually. This meeting is helpful in dealing with less communicative clients, as it presents a structured opportunity for requesting updated information. With more communicative clients a good deal of quantitative information may already have been furnished, but the meeting gives the planner an opportunity to confirm or clarify it. For both types of clients a major benefit of the annual meeting is the opportunity to renew the relationship between the client and the financial planner and the opportunity for the planner to reevaluate the client's conversation for changes in subjective information.

USE OF TAX PLANNING IN THE FINANCIAL PLANNING PROCESS

Because tax planning is a fundamental part of the comprehensive planning process, an understanding of the tax laws is necessary for financial planning to be effective. Without effective tax planning, comprehensive financial planning simply cannot be accomplished.

Nobody (not even a tax attorney) is an expert in all areas of taxation. In fact, tax attorneys are almost always highly specialized, most practicing in various subspecialties of tax law. This does not mean that a great deal cannot be learned about a particular area of taxation regardless of whether one has a legal or accounting background. It is a rare occasion, however, when anything other than the most simplistic tax planning can be done without the involvement of a competent tax attorney. Even if the financial planner has a legal and tax background, many planning cases will involve such sophisticated tax techniques that it will be necessary to obtain assistance and additional legal counsel from a practicing tax attorney.

Appropriate tax planning involves consideration of many planning techniques. Federal and state tax laws, as well as the different types of taxation within each system, must be considered. Unfortunately it is not unusual for clients (and many advisers) to lump all tax planning together into one broad category—taxes. This is an error that can leave clients confused and angry. For example, many clients are startled when they are told that the proceeds of their insurance policies are subject to federal estate taxes. "But my insurance agent told me that insurance proceeds were tax free," they say angrily. What the agent meant was that, as a general rule, the proceeds of life insurance are excluded from income taxation (IRC Sec. 101). Insurance proceeds, however, are not excluded from estate taxation if the decedent held any incidents of ownership in the insurance policy at death or if the life insurance policy had named the estate of the insured as the beneficiary (IRC Sec. 2042).

The Internal Revenue Code covers all forms of federal taxes. The primary types of taxes that financial planners deal with are income, gift, estate, and generation-skipping taxes, but the Code also deals with employment taxes and excise taxes that may be applicable in some planning cases.

The financial planner must learn to be precise in dealing with issues of taxation, and to do so requires spending sufficient time and study to recognize the existing systems of taxation and to understand that the rules for the imposition of the various types of taxes are often very different. Specific rules have been established by statute or case law to determine when taxation occurs and when tax liabilities arise. A taxable event occurs, as a general rule, when there is some transfer of property unless the Internal Revenue Code specifically provides otherwise. As noted in the above example concerning the federal taxation of life insurance proceeds, the income and estate tax rules are not always consistent. It is the task of the financial planner to understand the tax rules and to explain to the client the rules that are applicable to his or her situation.

After data gathering is complete, the planner analyzes the information for opportunities that would save the client income, estate, and gift taxes (and others if applicable). If the financial plan is being delivered for a fee, tax planning is a substantial portion of what the financial planner is being paid to do. Even when products are being offered for sale, it is the obligation of the financial planner to take a comprehensive and objective look at the client's situation and to save the client from costly tax blunders whenever possible. The time for product recommendations is after the client's affairs have been rearranged to maximize the benefits of the client's present holdings. For example, the best funding vehicle available for a stock-redemption agreement is of very little assistance if the agreement itself will have disastrous tax consequences or is legally unenforceable. The sale of a risky investment under the guise of comprehensive financial planning, without previous attention to the analysis and rearrangement of the client's current assets for maximum personal tax benefits, is not ethical.

One of the most important benefits of financial planning is educating the client to consider the tax benefits and costs of every transaction before engaging in it. Only before the transaction is consummated can the tax results be fully controlled through negotiation between the parties. Although it may be possible in some cases to restructure agreements to be more advantageous to the client, later repairs of completed transactions often are not feasible, as they are too expensive or would require the agreement of an adverse party. Each transaction should be structured in light of the client's tax, income, and cash-flow situation.

In most tax planning the timing and form of the transaction can mean everything. That is, by appropriately structuring the documents to control the form and the timing of the transaction, the drafter generally controls the tax result. Assume a client approaches the financial planner with a large potential taxable gain in a contemplated transaction. Assume the gain is $450,000. The first question in a discussion of the proposed transaction with a buyer will be how to structure the transaction so that the maximum amount of net proceeds from the sale will remain in the client's hands. The financial planner must be able to respond accurately to that question without unduly delaying negotiations. This may involve negotiating an agreement that allows reporting of the income on the installment method over 2 or more tax years. In reaching a conclusion on this issue, the factors that must be considered are the potential interest or other investment income or gain that will be forgone by stretching out the payments and the amount of taxes that will be saved by this technique. In some cases the savings are substantial. This is a simple example of how income tax planning is used in the comprehensive financial planning process.

Other taxes that are routinely considered are federal estate and gift taxes. Estate planning is an important part of financial planning, but it is only one part. Financial planning deals with all current assets of the client and all proposed acquisitions or dispositions of those assets during the client's life. It then seeks at the client's death to effect the transition of those assets through an orderly plan that is not only consistent with the owner's wishes but that is tax advantageous as well.

It is not unusual for a competent financial planner to save a client thousands of dollars in potential estate tax liabilities by effective utilization of the federal estate, gift, and generation-skipping tax laws. Generally it is not sufficient to save potential estate tax dollars only at the death of the first spouse. Unless there is some compelling family planning reason for not doing so, the financial planner should consider the total projected estate tax costs in the estates of both spouses and plan to minimize total taxes. The ultimate strategy is to transmit as much of the client's accumulated wealth as possible to the children or grandchildren at the death of the client and spouse. Most clients, of course, want a surviving spouse to continue to have most of the marital assets available in case of need but may want to assure that these assets cannot be squandered or diverted from their children. By utilizing appropriate estate planning techniques, marital assets can be made readily available to a surviving spouse, yet avoid inclusion in the surviving spouse's estate while ensuring that any assets that are unconsumed by the surviving spouse will be disposed of according to the client's wishes.

Although the comprehensive financial planner must know a great deal about tax issues and the tax laws to identify potential problem areas, most financial planners are not attorneys. For these financial planners the specter of a charge of unauthorized practice of law can be troubling.

Neither the American Bar Association's Model Rules of Professional Conduct nor its predecessor, the Code of Professional Responsibility, is helpful in this specific area. It is quite clear that no one other than a lawyer is permitted to engage in the practice of law. What constitutes the practice of law, however, is not clearly defined. The Model Rules of Professional Conduct takes the position that the definition of the practice of law is established by the law of the different jurisdictions and can therefore vary from jurisdiction to jurisdiction. The Code of Professional Responsibility stated that "It is neither necessary nor desirable to attempt the formulation of a single, specific definition of what constitutes the practice of law. Functionally the practice of law relates to the rendition of services for others that call for the professional judgment of a lawyer. The essence of the professional judgment of the lawyer is his or her educated ability to relate the general body and philosophy of law to a specific legal problem of a client."

Despite the American Bar Association's ambiguous definitions of what constitutes the practice of law, there are some activities that are universally regarded as the practice of law and as such are to be engaged in only by lawyers. One such activity is the drafting of legal documents.

The line between the unauthorized practice of law and the permissible giving of advice is much more difficult to ascertain, especially in fields such as accounting and financial planning. The pivotal question revolves around when the giving of tax advice or information about a particular proposed transaction or tax technique by a CPA or financial planner becomes "legal advice" and as such becomes the exclusive right of the lawyer. There is no absolute way to answer this question.

There is, however, some guidance available to assist the nonlawyer in avoiding potential problems in the unauthorized practice area. If the advice given is couched in general informational terms—for example, if the general principles of a technique are explained for the client's information, this should not be viewed as the unauthorized practice of law. Moreover, even advice that is specifically related to a client's situation should not constitute an unauthorized-practice violation as long as the subject matter of the advice is settled in the law and is a matter of common knowledge in the adviser's field.

The safest way to deal with the unauthorized-practice issue is to immediately involve an attorney as a member of the financial planning team. The attorney's involvement should continue throughout the planning process in those areas in which it is difficult to distinguish legal advice from advice or information that can be legitimately offered by someone who is not a lawyer.

USE OF INSURANCE IN THE FINANCIAL PLANNING PROCESS

After the client's current holdings have been analyzed for improved tax efficiency and the appropriate recommendations have been made in the area of tax planning, the emphasis in the financial planning process turns to an analysis of the client's exposure to potential loss of income or assets. There are three basic ways to deal with such exposures:

- The client bears the risk of the entire loss himself or herself (self-insurance).
- The client pays another to assume the risk for him or her (shifting the risk through insurance).
- The client utilizes some combination of both these strategies.

While insurance planning is as personal as the individual client, some general rules are applicable:

- Although life insurance is not the solution for all situations, current tax law does give permanent insurance products certain advantages that provide additional benefits to clients who need risk protection.
- Catastrophic risks should generally be insured against even when the probability of the occurrence of the loss is slight. Premium rates are usually low in these circumstances because rates are tied to the probability and magnitude of the loss.
- Small risks should generally not be insured against, especially when the probability of the occurrence of loss is high. Premium rates are usually relatively high and insurance is not cost effective.
- If the client has sufficient liquid assets to meet his or her stated objectives, it is a perfectly appropriate planning technique to fund these objectives from accumulated assets rather than from insurance proceeds.

- Insurance is essentially a device for shifting the risks of loss from the client and/or the family to an insurance company. Although many modern insurance products have substantial investment features, the primary function of insurance is still this risk-shifting function.
- Before the sale of additional (or replacement) insurance is recommended, the financial planner must be able to demonstrate to the client that it (a) meets a genuine need or objective of the client and (b) is a more cost-effective means of achieving that end than other planning techniques.
- Client objectives that will be met by the purchase of appropriate types and amounts of insurance coverage change over time. Insurance planning must be carefully reviewed and monitored along with the rest of the financial plan to assure that insurance coverage is adjusted as circumstances change.
- The need for insurance coverage does not always increase over time. Effective financial and estate planning techniques may result in a decreasing need for insurance because of asset accumulation over time.
- Insurance planning must always be coordinated with tax planning so that coverage is purchased in a tax-efficient manner and takes into account the tax impact of ownership and beneficiary designations.

Insurance, properly utilized, meets the client's need to minimize exposure to many types of serious losses as nothing else can. If it is improperly used, it drains the client's cash flow and consequently prevents the achievement of other objectives. Unless the coverage is positioned properly, it may needlessly aggravate estate tax problems and cost the client's family thousands of dollars in unnecessary estate tax liabilities. Judicious recommendations to purchase insurance contracts to insure against loss of income or assets can be a boon to the financial planning client. However, if recommendations are made by financial planners seeking only the planner's personal enrichment, the entire financial planning discipline suffers.

INVESTMENT RECOMMENDATIONS IN THE FINANCIAL PLANNING PROCESS

Investment analysis and recommendations are the final major areas addressed in the development of the client's financial plan. The purposes of investing generally fall into two categories. The first category includes the prefunding of anticipated expenditures such as retirement and education funding. The second category is discretionary in the sense that investments are made with the more general goal of adding to the stock of the client's assets rather than funding a specific need. Because investments are normally made from cash available after living expenditures, the appropriate time to ascertain the amount to be invested is after tax and insurance planning have been done. By assuring there is no cash drain because of poor tax or insurance planning, the maximum dollar amount will be available for investment.

Needless to say, the choice of appropriate investment vehicles can vary widely from client to client. Recommendations on investments must be based on the planner's assessment of the client's attitude toward risk and return. For example, it would not generally be appropriate to recommend trading in commodities futures to a risk-averse client whose previous investment choices have been federally insured savings deposits or CDs.

Within the limits of a particular client's risk/return tolerances, however, there may be considerable latitude in the choice of investment vehicles. To a great extent the choice among these vehicles will depend on the client's objectives.

As with insurance planning, investment planning should be carefully coordinated with the other aspects of the client's plan, and care should be taken to ensure that the investment recommendations made are those best suited to achieve the client's objectives.

ASCERTAINING THE VALUE OF TAX AUTHORITY

It is important for a financial planner to understand the sources of tax authority. In evaluating a potential recommendation, as well as in dealing with other members of the financial planning team or with the client's outside advisers, the planner must know both the source and the weight of the authority on which he or she is relying. There are three interrelated sources from which tax authority is derived:

- legislative
- administrative
- judicial

Legislative authority to enact a federal income tax law was granted to Congress by the Sixteenth Amendment to the Constitution of the United States in 1913. Under this authority Congress has enacted statutes that are the primary tax authority, subject only to a successful challenge of the constitutionality of the particular statute, an issue that is ultimately decided by the United States Supreme Court. The tax statutes enacted by Congress are codified in the Internal Revenue Code. Tax statutes (Code provisions) are cited in the following way: 26 U.S.C. 351, or more commonly IRC Sec.351—that is, the 26th title of the United States Code, Sec. 351, or Internal Revenue Code, Sec. 351. All section references in this book are to the Internal Revenue Code of 1986, as amended, and to the regulations thereunder unless otherwise noted.

After enactment, tax laws are subject to interpretation and explanation by both administrative bodies and the judicial system. The Internal Revenue Service (under delegated authority from the President of the United States or the

Congress through the Treasury Department) has responsibility for the actual formulation of the next tier of tax authority, the regulations. The Treasury Regulations are subject to final approval by the Treasury Department.

The purpose of the Treasury regulations is to explain how the tax laws are to be applied. In fact, the regulations may explain, exemplify, define, or even attempt to expand the Code provision. The regulations express the official Treasury (and thereby the Internal Revenue Service) interpretation of the Code provisions. After Treasury regulations are formulated, they are issued in proposed form to allow interested parties, such as representatives of the affected group or industry, as well as tax attorneys and accountants, to file comments or objections and to participate in public hearings before the regulations are adopted in final form. Once adopted, the final regulations become the official Internal Revenue Service's position on the particular Code section and are binding on IRS personnel. The general rule is that to the extent that the regulation is not inconsistent with the Code, it has the force and effect of law, unless and until it is overturned by a court of competent jurisdiction.

Regulations can be invalidated by courts on several grounds. A court may invalidate a Treasury regulation if (a) the regulation has incorrectly construed the Congressional intent of the statute or (b) the regulation exceeds the scope of the Code provision. It should be noted that courts give substantial weight to the regulations and are generally reluctant to invalidate them. This is generally considered to be good for taxpayers and tax advisers because it means that the regulations will not undergo constant change and therefore can generally be relied on for planning purposes.

One note of caution: Even if a court has ruled a regulation invalid, the Internal Revenue Service can still attempt to enforce the regulation against other taxpayers in other federal jurisdictions unless and until the decision to invalidate it has been upheld by the U.S. Supreme Court. Therefore a planner must be certain to clearly inform the client that the IRS could continue to enforce the regulation despite a contrary decision by the District Court or Circuit Court of Appeals in another jurisdiction. In fact, the IRS frequently attempts to get different results on the same issue from different Circuit Courts of Appeals, thereby creating a "conflict among the circuits" in an attempt to get the Supreme Court to hear the case and resolve the conflict.

Regulations are numbered in a manner consistent with the Internal Revenue Code sections for which they provide explanation or exemplification. For example, the income tax regulations for IRC Sec. 351 are cited as Regs. Sec. 1.351; estate tax regulations are cited as Regs. Sec. 20.2001; gift tax regulations are cited as Regs. Sec. 25.2501; and so on.

The next tier of tax authority consists of revenue rulings that are issued and published in response to a taxpayer's request for the Internal Revenue Service's interpretation of a particular point of law applied to a specific fact situation. When the request for interpretation is one involving an issue that is likely to affect a significant number of taxpayers, the IRS often issues a revenue ruling on the subject. The revenue ruling is a public announcement of the IRS's present position on the issue in question, and IRS personnel will act in accordance with that position.

The taxpayer, however, is not necessarily bound by the ruling. If his or her situation is substantially the same as that described in the revenue ruling and the result is favorable to the taxpayer, the ruling can be relied on in dealings with the IRS. If the facts of the case are substantially the same as those in the revenue ruling and the ruling is adverse to the taxpayer, the ruling can be challenged in the courts. Revenue rulings, unlike the regulations, are given no particular weight by the courts; that is, they are not necessarily presumed to be correct.

Unlike the regulations, revenue rulings are more often changed or modified by later revenue rulings. One should be especially careful when relying on such rulings to ascertain that the benefits they promise have not been diminished or eliminated by subsequent rulings.

Revenue rulings are cited in two ways. Those published recently are cited to the weekly publication in which they appear, the *Internal Revenue Bulletin*. For example, the 109th Revenue Ruling of 1992 appearing in the 36th weekly *Internal Revenue Bulletin* at page 14 would be cited as follows: Rev. Rul. 92-109, I.R.B. 36,14. Revenue rulings (and other administrative rulings by the IRS) are continuously collected by the U.S. Government Printing Office into bound volumes called *Cumulative Bulletins*. Each of these is compiled for a particular calendar year and may contain two or three volumes. If the revenue ruling has been printed in the *Cumulative Bulletin,* the citation is usually to that source and is slightly different in appearance. For example, the 50th Revenue Ruling of 1992 appears in volume two of the 1992 *Cumulative Bulletin* at page 205. The appropriate citation is Rev. Rul. 92-50, 1992-2 C.B. 205. Whether the citation is to the *Internal Revenue Bulletin* or to the *Cumulative Bulletin,* the degree of authority of an unsuperseded revenue ruling is the same.

Revenue rulings should not be confused with revenue procedures (Rev. Procs.), which are also published in the *Internal Revenue Bulletin* and collected in the *Cumulative Bulletin.* Revenue procedures usually relate to changes in procedures within the IRS. These changes include such items as limitations or additions in the areas in which the IRS will issue rulings, as well as changes in other internal techniques.

The following diagram shows the hierarchy of legislative and administrative authority.

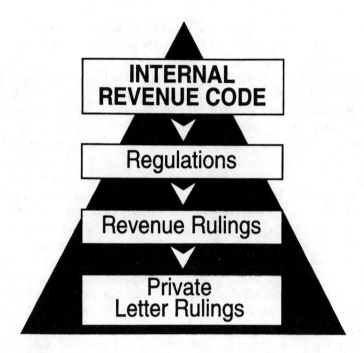

The final administrative tier of tax authority is that of the private letter rulings. Taxpayers can request a private ruling from the IRS that approves or interprets a transaction that has either not been consummated or for which a return has not been filed. The IRS will honor such requests if the transaction involves an issue upon which the IRS has decided to rule. (This decision is purely an administrative one, and the areas in which the IRS will rule have become much less numerous in recent years.) The private letter ruling is a personal response to a particular taxpayer and as such is determinative only in regard to the transaction it describes. Until recently private letter rulings were mailed directly to the taxpayer or an authorized representative, and public access to them was limited. However, they are now being released under the Freedom of Information Act and are published by private publishers after all confidential and identifying information has been deleted. While private letter rulings cannot be cited as authority by taxpayers other than the taxpayer obtaining the ruling, they are often helpful to tax practitioners as an indication of the IRS position on various issues. An example of how private letter rulings are cited is as follows: PLR 200001004. The first four numbers in the citation indicate the year in which the private ruling was issued.

The ultimate judicial authority for the interpretation of the law including tax law is the U.S. Supreme Court. Once the Supreme Court has decided an issue, the decision is binding on all taxpayers and the Internal Revenue Service and therefore must be adhered to unless Congress changes the relevant Code section or unless the Supreme Court later reverses its own decision. It is not possible, however, to take tax cases directly to the Supreme Court for determination. Tax cases must originate in lower courts and work their way up to the Supreme Court level. Even then, the Supreme Court has the discretion to agree or refuse to hear a tax case presented to it.

The choice of the lowest court in which tax cases are heard depends on whether the taxpayer, after exhausting the administrative appeal procedures of the IRS, can or will pay the tax and sue for a refund or seeks a judicial determination of the contested issues before the tax is paid. If the taxpayer wishes the court to rule on the correctness of the issue before paying the tax, the case will be tried in the Tax Court (known prior to 1942 as the United States Board of Tax Appeals). Cases in the Tax Court are tried without juries. Tax Court judges decide issues of law and fact. The party against whom the decision is made can appeal a Tax Court decision to the United States Court of Appeals in the circuit where the Tax Court decision was made. If the decision is adverse to the IRS, the Service may choose not to appeal the case but may also wish not to abandon the issue. The Service will usually indicate whether it will continue to litigate the particular issue involved by acquiescing or nonacquiescing in the decision. A nonacquiescence indicates that the Service disagrees with the decision and will continue to litigate the issue in future cases it believes are favorable to its position.

The Tax Court generally follows its own decisions as precedents; that is, a Tax Court in California is likely to consider the finding of a Tax Court in Massachusetts on a substantially similar issue extremely persuasive authority in determining the issue before it. This is true even if the Court of Appeals that reviewed the Massachusetts decision reversed the original Tax Court result.

Tax Court decisions that the court considers important or that express a new issue not previously dealt with in a published Tax Court opinion are collected and published by the Government Printing Office as Tax Court reports. These decisions are cited with volume number first, followed by T.C., and then page number. For example, a case appearing in the 72nd volume of the Tax Court reports at page 88 would be cited 72 T.C. 88. Other Tax Court decisions are called Tax Court Memorandum decisions and are presently available through private publishers. They are also cited by volume number, T.C.M., and page— for example, 49 T.C.M. 66. Tax Court decisions, published as either regular or memorandum decisions, carry the same degree of authority.

If the taxpayer pays the tax the IRS has assessed, the Tax Court will not determine whether the IRS acted correctly in assessing the tax. Instead, the taxpayer must take his or her case to a court that has jurisdiction over claims for refund. The taxpayer can choose either a United States District Court or the United States Claims Court. In a U.S. District Court the taxpayer can have a jury trial; in the U.S. Claims Court all trials are nonjury. Decisions from both the District Courts and the U.S. Claims Court are reported in a series called the *Federal Supplement,* which is cited as follows: 36 F. Supp. 103, meaning a particular case can be found in the 36th volume of the *Federal Supplement* beginning at page 103. However, the routes of appeal from the two courts are different—appeals from the U.S. District Courts are to the U.S. Courts of Appeals; appeals from the U.S. Claims Court are to the Court of Appeals for the Federal Circuit.

As already indicated, the party who loses in the Tax Court or the District Court can appeal the decision to the United States Court of Appeals in the circuit in which the Tax Court or District Court decision was rendered. The decision of the Court of Appeals is determinative of the issue before it (unless overturned by the Supreme Court), and therefore a Court of Appeals decision is higher authority than that of the Tax Court or a U.S. District Court. Cases from the U.S. Court of Appeals are reported in the *Federal Reporter* and are cited as follows: 72 F.2d 823 (7th Cir.), meaning that the 72d volume of the second series of the *Federal Reporter* at page 823 contains a decision by the 7th Circuit Court of Appeals.

The party who loses a case at the U.S. Court of Appeals or the Court of Appeals for the Federal Circuit can appeal the case to the U.S. Supreme Court. There is no guarantee, however, that the Supreme Court will grant a writ of certiorari (accept the case for a decision). If the Supreme Court refuses to hear the case, the decision of the Court of Appeals is determinative. If the Supreme Court hears the case, the Supreme Court's findings are the ultimate decision, and the issue is settled as a matter of law for all courts. Supreme Court decisions are officially cited as follows: 267 U.S. 972, meaning the 267th volume of the *Supreme Court Reports* at page 972.

The following diagram depicts the system of judicial authority for tax cases:

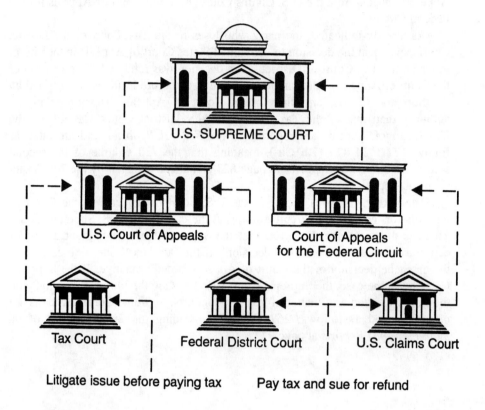

U.S. SUPREME COURT

U.S. Court of Appeals

Court of Appeals
for the Federal Circuit

Tax Court

Federal District Court

U.S. Claims Court

Litigate issue before paying tax

Pay tax and sue for refund

2

Developing the Outline for a Client's Plan

Chapter Outline

CASE NARRATIVE—CHARLES AND BARBARA WIGGINS 2.4

In this chapter you will review the data on the Wiggins family and proceed to develop preliminary outlines for their business and personal plans. The preliminary outline should note as many applicable techniques as possible for achieving the client's objectives, since the outline forms the basis for the planner's review of the client's case. Techniques that are undesirable will be eliminated when the preliminary outline is further refined. As the planner becomes more experienced, clearly undesirable techniques can usually be eliminated mentally, possibly during the data-gathering interview, so that an actual written preliminary outline may not be necessary.

Organizational outlines were discussed briefly in chapter 1. To reiterate, financial planning is generally first organized into two broad categories:

- *Personal planning*—lifetime and estate planning for the client's family and its individual members
  - Personal planning concerns will generally involve items such as personal income tax deferral or reduction; insurance needs; investment planning and strategies; effective retirement planning; educational objectives for children or grandchildren; the present titling and advice on correctly titling property; personal estate planning, including a review and analysis of the client's current plan, if any; and other personal topics raised by an examination of the client's interests or objectives.
- *Business planning*—planning for maximum income production as well as any business-ownership interest over which the client can exert sufficient control to effect a change in the business's operations or strategic direction

– Business planning can take into consideration many business and income-production areas. It may deal with employee benefit planning, including qualified and nonqualified deferred compensation; executive compensation packages; personal use of corporate assets; and the tax cost of corporate payments of certain quasi-personal expenses. Business planning may also deal with planning business transactions. Such transactions may include the client's personal ownership of certain assets that are leased to the business to provide personal income tax benefits, as well as the structuring of legally enforceable buy-sell agreements to effect a business transition at the death or disability of the owner. Business planning may also involve transferring an interest in a family-owned corporation to allow older-generation owners to turn over their day-to-day participation to their children or to convert the value of their interest into cash.

In cases where the bulk of the client's income or net worth is tied up in a business, particularly a closely held business, it is generally prudent to do a separate business plan and to prepare and present the business plan first. The personal planning can be prepared and presented as an ancillary plan, referring to the business plan as necessary for explanatory detail. This approach is preferable because the business and its success or failure largely control what is possible for the client to accomplish on the personal side.

In cases in which the client is a salaried person without significant control in policy-making areas, the plan may be viewed primarily as a personal plan with the "business planning" being limited to an investigation of existing salary and employee benefits. In such cases a separate business plan will be unnecessary.

The Wiggins family owns a partnership interest sufficiently substantial both in value and income production to warrant separate business planning treatment.

Before completing a preliminary outline for the business and personal plans for the Wiggins family, it is helpful to review the financial planning process as shown in the diagram on page 2.3.

To begin the process, prepare a written preliminary outline to recognize and consider the widest possible array of planning techniques available for achieving a particular objective. For example, the settled tax planning techniques for achieving a particular objective, such as income shifting for educating children, are finite in number. The astute planner should become acquainted with these methods and with their basic technical requirements. Once these have become familiar, it may be apparent at an early point in the relationship with the client that a particular technique will not meet the client's objective. At this point the preliminary outline has become a mental process for eliminating clearly unsuitable techniques, and many planners will dispense with the actual written form. The preliminary outline, however, whether a mental checklist or a written outline, continues to be a crucial part of the financial planning process.

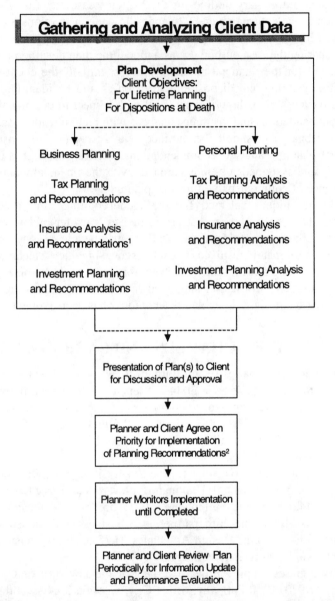

Gathering and Analyzing Client Data

Plan Development
Client Objectives:
For Lifetime Planning
For Dispositions at Death

Business Planning

Tax Planning
and Recommendations

Insurance Analysis
and Recommendations[1]

Investment Planning
and Recommendations

Personal Planning

Tax Planning Analysis
and Recommendations

Insurance Analysis
and Recommendations

Investment Planning Analysis
and Recommendations

Presentation of Plan(s) to Client
for Discussion and Approval

Planner and Client Agree on
Priority for Implementation
of Planning Recommendations[2]

Planner Monitors Implementation
until Completed

Planner and Client Review Plan
Periodically for Information Update
and Performance Evaluation

1. Investment planning may or may not be appropriate for a business interest, as many businesses reinvest profits in the business operation; that is, they invest primarily in themselves.

2. The client should be advised that he or she may enter the implementation phase with any planner of his or her choosing.

When the preliminary outline has been completed, it can be compared with the suggested preliminary outline for the Wiggins case that follows. Once that comparison is made, turn to page 2.26 and follow the instructions for preparing a working outline.

In preparing the case outline use as a model the plan development portion of the flowchart for the financial planning process. Initially the client's objectives for lifetime planning and dispositions at death should be identified and listed. Then the business plan should be outlined with respect to tax planning analysis with recommendations and insurance analysis with recommendations. Finally the client's personal plan should be outlined with respect to tax, insurance, and investment planning analyst recommendations. Working through a client's data thoroughly and systematically in accordance with the financial planning process is the essence of comprehensive financial planning.

In the techniques selected for the model outlines and case solutions, alternatives have been chosen that are settled as a matter of law or for which substantial authority exists, even though there may be a legal issue or issues that have not been ultimately resolved. In each instance in which a technique contains legal issues that are not presently resolved, this fact should be noted in the plan solution, and such information should always be disclosed to the client. The recommendation of highly speculative techniques has been avoided.

CASE NARRATIVE—CHARLES AND BARBARA WIGGINS

Your clients are Charles F. and Barbara B. Wiggins. They live at 421 Briarcliff Drive, Small City, Georgia 30341. Their home telephone number is (404) 555-2742. Charles is a professor of computer and decision sciences at Homestate Tech, a state university. His office address is Room 426, Commerce and Finance Hall, Homestate Tech, Small City, Georgia 30315, and his office telephone number is (404) 555-2550.

Barbara is a student counselor for the Small City School District. Her office address is Adams High School, Hickman Boulevard and Wavy Lane, Small City, Georgia 30344. Her business telephone is (404) 555-8000, extension 402.

Charles is also a one-third partner in a business and industrial computer consulting firm—Systems Design Associates. He founded the business 18 years ago with two of his university colleagues.

The Wigginses employ Edward L. Day of the law firm of Cox, Day and Elkins, Suite 920, 1000 Parkway, Small City, Georgia 30301, as their personal and business attorney. Edward Day's office number is (404) 555-9450.

Their CPA, Fred Granger, Suite 123, 888 Parkway, Small City, Georgia 30315, does their tax returns as well as the accounting work for Systems Design Associates. His office telephone number is (404) 555-6428. Assume that Granger has worked with you before on financial plans and that he recommended that Charles and Barbara see you for comprehensive financial planning.

Other advisers include

- administrative trust officer: Xavier Young, Universal Bank and Trust, New York, New York 10007, (212) 555-4000, who has responsibility for administering a trust of which Barbara is the beneficiary
- commercial banker: Helen Morgan, First National Bank, First National Bank Tower, Small City, Georgia 30301, (404) 555-9240
- life insurance agent: John King, CLU, Suite 903, 1000 Parkway, Small City, Georgia 30315, (404) 555-5000
- property and liability insurance agent: Larry Mincer, CPCU, 4220 Kingsway, Small City, Georgia 30322, (404) 555-1984
- securities broker: Nancy Osborne of the firm of Peters, Quigley and Rogers, 100 Broad Street, Small City, Georgia 30315, (404) 555-3622

None of these advisers has ever provided or offered to provide comprehensive financial planning for the Wiggins family. Neither Charles nor Barbara is displeased with any of their present advisers whom they feel have served them fairly well. They have asked that you cooperate with their existing advisers in developing their financial plan.

The biographical data on the Wigginses are as follows: Charles was born August 14, and is 38 years old. His Social Security number is 063-42-2221. Barbara Wiggins was born on June 5, and is 30 years old. Her Social Security number is 114-38-9370. Charles and Barbara were married 8 years ago shortly after Charles's divorce from Cynthia Crowley. Barbara had not been married previously. Barbara and Charles have one child, Charles F. Wiggins, Jr., born May 11, who is 7 years old. Charles has two children from his prior marriage: Stephanie R. Wiggins, born December 13, who is presently 14; and Caroline D. Wiggins, born August 25, presently 12. All the children attend public schools, and all the family is in good health.

Barbara's father is William B. Becker, born May 31, aged 59. He is an oral surgeon. Her mother, Susan A. Becker, was born March 11, and is 59 years old. She owns a gift shop. Barbara has a twin sister, Betty Becker, who is unmarried and is employed as a diplomatic courier for the United States State Department.

Both of Charles's parents are still living. His father, Ted Wiggins, was born July 4. He is 63 years old and is still employed as a machinist. His mother, Mary Wiggins, was born December 25; she is 62 and is a homemaker. Charles has a brother, James, aged 40, who is a self-employed contractor; he also had a brother, Edward, who was killed in an automobile accident many years ago at the age of 28.

Barbara and Charles are citizens of the United States. They file a joint tax return. Charles no longer pays alimony to Cynthia, who has remarried, but he does pay child support for his two daughters in the amount of $350 per child per month. He estimates that he provides for approximately 70 percent of their support with his child support payments. In accordance with the terms of the divorce decree Charles maintains a life insurance policy to provide for the payment of this child support in the event of his death. The face amount of the policy is $100,000. In addition, the divorce decree specifies that Charles can claim Stephanie and Caroline as dependents for income tax purposes.

Charles and Barbara have wills that they had drawn 4 years ago, but they have no prenuptial or postnuptial agreements. When asked to describe their basic estate plan, Charles tells you that his will leaves one-quarter of his estate to each of his two children by his previous marriage and one-half to Barbara if she survives him, otherwise to Charles, Jr. Should he die before his daughters reach the age of majority, the will creates trusts for their benefit. Barbara's will leaves all her property to Charles if he survives her. If he does not survive her, all her property is left to a trust for Charles, Jr., until he reaches 21 years of age. In their wills the Wigginses have designated a guardian for Charles, Jr., in the event of their death before his majority. They have chosen Barbara's sister, Betty Becker, who is a diplomatic courier with the U.S. State Department and lives in Apartment 3515, Parklane Towers, 100 Parklane Place, Washington, D.C. 20036. Neither Charles nor Barbara recalls notifying Betty of this fact when their wills were signed. No successor guardian was designated. The First National Bank of Small City is named executor of both their wills and trustee for the testamentary trusts.

Neither Charles nor Barbara has ever made a gift under the Uniform Gifts to Minors Act. Barbara is the present beneficiary of a trust created for her benefit by her paternal grandfather. Barbara also expects to receive a significant inheritance from her parents at their death. She estimates that her parents probably have a net worth well in excess of $2 million. Charles, on the other hand, does not expect to receive any significant inheritance or assistance from his family, nor does he believe that his family will require his assistance in the future.

Charles has a PhD in management and statistics, and Barbara has a master's degree in education. Neither Charles nor Barbara has ever served in the military.

When asked to rank a standardized list of general financial objectives in direct order of importance to their family (that is, the item numbered 1 has the highest priority and the item numbered 8 the lowest), Barbara and Charles responded in the following way:

• provide college education for all their children	1
• take care of the family in the event of the death of a breadwinner	2
• take care of self and family during a period of long-term disability	3
• reduce the tax burden	4
• maintain their standard of living	5
• enjoy a comfortable retirement	6
• invest and accumulate wealth	7
• develop an estate plan	8

Charles and Barbara tell you they have no formal monthly budget. They estimate that they save $8,000 annually from their combined take-home pay, $5,000 of which they put in investments other than savings accounts or CDs. They believe they should be able to save and invest 20 percent of their income after taxes. They would use their savings or investments for college expenses for the children and to build in a cushion for Barbara and the children in case of Charles's death or disability.

Neither Charles nor Barbara has ever given substantial gifts to family members or to educational institutions or charities. They have not made any specific bequests or bequests to charity in their wills. They indicate that they have been basically satisfied or somewhat satisfied with their previous investment results but feel that yields should be higher given current conditions. They have no commitment to any one particular form of investment.

Charles states that he feels Barbara is competent to handle money, and if he should die first, he believes that her judgment and emotional stability would probably serve the best interests of the family. He thinks the emotional and economic maturity of his children is about average for their ages. Charles states further that in the event of his death he believes Barbara will remarry, and he feels she should. Barbara hopes that Charles would remarry in the event of her death. Charles says he would probably like to retire from teaching at about age 65 but would not like to retire from his consulting business until at least age 70. Barbara would like to stop working at age 65.

Leaving tax considerations aside, Charles would like his estate to be utilized first to provide for Barbara and any minor children. After Barbara's death he would like any remaining assets distributed equally to his children. Barbara feels that her estate should provide for Charles first and then be left to Charles, Jr. Barbara and Charles are looking at financial planning as a cohesive method for understanding and managing their financial affairs on a long-range basis.

Charles and Barbara seem to have a successful marriage filled with a great deal of affection and mutual respect, and they experience very few of the typical stepfamily problems. Barbara admires and respects Charles's devotion to his daughters, who spend a lot of time with them, and they are fond of her. She feels that they have a very good relationship. Stephanie and Caroline are especially close to their half brother, Charles, Jr.

Charles is essentially a self-made man who put himself through school with part-time jobs and scholarships. He has had a successful career at Homestate Tech. Although he considers that his consulting business has been "moderately successful," he wishes it were more successful and is somewhat frustrated that his business-ownership position is not providing more current and long-term financial and tax advantages for himself and his family. As a practical matter, however, Charles seems perfectly capable of making the business even more successful, but it is already doing quite well despite the limited amount of time he and his two partners devote to managing it. Charles acknowledges this, but believes that the business could become even more efficient with some effective planning, which he and his partners never seem to address.

Barbara Wiggins is an intelligent, cultured woman whose father and mother provided every advantage for her and her twin sister, Betty. Barbara and Betty are beneficiaries of trusts their grandfather established for them many years ago. Barbara's trust is invested largely in low-yielding longer-term corporate bonds and has a current market value of about $200,000. The corpus of the trust is under management by Universal Bank and Trust in New York and yields about $14,000 in annual income. The dispositive provisions of the trust provide that one-half the principal is to be paid to Barbara at age 35 and the balance at age 45 if she is living. If she dies prior to distribution, the trust continues for her living children. If she has no children living, the trust is to be distributed to Betty. Barbara believes the terms of Betty's trust are identical.

Barbara also believes that she and Betty are equal remainder beneficiaries of her father's and mother's wills. As already noted, Barbara's father's estate is estimated to be quite large; however, Barbara knows almost nothing further about her father's financial affairs. She says that she lives without any conscious expectations that her father's estate may someday make her wealthy. She is accustomed to her present standard of living, which is based primarily on what she and Charles earn. She enjoys her career and takes a good deal of interest in both Charles's teaching career and his partnership. She says that she would not really feel comfortable questioning her parents specifically about their net worth or their estate plans at this time.

Both Charles and Barbara have felt for some time that they are paying higher than necessary income taxes, and one reason they are seeking financial planning advice is to explore means of reducing their tax obligation and of diverting more of their income toward their financial planning objectives. It is important to note that, although the Wigginses' family income is quite substantial, they are not saving and investing as much as they would like—or as much as they will need if they expect to achieve their objectives without cutting back on their standard of living. Because they do not wish to cut back, they are hoping to achieve their savings and investment objectives through other financial planning techniques.

One fringe benefit of Charles's employment is tuition-free education for both the undergraduate and graduate level at Homestate Tech for each of his children. Should Charles die while employed at the university, all three children would still be able to obtain a tuition-free education at Homestate Tech. Stephanie has indicated that she will probably want to attend Homestate Tech. Charles and Barbara estimate that 4 years of college for Stephanie, taking into account the free tuition, will cost no more than $12,000. For Caroline, who may not wish to go to Homestate Tech, they estimate college costs of approximately $40,000. They are estimating approximately $60,000 for Charles, Jr., on the chance that he will also go elsewhere. They are somewhat concerned that later one or more of the children may wish to attend a private college and that the costs they have projected may not be sufficient in an inflationary economy. In addition, they are projecting graduate or professional school costs of about $30,000, $35,000, and $50,000 respectively for each child. All these estimated college costs are stated in current dollars. Ideally they would like to be able to assist their children through their entire educational careers, including postgraduate work, even though they are not sure at present that these expenses will be necessary. To partially fund these costs Charles and Barbara have long-term CDs of $3,000 each for Caroline and Stephanie and $7,000 for Charles, Jr. These CDs will mature in 2 years.

In addition to the capital necessary for funding the children's educations, Charles and Barbara hope to build a comfortable vacation home on a lake in the nearby mountains. They expect to acquire the lot and begin construction in 4 years, and they project a cost of $120,000 in current dollars. They hope that they will be able to obtain conventional 30-year, fixed-rate financing for this project. For part of the down payment they have several long-term CDs worth $10,000, all of which mature in 3 1/2 years. Their goal is to accumulate an additional $8,000 for the down payment and closing costs. They believe that the mountain home would be a good investment and have discussed the possibility that it could be liquidated, if necessary, to provide additional funds for educating the children. If liquidation is not required for this purpose, they would like to keep the house permanently.

The Inventory of Assets (see table 2-1) for Charles and Barbara Wiggins consists of asset information they supplied. The stated values represent fair market value at the end of last year and yields for this year.

Several years ago Charles, along with two colleagues from the university, Steve Thomas and Ursula Von Waldhem, founded a private consulting firm, Systems Design Associates. Each owns a one-third interest in the partnership. Both of Charles's partners are in excellent health, and both are married. The business is located at 1773 Park Place, Small City, Georgia 30318. The business telephone number is (404) 555-2550. The principal business activity of the partnership is the design and development of management information and decision support computer systems for business and industrial use. None of the partners has an employment contract. The partnership is a calendar-year, cash-method taxpayer. Charles has a strong expectation that he and his partners will have a long-term relationship. They work together very smoothly and are committed to continuing the business.

The firm has three full-time, non-owner-employees whom the partners consider key employees. They are Tom Young, John Blake, and Sarah L. McIntyre. Charles considers the retention of these employees vital to the continued success of Systems Design. None has any insurability problem as far as Charles knows.

Charles Wiggins has expressed the following views about his interest in the firm:

- If he retires, he wants to sell his interest to the other two partners or to a new partner.
- If he becomes disabled, he may want to sell his interest.
- If he dies, he wants his interest sold to provide cash for his estate.

In case of disability, death, or retirement, Charles assumes that Ursula Von Waldhem will take over his functions in the business. Charles thinks that the business could be sold now as a going concern and that his one-third interest is worth $175,000. He himself would pay $450,000 for the firm if he were an outsider; he would also pay $275,000 for his two partners' interest. No objective valuation of the business has been made.

The largest single asset Systems Design Associates owns is the building that houses the business. The partnership purchased the building 6 years ago for a total price of $185,000, of which they financed $155,000 for 25 years at 9.5 percent interest. The present mortgage balance is $140,000. The purchase price was allocated in the purchase contract—$150,000 for the building and $35,000 for the land. The building has been depreciated under the original accelerated cost recovery system for tax purposes. Charles believes the building could be sold for $240,000.

The average indebtedness of the firm is $170,000, including the mortgage on the building it occupies; the highest indebtedness was $195,000 6 years ago when they bought their building; the lowest was $10,000 when the company was founded. None of the partners personally owns any equipment or other property that the business uses.

According to Charles the company has a strong market position and should command a good price if it was put up for sale. While it is conceivable that some larger firm might be interested in a merger, there is no indication of interest at this time. There is virtually no chance that the company will go public.

Charles and his two partners each expect $42,000 in net taxable income from the partnership this year. The partnership's three full-time key employees are each paid $30,000 annually. In addition, there are three clerical/support employees, each of whom earns $18,000 annually.

Although the partners have agreed among themselves that the remaining partners would want to purchase the interest of any one of them who might become disabled, retire, or die, they have no formal agreement to effect their wishes. In the event of death, disability, or retirement of one partner they have agreed that they would consider selling a one-third interest to a new partner only if the present partners were unable to purchase the interest and only if the "right person" could be found.

When Charles and his partners went into business, it was a fairly informal arrangement that was formalized 10 years ago by a simple partnership agreement under which partners share income and losses in direct proportion to their capital accounts, which are equal. The business has provided attractive extra income for all three partners (a welcome addition to their relatively low beginning salaries at the university). Their partnership arrangement has worked well, and the partners have never seriously considered incorporation before. However, they are looking for ways to use the business to provide themselves with maximum personal financial and tax advantages and have decided that they should look seriously at incorporation. They are wondering how the latest changes in the tax law might affect their decision.

TABLE 2-1
Inventory of Assets

	Cost or Basis	Fair Market Value	Current Return %	Current Return $	Form of Owner- ship*	Available for Liquidity	Collater- alized	Location
Checking accounts	$ 6,000	$ 6,000			JT	Yes	No	First National
Savings accounts	16,000	16,000			JT	Yes	No	First National
Money market funds	9,800	9,800	4.75	$ 760	JT	Yes	No	Safe-deposit box
Life ins. cash value	12,200	12,200	5.25	515	S(H)	Yes	No	Insurance company
Life ins. cash value	5,600	5,600			S(H)	Yes	No	Insurance company
200 shares of Home Products, Inc. (8 years)	4,000	16,000	4	600	S(H)	Yes	No	Safe-deposit box
400 shares of Octane Oil Co. (10 years)	2,000	12,000	5	640	JT	Yes	No	Safe-deposit box
100 shares of Growth Industries, Inc. (3 years)	3,000	6,000	2	300	JT	Yes	No	Safe-deposit box
1,000 shares of Computers Corp. (2 yrs.)	1,800	1,200	1	60	JT	Yes	No	Safe-deposit box
135 shares of Mega Growth Fund (3 years)	1,200	1,800	3	144	JT	Yes	No	Safe-deposit box
Long-term CDs	26,000	26,000	8	2,080	JT	No	No	Safe-deposit box
Pension/return benefits (vested) TDA	0	80,000	10	8,000	S(H)	No	No	Safe-deposit box
Personal residence (7 years)	80,000	150,000	—	—	JT	No	$65,500	
Personal assets household furnishings	25,000	20,000	—	—	JT	No	No	At home
auto (one year)	13,000	8,000	—	—	JT	No	No	At home
jewelry/furs (various dates of purchase)	15,000	28,000	—	—	S(W)	No	No	At home

*JT = joint tenants with right of survivorship; S = single ownership; H= husband; W = wife.

The liabilities of Charles and Barbara Wiggins as they provided them are shown in table 2-2. Charles and Barbara are uncertain about their income tax liability estimates.

In addition, Charles is responsible as a partner for approximately $52,000 of the $155,000 mortgage for the building that houses Systems Design Associates. (As a legal matter, of course, Charles is ultimately responsible for 100 percent of all partnership debts because of his status as a general partner. At present all partnership debts are being paid by the partnership.) Also he and Barbara plan to build a vacation home for which they expect to obligate themselves to a mortgage of not less than $100,000.

Charles and Barbara have provided you with income tax returns for the past 3 years. They have also provided the following data on their current year's income:

Charles	$82,000	(salary from Homestate Tech before TIAA/ CREF deduction)
	42,000	(net taxable income from Systems Design Associates)
Barbara	40,000	(salary from Small City School District)
	10,000	(trust income)

In addition, they expect to receive $1,746 in stock dividends, $515 in interest from money market funds, and $2,840 in interest from savings accounts and CDs. On a jointly filed return for last year they paid approximately $25,000 in federal income tax and $5,000 in state income tax.

Eight percent of Charles's gross salary from the university is deducted each year and contributed to a TIAA/CREF tax-deferred annuity. The university contributes an additional 6 percent dollar for dollar on a tax-deferred basis. One-half of each tax-deferred contribution is presently invested in a fixed-rate fund paying 8 percent, and one-half is invested in a common stock fund. The average combined yield has been about 10 percent annually for the past 3 years. The most recent statement from the plan projects a lifetime monthly benefit of $2,231 on a single life annuity on Charles. Joint and survivor annuities are available. This particular tax-deferred annuity does not permit withdrawals or loans to participants prior to their reaching retirement age. Several settlement options are available, but there is no provision for a participant to elect a lump-sum distribution. Charles has not yet selected a settlement option. Barbara is the named beneficiary of the account.

TABLE 2-2
Statement of Liabilities

Name of Creditor	Original Amount	Maximum Credit Available	Present Balance	Monthly/ Annual Repayment	Interest Rate	Maturity	Secured/ Insured
Various dept. stores and oil companies	—	$10,000	$ 1,000	Pay in full each mo.	18.0	—	No
Credit cards, bank	—	20,000	2,000	Pay in full each mo.	18.4	—	No
Federal income tax (current year projection)	$30,000	—	30,000	—	—	—	—
State income tax (current year projection)	5,400	—	5,400	—	—	—	—
Property taxes	—	—	3,000	—	—	—	—
1st National Bank (home mortgage)	72,000	—	65,500	$530/$6,360	8.0	2023	Secured, no ins.
Child support	—	—	42,000*	$700/$8,400	—	—	Yes

*At $4,200 per year for both Stephanie and Caroline until each reaches 18.

Charles puts his quarterly estimated income tax liability at $2,000. He does not expect any increase in his net income from the partnership unless he devotes significantly more time to its management. At present he has no plans to curtail his teaching duties to devote more time to Systems Design.

Charles and Barbara expect their combined annual income to be $174,000 next year and believe it could approach $190,000 the following year. Charles expects his university salary to increase by 5 percent over the next several years, and Barbara expects salary increases of not less than 4.5 percent annually.

From the income items recorded in their sources of income and their expenditures, you can prepare for Charles and Barbara a cash management (annualized income and expense) statement:

- income items as recorded in sources of income
- expenditures as noted below:

TABLE 2-3 Cash Management Statement		Percent Expected Increase over Next 3 Years
Home mortgage	$ 6,340	0
Clothing and cleaning	3,500	5
Life insurance	2,620	0
Vacations	4,500	5
Household furnishings	3,000	0
Education fund	2,000	0
Food	8,000	5
Utilities, fuel, and telephone	3,500	5
Income taxes (federal and state)	35,000	7
Property taxes	2,500	6
Transportation	1,500	5
Medical/dental/drugs/health insurance	2,480	5
House maintenance/repairs	2,000	5
Property & liability insurance	1,150	5
Recreation/entertainment	3,500	5
Contributions	1,000	5
Savings	1,000	0
Investments	5,000	0
Child support	8,400	0
Total annual expenditures	$96,990	

Although Charles and Barbara have not prepared a recent balance sheet, the data for their financial position statement comes from their inventory of assets and liabilities and from their business interest survey.

When asked to state his preference for or aversion to the various types of savings and investment vehicles below, Charles gave the following ratings from 0 to 5, with 0 representing an aversion and 5 representing a substantial preference:

Savings account	3
Money market fund	4
U.S. government bond	1
Corporate bond	3
Mutual fund (growth)	5
Common stock (growth)	5
Mutual fund (income)	3
Municipal bond	2
Real estate (direct ownership)	4
Variable annuity	2
Limited partnership units (real estate, oil and gas, cattle, equipment leasing)	1
Commodities, gold, collectibles	0

Barbara says she has so little investment experience and so little knowledge of investment vehicles that it would be pointless for her to rate the investments at this time. When asked to respond to a standardized list of personal financial concerns (5 indicating a very strong concern and 0 indicating no concern), Charles responded as follows:

Liquidity	3
Safety of principal	4
Capital appreciation	4
Current income	3
Inflation protection	4
Future income	4
Tax reduction/deferral	5

Barbara responded to the same concerns in the following manner:

Liquidity	4
Safety of principal	4
Capital appreciation	5
Current income	3
Inflation protection	3
Future income	5
Tax reduction/deferral	5

Charles and Barbara have provided you with all their individual life as well as personal property and liability insurance policies for review of policy provisions and cost. In addition, they have provided you with copies of their group insurance certificates. From these you have extracted the following information that is most relevant for financial planning purposes:

- Disability income
    Group policy #: W376701
    Ins. Co.: TIAA/CREF
    Insured: Charles Wiggins
    Owner: Homestate Tech
    Cost and pmt. period: fringe benefit, no employee contribution
    Definition of disability: own occupation, 2 yrs.; thereafter any occupation by virtue of training, education, or experience
    Monthly benefit: for illness or accident, 70 percent of salary, offset by Social Security for employee only
    Waiting period: 6 months (sickness or accident)
    Benefit period: to age 65 (sickness or accident)

    Group policy #: RJ42503
    Ins. Co.: GAMMA
    Insured: Barbara Wiggins
    Owner: Small City School District
    Cost and pmt. period: fringe benefit, no employee contribution
    Definition of disability: own occupation, 2 yrs.; thereafter any occupation by virtue of training, education, or experience
    Monthly benefit: for illness or accident, 70 percent of salary, offset by Social Security for employee only
    Waiting period: 1 year (sickness or accident)
    Benefit period: to age 65 (sickness or accident)

- Uninsured salary continuation plan
    Covered employee: Charles Wiggins
    Cost and pmt. period: fringe benefit, no employee contribution
    Definition of disability: own occupation
    Monthly benefit: 100 percent of salary, offset by any Social Security disability insurance benefits
    Waiting period: none
    Benefit period: 6 months.
    Covered employee: Barbara Wiggins
    Cost and pmt. period: fringe benefit, no employee contribution
    Definition of disability: own occupation
    Monthly benefit: 100 percent of salary for 3 months, 50 percent for next 9 months.

Waiting period: sickness, 7 days; accident, none
Benefit period: 1 year

- Medical expense
    Group policy #: W497321
    Ins. Co.: Blue Cross/Blue Shield
    Insured: Charles Wiggins
    Owner: Homestate Tech
    Cost and pmt. period: noncontributory fringe benefit for Charles; $40 per mo. payroll deduction for family coverage. Coverage for children terminates at 19 (23 if in college).
    Basic hospital: 90 days' coverage in semiprivate accommodations, most hospital extras covered in full
    Surgical: prevailing fee schedule
    Major medical: $200 deductible per person, 80/20 percentage participation, up to $10,000 of covered expense annually, lifetime maximum of $500,000 per person

- Life insurance
    Policy #: W216546
    Ins. Co.: AJAX
    Issue age: 25
    Insured: Charles F. Wiggins
    Owner: Charles F. Wiggins
    Type of policy: whole life, nonparticipating
    Cost and pmt. period: $720/annual
    Cash value: $5,600
    Extra benefits: waiver of premium, accidental death
    Amount of base policy: $50,000
    Net amount payable at death: $50,000 ($100,000 for accidental death)
    Beneficiaries and settlement options: first to Caroline and Stephanie Wiggins—lump sum; second to Barbara Wiggins—lump sum

    Group policy #: W927354
    Ins. Co.: TIAA
    Issue age: 28
    Insured: Charles F. Wiggins
    Owner: Homestate Tech
    Type of policy: term
    Cost and pmt. period: fringe benefit, no employee contribution
    Extra benefits: waiver of premium, accidental death and dismemberment
    Amount of base policy: $52,000 (equivalent to annual salary)

Net amount payable at death: $52,000 ($104,000 for accidental death)

Beneficiaries and settlement options: first to Barbara Wiggins—lump sum; second to Charles F. Wiggins, Jr.—lump sum

Policy #: W327621
Ins. Co.: ALPHA
Issue age: 29
Insured: Charles F. Wiggins
Owner: Charles F. Wiggins
Type of policy: whole life, nonparticipating
Cost and pmt. period: $1,900/annual
Cash value: $12,200
Amount of base policy: $100,000
Extra benefits: policy waiver of premium
Net amount payable at death: $100,000
Beneficiaries and settlement options: first to Stephanie and Caroline (to assure support to age of majority)—lump sum; second to Barbara Wiggins—lump sum

Group policy #: W541839
Ins. Co.: GAMMA
Issue age: 28
Insured: Barbara Wiggins
Owner: Small City School District
Type of policy: term
Cost and pmt. period: fringe benefit, no employee contribution
Extra benefits: waiver of premium, accidental death and dismemberment
Amount of base policy: $20,000
Net amount. payable at death: $20,000 ($40,000 for accidental death)
Beneficiaries and settlement options: first to Charles F. Wiggins—lump sum; second to Charles F. Wiggins, Jr.—lump sum

- Property and liability insurance
  Property insurance
  Policy #: W726495
  Ins. Co.: DELTA
  Address of property: 421 Briarcliff, Small City
  HO Form #: 3
  Coverage limits: dwelling, $125,000; personal property, $62,500; additional living expense, $25,000
  Deductible: $200 (for property coverage)

Cost and pmt. period: $500/annual
Liability included in homeowners: $25,000

- Automobile insurance
    Policy #: W526837
    Ins. Co.: EAGLE
    Automobile: 1996 Buick
    ID #: 464391 BUOY
    Named insured: Charles F. and Barbara Wiggins
    Bodily injury: $100,000/$300,000
    Property damage: $25,000
    No-fault benefits: unlimited medical payments; disability benefits
        up to $1,000 per month
    Uninsured motorist: $10,000/$20,000
    Collision deductible: $250
    Comprehensive deductible: $50
    Cost and pmt. period: $650/annual

- Home insurance
    Policy HO-3 #: 264185
    Ins. Co.: Eagle
    Named insured: Charles F. and Barbara Wiggins
    Dwelling: $120,000
    Liability: $300,000
    Inflation Guardian Endorsement
    Cost: $375/annual

- Umbrella
    Policy #: 198463
    Ins. Co.: Eagle
    Named insured: Charles F. and Barbara Wiggins
    Limit: $1 million
    Self-insured retention: $250
    Premium: $175

Charles has provided some information on the insurance policies of the partnership. While he has been involved in decisions concerning their purchase, this aspect of the partnership's affairs is handled primarily by Steve Thomas. Charles does know that the partnership carries errors and omissions coverage and fire insurance on its building as well as workers' compensation and general liability insurance. In addition, employees of the partnership are provided with a comprehensive plan of group medical expense insurance and $10,000 of group term life insurance. Both plans are noncontributory except for dependent medical expense coverage. Because contributions for the coverage of partners are not tax deductible and because they have employee benefits at their university jobs, the partners are not covered under these plans. Recently two of Systems Design's key employees have discussed with the partners their concerns about having no company retirement plan.

For their needs (in current dollars) in the event of disability, retirement, or the death of either of them, Barbara and Charles have concluded that in the event of Charles's disability they would need a monthly income of $9,500, and in the event of Barbara's $3,000 monthly. For Charles's retirement Charles and Barbara would need $9,000 per month. In the event of his premature death Charles estimates that his survivors would need $10,000 per month during an adjustment period of approximately one year, then $9,000 per month for another 14 years (or until Charles, Jr., is 22 years old), then $7,500 per month. Charles and Barbara estimate that in the event of her death he would need $3,000 per month of extra income for the full 15 years until Charles, Jr., is 22 years old and presumably self-supporting.

If Charles should become disabled or retire, his major medical and other health insurance can be continued, and his survivors can also convert these policies in the event of his death.

As noted earlier, all resource items shown below are in current pretax dollars. The final amount of several items depends on interest rate, dividend assumptions, and current levels in benefits from government programs such as Social Security, which may or may not be accurate at the time disability, retirement, or death actually occurs. (This is one of the main reasons why client financial plans must continuously be reviewed and updated.) For the purposes of this exercise all calculations for death and disability income resources assume that the specified contingency will happen tomorrow. In computing resources for retirement the accumulation amount in the qualified plan (TDA) to which ascertainable contributions are being made by a solvent employer has been projected to normal retirement age (65) to establish what amount in current dollars would be available monthly over the actuarial life expectancy of the client. Other resource items such as Social Security benefits, spousal earnings, and present investment returns have been listed at current levels.

In the event of disability Charles Wiggins could rely on the following resources:

<u>Monthly income</u>

Social Security	$1,738
Group disability income insurance	1,876
Continuing income from investments including spouse's trust income	1,258
Earnings of spouse	3,333
Total income	$8,205

If Charles retires at age 65, he can rely on the following resources:

Monthly income

Social Security benefits	$ 1,249
Pension plan (TDA)	2,708[1]
Continuing income from investments including spouse's trust income	1,258
Earnings of spouse	3,333
Total monthly income	$8,548

If he dies tomorrow, Charles's family can rely on the following resources:

Monthly income

Social Security benefits	$2,080[2]
Pension plan (TDA)	400[3]
Continuing income from investments including spouse's trust income	1,258
Earnings of spouse	3,333
Interest earnings on group term life insurance proceeds payable to spouse	260[3]
Total monthly income	$7,331

Lump-sum payments

Social Security	$ 255
Group life insurance	52,000
Personal life insurance	150,000[4]
Total	$202,255

---

1. Assumes total contributions at 14 percent of salary through 2006, level contributions of $8,508 from 2002 through retirement at age 65, and inflation-adjusted rates of return of 4.5 percent to date of retirement and 3 percent thereafter. Also assumes that principal and interest are liquidated over a life expectancy for Charles of 99 years.
2. In the event of death the maximum family benefit from Social Security for a typical wage earner at Charles's salary level and age is projected at $2,080. Assuming that both Barbara and Cynthia, Charles's former wife, continue to work, this maximum benefit would be allocated equally to the three surviving children.
3. Interest only—assumes 6 percent rate of return.
4. Of which $100,000 is payable to Stephanie and Caroline.

PRELIMINARY OUTLINE
[Suggested Solution]

I. Client's objectives

    A. For lifetime planning
        1. Fund college education for children.
        2. Reduce tax burden.
        3. Explore more efficient utilization of interest in Systems Design.
        4. Build vacation home.
        5. Assure comfortable retirement.

    B. For dispositions at death
        1. Provide for sale of business interest.
        2. Assure sufficient assets in estate to provide for Barbara and minor children in the event of Charles's premature death.
        3. Use estate assets to provide first for Barbara and any minor children; distribute assets remaining at Barbara's death equally among children.

II. Business planning

    A. Tax planning
        1. Present position
        2. Choosing the appropriate business form
            a. Proprietorship
            b. Partnership
            c. S corporation
            d. C corporation
            e. Limited liability corporation
            f. Recommendations
        3. Incorporation feasibility
            a. Legal requirements for incorporation
                • Professional corporations
            b. Tax implications of incorporation
                • Transfers of partnership interest to corporation in tax-free exchange (Sec. 351)
                • Taking advantage of Sec. 1244 stock
            c. Legal benefits of doing business as a corporation
            d. Tax benefits of doing business as a corporation
                • Reasonable compensation for shareholder-employees
                • Employment contracts
                • Qualified plans of deferred compensation
                • Borrowing from qualified plans
                • Group medical, disability, and life insurance plans
                • Personal use of company assets

- Employment of family members
- Buy-sell agreements to assure that the business interest is marketable in the event of death or disability

B. Insurance planning
1. Funding the buy-sell agreements
2. Selecting appropriate products and coverage amounts for group medical, disability, and life insurance plans
3. Nondiscrimination requirements
4. Selecting appropriate products and coverage amounts of property and liability insurance for the business

III. Personal planning

A. Tax planning
1. Present position
2. Fund college education for children
   a. Outright gifts
   b. UGMA and UTMA gifts
   c. 2503(b) trusts
   d. 2503(c) trusts
   e. Education IRAs (education savings accounts)
   f. Section 529 plans
   g. Family partnership
   h. Employment opportunities at Systems Design
   i. S corporation shares
   j. Borrowing from qualified plans
   k. Using Charles's university fringe benefit for free tuition
   l. Other considerations
   m. Using Barbara's trust distribution for payment
3. Assure adequate protection in case of disability
   a. Personal disability coverage
   b. Disability coverage provided by Systems Design after incorporation
4. Reduce tax burden
   a. Achieve personal objectives through income-splitting devices to reduce cost.
   b. Defer tax liability on portion of income from Systems Design through use of qualified plans.
   c. Structure future purchases (for example, vacation home) to maximize tax benefits.
5. Build vacation home—structure purchase agreements for use of maximum leverage consistent with available cash flow.
6. Assure comfortable retirement
   a. Continue TDA participation.

       b. Utilize qualified plans in Systems Design when incorporated.
  7. Dispositions at death—analysis of present estate plans
       a. Present plans do not carry out client's expressed wishes—explore differences with client.
       b. Review provisions for guardianship of Charles, Jr.
       c. QTIP trust
       d. Life insurance placement results in inclusion in gross estate for estate tax purposes; consider repositioning into life insurance trust(s) and naming the trustee as beneficiary of the life insurance policy proceeds, allowing the terms of the trust instrument to control distribution—a more flexible arrangement.

B. Insurance planning
  1. Recheck ownership, beneficiary designations, amounts of current life insurance, and available products against demonstrated needs after tax planning is completed.
  2. Recheck disability needs after tax planning is completed.
  3. Review other insurance coverage to assure adequacy of protection and cost effectiveness.

C. Investment planning
  1. Investment overview
       a. Characteristics of meaningful financial objectives
       b. Reasons for wealth accumulation
          • Emergency reserve fund
          • Retirement
          • Education funding
          • Other specified purposes
          • General wealth accumulation
       c. Sources of investment risk
       d. Risk and return
          • Investor attitudes
          • Investment products
  2. Client analysis
       a. Financial objectives
       b. Current position
       c. Funding for children's education
          • Determination of needs
          • Investment alternatives and selection
          • Funding vehicles
          • Recommendations
       d. Vacation home

    e.   Retirement funding
    f.   General wealth accumulation
    g.   Portfolio recommendations

INSTRUCTIONS

The next step in the planning process is to eliminate those alternatives that at this time appear clearly inappropriate to the client's situation and to further refine the plan outline, retaining those alternatives and techniques that require further investigation. In this regard review the suggested preliminary outline at this time and bracket or strike those items that are inappropriate for the Wiggins family situation. When this has been done, compare the result with the working outline that follows.

WORKING OUTLINE
[Suggested Solution]

I.   Client's objectives

A.   For lifetime planning
     1.   Fund college education for children.
     2.   Reduce tax burden.
     3.   Explore more efficient utilization of interest in Systems Design.
     4.   Build vacation home.
     5.   Assure comfortable retirement.

B.   For dispositions at death
     1.   Provide for sale of business interest.
     2.   Assure sufficient assets in estate to provide for Barbara and minor children in the event of Charles's premature death.
     3.   Use estate assets to provide first for Barbara and any minor children; distribute assets remaining at Barbara's death equally among children.

II. Business planning

A.   Tax planning
     1.   Present position
     2.   Choosing the appropriate business form
          a.   Proprietorship [The proprietorship is inappropriate on these facts because there is no expressed interest in Charles's leaving his colleagues. A proprietorship involves exclusive ownership.]
          b.   Partnership
          c.   S corporation
          d.   C corporation
          e.   Limited liability company
          f.   Recommendations
     3.   Incorporation feasibility
          a.   Legal requirements for incorporation
               •   Professional corporations
          b.   Tax implications of incorporation
               •   Transfers of partnership interest to corporation in tax-free exchange (Sec. 351)
               •   Taking advantage of Sec. 1244 stock
          c.   Legal benefits of doing business as a corporation
          d.   Tax benefits of doing business as a corporation
               •   Reasonable compensation for shareholder-employees

- Employment contracts
- Qualified plans of deferred compensation
- Borrowing from qualified plans
- Group medical, disability, and life insurance plans
- Personal use of company assets
- Employment of family members
- Buy-sell agreements to assure that the business interest is marketable in the event of death or disability

B. Insurance planning
1. Funding the buy-sell agreements
2. Selecting appropriate products and coverage amounts for group medical, disability, and life insurance plans
3. Nondiscrimination requirements
4. Selecting appropriate products and coverage amounts of property and liability insurance for the business

III. Personal planning

A. Tax planning
1. Present position
2. Fund college education for children
   a. Outright gifts
   b. UGMA and UTMA gifts
   c. 2503(b) trusts
   d. 2503(c) trusts
   e. Education IRAs (education savings accounts)
   f. Section 529 plans
   g. Family partnership [The Wigginses' assets are not appropriate for this vehicle at this time. Family partnerships with partners who are minors generally require that capital be a material income-producing factor to be fully effective.]
   h. Employment opportunities at Systems Design
   i. S corporation shares
   j. Borrowing from qualified plans
   k. Using Charles's university fringe benefit for free tuition
   l. Other considerations
   m. Using Barbara's trust distribution for payment
3. Assure adequate protection in case of disability
   a. Personal disability coverage
   b. Disability coverage provided by Systems Design after incorporation
4. Reduce tax burden
   a. Achieve personal objectives through income-splitting devices to reduce cost

       b. Defer tax liability on portion of income from Systems Design through use of qualified plans

       c. Structure future purchases (for example, vacation home) to maximize tax benefits

5. Build vacation home—structure purchase agreements for use of maximum leverage consistent with available cash flow

6. Assure comfortable retirement

       a. Continue TDA participation.

       b. Utilize qualified plans in Systems Design when incorporated.

7. Dispositions at death—analysis of present estate plans

       a. Present plans do not carry out client's expressed wishes—explore differences with client.

       b. Review provisions for guardianship of Charles, Jr.

       c. QTIP trust [A QTIP trust is not necessary based on the facts and circumstances of the Wigginses' case. A credit bypass residuary trust provides sufficient control without being subject to taxation in Barbara's estate.]

       d. Life insurance placement results in inclusion in gross estate for estate tax purposes; consider repositioning into life insurance trust(s) and naming the trustee as beneficiary of the life insurance policy proceeds, allowing the terms of the trust instrument to control distribution—a more flexible arrangement.

B. Insurance planning

  1. Recheck ownership, beneficiary designations, amounts of current life insurance, and available products against demonstrated needs after tax planning is completed.

  2. Recheck disability needs after tax planning is completed.

  3. Review other insurance coverage to assure adequacy of protection and cost effectiveness.

C. Investment planning

  1. Investment overview

       a. Characteristics of meaningful financial objectives

       b. Reasons for wealth accumulation

- Emergency reserve fund
- Retirement
- Education funding
- Other specified purposes
- General wealth accumulation

       c. Sources of investment risk

       d. Risk and return

- Investor attitudes
- Investment products

2. Client analysis
    a. Financial objectives
    b. Current position
    c. Funding for children's education
        •   Determination of needs
        •   Investment alternatives and selection
        •   Funding vehicle
        •   Recommendations
    d. Vacation home
    e. Retirement funding
    f. General wealth accumulation
    g. Portfolio recommendations

3

Preparing a Financial Plan for the Wiggins Family

Chapter Outline

Portfolio and Funding Recommendations   3.125

In chapter 2 you were introduced to the Wiggins family, given the information necessary to complete a financial plan for them, and asked to condense this information for planning purposes into a preliminary outline and then into a working outline. As in actual cases, you will note that there are some contradictions or inconsistencies in the information provided by the clients. Some resolution of these issues must be made before the clients' plan can be developed.

The primary contradictions occur in the area of property dispositions at death. For purposes of preparing the Wigginses' financial plan you may assume that, as in actual cases, further conversations with Charles and Barbara were necessary and that the result of those conversations was that Charles wishes his estate to be disposed of to take care of Barbara and his children as long as the children are minors. However, if the children are adults at the time of his death, he wants his assets distributed to take care of Barbara first and then his children. At Barbara's death any of his remaining assets should be divided equally among his children.

Barbara's trust distributions from her grandparents and her anticipated inheritance from her parents present another difficult issue. In some families with children from prior marriages, there would be little possibility of these children inheriting from a stepparent. However, in the Wiggins case no such animosity exists and Barbara is genuinely fond of her stepdaughters. As a result, this issue may be an even more complicated and delicate one. If Barbara feels that the funds she will inherit from her family should go to Charles, Jr., alone, will this create a problem with Charles in their marriage, or will it alienate her stepdaughters should that fact become known, as it ultimately must? On the other hand, if she decides that she is content to share her inheritance with Charles's daughters, will she be in conflict with her parents over the decision? Could that conflict be so significant that it irreparably damages their relationship and Barbara even ceases to be a beneficiary under their wills? The answer to both questions could be yes.

It is likely on the facts of this case that a compromise could be reached. Let us assume that Barbara has no objection to income or principal distributions from the trust of which she is a present beneficiary being used and invested in family endeavors and that she also has no objection to this amount's being ultimately shared with Charles's daughters, but she feels that the bulk of the remainder of her inheritance from her family should go to Charles, Jr., as that is what her parents would wish. When developing planning recommendations in this area, one must consider options that will not only effect these results but that also attempt to minimize confrontations among members of the families involved.

A further issue must be resolved in order to ensure that an effective estate plan can be implemented with appropriate documents according to Charles's wishes. That issue is the fact that most of Charles and Barbara's assets are being held as joint tenants with right of survivorship. As long as this is true, a will cannot control the disposition of such property. In fact, although Charles's current will provides that one-half of his assets are to go directly to his daughters, in reality they will take only one-half of the assets he owns in his own name, excluding the TDA account for which Barbara is the named beneficiary. All other items, except the life insurance of which they are the named beneficiaries, will pass directly to Barbara by operation of law. If these assets were to pass later under the terms of her current will, they would all pass to Charles, Jr.

A discussion of the various forms of property ownership is an appropriate subject for the final plan. However, one should not overlook the emotional issues that may be attached to property that is jointly held. For purposes of the Wiggins plan, let us assume that there is no underlying emotional basis to any form of property ownership on the part of either Charles or Barbara, although both feel that Barbara should own some assets because she contributes financially to the family through her employment.

PERSONAL FINANCIAL PLAN
FOR
CHARLES AND BARBARA WIGGINS
[Suggested Solution]

INSTRUCTIONS

After a review of the Wiggins case narrative and the working outline, develop a written financial plan that could be presented to Charles and Barbara Wiggins. The plan should explain the problems, the available techniques, the technical requirements for each technique, and the strengths and weaknesses of each technique in terms of achieving the Wiggins family's objectives; the plan should then make a recommendation that seems best suited to meet the needs of the Wiggins family as they have expressed them. Once the planning solution has been formulated, it can be compared to the following completed financial plan that coordinates and integrates these considerations for the Wiggins family. (Keep in mind that, for learning purposes, the material that follows is more lengthy and detailed than most plans would usually be.)

Note that a good deal of financial information has been omitted from the details of the partnership operation to facilitate the handling of this early case. Suggested recommendations will essentially be restricted to those that can be made on the information that has been given.

One word of warning: whenever there are multiple business owners, the financial planner runs the risk that advice given to one owner will be adverse to the interests of the others. In this case assume that the partners are harmonious and that advice given to Charles will also be beneficial to them. This is not an assumption that you can make in actual practice, so be especially careful to make it clear to the client that you represent only him or her and not the client's business associates. At the same time any advice that will have an adverse effect on business associates should be disclosed to the client, so that any decisions can be based on knowledge of all the consequences. Business associates, especially those in closely held businesses, are frequently longtime friends with strong social relationships.

CLIENTS' OBJECTIVES

A. For lifetime planning
   1. Fund college education for children.
   2. Reduce tax burden.
   3. Explore more efficient utilization of interest in Systems Design.
   4. Build a vacation home.
   5. Assure comfortable retirement.

B. For disposition at death
   1. Provide for sale of the business interest.
   2. Assure sufficient assets in the estate to provide for Barbara and the children in the event of Charles's premature death.
   3. Use estate assets to provide first for Barbara and any minor children; distribute assets remaining at Barbara's death equally among the children.

BUSINESS PLANNING: TAXES

Present Position

Charles and two of his colleagues from Homestate Tech began the business of Systems Design Associates in a very informal manner. Apparently, from a tax perspective, the business functioned as a partnership from its inception; that is, the three owners were engaged in a business venture other than a trust, estate, or corporation from which they shared profits (IRC Sec. 7701(a)(2)). For tax purposes this type of business entity is treated as a partnership, regardless of whether there is a partnership agreement. In fact, partnership agreements need not even be written but may be oral agreements between the parties or even implied from the way in which the business is carried on. In the Wiggins case the partnership was formalized by a written partnership agreement, although a simple one, a few years later. Written partnership agreements should always be utilized, since the terms of oral agreements are quite difficult to interpret or even to prove if the partners disagree.

The business has obviously prospered over the years, as can be seen by the amount of income it produces for the various partners and the number of people it employs. There are three partners, three other full-time key employees, and three part-time employees to carry on the day-to-day clerical tasks, customer service, and other duties. After paying for partnership expenses, including the mortgage and normal trade accounts, and supporting a payroll for six people other than the partners, as well as producing net taxable income of $42,000 per year per partner, the business does, in fact, enjoy a strong market position, as Charles has indicated. It also has substantial billings, almost certainly in the mid-to-high 6 figures per year.

In short, the business has provided substantial amounts of cash-flow income to the partners, considering that each devotes only a portion of his or her time to its success. Since Charles has indicated that he is not inclined to curtail his teaching duties at Homestate Tech in order to expand Systems Design Associates, the problem here is not how to make the business more successful but how to make the business interest as efficient a mechanism as possible for providing tax and other benefits that will further the personal objectives of Charles Wiggins and his family.

An illustration demonstrating 5-year projections of the Wigginses' tax, net worth, and cash-flow situation prior to the implementation of any planning recommendations follows.

It is important to remember that these projections are computer produced and illustrative only, and that there is not necessarily an expectation that these results will be duplicated.

[text continues on page 3.18]

BASE CASE

Assumptions

1. The checking account balance is maintained at approximately $6,000 and is noninterest bearing.

2. The savings account balance of $16,000 at the end of last year earns 4.75 percent interest annually. Interest is allowed to accumulate in the account.

3. The $26,000 in CDs earns 8 percent annually, and the CDs mature in December 2006.

4. The money market account pays 5.25 percent annually, and interest is accumulated in the account.

5. The Home Products stock, worth $16,000 at the end of last year, is expected to grow in value at 5 percent annually, and the dividend yield is 4 percent.

6. The Octane Oil stock with a year-end value of $12,000 is expected to appreciate at 6 percent annually, while yielding a 5 percent dividend.

7. The Growth Industries stock with a year-end value of $6,000 is expected to appreciate at 6 percent and yield 2 percent annually in dividends.

8. The Computers Corporation stock with a year-end value of $1,200 is not appreciating in value and is yielding one percent per year in dividends.

9. The Mega Fund shares with a year-end value of $1,800 are expected to increase in value at 8 percent per year and yield 3 percent.

10. The value of the personal residence ($150,000) will increase at 10 percent annually. The residence was purchased in January 1994. The original amount of the mortgage was $72,000 at an interest rate of 8 percent for 30 years.

11. The summer home will be purchased or constructed by May 2005 for $120,000. The down payment will be $12,000, and a $108,000 30-year mortgage at 8.5 percent will provide the remainder of the financing. The summer home will increase in value 5 percent annually. Property taxes for the vacation home are expected to be $400 per year.

12. The household furnishings will neither increase nor decrease in value.

13. Automobiles decrease in value at a rate of 15 percent per year.

14. Property taxes and maintenance costs on both the vacation home and the personal residence are expected to increase at 6 percent annually.

15. Charles's university salary is expected to increase 5 percent annually. Barbara's salary is expected to increase 4.5 percent annually.

16. The level of net taxable income from Systems Design Associates is set at $42,000 and will not increase over the 5-year period.

17. The value of Charles's partnership interest will increase 2.5 percent annually.

18. Contributions to Charles's TDA account will continue at 8 percent of his salary until 2007 and will not increase after that date.

19. Seventy-five percent of Charles's TDA contribution will be matched by the university, and the combined amount will earn 10 percent annually over the next 5 years.

20. Present expenditures for clothing, vacations, food, utilities, transportation, medical care, entertainment, property and liability insurance, and charitable contributions are projected to increase annually at the rate of 5 percent.

21. Investable cash earns 5.25 percent annually.

INCOME STATEMENT

CHARLES & BARBARA WIGGINS

BASE CASE	2002	2003	2004	2005	2006
Earned Income					
Salary - Charles	82,000	86,100	90,405	94,925	99,672
Partnership Income	42,000	42,000	42,000	42,000	42,000
Salary - Barbara	40,000	41,800	43,681	45,647	47,701
TDA-Charles Contrib	-6,560	-7,085	-7,652	-8,264	-8,925
	157,440	162,815	168,434	174,308	180,447
Interest/Dividends					
Cert Of Deposits	2,080	2,080	2,080	1,680	1,280
Home Products stock	672	699	727	756	786
Octane Oil Stock	636	668	701	736	773
Growth Indust Stock	120	122	125	127	130
Computer Corp Stock	12	12	12	12	12
Mega Fund Shares	58	60	62	63	65
Investable Cash	1,677	5,139	8,828	12,260	15,494
Saving/NOW Acts	760	796	834	874	915
Money Market Fund	515	542	570	600	631
	6,530	10,118	13,939	17,109	20,087
Other					
TrustIncome-Barbara	10,000	10,000	10,000	10,000	10,000
	10,000	10,000	10,000	10,000	10,000
Adjustments					
S.E. Tax Dedctn	563	563	563	563	563
	563	563	563	563	563
	========	========	========	========	========
Adj Gross Income	173,407	182,370	191,810	200,854	209,971
Deductions					
Charitable 50%	1,000	1,050	1,103	1,158	1,216
State Tax Paid	8,382	8,892	9,380	9,180	9,323
Property Tax - Home	2,500	2,650	2,809	2,978	3,156
PropertyTax-VacHome	0	0	0	400	424
Mortgage - Home	5,202	5,107	5,005	4,894	4,774
Vacation Home	0	0	0	6,106	9,102
Mortgage - Vac Home	0	0	0	6,106	9,102
Reductn for High Inc	-1,214	-1,379	-1,556	-1,718	-1,252
Gross Deductions	15,870	16,320	16,741	29,104	35,845
Standard Deduction	7,600	7,800	8,000	8,526	9,292
Allowed Deductions	15,870	16,320	16,741	29,104	35,845
Pers Exemptions	14,500	14,750	15,250	15,750	10,453
	========	========	========	========	========
Taxable Income	143,037	151,300	159,819	156,001	163,673
	========	========	========	========	========
Fed Income Tax	34,513	36,759	38,988	39,017	40,053
	========	========	========	========	========
Fed Tax Bracket-Ord Inc	30.0%	30.0%	29.0%	29.0%	28.0%

BALANCE SHEET

CHARLES & BARBARA WIGGINS

BASE CASE	2002	2003	2004	2005	2006
LIQUID ASSETS					
Cash Balance	6,005	6,038	6,002	6,061	6,075
Cash Deposits					
Investable Cash	65,571	135,335	209,802	269,509	336,226
Saving/NOW Acts	16,760	17,556	18,390	19,264	20,179
Cert Of Deposits	26,000	26,000	26,000	16,000	16,000
Money Market Fund	10,315	10,857	11,427	12,027	12,658
	118,646	189,748	265,619	316,800	385,063
Stocks & Bonds					
Home Products stock	16,800	17,640	18,522	19,448	20,421
Octane Oil Stock	12,720	13,483	14,292	15,150	16,059
Growth Indust Stock	6,360	6,742	7,146	7,575	8,029
Computer Corp Stock	1,200	1,200	1,200	1,200	1,200
Mega Fund Shares	1,944	2,100	2,267	2,449	2,645
	39,024	41,164	43,428	45,822	48,353
Life Insurance					
Life Ins-Charles #1	12,200	12,200	12,200	12,200	12,200
Life Ins-Charles #2	5,600	5,600	5,600	5,600	5,600
	17,800	17,800	17,800	17,800	17,800
	========	========	========	========	========
Liquid Assets	181,475	254,750	332,849	386,483	457,291
	========	========	========	========	========
NONLIQUID ASSETS					
Bus Interests					
Partnershp Interest	175,000	179,375	183,859	188,456	193,167
	175,000	179,375	183,859	188,456	193,167
Retirement Plans					
TDA-Charles Contrib	6,560	13,645	21,297	29,561	38,486
TDA-Employr Contrib	3,120	6,396	9,836	13,448	17,240
TDA Fund-Contrb+Int	88,000	96,800	106,480	117,128	128,841
	97,680	116,841	137,613	160,137	184,567
Personal Property					
Home	165,000	181,500	199,650	219,615	241,577
Vacation Home	0	0	0	120,000	126,000
Auto	6,800	5,780	4,913	4,176	3,550
Home Furnishings	20,000	20,000	20,000	20,000	20,000
Jewelry & Furs	28,000	28,000	28,000	28,000	28,000
	219,800	235,280	252,563	391,791	419,126
	========	========	========	========	========
Nonliquid Assets	492,480	531,496	574,035	740,384	796,861
	========	========	========	========	========
Total Assets	673,955	786,246	906,884	1,126,867	1,254,152

BALANCE SHEET (cont.)

CHARLES & BARBARA WIGGINS

BASE CASE	2002	2003	2004	2005	2006
LIABILITIES					
Mortgage Loans					
Mortgage - Home	64,395	63,162	61,827	60,381	58,815
Vacation Home	0	0	0	107,463	106,600
Mortgage - Vac Home	0	0	0	107,463	106,600
	64,395	63,162	61,827	275,307	272,015
	========	========	========	========	========
Total Liabilities	64,395	63,162	61,827	275,307	272,015
	========	========	========	========	========
Net Worth	609,560	723,084	845,057	851,560	982,137
	========	========	========	========	========

CASH FLOW STATEMENT

CHARLES & BARBARA WIGGINS

	2002	2003	2004	2005	2006
BASE CASE					
BEGINNING OF YEAR					
Idle Cash On Hand	6,000	6,005	6,038	6,002	6,061
SOURCES OF CASH					
Cash Income					
Salary - Charles	82,000	86,100	90,405	94,925	99,672
Partnership Income	42,000	42,000	42,000	42,000	42,000
Salary - Barbara	40,000	41,800	43,681	45,647	47,701
Interest+Dividends	3,578	3,641	3,707	3,375	3,047
TrustIncome-Barbara	10,000	10,000	10,000	10,000	10,000
	177,578	183,541	189,793	195,947	202,419
Sale/Withdrawals					
Cert Of Deposits	0	0	0	10,000	0
	0	0	0	10,000	0
Liab Incurred					
Cash Borwd-Vac Home	0	0	0	108,000	0
	0	0	0	108,000	0
Total Cash Inflow	177,578	183,541	189,793	313,947	202,419
Tot Cash Available	183,578	189,546	195,831	319,949	208,480
USES OF CASH					
Fully Tax Deductible					
TDA-Charles Contrib	6,560	7,085	7,652	8,264	8,925
Mortgage - Home	5,202	5,107	5,005	4,894	4,774
Vacation Home	0	0	0	6,106	9,102
Mortgage - Vac Home	0	0	0	6,106	9,102
	11,762	12,192	12,657	25,370	31,903
Partly Deductible					
Medical Care	2,480	2,604	2,734	2,871	3,014
Charity Contrb-50%	1,000	1,050	1,103	1,158	1,216
	3,480	3,654	3,837	4,029	4,230
Not Tax Deductible					
Education Fund	2,000	2,000	2,000	2,000	2,000
Child Support	8,400	8,400	8,400	8,400	8,400
Food	8,000	8,400	8,820	9,261	9,724
Clothing	3,500	3,675	3,859	4,052	4,254
Entertainment	3,500	3,675	3,859	4,052	4,254
Vacations	4,500	4,725	4,961	5,209	5,470
Transportation	1,500	1,575	1,654	1,736	1,823

CASH FLOW STATEMENT (cont.)

CHARLES & BARBARA WIGGINS

BASE CASE	2002	2003	2004	2005	2006
Life Ins Prem Pymnt	2,620	2,620	2,620	2,620	2,620
Prop Ins Prem Pymnt	1,150	1,208	1,268	1,331	1,398
Maint--Home/VacHome	2,000	2,120	2,247	2,382	2,525
Utility/Phone	3,500	3,675	3,859	4,052	4,254
New Furniture	2,000	2,000	2,000	2,000	2,000
ClosingCost-VacHome	0	0	0	6,000	0
	42,670	44,073	45,546	53,095	48,723
Taxes Paid					
Fed Tax Paid	34,513	36,759	38,988	39,017	40,053
State Tax Paid	8,382	8,892	9,380	9,180	9,323
FICA/Soc Sec Tax	9,234	9,431	9,638	9,853	10,079
Real Estate Tax	2,500	2,650	2,809	3,378	3,580
	54,629	57,732	60,815	61,428	63,035
Purchase/Deposits					
Purchase Vac Home	0	0	0	120,000	0
Investable Cash	63,894	64,625	65,639	47,447	51,223
	63,894	64,625	65,639	167,447	51,223
Liability Liquidation					
Mortgage - Home	1,138	1,233	1,335	1,446	1,566
Vacation Home	0	0	0	537	863
Mortgage - Vac Home	0	0	0	537	863
	1,138	1,233	1,335	2,520	3,292
	========	========	========	========	========
Tot Cash Outflow	177,573	183,508	189,829	313,888	202,406
	========	========	========	========	========
END OF YEAR					
Cash Balance	6,005	6,038	6,002	6,061	6,075
	========	========	========	========	========

SUPPORTING SCHEDULE

CHARLES & BARBARA WIGGINS

	JOINT 2002	JOINT 2003	JOINT 2004	JOINT 2005	JOINT 2006
BASE CASE					
Income					
Earned Income	157,440	162,815	168,434	174,308	180,447
Adj Gross Income	173,407	182,370	191,810	200,854	209,971
Allowed Deductions	15,870	16,320	16,741	29,104	35,845
Pers Exemptions	14,500	14,750	15,250	15,750	10,453
Taxable Income	143,037	151,300	159,819	156,001	163,673
Federal Tax Liab					
Regular Tax	33,388	35,634	36,840	35,503	36,367
Gross Fed Inc Tax	33,388	35,634	36,840	35,503	36,367
Alt Minimum Tax	0	0	1,023	2,389	2,561
AMT Credit C/Over	0	0	0	0	1,023
Disallowed	0	0	0	-1,023	-3,412
Self Employmt Tax	1,125	1,125	1,125	1,125	1,125
Fed Income Tax	34,513	36,759	38,988	39,017	40,053
Fed Tax Analysis-Ord Inc					
Indexing Factor	77	82	87	91	96
Fed Tax Bracket-Ord Inc	30.0%	30.0%	29.0%	29.0%	28.0%
$ to Next Bracket	27,763	23,950	19,981	28,499	25,627
Next Bracket	35.0%	35.0%	34.0%	34.0%	33.0%
Previous Bracket	27.0%	27.0%	26.0%	26.0%	25.0%
$ to Prev Bracket	30,987	36,300	41,819	34,951	39,473
Fed Effective Tax Rate	24.1%	24.3%	24.4%	25.0%	24.5%
Alt Minimum Tax					
Adj Gross Income	173,407	182,370	191,810	200,854	209,971
Contributions	-1,000	-1,050	-1,103	-1,158	-1,216
Home Mortg Int	-5,202	-5,107	-5,005	-17,106	-22,978
Adjusted AMTI	167,205	176,213	185,702	182,590	185,777
AMT Exemptions	-44,699	-42,447	-40,074	-36,852	-36,056
AMT Taxable Inc	122,506	133,766	145,628	145,738	149,722
Gross Alt Min Tx	31,852	34,779	37,863	37,892	38,928
Fed Tax Less FTC	-33,388	-35,634	-36,840	-35,503	-36,367
Alt Minimum Tax	0	0	1,023	2,389	2,561
Other Tax Liabs					
FICA/Soc Sec Tax	9,234	9,431	9,638	9,853	10,079
Adj Gross Inc	173,407	182,370	191,810	200,854	209,971
GA Adj Gross Inc	173,407	182,370	191,810	200,854	209,971
GA Standard Ded	3,000	3,000	3,000	3,000	3,000
GA Itemized Ded	15,870	16,320	16,741	29,104	35,845
GA Exemptions	13,500	13,500	14,400	14,400	14,400
GA Taxable Inc	144,037	152,550	160,669	157,351	159,727
GA Regular Tax	8,382	8,893	9,380	9,181	9,323
GA Income Tax	8,382	8,893	9,380	9,181	9,323
Georgia Tax	8,382	8,893	9,380	9,181	9,323
Tot State/Local Tx	8,382	8,893	9,380	9,181	9,323
Total Inc Tax	52,129	55,083	58,006	58,051	59,455

FINANCIAL SUMMARY

CHARLES & BARBARA WIGGINS

BASE CASE	2002	2003	2004	2005	2006
Gross Real Income					
Personal Earnings	164,000	169,900	176,086	182,572	189,372
Interest Income	5,032	8,557	12,312	15,414	18,320
Dividends Rcvd	1,498	1,561	1,627	1,695	1,767
TrustIncome-Barbara	10,000	10,000	10,000	10,000	10,000
	180,530	190,018	200,025	209,681	219,459
Income & Inflation					
Gross Real Inc	180,530	190,018	200,025	209,681	219,459
Total Inc Tax	-52,129	-55,083	-58,006	-58,051	-59,455
Net Real Income	128,401	134,935	142,019	151,630	160,004
Cur Real Inc =	128,401	131,742	135,170	138,686	142,295
At Infltn Rate of	3	3	3	3	3
Cash Flow					
Idle Cash On Hand	6,000	6,005	6,038	6,002	6,061
Norml Cash Inflow	177,578	183,541	189,793	313,947	202,419
Norml Cash Outflw	113,679	118,883	124,190	266,441	151,183
Cash Invested	63,894	64,625	65,639	47,447	51,223
Cash Balance	6,005	6,038	6,002	6,061	6,075
Net Worth					
Personal Assets	243,605	259,118	276,365	415,652	443,001
Investment Assets	430,350	527,128	630,519	711,214	811,151
Personal Liabilities	-64,395	-63,162	-61,827	-275,307	-272,015
Personal Net Worth	179,210	195,956	214,538	140,345	170,986
Investment Net Worth	430,350	527,128	630,519	711,214	811,151
Net Worth	609,560	723,084	845,057	851,560	982,137

Choosing the Appropriate Business Form

Remaining a Partnership

The Internal Revenue Code defines a partnership as any business carried on through joint ventures or enterprises other than trusts, estates, or corporations (IRC Sec. 7701(a)(2)). The partnership is not a tax-paying entity. While a partnership is a tax-reporting entity that has taxable income or loss, the business entity itself is a mere conduit; partnership income and losses are passed through to the partners themselves. This does not mean, however, that the partnership has no importance in determining the amount and type of taxes that the partners will pay. The characterization of income or loss is made at the partnership level and is passed on to the individual partners for reporting on their individual income tax returns. The partnership can pass through losses to the individual partners to offset income from other sources. It is also a very flexible form of business ownership, which can allow for a substantial amount of informality in business operations if the partners so desire. It is not without its problems, however.

One of the most troublesome problems encountered in operating a business in the form of a partnership is that as a matter of law, all the general partners are responsible for all the debts of the partnership and for the debts of other general partners arising out of the partnership business. For a group of sophisticated computer consultants (or other professionals such as physicians or lawyers), this means that a judgment against one partner will become the responsibility of each of the other partners to the full extent of the liability. In other words, if the person who made the error is unable to pay all the liability, each of the other partners will be fully liable for the payment of the remaining amount. In legal parlance each partner is "jointly and severally liable" for the total liabilities of the partnership and of the individual partners arising out of the partnership business. This joint-and-several liability is not restricted to matters of liability arising out of professional negligence but extends to all areas of liability arising out of the partnership business. For example, a partner who defaults on a partnership mortgage will trigger the same resulting liability to the other partners. The amount of a partner's liability is not limited to the assets that the partner has in the partnership but extends to personal assets as well. Each partner can lose everything he or she owns due to the joint and severable liability of the partnership form of business.

Technically, the death of a partner results in dissolution of the partnership. Although partnership interests can be inherited, the result is the formation of a new partnership.

As a matter of federal tax law, partnerships do not offer the opportunity to split income between a business entity and an individual. Because the partnership is not an entity that pays taxes, all income is taxed to the partners at their top marginal rate. In addition, if the partnership has taxable income, the partner must pay tax on his or her pro rata portion of that amount in the year in which it is recognized by the partnership regardless of whether it is actually distributed to the partner.

There are also benefits available to shareholder-employees of regular corporations (referred to as C corporations) on a tax-advantaged basis that are either limited or unavailable to partners. These benefits include

- group medical, disability, and life insurance plans
- permissible loans from qualified corporate plans of deferred compensation

S Corporations

Before 1982, S corporations were treated as corporations for tax purposes except that the income from such corporations was treated as if it had been earned or received as a dividend by the individual shareholders regardless of whether it was actually distributed to shareholders. Because of this tax treatment, a gift of S corporation stock to a minor was an effective way to shift income attributable to those shares to the recipient without raising issues of reasonable compensation. In view of these facts it is not surprising that S corporations have always been loosely compared to partnerships with regard to the taxation of their income, even though S corporations combine the tax treatment of regular corporations and partnerships. Since the enactment of the Subchapter S Revision Act of 1982, however, the rules governing the taxation of S corporation income are, in fact, much closer to the rules governing partnership income than to those governing the income of regular corporations. The S corporation is now treated for most federal tax purposes as if it were a partnership. There are significant differences between the formation and the eligibility requirements of an S corporation and those of a partnership, and it is important to keep these differences in mind.

Under IRC Sec. 1361, in order to elect Subchapter S status a corporation must be a domestic (that is, a U.S.) corporation that is not an ineligible corporation. Ineligible corporations include (a) affiliated corporations as defined in IRC Sec. 1504(a) regardless of whether they are eligible to file a consolidated return, (b) financial institutions that are allowed deductions for bad debts under IRC Sec. 585 or 593, (c) insurance companies subject to tax under Subchapter L, (d) corporations electing the Puerto Rico and possessions tax credit under IRC Sec. 936, as amended, and (e) DISCs (domestic international sales corporations) or former DISCs.

In addition, the corporation must satisfy the following requirements:

- The electing S corporation may have no more than a total of 75 shareholders; however, a husband and wife or their estates, each owning stock individually, are treated as one shareholder.

- Each individual shareholder must be a citizen or resident of the United States; that is, no shareholder can be a nonresident alien.
- Each shareholder must be an individual, an estate, or a specified type of trust. The definition of individual shareholders does not include corporations or partnerships. There are, however, four basic types of trusts that are permitted to be shareholders:

  - a trust all of which is treated as owned by an individual who is a citizen or resident of the United States (a grantor trust)
  - a trust that is characterized as a grantor trust immediately before the death of the deemed owner and that continues in existence after such death, but only for the 2-year period beginning on the day of the deemed owner's death. If a trust is a grantor trust and the entire corpus of the trust is includible in the gross estate of the deemed owner, the 2-year period applies.
  - a testamentary trust pursuant to the terms of a will, but only for a 2-year period beginning on the day on which S corporation stock is transferred to it
  - a trust created primarily to exercise the voting power of stock transferred to it

Two other permissible trusts (Qualified Sub-Chapter S Trusts and Electing Small Business Trusts) have technical regulations and are covered in a subsequent case.

- The corporation must have no more than one class of outstanding stock. One class of stock means that all shareholders have identical rights in the profits and assets of the corporation. Differences in voting rights among shares of common stock are permitted. Although the voting rights can differ, all shares must have identical rights with respect to distribution and liquidation proceeds. (Note that Treasury regulations make it relatively easy to inadvertently create a second class of stock.)

Any qualifying corporation (one that meets all four conditions noted above) can elect Subchapter S status. The election may be made at any time during the taxable year preceding the year the election is to go into effect or on or before the 15th day of the third month of the year in which the election is to be effective. If the corporation makes the election on or before the 15th day of the third month of the taxable year, the election will be applied retroactively; that is, it will be treated as if it had been made on the first day of the taxable year, and the corporation will be treated as an S corporation for the entire taxable year. If the corporation fails to make the election until after the 15th day of the third month of the year in which the election is intended to be effective, it will be treated as an election made for the succeeding tax year.

For example, assume that a corporation with a taxable year ending on December 31 makes a Subchapter S election on or before March 15, 2003. In this case the corporation will be an S corporation for the entire 2003 taxable year. If, on the other hand, the election is made after March 15, 2003, but on or before March 15, 2004, the election will become effective January 1, 2004. The consent of all shareholders on the day the election is made is required. In the case of an election made during the election year, the consent of anyone who was a shareholder during the preelection portion of the year is also necessary to effect the election.

New shareholders cannot revoke or effectively eliminate the Subchapter S election by refusing to affirmatively consent to the election within 60 days after acquiring the stock. The one exception to this rule is a new shareholder who owns more than 50 percent of the stock who elects to revoke the election. If a new shareholder owning 50 percent or less of the corporation's stock becomes a shareholder during the time that an S election is in effect, the new shareholder will be bound by the election.

Once a valid election for Subchapter S status is made, the election is in effect for the tax year for which it was made and continues in effect for all subsequent years unless it is terminated or voluntarily revoked. The S election may be terminated or revoked in any of the following ways:

- Shareholders owning more than 50 percent of the stock of the corporation consent to a voluntary revocation.
- The corporation does not continue to satisfy any one of the qualification requirements (for instance, it exceeds the allowable number of shareholders).
- More than 25 percent of the S corporation's gross receipts for 3 successive tax years is derived from certain types of passive income, and the corporation has accumulated earnings and profits from its days prior to the S corporation election.

S corporation status can be revoked on or before the 15th day of the third month of the current taxable year. It will be effective retroactively for that entire taxable year unless the revocation specifically requests a revocation date in the future, in which case the revocation will be effective on that future date. If no future date of revocation is specified but the revocation election is filed after the permissible period, the revocation is effective at the beginning of the following taxable year.

If S corporation status is voluntarily revoked, the corporation is prohibited from reelecting S corporation status for 5 years without obtaining IRS consent. In appropriate circumstances the IRS is permitted to waive the 5-year waiting period and permit the corporation to make a new election effective for the following taxable year. In the event of an inadvertent termination of the S election, the IRS may waive the effect of the inadvertent termination for any period, provided the corporation corrects the event that created the termination, and the corporation and its shareholders agree to be treated as if the election had been in effect for the entire period.

A new corporation is required to have a taxable year ending December 31 unless it can establish to the satisfaction of the IRS that it has a business purpose for choosing another taxable year, or unless it makes a special election under IRC Sec. 444 and agrees to make certain "required payments" to its shareholders annually under a complex formula.

Shareholder-employees of new S corporations who own (either individually or by attribution under IRC Sec. 318) more than 2 percent of the outstanding stock of the S corporation or stock having more than 2 percent of the voting power of all stock of the S corporation are not able to deduct the full cost of certain fringe benefits. In this instance, S corporation stockholders are treated in the same way as the partners in a partnership. These fringe benefits include group medical, disability, and life insurance benefits (IRC Sec. 1372 applying IRC Sec. 7701(a)(2)). S corporation shareholders are also prohibited from enjoying some of the benefits of qualified plans (such as loans) that have always been and continue to be available to shareholder-employees of regular corporations (IRC Sec. 4975(d)). Note that the effect of these provisions is to treat the S corporation the same as a partnership for determining the taxability of fringe benefits.

Income from an S corporation, with the exception of certain built-in capital gains and passive income (IRC Sec. 1374(a)), is not taxed at the corporate level. For tax years beginning after December 31, 1989, S corporations are required to make estimated tax payments for tax liability attributable to the built-in gains tax as well as excessive passive-investment income tax (IRC Sec. 1375(a)) and tax due by reason of investment credit recapture (IRC Sec. 1371(d)(2)). Other items of income and loss are passed through to the individual shareholders in proportion to their percentage of ownership and are taxed at the shareholder's individual tax rate. This eliminates any possibility of reducing a shareholder's tax burden by splitting income between the shareholder and the corporation. The fact that income is taxable to shareholders in direct proportion to their ownership interests also presents the opportunity for gifting S corporation stock, especially to minors, thereby taking advantage of the minors' lower tax brackets without involving most of the concerns about reasonable compensation encountered with C corporations. While this can be a particularly effective technique for an S corporation that is an operating business, it has significantly less utility in service corporations.

While the S corporation can work effectively, especially in passing through the start-up losses of a new business to offset other income of shareholders, and does limit the personal liability of shareholders, care should be taken not to make a Subchapter S election or to revoke such an election once it has been made without consideration of all the factors noted in this section.

Under the Revenue Reconciliation Act of 1993 the top tax rate for C corporations has been increased to 35 percent effective for tax years beginning in 1993. (A special surcharge applies to income between certain ranges in order to achieve a flat 35 percent rate.) The top tax rate for individuals in 2002 is 38.6 percent. Because of this change in the relationship between corporate and individual rates, many advisers reexamined Subchapter S elections. C corporations (other than "qualified personal service corporations") are still taxed at a rate of 15 percent on the first $50,000 of corporate taxable income and at a rate of 25 percent on corporate taxable income between $50,000 and $75,000. Therefore the first $75,000 of corporate taxable income will still be taxed at marginal rates that are most likely lower than the owner's marginal rate.

However, pursuant to the Revenue Act of 1987 taxable income of qualified personal service corporations is taxed at a flat rate of 35 percent. This provision denies the benefit of the graduated corporate rates to corporations that fall into this category. S elections may be available for some corporations that are now subject to the 35 percent flat rate.

C Corporations

There are few intricate rules for setting up a corporation that qualifies as a regular (or C) corporation for tax purposes. There is no limitation on the number or types of persons or entities that can be shareholders. Any business operating in a corporate form, as set forth by state law, as well as business entities that have chosen to be treated as corporations for federal tax purposes, are subject to the tax rules set forth in Subchapter C of the IRC. Unlike owner-employees (partners and sole proprietors), owners of regular corporations may also be employees of the corporations and as such are entitled to payment in the form of reasonable salaries and certain tax-free fringe benefits. Salary and benefit payments are deductible by the corporation.

The regular (or C) corporation is both a tax-reporting and a tax-paying entity. There are separate rates of corporate taxation, and the benefits of splitting the taxation of corporate profits between the corporation and the individual shareholders can be significant in some cases. As a general rule shareholders are taxed only on monies that are actually distributed to them from the C corporation. Leaving excessive funds in the corporation to avoid taxation at the individual level can lead to additional problems such as the accumulated-earnings penalty tax, which is a punitive tax carrying an additional tax on all accumulated taxable income (IRC Secs. 531-537). The accumulated-earnings tax is a penalty tax that is imposed in addition to regular corporate tax rates.

There is, however, a safe harbor amount of accumulated taxable income for capital-intensive, nonpersonal-service-type businesses of $250,000. For service businesses such as Systems Design the safe harbor amount is $150,000 (IRC Sec. 535(c)(2)). Note especially that "unreasonable" accumulations can consist not only of cash but also of many other corporate assets. This is a complex area of the tax law and the assistance of competent tax attorneys and accountants is crucial in determining whether an accumulated-earnings problem exists if the corporation has accumulations in excess of the safe harbor amounts.

In businesses that are essentially service businesses, such as Systems Design Associates, the corporate income tax can be minimized and accumulated-earnings tax problems eliminated by paying out the bulk of corporate taxable income in the form of salaries and tax-favored benefits to or for the benefit of the shareholders and other employees. Remaining corporate taxable income, however, will be taxable at a flat rate of 35 percent if the corporation is classified as a qualified personal service corporation.

Would Systems Design be subject to the 35 percent flat tax rate if it was incorporated as a C corporation? Since it would perform services in the area of consulting, it would be subject to it if each of the partners owned one-third of its stock. However, the regulations provide that a service corporation will not be treated as a qualified personal service corporation unless 95 percent or more of the value of the stock is held at all times during the taxable year by employees performing services for the corporation or by retired employees, their estates, or the beneficiaries of their estates during the first 2 years after death.

Stock owned by family members is not considered to be owned by the employee for this purpose (except for stock owned by a spouse solely by reason of community-property laws).

If Systems Design incorporated and was characterized for federal income tax purposes as a C corporation, its taxable income could probably be "zeroed out" by payments of compensation to the three principals. This means that after the payment of all expenses and salaries, the corporation would have no taxable income. However, reasonable compensation problems, the need for additional capital investment, or other factors could make it advisable to retain some taxable income within the corporation. In that event it would be helpful if the graduated corporate tax rates (beginning at 15 percent on the first $50,000 of taxable income and 25 percent on the next $25,000) could be used, rather than the 35 percent flat rate.

The Treasury regulations state clearly that if more than 5 percent of a corporation's stock is owned by an individual who is not an employee, retired employee, or beneficiary of a deceased employee's estate, the corporation will not be treated as a qualified personal service corporation. Sec. 11 of the Internal Revenue Code uses this definition to determine whether the flat tax rate will apply. Therefore if Charles were to give Barbara 6 percent of the stock in the corporation, or alternatively if each of the spouses of the three principals were given 2 percent, under the regulations Systems Design Associates would not be treated as a qualified personal service corporation. Presumably the business could then take advantage of the graduated corporate rates.

The Tax Reform Act of 1986 imposed some serious tax disadvantages on the liquidation of C corporations. Specifically a C corporation will now recognize gain on the distribution of appreciated property in complete liquidation of the corporation. In the case of a personal service corporation goodwill is very likely to be included as an appreciated asset that could give rise to significant tax liability when liquidation occurs. Goodwill will generally be considered an appreciated asset only if the shareholders of the liquidating corporation continue to practice the profession in the same geographic area so that the goodwill retains its value. A C corporation will also be taxed on the sale of its property pursuant to a plan of liquidation. Under prior law gain on such sales would not be recognized.

Since the shareholder of a C corporation is taxed on receipt of property in a liquidating distribution, the specter of double taxation looms when a C corporation liquidates. This is now an important consideration in evaluating the C corporation as a choice of business entity. For Charles this problem is not as onerous as it would be in many cases. Since he and his partners are strongly committed to continuing the business permanently, a liquidation of Systems Design Associates at any time in the foreseeable future is a very remote possibility. However, Charles should be made aware of this possible tax problem.

Clients should appreciate the fact that there are nontax considerations that also need to be examined when analyzing the corporate form.

A nontax advantage of the corporate form, whether it is an S corporation or a regular C corporation, is the limited personal liability of the shareholders. The general rule is that in a claim against the corporation the shareholder's potential liability is limited to the amount of money he or she has invested in the corporation. An employee-shareholder is, however, personally liable for his or her own negligence. Regarding the facts of the Wiggins case, that limited liability essentially means that if there was a civil judgment against Charles or one of his associates, the shareholders other than the negligent or offending party would have liability only to the extent of their investment in the corporation. This is a material benefit in most situations when more than one shareholder is a key employee. It should be noted that under Georgia law shareholders in a professional corporation may be held liable for the misdeeds of other shareholders. However, Systems Design would not be a professional corporation under Georgia law.

Regular corporations generally work best for operating businesses and are less appropriate for holding investments such as real estate, since they effectively build a tax wall around the tax benefits, trapping them inside the corporation. Benefits such as depreciation on real estate are thereby effectively denied for personal use by the individual shareholders.

As a general rule property can be transferred from a proprietorship or a partnership into a regular (or an S) corporation without the recognition of gain or loss on the transfer (IRC Sec. 351) provided the transferors (as a group) own, immediately after the transfer, 80 percent of the stock of the corporation.

The Limited Liability Company

The limited liability company (LLC) may be thought of as a mixture of both a corporation and a partnership since this type of enterprise has certain attributes of each. In essence, the limited liability company is an unincorporated entity that protects its members from personal liability for the firm's debts that may have been incurred through and during normal business operations. For tax purposes, an LLC is treated as a partnership and passes through items of income, deduction, and tax credit. Unlike a partnership, however, the LLC provides the corporate characteristic of limited liability to all of its members.

At this time, the limited liability company has become a very popular form of business association and all states have now approved its usage.

The limited liability company is created by the adoption of an operating agreement that sets forth the conditions upon which the entity will operate and do business. All members must generally be a party to this operating agreement by signing it. Participants in the venture (called "members") contribute something of value to the company such as cash, other property, or even services, and in return for such contribution, participants (members) receive a membership interest in the enterprise. Earnings and profits as well as losses incurred by the firm are apportioned in accordance with the proportionate value of the contributions originally made by the members of the LLC.

In December 1996 the IRS adopted the "Check-the-Box Regulations" for the tax classification of business entities. The check-the-box regulations replaced the old four-factor "Morrissey Test," which disregarded state-law characterization of a business entity and defined what a corporation was for federal tax purposes. Because an LLC is not a per se C corporation organized under state law, it will be classified as a partnership (if it has two or more members) or as a sole proprietorship (if it has only one member) for federal tax purposes unless it chooses to be taxed as a corporation by "checking the box." Prior to the adoption of the check-the-box regulations, setting up an LLC to achieve partnership tax treatment (the presumed goal when a business owner uses an LLC instead of a corporation) required careful (and expensive) drafting. Now that the IRS has settled the question of how an LLC will be taxed, it is likely to become a popular form of business organization in the future.

Recommendations

Congress has enacted several provisions discouraging the use of a C corporation by service businesses. As a result it is much more common for service businesses to operate as partnerships, limited liability companies, or S corporations in light of these changes. However, in this case there are balancing considerations. Assuming all three owners of Systems Design are in a 31 percent tax bracket, and assuming the corporation retains up to $75,000 of taxable income in a given year, C corporation status could produce a tax savings of up to $9,500 per year if the regular corporate tax rates (as opposed to the flat 35 percent, discussed above) are available. In addition, tax-advantaged fringe benefits and loans from a qualified plan operated by the company would then be available. Particularly helpful in Charles's case would be tax-free disability income coverage that a C corporation could provide to him with deductible dollars (discussed in a later section).

Both a C and an S corporation as well as the LLC generally provide a limited liability feature. Although there has not been a multitude of lawsuits brought against businesses such as Systems Design, there is a substantial possibility that lawsuits could occur in the future as the law in this area develops. Therefore incorporation in some form or the use of an LLC is advisable because of the limited liability feature.

Although the LLC would also provide limited liability protection, given the nature of the business and the goals of the owners, a corporation is probably more appropriate.

Therefore, it is recommended that Systems Design Associates incorporate as a C corporation. If at any time the corporation cannot or does not wish to zero out its taxable income, 6 percent of the corporation's stock should be transferred to a nonemployee-shareholder before the beginning of the taxable year. It may be preferable for Charles to give Barbara 6 percent of the stock in Systems Design, rather than have all three of the principals transfer 2 percent of the stock to each of their spouses. However, in either case the voting balance of the corporation would not be significantly affected, unless marital problems should occur. These alternatives could be discussed among the principals. Recall that gifts of stock to a spouse have no adverse federal gift tax consequences because of the unlimited federal gift tax marital deduction. (However, in any situation in which the donee-spouse is not a citizen of the United States, there is not a federal gift tax marital deduction but rather a special annual exclusion.)

In order to help minimize the harsh tax results of a partial or complete corporate liquidation, only the operating business should be incorporated. Charles and his partners should keep the office building in partnership form or transfer it to a newly created LLC to maximize tax-planning benefits.

In conclusion, a C corporation appears to be the best alternative for the operation of Systems Design Associates.

Incorporation Feasibility

Legal Requirements for Incorporation

The legal requirements for the incorporation of a business are a matter of local law. A corporation is required to have both officers and a board of directors. In Georgia the minimum number of members of the board of directors is one. However, the shareholders can be authorized to fix or change the number of directors. In the case of Systems Design there must be at least one member of the board of directors. However, it would be advisable to have all three owner-employees serve as directors of the corporation. The corporation will also have officers as described in its bylaws. Typically these will include a president, a secretary, and a treasurer. The owner-employees can assign these duties as they see fit.

The mechanics of incorporating also require, among other things, drawing up articles of incorporation and by-laws, reserving a corporate name, filing articles of incorporation with the Secretary of State's office, and publishing notice of incorporation.

In addition to the purely legal requirements for incorporation of the Systems Design partnership there are some requirements that can be described as organizational and operational formalities. These basically include changes in the method of operation necessitated by the change from the partnership form of business operation to the corporate form. The most basic change that will occur after incorporation is that the former partners will become employees of the corporation (recall that partners are not considered to be employees of their partnership). While this need not require any substantial difference in day-to-day job performance, certain differences must of necessity exist. For example, business cards, invoices, bank accounts, and methods of signing checks must be changed to a corporate form. Also income taxes, FICA, and FUTA will be withheld from the wages of the former partners just as they presently are for the partnership's employees. This should not materially affect the cash flow to the Wiggins family as it will also eliminate the necessity to budget for cash to pay a quarterly estimated tax liability. In addition, the amount of federal income tax withholding can and should be adjusted to take into account foreseeable itemized deductions so that withholding does not significantly exceed the Wigginses' anticipated tax liability. This can be accomplished when filling out the W-4 form that all employees must complete. The W-4 contains instructions for projecting the taxpayer's anticipated deductions and translating those withholding deductions into exemption equivalents.

In addition, certain decisions, probably the same types of decisions that Charles Wiggins and his partners made as a unit, will be made either directly by the board of directors or by the president of the corporation acting under delegated authority from the board. Generally the bylaws of the corporation will provide that the board of directors must have a regularly scheduled meeting at least annually. In the event that other meetings are required, special meetings can be called as necessary.

Professional Corporations. Under Georgia law computer systems consultants do not incorporate as professional corporations. However, most professionals, including doctors, dentists, lawyers, accountants, architects, and engineers, must comply with the special professional corporation rules if they wish to incorporate. These rules are not applicable to other corporations. For example, in order to qualify as a professional corporation in Georgia, only a person or persons who are licensed to practice the profession for which the corporation is organized and who, unless disabled, are actively engaged in such practice may hold shares in the professional corporation. In addition, the stock certificates of the corporation must (by law) bear a legend that discloses this restriction. The only exception to this rule is that after a shareholder retires or dies, his or her shares may be held by the retired shareholder or the deceased shareholder's estate or beneficiaries for not more than 6 months. Before that period ends, the shares must be redeemed, cancelled, or transferred to other professionals authorized to hold shares in the corporation. Also professional corporations can engage in the practice of only one profession.

In a professional corporation, at least one member of the board of directors and the president of the corporation must be licensed to practice the particular profession for which the corporation is organized. Persons who are not members of the profession are permitted to be board members or officers (other than president). However, nonprofessional management may not participate in decisions relating to professional considerations.

Another legal requirement of incorporating a professional corporation is that the corporation must use a designation that indicates it is operating as a corporation. The designation may be the same as that of any other corporation— for example, Warner and Stackpole, Inc. Many professionals choose instead an equally acceptable form under the law, such as Warner and Stackpole, P.C., to denote status as a professional corporation.

Tax Implications of Incorporation

Transfers of Partnership Interests to the Corporation in a Tax-Free Exchange (Sec. 351). As a general rule transfers of property to a corporation solely in exchange for the corporation's stock are tax-free exchanges that result in no recognition of gain to either the corporation or the transferor-shareholder provided that immediately after the transfer the transferor group is in control of the corporation (IRC Sec. 351). For this purpose control means the ownership of stock possessing at least 80 percent of the combined voting power of all classes of stock entitled to vote and at least 80 percent of the number of shares of all other classes of stock of the corporation (IRC Sec. 368(c)).

Partnership interests are property for purposes of IRC Sec. 351 (Rev. Rul. 70-239). As such, they may qualify for nonrecognition treatment under Sec. 351 if all the other requirements of Sec. 351 are met. On the facts of this case the only problem that could prevent the transfers of the partners' partnership interests into a corporation from being a tax-free exchange under Sec. 351 would be if the partners' liabilities in the partnership exceeded their basis in their partnership interests (IRC Sec. 357(c)). Although this information is not discussed in the case, let us assume for purposes of this exercise that liabilities do not exceed basis and will not prevent a successful tax-free Sec. 351 exchange for the partners' interests.

Although all the existing partnership interests can be contributed to the new corporation, it would be advisable to leave ownership of the business building in the hands of the individual partners. Ownership of real estate by a C corporation is not recommended. Charles, Ursula, and Steve could own the building as tenants in common and lease it to the business entity. Alternatively, Charles, Ursula, and Steve could transfer the building to a newly formed LLC owner in order to provide personal liability protection from claims arising from the building. Even if the lease merely provided that the business would pay rent equal to the mortgage payment, taxes, and a reasonable maintenance allowance—that is, the business's current level of expenditure—Charles, Ursula, and Steve could probably continue to utilize tax benefits such as interest and depreciation deductions on their personal returns.

There are strict limitations on the deductibility of so-called passive losses. Taxpayers who own rental real estate and actively participate in its management may still deduct losses from passive rental activities on their personal returns to the extent that the losses do not exceed $25,000. Taxpayers who have adjusted gross income over $100,000 must reduce this limitation by $1 for every $2 of adjusted gross income over $100,000. Therefore the $25,000 allowance is reduced to zero for taxpayers with adjusted gross income of $150,000 or more. Even though Charles and Barbara's adjusted gross income exceeds $100,000, they will still receive some tax benefits from personal ownership of the building. The Revenue Reconciliation Act of 1993 did ease some of the passive loss restrictions. Losses from rental real estate that have been realized by certain taxpayers involved in the real estate business are no longer subjected to as strict a standard as had previously been the case.

Note that there is insufficient information in the facts of the case to ascertain the exact tax consequences of the distribution of the building from the partnership, and a tax attorney should be consulted before such a transaction is undertaken. It is worth mentioning, however, that the distribution of property from a partnership can frequently be accomplished at little or no tax cost to the distributees.

Another consideration prior to the distribution of the building is whether such a transaction would have adverse effects on the present financing, such as triggering an acceleration of payment or requiring the acquisition of a new mortgage. If this would pose a problem, the building can be left in the partnership (after the operating business is transferred to the corporation).

If these considerations can be effectively managed, it would be much better not to contribute the building to the corporation since, in addition to depriving Charles, Ursula, and Steve of tax benefits, it would be virtually impossible to distribute the building later from a corporation without a substantial tax cost.

Using Sec. 1244 Stock. To assure ordinary-loss treatment rather than capital-loss treatment in the event that the stock in a corporation declines in value or becomes worthless, IRC Sec. 1244 provides that qualifying stock in small business corporations can be designated as Sec. 1244 stock. Usually in the case of a new corporation the stock is designated Sec. 1244 stock in the original documents of the corporation. Sec. 1244 treatment is available to allow an individual shareholder (or a partnership that is a shareholder of the corporation) to whom the stock is issued to deduct up to $50,000 ($100,000 in the case of a husband and wife filing a joint return) for losses sustained in the sale, exchange, or worthlessness of the qualifying stock. In the case of a partnership that is a shareholder, the applicable dollar limitation is determined separately for each partner (Treas. Reg. Sec. 1.1244(b)1(a)). Losses in excess of the statutory limits are treated as capital losses (Treas. Reg. Sec. 1.1244(b)). Shareholders that are trusts, estates, or corporations cannot qualify for ordinary-loss treatment under Sec. 1244 (IRC Sec. 1244(d)(4)).

In order to qualify as Sec. 1244 stock, the stock must be the stock of a domestic corporation and must also meet the following requirements:

- The issuing corporation must be a small business corporation (that is, a corporation in which the sum of all money and property received for stock as a contribution to capital and as paid-in surplus does not exceed $1 million at the time the stock is issued).
- The stock must have been issued in exchange for money or property but not for stock or securities. A partnership interest qualifies as property for this purpose (Rev. Rul. 70-239, 1970-1 C.B. 74).
- During the 5 most recent taxable years before the stock is disposed of by the shareholder, more than 50 percent of the corporation's gross income must have been other than passive income, such as rents, royalties, dividends, and interest.

Common stock is eligible for Sec. 1244 treatment and preferred stock issued after July 18, 1984, can also qualify.

There are absolutely no tax costs or disadvantages to designating qualifying stock as Sec. 1244 stock; for example, the shareholder does not risk ordinary-income treatment if the stock is sold at a gain.

Systems Design is a perfect candidate for Sec. 1244 stock, and if the shareholders take a loss on the disposition of their stock, the ordinary-loss treatment they could receive would allow them to offset the loss, within the statutory limits, against other income. This could save a significant amount in taxes in the year in which the loss occurred. There are significant limitations on utilizing capital losses to offset ordinary income. Capital losses can offset only $3,000 of ordinary income in any given year. This is the tax result the Systems Design shareholders would have without qualifying the stock as Sec. 1244 stock if it was later sold at a loss.

Legal Benefits of Doing Business as a Corporation

A major problem of doing business as a general partnership is the unlimited personal liability of the general partners for both the debts of the partnership and the liabilities of other general partners arising out of the partnership business. One of the primary legal benefits of doing business as a corporation is that it essentially limits the liability of a shareholder to his or her investment in the corporation in virtually all cases except those in which the liability arises from the personal negligence of the shareholder. In addition, a business carried on in a partnership form is legally dissolved at the death of a partner, whereas corporations have perpetual life. The death or disability of a corporate shareholder has no effect on the legal life of a business doing business as a corporation. Furthermore, as a practical matter it is often easier to dispose of shares in a corporation where liability is limited than it is to dispose of a going-concern partnership interest where the liability picture of the existing partners is unknown to the prospective purchaser.

Tax Benefits of Doing Business as a Corporation

Reasonable Compensation for Shareholder-Employees. Salaries are one method available to transfer funds from a corporation to shareholder-employees without subjecting them to double taxation—once at the corporate level and again at the individual level when the shareholder-employee receives them. To avoid this double taxation, the salary paid must be reasonable in amount and must be paid for personal services actually rendered (Sec. 162(a)(1)). If the salary meets this test, it is deductible by the corporation as an ordinary and necessary trade or business expense and is taxed only once—to the shareholder-employee who receives it.

As already indicated, the principal way in which salaries can lose their tax-favored status is through a determination by the Internal Revenue Service that some amount of the salary is "unreasonable compensation." The IRS takes the position that the "unreasonable" portion is not salary at all but a distribution of the corporation's earnings and profits—a dividend. If the IRS makes this determination, the deduction to the corporation is disallowed because dividends are not deductible.

The following example should illustrate this point: Assume taxpayer A owns 100 percent of the stock of Corporation Y, a regular corporation. A is also an employee of Y, devoting substantially his full time to its business. The corporation pays a salary of $100,000 in a particular year.

On audit the IRS seeks to disallow a portion (for example, $30,000) of the salary as unreasonable compensation. If the IRS is successful in the disallowance, the corporate deduction for the unreasonable amount is disallowed, and an additional $10,500 tax (assuming a 35 percent corporate tax rate) is due at the corporate level. The taxpayer will still have to report and pay tax on the $100,000 received from the corporation; $70,000 will be treated as wages and $30,000 will be treated as a dividend.

Tax Results of Reasonable Compensation

Corporation pays	$100,000
Corporation deducts	100,000
Additional taxable income	–0–
Multiplied by 35 percent (corporate rate)	x .35
Additional tax	–0–

Tax Results of Disallowance of $30,000
as Unreasonable Compensation

Corporation pays	$100,000
Corporation deducts	– 70,000
Additional corporate taxable income	30,000
Multiplied by 35 percent (corporate rate)	x .35
Additional tax	$ 10,500

The issue of unreasonable compensation is generally raised only in closely held corporations where there is a strong identity of interest between the role of employee and that of stockholder or where a member of the employee's family is a stockholder. The Internal Revenue Service's position appears to be that an arm's-length transaction setting the value of personal services and effectively eliminating the unreasonable compensation issue cannot exist in most closely held corporations. Obviously the closer the identity of interest between the corporation and the employee, the more vulnerable to IRS scrutiny compensation becomes; for example, the most vulnerable situation occurs between an employee and the employee's wholly owned corporation. Therefore it is important for anyone who is considering incorporating a closely held business to understand that compensation planning for shareholder-employees is an area that should be given thoughtful consideration.

It is only fair to say that effective planning in this area is very difficult, since there are no specific guidelines that have been uniformly applied. The appropriate test is to determine whether the compensation is reasonable under all the facts and circumstances of the particular case. That is, each case will be considered separately on its particular facts, and this may account to some extent for the fact that the court cases in this area are decidedly less than definitive.

This somewhat confusing state of affairs does not mean, however, that no general guidelines exist for setting compensation arrangements for shareholder-employees that can withstand IRS scrutiny. The following points are critical and should always be kept in mind when negotiating compensation arrangements:

- All compensation, present or deferred, will be considered together to determine if the total is reasonable.

- The compensation must be for services actually performed. Sometimes owners of closely held businesses will list spouses or other family members as employees and deduct payments to them as "salaries." In such cases a favorite IRS technique is to visit the business location and demand to see the office, desk, or other working environment of the family member.
- Technically the appropriate time for measuring the reasonableness of a compensation arrangement is the time the arrangement was entered into, not at some later point when circumstances may have changed so dramatically that compensation payments exceed the expectations of all the parties. Although this rule is often ignored by IRS agents conducting an audit, it is a decided advantage to the taxpayer in litigation if the compensation plan was set long before the IRS challenge arose.

As a practical matter compensation arrangements should always be set in advance. It is unwise to wait until the close of the corporate year to determine bonuses or other contingent amounts. An advance determination of compensation should set out all compensation (base salaries, bonus formulas, deferred compensation, automatic cost-of-living adjustments, and any other payments). If a bonus is to be used, the formula for computing the bonus should be predetermined. That formula should never be based on the percentage of shares held or net profits.

Especially in a consulting business such as Systems Design, the new corporation may wish to utilize a bonus formula in addition to base salaries to ensure that the corporation produces little or no taxable income. Contingent compensation, such as bonuses, is not unreasonable in itself. Bonuses can provide incentives for both shareholder-employees and other employees to increase corporate profitability and can also build in flexibility to allow total compensation to adjust to any cyclical nature of the business.

It would probably be appropriate in the case of Systems Design Associates to authorize a base salary and a bonus formula that would allow the board of directors to grant bonuses to the shareholder-employees up to the amount of the net billings of each. There is support for the position that consultants can reasonably take amounts up to their billings as salary.

If this authorization is given to the board of directors and base salaries are set at the low end of the range, Charles and the others should be aware that the result of these bonus payments could be a significant difference in income among the three shareholder-employees. This could produce unwanted conflict among them, particularly as they are accustomed to sharing income equally. A better idea would be to set the base salaries at or near the present level of income from the partnership—for example, $37,000, and then to authorize bonuses, if any, based on net billings in excess of that amount.

Corporate minutes and employment contracts can and should be used to document compensation arrangements and the reasons for establishing them at a particular level. Some helpful factors that should be included in employment contracts, corporate minutes, or both are that

- the employee's compensation is at or near the amount the employee earned in prior years. Charles and his associates should have little trouble justifying compensation in the $37,000 range because they were earning in excess of this amount when the business was operated as a partnership.
- compensation was set taking into consideration the employee's education, experience, skill, knowledge, standing in the industry, and other special qualifying attributes
- compensation was set taking into consideration responsibilities assigned to the employee
- outside activities, if any, of the employee are not expected to interfere with the performance of the duties enumerated in his or her employment contract, and such outside activities, if any, are reflected in the compensation arrangements
- the compensation arrangement reflects the standard compensation level in the profession

Employment Contracts. Employment contracts between employees and employer are often helpful in reducing misunderstandings about the rights and responsibilities of each party. In the case of a shareholder-employee of a closely held corporation, employment agreements are often utilized not only to clarify the employee's duties but also to describe compensation arrangements in an effort to support the reasonableness of compensation in the event of an IRS challenge.

In small, closely held corporations where the shareholder-employee is the sole or the majority shareholder, the principal reason for an employment contract may be to provide the documentation for supporting the reasonableness of that employee's compensation. In closely held corporations such as Systems Design Associates, where no single shareholder holds a majority of the stock, employment contracts can have increased importance and serve additional functions. For example, they can protect a shareholder in the event of shareholder dissension, since they can guarantee a compensation arrangement that could be enforced by the shareholder in the event of job termination. In addition, employment contracts can contain "covenants not to compete" that can prevent a disgruntled shareholder-employee from withdrawing from one corporation and starting another in direct competition just across the street. Courts will generally enforce "covenants not to compete" as long as they are not considered excessively broad—that is, as long as they are limited to a reasonable geographical area and a reasonable period of time.

Employment contracts can be entered into for any period of time, but care should be taken to treat the contract as if it were being entered into between the employee and an employer who is a stranger—that is, as an arm's-length bargain. For this reason contract periods are usually short, not exceeding 3 to 5 years, although some contain options to renew for an additional specified period.

For the reasons indicated, employment contracts covering corporate duties, compensation agreements, termination payments, and covenants not to compete should be implemented for the Systems Design shareholders. These documents must be prepared by an attorney.

Qualified Plans of Deferred Compensation. In the case of Charles and Barbara Wiggins there are actually two considerations regarding qualified plans. The first is the participation in the tax-deferred annuity available to Charles through Homestate Tech. Tax-deferred annuities are special types of deferred-compensation plans that are available primarily through educational and other nonprofit organizations and are known as 403(b) plans. A 403(b) plan allows an employee to elect to have a portion of his or her salary deducted and contributed to the tax-deferred annuity account. Such a voluntary contribution is treated as if it is excluded from gross income for federal income tax purposes. In many situations the employing organization agrees to match all or a portion of the voluntary employee contribution, as is the case here. The employer's contribution is taken into the tax-deferred annuity account without federal tax consequences at that time to the employee. The tax-deferred annuity account is invested, and earnings on the account are allowed to accumulate tax free during the period of the employee's working life.

An important difference to note is that 403(b) plans do not have any special tax benefits on the distributions. Distributions are taxed as ordinary income and cannot obtain the benefit of 10-year forward averaging that is available in certain qualified pension plans.

As an employee, Charles has no policy-making control over the design of the university's tax-deferred annuity account. A second area of control for plan participants is that many tax-deferred annuity plans permit the participant to make investment decisions that will influence the ultimate amount accumulated by retirement time. One decision is to choose between fixed and variable investments during the accumulation period. Often choice exists in both the fixed and variable areas, particularly the variable, where several mutual funds (or annuity accumulation funds of insurers) with different equity-based investment objectives are available. The total contribution does not have to be placed in one choice; however, some plans limit the number that can be selected or have minimum dollar amounts to any one choice for the purpose of reducing administrative expense and record keeping.

By participating in the plan, Charles now has an account balance of approximately $88,000. Assume the following: Charles continues to make contributions at 8 percent of his salary through 2007; the university makes matching contributions of 6 percent of his salary; total contributions are frozen in 2007 at the level of $7,974 through the time he is 65; and the internal inflation-adjusted yield of the fund from the present to the date of his retirement will be 4.5 percent. Having assumed all of this, the account balance when he is 65 will be $753,978 in today's dollars. If Charles chooses a settlement option that will liquidate the accumulated balance over the period from age 65 to age 99, he can expect to receive a monthly payment of approximately $2,708, assuming an inflation-adjusted earnings rate of 3 percent after he is 65. This is obviously a valuable plan for the Wiggins family, and Charles should continue to utilize it fully.

The second issue regarding qualified plans is one over which Charles and the other shareholders of Systems Design Associates, Inc., can exercise substantial control. It relates to the corporation's adoption of qualified plans. One of the reasons Charles and Barbara Wiggins agreed to engage in comprehensive financial planning was to reduce the amount of taxes they are paying. Although they earn a significant income, their tax bracket (currently 30 percent) is hampering their efforts to accumulate funds to achieve their personal objectives. The utilization of an appropriate qualified plan or a combination of qualified plans not only reduces the taxes that the Wiggins family is presently paying, it also accumulates earnings tax free on the amount in the plan until distribution. The tax-deferred accumulation within the plan can obviously allow assets to increase at a much more rapid rate than if taxes were currently payable. These benefits can be attained at absolutely no tax risk. In fact, qualified plans are specifically authorized by the Internal Revenue Code and, as such, are statutorily sanctioned tax shelters. In addition, qualified deferred-compensation plans can provide important incentives to nonshareholder key employees such as Tom Young, John Blake, and Sarah McIntyre to remain with Systems Design Associates.

There are two broad categories of qualified plans: defined-contribution plans and defined-benefit plans. The differences between the two types of plans are primarily related to the way in which benefits are funded and ultimately to whether the employer or the employee bears the risk of the plan's investment experience.

Defined-Benefit Plans. Defined-benefit plans are designed to assure a specific annual benefit up to a maximum statutory limit (in 2002 the lesser of $200,000 or 100 percent of the average compensation for the participant's high 3 years) to the plan participants at a specified retirement age, now generally age 67 for persons born after 1938. The amount of annual funding necessary to assure the annual benefit is initially computed under generally conservative investment assumptions by taking the present value of dollars promised to the plan participant at a specified retirement age. The necessary funding is then contributed to the plan in behalf of the participants and is deductible to the employer subject to an allowable maximum (IRC Sec. 404(a)(1)).

Obviously the lower the investment return assumptions and the shorter the time until a specified retirement date, the larger the amount of annual funding that is necessary to assure the participant's retirement benefits. Absent statutory constraints, employers that are closely held or wholly owned could adopt plans that assume very low investment returns and very early retirement dates to overfund the plan for the benefit of shareholder-employees who are plan participants. To prevent this type of overfunding, the Internal Revenue Code provides that the $200,000 maximum benefit limitation (or 100 percent of the average compensation for the participant's high 3 years, if less) will be allowed only if the retirement-age assumption is not less than age 67. These statutory limitations on benefits will be subject to cost-of-living adjustments. If the retirement-age assumption used is less than 67, the Social Security retirement age, the permissible annual benefit is actuarially reduced for the longer payout period. Further reductions in permissible annual benefits must be made for plan participants with less than 10 years of service with the employer (IRC Sec. 415(b)(5)).

As a further check against overfunding, the plan's actual investment experience must be evaluated on a regular basis, and that information must be factored into the funding formula. For example, if the plan's funding was initially computed utilizing a 5 percent investment return assumption, and the actual investment return was 10 percent, the present contribution amount necessary to fund the specified retirement benefits will be far less than originally projected. In that case the employer's contribution will be reduced accordingly. Conversely if investment return should be less than 5 percent, the employer's obligation for contributions will be increased. It is this feature that leads to the description of defined-benefit plans as plans in which the employer bears the risk of investment return experience. Because the defined-benefit plan is a pension plan, contributions are mandatory once the plan is established.

Since defined-benefit plans focus on allowing employer contributions sufficient to fund specific annual benefits, they can be particularly appropriate for older shareholder-employees (particularly those over 50) who have little or no assured retirement income and only a short time left to fund adequate benefits. It should be noted, however, that funding the maximum permissible benefit over 10 or 12 years can be very expensive to the employer, and care should be taken not to rush into adopting a defined-benefit plan even in this situation unless it is obvious that the employer corporation can afford to fund the necessary benefits.

As already noted, defined-benefit plans require that contribution levels be redetermined annually. This is an administrative cost to the plan, and because it generally involves the use of multiple actuarial assumptions, the cost can be significant.

In addition to being virtually the only way to assure an adequate retirement income to older shareholder-employees through qualified plans, defined-benefit plans are particularly appropriate when a client does not wish to assume the investment risk inherent in a defined-contribution plan but prefers the predictable certainty of retirement benefits that defined-benefit plans are designed to provide.

As a general rule defined-benefit plans are subject to additional regulation by the Pension Benefit Guaranty Corporation; however, certain exceptions do exist. The exception that would be important for Systems Design Associates, Inc., excludes all professional service employers who at no time after September 2, 1974, have had more than 25 active participants (ERISA Sec. 4021(c)(2)). While the PBGC does provide some protection to the participants of defined-benefit plans by assuring that a certain, if nominal, amount of benefits will be available, it also represents an additional tier of regulation as well as additional plan costs in the form of required premium payments. At this time it appears unlikely that Systems Design will be subject to regulation by the PBGC unless it dramatically increases the size of its operations.

Defined-Contribution Plans. Unlike defined-benefit plans that set an assured benefit level at a specified time in the future and work backward from that figure to determine what contribution in current dollars is necessary to fund that benefit, defined-contribution plans take a set or determinable contribution level and promise the participant only the amount that those funds have grown to when contributed to a tax-free trust and invested until the participant retires.

Thus in the defined-contribution plan, the employee bears the investment risk. That is, if the investment experience of the plan is greater than anticipated, the employee receives more at retirement, while if the investment experience is less than expected, the employee receives less. The employer's contribution is not affected by investment results. That is, once contribution levels are determined, the employer contributes and deducts those amounts within statutory limits. The funds are invested in a tax-free trust over the employee's working life, and the benefits available at retirement consist of the contributions that have been made to the plan, plus any forfeitures that have been allocated to the account, plus earnings on the account assets.

Defined-contribution plans basically fall into two categories: profit-sharing plans and money-purchase pension plans. Profit-sharing plans allow contributions to be made and deducted by the employer up to 25 percent of covered compensation (IRC Sec. 404(a)(3)) beginning in 2002. The maximum contribution for each employee is the lesser of 25 percent of covered compensation or a statutory maximum ($40,000) (IRC Sec. 415(c)(1)(A)). The profit-sharing plans specify how contributions will be allocated among the participants. A common approach is to allocate contributions based on compensation, which results in an allocation that is a level percentage of pay. However, other allocation formulas exist that can legitimately direct a larger portion of the total contribution to the business owner. Profit-sharing plans allow the maximum corporate flexibility, since there is no requirement that a set contribution be made every year. In fact, there is no requirement that any contribution be made in a particular year, although a number of successive years without contribution may result in IRS determination that the plan has terminated. Under current rules, an employer can make plan contributions regardless of whether there are actual profits. The flexibility afforded by profit-sharing plans makes them particularly appropriate for businesses that have cyclical or erratic business cycles.

The employer corporation's board of directors can decide not to make a contribution in any year in which corporate profits are absent or do not reach anticipated or desired levels. Since the amount of the contribution to a profit-sharing plan in a particular year is not fixed, the board of directors can contribute any amount between 0 and 25 percent of covered compensation to the plan in a given year. Contribution decisions can be based on the performance of the business or the necessity of keeping funds in the business for expansion or other business needs. It is not necessary for the corporation to make contribution decisions prior to knowing exactly what the corporation's position and cash needs are, since the corporation can take up to the due date for filing the corporate tax return (at least 2 1/2 months after the close of the corporation's taxable year and perhaps longer, because the permissible time includes extensions) to decide whether a contribution should be made to the profit-sharing plan and, if so, how much the contribution should be. If the contribution is made during the permissible period, the corporation can deduct the amount of the contribution exactly as if it had been made before the close of the prior taxable year (IRC Sec. 404(a)(6)).

Suppose that Systems Design Associates, Inc., implemented a 15 percent profit-sharing plan in 2001 and contributed the full 15 percent of Charles Wiggins's salary (assuming it stayed constant at $37,000 until Charles was 65 years old) and that the plan assets earned an inflation-adjusted rate of return of 4.5 percent annually over that period. Under those assumptions the corporation would contribute and deduct $5,550 annually in Charles's behalf, none of which would be taxable to Charles until distribution, and Charles would have $281,448 in his profit-sharing account at age 65.

The second type of defined-contribution plan that Systems Design Associates, Inc., might choose to adopt is a money-purchase pension plan. Employer contributions are tax deductible up to a maximum of 25 percent of covered compensation to all profit-sharing and money-purchase pension plans (not to exceed the statutory maximum, currently $40,000) (IRC Sec. 415(c)). The money-purchase pension plan functions in a slightly different fashion from the profit-sharing plan. Once it is adopted, as a general rule the contribution is mandatory each year at the level specified in the plan.

Another rule is that compensation that can be taken into account for purposes of deducting contributions to defined-contribution plans is limited to $200,000 (IRC Sec. 401(a)(17)). The $200,000 (2002 figure) is subject to annual cost-of-living adjustments. This provision is designed to prevent situations such as that of a controlling shareholder-employee with a $300,000 salary causing the corporation to contribute 10 percent of covered compensation to a qualified plan in order to reach the $40,000 statutory maximum available for him or her. For example, the employer must contribute 20 percent of covered compensation (limited to $200,000) in behalf of all plan participants in a money-purchase pension plan in order for the controlling shareholder-employee to receive the maximum $40,000 contribution. The dollar-amount limit on all defined-contribution plans is $40,000 (IRC Sec. 415(c)(1)).

If Systems Design Associates adopted and fully utilized both a profit-sharing plan and a money-purchase pension plan, the new corporation could contribute and deduct up to $9,250, based on Charles's $37,000 salary. At retirement the combined contributions of $9,250 annually, assuming a 4.5 percent inflation-adjusted earnings rate, would have accumulated $469,079 in Charles's accounts.

While contributions to this combination of qualified plans would result in a pretax cash-flow reduction to the Wiggins family of $9,250 a year, it would also save them approximately $2,775 in taxes, for a net cash-flow reduction of only $6,475, since their marginal tax bracket is 30 percent.

Of course, there are few tax benefits without some cost. In the area of qualified plans it is not possible to provide impressive tax-free benefits to Charles and the other shareholder-employees without providing benefits to the rank-and-file employees. In the case of Systems Design Associates it is probably prudent to furnish other employees with improved benefits since their present benefit package is sparse, and some key employees have already expressed their concern about the lack of retirement plans. Improved benefit packages are one important way to retain key employees.

In order to be eligible for qualified status—that is, the tax-preferred benefits that are inherent in qualified plans, no qualified plan can impermissibly discriminate in favor of highly compensated employees. In order to assure that impermissible discrimination does not occur, the Internal Revenue Code requires that the plan's coverage of employees either meet one of three specific mathematical tests or be able to demonstrate to the satisfaction of the IRS that the plan does not discriminate in favor of officers, shareholders, or highly compensated employees. The mathematical tests that a plan must meet are expressed as a percentage requirement to measure participation in the plan. For this purpose the plan must meet one of the following percentage tests:

- The plan must cover at least 70 percent of employees who are not highly compensated—*the percentage test.*
- The plan must cover a percentage of nonhighly compensated employees that is at least 70 percent of the percentage of highly compensated employees covered—*the ratio test.*
- The plan must meet the *average benefits test.* This is a combination of the old nondiscriminatory classification test of prior law, with an additional requirement that the contributions or benefits under all qualified plans of the employer be a nondiscriminatory percentage of compensation.

Highly compensated employees include

- individuals who are 5 percent owners during the current or previous year and
- individuals who earned $85,000 (as indexed in 2001) in the preceding year. (The employer can elect to limit this group to employees whose compensation puts them in the top 20 percent of payroll.)

The following persons can be excluded (that is, not considered employees) under the eligibility rules:

- those under the age of 21
- those who have not completed a year of service
- part-time employees (generally employees with less than 1,000 hours of service within a 12-month period)
- members of certain collective bargaining units that have already bargained in good faith with the employer regarding retirement benefits

Be cautious in the case of Systems Design Associates, as the shareholder-employees may not be covered by the plan if it is designed to exclude part-time employees—that is, those with less than 1,000 hours of service in a 12-month period, since it appears that only Charles and his fellow shareholder-employees may be "part-time" employees under this definition. Participation requirements can be more liberal, but not more restrictive, than those enumerated.

When both age and service conditions have been met, the employee must begin participation in the plan no later than the earlier of the following times: a) the first day of the first plan year beginning after the date on which the employee satisfied the age and service requirements or (b) the day 6 months after the date on which the employee satisfied the requirements.

The vesting of plan benefits refers to the point in time at which benefits become nonforfeitable to the plan participants with certain exceptions. In the past a plan could be designed to provide that the death of a plan participant prior to reaching retirement age would result in a loss of all benefits attributable to employer contributions. This was not considered a forfeiture.

As a general rule under current law qualified plans are required to offer preretirement survivor annuities. These preretirement annuities must be offered automatically and will be effective unless the plan participant and his or her spouse waive them. In addition, such a waiver can be revoked at any time. Very few responsible designers of small plans (such as one that would be appropriate for Systems Design) would recommend a provision allowing preretirement death forfeitures because the shareholder-employees would not wish to subject their families to a risk of losing their accumulated account balances. However, the law provides this additional safeguard.

Qualified plans can be very liberal and provide for immediate vesting of all contributions for all employees, or they can require 2 years of service before an employee becomes a plan participant if the employee is then 100 percent vested in all contributions. These are generally very expensive types of vesting schedules because employees who leave the business are usually entitled to continue their vested interest in the plan regardless of whether they can actually withdraw their account balances. However, before deciding to take a more restrictive approach to vesting, it is important to remember that there cannot be one vesting schedule for rank-and-file employees and another for owner-employees. In other words, the owner-employees must abide by the same vesting schedule as everyone else.

The following are permissible vesting schedules under current law:

- 100 percent vesting after 3 years of service (referred to as cliff vesting)
- 2- to 6-year vesting, illustrated below (referred to as graded vesting):

Years of Service	Vested Percentage
2	20%
3	40
4	60
5	80
6 or more	100

To be permissible, a vesting schedule must be no slower than one of the two indicated above. Of course, vesting schedules that are faster than the statutory schedules are allowed.

While it is not required that a favorable determination letter be obtained from the Internal Revenue Service in order for a plan to be qualified and therefore to be eligible for favorable tax treatment, it is important to understand that the discrimination provisions that prohibit discrimination of contributions or benefits in favor of officers, shareholders, or highly compensated personnel are tested by the IRS at two points. One is on the face of the plan document. The IRS can apply the other test to see whether the plan actually operates in a discriminatory manner despite the plan document's being nondiscriminatory on its face in favor of highly compensated personnel. According to the Committee Reports a determination letter purports to protect a plan from continuous IRS scrutiny (in the absence of actual abuse) to determine whether discrimination regarding vesting is present in practice. Such discrimination can take the form of firing employees just before their interests are vested. This is a very important consideration in the case of small corporations because nonshareholder-personnel, such as clerical and other support staff, can have a high rate of turnover despite no wrongdoing on the part of the shareholder-employees. Absent a favorable determination letter, natural attrition, which is in no way the fault of the shareholder-employees, could result in a challenge from the IRS and a determination that the plan is discriminatory in practice, causing the plan to lose its qualified status. Therefore it is important to obtain a determination letter, especially in small corporations such as Systems Design Associates.

Top-heavy Plans. By definition a plan is top-heavy if it provides more than 60 percent of its aggregate accumulated benefits or account balances to key employees. A key employee is an employee who is either

- an officer of the employer whose annual compensation from the employer is in excess of $130,000 (subject to inflation adjustments after 2002) or
- a 5 percent owner of the employer or
- a one percent owner of the employer earning more than $150,000 a year from the employer (IRC Sec. 416(i))

The Economic Growth and Tax Relief Reconciliation Act of 2001 eliminated the 4-year look-back period.

Many small plans will be subject to the top-heavy rules, and there are significant changes from the general rules for corporate qualified plans if the plan is deemed to be a top-heavy plan. In particular there is mandatory accelerated vesting for top-heavy plans. Top-heavy plans must meet one of two new statutory vesting standards: the plan must either provide that participants be 100 percent vested at the end of their third year of service or adopt the alternative 6-year-graded vesting schedule. Under 6-year-graded vesting at least 20 percent of the accrued benefit must vest in the participant by the end of the second year of service with additional vesting of 20 percent in each succeeding year and with full vesting at the end of 6 years (IRC Sec. 416(b)).

The 6-year-graded vesting schedule is illustrated below:

If Years of Service Equal or Exceed	Nonforfeitable Percentage Is
1	0
2	20
3	40
4	60
5	80
6	100

Note that the older top-heavy vesting schedules are still more accelerated than the new regular vesting schedules under the Tax Reform Act of 1986. Therefore even though the top-heavy vesting schedules were enacted prior to the 1986 act, they are still permissible under both the older top-heavy rules and the newer rules of the 1986 act. After enactment of the Economic Growth and Tax

Relief Reconciliation Act of 2001, there is no difference between required vesting schedules for top-heavy plans and those allowed for other plans.

Another rule applicable to top-heavy plans is a minimum-contribution rule, which assures that nonkey employees will be provided with plan contributions. You will remember that contributions to profit-sharing plans may be made at the discretion of the corporate board of directors. However, if the profit-sharing plan is the employer's only plan, the employer must make minimum contributions of at least 3 percent of compensation in behalf of nonkey employees (IRC Sec. 416(c)(2)(A)). The only exception to the minimum-contribution rule occurs if contributions of less than 3 percent of covered compensation of less than $150,000 are made in behalf of key employees. In that event the minimum contribution for nonkey employees may be the same percentage as that for key employees. In the event that an employer maintains more than one plan, it appears that the minimum contribution requirement will be satisfied by a 3 percent contribution to one of the plans (IRC Sec. 416(f)). The portion of FICA that employers pay in behalf of employees cannot be counted against the minimum-contribution requirement (IRC Sec. 416(e)).

To determine whether a plan is top-heavy, key employees as statutorily defined must first be identified. In this case key employees are Charles Wiggins, Ursula Von Waldhem, and Steve Thomas. If one assumes that their salary levels are set at $37,000 each per year, with the other three key employees listed in the case narrative each being paid $30,000 a year, and each of the remaining clerical and support staff being paid $18,000 per year, the covered compensation for Systems Design Associates would be $255,000 per year. If Systems Design Associates, Inc., adopts a 15 percent profit-sharing plan, a contribution could be made on the part of all the plan participants in the amount of $38,250 in the first plan year. Of that amount $16,650 ($5,550 each for Charles, Ursula, and Steve) would be contributed in behalf of key employees. This results in approximately 44 percent of the plan contributions being made in behalf of key employees under these assumptions.

At this point the plan is not top-heavy. However, the test is measured not by contributions but rather by accumulated benefits or account balances. If there is any significant turnover in Systems Design Associates' clerical support staff that would result in forfeitures being allocated to the account balances of shareholder-employees, it is likely that Systems Design Associates' plan will become a top-heavy plan. Since this is the case, it is best to prepare the client to expect to comply with the top-heavy rules at some point. At any rate all plans must contain top-heavy provisions, regardless of whether they are presently top-heavy. Failure to do so can cause the plan to lose its tax-qualified status.

The top-heavy rules are less burdensome than other qualified plans after the Tax Reform Act of 1986 (TRA '86). Therefore if Systems Design Associates' plan does become top-heavy, the additional restrictions will not have a dramatic effect.

A preceding paragraph referred to forfeited account balances. Forfeitures occur when employees leave the employer while all or a portion of the contributions made in their behalf has not become fully vested. These nonvested account balances are forfeited by the employee. Forfeitures in profit-sharing plans are usually allocated among the remaining participants at the end of the plan year. Such allocations are generally made pro rata based on compensation, with the result that the employee with the longest employment and the highest compensation is allocated the bulk of the forfeited funds. Under TRA '86 money-purchase pension plans may also reallocate forfeitures among participants.

As already noted, forfeitures can result in a plan's becoming a top-heavy plan. Forfeited amounts also reduce the statutory maximum that can be contributed in behalf of an employee. For example, assume an employee is covered by a 15 percent profit-sharing plan and is compensated at the rate of $200,000 per year. If a 20 percent contribution is made to the profit-sharing plan, the statutory annual maximum of $40,000 is reached for that employee. If the employee has had forfeited amounts of $4,000 allocated to his or her account balance in the plan year, the permissible contribution is reduced by that amount. In other words, in that year the employer may contribute and deduct only $36,000 in behalf of the employee.

Forfeitures are treated differently in defined-benefit plans. They are not allocated among remaining participants but go to reduce the mandatory corporate contributions in the next year.

Recommendation for Qualified Plans for Systems Design Associates. Based on our facts Systems Design Associates should implement a qualified profit-sharing plan at this time. It should be designed to begin with the 2- to 6-year vesting schedule (the slowest vesting schedule permitted) and participation-eligibility provisions that are sufficiently liberal to allow the participation of the three shareholder-employees, based on the hours of service they actually provide in a 12-month period. The plan must also be designed to comply automatically with the top-heavy rules should the plan become top-heavy. The following is a 5-year projection of the Wigginses' tax, net worth, and cash-flow situation if Systems Design is incorporated early in 2002 and if a 15 percent profit-sharing plan is adopted, implemented immediately, and fully utilized by Systems Design.

[text continues on page 3.56]

CASE II
Projections Utilizing a 15 Percent Profit-Sharing Plan

New Assumptions

1. In 2003 Systems Design Associates incorporates and implements a 15 percent profit-sharing plan whose assets earn an average of 8 percent annually over the 5-year period.

2. The value of the Systems Design Associates stock will increase 2.5 percent annually. Pending further information on the tax consequences of distributing the business building, the entire partnership interest is considered to have been contributed to the corporation for this purpose only.

3. The level of income from Systems Design Associates is set at $37,000 and will not increase over the 5-year period. (This is a decrease of $5,000 from the amount of partnership income.)

Continuing Assumptions

1. The checking account balance is maintained at approximately $6,000 and is noninterest bearing.

2. The savings account balance of $16,000 at the end of last year earns 4.75 percent interest annually. Interest is allowed to accumulate in the account.

3. The $26,000 in CDs earns 8 percent annually, and the CDs mature in December 2006.

4. The money market account pays 5.25 percent annually, and interest is accumulated in the account.

5. The Home Products stock, worth $16,000 at the end of last year, is expected to grow in value at 5 percent annually, and the dividend yield is 4 percent.

6. The Octane Oil stock with a year-end value of $12,000 is expected to appreciate at 6 percent annually, while yielding a 5 percent dividend.

7. The Growth Industries stock with a year-end value of $6,000 is expected to appreciate at 6 percent and yield 2 percent annually in dividends.

8. The Computers Corporation stock with a year-end value of $1,200 is not appreciating in value and is yielding one percent per year in dividends.

9. The Mega Fund shares with a year-end value of $1,800 are expected to increase in value at 8 percent per year and yield 3 percent.

10. The value of the personal residence ($150,000) will increase at 10 percent annually. The residence was purchased in January 1994. The original amount of the mortgage was $72,000 at an interest rate of 8 percent for 30 years.

11. The summer home will be purchased or constructed by May 2005 for $120,000. The down payment will be $12,000, and a $108,000 30-year mortgage at 8.5 percent will provide the remainder of the financing. The summer home will increase in value 5 percent annually. Property taxes for the vacation home are expected to be $400 per year.

12. The household furnishings will neither increase nor decrease in value.

13. Automobiles decrease in value at a rate of 15 percent per year.

14. Property taxes and maintenance costs on both the vacation home and the personal residence are expected to increase at 6 percent annually.

15. Charles's university salary is expected to increase 5 percent annually. Barbara's salary is expected to increase 4.5 percent annually.

16. Contributions to Charles's TDA account will continue at 8 percent of his salary until 2007 and will not increase after that date.

17. Seventy-five percent of Charles's TDA contribution will be matched by the university, and the combined amount will earn 10 percent annually over the next 5 years.

18. Present expenditures for clothing, vacations, food, utilities, transportation, medical care, entertainment, property and liability insurance, and charitable contributions are projected to increase annually at the rate of 5 percent.

19. Investable cash earns 5.25 percent annually.

INCOME STATEMENT

CHARLES & BARBARA WIGGINS

CASE II	2002	2003	2004	2005	2006
Earned Income					
Salary - Charles	82,000	86,100	90,405	94,925	99,672
Partnership Income	42,000	0	0	0	0
Corporation Income	0	37,000	37,000	37,000	37,000
Salary - Barbara	40,000	41,800	43,681	45,647	47,701
TDA-Charles Contrib	-6,560	-7,085	-7,652	-8,264	-8,925
	157,440	157,815	163,434	169,308	175,447
Interest/Dividends					
Cert Of Deposits	2,080	2,080	2,080	1,680	1,280
Home Products stock	672	699	727	756	786
Octane Oil Stock	636	668	701	736	773
Growth Indust Stock	120	122	125	127	130
Computer Corp Stock	12	12	12	12	12
Mega Fund Shares	58	60	62	63	65
Investable Cash	1,596	4,807	8,152	11,365	14,565
Saving/NOW Acts	760	796	834	874	915
Money Market Fund	515	542	570	600	631
	6,449	9,786	13,263	16,214	19,158
Other					
TrustIncome-Barbara	10,000	10,000	10,000	10,000	10,000
	10,000	10,000	10,000	10,000	10,000
Adjustments					
S.E. Tax Dedctn	563	496	496	496	496
	563	496	496	496	496
	========	========	========	========	========
Adj Gross Income	173,326	177,105	186,201	195,026	204,109
Deductions					
Charitable 50%	1,000	1,050	1,103	1,158	1,216
State Tax Paid	8,443	8,652	9,102	9,235	9,549
Property Tax - Home	2,500	2,650	2,809	2,978	3,156
PropertyTax-VacHome	0	0	0	400	424
Mortgage - Home	5,202	5,107	5,005	4,894	4,774
Mortgage - Vac Home	0	0	0	6,106	9,102
Reductn for High Inc	-1,211	-1,221	-1,388	-1,543	-1,135
Gross Deductions	15,934	16,238	16,631	23,228	27,086
Standard Deduction	4,550	4,650	4,800	4,900	5,050
Allowed Deductions	15,934	16,238	16,631	23,228	27,086
Pers Exemptions	9,570	9,735	9,455	9,135	11,093
	========	========	========	========	========
Taxable Income	147,822	151,132	160,115	162,664	165,930
	========	========	========	========	========
Fed Income Tax	40,200	40,906	42,914	44,336	46,334
	========	========	========	========	========
Fed Tax Bracket-Ord Inc	35.0%	35.0%	34.0%	34.0%	33.0%

BALANCE SHEET

CHARLES & BARBARA WIGGINS

CASE II	2002	2003	2004	2005	2006
LIQUID ASSETS					
Cash Balance	5,827	5,862	6,003	6,053	6,064
Cash Deposits					
Investable Cash	62,400	125,515	193,190	251,110	318,315
Saving/NOW Acts	16,760	17,556	18,390	19,264	20,179
Cert Of Deposits	26,000	26,000	26,000	16,000	16,000
Money Market Fund	10,315	10,857	11,427	12,027	12,658
	115,475	179,928	249,007	298,401	367,152
Stocks & Bonds					
Home Products stock	16,800	17,640	18,522	19,448	20,421
Octane Oil Stock	12,720	13,483	14,292	15,150	16,059
Growth Indust Stock	6,360	6,742	7,146	7,575	8,029
Computer Corp Stock	1,200	1,200	1,200	1,200	1,200
Mega Fund Shares	1,944	2,100	2,267	2,449	2,645
	39,024	41,164	43,428	45,822	48,353
Life Insurance					
Life Ins-Charles #1	12,200	12,200	12,200	12,200	12,200
Life Ins-Charles #2	5,600	5,600	5,600	5,600	5,600
	17,800	17,800	17,800	17,800	17,800
	========	========	========	========	========
Liquid Assets	178,126	244,754	316,238	368,076	439,369
	========	========	========	========	========
NONLIQUID ASSETS					
Bus Interests					
Partnershp Interest	175,000	0	0	0	0
Corporat'n Interest	0	179,375	183,859	188,456	193,167
	175,000	179,375	183,859	188,456	193,167
Retirement Plans					
TDA-Charles Contrib	6,560	13,645	21,297	29,561	38,486
TDA-Employr Contrib	3,120	6,396	9,836	13,448	17,240
Mortgage - Home	88,000	96,800	106,480	117,128	128,841
	97,680	116,841	137,613	160,137	184,567
Benefit Plans					
PS--Charles contrib	0	5,550	11,100	16,650	22,200
	0	5,550	11,100	16,650	22,200
Personal Property					
Home	165,000	181,500	199,650	219,615	241,577
Vacation Home	0	0	0	120,000	126,000
Auto	6,800	5,780	4,913	4,176	3,550
Home Furnishings	20,000	20,000	20,000	20,000	20,000
Jewelry & Furs	28,000	28,000	28,000	28,000	28,000
	219,800	235,280	252,563	391,791	419,126
	========	========	========	========	========
Nonliquid Assets	492,480	537,046	585,135	757,034	819,061
	========	========	========	========	========
Total Assets	670,606	781,800	901,373	1,125,110	1,258,430

BALANCE SHEET (cont.)

CHARLES & BARBARA WIGGINS

CASE II	2,002	2,003	2,004	2,005	2,006
LIABILITIES					
Mortgage Loans					
Mortgage - Home	64,395	63,162	61,827	60,381	58,815
Mortgage - Vac Home	0	0	0	107,463	106,600
	64,395	63,162	61,827	167,844	165,415
	========	========	========	========	========
Total Liabilities	64,395	63,162	61,827	167,844	165,415
	========	========	========	========	========
Net Worth	606,211	718,638	839,546	957,266	1,093,015
	========	========	========	========	========

CASH FLOW STATEMENT

CHARLES & BARBARA WIGGINS

CASE II	2002	2003	2004	2005	2006
BEGINNING OF YEAR					
Idle Cash On Hand	6,000	5,827	5,862	6,003	6,053
SOURCES OF CASH					
Cash Income					
Salary - Charles	82,000	86,100	90,405	94,925	99,672
Partnership Income	42,000	0	0	0	0
Corporation Income	0	37,000	37,000	37,000	37,000
Salary - Barbara	40,000	41,800	43,681	45,647	47,701
Interest+Dividends	3,578	3,641	3,707	3,375	3,047
TrustIncome-Barbara	10,000	10,000	10,000	10,000	10,000
	177,578	178,541	184,793	190,947	197,419
Sale/Withdrawals					
Cert Of Deposits	0	0	0	10,000	0
	0	0	0	10,000	0
Liab Incurred					
Cash Borwd-Vac Home	0	0	0	108,000	0
	0	0	0	108,000	0
Total Cash Inflow	177,578	178,541	184,793	308,947	197,419
Tot Cash Available	183,578	184,368	190,654	314,950	203,472
USES OF CASH					
Fully Tax Deductible					
TDA-Charles Contrib	6,560	7,085	7,652	8,264	8,925
Mortgage - Home	5,202	5,107	5,005	4,894	4,774
Mortgage - Vac Home	0	0	0	6,106	9,102
	11,762	12,192	12,657	19,264	22,801
Partly Deductible					
Medical Care	2,480	2,604	2,734	2,871	3,014
Charity Contrb-50%	1,000	1,050	1,103	1,158	1,216
	3,480	3,654	3,837	4,029	4,230
Not Tax Deductible					
Education Fund	2,000	2,000	2,000	2,000	2,000
Child Support	8,400	8,400	8,400	8,400	8,400
Food	8,000	8,400	8,820	9,261	9,724
Clothing	3,500	3,675	3,859	4,052	4,254
Entertainment	3,500	3,675	3,859	4,052	4,254
Vacations	4,500	4,725	4,961	5,209	5,470
Transportation	1,500	1,575	1,654	1,736	1,823

CASH FLOW STATEMENT (cont.)

CHARLES & BARBARA WIGGINS

CASE II	2002	2003	2004	2005	2006
Life Ins Prem Pymnt	2,620	2,620	2,620	2,620	2,620
Prop Ins Prem Pymnt	1,150	1,208	1,268	1,331	1,398
Maint--Home/VacHome	2,000	2,120	2,247	2,382	2,525
Utility/Phone	3,500	3,675	3,859	4,052	4,254
New Furniture	2,000	2,000	2,000	2,000	2,000
ClosingCost-VacHome	0	0	0	6,000	0
	42,670	44,073	45,546	53,095	48,723
Taxes Paid					
Fed Tax Paid	40,200	40,906	42,914	44,336	46,334
State Tax Paid	8,443	8,652	9,102	9,235	9,549
FICA/Soc Sec Tax	6,754	6,839	6,929	7,023	7,122
Real Estate Tax	2,500	2,650	2,809	3,378	3,580
	57,897	59,047	61,754	63,972	66,585
Purchase/Deposits					
Purchase Vac Home	0	0	0	120,000	0
Investable Cash	60,804	58,308	59,523	46,555	52,640
	60,804	58,308	59,523	166,555	52,640
Liability Liquidation					
Mortgage - Home	1,138	1,233	1,335	1,446	1,566
Mortgage - Vac Home	0	0	0	537	863
	1,138	1,233	1,335	1,983	2,429
	========	========	========	========	========
Tot Cash Outflow	177,751	178,506	184,652	308,897	197,408
	========	========	========	========	========
END OF YEAR					
Cash Balance	5,827	5,862	6,003	6,053	6,064
	========	========	========	========	========

SUPPORTING SCHEDULE

CHARLES & BARBARA WIGGINS

CASE II	SINGLE 2002	SINGLE 2003	SINGLE 2004	SINGLE 2005	SINGLE 2006
Income					
Earned Income	157,440	157,815	163,434	169,308	175,447
Adj Gross Income	173,326	177,105	186,201	195,026	204,109
Allowed Deductions	15,934	16,238	16,631	23,228	27,086
Pers Exemptions	9,570	9,735	9,455	9,135	11,093
Taxable Income	147,822	151,132	160,115	162,664	165,930
Federal Tax Liab					
Regular Tax	39,075	39,915	41,418	41,958	41,374
Gross Fed Inc Tax	39,075	39,915	41,418	41,958	41,374
Alt Minimum Tax	0	0	505	1,387	3,969
AMT Credit C/Over	0	0	0	0	505
Disallowed	0	0	0	-505	-1,892
Self Employmt Tax	1,125	991	991	991	991
Fed Income Tax	40,200	40,906	42,914	44,336	46,334
Fed Tax Analysis-Ord Inc					
Indexing Factor	77	82	87	91	96
Fed Tax Bracket-Ord Inc	35.0%	35.0%	34.0%	34.0%	33.0%
$ to Next Bracket	157,228	161,868	161,035	166,836	172,120
Next Bracket	38.6%	38.6%	37.6%	37.6%	35.0%
Previous Bracket	30.0%	30.0%	29.0%	29.0%	28.0%
$ to Prev Bracket	7,522	7,182	12,415	11,164	10,480
Fed Effective Tax Rate	27.2%	27.1%	26.8%	27.3%	27.9%
Alt Minimum Tax					
Adj Gross Income	173,326	177,105	186,201	195,026	204,109
Contributions	-1,000	-1,050	-1,103	-1,158	-1,216
Home Mortg Int	-5,202	-5,107	-5,005	-11,000	-13,876
Adjusted AMTI	167,124	170,948	180,093	182,868	189,017
AMT Exemptions	-22,094	-21,138	-18,852	-16,158	-14,621
AMT Taxable Inc	145,030	149,810	161,241	166,711	174,397
Gross Alt Min Tx	37,708	38,951	41,923	43,345	45,343
Fed Tax Less FTC	-39,075	-39,915	-41,418	-41,958	-41,374
Alt Minimum Tax	0	0	505	1,387	3,969
Other Tax Liabs					
FICA/Soc Sec Tax	6,754	6,839	6,929	7,023	7,122
Adj Gross Inc	173,326	177,105	186,201	195,026	204,109
GA Adj Gross Inc	173,326	177,105	186,201	195,026	204,109
GA Standard Ded	2,300	2,300	2,300	2,300	2,300
GA Itemized Ded	15,934	16,238	16,631	23,228	27,086
GA Exemptions	13,500	13,500	14,700	14,700	14,700
GA Taxable Inc	143,892	147,367	154,870	157,099	162,323
GA Regular Tax	8,443	8,652	9,102	9,235	9,549
GA Income Tax	8,443	8,652	9,102	9,235	9,549
Georgia Tax	8,443	8,652	9,102	9,235	9,549
Tot State/Local Tx	8,443	8,652	9,102	9,235	9,549
Total Inc Tax	55,397	56,397	58,945	60,594	63,005

FINANCIAL SUMMARY

CHARLES & BARBARA WIGGINS

CASE II	2002	2003	2004	2005	2006
Gross Real Income					
Personal Earnings	164,000	164,900	171,086	177,572	184,372
Interest Income	4,951	8,225	11,636	14,519	17,391
Dividends Rcvd	1,498	1,561	1,627	1,695	1,767
TrustIncome-Barbara	10,000	10,000	10,000	10,000	10,000
	180,449	184,686	194,349	203,786	213,530
Income & Inflation					
Gross Real Inc	180,449	184,686	194,349	203,786	213,530
Total Inc Tax	-55,397	-56,397	-58,945	-60,594	-63,005
Net Real Income	125,052	128,289	135,404	143,192	150,525
Cur Real Inc =	125,052	128,305	131,643	135,068	138,582
Purch Power Drop	0	16	0	0	0
At Infltn Rate of	3	3	3	3	3
Cash Flow					
Idle Cash On Hand	6,000	5,827	5,862	6,003	6,053
Norml Cash Inflow	177,578	178,541	184,793	308,947	197,419
Norml Cash Outflw	116,947	120,198	125,129	262,342	144,768
Cash Invested	60,804	58,308	59,523	46,555	52,640
Cash Balance	5,827	5,862	6,003	6,053	6,064
Net Worth					
Personal Assets	243,427	258,942	276,366	415,644	442,991
Investment Assets	427,179	522,858	625,007	709,465	815,440
Personal Liabilities	-64,395	-63,162	-61,827	-167,844	-165,415
Personal Net Worth	179,032	195,780	214,539	247,800	277,576
Investment Net Worth	427,179	522,858	625,007	709,465	815,440
Net Worth	606,211	718,638	839,546	957,266	1,093,015

At this time the implementation of a 10 percent money-purchase pension plan is not recommended, particularly since the maximum amount that could be contributed in behalf of each of the shareholder-employees based on their compensation is only $3,700 each per year. The cost of this $3,700 contribution is the inclusion of all the other employees in the plan and contributions in their behalf. A further consideration is the mandatory employer contribution, which can be burdensome, especially in small businesses.

If at some time in the future Systems Design Associates becomes more profitable and the shareholder-employees believe they can forgo another 10 percent of their cash income from Systems Design, implementation of a money-purchase pension plan or an increase in the profit-sharing plan contribution percentage could be considered. As previously discussed, use of a 10 percent money-purchase pension plan in combination with the profit-sharing plan, or a 25 percent contribution-rate profit-sharing plan would allow the corporation to deduct total contributions of $9,250 annually for Charles's retirement, based on his present salary.

Borrowing from Qualified Plans. One of the important benefits of closely held businesses to shareholder-employees is the ability to borrow from qualified plans for personal objectives. Interest deductions to the borrower, are, of course, subject to the restrictions on deductibility applicable to various types of interest payments. In addition, key employees may not deduct interest on plan loans, as discussed below. Interest paid into the plan is received tax free to accumulate with the remainder of the shareholder-employee's account balance.

In order to take advantage of the possibility of borrowing from qualified plans, the plan document must specifically provide authorization for such loans. As a general rule, while there are some statutory restrictions that prohibit transactions between shareholder-employees (and other disqualified persons) and qualified plans, shareholder-employees of regular C corporations may participate in loan programs if certain conditions are met with respect to the loans (IRC Sec. 4975(d)). These conditions are as follows:

- The loans must be made available to all participants or beneficiaries of participants on a reasonably equivalent basis.
- Loans may not be made available to highly compensated employees in an amount greater than the amount made available to other employees. (This requirement is satisfied if a percentage of the account balance can be borrowed and is not a dollar-for-dollar limitation.)
- Loans must be made in accordance with the specific provisions regarding such loans as set forth in the plan documents.
- The loan must bear a reasonable rate of interest.
- The loan must be adequately secured. Such security may include the employee's vested accrued benefit or account balance under the plan or plans.

The general rule with regard to borrowing from qualified plans is that plan loans are taxable distributions under the annuity rules of IRC Sec. 72. This means that employer contributions would be fully taxable as ordinary income in the year received. The general rule, however, is subject to an important exception, which states that the treatment as a taxable distribution will apply only to the extent that the outstanding principal on loans from qualified plans exceeds the lesser of $50,000 or 50 percent of the nonforfeitable accrued benefit or vested account balance. Note that deductible employee contributions are not considered vested benefits or account balances for this purpose and that loans of these deductible employee contributions will always be a taxable distribution. However, the statute does provide a safe harbor. All participants can borrow up to $10,000 regardless of their accrued benefit or vested account balance as long as the above conditions are met.

A rapid repayment schedule is required to avoid treatment as a taxable distribution for all loans except those for the acquisition or construction of a principal residence of the plan participant or a member of his or her family (IRC Sec. 72(p)(1)(B)(ii)). The time requirement for repayment of all loans except those for a principal residence described in the preceding sentence may not exceed 5 years for both the loan and any extensions of the loan. If the loan term exceeds 5 years, but the loan is in fact repaid before the 5-year period expires, it will still be treated as a taxable distribution.

Current federal tax laws have further tightened up the rules regarding loan balances with the following additional requirements:

- The $50,000 loan limit is reduced by the highest outstanding loan balance during the one-year period ending the day before the loan date.
- Level amortization of the loan is required.
- Interest deductions, even if otherwise allowable, are denied for a loan to a key employee.

The law's reduction for the highest outstanding loan balance during the prior 12 months is designed to prevent participants from effectively avoiding the 5-year repayment requirement by simply renewing the loan every 5 years. For example, if a participant repays a $50,000 loan on January 1, 2003, that participant cannot borrow from the plan until 2004. Under prior law the participant could have immediately reborrowed $50,000 with a new 5-year repayment provision.

Despite the significant limitations on the capability of C corporation shareholder-employees to borrow from qualified plans, such borrowing can still provide needed funds for the achievement of personal objectives and can be especially helpful for more or less short-term cash-flow deficiencies. For example, a $10,000 loan to the Wiggins family could be a part of the down payment on their vacation home if other funding mechanisms unexpectedly fall short of their objectives. For this reason when the profit-sharing plan is designed, it should contain a provision that allows for loans to plan participants within the present statutory limits.

Pursuant to the Economic Growth and Tax Relief Reconciliation Act of 2001, self-employed individuals now qualify to use plan loans. Sole proprietors, partners, and S corporation shareholder-employees who hold more than 5 percent of the outstanding stock of an S corporation are self-employed for this purpose (IRC Sec. 4975(d)).

Group Medical, Disability Income, and Life Insurance Plans. The Internal Revenue Code provides that medical, disability income, and life insurance plans within certain limits can be made available to employees and the costs can be deducted by the corporation (except an S corporation for owner-employees) without being included in the gross income of the employees. In the case of life insurance an employer or employers can provide up to $50,000 of group term life insurance on a tax-free basis unless the plan is discriminatory. In the event that a plan is discriminatory, the entire actual cost of their group term insurance is taxable to highly compensated employees.

Under IRC Sec. 106 the employee's gross income does not include contributions by the employer to accident or health plans to provide compensation (through insurance or otherwise) to his or her employees for personal injuries or sickness. The tax consequences of the amounts received under those plans are governed by IRC Sec. 104 for personal injury and sickness and by IRC Sec. 22 for disability payments.

As a general rule Sec. 104 provides that the employee's gross income does not include medical expenses that are paid to the employee or to care providers on his or her behalf if such amounts have not been deducted under Sec. 213 as medical expenses in a prior year.

There is a limited tax credit that is a modification of the former credit for the elderly. This current credit is called the credit for the elderly and the permanently and totally disabled (IRC Sec. 22).

Under Sec. 22 there is a 15 percent tax credit computed on the Sec. 22 amount for the taxable year. The Sec. 22 amount is computed by taking an initial amount not in excess of disability income includible in the gross income of the taxpayer (unless one or both of the taxpayers filing a joint return are 65 and disabled) and reducing that amount by Social Security disability payments and certain other payments excludible from gross income (IRC Sec. 22(c)(3)). There is a further reduction for taxpayers with adjusted gross incomes in excess of certain limits. These limits are $7,500 for single taxpayers, $10,000 for married taxpayers filing a joint return, and $5,000 for a married taxpayer filing a separate return. If the taxpayer's adjusted gross income exceeds these levels, the Sec. 22 amount is further reduced by one-half of the excess of the adjusted gross income over these levels. When these adjustments have been made, the credit is 15 percent of the resulting amount.

Personal Use of Company Assets. The facts of this case disclose that Charles Wiggins is already utilizing a business asset—namely, a company car. An employee's personal use of business assets results in taxable income to the employee. The amount of taxable income, however, is not the asset's total value. Instead the general rule is that the amount of income taxable to the employee will be the fair rental value of the personally used corporate assets for the time of the personal use. For example, if the personal use of the company car is approximately 40 percent, Charles will have taxable income in the amount of 40 percent of the rental value of the car for the entire year. Nevertheless, it is often helpful from a cash-flow standpoint to have the employer corporation pay for and deduct the use of assets that are ordinary trade and business expenses to the corporation and to have the employee responsible for only the tax liability for the time apportioned for personal use.

The tax treatment by business entities of business assets used partially for business and partially for personal use has been restricted repeatedly by continuous changes in the tax law. These changes particularly affect automobiles (although some of the rules apply to other kinds of "mixed-use" property). The types of property affected by the current tax laws are referred to as listed property and are

- any passenger automobile as defined in IRC Sec. 280F(d)
- any other property used as a means of transportation
- any property of a type generally used for purposes of entertainment, recreation, or amusement
- any computer or peripheral computer equipment (except one used exclusively at a regular business establishment or bona fide home office)
- any other property specified by the secretary in the regulations (IRC Sec. 280F(d)(4))

The general rule for listed property is that it must be used more than 50 percent for business before the ACRS (accelerated cost recovery system) for depreciation can be utilized. If the property is used 50 percent or less for business, depreciation can still be taken for the proportion of business use. However, the depreciation must be computed on a straight-line method over a period longer than ACRS (IRC Sec. 280F(b)).

For automobiles there are additional limitations even if the automobiles are used 100 percent for business purposes. For automobiles placed in service after December 31, 1988, the maximum allowable cost recovery deduction is limited to $3,060 in the first year of the recovery period, $5,000 in the second year of the recovery period, $2,950 in the third year, and $1,775 for each remaining year. If the automobile is used partly for business and partly for personal use, these amounts must be reduced by the proportion of personal use.

The extent of business use of such property is an area in which there have traditionally been a great many factual disputes between taxpayers and the IRS, and the area is likely to become an audit point for the individual taxpayer and also for the corporation. Without appropriate documentation the IRS has usually been successful in prevailing in its position in an audit in this area. Failure to keep the required records results in the loss of the claimed deduction (IRC Sec. 274(d)(4)). It is very important to maintain appropriate documentation on personal usage in order to apportion correctly the percentage of usage between the corporation and the individual employee. A log completed at or near the time of use is the recommended method.

Employment of Family Members. A closely held business such as Systems Design Associates often provides important fringe benefits not only for the shareholder-employees but for their families as well. One area that Charles Wiggins should explore for reducing the family's net tax liability while providing some funding for his children's education or other expenses is the employment of the children with Systems Design Associates during summer vacations or after school. Stephanie, in particular, will be 15 next summer and could be expected to receive a work permit for vacation periods. The bona fide employment of family members can provide not only needed funds that are taxed at the children's lower tax bracket but also work experience that will prove valuable in the children's later life. As already noted in the section on reasonable compensation, it would not be permissible for Systems Design Associates to pay the children and deduct the payments as salary unless the children are actually providing services for the corporation. If, however, there are delivery, courier, or clerical jobs for which the Wiggins children could qualify as they become old enough to be employed, this could provide the beginnings of a college fund of their own. It is important to note here that, although we are not given enough facts about the other two shareholders of Systems Design Associates to know whether they also have children of like ages and with similar problems, there could be a conflict among the shareholders if there are children of the other shareholders and a limited number of vacation and summer jobs. This is an area that will merit further consideration.

Buy-Sell Agreements to Assure That the Business Interest Is Marketable at Death or Disability. One of the largest assets that the Wiggins family owns is Charles's interest in Systems Design Associates. However, there is no guarantee that this business interest could be translated into cash within a reasonable time after his death or disability, because of the difficulty of selling closely held business interests and because Charles and his former partners have never implemented a legally enforceable agreement to take effect at the death or disability of any of them. The failure to implement a legally enforceable buy-sell agreement that is appropriately funded often causes the destruction of closely held businesses, particularly service businesses. In this case Charles's present estate plan calls for his business interest to pass under his will. This means that one-half of his business interest would go to Barbara and one-quarter to each of his daughters by his prior marriage.

It was noted earlier that the death of a partner results in a technical dissolution of a partnership under state partnership law. Unless a way is found to fund the buyout of the interests of Barbara, Stephanie, and Caroline, Systems Design could be effectively crippled as a going business.

In the event that Charles becomes disabled, his business interest should be convertible to cash to provide him with additional monies throughout the period of his disability. These objectives can be achieved only through the design and implementation of a buy-sell agreement.

Buy-sell agreements are usually of two types:

- redemption agreements in which the corporation and the shareholder enter into an agreement containing the provision that the corporation will purchase (redeem) the shareholder's stock upon death, disability, or some other preestablished event
- cross-purchase agreements that are agreements between and among the shareholders that in the event of death, disability, or some other preestablished event, one or more of the remaining shareholders will purchase the deceased or disabled shareholder's interest

Redemption agreements can cause problems for tax purposes. Because of the constructive ownership rules of Code Sec. 318, redemptions in family-owned corporations may result in dividend treatment rather than capital-gain treatment. This will substantially increase the tax liability resulting from a redemption from a deceased shareholder's estate.

Dividend treatment prevents the estate from recovering its basis in the redeemed stock free of federal income tax. This is particularly important for redemptions from estates, since the estate generally has a basis in the stock equal to its fair market value on the date of the stockholder's death (IRC Sec. 1014). Therefore a redemption of such stock that is treated as a capital transaction rather than as a dividend will result in little or no income tax liability, since the estate's basis in the stock will be approximately equal to the redemption price. Dividend treatment, on the other hand, will result in the full amount of redemption proceeds being taxable to the extent of the corporation's current and accumulated earnings and profits.

In addition, such agreements are typically funded by insurance. The receipt of insurance proceeds may result in an income tax liability to the corporation under the concept known as book income preference to the alternative minimum tax. The details of this book income preference are beyond the scope of this discussion. Briefly, however, insurance proceeds may subject a corporation to the alternative minimum tax. Such a tax could be imposed on as much as one-half of insurance proceeds received by a corporation, resulting in an effective tax rate of 10 percent on the total proceeds. Prior to the 1986 act the receipt of insurance proceeds by a corporation generally did not give rise to income tax liability. The book income preference under the alternative minimum tax should be considered whenever corporate-owned life insurance is being used as part of a business plan.

A redemption agreement also does not result in an increase in the surviving stockholders' tax basis in their ownership interest in the corporation when a stockholder dies. In a cross-purchase agreement the purchasing stockholder's basis in his or her stock interest is increased to include the cost of the purchased interest. This can reduce the tax liability on a subsequent sale of the stock by the surviving shareholder.

Another possible problem with redemption agreements is that any accumulation of corporate funds to fund a redemption agreement can result in an "unreasonable accumulation" for tax purposes. This can make the corporation subject to the accumulated-earnings tax if the redemption is determined to be for the benefit of the shareholders rather than for the business of the corporation itself (IRC Secs. 531–537).

Cross-purchase agreements are problematic when there are a large number of shareholders, when shareholders are of widely disparate ages, or if there is a shareholder whose health is impaired, because such agreements are usually also funded wholly or partially with life insurance. The difference in ages or health conditions can result in the younger or healthier shareholders' being forced to personally pay high nondeductible premiums for insurance on the life of the older or impaired shareholder. Another aspect of cross-purchase agreements is that on the death of one of the shareholders the deceased shareholder's estate will own policies on the lives of the surviving shareholders. If these policies are sold to a shareholder other than the insured to fund a new or continuing buy-sell agreement, the transfer is a transfer-for-value that can result in regular income tax liability on receipt of the policy proceeds. With a redemption agreement, however, the corporation can continue to hold the insurance policies on the lives of the surviving shareholders to fund a continuing redemption agreement without creating a transfer-for-value problem.

Given the closeness of the ages of the owners of Systems Design Associates, and taking into account the factors just described, a cross-purchase agreement would appear to offer more advantages to Charles and his associates than a redemption agreement. Therefore one recommendation is that the shareholders adopt a cross-purchase buy-sell agreement.

Since there is no set formula that is equally successful for every corporation, the buy-sell agreement may contain whatever provisions are of importance to the shareholders of a particular corporation. It is neither unusual nor improper for such agreements to be very personal to the corporation and to the shareholders' particular situations.

However, the agreement must provide for the surviving shareholders to become obligated to purchase the shares of a deceased or disabled shareholder. At the death of the shareholder there are no arguable facts to impede the buy-sell agreement's becoming operative. In fact, the event is known and ascertainable from the moment it occurs.

In the event of disability, however, the definition of disability that will make the buy-sell operative must be contained within the document to make the document totally effective. If disability insurance is used to fund the buy-sell agreement, the same definition of disability and the waiting period that is contained within the insurance policy that funds the agreement should be embodied within the buy-sell agreement itself.

The buy-sell should not be designed to provide for the immediate buyout of a disabled shareholder. An appropriate waiting period should be adopted to balance the client's need for disability income and the time at which the client can psychologically deal with the fact that he or she will be unable to resume former duties.

There are basically three ways to deal with funding buy-sell agreements. The first is that the buy-sell agreement will be paid for by an installment sale arrangement between the stockholders. One disadvantage of this arrangement is that the deceased stockholder's heirs will not receive the value of the deceased's stock in cash immediately but will receive only installment payments, which may cease if the surviving shareholders encounter financial difficulties.

Another significant disadvantage is that the surviving stockholders' interest payments under the installment arrangement will be subject to the limitations on investment interest expenses under the current federal tax laws if the corporation is a C corporation.

The IRS has indicated that these interest payments are deductible as a business interest expense if the business interest being purchased is an interest in a partnership or an S corporation. This may make an S election more favorable for certain corporations.

The second method of funding a buy-sell agreement requires the establishment of a sinking fund. This is roughly the equivalent of a savings account to assure that the survivors will have adequate funds when the buy-sell becomes operative. There can be practical problems with this approach because death or disability may occur before the targeted amount for the fund has been fully accumulated, requiring part of the purchase to be made with other assets of the survivors.

The third (and usually the best) method of funding buy-sell agreements is full or partial funding through the purchase of life and disability insurance on the corporate shareholder.

If insurance is used to fund the corporate buy-sell agreement, a common provision embodied in the buy-sell agreement itself requires that the survivors pay the amount of the proceeds of such insurance in a lump sum to the disabled shareholder or to the estate or beneficiaries of a deceased shareholder. Inclusion of such a provision would be advisable in Systems Design Associates' cross-purchase agreement.

Because of the step-up in basis at the death of a shareholder there is usually little or no federal income tax liability to the estate of the deceased shareholder. Under a disability buyout, however, there is a possibility of federal income tax liability. The tax could possibly be reduced or deferred by having the still actively involved shareholders buy the stock on an installment-sale basis. However, considerations of the safety of the principal may outweigh the potential tax savings. In addition, the interest on the payments will probably not be fully deductible, as discussed above. It is advisable, then, to have both the death and disability buyout provisions as fully funded by insurance as is possible.

Generally the most difficult portion of any buy-sell agreement is deciding on a valuation for the business interest. Of course the surest way to ascertain the value of a going business is to have the business appraised by an appropriate professional. In many cases, however, closely held business owners are reluctant to engage an appraiser because of the expense. In addition, even if an appraisal is made this year and a firm dollar value is entered into the buy-sell agreement, it is likely that the agreement may not become operative for many years. In that event the appraisal figure is meaningless because it is totally outdated. That does not mean, however, that the parties to the buy-sell agreement can ignore the stated dollar figure. In fact, the value of the business could have risen tenfold, and if the dollar figure stated in the buy-sell agreement was not revised, the corporation is obligated to pay only the original price (10 percent of the current value) as stated in the buy-sell agreement. This can result in significant hardships to the estate or beneficiaries of the closely held business owner.

It is human nature to expect that even with a buy-sell in effect, most closely held business owners will not revalue the valuation figure on a regular basis. They are usually preoccupied with their lives and just never get around to doing a routine revaluation. Therefore absolute dollar figures are quite likely to become outdated and should be avoided whenever possible.

In the case of a personal service business such as Systems Design, if the client can be persuaded to obtain an appraisal on the current value of the business, that value can be used as the starting point for the valuation of the buy-sell agreement. Furthermore, the appraisal may provide a formula approach to valuing the business based on billings, accounts receivable, and other items that will provide a framework upon which an appropriate valuation formula can be built. Such a formula should be included in the buy-sell agreement in lieu of a stated dollar figure. In the absence of such a formula, the buy-sell agreement may provide that the shareholders will meet at regular intervals, not to exceed every 2 years, and will redetermine the value of the corporation for purposes of the buy-sell agreement. The formula approach is preferable as it allows the value of the corporation to be determined at any point in time and requires no affirmative action on the part of the corporate shareholders. As long as three conditions are met, the IRS will accept the value determined by the formula. The three conditions are (1) the estate must be legally obligated to sell the business interest, (2) there can be no disparity between the purchase price in a lifetime sale setting versus at death, and (3) the pricing mechanism must be based on data arrived at as the result of arm's-length basis.

Any arrangement agreed to between Charles and the owners would need to include some consideration of the fact that each owner holds a minority interest in the business. Due to the enactment of estate freeze prohibitions, a buy-sell agreement executed by and between family members will not be successful in freezing the value of the business interest.

To be legally binding the shares of stock in the corporation must bear an appropriate legend—that is, a statement that says in substance that the stock is restricted stock and is subject to an agreement among the shareholders dated on the date of the buy-sell agreement.

In the Wiggins case a buy-sell agreement—specifically, a cross-purchase agreement—should be entered into by Charles and his associates. The agreement should be funded by insurance. A realistic value for the stock should be established, preferably by an appraisal, and should be required by contract to be maintained by a formula throughout the life of the buy-sell agreement.

BUSINESS PLANNING: INSURANCE

Funding the Buy-Sell Agreement

As already indicated, insurance is the recommended vehicle for funding the buy-sell agreement. (The amount of coverage indicated below assumes that the business building has been successfully distributed to Charles, Ursula, and Steve prior to incorporation.)

If the buy-sell is triggered by the death of a shareholder (Charles), both Steve and Ursula can fund their obligation by obtaining a life insurance policy in the amount of $75,000 on Charles's life. If policies are obtained for a death benefit of $150,000 and the total $150,000 amount is in excess of the amount necessary to fund the buy-sell at Charles's death, any remaining proceeds can be used as the surviving shareholders see fit. Insurance on each shareholder should be purchased by the other two shareholders in a similar fashion.

If a cash value type of policy is used to fund the buy-sell agreement, the cash value can also be used to help purchase the ownership interest of a retiring corporate shareholder. Buy-sell agreements can also be funded with term insurance that will increase in cost with age and must be kept in force until the shareholder dies or retires.

The other element that must be considered in funding the buy-sell agreement is the appropriate coverage if the disability of a shareholder-employee triggers the buy-sell.

Insurers are willing to provide coverage with lump-sum benefits for the disability buyout. As a general rule such coverage is limited to 80 percent of the value of the business interest. In this case Charles could probably get insurance based on $150,000 for his ownership rights and thereby be assured of $120,000 of lump-sum coverage.

Important issues concerning disability buyout insurance include the definition of disability and the elimination period (waiting period). The definition of disability and the length of the elimination period in the insurance contract used for funding should match the terms set forth in the buy-sell agreement. Coverage with 12-month, 18-month, 24-month, or 36-month elimination periods is available. The annual premiums for a $100,000 policy with 80 percent disability buyout coverage for these elimination periods would be approximately $1,200, $1,050, $975, and $825, respectively.

There is a real danger in selecting too short an elimination period. Not only is it more expensive, but it could result in a mandatory sale of the business interest because of a disability that is relatively short-term but that lasts longer than the elimination period. It would probably be advisable to have at least a 24-month elimination period for the lump-sum buy-out coverage. This coverage is available in addition to the monthly disability income coverage. If the disability coverage for the buy-sell is triggered and $120,000 is paid out in a lump sum, earning 7 percent annually before taxes, this would add an additional $700 per month in disability income for Charles.

Selecting Appropriate Products and Coverage Amounts for Group Medical, Disability, and Life Insurance Plans

If Systems Design Associates (currently a partnership) does not become a corporation, there appear to be no significant advantages for having the existing partnership provide benefits to the partners. Partners are not considered "employees" of the partnership for most tax purposes, and therefore contributions in behalf of partners would produce no tax advantages.

The major advantages of employee benefits lie in the fact that their cost is tax deductible to the employer and not included in the income of the employee. Another important advantage is that benefits can usually be purchased on a group basis at a lower cost than is available to individual employees in the individual insurance marketplace.

Medical Expense Insurance

Although the medical expense coverage under Charles's existing group insurance policies seems reasonably adequate, two factors are worthy of discussion. The first is the $500,000 lifetime maximum for each person. The stated limit falls within a "normal" range, but limits of $1 million or unlimited benefits are no longer uncommon. In fact, the limit of $500,000 may be too low for a serious illness. Second, no mention is made of any type of stop-loss provision under the medical expense plan. If medical expenses were severe, the Wigginses' 20 percent participation could become substantial.

There is a type of policy sold in the individual marketplace designed to supplement these kinds of inadequacies in group medical expense protection. Sold primarily by companies in the property and liability business, this policy is a form of major medical coverage that provides broad benefits for medical expenses that exceed a specified deductible and that are not covered by underlying medical expense contracts. Covered medical expenses are paid without coinsurance but are subject to the other usual types of limitations found in major medical contracts.

This type of policy is not standardized, and numerous variations in policy provisions and price exist among companies. However, for an annual cost ranging from $100 to $500 per policy, Systems Design Associates could buy such a policy for the Wigginses and the other employees. For example, such a policy could provide an additional $500,000 or $1 million of protection per person with a $1,000 annual deductible per person. Thus if one member of the family had $50,000 in medical expenses, the existing group coverage would pay 80 percent of $49,800, or $39,840. Of the $10,160 not covered by the existing group policy, all but $1,000 would then be covered by the supplemental contract.

Charles and his associates should consider whether the savings generated by providing such coverage on a tax-advantaged group basis is worth the additional cost of including the three other full-time employees in such a plan. Charles may be interested in providing the employees with such benefits or with more comprehensive medical coverage to provide motivation. On the other hand, it may be less expensive overall for Charles to simply purchase such coverage individually. This particular question should be discussed further with Charles.

Disability Income Insurance

Although Charles has a very generous disability income protection package from Homestate Tech relative to his teaching salary, it is not sufficient to fund all his income objectives in case of total disability. Charles can look forward to about $8,205 per month from current ascertainable sources, which include Social Security disability benefits, current disability insurance, and the income Barbara earns, supplemented by her trust income. This is still over $1,295 short of the $9,500 per month objective. It will not be possible to fully satisfy this objective solely with disability income protection because insurers will not provide such a high ratio of coverage to total income. The maximum amount of coverage available will be based on Charles's combined income from teaching and the consulting business. The amount of additional disability income insurance available will be the difference between the amount already provided and the underwriting limit on the combined incomes for Charles. The upper limit is higher if the employer provides the coverage than it is if the individual purchases the coverage. The overall limit will be approximately $4,300 per month of benefits through the employer or $3,600 monthly if purchased individually.

Since there are already monthly benefits of $3,614 in place ($1,876 group disability plus $1,738 Social Security), the insurers will limit additional coverage to approximately $1,500 monthly for employer-purchased coverage and $1,000 monthly for personal employee purchases. The price for these coverages depends on both the waiting period (elimination period) before benefits begin and the benefit duration. This is very close to the $1,295 per month shortfall that exists without this coverage.

Comprehensive disability coverage with a 6-month elimination period and a lifetime benefit period should be available for an annual premium of $37 per $100 of monthly benefit. In other words, the $1,500 of additional monthly coverage is available for approximately $555 annually. The following table shows other prices based on different elimination and benefit periods.

Elimination Period	Benefit Period	
	To Age 65	For Life
6 months	$30.00	$37.00
12 months	27.00	34.00
24 months	23.00	30.00

Because of the additional coverage amounts available through the corporation, our recommendation would be that disability income coverage with a 6-month waiting period be provided to shareholder-employees through Systems Design Associates.

Group Life Insurance Plan

Although it appears likely that Charles will need some additional life insurance protection, his group term coverage from the university, which is tied to his salary, exceeds the $50,000 aggregate limit for tax-favored group term coverage. Because of the level of his salary he will be unable to obtain any tax-favored additional coverage from his employment. Therefore it would perhaps be best for Charles to obtain any needed insurance personally.

Additional amounts of personal life insurance will be discussed further in the insurance planning section of the personal plan.

Property and Liability Insurance for the Business

With little information given in the case narrative about the business assets to be covered by property and liability insurance, it is difficult to make any recommendations other than noting the necessity of having these coverages thoroughly reviewed by a professional in the field of property and liability insurance.

PERSONAL PLANNING: TAXES

Present Position

Although Charles and Barbara Wiggins enjoy a respectable income, because of taxes and inflation they are accumulating and saving assets at a slower rate than they find desirable.

Charles and Barbara have indicated that they would like to reduce the amount of taxes they are paying and to devote their tax savings to funding their personal objectives. Some suggestions in that regard have already been made in the business planning section, particularly concerning the establishment, implementation, and utilization of a qualified plan of deferred compensation. While this will add to their retirement security without severely impairing their lifestyle, it will not materially assist them in achieving their accumulation objectives in the short term.

Fund College Education for Children

The Wigginses' first personal financial priority is funding college education for their children. Some assets have already been accumulated for that purpose and a systematic savings plan has been implemented.

The amounts that the Wigginses have projected as necessary for their children's education are significant by any standards. Since they are in a high marginal federal tax bracket and since funding for children's education is not a tax-deductible item for federal tax purposes, each dollar they accumulate to spend for their children's education will actually cost them considerably more than $1 in pretax income. Obviously the most advantageous way to accumulate the sum needed for education is with tax-advantaged dollars. One of the ways this can be accomplished in harmonious family situations is through tax-free opportunities to save for education or through the mechanisms of income shifting or gift giving.

Tax-Free Growth Options

Since 1997 two planning options have emerged that allow individuals to set aside money for education costs that can grow on a tax-free basis. These planning options are Coverdell Education Savings Accounts (formerly known as Education IRAs) and Sec. 529 plans. Provided that the accumulations inside of these vehicles are used for qualified education expenses, the growth and income on amounts contributed to the plans are excluded from income.

Coverdell Education Savings Accounts allow individuals to contribute up to $2,000 per year to a fund dedicated for educational expenses. The ability to contribute is phased out for high income individuals; consequently the Wigginses will not be able to personally contribute to a Coverdell Education Savings Account for the benefit of their children. If other family members (parents, brothers, sisters) meet the contribution limitations, it may be possible to have them set up the accounts for Charles and Barbara's children. If Coverdell Education Savings Accounts are created, any amounts remaining in the account that have not been used for qualified education expenses must either be distributed to the named beneficiary by age 30 (at which point the distribution in excess of basis is subject to income tax plus a penalty) or rolled over to a Coverdell Education Savings Account for the benefit of a related party of the beneficiary.

Sec. 529 plans also allow for tax-free growth of amounts used for qualified education expenses, but they provide more flexibility. An individual can make a lump-sum contribution to a Sec. 529 plan that is treated as five annual exclusion gifts to the beneficiary. This allows an individual to contribute a significant amount to the plan, in contrast to the maximum $2,000 annual contribution limit to a Coverdell Education Savings Account. Another advantage of the Sec. 529 plan is that there is no mandatory payout requirement when the beneficiary reaches age 30. Any amounts remaining at that point can be left in the account to cover future educational expenses of the beneficiary. Furthermore, there are no income limitations imposed on an individual's ability to make contributions to the plan. Some states also allow a state income tax deduction for contributions to certain Sec. 529 plans.

For the Wigginses, a Sec. 529 plan for the benefit of their children, particularly the younger children, is probably their best option. For illustrative purposes, however, we will illustrate other funding options for education as the proposed solution to this case.

Gifting

Outright Gifts. Under the current gift tax provisions a person (donor) can give any other person (donee) up to $11,000 per year per donee, gift tax free (IRC Sec. 2503(b)). That amount can be doubled if the spouse agrees to consent to the gift regardless of whether the spouse actually contributes any portion of the gift (IRC Sec. 2513). Although this can be an attractive proposition for some very affluent clients, the Wigginses simply do not have sufficient assets to repeatedly gift this amount to their children. In any event outright gifting presents some significant problems. The person giving the gift (the donor) must part forever with all control over the property that is gifted, including any earning capacity that it has. The outright gifting of property to a minor child may also necessitate the appointment of a guardian of the minor's property. Consequently, while a gifting program has the potential of providing substantial benefits, significant outright gifting at this time is not appropriate for Charles and Barbara.

UGMA and UTMA Gifts. The Uniform Gifts to Minors Act (UGMA) or the Uniform Transfers to Minors Act (UTMA) provides a mechanism by which a donor can give a gift to a minor without the appointment of a guardian of the minor's property. Instead a custodian of the gift, who has full powers over the gifted property and its income on behalf of the minor child, is designated. In many cases the donor is the minor child's parent, who also functions as the custodian of the UGMA or UTMA account. Gifts under the Uniform Acts qualify under the gift tax provisions as present-interest gifts (without the necessity of withdrawal rights or annual payments of income) and as such are subject to the $11,000 per-year-per-donee gift tax exclusion (IRC Sec. 2503(b)). Many states have adopted the newer Uniform Transfers to Minors Act.

There are, however, some problems with UGMA and UTMA gifts:

- If the donor is the parent of the minor and also the custodian of the account and dies while still the custodian, the total amount of the account will be included in the donor's estate for estate tax purposes because of the control he or she can exercise over the account (IRC Sec. 2036(a)).

- The type of property that can be transferred effectively under either Uniform Act is severely restricted in some states. In other words, the Uniform Acts are not uniform from state to state. When the original UGMA was considered by the states, the most effective lobbying group consisted primarily of securities dealers attempting to facilitate gifts of stock and securities to minors. The result of this lobbying effort was that many of the UGMA statutes enacted by the various states restrict UGMA gifts to money, securities, life insurance, or annuity contracts. In other words, other types of property such as real estate cannot be effectively transferred by UGMA gifts in many states. In states that have adopted the Uniform Transfers to Minors Act, there is more flexibility regarding the types of assets that may be transferred.

- As a general rule the custodianship terminates when the minor attains either age 21 or the local legal age of majority. At that time all funds in the custodial account must be distributed to the beneficiary. This gives the 18-, 19-, or 21-year-old (depending on local law) unfettered discretion over the disposition of the assets, which may result in the assets being squandered rather than being used for the purpose for which the custodianship was established, such as education.

- Income from assets in these accounts will be subject to the kiddie tax for minors under 14 years if the minor has more than $1,500 (in 2002) of unearned income, regardless of whether the income is distributed to the minor. This is so because the UGMA or UTMA account, unlike a trust, is not a separate taxpayer from the minor beneficiary.

Primarily because of the potential kiddie tax problems and the possible adverse estate tax consequences, these types of gifts are often less desirable than other alternatives for gifting significant amounts of money.

Income Shifting

One of the most effective ways to accumulate assets for objectives such as education is to use a technique that splits income from family assets between highly taxed adults in the family and the children who are taxed in lower brackets, if at all. It has long been settled in the law that one cannot assign a portion of the income that one earns to another and avoid taxation (*Lucas v. Earl,* 281 U.S. 111 (1930)). One can, however, assign property one owns to another and have the income from the property taxed to the donee or assignee. The techniques for accomplishing this are called income-shifting techniques and can result in substantial net family tax savings. The following discussion covers those income-shifting possibilities that have survived multiple tax law changes.

2503(b) Trusts. A trust device that can be utilized to provide gifts to minors is the IRC Sec. 2503(b) trust, which provides certain advantages not available under the Sec. 2503(c) trusts, discussed later in this section. Unlike the UGMA, there are no statutory restrictions concerning the type of property transferred to this trust. The 2503(b) trust also presents certain disadvantages that are not present in the Sec. 2503(c) trust. The principal advantage of the Sec. 2503(b) trust is that it need not terminate at the beneficiary's attaining the age of 21. A principal disadvantage is that the trust must pay the net income to the beneficiary annually or in more frequent installments. That is, the trust cannot accumulate income even during the minority of the beneficiary. This means that trust income that is paid to beneficiaries under the age of 14 will be taxed at the marginal federal income tax rate of the beneficiary's parents, generally to the extent that such income exceeds $1,500 per year (the kiddie tax threshold for 2002). This substantially reduces the income-shifting benefits of the 2503(b) trust.

Another disadvantage of the Sec. 2503(b) trust is that the value of the income interest and the value of the remainder interest (the value of the property that composes the principal of the trust) are computed separately for gift tax purposes. Only the value of the income interest is eligible for the $11,000 per-year-per-donee annual gift tax exclusion.

The Sec. 2503(b) trust, to qualify for the annual gift tax exclusion, must provide a specified level of income to every beneficiary for whom an annual exclusion is desired. In addition, there can be no unreasonable delay in commencing the payment of the net income of the trust. If there are any restrictions on distribution of trust income—for example, if the income is conditional or discretionary in any way, the annual exclusion will be unavailable.

Obviously the mandatory payment of the trust income can be a major tax and nontax disadvantage when the beneficiary is a minor. This is especially true if significant sums are involved, since it could necessitate the appointment of a guardian of the minor's property. This procedure is both expensive and tedious, as guardians are subject to court supervision in handling the funds of the minor and are statutorily prohibited from entering into certain investment transactions.

Because of the mandatory payment requirement and the fact that the Wiggins children are minors—and especially in the case of the Wiggins children under age 14—it would not be advisable in this case to utilize the Sec. 2503(b) trust to fund the college education for the children.

Sec. 2503(c) Trusts. If a trust is structured according to the terms of IRC Sec. 2503(c), gifts to the trust qualify for the $11,000 per-year-per-donee gift tax exclusion without giving the beneficiary a right to withdraw the funds or the necessity for paying the beneficiary the income at least annually. Therefore the trust may accumulate income. The Sec. 2503(c) trust can be more advantageous than transfers to UGMA custodianship because no statutory restriction on the type of property transferred is applicable in the case of 2503(c) trusts. In addition, the property can be maintained in the trust at least until the beneficiary reaches age 21, regardless of whether the age of legal majority in the state of the trust situs is less than 21. There is no return of the Sec. 2503(c) trust principal to the donor.

The Internal Revenue Code requires that both the property and the income from the property be available to be expended by or for the benefit of the beneficiary during the time before reaching age 21. In addition, to the extent that it has not already been expended by or for the beneficiary before he or she becomes 21, the property and the income from it must pass to the beneficiary when age 21 is attained. If the beneficiary fails to live to the age of 21, the income and the principal must be payable to the beneficiary's estate unless he or she can appoint it to another under a general power of appointment.

Let us examine separately each of the statutory requirements for qualification for a 2503(c) trust. As already noted, the statute requires that the principal and income must be available for distribution in the time period before the donee is 21. The regulations, however, go further. Treas. Reg. Sec. 25.2503-4(b)(1) prohibits "substantial restrictions" on the trustee's power to make distributions of trust income and principal. This might prohibit provisions in the trust instrument that specifically restrict the distributions of income and principal to certain specified purposes, such as illness or education. However, as a practical matter the trustee can make distributions or accumulate income for the purposes intended by the donor in his or her discretion as trustee.

In addition, the Sec. 2503(c) trust cannot be used for the benefit of a class of beneficiaries—that is, more than one beneficiary. (There is no similar restriction when using the Sec. 2503(b) trust.)

Another statutory requirement of the Sec. 2503(c) trust is that the trust cannot extend beyond the beneficiary's 21st birthday. The regulations, however, provide that the trust will not be disqualified provided that the donee (beneficiary) has the right to extend the term of the trust upon reaching the age of 21 (Treas. Reg. Sec. 25.2503-4(b)(2)). The right to continue the trust can apparently require the beneficiary to take an affirmative action to compel distribution at age 21 (Rev. Rul. 74-43, 1974-1 C.B. 285). The right to compel distribution at age 21 may exist for only a limited period of time, as long as the period of time is reasonable. Thirty to 60 days has been deemed reasonable in a number of private letter rulings (PLR 7824035; PLR 7805037). If the beneficiary fails to compel the distribution from the trust during the permissible period or otherwise affirmatively allows the trust to continue, the trust will continue until it terminates under the terms of the trust instrument.

The next statutory section addresses the death of the beneficiary before attaining age 21. It is often undesirable to allow the trust principal and accumulated income, if any, to pass through the estate of a minor, since the minor may be legally incompetent to make a will and the fund must pass by intestacy. However, the regulations provide that if the beneficiary is given a general power of appointment over the trust principal and accumulated income and fails to exercise this power of appointment, regardless of whether the beneficiary as a minor is competent to do so under local law, the trust continues to qualify for the annual exclusion. In fact, the trust instrument may provide that in the absence of the exercise of the power of appointment there is a gift in default of the exercise of the power. This gift-over may be made to whomever the grantor of the trust desires, including his or her other children. Since this is an especially advantageous provision, consideration should be given to including it in any Sec. 2503(c) trust. It is especially appropriate in the case of trusts for the benefit of Stephanie and Caroline to prevent trust funds from passing partially to Cynthia (Charles's former wife) should one of his daughters die during the trust term.

The practical use of the 2503(c) trust involves several important factors. If the income is accumulated until the child reaches age 14, there is no kiddie tax problem with this arrangement. The income of the trust will be taxed at the trust's marginal federal income tax rate and not the marginal rate of the parents (unless the trustee distributes income to the child). The following schedule of taxable income and tax rates applicable to trusts and estates was established by the Revenue Reconciliation Act of 1993 and is indexed for inflation annually. The tax rates for trusts in 2002 are as follows:

If Taxable Income Is:	The Tax Is:
Not over $1,850	15% of taxable income
Over $1,850 but not over $4,400	$277.50 plus 27% of the excess over $1,850
Over $4,400 but not over $6,750	$966.00 plus 30% of the excess over $4,400
Over $6,750 but not over $9,200	$1,671.00 plus 35% of the excess over $6,750
Over $9,200	$2,528.50 plus 38.6% of the excess over $9,200

The first $1,850 of trust income is taxed at a rate of 15 percent. Therefore the parents can save up to 23.6 percent in taxes on the income if they are in a 38.6 percent bracket. Also, even though the child must be given access to both income and principal no later than age 21, smart parents can minimize the amount of money they must transfer. If the trust invests in fixed rate-of-return investments such as bonds, a precise calculation can be made to determine how much should be contributed annually to the trust to fund a specific dollar-amount funding objective. In this way the trust fund can be fully exhausted to pay education expenses so that there is no money left in the trust when the child finishes college. The only actual risk taken by the parents in transferring funds is that the child does not use the money for college education but instead drops out of school and squanders the money after turning 21.

Having the first dollars of trust income taxed at lower rates than those applicable to the donors may not seem like a substantial tax savings. However, if the trust is funded when the beneficiary is young, savings can be significant.

The numbers in the following table are based on these assumptions:

- The trust accumulates income until the beneficiary reaches age 18.
- The contributions are made annually beginning at the stated age.
- The trust funds earn 8 percent annually.
- The parents' marginal tax rate is 30 percent.

Tax Savings from the 2503(c) Trust
When the Beneficiary Reaches Age 18

Annual Gift to Trust	Age of Beneficiary When Trust Is Established		
	5	10	15
$ 1,000	$2,166	$ 751	$ 136
5,000	5,366	2,692	678
10,000	3,455	3,178	1,062
20,000	(5,402)	1,107	1,354

These savings are calculated on the assumption that without the trust the same income would be taxed at the parents' rate. The calculations do not include allowances for the cost of establishing and managing the trust.

The effect of the changes in the income tax rates for trusts and estates, as well as those for individual taxpayers, that were an integral part of the 1993 tax act is to significantly reduce the tax savings for some individuals who use 2503(c) trusts for accumulating the funds for any purpose, including funding children's future education expenses. As the above data show, the actual tax benefit is negative (that is, income taxes are higher with a trust) if the Wigginses contribute $20,000 a year to a trust for 13 years. Funding the trust at $10,000 a year results in less tax savings than if the trust was funded with $5,000 a year if the funding period is 13 years. Funding the trust with $10,000 a year yields only $486 more in tax savings than a funding level of $5,000 a year would produce if the funding period is for 8 years. These results would be different if the marginal tax rate applicable to the Wigginses was higher, such as 35 or 38.6 percent.

However, if Charles and Barbara's attorney can set up a trust for each child for whom a trust is appropriate, act as a trustee, and work with their CPA to file estimated and annual tax returns (a relatively simple procedure), the tax benefits should still substantially outweigh the total costs. Since an attorney will typically not charge a full fee for each separate trust if more than one is used, Charles and Barbara should be able to set up 2503(c) trusts for one or more of their children at a total cost of $1,500 to $2,500. Annual administration and tax return preparation expenses must be paid, but these costs should be modest and substantially less than the tax savings that can be realized.

Despite its complexities the Sec. 2503(c) trust is often the best vehicle for families to utilize as an income-shifting device. Specific recommendations for use of the trust will be discussed in the investment planning section.

Employment Opportunities at Systems Design

The business plan has already discussed the possibility that as the Wiggins children reach the age when they can work, it may be possible to provide them with an independent source of income that would not be subject to the high income tax rates that Charles and Barbara have each year. Of course, the amount of money that could be earned in this manner while the children are in their precollege years may not be great, but it could be significant enough to provide needed extras during college or to begin accumulating separate funds for the later purchase of a home, a car, or some other desirable item.

As already noted, our facts do not clarify the availability of employment opportunities at Systems Design. However, it is a rare closely held business that does not need some part-time, summer, or vacation help. In addition to the financial aspects of employment with Systems Design Associates, it is often the case that employment in a family-owned business allows the owner's children to experience firsthand the conditions of the business and to decide whether they have an interest or would have an interest at a later date in participating in that business or profession. While this does not immediately translate into a financial gain for the family, it may indeed be an important method by which children of closely held business owners demonstrate whether they have an aptitude or an interest in a family business or profession. In addition, this practical experience could save owners (parents) innumerable dollars in tuition for professional schools.

As appropriate employment opportunities at Systems Design materialize, a strong recommendation would be to involve the Wiggins children to the extent that they have the interest and ability to meet the needs of the business.

S Corporation Shares

While it is possible in this case to incorporate and elect S corporation status, it has not been recommended that Systems Design do so. However, many corporations make S elections in order to allow older shareholders (parents) to gift corporate shares to their children. This can be advantageous as an intrafamily income-splitting device since the taxable income of the S corporation is taxed to the shareholders in proportion to their shareholdings, and the children would normally be in lower tax brackets than their parents. However, in the case of a corporation engaged in a service business, this approach is treated as a pure assignment of income and is therefore unacceptable.

Borrowing from Qualified Plans

The federal income tax rules for borrowing from qualified plans have already been discussed in the business plan. Since the law contains a provision allowing a plan participant to borrow up to the lesser of one-half of his or her vested account balance or $50,000 (and not less than $10,000 regardless of the vested account balance), the option to borrow from qualified plans to assist with meeting personal objectives still remains significant. Because any loans from qualified plans must be repaid within 5 years of the borrowing (as already noted in the business planning section), this would mean a relatively short-term remedy at best. In addition, Charles could not deduct interest payments on plan loans since he is a key employee. Plan loans should not, however, be overlooked in the event of an emergency or an unusually attractive investment opportunity.

Using Charles's University Fringe Benefit for Free Tuition

While the facts indicate that two of the Wiggins children are undecided about whether they will attend Homestate Tech, it is important to keep in mind that with Charles's free tuition benefit the Wiggins children can attain a college education at a nominal cost. In fact, if the Wigginses encounter unexpected financial difficulties and are unable to fully fund the amounts they have projected for their children's college education, it is nevertheless possible that their children will not have to become self-supporting while still in college.

Some universities that offer free tuition benefits to their faculty members' children also provide an equivalent amount of money to be applied to tuition at other universities. If employer universities do not offer an equivalent amount of money to be applied to tuition, other universities may offer reciprocal free or reduced tuition privileges. Unfortunately, Homestate Tech does not provide benefits of this nature. Since the plans for Caroline and Charles, Jr., are for them to attend schools other than Homestate Tech, the funding recommendations will be made as though no such benefits will be available to offset some of their tuition costs.

Other Considerations Regarding Payment of Education Expenses

Any individual can make direct payments of tuition gift tax free in any amount under IRC Sec. 2503(e). Therefore if any shortfall in advance funding occurs, Charles and Barbara would at least be able to use current cash flows to pay for the children's higher education without reducing their unified credit.

In addition, under current tax law taxpayers may deduct interest payments on home equity loans for second mortgages secured by their principal residence or one vacation home to the extent such loans do not exceed $100,000 in principal amount. Therefore if borrowing should be needed to make up any shortfall in advance education funding, the loan should be a home equity loan rather than, for example, a loan from a qualified plan, in order to make the interest payment on the loan deductible for federal income tax purposes.

Using Barbara's Trust Distribution for Payment of Education Expenses

Under the terms of the trust Barbara's grandfather set up for her years ago, when she reaches age 35 in 5 years, she is entitled to receive one-half the principal of the trust in a lump-sum distribution in the amount of $75,000. The remaining $75,000 will be paid to Barbara outright when she reaches age 45, at which point the trust will terminate. As Barbara has indicated, she has no concern about these funds being expended for the benefit of the family or being commingled with Charles's funds. While under local law this commingling would make the funds much more difficult to retrieve in the event of a divorce, these funds could be allocated to the education of the three children, if this is not inconsistent with Barbara's wishes. However, it would be more advantageous to utilize some income-splitting device to allow income to begin to accumulate and be taxed at the children's lower brackets. In addition, it may be that while Barbara has no objection to the distributions from her trust fund being expended for her and Charles's lifestyle, she may have some objection to spending the money to educate Charles's daughters by his prior marriage. Since that may be the case, the recommendation for use of the distribution from Barbara's trust fund for educational objectives would be appropriate in our judgment only on an emergency basis.

Recommendations for funding the educations of the Wiggins children will be discussed in the investment planning section.

Assure Adequate Protection in Case of Disability

Design the Buy-Sell Agreement to Become Operative in the Event of Disability

The discussion of the buy-sell agreement in the business plan has indicated that buy-sell agreements can be designed to become operative in the event of the death or disability of a shareholder. The agreement that has been recommended for Systems Design Associates has in fact been designed to become operative in the event of disability, with the definition of disability and the elimination period in the agreement matching the definition of disability and the elimination period in the insurance contracts that are chosen to fund the agreement.

The fact-finding data clearly illustrates that there is a significant gap between the Wigginses' projection of required income in the event of Charles's disability and the resources presently available to provide that income. A portion of this gap could be filled by the sale of Charles's interest in Systems Design Associates according to the terms of an appropriate buy-sell agreement. The amount of funding that is available to fund buy-sell agreements for disability is approximately 80 percent of the value of the business interest. In this case if the value of the business interest for this purpose were set at $150,000 (again assuming the business building is distributed prior to incorporation), the applicable total coverage would be $120,000. If this amount were obtained through the use of insurance to fund the buy-sell in the event of disability and paid out as a lump sum, it could yield an additional $8,400 per year at a pretax yield of 7 percent. This would add an additional $700 to the monthly income Charles and his family could anticipate in the event of a disability. Since information in the case narrative indicates that other available resources would be $8,205, this amount would increase the total income available at disability to approximately $8,905 a month. While this is a significant income, it does fall short of the $9,500 monthly income Charles and Barbara have projected they would need in the event of Charles's disability. This shortfall can be covered by disability income insurance through the corporation, as has already been discussed in the business plan. If that coverage provides $1,000 per month of additional benefits, the shortfall will be covered, with a cushion of over $400 per month.

Personal Disability Coverage

The primary advantage of personally acquired disability income coverage is that the proceeds are received tax free. The primary disadvantage of personal disability income coverage is that the premiums for such coverage are not tax deductible.

Disability Coverage Provided by Systems Design after Incorporation

As discussed in the business planning section, one of the benefits of incorporation is to allow the corporation to provide a disability income plan to employees of the corporation without the premium payments being taxed to the employee. The corporation can pay the premium and deduct it as an ordinary and necessary business expense. There is, however, a tax cost to the employee. The benefits are generally taxable when paid.

This result may be acceptable because it may be more economical in the long run than attempting to purchase disability benefits personally with after-tax dollars. An increased amount of coverage is also available under the corporate plan.

In this case it is recommended that Systems Design Associates purchase additional disability income insurance through an employer plan.

Reduce the Tax Burden

Achieve Objectives through Income-Splitting Devices to Reduce Cost

As has already been discussed, the use of income-splitting devices allows income from certain assets to be taxed to lower-bracket family members. The use of an outright gift of a fairly nominal sum (when compared to the required accumulation amount) to a Sec. 2503(c) trust or UGMA account to fund the college education objectives of the Wiggins children is such an income-splitting device. The appropriate vehicles and investment techniques will be discussed in the investment planning section.

Defer Tax Liability on a Portion of the Income from Systems Design through the Use of Qualified Plans

The Wiggins family is presently paying federal income taxes at a marginal bracket of 30 percent. This effectively means that the $42,000 a year that Charles earns from Systems Design Associates nets the family (after tax) slightly less than $30,000. When the business incorporates, as has been recommended, and implements a qualified profit-sharing plan (with a company-imposed maximum percentage of 15 percent), the corporation can make tax-deductible contributions of $5,550 per year in Charles's behalf, assuming he earns $37,000 a year as an employee. This contribution will not be taxable to Charles until it is distributed to him. The plan proceeds can become available without penalty to the participant or the beneficiaries upon the disability, retirement, or death of the participant.

Structure Future Purchases (for example, the Vacation Home) to Maximize Tax Benefits

An understanding of the appropriate use of leverage is important in structuring transactions such as the purchase of a vacation home or other major asset. For example, in the case of the purchase (or construction) of a vacation home the mortgage interest would be a deductible item for the Wiggins family. Primarily because the Wiginses have significant other personal objectives to achieve, it is not advantageous for them to take a large equity position in the second home. The down payment would be tied up in a non-income-producing property, although the vacation home might indeed be an appreciating asset. A balance between a high mortgage payment and a high equity position that is consistent with the Wigginses' cash-flow position should be taken. In this particular case a mortgage interest rate of 8.75 percent would have an after-tax cost to the Wigginses of only about 6.3 percent. A down payment of approximately 10 percent of the value of the vacation home would be appropriate in this case.

Build Their Vacation Home

In purchasing the lot for the vacation home, there may be a trade-off between the price of the lot and the rate of interest charged if the purchase is being made with a purchase-money mortgage from a private seller. The Wigginses may be willing to pay a higher interest rate in return for a reduction in the purchase price, because the interest payment is deductible while the principal payment is not.

Taxpayers are permitted to deduct mortgage interest payments on loans up to $1 million used to acquire a principal residence plus one vacation home. The amount of interest that may be deducted on a second mortgage secured by a residence and one vacation home, however, is lower. The limitation is generally $100,000 of principal for all such loans owned by the taxpayer.

Interest on debt incurred with respect to property held for investment is subject to more detailed and comprehensive limitations under the current federal tax laws. The seller must report any interest payments received under a purchase-money mortgage as ordinary income. Payments of principal receive capital-gains tax treatment to the seller.

The relationship between purchase price and the interest rate is an important negotiating point. Because of the exclusion amount for long-term capital gains enacted under the Taxpayer Relief Act of 1987, a seller of property will be motivated to allocate as much of the purchase price as possible to gain on the sale of property, not interest. Therefore it will be difficult from a negotiating standpoint to persuade a prospective seller to accept an increase in interest payments in return for a corresponding reduction in the principal amount. This would, however, provide a greater tax benefit for Charles and Barbara, resulting in a lower net cost for the land. Since the Wigginses do not anticipate the construction of their summer house to begin until 2005, it might be appropriate for them to use this strategy to purchase the lot sometime before the beginning of construction.

Assure a Comfortable Retirement

In computing the amounts of assets that are projected to be available at retirement, one should consider that while all projections involve assumptions that may or may not be operative at the target date, retirement planning is the most problematic because it requires assumptions in a large number of areas and usually involves projections over a relatively long period of time. It is important to understand, therefore, that it is impossible to project with any degree of precision the exact retirement benefit a client will receive in 25 to 30 years. It is possible, however, to look at all the client's resources today, assuming that the retirement plan was fully funded and growing at a specified rate. If that amount is short of the client's estimate of retirement income needs, it is an indication that the client's investments should be managed or repositioned to meet the shortfall. However, the numbers provide only an indication of adequacy or inadequacy at retirement and are not material in themselves. Absolute dollar amounts are best tracked and determined in intermediate (3- to 5-year) planning throughout the planner's relationship with the client.

Keeping these caveats in mind, the Wiggins family appears to be adequately protected if Charles lives to retirement and continues to participate in his tax-deferred annuity account at or near the total contribution level of 14 percent of salary per year. In addition, if a profit-sharing plan is implemented for Systems Design Associates and is fully utilized, this amount will add another $281,448-plus to his retirement account, as already noted in the business plan. It appears, therefore, that the Wigginses will be able to enjoy a comfortable retirement if most of the assumptions that have been used in making the calculations hold. If we assume that the $281,448 earns an inflation-adjusted rate of return of 3 percent after retirement and is liquidated over a life expectancy to age 99 for Charles, his monthly retirement income from the plan will be $1,110. Currently his projected available retirement income is $8,548 per month. This would bring his total monthly retirement income to $9,648, which would exceed the $9,500-per-month objective for Charles and Barbara.

Dispositions at Death

Analysis of Present Estate Plans

On the facts of our case the Wiggins family presently appears to have not one estate plan but three. Charles's will, executed in June of 1995, provides that one-quarter of his estate goes to Stephanie, one-quarter goes to Caroline, and one-half goes to Barbara if she survives him, otherwise to Charles, Jr. Should Charles die before his daughters reach the age of majority, the will creates trusts for their benefit. Barbara's will, executed on the same date, provides that all her property will go to Charles if he survives her, and if he fails to survive her, to Charles, Jr. In further discussing the matter, Charles stated that he wishes his estate to be used first to provide for Barbara and any of his children while they are minors and that any amount not consumed in this manner be continued as support for Barbara until her death, at which time it is to be divided equally among all his children.

Barbara's expressed wishes about her estate plan are apparently carried out in her will, as she has said that she wishes her assets to take care of Charles first; if he fails to survive her or at his death, the assets are to go to Charles, Jr.

Unfortunately few of either Charles's or Barbara's expressed wishes regarding the disposition of their property at death will be carried out because most of their assets are held as joint tenants with right of survivorship. No will can control the distribution of such property at the death of the first joint tenant. When property is titled jointly with rights of survivorship the surviving joint tenant automatically takes the entire property at the death of the first tenant by operation of law. Therefore the bulk of Charles's property will go to Barbara automatically by operation of law if he should die first, and at her later death that property will be controlled by her will, under the terms of which the property will be left solely to Charles, Jr.

The partial solution to Charles and Barbara's situation is to allow one spouse or the other (usually the husband) to own most of the family's assets solely in his name. This does not mean that Barbara cannot and should not own particular assets in her name. The facts of the case have indicated that neither Charles nor Barbara would have a problem with returning the assets to single ownership. This can be done in whatever proportion the couple wishes once they understand the difficulties of ownership as joint tenants with right of survivorship. These difficulties have already been demonstrated in the preceding paragraph and are accentuated in families with children from prior marriages.

If Barbara were not expecting to inherit a substantial amount from her family, it would be appropriate to divide the assets fairly equally and to assure that Barbara had at least sufficient assets so that her estate could take advantage of the unified credit should she predecease Charles. However, as she is virtually assured of receiving at least $150,000 in trust distributions by her 45th birthday, this amount should be taken into consideration in deciding which assets should be transferred into Charles's name. The facts of our case also indicate that it is highly likely that Barbara will eventually inherit a very substantial amount of assets from her parents at some undetermined future time. This would indicate that, to the extent that these inheritances are outright to Barbara, she will probably have a large enough estate to be subject to significant estate tax liabilities. As assets are acquired in the future, this fact should also be kept in mind when considering whether these assets should be titled in Barbara's name.

Any assets owned as joint tenants with right of survivorship can be returned to the sole ownership of either spouse without federal gift tax consequences because of the unlimited gift tax marital deduction. As long as the consequences of property ownership are understood, some assets, such as the personal residence, can be left in a joint tenancy with right of survivorship, since it is likely that upon the death of the first spouse, married couples usually want the house to go outright to the surviving spouse.

Because of the unlimited marital deduction, some advisers have advocated the full utilization of the unlimited marital portion by the first spouse to die, thereby deferring all federal estate taxes until the time of the second death. However, the unified credit should be utilized in conjunction with the unlimited marital deduction in estates that, when combined, are larger than the amount of a single unified credit exemption equivalent of $1 million in 2002–2003.

In estate planning the crucial problem is to plan not only the estate of the first spouse to die but the estate of the surviving spouse as well. If the unlimited marital deduction is utilized by leaving all assets to a surviving spouse, the unified credit of the first spouse to die is wasted, and the entire value of marital deduction assets will be taxed in the estate of the surviving spouse. If the surviving spouse has or expects to inherit substantial assets, the addition of marital deduction assets can cause an unnecessarily high estate tax liability at the second death.

In lieu of the unlimited marital deduction, at least the amount of assets equal to the unified credit equivalent can be directed by a properly drawn will to a trust that gives the surviving spouse access to the funds without being included in the surviving spouse's estate. That access to the trust income and principal can be virtually unrestricted or it can be quite restrictive, depending on the client's preference.

In the case of Charles and Barbara let us assume for the sake of simplicity that all jointly held assets will be returned to Charles. In that case the house, household furnishings, automobile, and personal effects should probably be left to Barbara as outright bequests in Charles's will. Also a simultaneous death provision should be included in order to preserve the marital deduction.

An appropriate design for a new estate plan for Charles that will contain these provisions and a credit shelter residuary trust could read substantially as follows:

1. Any interest I (Charles) own in my personal residence at my death, I leave to my wife, Barbara, outright, subject to any indebtedness secured thereby.
2. Any interest in household furnishings, automobiles, and personal effects that I own at my death, I leave to my wife, Barbara, outright.
3. If my wife, Barbara, survives me (and if we die under such circumstances that it is difficult or impossible to determine which died first, it shall be presumed that she survives me and that this bequest shall be effective), I give, devise, and bequeath to my wife an amount determined as follows:
   a. Ascertain the maximum marital deduction allowable in determining the federal estate tax payable by reason of my death, taking into account any election my executor makes for tax purposes.
   b. Deduct therefrom the value of any and all other property that passes or has passed to my wife either outside this will or under any other item of this will in such manner as to qualify for the marital deduction.
   c. From that figure deduct that amount, if any, needed to increase my taxable estate to the largest amount that, after allowing for the

unified credit, will result in no federal estate tax being imposed upon my estate. The resulting amount shall be the amount bequeathed in this item. No reduction shall be made in this bequest, however, and no charge shall be made against any bequest or the beneficiary thereof because of any estate or inheritance tax imposed on my estate or this bequest.

4. All the rest, residue, and remainder of my property of every kind and description and wherever located, including any lapsed or void legacy or devise (but not including any property over which I may have a power of disposition or appointment), I give, devise, and bequeath to the First National Bank of Small City as trustee. (The recommended provisions for this residuary trust are described below.)

This method employs a pecuniary (or specific dollar-amount) bequest to utilize the marital deduction and a residuary bequest for determining the amount going to the credit shelter trust. This type of arrangement can also be made by using a pecuniary bequest for the credit shelter trust and creating the marital deduction amount through the use of a residuary bequest.

The residuary credit shelter trust could provide that the net income from the trust be paid to Barbara, Caroline, Stephanie, and Charles, Jr., as necessary, in the sole discretion of the trustee during the period the children are minors. In addition, the trustee could be empowered to invade the principal of this residuary trust for the same beneficiaries as long as the children are minors. Note that some states, such as Pennsylvania, will impose an inheritance tax on the value of property left to a credit shelter trust if anyone other than the surviving spouse could have access to the funds during the surviving spouse's lifetime.

At the majority of each child the trust provisions can provide that further distributions of the trust income and principal can be made for that child only in the event of an exceptional circumstance, such as illness, accident, purchase of a home, beginning of a business, and other specified occurrences. Barbara can continue to be the primary income and principal beneficiary under this trust until she dies, at which time the trust will terminate and any remaining assets will be divided equally among Charles's living children and children of a deceased child, per stirpes.

It is also possible to allow Barbara to remain a beneficiary under the residuary trust only until she remarries. This decision is purely a personal one. There is no tax difference whether the residuary trust described here is terminated at the death of the surviving spouse or at his or her remarriage. It is not unusual to expect that the surviving spouse in such cases would prefer to continue to be an income and principal beneficiary of the residuary trust until his or her death, regardless of whether he or she remarries. Naturally this delays the termination of the trust and the eventual distribution of the assets to the children. It does not, however, preclude the children's having the advantage of the monies in trust in the event of genuine need.

Many spouses object particularly to having all their inheritance tied up in trusts, as they feel they must deal continuously with bank trust officers who may be less than sympathetic to their wishes. The marital portion of the bequest can be left in certain types of trusts and can still qualify for the marital deduction. The most common type of marital deduction trust is described as a power-of-appointment trust. A power-of-appointment trust qualifies for the estate tax marital deduction provided that the trust is required to pay all the income from the trust to the surviving spouse in annual or more frequent payments and that the surviving spouse is given a general power of appointment (for example, if the surviving spouse is the wife, the power to appoint the property to herself, her estate, her creditors, creditors of her estate, and any other appointee exercisable either during her life or by specific reference to the power in her will, or both). In other words, the surviving spouse (in this case the wife) can either be allowed to appoint property as she sees fit to herself or others during lifetime (a very liberal provision), or she can be effectively restricted from withdrawing the principal of the marital trust until the time of her death by the use of a testamentary general power.

Even if the decision to use a marital trust seems indicated, and that does not appear to be the case on our facts, there are some assets, primarily the decedent's principal residence, that should not be included in the marital trust. If the residence is included in the marital trust, the nonrecognition-of-gain provisions from the sale of the principal residence will be lost unless the beneficiary seeking to take advantage of these provisions has the sole power to vest the trust property in himself or herself and is therefore treated as the owner of the trust for income tax purposes under the Internal Revenue Code. In addition, a trustee's management of a residence may present practical administrative problems. For these reasons it is usually advisable to convey the house as a separate outright bequest of all the decedent's interest to the spouse.

In this case we are recommending an outright bequest of the residence, household furnishings, automobiles, and personal effects to the spouse; an outright bequest of the remaining marital portion determined under the formula already described; and a residuary trust of which Barbara is a continuing beneficiary either for the entirety of her life or until she remarries. This type of will design meets Charles's stated objectives in the disposition of his assets at his death. Note that it protects Barbara and all his children equally as long as a child or children are minors. After that point Barbara becomes the primary beneficiary, and the children continue to be protected but only under certain, more or less exceptional, circumstances. At Barbara's death or remarriage, depending on which event occurs, the trust will terminate and the principal remaining in the trust will be divided equally among Charles's three children, if living. The will should be designed so that if a child has died but leaves living children, the child's portion goes to his or her living children, per stirpes. If the child leaves no living children, the assets will be shared by Charles's remaining children.

In estates the size of Charles and Barbara's the maximum use of the residuary trust to absorb the federal estate tax credit can result in a significant reduction of the marital portion (other than items that are specific bequests, such as the interest in the house and items passing outside the will such as the TDA account), since the exemption equivalent for the unified credit is $1 million (in 2002–2003). In this case because Barbara is the anticipated beneficiary of a significant amount of money from her parents, this reduction of the marital portion will probably produce a very desirable result, because any funds left to her in the marital deduction portion will be subject to taxation in her estate at her death.

Guardianship of Charles, Jr.

Barbara's sister has been designated the guardian for Charles, Jr., in the event that Charles and Barbara should die while Charles, Jr. is a minor. It is wise to check with the proposed guardian before including him or her in an estate plan. On the facts of this case it appears that Betty Becker's lifestyle, particularly due to the nature of her job, is not an ideal one for assuming the care of a child. Sometimes more distant relatives or even family friends are preferable as guardians if their lifestyles or work activities are better suited to rearing a child. Also an alternate or successor guardian should always be named.

Life Insurance

At present Charles has $202,000 in life insurance death benefits. In each of the three policies constituting that amount, there are significant problems. First, Charles is the owner of each of the personally owned policies and retains incidents of ownership in the group coverage, so the proceeds will be includible in his estate for estate tax purposes at his death (IRC Sec. 2042(2)). Second, each of the insurance contracts is payable to a specific beneficiary or beneficiaries and consequently can serve only one purpose. Third, some of the named beneficiaries are minors. Fourth, the insurance coverage is inadequate at present to assure that Charles's family will have sufficient assets to achieve their financial objectives should he die within the next few years. Fifth, the $100,000 policy that Charles is carrying is expensive coverage per $1,000 of death benefits.

The specific amounts of coverage needed and the replacement of insurance coverage will be discussed further in the insurance planning section.

The positioning of the insurance policies can become very important as Charles's estate grows, since inclusion of life insurance proceeds in his taxable estate will result in unnecessary additional estate tax liabilities. Also in order to practice maximum economy with life insurance proceeds, each dollar should be available to meet several financial needs or contingencies should the occasion arise. These objectives can be achieved by the utilization of an irrevocable life insurance trust to apply for, own, and be the beneficiary of the life insurance coverage. The terms of the trust instrument can control the distribution of the proceeds. This is a much more flexible arrangement than the use of individual beneficiary designations.

Structuring the Irrevocable Insurance Trust

In the usual case the terms of the irrevocable life insurance trust are tailored much like those in the credit shelter trust under the client's estate plan. Although this type of design is not required, it is recommended in this case because it would result in making the entire amount of the insurance proceeds available to Barbara and to the minor children until they reach adulthood.

Because of the court order to continue insurance protection in an amount sufficient to assure funding of the child support obligation for Caroline and Stephanie, one difference in the trust terms is necessary. The trust must specify that child support payments for Stephanie and Caroline should be paid prior to any other distributions from the trust until they reach majority. Support payments can be made from income if available; if not, the principal can be invaded. Any income in addition to the amount required for the child support payments can be distributed to either Barbara or the minor children as necessary until the children reach adulthood. At that time provisions providing for distributions for exceptional circumstances or in the event of emergencies for the adult children, as already noted in the discussion of the residuary trust, can be substituted. This trust can also terminate on either Barbara's death or remarriage, depending on the family's decision.

An additional provision that is often advantageous in life insurance trusts is a provision that allows but does not require the trustee to loan money to the estate of the deceased or the deceased's spouse or to purchase assets from the estate of the deceased or the deceased's spouse. This can provide needed liquidity to the estate. However, it is important that the trust instrument does not require such loans or purchases, since the Internal Revenue Service has construed such requirements as making the proceeds available to the executor for the use of the estate and has included them in the estate tax valuation of the decedent's gross estate. This would defeat the purpose of the insurance trust, which is to protect the insurance proceeds from estate taxation (Treas. Reg. Sec. 20.2042-1(b)(1)). When the recommended design is implemented, the insurance proceeds are protected from estate taxation in both spouses' estates. Furthermore, as a general rule the proceeds of life insurance in a life insurance trust are not subject to the claims of either the insured's or the beneficiaries' creditors.

One potential estate tax problem remains—the fact that gifts of life insurance policies within 3 years of death will result in inclusion of the proceeds of the policy in the insured decedent's estate (IRC Sec. 2035(d)(2)). To avoid this result, the insured can set up an irrevocable insurance trust that will apply for, own, and be the beneficiary of the insurance policy. The insured will gift money to the trust to pay the premiums on the policy. To avoid any attempt by the IRS to allege a deemed transfer, the insured should be cautioned to sign the application only as the insured.

In addition to avoiding the estate tax pitfalls just mentioned, it is also important to consider the gift tax consequences of gifts of insurance policies or funds to pay premiums on insurance policies to an irrevocable life insurance trust.

If restrictions are placed on the beneficiaries' rights to exercise immediate ownership rights on the policies or the funds to pay premiums on the policies, the gift is a gift of a future interest and the $11,000 per-year-per-donee annual exclusion does not apply. The result is that an immediate gift tax liability arises. This problem can be avoided by the use of a withdrawal right in the beneficiaries called a Crummey provision (*Crummey v. Comm'r,* 397 F.2d 82 (1968)), which gives the trust beneficiaries the noncumulative right to demand that annual gifts to the trust be paid to them. The right to withdraw such gifts usually lasts for only a short period of time and then lapses. The safest course of action is to limit the withdrawal right to $5,000 per year. This will avoid adverse federal gift tax consequences if the right should lapse. The period of time must be reasonable—usually 30 to 60 days are sufficient—and there is authority that notice of the withdrawal right must be given to the beneficiary. The fact that the beneficiary is a minor without an appointed guardian has not been held to be an impediment to the effectiveness of the Crummey provision.

There are also income tax consequences to a grantor of a trust that is empowered to use the trust income to pay premiums on policies of insurance on the life of the grantor or the grantor's spouse (IRC Sec. 677(a)(3)). However, in the case of most irrevocable insurance trusts there is little or no trust income to be taxable to the grantor.

PERSONAL PLANNING: INSURANCE

Life Insurance

Existing Policies

Examination of the Wigginses' existing assets reveals that Charles needs approximately $700,000 of life insurance to fund his objectives in case of his premature death. Not only is his existing coverage inadequate, but $150,000 of the coverage is positioned poorly and $100,000 of the coverage is very expensive. The $52,000 of group term coverage is also positioned poorly for federal estate tax purposes. His personally owned $100,000 insurance policy should be replaced with new lower-cost coverage.

The reductions in life insurance premiums in recent years have shed a new perspective on policy replacement. Although it has generally been accepted in the past that policy replacements were not in the policyowner's best interest, it is now likely that some policy replacements may be beneficial to the policyowner.

The competitive force in the insurance marketplace has spawned new lower-cost policies that may be appropriate for replacement, especially if the existing policy is a nonparticipating policy with high premiums and mediocre growth of the cash value. Many older policies did not anticipate current levels of investment earnings or improvements in actuarial life expectancy.

Each potential replacement should be evaluated on the individual merits of the existing policy and the proposed policy. Both policies should be compared on the basis of after-tax, out-of-pocket costs relative to death benefits and cash-value growth. The differences in policies are very often a direct result of the investment results of the insurers. Meaningful policy comparisons must evaluate both policies under similar configurations and tax treatment. Although there are many justifiable replacements, not all existing policies are candidates for replacement.

Both individual policies currently covering Charles are nonparticipating policies. The premium level for the $100,000 policy is in excess of those required on new policies now being issued at Charles's attained age, which is 13 years older than the issue age for the existing policy. Charles can reduce his premium outlay $5.50 per thousand dollars of coverage and still have the assurance of level premium cash value coverage. This amounts to annual savings of $550.

Needed Insurance

As already noted, Charles should consider the purchase of individual insurance to provide the necessary $700,000 of coverage. This total results from a $700,000 shortfall in the survivors' coverage objectives when discounted at 7 percent. The calculation is based on discounted values after recognition of existing resources available if Charles were to die tomorrow.

The selection of life insurance products involves choices between many available designs. Material changes made by recent federal tax legislation in the context of the modified endowment contract will also need to be considered.

The Concept of the Modified Endowment Contract (MEC). With the growth and popularity of interest-sensitive life insurance products in which the policy cash value can earn interest at a highly competitive rate, the Internal Revenue Service urged the adoption of specialized and complex rules to impose federal income taxation on life insurance in certain situations. Before the enactment of federal tax legislation addressing this issue, it was possible for the cash value of an interest-sensitive life insurance policy to grow at a very attractive rate free of federal income taxation. Because this inside buildup in the policy has traditionally escaped the imposition of federal income taxation, the Internal Revenue Service urged Congress to take steps to reverse that treatment.

Under current federal income tax law, if an insurance policy is characterized as a *modified endowment contract,* any withdrawals, including policy loans, will be treated as interest first and then as principal. In order for a life insurance policy to avoid the characterization as a modified endowment contract, it must pass a "7-pay test." This test is applicable to all cash value life insurance policies and can even apply when there is a change in either the amount of the annual premium or the face amount of the policy. If at any time the accumulated amount of the first 7 years' premiums paid on the policy exceeds the accumulated amount of the so-called net level premiums that would have been paid by that time, then the policy will be classified as a modified endowment contract, and any withdrawals, including policy loans, will be treated as interest first and then as principal. The withdrawal (or loan) treated as interest will be currently taxable. In addition, a 10 percent penalty tax on the amount of the taxable distribution will generally apply to taxpayers under age 59 1/2.

Modified endowment contract rules state that if there is a material change in the benefits or other terms of a contract that had not been reflected in any prior determination under the 7-pay test, the contract will then be treated as a new contract entered into on the day the material change takes effect. Adjustments must then be made in the application of the 7-pay test to take the cash surrender value of the contract into account. Under the MEC rules it is clear that a material change includes (1) any increase in the death benefit under the contract of insurance or (2) any increase in or addition of a qualified additional benefit under the contract.

It is also clear that a material change will not include any increase in the death benefit provided under a contract if the increase is attributable to (1) the premiums paid to fund the lowest death benefit payable in the first 7 contract years or (2) the crediting of interest or other earnings regarding such premiums. For this purpose if each premium paid before the death benefit increase is necessary to fund the lowest death benefit payable in the first 7 contract years, then the death benefit increase may be viewed as being directly attributable to the payment of premiums necessary to fund the lowest death benefit payable in the first 7 contract years or the crediting of interest or other earnings with respect to such premiums.

The definition of a modified endowment contract has been broadened to discourage the acquisition or purchase of certain types of "second-to-die" policies. Specifically if a qualified life insurance contract is payable only upon the death of one insured following the death of another insured, and there is a reduction of such death benefit below the lowest level of such death benefit provided under the policy during the first 7 contract years (that is, the 7-pay test), then IRC Sec. 7702A will be applied for the first 7 years of the contract as though the policy had been issued at the reduced benefit level.

Charles should consider using one of the following types of policies to provide the additional survivor protection needed:

- *ordinary whole life insurance.* This form of insurance is based on the assumption that premiums will be paid on a level annual basis throughout the lifetime of the insured. Variations are available on which premiums are paid for a specified period. In the early years of the policy the premium exceeds the cost of protection, thereby providing the basis for cash values within the policy. The cash values of a policy depend on the size of the policy, the insured's age at the time of issue, and whether the policy is rated. Cash values are guaranteed by the contract and can be borrowed at a rate explicitly stated therein or based on a specified index. In addition, the increase in cash value each year is not taxable to the policyowner. Even though the assumption is that the premium will be paid over the life of the insured, many owners often convert their policies to either a reduced paid-up policy when the need for this protection decreases, such as when children become self-supporting, or to an annuity on retirement of the insured.

- *variable life policy.* This is also a fixed, level premium policy for the lifetime of the insured. With variable life the insured selects the investment medium used within the policy, usually with a choice restricted to specific funds managed by the insurer. This policy differs from the ordinary whole life policy in that the face amount of the policy changes with the investment performance of the investment instrument chosen by the insured. Often a minimum guaranteed floor below which the policy's face value will not fall is an integral part of the policy.

  However, all investment risk, except for the minimum death benefit floor, shifts to the policyowner. Since the investment risk is transferred to the owner, no guarantees are included as to the amount of the policy's cash values. If cash values do exist within the policy, borrowing of these values is permissible. Some policies specify a variable interest rate on the borrowing that fluctuates with changes in some previously established standard interest-rate index. Other policies do have fixed borrowing rates. However, these policies generally have a substantial surrender charge during their early years. Therefore the client should realize that a long-term commitment is being made if this type of policy is chosen.

  In addition, the insured needs to monitor carefully the performance of the investment instrument(s) selected. If the initial choice is incorrect, or if the insured fails to shift funds when economic conditions change, the amount of protection can fall sizably. This form of fluctuating death benefit might not be suitable to the client when the primary reason for acquiring additional insurance at this time is protection for survivors.

- *universal life policy.* This policy differs from the previous two policies in that it has a flexible premium. In addition, universal life may feature either a level or an increasing death benefit. (Certain increasing death benefits may cause the policy to be treated as a MEC, however.) The insured has the option to either increase or decrease, or even omit, the premium. However, all premiums when paid are added to the policy's cash value account, and all mortality charges are deducted from the same account. Interest is credited to this account with a minimum guarantee. Another characteristic of this policy is that some mortality risk is shifted to the insured by virtue of the variability of the deduction from the cash value account. Also a minimum interest on the cash value is guaranteed, and interest in excess of the guarantee depends on investment performance and insurer discretion. Any interest buildup in the policy is currently tax free. Although borrowings can be made from the cash values, the insured can also make withdrawals from the cash values that are not considered a loan by the insurance company. Therefore no interest need be paid to the insurer for the funds, and the funds need not be repaid to the insurer. However, there will be income tax consequences associated with such withdrawals if the policy is a MEC, or if the withdrawals are associated with a reduction in the death benefit. As with the variable life policy, there are significant surrender charges during the early years.

- *variable-universal life policy.* A variable universal life insurance policy is essentially a universal life insurance policy that gives the insured the ability to direct the investment of cash values. Like a variable life policy, cash values are not guaranteed. Variable-universal life insurance policies are often useful for healthy, young insureds who plan on using a maximum premium funding approach.

- *term policy.* This policy has an increasing premium used solely to provide life insurance protection over the lifetime of the insured. Important features of this policy are its guaranteed renewability, convertibility of the policy to permanent insurance up to age 65, and no cash value buildup over the life of the insured.

The cost ranges of acquiring either an ordinary whole life insurance policy, a variable life insurance policy, or a universal life insurance policy are approximately the same: between $11 and $15 per $1,000 of insurance per year. The cost of one-year guaranteed renewable, convertible term insurance at age 38 is approximately $1 per $1,000 of death benefit per year. However, the annual premium on the term insurance will rise significantly as Charles gets older.

Charles should keep in mind that even though the investment features and tax advantages of some of the permanent forms of insurance are attractive, the primary function of insurance is to protect survivors. However, Charles could still use additional permanent life insurance as part of his planning for the protection of his survivors. Permanent insurance is almost always the best choice for providing estate liquidity or funding the eventual payment of estate taxes. As a rule of thumb, if insurance is purchased and will remain in force for at least 10 years, it is generally better to purchase some form of permanent policy.

Charles does have some need for temporary insurance to provide for his survivors, at least until the children are finished with their college education. For this purpose term insurance would provide the necessary protection at the lowest cost. However, he does have some need for permanent survivorship protection extending beyond the time the children have finished their education and are self-supporting. For this purpose he might consider one of the four forms of permanent life insurance just discussed. Charles should work with his life insurance agent for the best choice of policies and combination thereof to meet his life insurance needs.

Disability Income Insurance

As already discussed, Charles's present disability income of $8,205, supplemented by an employer plan through Systems Design Associates, Inc., for an additional $1,000 per month, and the lump-sum payment provided through the funded buy-sell agreement, yielding another $700 monthly, bring Charles's disability income resources to approximately $9,905 monthly. This amount is approximately $405 more than his estimate of his family's needs ($9,500) and is based only on his utilizing the earnings on the lump-sum payment for the buy-sell and not on any invasion of the principal. Therefore Charles's position should be fairly strong should disability occur after implementation of the plan elements.

Property and Liability Insurance

The information in the case indicates that the homeowners policy is appropriate for the clients' needs, with the exception of the low limit for the liability coverage. The homeowners policy is designed for the average person, and endorsements to the contract are often necessary to meet a client's own particular circumstances. However, the facts of the case mention no circumstances that would call for such endorsements. The automobile insurance policy again seems adequate with the exception of the liability limits.

In light of judgments currently being awarded by some juries, it would be difficult to recommend liability limits under $100,000 or $300,000 for the homeowners policy and $100,000/$300,000/$50,000 or $250,000/$500,000/$100,000 for the automobile insurance policy.

An even better recommendation is to purchase a personal umbrella liability policy. Because this type of policy is not highly standardized and so many differences exist among companies, few specific comments can be made here. The personal umbrella policy provides excess liability coverage over the regular personal liability coverage that is found in the homeowners and the automobile liability insurance policies. Not only does the policy provide additional amounts of liability coverage for the same situations that are covered under the homeowners and automobile policy, it also provides protection for most other types of liability situations of a personal (rather than a business) nature. Umbrella policies can be readily purchased with limits of $1 million to $5 million, and the premium is quite reasonable, typically in the $200 to $300 annual range. There is a requirement, however, that certain underlying limits be carried under an individual's homeowners and automobile liability coverages. This limit may vary from $100,000 to $300,000 for the homeowners coverage and from $100,000/$300,000/$50,000 to $250,000/$500,000/$100,000 (or $300,000 to $500,000 if single-limit coverage is carried) for the automobile coverage. In those cases when the umbrella policy provides coverage for liability situations not covered by the underlying policies, there is a deductible, commonly ranging from $250 to $1,000.

PERSONAL PLANNING: INVESTMENT

General Investment Planning Considerations

Characteristics of Meaningful Financial Objectives

The first step in the development of a client's financial plan is to establish definitive and realistic financial objectives. While this is one of the most important steps in the process, it probably receives less formal consideration than any other step in comprehensive financial planning. Too frequently objectives are established by stating broad, general goals within a verbal, nonquantified framework. For instance, a client may want "enough life insurance to provide my family with the lifestyle they presently enjoy" or "the value of invested capital to be adequate to fund my children's college education." Both of these comments represent a loose statement of objectives, and neither provides sufficient information on which to construct an operable plan. The funding of children's college education is a common objective, but unless some systematic analysis of financial need is undertaken, the objective cannot be planned for. Therefore planning for each objective must incorporate the following characteristics:

- *quantitative statement of financial objective.* This refers to the dollar amount needed to meet the objective. For example, the college funding objective referred to above would be improved if it was expressed as "to have $15,000 per year for 4 years (to fund the college education) for each of my three children." This dollar target provides the planner with a basis to begin developing the necessary plan to meet the client's needs.
- *time horizon for each objective.* To merely quantify the objective is not sufficient. Each objective must have a time frame or horizon indicating when the funds will be needed. To illustrate: for college education for child one a given client may need $15,000 each year for 4 years beginning in 2003; for child two $15,000 each year for 4 years beginning in year 2007, and so forth. This provides a time frame showing when the target amount of funds must be available and aids in establishing premises for financial accumulation purposes.
- *priority ranking of objectives.* Most clients have several financial objectives and insufficient resources to meet all their particular

objectives. This limited amount of money and the resulting competition of several objectives require that a priority ranking of objectives be made. Not all clients will assign the same priority to any particular objective, but each client must set priorities, nevertheless.

When all three characteristics have been specified, the planner has meaningful objectives for developing various funding proposals. Also the financial objectives should be designed to complement each other. A balance or blend of activity to obtain all or most of the objectives should be stressed. It would not be prudent financial planning, for example, for a young family to allocate all its discretionary cash flows to retirement funding while sacrificing the funding necessary for other financial objectives.

Reasons for Accumulating Capital

Individuals have specific purposes for which they want to accumulate funds. These purposes typically include the following:

- *emergency reserve fund.* As the name implies, the purpose of this fund is to provide the necessary liquidity should either an unexpected expense or an unexpected reduction in income occur. Most people at some time experience an unexpected major expenditure such as repairs to a home or auto, unbudgeted medical expenses, or unanticipated changes in current educational expenses. In addition, the potential loss of employment exists as businesses react to changing economic conditions. Because of these eventualities most financial planners recommend that this fund be equal to 3 to 6 months of disposable (after-tax) income. As an alternative, in the event that a client does not spend all of his or her disposable income, a reserve of 3 to 6 months of living expenses may be adequate.

  Whether the fund should be at the lower or upper end of the 3- to 6-month range depends on numerous factors associated with the client. Some clients will have multiple sources of income, including wages, interest, and dividends, that permit holding a smaller emergency reserve. For such clients the likelihood that both employment and other income will decline simultaneously is less than if the client depended solely on one of these sources of income. Also the nature of the client's income from employment is critical. A client whose income is in the form of commissions could experience fluctuations in month-to-month employment income flows. On the other hand, a client who has a salaried position will not experience the fluctuations. Because of the potential for low-income months, the client who is paid a commission needs to maintain a higher emergency cash reserve than a salaried client. Other factors that can determine the size of the emergency reserve fund are (1) employment of the client's spouse, (2) family size, (3) health, and (4) the client's age. Each of these items can either increase or decrease the relative size of the client's emergency reserve. For example, a client in poor health would need a larger emergency reserve for potential medical expenses than an otherwise healthy client would require. In addition, the client might experience periods of unemployment or reduced income while on sick leave, and the emergency reserve would provide the funds for normal living expenses at these times. For a client in poor health an emergency reserve near or at (or even exceeding) the 6-month level would probably be necessary.

- *retirement fund.* This is an objective for all clients, but one for which each client will have different time periods for accumulation. Although some funding, such as pension contributions, will take place concurrently with the funding of other objectives, many clients may want the major contributions to this fund to be made after funding other objectives has been accomplished. However, the sooner funds can be set aside for this purpose, the smaller will be the annual contribution needed to accumulate a specific sum by retirement.

  Critical factors for determining the size of the retirement fund include estimates of income needs during retirement based on the client's current or expected standard of living and inflation rates and estimates of income flow from pension plans, Social Security, and other sources of income.

- *education fund.* Most clients who have dependent children will specify college education for their children as one of their objectives. In addition, some clients may also wish to fund private school education for grade school or high school or both. Since the purpose of this fund is to have adequate accumulated capital at the time the education expenses will begin, the time horizon depends on the children's ages. For some clients the period available to fund this objective is only a few years; for others the accumulation period may approach 18 years. The unique aspect of this objective is the inability to defer the expenditures. If we are focusing on funding for college education, the expenditures will commence virtually immediately after each child graduates from high school.

  Since the expenditures are not deferrable, the funding media cannot be overly risky and must ensure that the principal and accumulated income will be available during those specific college years and in the targeted amounts. Since the need is usually some years in the future, it is critical to make an estimate of the inflation of education costs in determining the size of the fund.

- *other specified purpose fund.* This category includes the accumulation of funds for various purposes, such as acquiring a vacation home or a yacht, taking a 90-day cruise around the world, or for whatever other purpose the client may require substantial funds at some specific time.

Since the above illustrations, as well as other possible reasons for accumulation, approach the luxury category, some flexibility and/or deferral as to when the expenditures will be made is generally possible, depending on the priority of the client's other objectives.

- *general wealth accumulation fund.* This last category seeks to achieve maximum possible accumulation of assets or wealth in addition to any funds amassed for more specific purposes. The additional income can be used to increase the client's standard of living later in life, to make gifts on an occasional basis to help children acquire homes or other assets, or solely for the purpose and comfort of being financially independent.

Sources of Investment Risk

Risk is the chance that the actual return from an investment may differ from its expected return because of changes within the economic environment. Each source of change creates a somewhat distinct risk. These sources are as follows:

- *business risk (or credit risk).* Changes in consumer preferences, economic conditions, foreign competition, or a failure to keep up with competition can result in a decline in an organization's earning power and its ability to pay interest, dividends, or other payments to owners of its securities. This will cause the market value of the securities to fall. Any investor who purchased these securities would fail to realize the expected return.

- *purchasing power risk.* Changes in the price level alter the real purchasing power of money. When inflation occurs, the real purchasing power of money earned from an investment declines. Fixed-return investments are more susceptible to this investment risk than are those with variable returns; however, unless the variable return associated with some investments rises at a rate equal to inflation, the real return on these investments would also decline.

- *interest-rate risk.* Changes in interest rates cause opposite or inverse changes in the value of investments. When interest rates rise, most investments, particularly fixed-return investments, decline in value.

- *market risk.* Changes in investor preferences, attitudes, or psychology can cause a security's price to decline regardless of any fundamental change in the earning power of the security or its issuer.

- *tax risk.* Changes in tax laws or regulations that reduce or remove the tax attractiveness of certain investment media can lead to reductions in the prices of those investments.

- *event risk.* An unfavorable action, such as an unfriendly takeover attempt, the silicon breast implant danger, or an oil spill, can negatively affect the value of one firm's or an entire industry's securities. The impetus for many of these unfavorable occurrences arises both unexpectedly and rapidly. In the short run the issuer's securities fall sharply in price. Often, they recover most of that initial decline.

- *foreign exchange risk.* If the dollar rises in value relative to the Euro, an American investor who owns European securities could suffer. For example, suppose that 6 months after an investor purchases shares in a French firm for 300 Euros per share, the rate of exchange changes from 100E = $1 (one Euro = one cent) to 150E = $1 (one Euro = 2/3 of one cent). If the stock rises to 375 Euros per share, those Euros when returned to the United States will convert to only $2.50—a loss of 16.67 percent of the initial investment even though the stock rose in value by 25 percent. Of course if the dollar falls relative to the Euro, the investor gains. Investors who own foreign securities, either directly or through mutual funds, in addition to monitoring performance of the company, must be alert to potential changes in the price of the dollar relative to other currencies.

These changes may reduce the investor's ability to quickly convert an investment to cash without incurring an economic loss. If a loss on sale does occur, then the actual return does not equal the expected return. The ability to convert an investment to cash without loss is the essence of liquidity, an essential feature for some portion of an investor's portfolio.

Investor Risk Attitudes

Although every client would enjoy having a 100 percent increase in the value of an investment within a short period, not all clients possess the requisite risk tolerance to use investment instruments whose risk/return characteristics can result in such a level of performance. Effective financial planning requires ascertaining the client's risk-taking propensity and recommending investment media consistent with that risk profile, as well as with the client's priorities, target amounts, or time frame for each financial objective.

The Risk/Return Trade-off

Using the media available within the financial markets, numerous portfolios can be developed, each having a different degree of risk and return. Figure 3-1 represents such an array. The only way to obtain higher returns is to accept greater risk, as is shown in figure 3-1.

Figure 3-2 depicts the risk/return preferences for three different investors. Investor A is risk-averse and requires more than proportional increases in expected returns before accepting any additional risk. Investor B is risk-indifferent and accepts proportional increases in expected returns in exchange for accepting higher risks. Investor C, a risk taker, will accept smaller increases in expected returns in exchange for accepting higher risks.

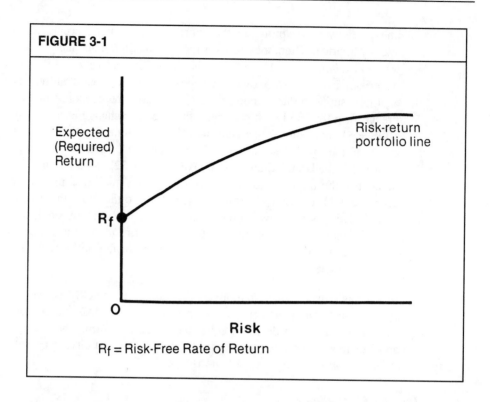

FIGURE 3-1

Expected
(Required)
Return

Risk-return
portfolio line

R_f

O

Risk

R_f = Risk-Free Rate of Return

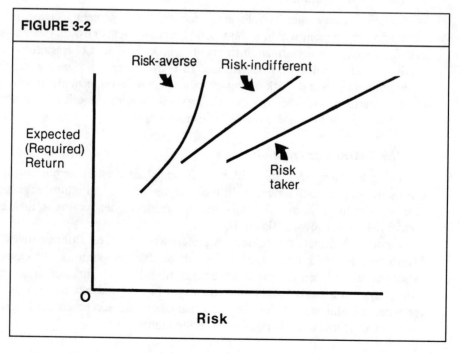

FIGURE 3-2

Risk-averse   Risk-indifferent

Expected
(Required)
Return

Risk
taker

O

Risk

Combining figures 3-1 and 3-2, as shown in figure 3-3, indicates that for a given portfolio line, the risk averter will select a portfolio having a small amount of risk, such as OA in figure 3-3, and earn a return only slightly above the return earned on a risk-free portfolio. The risk taker chooses a portfolio containing a higher amount of risk, such as OC in figure 3-3, and expects to receive a higher return from the portfolio than does the risk averter. The risk-indifferent client falls in between the risk averter and the risk taker. Any investment portfolio or revisions to an existing portfolio recommended to meet a particular objective must match the client's risk profile.

Change in Investor Risk Attitudes. The preceding description of investor risk attitudes assumes reasonable stability in the forces that shape an investor's willingness to accept varying degrees of risk in investments. The economic events surrounding this decision-making process may change. Such changes, which include expectations of future employment or business income and observed changes in the securities or real estate markets, result in reassessments

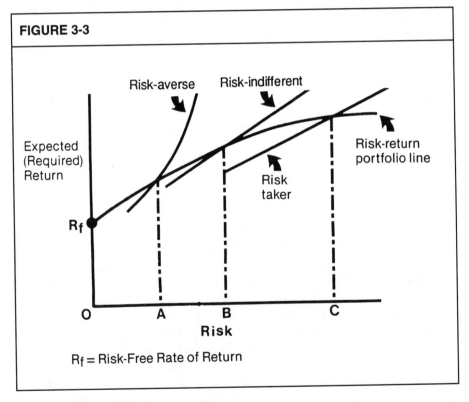

FIGURE 3-3

in an individual's degree of willingness to accept risk. Even the simple fact of aging tends to create a reduced willingness to undertake risk. Figure 3-4 shows a hypothetical shift in investor risk attitudes. The large decline in the Dow Jones Industrial Average (DJIA) in October 1987 could easily cause such a shift. The economic environment in 2001 could lead to the same shift. Even if an investor did not own any stocks at those times, the pessimism those events created could easily have affected attitudes toward other investments. For any risk profile the leftward shifts of the three risk curves suggest that for any investment to be retained, its expected (required) return must increase. As a result of the surging bull market of the 1990s, investors' willingness to take risk seems to have increased.

FIGURE 3-4

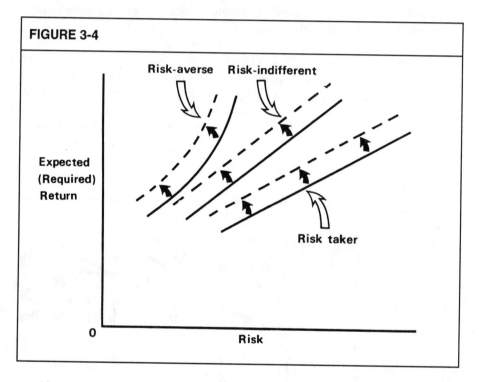

If the expected return does not increase, the investor would reposition assets to reflect this lessened willingness to undertake risk. Such a repositioning would result in a portfolio having both less risk and a reduced expected return. However, the reverse could occur. Investors could decide to undertake greater risk for any expected level of return, thus shifting their preference curves (rightward rather than leftward as shown on the graphs), resulting in portfolio compositions that accept greater risk for the same return.

The effective financial planner does not assume that the client's risk profile is constant, but he or she carefully monitors changes in both the economic environment and the client's situation and attitude. Based on these changes, the financial planner might suggest that some repositioning is desirable. Whenever this occurs, the underlying premises concerning the assumed returns and the amounts of funds being set aside for specific client objectives need to be reviewed.

The Time Frame. In addition to an investor's general propensity to accept or not accept risk, the time dimension is an additional factor contributing to the decision process. How long does the investor have before the funds are needed? How certain is the need for the funds at that specific time? These two dimensions are important considerations in developing a recommended portfolio for a client. If the accumulation period is relatively short—3 years, for example—and the planned expenditure of the funds at that time is quite certain, then high-risk investments would be inappropriate, and a relatively conservative investment should be chosen. On the other hand, if the expenditure planned for in a 3-year accumulation period is deferrable, then a somewhat higher risk/return investment could be considered.

Implications for Portfolio Selection. Applying this framework of a time dimension to an investor's several accumulation objectives, the following guidelines can be established:

- *emergency fund.* Since the funds could be needed at almost any time, safety of principal is primary and return is secondary. Investments that contain very low risk and low return fulfill these requirements.
- *retirement fund.* Since the need for these funds is somewhat distant for many clients and in some situations the expected retirement date can be delayed, investments carrying higher risk but consistent with the client's risk profile can be used. Indeed, except for those clients who are near their retirement date, this fund should hold investments containing higher risk/return trade-offs than would be acceptable for a client's emergency or education fund. The longer time frame until the funds are needed for retirement also permits changes in annual funding amounts and investment media should investment returns be more or less than expected.
- *education funds.* Due to the lack of deferability of the planned expenditures, these funds should be placed in relatively conservative investments even if they are not needed for 10 or more years. The need for these monies at a specified time is too definite to permit investing in instruments that carry a high degree of uncertainty as to their returns or their market value.
- *other specific objectives.* Since these objectives tend to be luxurious in nature and are somewhat deferrable, a client could use a higher-risk/return portfolio to accumulate funds for these purposes. This funding could be accomplished with a portfolio containing the highest risk/return trade-off consistent with the investor's risk profile.

Risk/Return Considerations of Investment Media

The preceding section developed the risk/return trade-off for a client's portfolio (mix) of assets. Most portfolios are comprised of several different

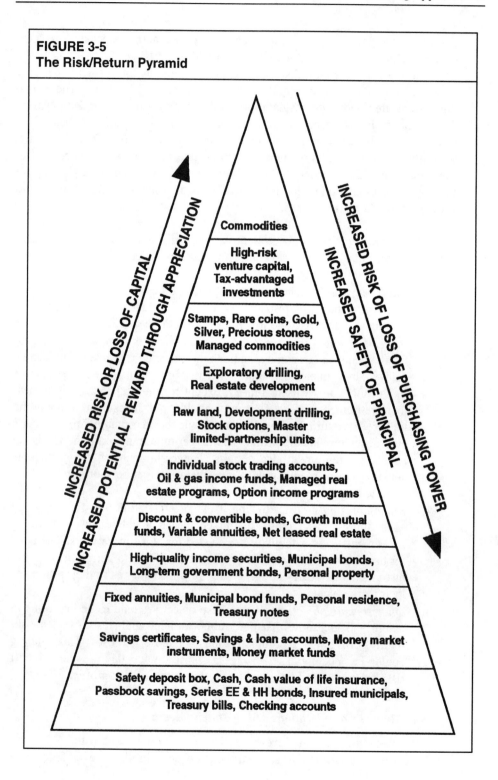

FIGURE 3-5
The Risk/Return Pyramid

investments, each of which contains its own risk/return characteristics. Figure 3-5 shows some of the frequently used investment vehicles arranged in a pyramid with the most conservative, least risky, and lowest-yielding vehicles at the base of the pyramid. To encourage individuals to accept any increased risk associated with a particular investment, the potential for higher expected returns must exist. As a consequence investments become progressively riskier as the pyramid is ascended.

All private sector investment media contain some of the risks in varying—business, market, interest rate, tax, purchasing power, event, and possibly foreign exchange risk. Public sector investments such as municipal bonds do not involve business risk as such but do have a default risk linked to the taxing power of the issuer. All long-term debt instruments—private sector, municipal, or U.S. government—contain the interest rate and purchasing power risks. The potential negative effect of all of these seven risks determines the location of an investment medium within the pyramid. The greater the possible effect of these risks on an investment, the greater must be the expected return. All decisions concerning the choice of funding vehicles involve trade-offs between risk and return. The financial planner must recommend and the client must choose those investment media most closely suited to both the latter's financial objectives and his or her willingness (or unwillingness) to accept risk. To reiterate an earlier point, due to either the inability to defer the expenditure or the time available to accumulate the funds, certain client objectives will require the use of investment media in the lower portion of the pyramid, regardless of a willingness to accept high risk.

Client Analysis

Investment planning develops the following considerations and applies them to the specific client situation. The planning is composed of two basic phases. The first phase involves determining client potential investment and accumulation objectives, setting priorities among these objectives, and ascertaining risk attitudes and general personal financial concerns. The second phase involves making and executing actual plans: selecting appropriate investment vehicles; allocating investment resources to specific objectives and funding vehicles; implementing a funding schedule that is consistent with currently available investment resources, standard-of-living objectives, and anticipated future investment resources; and designing an overall investment portfolio that is consistent with risk attitudes and personal financial concerns.

Financial Objectives

Among the Wigginses' general financial objectives are five items directly related to investment planning (listed in order of priority):

- funding their children's educations
- reducing their tax burden
- maintaining their standard of living
- attaining financial security at retirement (at a level comparable to the standard of living before retirement)
- accumulating wealth generally (they would like to save and invest 20 percent of their income after taxes)

The Wigginses have also indicated that they hope to build a vacation home by 2005. They feel this investment might serve several potential purposes. If necessary, they are willing to liquidate the investment to provide education funding; if not needed for education funding, the vacation home may serve as a permanent residence for their retirement years.

The Wigginses have listed the following personal financial concerns or attitudes toward various characteristics of potential investment vehicles (5 indicates a very strong concern and 0 indicates no concern):

Objective	Charles	Barbara	Average	Combined Rank Order
Tax reduction/deferral	5	5	5	1
Capital appreciation	4	5	4.5	2
Future income	4	5	4.5	2
Safety of principal	4	4	4	4
Inflation protection	4	3	3.5	5
Liquidity	3	4	3.5	5
Current income	3	3	3	7

As stated in the introduction to the Wiggins case (chapter 2), Barbara declined to rate investments. Charles did rate his preference for or aversion to specific types of savings and investment instruments as follows (5 indicates substantial preference and 0 indicates an aversion):

Investment Instrument	Rating	Rank Order
Mutual fund (growth)	5	1
Common stock (growth)	5	1
Real estate (direct ownership)	4	3
Money market fund	4	3
Mutual fund (income)	3	5
Savings account	3	5
Corporate bond	2	7
Municipal bond	2	7
Variable annuity	2	7

Investment Instrument	Rating	Rank Order
Limited partnership units	1	10
U.S. government bonds	1	10
Commodities, gold, collectibles	0	12

Furthermore, the Wigginses expressed their feeling that yields on their investments should be higher than they have been.

Charles and Barbara express almost total agreement on their financial objectives. Only a slight difference appears between their concerns for inflation protection and liquidity.

Analysis

Before specific accumulation and investment plans are discussed, several general observations are warranted. Tax reduction/deferral, capital appreciation, and future income are the Wigginses' primary financial concerns. These concerns are complementary, since investment vehicles that provide capital growth opportunities generally provide tax deferral. The tax on any capital appreciation is not paid until the year in which appreciated assets are sold and the gains are recognized. However, the full amount of the gain is includible in their gross income for federal tax purposes under current law although taxed at a maximum rate of 20 percent under most client circumstances. Future income needs can be met simply by converting growth-oriented assets to income-producing investments at a later date when income is desired. Until the conversion is made, income taxes are not paid on the amount of the annual appreciation.

Safety of principal is also a highly ranked financial concern and does not generally complement capital appreciation and tax reduction/deferral. Investments that maximize safety of principal generally have minimal capital appreciation and tax reduction/deferral, and vice versa. Thus the Wigginses' investment portfolio should contain investments that balance these opposing financial concerns.

Charles's preference ratings for investment vehicles are consistent with the Wigginses' financial concerns. Growth stocks and growth mutual funds, which may provide capital appreciation and tax deferral opportunities, are ranked the highest. Direct ownership of real estate, which may also provide capital appreciation potential and some tax reduction/deferral opportunities, especially when leveraged, is ranked third. Charles ranks limited partnership units very low. Although limited partnerships may provide some opportunities for tax reduction or deferral, their safety of principal and their liquidity are often minimal. In contrast, Charles gives a high rating to money market funds, which are safe and liquid but offer no tax advantages. These investment preference rankings taken together seem to reflect Charles's desired balance between capital appreciation and tax reduction/deferral on one hand, and safety of principal on the other.

As a general rule, most investment counselors recommend that clients maintain their emergency reserve fund in a safe and liquid investment vehicle. In the Wigginses' case this reserve could be maintained in money market funds or other safe and liquid savings vehicles such as cash values of whole life insurance policies. For the remainder of their investment portfolio the Wigginses seem willing to accept some risk of principal to the extent necessary to achieve greater capital appreciation and tax reduction/deferral.

Education Funding

Estimated Education Expenditures

The Wigginses' foremost objective is education funding for their children. The estimated college expenses in current dollars are $12,000 for Stephanie, who will begin college in 4 years; $40,000 for Caroline, who will begin college in 6 years; and $60,000 for Charles, Jr., who will begin college in 11 years. They have also mentioned a potential need to fund their children's graduate educations, which they estimate at $30,000 for Stephanie, $40,000 for Caroline, and $60,000 for Charles, Jr., in current dollars. They are also concerned that these estimated costs may be insufficient in an inflationary environment.

The first step in determining their education funding plans is to adjust these estimated costs for inflation and to plot their incidence over time. Assuming an 8 percent inflation factor, and assuming that graduate studies will last 3 years, the time profile of education costs as shown in table 3-1 can be developed.

Investment Alternatives for Education Funding

The second step in this phase is to evaluate the suitability of various investment media for meeting the objective. In this situation the Wigginses recognize that relatively conservative investment instruments must be used for each child's education fund. Although their choice of CDs as a funding mechanism is reasonable, numerous other instruments are available to fulfill this objective.

Savings Instruments. The question of investing in savings instruments such as savings accounts, NOW accounts, or certificates of deposit may arise. Generally these instruments offer the saver a high degree of liquidity and safety of principal but at the cost of a low return.

Perhaps the most important advantage of these instruments is, within limits, their FDIC insurance. For the most conservative of investors this assurance is highly important. Given their typically low returns, these instruments are inappropriate for long-term funding objectives whose target date is more than a year or two away, since the amount of annual funding needed would be greater

TABLE 3-1
Projected College and Graduate School Costs in Dollars, Assuming 8 Percent Inflation Payment in Full September 1 of Each Year

	2006	2007	2008	2009	2010	2011	2012	2013	2014	2015	2016	2017	2018	2019
College expenses:														
Stephanie	4,082	4,408	4,761	5,141	—	—	—	—	—	—	—	—	—	—
Caroline	—	—	15,869	17,138	18,509	19,990	—	—	—	—	—	—	—	—
Charles, Jr.	—	—	—	—	—	—	—	34,975	37,773	40,794	44,058	—	—	—
Total college expenses	4,082	4,408	20,630	22,279	18,509	19,990	—	34,975	37,773	40,794	44,058	—	—	—
Graduate expenses:														
Stephanie	—	—	—	—	18,509	19,990	21,589	—	—	—	—	—	—	—
Caroline	—	—	—	—	—	—	25,118	27,203	29,379	—	—	—	—	—
Charles, Jr.	—	—	—	—	—	—	—	—	—	—	—	52,869	57,099	61,667
Total graduate expenses	—	—	—	—	18,509	19,990	46,707	27,203	29,379	—	—	52,869	57,099	61,667
Total education expenses	4,082	4,408	20,630	22,279	37,018	39,980	46,707	62,178	67,152	40,794	44,058	52,869	57,099	61,667

than that needed with a higher-return investment. However, occasionally long-term CDs may provide a somewhat more attractive rate of return. The advantages of these savings instruments, liquidity and safety, can also be combined with a higher rate of return by investing in other conservative investment media.

Money Market Mutual Funds or Accounts. Whether the investor uses the money market mutual fund (MMMF) or a money market deposit account (MMDA) at a bank or a savings and loan, the primary advantage of either form of account is that the rate of return is higher than might be available from the short-term savings instruments described above. Intermediate and long-term CDs pay a higher return than either MMDAs or MMMFs. Both of these investment media (MMDAs and MMMFs) possess a high degree of safety and liquidity and consequently have a relatively low yield. However, the FDIC insurance rules apply only to the MMDAs. They are satisfactory as short-term depositories for funds until sufficient monies are accumulated for purchasing other investment media, but like saving instruments they do not adequately serve longer-term objectives, such as the Wigginses' education funding, since their return is relatively low.

T-Bills. Treasury bills possess the same characteristics as other forms of savings instruments—that is, high liquidity, excellent safety of principal since they are issued by the federal government, little risk of default, and a high certainty that the income will be paid when due. However, Treasury bills are a short-term investment maturing in 90 days to one year from date of issue and require constant management and reinvestment. In addition, because they have a high degree of safety, their return is not satisfactory for long-term funding objectives.

Treasury Notes. These government securities are usually issued with 3-, 7-, and 10-year maturities. The interest rate earned on these notes would be somewhat higher than on the Treasury bills. But with their longer maturity they provide a greater degree of interest-rate risk than do the Treasury bills. The other characteristics of low-default risk and assurance that interest will be paid are unchanged.

Corporate Bonds. Individual issues of selected high-quality corporate bonds are a potential investment for the Wigginses' education funding.

There are several advantages to individual corporate bonds that make them desirable for education funding. As has already been mentioned, they will generate a higher return than the previously described investment vehicles. Another major advantage occurs if the Wigginses or their trustee chooses selected issues that mature simultaneously with the payment of college expenses for each child and if the bonds are held until maturity. If this is their strategy, then the rate of return on the bonds and their redemption value are known with certainty. Thus there is a high degree of predictability for this investment's performance, which is desirable for the purpose of the funding. Assuming that bonds of at least AA quality—investment-grade bonds issued by large, financially stable corporations dominant in their industry—are purchased, another advantage would be low risk. These bonds would be registered in the owner's name. In addition, there would be little, if any, administrative effort and expense involved in their ownership. This slight administrative effort could be further reduced by purchasing zero coupon bonds that will mature when the education expenses are incurred.

There are five disadvantages of choosing individual issues of corporate bonds. Perhaps the greatest disadvantage is that the bonds lack an inflationary hedge. This lack of an inflationary hedge is common to all fixed-income issues and must be considered, especially since the Wigginses have specified a desire for such a hedge.

Another disadvantage is the possibility of the bond being called by the issuer. The Wigginses can eliminate or minimize the danger of any bonds being called by buying issues that have a deferred-callability feature, that are noncallable, or that are not likely to be called.

A third disadvantage of individual bonds is the interest-rate risk, which applies only when interest rates have risen and bonds are sold prior to their maturity date. This is not too great a concern in this situation since bonds that mature to meet their children's educational expenses will be selected, and the bonds will be held until that maturity occurs.

The fourth disadvantage can occur if the issuing corporation becomes the object of a leveraged buyout by outside interests or by existing management. If the corporation issues the bonds used in the leveraged buyout or guarantees the bonds of the buying corporation, the rating services will downgrade the quality rating of its previously issued bonds. This results in the bondholder's having a high-risk, low-grade bond but earning the interest rate associated with bonds of lesser risk. Although a put clause that allows the bondholder to put the bond for redemption at face value at any time would be desirable, few bonds with this provision are available in the marketplace.

Selected issues of high-quality corporate bonds from financially secure and dominant firms appear to be an excellent vehicle for college education funding. Interest-rate risk is not really a problem in this situation if maturity dates of the bonds match starting dates for education expenses. The danger of the bonds being called can be minimized or eliminated by selecting new issues or issues that are noncallable. Their failure to provide a hedge against inflation is their most serious shortcoming.

The fifth disadvantage involves the problem of reinvesting small sums of annual income to keep the funds productive. Unless the reinvested funds earn the anticipated return, the expected terminal values will not be achieved. Obviously zero coupon bonds are one way to eliminate this disadvantage.

The last disadvantage arises when zero coupon bonds are used. Income for tax purposes must be recognized annually, and cash is needed to pay federal and/or state income taxes.

Bond Funds. Mutual funds that invest in corporate bonds are another alternative to financing the children's education. Generally the advantages and disadvantages mentioned previously for specific bond issues also apply to a bond fund. However, there are some additional factors that must also be mentioned.

First, the same before-tax rate of return available through direct ownership of corporate bonds is also currently obtainable through a variety of highly regarded bond funds, thus making the current return from bond funds attractive. Other advantages of a bond fund are professional management and the portfolio diversification characteristic of the mutual-fund concept. Another advantage, although not nearly as important as those already mentioned, is the ease of bookkeeping, since complete data is provided to owners of bond funds.

Perhaps the major disadvantage of a bond fund is the lack of predictability regarding the value of the fund shares at some future date. The fund managers are continuously purchasing new bonds for the portfolio and selling bonds from the portfolio, thus resulting in reported capital gains or losses that create a fluctuating tax liability during the accumulation period. With direct ownership of a bond and a known date for maturity, the Wigginses will know with absolute certainty the value of that bond as of the maturity date. This is not true of ownership interests in a bond fund because the per-share value is determined by the fund's net asset value, which is unpredictable for any future time and hence not a certainty at the time the monies are needed for education expenses. Because of this unpredictability bond funds are not recommended for the Wigginses.

Stripped Bonds or Strips. Several investment brokerage firms have put together a relatively new investment instrument. The brokerage firm acquires a portfolio of high-grade corporate (or Treasury) bonds, and then the two financial parts, the income stream over the duration of the bond and the maturity value of the bond, are sold to investors. Purchasing the income stream from the bonds would provide a cash flow every year. The income stream purchased could have a duration equivalent to the funding horizon for each child's education expenses. This approach also provides additional cash that would have to be reinvested each year. If only the maturity value of the bond was purchased, there would be no stream of cash income. However, the accrued increase in the value of the security on a year-by-year basis must be recognized for tax purposes, without having any cash flow from the investment. Either additional funding by the Wigginses for the purpose of paying income taxes or owning a portfolio that is a combination of the income stream from a bond portfolio and the maturity value of a different portfolio of stripped bonds would be necessary.

These two investment media have the other advantages and disadvantages that were discussed with respect to corporate bonds. However, if properly used, they would assure the Wigginses of having the expected dollar amounts available as planned.

Common Stocks and Common Stock Mutual Funds. Common stocks may appear to be an ideal investment vehicle for funding the educational objective for a variety of reasons. The most obvious reason for selecting common stocks or a common stock mutual fund is the unlimited potential for gain if the issuing firm or the mutual fund's portfolio prospers. There is also a high degree of marketability with these investment vehicles in that they can be converted to cash quickly and relatively inexpensively. Another advantage to these investments is that they can be an effective inflationary hedge. As the general price level rises, the value of high-quality common stocks or a high-quality common stock portfolio held by a mutual fund should increase with the price level over long periods of time, hence providing the investor with some protection from inflation. For short periods of time this relationship between common stock prices and inflation might not exist. But over a long time frame common stocks or a common stock mutual fund is consistent with the Wigginses' preference for an inflationary hedge and capital appreciation. Unfortunately all the advantages of these media are accompanied by two serious disadvantages that preclude their use for education funding. Since the Wigginses want to realize a specific amount at a particular time to fund their children's education, the proper investment, as previously noted, would be one with a high degree of predictability. One of the disadvantages of both common stocks and common stock mutual funds is that the future value of the education fund cannot be predicted with any degree of certainty. A reduction in value as a result of uncontrollable and unpredictable factors is the greatest disadvantage of common stock investments and is precisely what the Wigginses should avoid in this situation.

In addition, the income stream from dividends on common stocks can be uncertain due to changes in corporate profitability or dividend policy. As a consequence the expected return from the portfolio of either common stocks or a common stock mutual fund may not be realized. For these reasons common stocks and mutual funds invested in common stocks are generally unacceptable investments for a portfolio that must be worth a specific dollar amount at a specified time. Indeed the only acceptable investments for objectives such as these are the various fixed-income investments whose income stream and ending value can be predicted with a high degree of certainty.

However, if individuals are willing to accept some of the risk of owning common stocks in their programs for funding specific future financial objectives, somewhat higher returns can be achieved. If investments are made in an index fund whose portfolio represents a specific market index, such as the S&P 500, the risk will equal the risk of the market as a whole. Since the end of World War

II (1945) to the present, the time required for the market index to recover to the level of the prior peak has exceeded 3 years only once (and that was slightly more than 3 years). Thus the indication is that an index fund could achieve the desired accumulation goal. The user of this technique should carefully monitor the fund's performance and be prepared to withdraw some or all of the investment approximately 3 years prior to the date the money is needed. For college education purposes, perhaps a withdrawal to cover the first 2 years of college costs would cope with the possibility that the recovery would take longer than 3 years. (Note: In the last 50 years most of the recoveries to the prior peaks have taken less than 2 years. The recommended 3-year period for withdrawals is a conservative investment strategy.)

Life Insurance Products. Numerous products of the life insurance industry such as single-premium whole life, variable, and universal life insurance are instruments that can be employed to accumulate funds in a tax-advantaged manner. In these policies there is no current income taxation on the annual buildup of the cash values, as previously discussed. This advantage of tax-free buildup can be attractive to clients in the top tax bracket. However, if the policy is surrendered and the cash values are received at that time, any gain will be subject to income taxation.

It is not recommended that permanent insurance be employed as the primary funding mechanism for several reasons. First, the primary reason for purchasing any policy should be the need for death protection. Second, the commission structure and mortality charges reduce the amount of funds working for accumulation purposes. Third, the guaranteed return on cash values is generally relatively low. Fourth, equity-based life insurance products such as variable life are not suitable for an objective that requires a near certainty of the availability of funds at a specified time. Last, the tax penalties that can be imposed on withdrawals (surrenders) of annuities or MECs can be sizable. However, it is certainly appropriate to consider using the cash values in permanent insurance as a means of making up any shortfall that may occur in the education funds when the expenses come due.

Investment Media Selection

For the Wigginses' education funding goal it is recommended that high-quality, investment-grade corporate bonds be used as the investment medium for the children's educational expenses (to the extent that education expenses are not funded through use of education IRAs and Sec. 529 plans). This choice fulfills the objectives of having a known return during the accumulation period and a known value upon maturity, and therefore the specific amounts of monies will be available when needed. Since the Wigginses' primary goal is education funding, and they rate both safety of principal and growth of capital as important, it seems appropriate to place the education funds in a vehicle where safety of principal is predominant. Growth can be achieved in other investments, possibly in their retirement portfolios.

During the last 30 years AAA corporate bonds yielded a before-tax compound rate of return of 8.35 percent. Currently investment-grade bonds are providing an 8.6 percent before-tax return, and it is anticipated that this return, as an average, is sustainable during the funding period.

Funding Vehicles

The third step in this planning process is to determine how much investment capital the Wiginses would have to allocate to this objective if they were to fund the objective today in its entirety. They may not want to fully fund this objective now, and they may not, in fact, be able to do so, but this calculation is necessary to determine how much of their currently available investment resources can be allocated to this objective as compared with other objectives and to determine a funding schedule for future contributions.

The amount of investment capital required today to fund their education objectives will depend, of course, on the assumed after-tax rate of return on investment, which will depend in turn on the choice of investment instruments, funding vehicles, and tax rates. The tax rate will depend on who nominally owns or receives the investment assets.

For example, if Charles and Barbara fund their children's education expenses without transferring investment assets to their children, they need to invest the following amounts today for each child, assuming that invested assets earn 8.6 percent before tax and, conservatively, that earnings will be taxed at a 31 percent rate.

Present Value of Education Costs
8 Percent Inflation for College Expenses
5.9 Percent After-tax Return
Charles and Barbara Retain Ownership of Funds

	College	Graduate	Total
Stephanie	$ 13,372	$ 35,803	$ 49,175
Caroline	46,357	43,405	89,762
Charles, Jr.	76,710	68,463	145,173
	$136,439	$147,671	$284,111

In other words, $136,439 ($13,372 for Stephanie, $46,357 for Caroline, and $76,710 for Charles, Jr.) invested by Charles and Barbara today at 8.6 percent before tax will accumulate enough money after tax, if both earnings and principal are liquidated, to pay their children's estimated college expenses (as shown in the preceding table) as they come due. Similarly, $147,671 will fully fund their children's graduate school expenses as they come due.

2503(c) Trusts. As discussed previously, a 2503(c) accumulation trust is one potential vehicle to achieve the desired income shifting during the time Charles and Barbara will be accumulating funds for their children's education. Three separate trusts, one for each child, could be established. Income earned by each trust would be taxed to the trust at the trust's marginal tax rates. For Stephanie's trust, the 15 percent rate would apply for both the funding and liquidation periods. Caroline's trust would be in the 28 percent bracket for a few of the years. Therefore Charles and Barbara could fund these trusts in their entirety either in full today or over a period of years with assets earning an after-tax return of 7.3 percent [8.6 − (.15 x 8.6)]. For Charles, Jr., this is not the case. After several years, annual trust income would exceed $6,750, and the 35 percent tax rate would apply. Based on an approximation of the average annual tax rate to which the trust would be subject, a reasonable estimate of an after-tax return on instruments yielding 8.6 percent before tax would be 6.8 percent for Charles, Jr.'s trust. The following table is based on the after-tax return of 7.3 percent for Stephanie's and Caroline's trusts and the approximate 6.8 percent for Charles, Jr.'s trust. Note that these two rates will apply to the inserts on the following pages that are used to determine the annual funding rather than the lump-sum funding needed to accomplish the accumulation for the college expenses objective.

Present Value of Education Costs
8 Percent Inflation for College Expenses
7.3 Percent After-tax Return for Stephanie and Caroline
and 6.8 Percent After-tax Return for Charles, Jr.
2503(c) Trust

	College	Graduate	Total
Stephanie	$ 12,437	$ 31,802	$ 44,239
Caroline	42,000	37,561	79,561
Charles, Jr.	68,909	64,454	133,363
	$123,346	$133,817	$257,163

The tax saving for the expected college education costs attained by shifting income from Charles and Barbara (at their marginal tax rate) to the trusts (at the trust's marginal tax rate) has a present value of $13,276 ($136,439 − $123,346). The Wigginses do not have the necessary assets to fully fund the three trusts at this time. Nor would it be desirable to do so even if sufficient assets were available since gift taxes would be incurred (or part of the unified credit used) for a portion of the funds placed in trust for Caroline and Charles, Jr. Instead level annual funding would be more appropriate for the clients. Only the 4-year college education of each child should be funded at this time. Graduate education plans are too uncertain for children of these ages, in the absence of strong client sentiment to the contrary. In addition, the Wigginses' cash flow is insufficient to do graduate school funding at this time, given their other obligations and objectives.

Charles and Barbara initially need $15,118 per year for these educational funding requirements. This amount would be allocated as follows: $1,982 to Stephanie's trust, $5,784 to Caroline's trust, and $7,352 to Charles, Jr.'s trust. The funding for Stephanie will end in 2009, for Caroline in 2011, and for Charles, Jr., in 2016.

In addition, the establishment and continuance of these trusts will generate some expenses. First, between $1,500 and $2,500 of expense will be incurred to have an attorney draft the trust instruments. If feasible, the attorney may also be named as trustee and work with the Wigginses' CPA to prepare the annual income tax returns for the trusts. A portion of the expense of establishing (but not maintaining) the three trusts qualifies as a tax planning expense and therefore will be tax deductible by Charles and Barbara in the year the trusts are established. Also the annual expenses incurred for trust-asset management and income tax preparation should be reasonable and substantially less than the tax savings that the three trusts generate. These expenses are tax deductible to the trusts. Each trust would deduct its portion of the annual expense against trust income for that year. As a consequence Charles and Barbara may wish to increase their annual contributions to meet these expenses. An estimate of the educational funding and payment schedule for each of the three children if the trusts are utilized is shown on the following pages.

[text continues on page 3.121]

EDUCATION FUNDING SCHEDULE

Stephanie's Education Fund 2002–2010
School Starting Date Sept. 1, 2006
7.30 Expected Rate of Return
Monthly Payments of $165 Made until School Ends

Charles and Barbara Wiggins
Annual Cash Flow Statement
Monthly Payments until School Ends
Invest $165 Each Month from Jan 2002 through June 2010

Year	Investment Needed	Education Expenses	Investment Earnings	Balance in Fund
2002	1,982	0.00	80.00	2,063
2003	1,982	0.00	236.00	4,281
2004	1,982	0.00	403.00	6,666
2005	1,982	0.00	583.00	9,232
2006	1,982	2,184.00	730.00	9,761
2007	1,982	4,638.00	632.00	7,737
2008	1,982	5,023.00	464.00	5,159
2009	1,982	5,440.00	252.00	1,954
2010	991	2,887.00	32.00	90
	16,850	20,173.00	3,413.00	

EDUCATION FUNDING SCHEDULE

Caroline's Education Fund 2002–2012
School Starting Date Sept. 1, 2008
7.30 Expected Rate of Return
Monthly Payments of $482 Made until School Ends

Charles and Barbara Wiggins
Annual Cash Flow Statement
Monthly Payments until School Ends
Invest $482 Each Month from Jan 2002 through June 2012

Year	Investment Needed	Education Expenses	Investment Earnings	Balance in Fund
2002	5,784	0.00	234.00	6,018
2003	5,784	0.00	688.00	12,490
2004	5,784	0.00	1,177.00	19,451
2005	5,784	0.00	1,702.00	26,937
2006	5,784	0.00	2,267.00	34,989
2007	5,784	0.00	2,875.00	43,648
2008	5,784	8,535.00	3,346.00	44,244
2009	5,784	18,126.00	2,850.00	34,752
2010	5,784	19,630.00	2,073.00	22,979
2011	5,784	21,260.00	1,120.00	8,623
2012	2,892	11,283.00	140.00	373
	60,732	78,834.00	18,474.00	

EDUCATION FUNDING SCHEDULE

Charles, Jr.'s Education Fund 2002–2017
School Starting Date Sept. 1, 2013
6.80 Expected Rate of Return
Monthly Payments of $613 Made until School Ends

Charles and Barbara Wiggins
Annual Cash Flow Statement
Monthly Payments until School Ends
Invest $613 Each Month from Jan 2002 through June 2017

Year	Investment Needed	Education Expenses	Investment Earnings	Balance in Fund
2002	7,352	0.00	276.00	7,628
2003	7,352	0.00	812.00	15,791
2004	7,352	0.00	1,384.00	24,527
2005	7,352	0.00	1,997.00	33,876
2006	7,352	0.00	2,653.00	43,881
2007	7,352	0.00	3,355.00	54,588
2008	7,352	0.00	4,106.00	66,046
2009	7,352	0.00	4,910.00	78,308
2010	7,352	0.00	5,771.00	91,430
2011	7,352	0.00	6,691.00	105,473
2012	7,352	0.00	7,676.00	120,501
2013	7,352	19,077.00	8,351.00	117,126
2014	7,352	40,514.00	6,989.00	90,952
2015	7,352	43,877.00	5,028.00	59,455
2016	7,352	47,519.00	2,683.00	21,970
2017	3,676	25,219.00	329.00	757
	113,950	176,206.00	63,013.00	

UGMA Gifts. Another vehicle to fund the children's educational objectives could be the UGMA custodial account. Charles and/or Barbara could be the named custodian(s) and they can then use their discretion in the investment media chosen for the account. For example, the account could be maintained with a securities brokerage firm that would invest the funds as Charles and Barbara direct. Or a banking institution could be selected and investment media available through the bank, such as CDs, bank money market accounts, or similar investment media, could be chosen. The major advantage of UGMA gifts as compared to trusts is that the UGMA gift is inexpensive and convenient. The major disadvantage is the fact that the kiddie tax will apply to the income from these accounts for each child under age 14 who has more than $1,500 of unearned income (inflation adjusted) in a year. Since the Wigginses are in the 30 percent bracket, unearned income of Charles, Jr., in excess of the inflation-adjusted $1,500 would be taxed at that rate. However, since Stephanie is already 14, this provision would not apply to income earned in an account for her benefit; rather, the income would be taxed to her at her rates. Caroline is 12, so for 2 years the kiddie tax would apply to her unearned income in excess of $1,500. Since Caroline is living with Charles's former wife, Cynthia, her kiddie tax would be calculated at the tax rate of Cynthia and her husband.

Since Charles and Barbara are not the custodial parents for the two girls, they are probably not in a position to make recommendations concerning the girls' tax situation.

For both Stephanie and Caroline the annual trust funding amounts shown on the preceding pages are quite close to what would be needed if corporate bonds were instead placed in UGMA accounts, one for each girl. There would be slight differences due to Stephanie's and Caroline's standard deduction amount and the potential kiddie tax payable by Caroline. This difference should not exceed approximately $200 per year and will be ignored for illustrative purposes. Charles, Jr., presents a different funding scenario. If it is assumed that the after-tax rate of return would be 5.9 percent (the Wigginses' after-tax rate) over the duration of the education funding period for Charles, Jr., the present value of his education expenses will be $76,710 and will require $8,202 funding each year (instead of $7,521 if the trust is used) if the Wigginses use their own funds for him.

If the UGMA account is used for Charles, Jr., the Wigginses will incur a substantial kiddie tax until Charles, Jr., reaches age 14. The result will be a lower after-tax rate of return much closer to that resulting from the use of their own funds than the higher rate that would result from the use of a Sec. 2503(c) trust, which could avoid the kiddie tax.

Recommendations

The Wigginses should use UGMA gifts for both Stephanie's and Caroline's education funding purposes. The difference in annual funding needed, even though Caroline's account may be subject to the kiddie tax for 2 years, is minor compared with the use of a trust. The accounts could be established with a brokerage firm where access to corporate bonds such as the funding instrument would be available. Tax-exempt investments could be used for Caroline until she reaches age 14 if the kiddie tax is a problem for her custodial parents.

For Charles, Jr., the potential annual saving of over $400 each year justifies establishing a 2503(c) trust for his educational needs. This is also the case because the numerous compliance problems of the kiddie tax are avoided by using the trust instead of UGMA gifts. Even though this approach results in somewhat different treatment for the children, it provides a practical method of arranging funding for the girls' education, whose dates for beginning college are more immediate. When the funding needed is greater and the benefits of longer-term shifting of income more substantial, as is the situation for Charles, Jr., then the trust vehicle should be used.

Alternatively, a split arrangement for Charles, Jr.'s education funding needs could be considered. For the years that the kiddie tax would apply, Charles and Barbara could make contributions to the trust until Charles, Jr., reaches age 14. Then an UGMA could be established, and its income would be taxed at Charles, Jr.'s rate, which currently would be less than that of the trust.

Vacation Home

The Wigginses have a second quantifiable accumulation objective, which is to build a vacation home by May 2005. They project a cost of $120,000. As discussed previously, given the Wigginses' projected income, tax rate, and other accumulation objectives, they should minimize their equity position in the vacation home and finance the rest through mortgage debt. The interest payments on the debt will be tax deductible, thus reducing the after-tax cost of borrowing by about 30 percent. They can reasonably expect the vacation home to maintain its value or, more likely, to increase in value. Therefore the greater the leverage, the greater the potential return on the vacation home if they choose to liquidate it at some future time. Furthermore, by increasing their leverage on the vacation home they may free up resources for other investment objectives.

It is impossible to project mortgage interest rates for 2005 at this time, and certainly the cost of funds should play a role in determining the appropriate amount of mortgage debt at the time the vacation home is purchased. However, it is likely that a down payment of approximately 10 percent would be appropriate and that an 8 percent interest rate on the amount financed might be a possibility.

A 10 percent down payment of $12,000, based on a projected purchase price of $120,000, will be required in about 3 years. In addition, the Wigginses should anticipate closing costs of about 4 percent of the cost of the vacation home, or an additional $4,800. Since this is a relatively short-term and certain accumulation objective, the investment instruments funding this objective should have relatively certain future values. For example, 36-month CDs would satisfy this criterion. Currently 36-month CDs at a savings and loan earn about 6 percent.

A better alternative, considering the Wigginses' tax rate, would be to purchase tax-exempt municipal notes or intermediate-term municipal bonds maturing in late 2004 or early 2005. The yield on high-quality municipals is currently about 70 percent of the yield on comparable-risk taxable issues with the same maturity. Therefore any investor in a tax bracket over 30 percent who is considering bond investments will generally be better off purchasing municipals rather than taxable bonds or small-saver certificates.

For the current year, yields on high to intermediate investment-quality short-term municipals range from about 5.75 to 6.25 percent. If the Wigginses invest in municipal issues yielding 6 percent (coupons paid semiannually) and reinvest the coupons in a money market mutual fund yielding 6 percent taxable (4 percent after tax), they need to purchase five $1,000 face-value bonds. After 3 years this $5,000 investment will accumulate to $5,950, with the $10,000 of CDs maturing at the end of 2000, when a total of $15,950 will be available. The actual down payment and closing costs may vary somewhat from the estimated $16,800, but the anticipated $900 deficit should present no serious problems. The Wigginses should be able to cover the actual required residual amount out of earnings or other savings in 2005. In the meantime resources may be released for investment in longer-term high-yielding instruments to fund other objectives, such as the children's college educations.

Retirement Income

Plans for funding the Wigginses' retirement income objectives have been discussed previously. In summary, it has been suggested that a profit-sharing plan that could add approximately $281,448 to Charles's retirement funds be instituted at Systems Design Associates. Charles should continue his tax-deferred annuity account at the 8 percent salary reduction level (plus the 6 percent university contribution per year). With this combination of instruments and with the projected contributions each year, Charles and Barbara should have adequate funds to maintain their standard of living in their retirement years.

Reducing the Tax Burden; Maintaining Their Standard of Living; General Wealth Accumulation

These three remaining investment/accumulation objectives have been implicitly or explicitly addressed in the discussions above. To the extent possible, plans have been designed to reduce taxes and fund objectives while maintaining the Wigginses' standard of living. The projected balance sheets and cash-flow statements reflect the expenditures required to maintain their standard of living. Given these expenditure projections, the Wigginses still have substantial projected residual discretionary cash flows in years 2002 through 2006 to fund their accumulation objectives.

Available Investments

For the reinvestable cash flow available for the clients' wealth accumulation, investments that provide capital appreciation (growth), tax reduction or deferral, and future income potential are appropriate and would be consistent with their stated objectives.

Zero Coupon Municipal Bonds. These bonds, sold at a discount, do not generate taxable income and will grow to a predictable value in a specified number of years, at which time they can be converted to income-producing assets. To obtain maximum benefit from owning these bonds, the Wigginses should include in the portfolio only "public purpose" bonds issued by a state or local government or agency to meet essential government functions such as highway construction or school financing. These bonds will retain the fully tax-exempt feature for interest income and will not create any potential alternative minimum tax consequences. Also they should acquire issues that are of an investment grade such as BBB or above, are obligations backed by the full faith and taxing power of the issuer, and, if possible, are insured by one of the five private insurance companies that provide this guarantee.

Municipals are currently yielding 6.1 to 6.75 percent, which for investors in the 28 percent tax bracket, like the Wigginses, equates to a before-tax rate between 8.47 and 9.4 percent.

The disadvantages are that these bonds provide no potential for capital appreciation and, like all debt instruments, are subject to both the interest-rate risk and the purchasing-power risk.

Growth Common Stocks. These are stocks issued by corporations that have experienced and will continue to experience consistently high rates of growth in corporate earnings. In addition growth common stocks frequently are associated with new or smaller-sized firms. However, even if the firm is large, these stocks sell at price/earnings ratios (P/Es) significantly higher than the P/Es of firms experiencing average growth rates. Should a downturn in the market occur, these growth stocks could experience a larger percentage decline than average stocks, or of the index as a whole. Another characteristic is that these stocks pay little or no current dividends. The corporation's earnings are reinvested in the business to finance the firm's future growth. Therefore the major source of return that an investor in these stocks can expect is that of price appreciation. However, there is an element of risk due to the uncertainty of the success of the reinvested earnings within the firm. This risk can be acceptable in view of the relatively high potential returns these securities offer.

Growth Stock Mutual Funds. As their primary investment objective these aggressive stock funds seek capital appreciation by acquiring a portfolio consisting largely of growth common stocks. Investments in these funds have the same advantages and disadvantages as does direct ownership of growth common stocks; however, the fund concept has two distinct advantages. First, the diversification available from its portfolio reduces risk compared to directly owning one or two growth common stocks. Clients who do not have large sums of money for investment purposes are unable to achieve the needed diversification of their investment. Mutual funds provide this spreading of the business risk. Second, the professional selection of securities and management of the portfolio can be desirable for someone as busy as Charles is with his teaching and business activities.

Index Funds. This type of mutual fund establishes as its investment objective the holding of a portfolio that will replicate the performance of a specified stock market index, such as the Standard & Poor's 500 or the Wilshire 5000. An investment in this type of fund provides a total return (less administration fees) equal to the average earned by the market (with market defined as the index the fund replicates). By their design these funds provide diversification. Their professional management needs are relatively slight since restructuring to match relative changes in the importance of particular securities in the index is done largely through computer programming. The result is that the annual administrative fees of these funds are typically less than those of funds whose portfolios are actively managed. As a means of benefiting from long-term growth in stock values, these funds could be attractive to the Wigginses, provided they are willing to accept a return equal to the average of the index.

In addition to the index funds that replicate a measure of stock market performance, several bond index funds are available that are designed to match the performance of intermediate or long-term bond measures.

International Funds. These specialized mutual funds hold portfolios consisting only of foreign bonds or stocks. Since foreign securities markets have outperformed American markets during the period 1980 to the present, these funds have the potential to provide American investors with the opportunity to capture these higher returns. In addition, the investor benefits from further portfolio diversification. The Wigginses might consider placing some of their investable cash flow into one of these funds.

Although the Wigginses still need a portfolio manager to select the appropriate fund and monitor its performance, the use of mutual funds would demand less of their time than would direct ownership of the stocks.

Portfolio and Funding Recommendations

The final step in the investment planning process is to allocate investment resources and future income to specific accumulation objectives and to construct an investment portfolio that is consistent with the Wigginses' financial concerns and risk attitudes.

We have determined that Charles and Barbara should maintain an emergency reserve comprised of relatively safe and liquid investments amounting to 3 to 6 months of disposable income. The insurance plans have addressed potential emergency areas such as disability, death, medical expenses, and property losses. Consequently they should probably maintain an emergency reserve toward the lower end of this range. In 2002 the Wiginses' after-tax income will be about $124,618. As a result they should have an emergency fund of between $31,154 and $62,300. A reserve of $32,000 would not be inappropriate in their case. The Wiginses can maintain a reserve toward the lower end of the recommended range for several reasons. First, Charles's basic income from teaching is relatively secure since he is a tenured faculty member. Second, Charles has another source of income from Systems Design, and Barbara is also employed. Finally, they have other income from Barbara's trust and from some income-producing assets. The combination of these several sources of income produces a rather secure situation since it is quite unlikely that all family sources of income would be significantly reduced or eliminated simultaneously. The loss of one income flow, when coupled with the protection available from a minimum-size emergency fund, should leave adequate protection for Charles and Barbara.

The $17,800 of cash value in Charles's life insurance policies could serve as the major segment of their emergency reserve. An additional $5,000 of this reserve can be the money in the money market mutual fund. To avoid prepayment penalties the $26,000 of CDs should be left untouched until they mature. If needed for emergency purposes they could be redeemed. When they mature, some investment planning will be needed.

As recommended earlier, the funding for their children's college education should be on an annual basis, with the funds for this purpose coming from their surplus cash flow available for investment each year. This will require a total contribution of approximately $15,118 per year.

Stephanie	$1,982 per year for 7 years, $991 in year 8
Caroline	$5,784 per year for 9 years, $2,892 in year 10
Charles, Jr.	$7,352 per year for 14 years, $3,676 in year 15

Depending on the effects of inflation on educational expenses and rates of return earned on the invested funds, the Wiginses need to periodically review this annual funding program.

This funding schedule avoids any gift tax consequences to Charles and Barbara since the annual gift to any child's trust or education account is less than their combined $22,000 annual gift tax exclusion.

Both the custodial accounts and the trust used for educational funding should acquire as many corporate bonds as possible each year, using the annual contribution and any interest earnings for that purpose. Idle funds, because of the interest income and the excess of the contribution over the value of any bonds that can be purchased, can be placed in a money market fund until such time as sufficient funds are accumulated to make additional bond purchases. The use of zero coupon bonds can solve the problem of reinvestment of annual income. However, some provision must be made for paying the annual income taxes due on the accrued income.

The maturity schedules for the bonds will recognize the annual contribution being made as well as any interest earnings. For example, Stephanie's account will have approximately 7 bonds (approximately $7,000 in value) as assets when she enters college. Her estimated costs are $2,184 for her first year, 2006. The annual funding will approximate $1,982, and the account will earn about $730 interest. Thus Stephanie's account will have a cash inflow of almost $2,712. The next year, 2007, the inflow will be almost $2,614 but the outflow will be $4,638. Two bonds must mature that year to provide the necessary education money. In line with this approach the following maturity schedule can be established as a guide to facilitate the investment activities for the education funds:

Maturity Schedule for Bonds in Each Child's Education Fund

Stephanie		Caroline		Charles, Jr.	
Year	No. of Bonds	Year	No. of Bonds	Year	No. of Bonds
2006	0	2008	0	2013	3
2007	2	2009	9	2014	24
2008	3	2010	11	2015	28
2009	2	2011	13	2016	34
2010	1	2012	7	2017	19

Some repositioning of Charles and Barbara's stock portfolio also appears to be appropriate. Some of Charles and Barbara's stocks—in particular, Growth Industries and Computers Corporation—do not seem to meet their investment growth objectives since they are expected to appreciate annually at only 4 and 2 percent respectively.

Charles and Barbara should probably sell their shares in Computers Corporation. Their cost basis is $1,800, and their sales proceeds will be $1,200; thus they will recognize a long-term loss of $600. This loss is deductible against ordinary income or against their capital gains for the year (see below).

It is also recommended that Charles and Barbara consider selling their shares in Growth Industries since the growth potential and expected overall performance are not comparable to their other investments. Their cost basis is $3,000, and the sales proceeds should be at least $6,360. They will recognize a long-term gain of $3,360. Assuming that the Computers Corporation shares are also sold this year, the Wigginses will have a net long-term capital gain of $2,760.

To meet their general wealth accumulation objectives of tax deferral, long-term growth, and future income, and to have a portfolio with which they would be comfortable based on their ratings and rank order of the various investment instruments, the proceeds from the sale of Growth Industries and Computers Corporation plus the investable cash available to the Wigginses should be invested as follows: one-third should be placed in a growth mutual fund, and one-third should be used to purchase three or four different issues of growth common stocks. Additional growth stocks can be acquired in subsequent years. Although the Wigginses have not expressed an interest in any municipal bonds, placing the remaining one-third of this money into zero coupon municipals is also recommended at this time since the income accrues tax free and is consistent with their need for preservation of capital.

The tax, net worth, and cash-flow projections on the following pages show the Wiggins family's position over a 5-year period if the following recommendations are adopted:

- Systems Design is incorporated and a 15 percent profit-sharing plan is implemented and fully utilized.
- Funding for the children's college education is accomplished through annual funding gifts for a period of years, and the funds are invested in high-quality corporate bonds.
- The additional down payment and closing costs for the summer home are funded through the purchase of short-term tax-free municipal bonds that mature in 2004 or 2005.
- The shares in Growth Industries and Computers Corporation are sold in this year.

CASE III
Projections Based on Funding Educational Objectives

New Assumptions

1. Beginning in 2002, $7,352 per year is transferred to a 2503(c) trust for Charles, Jr., to meet educational funding objectives.

2. Beginning in 2002, $7,766 per year is transferred to separate UGMA accounts for Stephanie and Caroline to meet educational funding objectives.

3. In 2003, the Computers Corporation stock is sold for $1,200.

4. In 2003, the Growth Industries stock is sold for $6,360.

5. In 2003, $9,000 is invested in 6 percent tax-free municipal bonds that mature in 2004.

Continuing Assumptions

1. In 2003 Systems Design Associates incorporates and implements a 15 percent profit-sharing plan whose assets earn an average of 8 percent annually over the 5-year period.

2. The checking account balance is maintained at approximately $6,000 and is noninterest bearing.

3. The savings account balance of $16,000 at the end of last year earns 4.75 percent interest annually. Interest is allowed to accumulate in the account.

4. The $26,000 in CDs earns 8 percent annually, and the CDs mature in December 2006.

5. The money market account pays 5.25 percent annually, and interest is accumulated in the account.

6. The Home Products stock, worth $16,000 at the end of last year, is expected to grow in value at 5 percent annually, and the dividend yield is 4 percent.

7. The Octane Oil stock with a year-end value of $12,000 is expected to appreciate at 6 percent annually, while yielding a 5 percent dividend.

8. The Growth Industries stock with a year-end value of $6,000 is expected to appreciate at 6 percent and yield 2 percent annually in dividends.

9. The Computers Corporation stock with a year-end value of $1,200 is not appreciating in value and is yielding one percent per year in dividends.

10. The Mega Fund shares with a year-end value of $1,800 are expected to increase in value at 8 percent per year and yield 3 percent.

11. The value of the personal residence ($150,000) will increase at 10 percent annually. The residence was purchased in January 1994. The original amount of the mortgage was $72,000 at an interest rate of 8 percent for 30 years.

12. The summer home will be purchased or constructed by May 2005 for $120,000. The down payment will be $12,000, and a $108,000 30-year mortgage at 8.5 percent will provide the remainder of the financing. The summer home will increase in value 5 percent annually. Property taxes for the vacation home are expected to be $400 per year.

13. The household furnishings will neither increase nor decrease in value.

14. Automobiles decrease in value at a rate of 15 percent per year.

15. Property taxes and maintenance costs on both the vacation home and the personal residence are expected to increase at 6 percent annually.

16. Charles's university salary is expected to increase 5 percent annually. Barbara's salary is expected to increase 4.5 percent annually.

17. The level of income from Systems Design Associates is set at $37,000 and will not increase over the 5-year period. (This is a decrease of $5,000 from the amount of partnership income.)

18. The value of the Systems Design Associates stock will increase 2.5 percent annually. Pending further information on the tax consequences of distributing the business building, the entire partnership interest is considered to have been contributed to the corporation for this purpose only.

19. Contributions to Charles's TDA account will continue at 8 percent of his salary until 2007 and will not increase after that date.

20. Seventy-five percent of Charles's TDA contribution will be matched by the university, and the combined amount will earn 10 percent annually over the next 5 years.

21. Present expenditures for clothing, vacations, food, utilities, transportation, medical care, entertainment, property and liability insurance, and charitable contributions are projected to increase annually at the rate of 5 percent.

22. Investable cash earns 5.25 percent annually.

INCOME STATEMENT

CHARLES & BARBARA WIGGINS

CASE III	2002	2003	2004	2005	2006
Earned Income					
Salary - Charles	82,000	86,100	90,405	94,925	99,672
Partnership Income	42,000	0	0	0	0
Corporation Income	0	37,000	37,000	37,000	37,000
Salary - Barbara	40,000	41,800	43,681	45,647	47,701
TDA-Charles Contrib	-4,160	-4,493	-4,852	-5,240	-5,660
	159,840	160,407	166,234	172,331	178,713
Interest/Dividends					
Cert Of Deposits	2,080	2,080	2,080	1,680	1,280
Home Products stock	672	699	727	756	786
Octane Oil Stock	636	668	701	736	773
Growth Indust Stock	120	0	0	0	0
Computer Corp Stock	12	0	0	0	0
Mega Fund Shares	58	60	62	63	65
Investable Cash	1,631	4,462	7,045	9,893	12,873
Saving/NOW Acts	760	796	834	874	915
Money Market Fund	515	542	570	600	631
	6,484	9,306	12,019	14,603	17,323
Other					
TrustIncome-Barbara	10,000	10,000	10,000	10,000	10,000
	10,000	10,000	10,000	10,000	10,000
Net Capital Gain	0	2,400	0	0	0
Adjustments					
S.E. Tax Dedctn	563	496	496	496	496
	563	496	496	496	496
	========	========	========	========	========
Adj Gross Income	175,761	181,618	187,756	196,438	205,540
Deductions					
Charitable 50%	1,000	1,050	1,103	1,158	1,216
State Tax Paid	8,585	8,915	9,192	9,663	10,147
Property Tax - Home	2,500	2,650	2,809	2,978	3,156
PropertyTax-VacHome	0	0	0	400	424
Mortgage - Home	5,202	5,107	5,005	4,894	4,774
Reductn for High Inc	-1,284	-1,357	-1,434	-1,585	-1,164
Gross Deductions	16,003	16,365	16,675	17,507	18,553
Standard Deduction	4,550	4,650	4,800	4,900	5,050
Allowed Deductions	16,003	16,365	16,675	17,507	18,553
Pers Exemptions	9,280	9,145	9,150	8,820	10,880
	========	========	========	========	========
Taxable Income	150,478	156,107	161,932	170,111	176,107
	========	========	========	========	========
Fed Income Tax	41,130	42,287	43,419	46,801	50,009
	========	========	========	========	========
Fed Tax Bracket-Ord Inc	35.0%	35.0%	34.0%	34.0%	33.0%

BALANCE SHEET

CHARLES & BARBARA WIGGINS

CASE III	2002	2003	2004	2005	2006
LIQUID ASSETS					
Cash Balance	5,825	5,881	6,009	6,016	6,033
Cash Deposits					
Investable Cash	63,765	110,679	164,750	222,027	281,231
Saving/NOW Acts	16,760	17,556	18,390	19,264	20,179
Cert Of Deposits	26,000	26,000	26,000	16,000	16,000
Money Market Fund	10,315	10,857	11,427	12,027	12,658
	116,840	165,092	220,567	269,318	330,068
Stocks & Bonds					
Municipal Bonds	0	9,000	9,000	0	0
Home Products stock	16,800	17,640	18,522	19,448	20,421
Octane Oil Stock	12,720	13,483	14,292	15,150	16,059
Growth Indust Stock	6,000	0	0	0	0
Computer Corp Stock	1,200	0	0	0	0
Mega Fund Shares	1,944	2,100	2,267	2,449	2,645
	38,664	42,223	44,082	37,047	39,124
Life Insurance					
Life Ins-Charles #1	12,200	12,200	12,200	12,200	12,200
Life Ins-Charles #2	5,600	5,600	5,600	5,600	5,600
	17,800	17,800	17,800	17,800	17,800
	========	========	========	========	========
Liquid Assets	179,129	230,996	288,458	330,181	393,025
	========	========	========	========	========

NONLIQUID ASSETS

	2002	2003	2004	2005	2006
Bus Interests					
Partnershp Interest	175,000	0	0	0	0
Corporat'n Interest	0	179,375	183,859	188,456	193,167
	175,000	179,375	183,859	188,456	193,167
Retirement Plans					
TDA-Charles Contrib	4,160	8,653	13,505	18,745	24,405
TDA-Employr Contrib	6,560	13,645	21,297	29,561	38,486
Mortgage - Home	88,000	96,800	106,480	117,128	128,841
	98,720	119,098	141,282	165,434	191,732
Benefit Plans					
PS--Charles contrib	0	5,550	11,100	16,650	22,200
	0	5,550	11,100	16,650	22,200
Personal Property					
Home	165,000	181,500	199,650	219,615	241,577
Vacation Home	0	0	0	120,000	126,000
Auto	6,800	5,780	4,913	4,176	3,550
Home Furnishings	20,000	20,000	20,000	20,000	20,000

B A L A N C E   S H E E T (cont.)

CHARLES & BARBARA WIGGINS

CASE III	2002	2003	2004	2005	2006
Jewelry & Furs	28,000	28,000	28,000	28,000	28,000
	219,800	235,280	252,563	391,791	419,126
	========	========	========	========	========
Nonliquid Assets	493,520	539,303	588,804	762,331	826,226
	========	========	========	========	========
Total Assets	672,649	770,299	877,262	1,092,512	1,219,251

LIABILITIES

Mortgage Loans

	2002	2003	2004	2005	2006
Mortgage - Home	64,395	63,162	61,827	60,381	58,815
	64,395	63,162	61,827	60,381	58,815
	========	========	========	========	========
Total Liabilities	64,395	63,162	61,827	60,381	58,815
	========	========	========	========	========
Net Worth	608,254	707,137	815,435	1,032,131	1,160,436
	========	========	========	========	========

CASH FLOW STATEMENT

CHARLES & BARBARA WIGGINS

CASE III	2002	2003	2004	2005	2006
BEGINNING OF YEAR					
Idle Cash On Hand	6,000	5,825	5,881	6,009	6,016
SOURCES OF CASH					
Cash Income					
Salary - Charles	82,000	86,100	90,405	94,925	99,672
Partnership Income	42,000	0	0	0	0
Corporation Income	0	37,000	37,000	37,000	37,000
Salary - Barbara	40,000	41,800	43,681	45,647	47,701
Interest+Dividends	3,578	3,506	3,570	3,236	2,904
Municipal Bonds	0	270	540	270	0
Other Income-Csh	10,000	10,000	10,000	10,000	10,000
	177,578	178,676	185,196	191,077	197,277
Sale/Withdrawals					
Growth Indust Stock	0	6,000	0	0	0
Computer Corp Stock	0	1,200	0	0	0
Municipal Bonds	0	0	0	9,000	0
Cert Of Deposits	0	0	0	10,000	0
	0	7,200	0	19,000	0
Liab Incurred					
Chas Borwd-Vac Home	0	0	0	108,000	0
	0	0	0	108,000	0
	========	========	========	========	========
Total Cash Inflow	177,578	185,876	185,196	318,077	197,277
	========	========	========	========	========
Tot Cash Available	183,578	191,702	191,077	324,086	203,292
	========	========	========	========	========
USES OF CASH					
Fully Tax Deductible					
TDA-Charles Contrib	4,160	4,493	4,852	5,240	5,660
Mortgage - Home	5,202	5,107	5,005	4,894	4,774
	9,362	9,600	9,857	10,134	10,434
Partly Deductible					
Medical Care	2,480	2,604	2,734	2,871	3,014
Charity Contrb-50%	1,000	1,050	1,103	1,158	1,216
	3,480	3,654	3,837	4,029	4,230
Not Tax Deductible					
Education Fund	2,000	2,000	2,000	2,000	2,000
Educ--2503(c) Trust	0	7,352	7,352	7,352	7,352
Educ--UGMA Accounts	0	7,766	7,766	7,766	7,766
Child Support	8,400	8,400	8,400	8,400	8,400

CASH FLOW STATEMENT(cont.)

CHARLES & BARBARA WIGGINS

CASE III	2002	2003	2004	2005	2006
Food	8,000	8,400	8,820	9,261	9,724
Clothing	3,500	3,675	3,859	4,052	4,254
Entertainment	3,500	3,675	3,859	4,052	4,254
Vacations	4,500	4,725	4,961	5,209	5,470
Transportation	1,500	1,575	1,654	1,736	1,823
Life Ins Prem Pymnt	2,620	2,620	2,620	2,620	2,620
Prop Ins Prem Pymnt	1,150	1,208	1,268	1,331	1,398
Maint--Home/VacHome	2,000	2,120	2,247	2,382	2,525
Utility/Phone	3,500	3,675	3,859	4,052	4,254
New Furniture	2,000	2,000	2,000	2,000	2,000
ClosingCost-VacHome	0	0	0	6,000	0
	42,670	59,191	60,664	68,213	63,841
Taxes Paid					
Fed Tax Paid	41,130	42,287	43,419	46,801	50,009
State Tax Paid	8,585	8,915	9,192	9,663	10,147
FICA/Soc Sec Tax	6,754	6,839	6,929	7,023	7,122
Real Estate Tax	2,500	2,650	2,809	3,378	3,580
	58,969	60,691	62,349	66,865	70,858
Purchase/Deposits					
Municipal Bonds	0	9,000	0	0	0
Purchase Vac Home	0	0	0	120,000	0
Investable Cash	62,134	42,452	47,026	47,384	46,331
	62,134	51,452	47,026	167,384	46,331
Liability Liquidation					
Mortgage - Home	1,138	1,233	1,335	1,446	1,566
	1,138	1,233	1,335	1,446	1,566
	========	========	========	========	========
Tot Cash Outflow	177,753	185,820	185,068	318,071	197,259
	========	========	========	========	========
END OF YEAR					
Cash Balance	5,825	5,881	6,009	6,016	6,033
	========	========	========	========	========

SUPPORTING SCHEDULE

CHARLES & BARBARA WIGGINS

CASE III	SINGLE 2002	SINGLE 2003	SINGLE 2004	SINGLE 2005	SINGLE 2006
Income					
Earned Income	159,840	160,407	166,234	172,331	178,713
Adj Gross Income	175,761	181,618	187,756	196,438	205,540
Allowed Deductions	16,003	16,365	16,675	17,507	18,553
Pers Exemptions	9,280	9,145	9,150	8,820	10,880
Taxable Income	150,478	156,107	161,932	170,111	176,107
Capital Gains					
Growth Indust Stock	0	3,000	0	0	0
Computer Corp Stock	0	-600	0	0	0
Net Capital Gain	0	2,400	0	0	0
LTCG Txd at Max Rt	0	2,400	0	0	0
Capital Gains-AMT	0	2,400	0	0	0
Federal Tax Liab					
Regular Tax	40,005	41,656	42,036	44,490	44,733
Max Tax on Cap Gn	0	480	0	0	0
Gross Fed Inc Tax	40,005	41,296	42,036	44,490	44,733
Alt Minimum Tax	0	0	392	1,320	4,285
AMT Credit C/Over	0	0	0	0	392
Disallowed	0	0	0	-392	-1,712
Self Employmt Tax	1,125	991	991	991	991
Fed Income Tax	41,130	42,287	43,419	46,801	50,009
Fed Tax Analysis-Ord Inc					
Indexing Factor	77	82	87	91	96
Fed Tax Bracket-Ord Inc	35.0%	35.0%	34.0%	34.0%	33.0%
$ to Next Bracket	154,572	159,293	159,218	159,389	161,943
Next Bracket	38.6%	38.6%	37.6%	37.6%	35.0%
Previous Bracket	30.0%	30.0%	29.0%	29.0%	28.0%
$ to Prev Bracket	10,178	9,757	14,232	18,611	20,657
Fed Capital Gain Rate	.0%	20.0%	.0%	.0%	.0%
Fed Effective Tax Rate	27.3%	27.1%	26.8%	27.5%	28.4%
Alt Minimum Tax					
Adj Gross Income	175,761	181,618	187,756	196,438	205,540
Contributions	-1,000	-1,050	-1,103	-1,158	-1,216
Mortgage - Home	-5,202	-5,107	-5,005	-4,894	-4,774
Adjusted AMTI	169,559	175,461	181,648	190,386	199,550
Net Capital Gain	0	-2,400	0	0	0
Capital Gains-AMT	0	2,400	0	0	0
AMT Exemptions	-21,485	-20,010	-18,463	-14,278	-11,987
AMT Taxable Inc	148,074	155,451	163,185	176,108	187,563
Gross Alt Min Tx	38,499	40,273	42,428	45,810	49,018
Fed Tax Less FTC	-40,005	-41,296	-42,036	-44,490	-44,733
Alt Minimum Tax	0	0	392	1,320	4,285
Other Tax Liabs					
FICA/Soc Sec Tax	6,754	6,839	6,929	7,023	7,122
Adj Gross Inc	175,761	181,618	187,756	196,438	205,540
GA Adj Gross Inc	175,761	181,618	187,756	196,438	205,540
GA Standard Ded	2,300	2,300	2,300	2,300	2,300
GA Itemized Ded	16,003	16,365	16,675	17,507	18,553
GA Exemptions	13,500	13,500	14,700	14,700	14,700
GA Taxable Inc	146,258	151,752	156,382	164,231	172,287
GA Regular Tax	8,585	8,915	9,192	9,663	10,147
GA Income Tax	8,585	8,915	9,192	9,663	10,147
Georgia Tax	8,585	8,915	9,192	9,663	10,147
Tot State/Local Tx	8,585	8,915	9,192	9,663	10,147
Total Inc Tax	56,469	58,041	59,540	63,487	67,278

FINANCIAL SUMMARY

CHARLES & BARBARA WIGGINS

CASE III	2002	2003	2004	2005	2006
Gross Real Income					
Personal Earnings	164,000	164,900	171,086	177,572	184,372
Interest Income	4,986	7,880	10,529	13,047	15,699
Dividends Rcvd	1,498	1,426	1,490	1,556	1,624
TrustIncome-Barbara	10,000	10,000	10,000	10,000	10,000
Municipal Bonds	0	270	540	270	0
	180,484	184,476	193,645	202,444	211,696
Income & Inflation					
Gross Real Inc	180,484	184,476	193,645	202,444	211,696
Total Inc Tax	-56,469	-58,041	-59,540	-63,487	-67,278
Net Real Income	124,015	126,435	134,105	138,957	144,418
Cur Real Inc =	124,015	127,242	130,552	133,949	137,434
Purch Power Drop	0	806	0	0	0
At Infltn Rate of	3	3	3	3	3
Cash Flow					
Idle Cash On Hand	6,000	5,825	5,881	6,009	6,016
Norml Cash Inflow	177,578	185,876	185,196	318,077	197,277
Norml Cash Outflw	115,619	143,368	138,042	270,687	150,928
Cash Invested	62,134	42,452	47,026	47,384	46,331
Cash Balance	5,825	5,881	6,009	6,016	6,033
Net Worth					
Personal Assets	243,425	258,961	276,372	415,607	442,959
Investment Assets	429,224	511,338	600,890	676,905	776,291
Personal Liabilities	-64,395	-63,162	-61,827	-60,381	-58,815
Personal Net Worth	179,030	195,799	214,545	355,226	384,144
Investment Net Worth	429,224	511,338	600,890	676,905	776,291
Net Worth	608,254	707,137	815,435	1,032,131	1,160,436

4

Planning for the Younger Client

Chapter Outline

Perhaps the young couple best typifies the client who has potential for the accumulation of substantial assets but presently has few. Comprehensive financial planning for a client without a significant asset base is more difficult than it appears. In most of these cases there is little discretionary cash, and not all personal or financial objectives can be pursued at one time. In almost every instance there will be hard choices for the client to make, particularly in regard to the priority of objectives to be pursued with the available resources. The financial planner must be especially sensitive to the client's concerns and intentions in such cases in order to assist the client in setting realistic and achievable goals as well as in establishing priorities among objectives.

Planning for those with few accumulated assets may be necessary for persons other than young couples. However, the concerns and objectives of the client will necessarily be different, and the planning recommendations will be markedly different. Despite differing concerns and objectives, the problems of asset allocation to achieve the objectives of clients without substantial assets are generally similar. All planning is a decision-making process about the allocation of inherently scarce resources. Few, if any, clients have sufficient resources to pursue all their objectives at one time, but the greater the resource base, the fewer the objectives that must be given low priority because of funding problems. The converse is also true: the fewer the resources of a client, the greater the number of objectives that must be deferred, in whole or in part, until resources are available.

CASE NARRATIVE

Dick Johnson is now 26 years old and Jane is 25. They have been married for 4 years. Dick completed college just before their wedding, and Jane completed her last year of college after their marriage.

Jane is an assistant manager for a major hotel chain and earns approximately $35,000 per year. Dick is a paralegal and earns $30,000 annually. They both expect annual salary increases of approximately 5 percent.

They live in a comfortable but not luxurious two-bedroom apartment, for which they pay $800 per month in rent plus utilities. Since Jane recently had to have a new car, they purchased a small sedan for $10,700 in November 2000, financing $9,000 at 6 percent for 4 years. They estimate that the car is now worth about $8,600. Dick's car, which is 3 years old and paid for, is presently worth approximately $4,000 in Dick's estimation.

Shortly after they were married, Dick and Jane bought tasteful but not extravagant furniture, which is now fully paid for. No major appliance purchases were necessary, since the apartment supplied such items. The Johnsons estimate the replacement value of their household furnishings at $14,000.

Jane borrowed $4,000 under the government-guaranteed student loan program to help her complete her undergraduate education. The loans were made in 1996 and 1997 at a 9 percent simple interest rate and became payable over a period of 10 years beginning in 1999, the year following her graduation. As is common with loans of this type, no interest accrued until repayment began.

Dick and Jane have saved almost $16,000 since their marriage. These savings are presently invested in a money market fund that has earned a high of 7 percent and a low of 3 percent over the past 3 years. Its annualized yield for 2001 was approximately 4 percent. In addition to their money market funds, they have approximately $4,500 in a joint checking account.

They feel their next investment should be a house and wonder if they can afford a mortgage. They are also concerned about how to support their lifestyle when they start having children if either Dick or Jane stays home with their child(ren), particularly if they have purchased a home by then.

Both like the idea of owning a house. They are aware of the escalation in prices for houses over the last decade and feel that they should invest in a house now. However, they are also concerned about the debt involved in buying a house. Jane's upbringing instilled in her a distrust of owing money, a practice her father still preaches assiduously. She recognizes that the purchase of a home is usually a young person's or a young couple's first significant investment but has a difficult time overcoming her fear of indebtedness. After looking at houses for some time, Dick and Jane are most attracted to those in the $90,000 to $120,000 range but wonder if they will be able to afford a house of this price.

Dick and Jane, although just starting out, realize they must give due consideration to their long-term financial well-being by owning more than a home and money market accounts. However, they have not had any experience in investments, since each grew up in a family of modest means, and neither studied the subject of investments in college. Jane was an English major and Dick majored in history/political science. Since they feel they are working hard to accumulate money, at this time they are apprehensive about placing their savings at any great degree of risk and describe themselves as risk averse. They have furnished the following information about their annual expenditures:

TABLE 4-1
Estimate of Johnsons' Current Annual Expenditures and Anticipated Annual Increase

	Estimate of Annual Expenditures	Anticipated Annual Increase in Next 3–5 Years
Food	$ 4,800	4%
Rent	9,600	5
Utility/phone	2,100	6
Car payment	2,383	0
Clothing	1,800	4
Student loans	608	0
FICA	4,973	—
Fed. income tax	8,055	—
Ga. income tax	3,186	—
Entertainment	1,500	6
Auto insurance	800	8
Gas, oil, repair (automobile)	600	6
Medical insurance (Dick)	240	8
Medical and dental care	1,100	8
Tenant's insurance	250	8
Charitable contributions	200	5
Savings	2,000	
Total	$44,195	

Dick and Jane would like to start their family during the next 2 or 3 years. They would like to have at least two children and would not object to having as many as four. Both are from large families and enjoyed warm family relationships. However, they are concerned about whether they will truly be able to afford children and give them more than just the basic necessities, a fact they feel will probably keep their family smaller than if they had greater resources.

At present Dick's and Jane's parents are all living. In fact, both families still have younger children at home. Their family backgrounds are economically modest, and they receive no continuing support from their families, nor does either expect a significant inheritance from his or her parents. Their families have occasionally helped them with small gifts of cash, some of which have been used to purchase furniture and some of which they have saved.

Neither Dick nor Jane has any health problems, but an investigation into the health of their parents reveals that Dick's mother has severe allergies that have been life threatening on occasion. While they do not anticipate any significant assistance or inheritances from their parents, neither Dick nor Jane can foresee the necessity of assisting them financially at the present time. They do recognize, however, that such a possibility exists as their parents grow older.

The Johnsons have never seen a lawyer about estate planning. Neither has a will. Jane has named Dick the beneficiary of her group life insurance, and she has named her estate the beneficiary of her pension plan proceeds. Dick has named his estate the beneficiary of his group life insurance policy and of his profit-sharing plan. Both Dick and Jane say they would like to plan to preserve the lifestyle of the other should one predecease. If there are children, they would want them provided for. Both say they would expect the other to remarry if one died.

Dick and Jane have medical insurance and some disability insurance through their respective employers. They do not carry additional life insurance or additional medical or disability protection.

Jane's employee benefit plan is very generous and includes the following coverages:

- *group term life insurance equal to 2 1/2 times salary.* Dick is the beneficiary.
- *short-term disability benefits under a salary continuation plan.* During the first 4 months of disability her salary will be continued in full; during the next 2 months 50 percent of her salary will be paid. However, after 6 years of service, her salary will be continued in full for the entire 6 months.
- *group long-term disability insurance.* Benefits commence after a 6-month elimination period and are paid until age 65 as long as Jane is unable to perform her regular job. Benefits are equal to 60 percent of salary reduced by her primary disability benefit under Social Security.

- *group comprehensive major medical insurance.* Unlimited medical benefits are provided subject to a $100 calendar-year deductible and copayments of 20 percent for most medical expenses (some expenses are covered in full). The plan contains a stop-loss limit so that all expenses are paid in full for the remainder of a calendar year in which Jane has had out-of-pocket medical expenses of $2,000.
- *group scheduled dental insurance.* The maximum annual benefit is limited to $1,000.
- *maternity leave.* Jane will be paid for up to 4 months' maternity leave.

Jane is a participant in a defined-benefit pension plan, under which she can retire at age 65 with benefits equal to 70 percent of the average of her high 3 of the last 5 years' salary.

All Jane's plans are noncontributory for the employee's coverage. Dependent coverage is available for the medical and dental coverage. The cost is $65 per month, which reflects a 50 percent employer contribution. Jane has not elected dependent coverage, but she and Dick have considered the possibility because of his more limited coverage.

Dick's employer provides him with the following benefits, all of which are noncontributory except the major medical coverage, which costs him $20 per month:

- *group term life insurance in a flat amount of $10,000.* His estate is the beneficiary.
- *10 days of sick pay annually at full pay.* Unused sick pay can be carried over, up to a maximum of 100 days. Currently Dick has 9 unused days from previous years.
- *group major medical insurance.* A lifetime benefit of $250,000 is provided subject to a $200 annual deductible and 20 percent copayments for all expenses. There is no stop-loss limit.

INSTRUCTIONS

After considering all these facts, prepare a working outline and a financial plan for the Johnsons. After you have completed your answers, you can compare them with the suggested working outline and the completed financial plan for the Johnsons that follow.

WORKING OUTLINE
[Suggested Solution]

I. Clients' objectives

    A. For lifetime planning
        1. Purchase an affordable first home.
        2. Plan for Jane or Dick to stay home if possible after children are born.

    B. For dispositions at death: provide for the orderly continuation of lifestyle of a surviving spouse and children, if any.

II. Personal planning

    A. Tax planning
        1. Present situation
        2. Purchasing a house with tax-deductible dollars
        3. Tax implications of home ownership
        4. Nontax considerations
        5. Other factors to consider when purchasing a home
        6. Choosing the appropriate financing for the purchase of a residence
            a. Creative financing
            b. Conventional financing
            c. Subsidized or guaranteed financing
            d. Financing major appliances and fixtures with the house
            e. Purchasing a house for rehabilitation
        7. Financing recommendations
            a. 15-year mortgage with balloon payment
            b. Fully amortized 30-year mortgage
        8. Extent to which purchase of a home will preclude Jane or Dick staying at home with children
        9. Estate planning

B. Insurance planning
    1. Disability income insurance
    2. Medical insurance
    3. Life insurance
    4. Property and liability insurance

C. Investment planning
    1. Purchasing a home
    2. Emergency fund
    3. Investable funds
    4. Client characteristics
    5. Recommendations

PERSONAL FINANCIAL PLAN
FOR
DICK AND JANE JOHNSON
[Suggested Solution]

CLIENTS' OBJECTIVES

A. For lifetime planning
   1. Purchase an affordable first home.
   2. Plan for Jane or Dick to stay home if possible after children are born.

B. For dispositions at death: provide for the orderly continuation of lifestyle of a surviving spouse and children, if any.

C. Start an investment program.

BASE CASE

Assumptions

1. The checking account balance is maintained at $4,500; the account is noninterest bearing.

2. Dick's and Jane's salaries are increased at 5 percent annually.

3. Money market funds earn 4 percent interest annually.

4. Investable cash earns 5.25 percent annually.

5. Expenditures for food and clothing will increase annually at 4 percent.

6. Expenditures for rent and charitable contributions will increase 5 percent annually.

7. Expenditures for utilities, telephone, entertainment, and automobile gas and repairs will increase 6 percent annually.

8. Expenditures for medical insurance and other medical care, as well as both automobile and tenant's insurance, will increase by 8 percent annually.

9. Decreases in value of furniture have been ignored.

10. Automobiles decrease in value at a rate of 15 percent annually.

11. The inflation rate for taxes is 3.5 percent annually.

INCOME STATEMENT

DICK & JANE JOHNSON

BASE CASE	2002	2003	2004	2005	2006
Earned Income					
Jane's Salary	35,000	36,750	38,588	40,517	42,543
Dick's Salary	30,000	31,500	33,075	34,729	36,465
	65,000	68,250	71,663	75,246	79,008
Interest/Dividends					
Money Market Fund	640	666	692	720	749
Investable Cash	594	1,830	3,174	4,725	6,491
	1,234	2,496	3,866	5,445	7,240
	========	========	========	========	========
Adj Gross Income	66,234	70,746	75,529	80,691	86,248
Deductions					
Charitable 50%	200	210	221	232	243
State Tax Paid	3,186	3,441	3,711	4,003	4,317
Gross Deductions	3,386	3,651	3,932	4,235	4,560
Standard Deduction	7,600	7,850	8,100	8,787	9,568
Allowed Deductions	7,600	7,850	8,100	8,787	9,568
Pers Exemptions	5,800	6,000	6,200	6,400	6,700
	========	========	========	========	========
Taxable Income	52,834	56,896	61,229	65,504	69,980
	========	========	========	========	========
Fed Income Tax	8,055	8,954	9,808	9,701	10,661
	========	========	========	========	========
Fed Tax Bracket-Ord Inc	27.0%	27.0%	26.0%	26.0%	25.0%

BALANCE SHEET

DICK & JANE JOHNSON

BASE CASE	2002	2003	2004	2005	2006
LIQUID ASSETS					
Cash Balance	4,469	4,477	4,486	4,492	4,498
Cash Deposits					
Investable Cash	23,236	48,326	75,752	108,986	144,787
Money Market Fund	16,640	17,306	17,998	18,718	19,467
	39,876	65,632	93,750	127,704	164,254
	========	========	========	========	========
Liquid Assets	44,345	70,109	98,236	132,196	168,752
	========	========	========	========	========
NONLIQUID ASSETS					
Personal Property					
Dick's car	3,400	2,890	2,457	2,088	1,775
Jane's car	9,095	7,731	6,571	5,585	4,748
Furniture/Fixture	14,000	14,000	14,000	14,000	14,000
	26,495	24,621	23,028	21,673	20,522
	========	========	========	========	========
Nonliquid Assets	26,495	24,621	23,028	21,673	20,522
	========	========	========	========	========
Total Assets	70,840	94,730	121,264	153,869	189,274
LIABILITIES					
Notes Payable					
Jane's Student Loan	3,149	2,811	2,441	2,036	1,593
Jane's Car Loan	4,836	2,382	0	0	0
	7,985	5,193	2,441	2,036	1,593
	========	========	========	========	========
Total Liabilities	7,985	5,193	2,441	2,036	1,593
	========	========	========	========	========
Net Worth	62,855	89,537	118,823	151,833	187,681
	========	========	========	========	========

CASH FLOW STATEMENT

DICK & JANE JOHNSON

BASE CASE	2002	2003	2004	2005	2006
BEGINNING OF YEAR					
Idle Cash On Hand	4,500	4,469	4,477	4,486	4,492
SOURCES OF CASH					
Cash Income					
Jane's Salary	35,000	36,750	38,588	40,517	42,543
Dick's Salary	30,000	31,500	33,075	34,729	36,465
	65,000	68,250	71,663	75,246	79,008
	========	========	========	========	========
Total Cash Inflow	65,000	68,250	71,663	75,246	79,008
	========	========	========	========	========
Tot Cash Available	69,500	72,719	76,139	79,732	83,500
	========	========	========	========	========
USES OF CASH					
Partly Deductible					
Med Ins Prem - Dick	240	259	280	302	327
Other Medical	1,100	1,188	1,283	1,386	1,497
Charity Contrb-50%	200	210	221	232	243
	1,540	1,657	1,783	1,920	2,066
Not Tax Deductible					
Jane's Student Loan	298	270	238	203	165
Jane's Car Loan	366	223	72	0	0
Food	4,800	4,992	5,192	5,399	5,615
Clothing	1,800	1,872	1,947	2,025	2,106
Entertainment	1,500	1,590	1,685	1,787	1,894
Auto Insurance	800	864	933	1,008	1,088
Tenant's Insurance	250	270	292	315	340
Rent	9,600	10,080	10,584	11,113	11,669
Auto Gas/Oil/Repair	500	530	562	596	631
Utility/Phone	2,100	2,226	2,360	2,501	2,651
	22,014	22,917	23,864	24,946	26,160
Taxes Paid					
Fed Tax Paid	8,055	8,954	9,808	9,701	10,661
State Tax Paid	3,186	3,441	3,711	4,003	4,317
FICA/Soc Sec Tax	4,973	5,221	5,482	5,757	6,045
	16,214	17,616	19,001	19,461	21,023
Purchase/Deposits					
Investable Cash	22,642	23,260	24,252	28,509	29,310
	22,642	23,260	24,252	28,509	29,310

CASH FLOW STATEMENT (cont.)

DICK & JANE JOHNSON

BASE CASE	2002	2003	2004	2005	2006
Liability Liquidation					
Jane's Student Loan	310	338	370	405	443
Jane's Car Loan	2,311	2,454	2,382	0	0
	2,621	2,792	2,752	405	443
	========	========	========	========	========
Tot Cash Outflow	65,031	68,242	71,653	75,240	79,002
	========	========	========	========	========
END OF YEAR					
Cash Balance	4,469	4,477	4,486	4,492	4,498
	========	========	========	========	========

SUPPORTING SCHEDULE

DICK & JANE JOHNSON

BASE CASE	JOINT 2002	JOINT 2003	JOINT 2004	JOINT 2005	JOINT 2006
Income					
Earned Income	65,000	68,250	71,663	75,246	79,008
Adj Gross Income	66,234	70,746	75,529	80,691	86,248
Allowed Deductions	7,600	7,850	8,100	8,787	9,568
Pers Exemptions	5,800	6,000	6,200	6,400	6,700
Taxable Income	52,834	56,896	61,229	65,504	69,980
Federal Tax Liab					
Regular Tax	8,053	8,948	9,808	9,706	9,935
Gross Fed Inc Tax	8,055	8,954	9,808	9,701	9,936
Alt Minimum Tax	0	0	0	0	725
Fed Income Tax	8,055	8,954	9,808	9,701	10,661
Fed Tax Analysis-Ord Inc					
Indexing Factor	79	85	92	98	105
Fed Tax Bracket-Ord Inc	27.0%	27.0%	26.0%	26.0%	25.0%
$ to Next Bracket	60,216	60,104	59,872	59,846	59,770
Next Bracket	30.0%	30.0%	29.0%	29.0%	28.0%
Previous Bracket	15.0%	15.0%	15.0%	15.0%	15.0%
$ to Prev Bracket	6,084	8,496	11,128	9,704	9,953
Fed Effective Tax Rate	15.3%	15.7%	16.0%	14.8%	15.2%
Alt Minimum Tax					
Adj Gross Income	66,234	70,746	75,529	80,691	86,248
Contributions	-200	-210	-221	-232	-243
Adjusted AMTI	66,034	70,536	75,308	80,459	86,005
AMT Exemptions	-49,000	-49,000	-49,000	-45,000	-45,000
AMT Taxable Inc	17,034	21,536	26,308	35,459	41,005
Gross Alt Min Tx	4,429	5,599	6,840	9,219	10,661
Fed Tax Less FTC	-8,055	-8,954	-9,808	-9,701	-9,936
Alt Minimum Tax	0	0	0	0	725
Other Tax Liabs					
FICA/Soc Sec Tax	4,973	5,221	5,482	5,757	6,045
Adj Gross Inc	66,234	70,746	75,529	80,691	86,248
GA Adj Gross Inc	66,234	70,746	75,529	80,691	86,248
GA Standard Ded	3,000	3,000	3,000	3,000	3,000
GA Itemized Ded	3,386	3,651	3,932	4,235	4,560
GA Exemptions	5,400	5,400	5,400	5,400	5,400
GA Taxable Inc	57,448	61,695	66,197	71,056	76,288
GA Regular Tax	3,186	3,441	3,711	4,003	4,317
GA Income Tax	3,186	3,441	3,711	4,003	4,317
Georgia Tax	3,186	3,441	3,711	4,003	4,317
Tot State/Local Tx	3,186	3,441	3,711	4,003	4,317
Total Inc Tax	16,214	17,616	19,001	19,461	21,023

FINANCIAL SUMMARY

DICK & JANE JOHNSON

BASE CASE	2002	2003	2004	2005	2006
Gross Real Income					
Personal Earnings	65,000	68,250	71,663	75,246	79,008
Interest Income	1,234	2,496	3,866	5,445	7,240
	66,234	70,746	75,529	80,691	86,248
Income & Inflation					
Gross Real Inc	66,234	70,746	75,529	80,691	86,248
Total Inc Tax	-16,214	-17,616	-19,001	-19,461	-21,023
Net Real Income	50,020	53,130	56,527	61,230	65,225
Cur Real Inc =	50,020	51,771	53,582	55,458	57,399
At Infltn Rate of	4	4	4	4	4
Cash Flow					
Idle Cash On Hand	4,500	4,469	4,477	4,486	4,492
Norml Cash Inflow	65,000	68,250	71,663	75,246	79,008
Norml Cash Outflw	42,389	44,982	47,401	46,731	49,692
Cash Invested	22,642	23,260	24,252	28,509	29,310
Cash Balance	4,469	4,477	4,486	4,492	4,498
Net Worth					
Personal Assets	30,964	29,097	27,514	26,165	25,020
Investment Assets	39,876	65,632	93,750	127,704	164,254
Personal Liabilities	-7,985	-5,193	-2,441	-2,036	-1,593
Personal Net Worth	22,979	23,904	25,073	24,129	23,427
Investment Net Worth	39,876	65,632	93,750	127,704	164,254
Net Worth	62,855	89,537	118,823	151,833	187,681

PERSONAL PLANNING: TAXES

Present Situation

Dick and Jane are 26 and 25 years old respectively and have been married for 4 years. Jane is an assistant manager for a major hotel chain and currently earns $35,000 a year. Dick is a paralegal earning $30,000 per year. They anticipate that their salaries will increase approximately 5 percent annually in the foreseeable future. At present they rent an apartment for $800 a month plus utilities. They feel that the apartment rent will increase at least 5 percent annually.

Their major assets are almost $16,000 in a money market fund, about $10,000 of net investable cash flow, $4,500 in a joint checking account, and their household furnishings that are fully paid for and whose replacement value they project at $14,000. The household furnishings do not include any major appliances since such appliances are furnished with the apartment.

Their other major assets are two cars, one of which Jane purchased for $10,700 in November 2000. They made a $1,700 down payment and financed $9,000 at 6 percent for 4 years. They estimate its present value at $8,600. Dick's car, which is paid for, is 3 years old and is worth approximately $4,000.

The Johnsons' primary financial planning objectives at present are to ascertain whether they can realistically afford the purchase of a home and, if so, what would be the best way to accomplish their goal. One of their most pressing concerns is that it will probably require both their salaries to purchase and maintain a home, but there is the possibility, even the likelihood, that either Jane or Dick would prefer to stay home with their children. They would like to start their family within the next 2 years.

As already noted, since their marriage 4 years ago the Johnsons have accumulated almost $16,000 in savings, presently invested in money market funds that are paying about 4 percent, and $10,000 of investable cash flow in 2001. Other than the car loan their only significant liabilities are Jane's two government-guaranteed student loans in the total amount of $4,000. The loans became payable in 1999 at 9 percent simple interest and are payable over 10 years.

The tax, cash-flow, and net worth projections in the base case illustrate the Johnsons' financial position over the next 5 years if they make no changes in their present lifestyle.

Purchasing a House with Tax-Deductible Dollars

It seems appropriate that the Johnsons begin to consider the purchase of a principal residence at this time, since such a purchase would provide them with tax-deductible interest and real estate tax payments that could offset any increased amount of cash flow necessary to support the cost of the home. In computing the actual cost of a home purchase, it is important to remember that if the purchase is leveraged, as most home purchases are, the interest payment portion of the total payment is fully deductible as long as the first mortgage does not exceed $1 million. In addition, property tax payments are fully deductible.

In the Johnsons' case, if mortgage financing were available at a rate of 8.75 percent, the effective after-tax rate would be reduced due to the tax deductibility of the home mortgage interest payments. The Johnsons' itemized deductions, before consideration of the mortgage interest, are $3,386. Since the standard deduction currently is $7,600, the first $4,214 of mortgage interest will not provide them any tax advantages. Only the interest and property (real estate) taxes in excess of $4,214 will effectively reduce their income taxes. If we assume that their taxable income places the Johnsons in the 27 percent tax bracket, then their effective after-tax mortgage interest rate will be 7.69 percent, as determined by the following calculation:

$$
\begin{aligned}
\text{Effective after-tax interest rate} &= \text{nominal interest rate (as percent)} \left[1 - \left(\frac{\text{marginal tax rate (as decimal)} - \left(\text{total itemized deductions} - \text{standard deduction} \right)}{\text{standard deduction}} \right) \right]
\end{aligned}
$$

$$
= 8.75\% \left[1 - \left(\frac{.27 \times (\$11,022 - \$7,600)}{\$7,600} \right) \right]
$$

$$
= 8.75\% \left[1 - \left(\frac{\$923.94}{\$7,600} \right) \right]
$$

$$
= 7.69\%
$$

Tax Implications of Home Ownership

Clients, such as the Johnsons, who are contemplating the ownership of their first home often need information on the tax benefits of home ownership. All too frequently they view their mortgage and property tax payments as rent—that is, a personal expense without income tax ramifications. However, ownership of a primary or principal residence provides significant tax advantages, some of which also apply to the ownership of a second home.

Once clients decide that home ownership is part of a desirable lifestyle, then their concern should focus on its financial feasibility. A paramount consideration should be the advantage of leverage gained from the beneficial effect the income tax code accords home ownership.

Rarely does someone acquire a first (or subsequent) principal or secondary residence by paying the entire purchase price from savings. Rather, the down payment and the closing costs frequently consume much of the buyer's available assets, and borrowing the balance is the only feasible alternative.

Benefit of Leverage

Since home mortgages do not have an equity-kicker clause benefiting the lender, the full benefit of any increase in home prices accrues to the debtor/owner. Borrowing a portion of the acquisition price results in financial leverage that enables the homeowner to reap sizable returns on his or her equity in the home should its price rise. This gain realized on the amount invested (that is, on the equity in the property) exceeds the percentage increase in the property's market price. If the owner invests $20,000 and borrows $80,000 to acquire a $100,000 residence that then increases in net value (net of buying and selling expense) by 5 percent, or $5,000 ($100,000 x .05), the owner reaps a 25 percent gain ($5,000 ÷ $20,000) on the equity investment.

Tax Advantages

Homeowners also benefit from various tax advantages found in the Internal Revenue Code. Some of the tax advantages associated with owning a home are the following:

- deductibility of interest paid on a home mortgage
- deductibility of state and local property taxes assessed on the home
- tax exemption of the realized gain when a principal residence is sold (subject to limitations discussed below)
- step up in basis for ownership interest of homeowner

Deductibility of Interest Paid on a Home Mortgage. As a general rule, an individual who itemizes deductions in lieu of using the standard deduction may deduct against adjusted gross income the interest paid on the mortgage on the principal residence in the year when payment is made. Likewise, interest payments for a mortgage on a second home (a vacation home whose owner is the sole user) also qualify as a deduction against adjusted gross income.

In addition, if at the time of the initial acquisition the buyer pays points (one point being one percent of the face amount of the loan) to the lender to facilitate granting the mortgage for either a primary or a second home, the points are deemed to be interest and are deductible. Exceptions to the general rule of deductibility of interest and points paid are as follows:

- *a limit on the acquisition indebtedness that may be deducted as qualified residence interest.* For any tax period, the amount of qualified residence interest that may be deducted as acquisition indebtedness may not exceed the interest paid on a maximum of $1 million of home acquisition indebtedness (or $500,000 each for a married couple filing separate returns). The limit is the total indebtedness of both the primary and other qualified residences.

- *a limit on the home equity indebtedness interest that may be deducted as qualified residence interest.* For any tax period, the amount of qualified residence interest that may be deducted as home equity indebtedness (other than acquisition indebtedness) may not exceed the interest paid on the fair market value of the qualified residence less the amount of the property's acquisition indebtedness. Further, the maximum amount of home equity loan interest that may be deducted as qualified residence interest may not exceed the interest paid on a home equity loan of $100,000 ($50,000 in the case of separate returns by a married couple).

- *nondeductibility of points paid to refinance a qualified residence.* Although the dollar amount of any points paid to acquire the initial mortgage on a qualified residence is fully deductible for the year in which the points are paid, the dollar amount of points paid as a consequence of refinancing an existing indebtedness on a residence must be allocated ratably over the life of the new mortgage. Should the indebtedness be paid off prior to its full term, any points not so allocated are deductible at the time of payoff.

- *the manner in which the taxpayer uses the property.* The deductibility of interest applies only to properties that qualify as residences. For property to qualify as a residence for any one year the taxpayer (or a qualifying member of the taxpayer's family) must use it for personal purposes for a number of days exceeding the greater of 14 days or 10 percent of the days during the year that the property is rented at a fair rental. If the taxpayer (or a member of the taxpayer's family) uses the property during any part of any day that the unit was rented, that day is considered a personal use, not a rental, day.

For the taxpayer who uses the property as his or her principal place of business, the interest allocable to the portion of the dwelling used exclusively for business purposes is not deductible as acquisition or home equity interest. (If other requirements are met, it would qualify as a deductible business expense.)

Deductibility of State and Local Property Taxes. The general rule is that state and local property taxes qualify as a deduction in the year paid in the same way as interest payments for both the principal and second homes do. Deductibility of taxes on a second home is restricted in a manner similar to limitations on interest deductibility.

Exclusion of Realized Gain from Sale of the Principal Residence. The Taxpayer Relief Act of 1997 changed the traditional rules dealing with the sale of a taxpayer's principal residence and created an income tax exclusion, within limits, for the profit made on the sale of the home.

A single taxpayer, or a married taxpayer filing a joint return, who sells a home that was used as a principal residence for 2 out of the last 5 years may exclude $250,000 of the gain from income. This limit is doubled for married taxpayers filing jointly if both spouses meet the ownership and use requirements. Individuals residing in nursing homes because they are incapable of self-care may treat their stay in the nursing home as "use" of their principal residence for up to one year for purposes of meeting the 2-year requirement.

This exclusion may be used only once every 2 years. A reduced exclusion, based on the ratio of the amount by which the period of ownership and use compares to 2 years, may be available if the sale of the home is due to a change in employment, a change in health, or other unforeseen circumstances defined as IRS regulations. The exclusion may be used by the taxpayer multiple times, allowing taxpayers to plan for the disposition of primary residences and vacation homes (by converting the vacation home to the primary residence) during their lifetime or at retirement.

For sales of residences after August 4, 1997, taxpayers are no longer permitted to roll over the gain on the sale of the residence into a new principal residence. Consequently, gain in excess of the $250,000 or $500,000 exclusion limit will be subject to tax whether or not the taxpayer purchases a replacement residence.

Step Up in Basis at Death of Homeowner

A residence, like other assets owned by individuals, qualifies for the tax-free step up in basis upon the taxpayer's death. Thus any capital gain resulting from ownership of one or more qualified residences escapes income taxation.

The proportion of the residence owned by the deceased receives the step up in basis. When the residence is owned jointly with the spouse, the deceased (spouse) is assumed to own one-half. The surviving spouse will then own the property, with a basis in his or her hands equal to the sum of the survivor's basis plus the stepped-up value of the deceased spouse.

Note that the step up in basis provision provides no benefit for individuals or married couples whose home has not appreciated more than the exclusion amount allowed for personal residences as discussed above.

Keep in mind that this discussion focuses on the general rules concerning the deductibility of expenditures associated with home ownership and the income tax exclusion applicable to personal residence sales. Each of these elements must be examined for every client.

Tax Disadvantages

As detailed in the previous section, the Internal Revenue Code provides homeowners with numerous federal income tax advantages. But two major tax disadvantages exist. The tax code treats the personal residence(s) as it does other personal property when it is sold at a loss; that is, the loss is not deductible against any of the taxpayer's income.

Another tax disadvantage occurs from the fact that not all state income tax laws treat the sale of residences in the same manner as does the federal tax code. Some states permit rollover of capital gains and others do not. Some allow a one-time exclusion of $125,000 of any realized gain for taxpayers aged 55 or older and others either do not have an exclusion or have a different dollar amount exclusion. The result of these differences requires the homeowner to keep two sets of financial records for determining the basis in the property for federal and state income tax purposes. This record keeping becomes more complex if the client changes his or her state of domicile.

Nontax Considerations

Although the tax advantages of owning one's personal residence are numerous, for many individuals non-tax reasons are the consideration in determining whether to purchase a home:

- *privacy.* Most nonhomeowners live in some form of multiple dwelling such as apartment houses or converted single family homes where common walls, ceilings, or floors do not guarantee privacy. (Some owner-occupied homes, such as townhouses and condominium apartments, have similar privacy constraints.)
- *security.* Owning one's residence, even if subject to a mortgage, can provide financial security as well as psychological benefits. Economic well-being is enhanced since a part of each payment decreases the homeowner's debt and increases the equity. There is psychological security from the fact that the property belongs to its owner and that the law protects this ownership interest.
- *preference.* Many individuals realize benefits through demonstrating their pride of ownership by making both the interior and exterior reflect their own tastes (within limits of zoning requirements). They also enjoy being able to make redecorating decisions themselves.
- *space.* Owner-occupied homes generally are larger than all but the most elegant rental units. The additional interior space, as well as the exterior grounds, enable individuals to develop and enjoy their lifestyle activities.

Other Factors to Consider When Purchasing a Home

Young clients like the Johnsons who have not been homeowners need information in addition to tax factors in order to make an informed decision. Given Jane's job, it is quite likely that she will be transferred by the hotel chain during her career. Because of this possibility, the Johnsons should consider the potential salability of any home they purchase in the near future. (Note: Most hotel chains provide the hotel manager with an apartment in the hotel so that the person is available "around the clock" to cater to unexpected customer needs. This does not appear to be a factor the Johnsons must consider at this time.) Some features that affect the marketability of a residence are the following:

- *location.* According to real estate experts, "location, location, and location" are the three important variables in determining the value of a particular parcel of real estate. Particularly if resale at some not-too-distant time is highly likely, the location of residential property is especially important. A secluded home down a long country road or one that has a bridge over a stream could be difficult to sell.

  Location also includes the general ambiance of the community, the quality of its schools and other municipal services, the level of local taxes relative to other nearby communities, and its proximity to work, public transportation, and highway networks. These are some of the more important features that the Johnsons should consider when making their selection.

- *lifestyle features.* For ease of marketability, the home chosen should have appeal to a wide spectrum of potential buyers. Housing styles and consumer preferences change, and any home the Johnsons acquire should be within the mainstream of homebuyers' preferences. Likewise the property should have "eye" or "curb appeal," since prospective buyers' first impressions are highly important. Amenities of the property, such as decks and attractive gardens and shrubs as well as the interior design and rooms that most purchasers desire, also facilitate its resale.

Choosing Appropriate Financing for Purchase of a Residence

Creative Financing

In seeking out a house to purchase, it may be advantageous for the Johnsons to consider various means of both conventional and creative financing. For example, home loans have traditionally been made with a down payment of 20 percent and the balance financed by a fixed-rate mortgage usually for a term of 20, 25, or 30 years. However, two changes have resulted in a rather major difference in the financing of residences.

The first change has been the securitization of home mortgages, which developed as more and more banks and savings and loans desire to sell their acquired home mortgages shortly after they are generated. The buyers of these mortgages want somewhat standardized terms, particularly regarding mortgage duration. Consequently in many parts of the country potential homebuyers can only choose between a 15-year and a 30-year mortgage.

The second change is a result of changes in interest rates. During periods of high interest rates, various other types of mortgages have become available, such as variable- or adjustable-rate mortgages in which the interest rate either floats continuously or is set for a period of years and then reset based on a specified index at the time of the adjustment. This type of financing does not lock in a fixed-dollar amount for a house payment that a young couple can depend on for the entire term of the mortgage.

To make variable-rate mortgages more appealing to consumers, some financial institutions have introduced the convertible residential mortgage. This vehicle typically permits the borrower on any one of the first 5 years' anniversary dates of the loan to convert the variable-rate mortgage to a fixed-rate mortgage at the then-prevailing rate for home mortgages, usually specified as the lender's then-current rate for similar mortgages (although it could be linked to some other measurable market interest rate). If not converted, the mortgage retains its variable-interest-rate feature. When mortgage rates are high, the borrower can probably expect to see lower market interest rates at one of those first 5 anniversary dates, thereby making conversion worthwhile. In addition, the typical interest-rate changes as specified in the contract on a year-to-year basis are often tied to the Treasury bill index and can have an annual cap of 2 percent and a life-of-the-loan cap of 6 percent. A further attractive feature is that, as with other variable-rate mortgages, the initial interest charged the borrower is about 2 percent less than that for a fixed-rate mortgage at the time the contract is initiated. Finally, the cost of converting the mortgage is specified in the mortgage and is currently about $750, a sum far less than the cost of refinancing through the acquisition of a replacement mortgage that could entail the payment of points, legal fees, and other attendant expenses associated with obtaining a new mortgage. Despite the attractiveness of this set of features, some disadvantages do exist. First, the interest rate will be slightly higher than that charged on a nonconvertible, variable-rate mortgage. In addition, interest rates could rise steadily over the 5 years, and the borrower would have to either convert to a higher fixed rate than was available at the inception of the mortgage or continue to face the uncertain variable-rate provisions for the duration of the mortgage unless refinanced. Also the maximum 6 percent increase in the rate over the life of the mortgage could significantly raise the monthly payment needed to amortize the loan, placing a heavy strain on the borrower's budget. Other drawbacks include conversion issues such as inadvertent nonexercise of the option or converting just before a significant decline in interest rates.

For these and many other reasons, specifically the inability to assure the level of payments required for retiring the mortgage indebtedness, variable- or adjustable-rate mortgages are not recommended for the Johnsons if there are other alternatives available. If these alternatives are not available, a variable- or adjustable-rate mortgage that has reasonable limits on interest-rate increases could be considered.

Some sellers of homes will either finance the entire purchase or take back a second mortgage at less than the market rate of interest. If a suitable property can be found, especially one with an assumable loan at an advantageous interest rate, and the seller is willing to take back a second mortgage for most or all of the remaining balance of the purchase price, this type of arrangement can result in a significantly less expensive interest rate and a net saving to the buyer. One disadvantage of this type of financing is that the term on the second mortgage is frequently short, usually no more than 5 to 7 years, requiring substantial cash-flow expenditures in the initial years of the home purchase. While this financing technique should not be ignored, any creative financing arrangement should be carefully explored in detail with a competent attorney prior to the signing of a purchase agreement.

Where possible, the typical home purchaser has rejected the variable- or adjustable-rate mortgage, preferring to have the certainty of a fixed payment during the period of indebtedness. Lenders, on the other hand, do not like to be locked into a fixed-rate loan for a period as long as 25 or 30 years. One compromise some financial planners recommend is a 15-year, fully amortized loan. If the client can afford the higher monthly payments, this can be a viable approach. However, not all clients can afford the larger payments, and many who could might prefer not to be so financially squeezed that way. Another alternative attracting some home-purchaser acceptance is the 15-year, fixed-rate mortgage with a predetermined balloon payment. The full amount of such a loan is not paid off during its term, and the borrower must seek refinancing some time before the end of the loan. This creates an uncertainty for the borrower as to the level of interest to be paid to refinance the balloon payment, thereby increasing the risk to the borrower. But since the lender accepts a slightly lower interest rate due to the shorter term of the loan, this form of loan arrangement can have attractive features for the borrower.

The first attractive feature of this type of mortgage arrangement is that the borrower does have the benefit of a fixed payment during the life of the loan. A second feature is that the interest rate is slightly lower because of the shorter duration. Third, the loan can be structured to result in a manageable monthly payment, perhaps only slightly higher than would be the case with a conventional 30-year loan. These factors will result in a significantly larger portion of the total indebtedness being paid off during the initial 15-year period. A fourth advantage is that the shorter structure meshes with the fact that the typical mortgage is paid off before 15 years because homeowners tend to either trade up to a larger home or move to another geographic location. Fifth, it could be possible to arrange terms permitting additional principal payments without penalty on an irregular basis that will result in a further reduction of the balloon payment due at the end of the 15-year term. Sixth, in this particular situation, 15 years from now Jane and Dick will most likely have received salary increases, thereby not making refinancing of the amount required to meet the balloon payment a financial hardship even if mortgage interest rates are significantly higher at that time.

Conventional Financing

Other more conventional avenues of financing are still generally available. These financing techniques include so-called conventional 80, 90, and 95 percent loans. These loans, especially those of 90 and 95 percent of the purchase price, may require the payment of discount points by the buyer and the purchase of personal mortgage insurance for the protection of the lending institution. Paying these points to the lender results in a higher effective interest rate being charged to the borrower. Private mortgage insurance is required because lending institutions are fearful that borrowers with minimal equity invested in a residence might simply walk away from the property and forfeit the equity in such a property if it becomes difficult to meet the mortgage payments, leaving the lending institution in a foreclosure position. Mortgage insurance is usually paid for as part of the monthly mortgage payment and insures lenders against a loss should they encounter a foreclosure situation and be unable to recover the balance of the mortgage amount.

Subsidized or Guaranteed Financing

A most attractive option, especially for the Johnsons and people who are similarly situated—that is, first-time homebuyers or homebuyers who have limited cash to invest in a home—exists in the form of subsidized or guaranteed mortgages, most familiarly known as VA (Veterans Administration) and FHA (Federal Housing Administration) loans. In addition, locally subsidized mortgage loans are periodically made available for first-time buyers in many areas.

The VA loan requires no down payment and is available to persons who have served in the U.S. military. Our facts indicate that neither Dick nor Jane has any military service, so a VA loan would not be an option. FHA loans, on the other hand, are available without regard to military service and require down payments of approximately 3 percent of the purchase price of the residence up to $25,000 and 5 percent for any remaining amount. There is a maximum amount available for FHA loans, as they are designed primarily to assist low- and middle-income families in acquiring homes. These maximum amounts are set by geographical region based on the prevailing cost of moderate-priced housing. Housing in the price range that the Johnsons are discussing would not exceed the maximum amount available under an FHA loan.

At one time there were additional benefits of FHA financing to the buyer. Interest rates were subject to a maximum set by the FHA and were often significantly below the current market rate. In addition, the seller and not the buyer was required to pay the points on the loan. Although the cost of the points was often implicitly included in pricing a property that was sold under an FHA contract, such an arrangement did not require an immediate cash outlay, as the cost was merely added to the mortgage amount and amortized over the life of the loan. While this resulted in additional long-term costs over the life of the loan, it did not require that the purchaser have these funds available in addition to down payment and closing costs at the time the sales transaction was closed.

The FHA can no longer control the maximum interest rates that lenders can charge on FHA loans. Also points are no longer required to be paid by the seller but are negotiable between the buyer and seller. In addition, variable-rate mortgages can qualify for FHA guarantees. FHA financing may still carry a slightly lower interest rate than conventional mortgages because of the safety of the loans due to the FHA guarantees.

Since the financing arrangements for a home purchase can be so critical, the Johnsons should be aware that some sellers do not choose to offer their homes for sale under an FHA contract, because for purchases with FHA financing the seller is obligated to make necessary repairs to meet the FHA's standards before the loan will be approved. In selecting houses to consider for purchase, the Johnsons will want to alert their real estate agent or broker or both to the fact that they prefer FHA financing for their purchase. Of course it is possible to offer an FHA contract to a seller who has not indicated that he or she will accept FHA financing; however, this type of contract may be rejected purely on the basis of the additional costs to the seller. It is frequently more time efficient to ask the real estate agent or broker to ascertain whether FHA financing is available for a specific house.

A third form of government-subsidized mortgage that might be available to the Johnsons is state-subsidized (or city-subsidized) mortgage financing. Those qualifying for the subsidized program receive mortgages at 2 or 3 percentage points below the going rate. To qualify, the homebuyer typically must be a resident of the state (or city), be a first-time purchaser, and have an income at or below a specified level. These mortgage loans are of the fixed-rate form and are of relatively long duration (25 to 30 years). Depending on where the Johnsons reside, they might qualify for this form of loan.

Financing Major Appliances and Fixtures with the House

Another advantage in financing and furnishing a home can be obtained if items such as lighting fixtures, window treatments (curtains, drapes, and blinds), and particularly major appliances are being sold with the property. This is especially true of decorative items such as lighting fixtures and window treatments if the purchaser thinks they are attractive or, at the very least, would be content to live with them temporarily. Acquiring basic appliances such as a refrigerator, washer, dryer, and dishwasher can run well over $2,000. If these appliances are purchased as separate items from retail sources, there is a further cash drain at a time when most young couples with limited assets are least able to afford it. Even if the house is being offered for sale without appliances, it may be possible to negotiate with the owner so that for an additional amount included in the contract-offering price, all or certain specified appliances are left with the property. Any items such as appliances or window treatments that are included in the offering price must be specified in the offering contract.

If one is able to obtain the owner's agreement in the matter of leaving appliances, at the very least an immediate and significant cash-flow expenditure is avoided. If the assets to pay cash for the appliances are lacking, finance charges at retail levels that may be considerably above the effective mortgage rate can also be eliminated. If the cost of the appliances is added to the purchase price of the residence, the price can be effectively absorbed into the mortgage costs by increasing monthly payments by a nominal amount. While this approach may again result in overall higher costs over the term of the mortgage, it does prevent a severe cash-flow deficiency in the year in which the house is purchased when expenditures are already at a high level. It can also save a significant amount in the cost of the appliances themselves, since the cost of used appliances, even though relatively new and quite serviceable, is significantly less than the cost of new appliances of the same type. Such a plan may also save in delivery charges and time away from work, as delivery and installation are required on new purchases. The same principle is true regarding the purchase of lawnmowers, yard tools, and any other equipment necessary to maintain the residence if the seller is willing to negotiate on these items. At the very least, if yard equipment or tools are not included in the mortgage amount as a part of the residential purchase package, a separate offer can be made to the seller to purchase these items, provided they are serviceable, for a nominal sum. Frequently these offers are accepted, especially if the seller is making a long-distance move in which the transportation costs of packing and moving the items may exceed their value or if the present owner is moving to a different type of residence, such as a move from a single-family house with a substantial yard into a condominium or an apartment.

In short, young couples such as the Johnsons should be alert to the most advantageous methods of financing, from a cash-flow standpoint, and the opportunity to acquire the appliances, decorative fixtures, and equipment necessary to furnish and maintain the property that they are purchasing. These items may be less than perfect for their purposes but can be replaced one by one as their usefulness deteriorates or their maintenance becomes a problem. This gives the first-time home purchaser the opportunity to spread the acquisition of new major appliances over a number of years rather than making all purchases at once.

Purchasing a House for Rehabilitation

An additional option for the Johnsons could be to seek out a house that has not been maintained and/or redecorated and to rehabilitate that house into a residence they would enjoy. This concept is particularly appealing to some first-time home purchasers, since these dwellings frequently lack the visual appeal to command a premium price and consequently can be acquired at considerable savings. It is not unusual for a house that sells in the $90,000 to $100,000 range to sell unrenovated in the high $60,000 to low $70,000 range or even less, depending on the renovation required.

Unless the first-time home purchaser, or indeed any other purchaser, has some experience in rehabilitating a house, the project can become quite a chore. In choosing a house for renovation, the first step is to select one whose space and basic layout meet the family's needs and whose appearance appeals to the family. As a general rule persons undertaking a renovation project for the first time should probably restrict their purchase to buildings requiring only cosmetic changes. The exception to this rule might be if one or both of the purchasers are exceptionally adept at or interested in home repair. Even if either of the Johnsons is exceptionally handy or interested in rehabilitation, it would probably be best to avoid a total rehabilitation that includes a number of structural changes in the proposed dwelling. These types of changes can actually be quite expensive while appearing deceptively inexpensive to an amateur. For the present, if the Johnsons choose to consider the rehabilitation of an existing dwelling, they should limit their choices to those dwellings that are structurally sound, in which all major systems are functional, and that require only paint, wallpaper, and some redecorating.

To assure the structural soundness of an existing dwelling, the services of a building engineer should always be utilized to provide a written report covering structural soundness and the soundness of all major systems—plumbing, heating, cooling, and electrical. Frequently the charges for an inspection report are surprisingly nominal, usually not exceeding a few hundred dollars, while the information provided by such a report can be invaluable.

If a rehabilitation approach is undertaken, there are basically two ways to accomplish the project. The first is to engage a contractor or decorator to make the necessary or desired improvements, and the second is to attempt many or most of the improvements oneself. For those with limited resources, the latter may be the only viable alternative. As long as the dwelling has been carefully chosen, and the purchaser understands the types of necessary improvements, it is not uncommon for the purchaser to successfully redo a dwelling to a great monetary advantage. Basic redecorating such as painting and wallpapering is achievable even by the inexperienced person if he or she is diligent and patient.

A person considering the purchase of a dwelling to rehabilitate should be aware that the availability of financing, specifically FHA financing, may be contingent on the building's being in a certain state of functional repair. Although the precise standards that the structure must meet to be eligible for such financing can vary according to the area of the country, at a minimum the acquisition of FHA financing requires that the building is structurally sound and that all major systems are functional. Since these are the minimum criteria that have already been recommended in the event that a dwelling is purchased for rehabilitation, no problems should arise if the Johnsons decide to attempt a rehabilitation project. However, purchasing a home for rehabilitation is a major project involving a substantial time commitment. The Johnsons may want to consider this alternative but have not specifically expressed interest in this type of project.

Financing Recommendations

The following analysis presumes the Johnsons purchase a $90,000 home with a down payment of $12,000.

15-Year Mortgage with Balloon Payment

In contrast to a fully amortized 30-year mortgage of $78,000, the Johnsons could consider one that would amortize $38,000 over a 15-year period and would require a $40,000 balloon payment at the end of the 15 years.

The Johnsons would incur more risk with this set of mortgage terms due to having to meet the balloon payment in 15 years. The lender would experience somewhat less interest-rate risk due to the shorter term of the loan. Because of the altered risk distribution the Johnsons could arrange for a slightly lower interest rate on the loan.

If an 8.25 percent, fixed-rate, 15-year mortgage with a balloon payment of $40,000 at the end of year 15 is considered, the annual payment of $7,724 ($643.65 monthly) would amortize the $38,000 and pay the monthly interest on the $40,000. A 30-year fully amortized $78,000 loan at 8.75 percent would require an annual payment of $7,364. The difference in the higher annual payment with the 15-year loan, approximately $360 ($7,724 − $7,364), would result in the Johnsons' reducing their outstanding indebtedness at the end of 15 years by approximately $21,396 more than with a 30-year conventional loan. This results from a combination of the lower interest rate and the slightly higher monthly payments. (At 8.50 percent the annual payment will be approximately $530 more than the conventional loan of 30 years to achieve the same $40,000 unpaid balance at the end of 15 years.)

Given this relatively small difference, the Johnsons might consider this alternative financing arrangement. They should recognize that their incomes should continue to rise and, barring an unforeseen economic or personal financial disaster at that distant time, the Johnsons most likely would incur little difficulty in refinancing the balloon payment. At that future time an 8.75 percent, 15-year, fixed-rate loan for $40,000 would require $4,800 annually ($400 monthly) for its amortization. At 12 percent the loan would require an annual payment of $5,760 ($480 monthly). The reduced payments for the second 15-year period would at that time free additional income for other objectives, such as college education for the children they plan to have.

Fully Amortized 30-Year Mortgage

Based largely on the economics of the financing, the 15-year mortgage is very attractive. However, the planner must consider the clients' total situation.

The Johnsons are inexperienced in financial matters, and they describe themselves as having an aversion to any risk. The Johnsons should obtain an FHA loan if possible. The uncertainty associated with the 15-year mortgage with balloon payment may not provide the requisite peace of mind for Dick and Jane. To relieve Jane's concern about debt, the mortgage terms should permit reduction of principal without penalty on an irregular or regular basis. This permits some of any excess cash to be channeled toward debt reduction. Therefore in light of the total situation the 30-year, fixed-rate, fully amortized mortgage is the recommended choice.

The following projections of the Johnsons' tax, cash-flow, and net worth positions over the next 5 years represent an assumption that the Johnsons buy a residence for a purchase price of $90,000 in September 2003, make a down payment of $12,000 on the purchase, and finance the balance with fully amortized financing at a fixed rate of 8.75 percent over a period of 30 years. These projections assume that the Johnsons are able to purchase major appliances with the property.

[text continues on page 4.39]

CASE II
$90,000 Residence Purchased

New Assumptions

1. The Johnsons purchase a house in September 2003 for $90,000, making a $12,000 down payment and financing the balance of $78,000 with an 8.75 percent fixed-rate mortgage with a term of 30 years.

2. Closing costs for the home purchase are 5 percent of the amount of the mortgage.

3. Property taxes on the home are $950 and increase 5 percent annually.

4. The residence increases in value at 3 percent annually.

5. Homeowners insurance will replace the existing tenant's insurance and will cost $500 a year.

Continuing Assumptions

1. The checking account balance is maintained at $4,500; the account is noninterest bearing.

2. Dick's and Jane's salaries are increased at 5 percent annually.

3. Money market funds earn 4 percent interest annually.

4. Investable cash earns 5.25 percent annually.

5. Expenditures for food and clothing will increase annually at 4 percent.

6. Expenditures for rent and charitable contributions will increase 5 percent annually.

7. Expenditures for utilities, telephone, entertainment, and automobile gas and repairs will increase 6 percent annually.

8. Expenditures for medical insurance and other medical care, as well as both automobile and tenant's insurance, will increase by 8 percent annually.

9. Decreases in value of furniture have been ignored.

10. Automobiles decrease in value at a rate of 15 percent annually.

11. The inflation rate for taxes is 3.5 percent annually.

INCOME STATEMENT

DICK & JANE JOHNSON

CASE II	2002	2003	2004	2005	2006
Earned Income					
Jane's Salary	35,000	36,750	38,588	40,517	42,543
Dick's Salary	30,000	31,500	33,075	34,729	36,465
	65,000	68,250	71,663	75,246	79,008
Interest/Dividends					
Money Market Fund	640	666	692	720	749
Investable Cash	594	1,747	3,102	4,859	6,876
	1,234	2,413	3,794	5,579	7,625
	========	========	========	========	========
Adj Gross Income	66,234	70,663	75,457	80,825	86,633
Deductions					
Charitable 50%	200	210	221	232	243
State Tax Paid	3,186	3,254	3,267	3,570	3,898
Property Taxes	0	950	998	1,047	1,100
Home Mortgage	0	2,274	6,786	6,735	6,676
Gross Deductions	3,386	6,688	11,272	11,584	11,917
Standard Deduction	7,600	7,850	8,100	8,787	9,568
Allowed Deductions	7,600	7,850	11,272	11,584	11,917
Pers Exemptions	5,800	6,000	6,200	6,400	6,700
	========	========	========	========	========
Taxable Income	52,834	56,813	57,985	62,840	68,016
	========	========	========	========	========
Fed Income Tax	8,055	8,932	8,965	9,008	9,445
	========	========	========	========	========
Fed Tax Bracket-Ord Inc	27.0%	27.0%	26.0%	26.0%	25.0%

BALANCE SHEET

DICK & JANE JOHNSON

CASE II **LIQUID ASSETS**	2002	2003	2004	2005	2006
Cash Balance	4,469	4,481	4,489	4,497	4,510
Cash Deposits					
Investable Cash	23,236	45,063	76,220	113,728	155,088
Money Market Fund	16,640	17,306	17,998	18,718	19,467
	39,876	62,369	94,218	132,446	174,555
	========	========	========	========	========
Liquid Assets	44,345	66,850	98,707	136,943	179,065
	========	========	========	========	========
NONLIQUID ASSETS					
Personal Property					
Residence	0	90,000	92,700	95,481	98,345
Dick's car	3,400	2,890	2,457	2,088	1,775
Jane's car	9,095	7,731	6,571	5,585	4,748
Furniture/Fixture	14,000	14,000	14,000	14,000	14,000
	26,495	114,621	115,728	117,154	118,868
	========	========	========	========	========
Nonliquid Assets	26,495	114,621	115,728	117,154	118,867
	========	========	========	========	========
Total Assets	70,840	181,471	214,435	254,097	297,932
LIABILITIES					
Mortgage Loans					
Home Mortgage	0	77,819	77,241	76,612	75,924
	0	77,819	77,241	76,612	75,924
Notes Payable					
Jane's Student Loan	3,149	2,811	2,441	2,036	1,593
Jane's Car Loan	4,836	2,382	0	0	0
	7,985	5,193	2,441	2,036	1,593
	========	========	========	========	========
Total Liabilities	7,985	83,012	79,682	78,648	77,517
	========	========	========	========	========
Net Worth	62,855	98,459	134,753	175,449	220,415
	========	========	========	========	========

CASH FLOW STATEMENT

DICK & JANE JOHNSON

CASE II	2002	2003	2004	2005	2006
BEGINNING OF YEAR					
Idle Cash On Hand	4,500	4,469	4,481	4,489	4,497
SOURCES OF CASH					
Cash Income					
Jane's Salary	35,000	36,750	38,588	40,517	42,543
Dick's Salary	30,000	31,500	33,075	34,729	36,465
	65,000	68,250	71,663	75,246	79,008
	========	========	========	========	========
Total Cash Inflow	65,000	68,250	71,663	75,246	79,008
	========	========	========	========	========
Tot Cash Available	69,500	72,719	76,144	79,735	83,505
	========	========	========	========	========
USES OF CASH					
Fully Tax Deductible					
Home Mortgage	0	2,274	6,786	6,735	6,676
	0	2,274	6,786	6,735	6,676
Partly Deductible					
Med Ins Prem - Dick	240	259	280	302	327
Other Medical	1,100	1,188	1,283	1,386	1,497
Charity Contrb-50%	200	210	221	232	243
	1,540	1,657	1,783	1,920	2,066
Not Tax Deductible					
Jane's Student Loan	298	270	238	203	165
Jane's Car Loan	366	223	72	0	0
Food	4,800	4,992	5,192	5,399	5,615
Clothing	1,800	1,872	1,947	2,025	2,106
Entertainment	1,500	1,590	1,685	1,787	1,894
Auto Insurance	800	864	933	1,008	1,088
Tenant's Insurance	250	250	0	0	0
Rent	9,600	10,080	0	0	0
Auto Gas/Oil/Repair	500	530	562	596	631
Utility/Phone	2,100	2,226	2,360	2,501	2,651
	22,014	22,897	12,988	13,518	14,151
Taxes Paid					
Fed Tax Paid	8,055	8,932	8,965	9,008	9,445
State Tax Paid	3,186	3,254	3,267	3,570	3,898
FICA/Soc Sec Tax	4,973	5,221	5,482	5,757	6,045
Real Estate Tax	0	950	998	1,047	1,100
	16,214	18,357	18,712	19,382	20,487

CASH FLOW STATEMENT(cont.)

DICK & JANE JOHNSON

CASE II **Purchase/Deposits**	2002	2003	2004	2005	2006
Investable Cash	22,642	20,080	28,055	32,649	34,484
	22,642	20,080	28,055	32,649	34,484
Liability Liquidation					
Jane's Student Loan	310	338	370	405	443
Jane's Car Loan	2,311	2,454	2,382	0	0
Home Mortgage	0	181	578	629	688
	2,621	2,973	3,330	1,034	1,131
	========	========	========	========	========
Tot Cash Outflow	65,031	68,238	71,655	75,238	78,995
	========	========	========	========	========
END OF YEAR					
Cash Balance	4,469	4,481	4,489	4,497	4,510
	========	========	========	========	========

SUPPORTING SCHEDULE

DICK & JANE JOHNSON

	JOINT 2002	JOINT 2003	JOINT 2004	JOINT 2005	JOINT 2006
CASE II					
Income					
Earned Income	65,000	68,250	71,663	75,246	79,008
Adj Gross Income	66,234	70,663	75,457	80,825	86,633
Allowed Deductions	7,600	7,850	11,272	11,584	11,917
Pers Exemptions	5,800	6,000	6,200	6,400	6,700
Taxable Income	52,834	56,813	57,985	62,840	68,016
Federal Tax Liab					
Regular Tax	8,053	8,935	8,963	9,004	9,447
Gross Fed Inc Tax	8,055	8,932	8,965	9,008	9,445
Fed Income Tax	8,055	8,932	8,965	9,008	9,445
Fed Tax Analysis-Ord Inc					
Indexing Factor	79	85	92	98	105
Fed Tax Bracket-Ord Inc	27.0%	27.0%	26.0%	26.0%	25.0%
$ to Next Bracket	60,216	60,187	63,115	62,510	61,734
Next Bracket	30.0%	30.0%	29.0%	29.0%	28.0%
Previous Bracket	15.0%	15.0%	15.0%	15.0%	15.0%
$ to Prev Bracket	6,084	8,413	7,885	7,040	7,989
Fed Effective Tax Rate	15.3%	15.7%	15.5%	14.3%	13.9%
Alt Minimum Tax					
Adj Gross Income	66,234	70,663	75,457	80,825	86,633
Contributions	-200	-210	-221	-232	-243
Home Mortgage	0	-2,274	-6,786	-6,735	-6,676
Adjusted AMTI	66,034	68,179	68,450	73,858	79,714
AMT Exemptions	-49,000	-49,000	-49,000	-45,000	-45,000
AMT Taxable Inc	17,034	19,179	19,450	28,858	34,714
Gross Alt Min Tx	4,429	4,987	5,057	7,503	9,026
Fed Tax Less FTC	-8,055	-8,932	-8,965	-9,008	-9,445
Other Tax Liabs					
FICA/Soc Sec Tax	4,973	5,221	5,482	5,757	6,045
Adj Gross Inc	66,234	70,663	75,457	80,825	86,633
GA Adj Gross Inc	66,234	70,663	75,457	80,825	86,633
GA Standard Ded	3,000	3,000	3,000	3,000	3,000
GA Itemized Ded	3,386	6,688	11,272	11,584	11,917
GA Exemptions	5,400	5,400	5,400	5,400	5,400
GA Taxable Inc	57,448	58,575	58,785	63,840	69,316
GA Regular Tax	3,186	3,254	3,267	3,570	3,898
GA Income Tax	3,186	3,254	3,267	3,570	3,898
Georgia Tax	3,186	3,254	3,267	3,570	3,898
Tot State/Local Tx	3,186	3,254	3,267	3,570	3,898
Total Inc Tax	16,214	17,407	17,714	18,335	19,388

FINANCIAL SUMMARY

DICK & JANE JOHNSON

CASE II	2002	2003	2004	2005	2006
Gross Real Income					
Personal Earnings	65,000	68,250	71,663	75,246	79,008
Interest Income	1,234	2,413	3,794	5,579	7,625
	66,234	70,663	75,457	80,825	86,633
Income & Inflation					
Gross Real Inc	66,234	70,663	75,457	80,825	86,633
Total Inc Tax	-16,214	-17,407	-17,714	-18,335	-19,388
Net Real Income	50,020	53,256	57,742	62,490	67,245
Cur Real Inc =	50,020	51,771	53,582	55,458	57,399
At Infltn Rate of	4	4	4	4	4
Cash Flow					
Idle Cash On Hand	4,500	4,469	4,481	4,489	4,497
Norml Cash Inflow	65,000	68,250	71,663	75,246	79,008
Norml Cash Outflw	42,389	48,158	43,600	42,589	44,511
Cash Invested	22,642	20,080	28,055	32,649	34,484
Cash Balance	4,469	4,481	4,489	4,497	4,510
Net Worth					
Personal Assets	30,964	119,102	120,217	121,651	123,377
Investment Assets	39,876	62,369	94,218	132,446	174,555
Personal Liabilities	-7,985	-83,012	-79,682	-78,648	-77,517
Personal Net Worth	22,979	36,090	40,535	43,003	45,860
Investment Net Worth	39,876	62,369	94,218	132,446	174,555
Net Worth	62,855	98,459	134,753	175,449	220,415

A comparison of the cash-flow expenditures necessary for the purchase of a residence and the cost of the continuing rental of the apartment they presently occupy should be carefully pointed out to the Johnsons. This comparison should be especially reassuring to Dick and Jane because it indicates that the difference is quite small. When the tax advantages and the equity buildup in a home are considered, the purchase of a home is a recommendation with substantial merit.

It is also important to point out to Dick and Jane not only that the purchase of a home does not materially increase their necessary annual cash outlay but also that the residence might well be an excellent investment for them, as residential real estate has historically been a good investment. Over the last several decades it has increased in value at a rate at least equal to inflation. Although housing is not currently increasing with the rate of inflation in certain areas of the country, the real estate market appropriate for the Johnsons continues to experience the historical price appreciation-inflation relationship. It is important for them to understand that they are benefiting not only by increasing equity through retirement of the principal mortgage amount but also by the long-term rising price of homes. If the property has been carefully chosen in a stable neighborhood and is structurally and functionally sound, it is unlikely that Dick and Jane will lose money on their investment. In addition, by purchasing a home with a fixed-rate mortgage they will effectively freeze their direct housing costs, which will not be possible if they continue to live in an apartment. All these factors taken together may be sufficient to allow Jane to convince herself that the risks involved in borrowing to achieve home ownership are more than balanced by the potential rewards. In this particular situation, however, the long-term benefits of home ownership might not accrue to the Johnsons since the possibility exists that Jane could be transferred to a distant location, necessitating the sale of this house.

The Johnsons must decide whether they want to title their home in Dick's or Jane's name alone or jointly. Since the enactment of the unlimited gift tax marital deduction and the new special rules for marital joint tenancies with right of survivorship, there are no significant tax pitfalls in joint ownership between spouses. Although a will does not control disposition of joint property, typically it is the wish of each spouse to have the survivor take ownership of the home upon the first death.

Since the lender will no doubt want both Dick and Jane to sign the note for the mortgage, our recommendation is that they take title to the property as joint tenants with right of survivorship.

Effect of Home Purchase on Staying Home with Child(ren)

Both Dick and Jane believe that, if at all financially feasible, a parent should be the care-provider for their offspring until enrollment in primary school. They have discussed how best to achieve this result in light of their situation. Jane's career would probably come to a halt if she were to resign her position to care for their child(ren). In addition, she has a higher level of income than Dick does and has a bright career potential.

Dick, on the other hand, holds a position that has little upward potential. He lacks any interest in studying law but would like to prepare for a career teaching history and other social science courses at the high-school level. To achieve this goal he needs the requisite education courses at the college/university level since he did not take them in college. In addition, he would like to earn a master's degree in history. They have agreed that he should start obtaining the necessary education credits as soon as feasible. They expect that he will complete these courses, at night and on Saturdays, prior to the birth of their first child. At some later time, he can begin graduate studies for the master's degree.

Under the Family Medical Leave Act of 1993, both Dick and Jane would qualify for time away from their work to care for a newborn. This law specifies that employees are entitled to 12 weeks of unpaid leave for this purpose. Since they are employed by different firms, each is eligible for this leave during the 12-month period following the child's birth. The 12 weeks must be taken all at one time. During the leave, benefits must continue, but the employee is responsible for paying the cost of any contributory benefit plans. Usually a request for this parental leave must be submitted in writing a reasonable time in advance of the starting date.

In the Johnsons' case it would be possible for Jane to take a 3-month maternity leave while Dick continues to work. When Jane returns to work at the end of her leave, Dick could start his unpaid 12-week leave. Afterward he can begin studying for the master's degree, they hope with a tuition scholarship from the university. Dick's conversation with the university indicates a good possibility for the scholarship. He also learned that the university maintains a day-care center, at nominal charge, for the children of graduate students. This situation appeals to the Johnsons. Dick could arrange his schedule generally around Jane's, relying on the day care as a backup.

After completing the requisite education courses, Dick might be able to occasionally substitute-teach at nearby high schools. No estimate of his potential income from this source is made at this time. The Johnsons would also incur child-care expenses when Dick is teaching. When their child starts kindergarten, Dick will seek a full-time high-school teaching position.

On the following pages 5-year tax, cash-flow, and net worth projections of the Johnsons' position have been run under two assumptions. The first set of projections (Case III) assumes that Dick and Jane purchase a $90,000 house in September 2003 and finance it with a mortgage of $78,000 at a fixed rate of 8.75 percent for 30 years, that Dick and Jane have their first child in early 2005, and that Jane returns to work after her maternity leave and Dick stays home with the child. Dick will be covered under Jane's health insurance.

The second set of projections (Case IV) again assumes the purchase of an $90,000 home with the same mortgage of $78,000 at the same terms. Under the second set of assumptions Dick and Jane have their first child early in 2005, and Dick stays home with the child for a period of one year. He then obtains a high-school teaching position that pays an estimated salary of $40,000 a year. He will complete his master's degree studies as a part-time night student. Upon his return to work, the assumption is that Dick and the child will continue to be covered under Jane's health plan.

[text continues on page 4.58]

CASE III
$90,000 Residence Purchased;
Dick Leaves Work

New Assumptions

1. The Johnsons will have their first child in 2005, and Dick will not return to work.

2. Dick will be covered under Jane's health insurance at a cost of $780 annually, which will increase at 8 percent annually. This is effective July 1, 2005.

Continuing Assumptions

1. The Johnsons purchase a house in September 2003 for $90,000, making a $12,000 down payment and financing the balance of $78,000 with an 8.75 percent fixed-rate mortgage with a term of 30 years.

2. Closing costs for the home purchase are 5 percent of the amount of the mortgage.

3. Property taxes on the home are $950 and increase 5 percent annually.

4. The residence increases in value at 3 percent annually.

5. Homeowners insurance will replace the existing tenant's insurance and will cost $500 a year.

6. The checking account balance is maintained at $4,500; the account is noninterest bearing.

7. Dick's and Jane's salaries are increased at 5 percent annually.

8. Money market funds earn 4 percent interest annually.

9. Investable cash earns 5.25 percent annually.

10. Expenditures for food and clothing will increase annually at 4 percent.

11. Expenditures for rent and charitable contributions will increase 5 percent annually.

12. Expenditures for utilities, telephone, entertainment, and automobile gas and repairs will increase 6 percent annually.

13. Expenditures for medical insurance and other medical care, as well as both automobile and tenant's insurance, will increase by 8 percent annually.

14. Decreases in value of furniture have been ignored.

15. Automobiles decrease in value at a rate of 15 percent annually.

16. The inflation rate for taxes is 3.5 percent annually.

INCOME STATEMENT

DICK & JANE JOHNSON

CASE III	2002	2003	2004	2005	2006
Earned Income					
Jane's Salary	35,000	36,750	38,588	40,517	42,543
Dick's Salary	30,000	31,500	33,075	0	0
	65,000	68,250	71,663	40,517	42,543
Interest/Dividends					
Money Market Fund	640	426	203	211	219
Investable Cash	594	1,433	2,454	3,515	4,112
	1,234	1,859	2,657	3,726	4,331
	========	========	========	========	========
Adj Gross Income	66,234	70,109	74,320	44,243	46,874
Deductions					
Charitable 50%	200	210	221	232	243
State Tax Paid	3,186	3,223	3,202	1,329	1,478
Residence	0	950	998	1,047	1,100
Residence	0	2,274	6,786	6,735	6,676
Gross Deductions	3,386	6,657	11,207	9,343	9,497
Standard Deduction	7,600	7,850	8,100	8,787	9,568
Allowed Deductions	7,600	7,850	11,207	9,343	9,568
Pers Exemptions	5,800	6,000	6,200	9,600	10,050
	========	========	========	========	========
Taxable Income	52,834	56,259	56,913	25,300	27,256
	========	========	========	========	========
Fed Income Tax	8,055	8,782	8,686	3,195	3,488
	========	========	========	========	========
Fed Tax Bracket-Ord Inc	27.0%	27.0%	26.0%	15.0%	15.0%

BALANCE SHEET

DICK & JANE JOHNSON

CASE III	2002	2003	2004	2005	2006
LIQUID ASSETS					
Cash Balance	4,469	4,498	4,484	4,508	4,509
Cash Deposits					
Investable Cash	23,236	32,788	63,162	74,275	86,484
Money Market Fund	16,640	5,066	5,269	5,480	5,699
	39,876	37,854	68,431	79,755	92,183
	========	========	========	========	========
Liquid Assets	44,345	42,352	72,915	84,263	96,692
	========	========	========	========	========
NONLIQUID ASSETS					
Personal Property					
Residence	0	90,000	92,700	95,481	98,345
Dick's car	3,400	2,890	2,457	2,088	1,775
Jane's car	9,095	7,731	6,571	5,585	4,748
Furniture/Fixture	14,000	14,000	14,000	14,000	14,000
	26,495	114,621	115,728	117,154	118,868
	========	========	========	========	========
Nonliquid Assets	26,495	114,621	115,728	117,154	118,867
	========	========	========	========	========
Total Assets	70,840	156,973	188,643	201,417	215,559
LIABILITIES					
Mortgage Loans					
Residence	0	77,819	77,241	76,612	75,924
	0	77,819	77,241	76,612	75,924
Notes Payable					
Jane's Student Loan	3,149	2,811	2,441	2,036	1,593
Jane's Car Loan	4,836	2,382	0	0	0
	7,985	5,193	2,441	2,036	1,593
	========	========	========	========	========
Total Liabilities	7,985	83,012	79,682	78,648	77,517
	========	========	========	========	========
Net Worth	62,855	73,961	108,961	122,769	138,042
	========	========	========	========	========

CASH FLOW STATEMENT

DICK & JANE JOHNSON

CASE III	2002	2003	2004	2005	2006
BEGINNING OF YEAR					
Idle Cash On Hand	4,500	4,469	4,498	4,484	4,508
SOURCES OF CASH					
Cash Income					
Jane's Salary	35,000	36,750	38,588	40,517	42,543
Dick's Salary	30,000	31,500	33,075	0	0
	65,000	68,250	71,663	40,517	42,543
Sale/Withdrawals					
Money Market Fund	0	12,000	0	0	0
Home Closing Costs	0	3,900	0	0	0
	0	15,900	0	0	0
Liab Incurred					
Cash Borrowed-Home	0	78,000	0	0	0
	0	78,000	0	0	0
Total Cash Inflow	65,000	162,150	71,663	40,517	42,543
Tot Cash Available	69,500	166,619	76,160	45,001	47,050
USES OF CASH					
Fully Tax Deductible					
Residence	0	2,274	6,786	6,735	6,676
	0	2,274	6,786	6,735	6,676
Partly Deductible					
Med Ins Prem - Dick	240	259	280	0	0
Med Ins Prem - Dick	0	0	0	780	842
Other Medical	1,100	1,188	1,283	1,386	1,497
Charity Contrb-50%	200	210	221	232	243
	1,540	1,657	1,783	2,397	2,582
Not Tax Deductible					
Jane's Student Loan	298	270	238	203	165
Jane's Car Loan	366	223	72	0	0
Food	4,800	4,992	5,192	5,399	5,615
Clothing	1,800	1,872	1,947	2,025	2,106
Entertainment	1,500	1,590	1,685	1,787	1,894
Auto Insurance	800	864	933	1,008	1,088
Home Insurance	0	250	500	540	583
Tenant's Insurance	250	125	0	0	0
Rent	9,600	10,080	0	0	0
Auto Gas/Oil/Repair	500	530	562	596	631
Utility/Phone	2,100	2,226	2,360	2,501	2,651
	22,014	23,022	13,488	14,058	14,734

CASH FLOW STATEMENT (cont.)

DICK & JANE JOHNSON

CASE III	2002	2003	2004	2005	2006
Taxes Paid					
Fed Tax Paid	8,055	8,782	8,686	3,195	3,488
State Tax Paid	3,186	3,223	3,202	1,329	1,478
FICA/Soc Sec Tax	4,973	5,221	5,482	3,100	3,255
Residence	0	950	998	1,047	1,100
	16,214	18,176	18,368	8,671	9,321
Purchase/Deposits					
Home Down Payment	0	12,000	0	0	0
Home Closing Costs	0	3,900	0	0	0
Purchases Made-Home	0	90,000	0	0	0
Investable Cash	22,642	8,119	27,920	7,598	8,097
	22,642	114,019	27,920	7,598	8,097
Liability Liquidation					
Jane's Student Loan	310	338	370	405	443
Residence	0	181	578	629	688
Jane's Car Loan	2,311	2,454	2,382	0	0
	2,621	2,973	3,330	1,034	1,131
	========	========	========	========	========
Tot Cash Outflow	65,031	162,121	71,676	40,494	42,541
	========	========	========	========	========
END OF YEAR					
Cash Balance	4,469	4,498	4,484	4,508	4,509
	========	========	========	========	========

SUPPORTING SCHEDULE

DICK & JANE JOHNSON

CASE III	JOINT 2002	JOINT 2003	JOINT 2004	JOINT 2005	JOINT 2006
Income					
Earned Income	65,000	68,250	71,663	40,517	42,543
Adj Gross Income	66,234	70,109	74,320	44,243	46,874
Allowed Deductions	7,600	7,850	11,207	9,343	9,568
Pers Exemptions	5,800	6,000	6,200	9,600	10,050
Taxable Income	52,834	56,259	56,913	25,300	27,256
Federal Tax Liab					
Regular Tax	8,053	8,786	8,690	3,199	3,491
Gross Fed Inc Tax	8,055	8,782	8,686	3,195	3,488
Fed Income Tax	8,055	8,782	8,686	3,195	3,488
Fed Tax Analysis-Ord Inc					
Indexing Factor	79	85	92	98	105
Fed Tax Bracket-Ord Inc	27.0%	27.0%	26.0%	15.0%	15.0%
$ to Next Bracket	60,216	60,741	64,187	30,500	32,771
Next Bracket	30.0%	30.0%	29.0%	26.0%	25.0%
Previous Bracket	15.0%	15.0%	15.0%	10.0%	10.0%
$ to Prev Bracket	6,084	7,859	6,813	13,300	15,256
Fed Effective Tax Rate	15.3%	15.6%	15.3%	12.6%	12.8%
Alt Minimum Tax					
Adj Gross Income	66,234	70,109	74,320	44,243	46,874
Contributions	-200	-210	-221	-232	-243
Residence	0	-2,274	-6,786	-6,735	-6,676
Adjusted AMTI	66,034	67,625	67,313	37,276	39,955
AMT Exemptions	-49,000	-49,000	-49,000	-45,000	-45,000
AMT Taxable Inc	17,034	18,625	18,313	0	0
Gross Alt Min Tx	4,429	4,843	4,761	0	0
Fed Tax Less FTC	-8,055	-8,782	-8,686	-3,195	-3,488
Other Tax Liabs					
FICA/Soc Sec Tax	4,973	5,221	5,482	3,100	3,255
Adj Gross Inc	66,234	70,109	74,320	44,243	46,874
GA Adj Gross Inc	66,234	70,109	74,320	44,243	46,874
GA Standard Ded	3,000	3,000	3,000	3,000	3,000
GA Itemized Ded	3,386	6,657	11,207	9,343	9,497
GA Exemptions	5,400	5,400	5,400	8,400	8,400
GA Taxable Inc	57,448	58,052	57,713	26,500	28,977
GA Regular Tax	3,186	3,223	3,202	1,329	1,478
GA Income Tax	3,186	3,223	3,202	1,329	1,478
Georgia Tax	3,186	3,223	3,202	1,329	1,478
Tot State/Local Tx	3,186	3,223	3,202	1,329	1,478
Total Inc Tax	16,214	17,226	17,370	7,624	8,221

FINANCIAL SUMMARY

DICK & JANE JOHNSON

CASE III	2002	2003	2004	2005	2006
Gross Real Income					
Personal Earnings	65,000	68,250	71,663	40,517	42,543
Interest Income	1,234	1,859	2,657	3,726	4,331
	66,234	70,109	74,320	44,243	46,874
Income & Inflation					
Gross Real Inc	66,234	70,109	74,320	44,243	46,874
Total Inc Tax	-16,214	-17,226	-17,370	-7,624	-8,221
Net Real Income	50,020	52,883	56,949	36,619	38,652
Cur Real Inc =	50,020	51,771	53,582	55,458	57,399
Purch Power Drop	0	0	0	18,839	18,747
At Infltn Rate of	4	4	4	4	4
Cash Flow					
Idle Cash On Hand	4,500	4,469	4,498	4,484	4,508
Norml Cash Inflow	65,000	162,150	71,663	40,517	42,543
Norml Cash Outflw	42,389	154,002	43,756	32,896	34,444
Cash Invested	22,642	8,119	27,920	7,598	8,097
Cash Balance	4,469	4,498	4,484	4,508	4,509
Net Worth					
Personal Assets	30,964	119,118	120,212	121,662	123,377
Investment Assets	39,876	37,854	68,431	79,755	92,183
Personal Liabilities	-7,985	-83,012	-79,682	-78,648	-77,517
Personal Net Worth	22,979	36,106	40,530	43,014	45,860
Investment Net Worth	39,876	37,854	68,431	79,755	92,183
Net Worth	62,855	73,961	108,961	122,769	138,042

CASE IV
$90,000 Residence Purchased;
Dick Leaves Work When Child Is Born
and Returns to Work the Following Year

New Assumptions

1. The Johnsons will have their first child in 2005, and Dick will not work in 2005 but will return to work in 2006.

2. In 2006 the Johnsons will incur $150 per week in child-care expenses.

3. Dick and the child will continue to be covered under Jane's health insurance.

Continuing Assumptions

1. The Johnsons purchase a house in September 2003 for $90,000, making a $12,000 down payment and financing the balance of $78,000 with an 8.75 percent fixed-rate mortgage with a term of 30 years.

2. Closing costs for the home purchase are 5 percent of the amount of the mortgage.

3. Property taxes on the home are $950 and increase 5 percent annually.

4. The residence increases in value at 3 percent annually.

5. Homeowners insurance will replace the existing tenant's insurance and will cost $500 a year.

6. The checking account balance is maintained at $4,500; the account is noninterest bearing.

7. Dick's and Jane's salaries are increased at 5 percent annually.

8. Money market funds earn 4 percent interest annually.

9. Investable cash earns 5.25 percent annually.

10. Expenditures for food and clothing will increase annually at 4 percent.

11. Expenditures for rent and charitable contributions will increase 5 percent annually.

12. Expenditures for utilities, telephone, entertainment, and automobile gas and repairs will increase 6 percent annually.

13. Expenditures for medical insurance and other medical care, as well as both automobile and tenant's insurance, will increase by 8 percent annually.

14. Decreases in value of furniture have been ignored.

15. Automobiles decrease in value at a rate of 15 percent annually.

16. The inflation rate for taxes is 3.5 percent annually.

INCOME STATEMENT

DICK & JANE JOHNSON

CASE IV **Earned Income**	2002	2003	2004	2005	2006
Jane's Salary	35,000	36,750	38,588	40,517	42,543
Dick's Salary	30,000	31,500	33,075	0	40,000
	65,000	68,250	71,663	40,517	82,543
Interest/Dividends					
Money Market Fund	640	426	203	211	219
Investable Cash	594	1,433	2,454	3,499	4,618
	1,234	1,859	2,657	3,710	4,837
	========	========	========	========	========
Adj Gross Income	66,234	70,109	74,320	44,227	87,380
Deductions					
Charitable 50%	200	210	221	232	243
State Tax Paid	3,186	3,223	3,202	1,498	3,941
Property Taxes	0	950	998	1,047	1,100
Home Mortgage	0	2,274	6,786	6,735	6,676
Gross Deductions	3,386	6,657	11,207	9,512	11,960
Standard Deduction	7,600	7,850	8,100	8,787	9,568
Allowed Deductions	7,600	7,850	11,207	9,512	11,960
Pers Exemptions	5,800	6,000	6,200	6,400	6,700
	========	========	========	========	========
Taxable Income	52,834	56,259	56,913	28,315	68,720
	========	========	========	========	========
Fed Income Tax	8,055	8,782	8,686	3,647	9,621
	========	========	========	========	========
Fed Tax Bracket-Ord Inc	27.0%	27.0%	26.0%	15.0%	25.0%

BALANCE SHEET

DICK & JANE JOHNSON

CASE IV	2002	2003	2004	2005	2006
LIQUID ASSETS					
Cash Balance	4,469	4,498	4,484	4,510	4,499
Cash Deposits					
Investable Cash	23,236	32,788	63,162	73,636	106,908
Money Market Fund	16,640	5,066	5,269	5,480	5,699
	39,876	37,854	68,431	79,116	112,607
	========	========	========	========	========
Liquid Assets	44,345	42,352	72,915	83,626	117,106
	========	========	========	========	========
NONLIQUID ASSETS					
Personal Property					
Residence	0	90,000	92,700	95,481	98,345
Dick's car	3,400	2,890	2,457	2,088	1,775
Jane's car	9,095	7,731	6,571	5,585	4,748
Furniture/Fixture	14,000	14,000	14,000	14,000	14,000
	26,495	114,621	115,728	117,154	118,868
	========	========	========	========	========
Nonliquid Assets	26,495	114,621	115,728	117,154	118,867
	========	========	========	========	========
Total Assets	70,840	156,973	188,643	200,780	235,973
LIABILITIES					
Mortgage Loans					
Home Mortgage	0	77,819	77,241	76,612	75,924
	0	77,819	77,241	76,612	75,924
Notes Payable					
Jane's Student Loan	3,149	2,811	2,441	2,036	1,593
Jane's Car Loan	4,836	2,382	0	0	0
	7,985	5,193	2,441	2,036	1,593
	========	========	========	========	========
Total Liabilities	7,985	83,012	79,682	78,648	77,517
	========	========	========	========	========
Net Worth	62,855	73,961	108,961	122,132	158,456
	========	========	========	========	========

CASH FLOW STATEMENT

DICK & JANE JOHNSON

CASE IV	2002	2003	2004	2005	2006
BEGINNING OF YEAR					
Idle Cash On Hand	4,500	4,469	4,498	4,484	4,510
SOURCES OF CASH					
Cash Income					
Jane's Salary	35,000	36,750	38,588	40,517	42,543
Dick's Salary	30,000	31,500	33,075	0	40,000
	65,000	68,250	71,663	40,517	82,543
Sale/Withdrawals					
Money Market Fund	0	12,000	0	0	0
Home Closing Costs	0	3,900	0	0	0
	0	15,900	0	0	0
Liab Incurred					
Cash Borrowed-Home	0	78,000	0	0	0
	0	78,000	0	0	0
	========	========	========	========	========
Total Cash Inflow	65,000	162,150	71,663	40,517	82,543
	========	========	========	========	========
Tot Cash Available	69,500	166,619	76,160	45,001	87,052
	========	========	========	========	========
USES OF CASH					
Fully Tax Deductible					
Home Mortgage	0	2,274	6,786	6,735	6,676
	0	2,274	6,786	6,735	6,676
Partly Deductible					
Med Ins Prem - Dick	240	259	280	0	0
Med Ins Prem - Dick	0	0	0	780	842
Other Medical	1,100	1,188	1,283	1,386	1,497
Charity Contrb-50%	200	210	221	232	243
	1,540	1,657	1,783	2,397	2,582
Not Tax Deductible					
Jane's Student Loan	298	270	238	203	165
Jane's Car Loan	366	223	72	0	0
Food	4,800	4,992	5,192	5,399	5,615
Clothing	1,800	1,872	1,947	2,025	2,106
Entertainment	1,500	1,590	1,685	1,787	1,894
Auto Insurance	800	864	933	1,008	1,088
Tenant's Insurance	250	125	0	0	0
Home Insurance	0	250	500	540	583
Rent	9,600	10,080	0	0	0
Auto Gas/Oil/Repair	500	530	562	596	631
Utility/Phone	2,100	2,226	2,360	2,501	2,651
Child Care Expenses	0	0	0	0	7,800
	22,014	23,022	13,488	14,058	22,534

CASH FLOW STATEMENT (cont.)

DICK & JANE JOHNSON

CASE IV	2002	2003	2004	2005	2006
Taxes Paid					
Fed Tax Paid	8,055	8,782	8,686	3,647	9,621
State Tax Paid	3,186	3,223	3,202	1,498	3,941
FICA/Soc Sec Tax	4,973	5,221	5,482	3,100	6,315
Property Taxes	0	950	998	1,047	1,100
	16,214	18,176	18,368	9,292	20,976
Purchase/Deposits					
Home Down Payment	0	12,000	0	0	0
Home Closing Costs	0	3,900	0	0	0
Purchases Made-Home	0	90,000	0	0	0
Investable Cash	22,642	8,119	27,920	6,975	28,654
	22,642	114,019	27,920	6,975	28,654
Liability Liquidation					
Jane's Student Loan	310	338	370	405	443
Home Mortgage	0	181	578	629	688
Jane's Car Loan	2,311	2,454	2,382	0	0
	2,621	2,973	3,330	1,034	1,131
	========	========	========	========	========
Tot Cash Outflow	65,031	162,121	71,676	40,492	82,553
	========	========	========	========	========
END OF YEAR					
Cash Balance	4,469	4,498	4,484	4,510	4,499
	========	========	========	========	========

SUPPORTING SCHEDULE

DICK & JANE JOHNSON

CASE IV	JOINT 2002	JOINT 2003	JOINT 2004	JOINT 2005	JOINT 2006
Income					
Earned Income	65,000	68,250	71,663	40,517	82,543
Adj Gross Income	66,234	70,109	74,320	44,227	87,380
Allowed Deductions	7,600	7,850	11,207	9,512	11,960
Pers Exemptions	5,800	6,000	6,200	6,400	6,700
Taxable Income	52,834	56,259	56,913	28,315	68,720
Federal Tax Liab					
Regular Tax	8,053	8,786	8,690	3,649	9,622
Gross Fed Inc Tax	8,055	8,782	8,686	3,647	9,621
Fed Income Tax	8,055	8,782	8,686	3,647	9,621
Fed Tax Analysis-Ord Inc					
Indexing Factor	79	85	92	98	105
Fed Tax Bracket-Ord Inc	27.0%	27.0%	26.0%	15.0%	25.0%
$ to Next Bracket	60,216	60,741	64,187	27,486	61,030
Next Bracket	30.0%	30.0%	29.0%	26.0%	28.0%
Previous Bracket	15.0%	15.0%	15.0%	10.0%	15.0%
$ to Prev Bracket	6,084	7,859	6,813	16,314	8,693
Fed Effective Tax Rate	15.3%	15.6%	15.3%	12.9%	14.0%
Alt Minimum Tax					
Adj Gross Income	66,234	70,109	74,320	44,227	87,380
Contributions	-200	-210	-221	-232	-243
Home Mortgage	0	-2,274	-6,786	-6,735	-6,676
Adjusted AMTI	66,034	67,625	67,313	37,260	80,461
AMT Exemptions	-49,000	-49,000	-49,000	-45,000	-45,000
AMT Taxable Inc	17,034	18,625	18,313	0	35,461
Gross Alt Min Tx	4,429	4,843	4,761	0	9,220
Fed Tax Less FTC	-8,055	-8,782	-8,686	-3,647	-9,621
Other Tax Liabs					
FICA/Soc Sec Tax	4,973	5,221	5,482	3,100	6,315
Adj Gross Inc	66,234	70,109	74,320	44,227	87,380
GA Adj Gross Inc	66,234	70,109	74,320	44,227	87,380
GA Standard Ded	3,000	3,000	3,000	3,000	3,000
GA Itemized Ded	3,386	6,657	11,207	9,512	11,960
GA Exemptions	5,400	5,400	5,400	5,400	5,400
GA Taxable Inc	57,448	58,052	57,713	29,315	70,020
GA Regular Tax	3,186	3,223	3,202	1,498	3,941
GA Income Tax	3,186	3,223	3,202	1,498	3,941
Georgia Tax	3,186	3,223	3,202	1,498	3,941
Tot State/Local Tx	3,186	3,223	3,202	1,498	3,941
Total Inc Tax	16,214	17,226	17,370	8,245	19,877

FINANCIAL SUMMARY

DICK & JANE JOHNSON

CASE IV	2002	2003	2004	2005	2006
Gross Real Income					
Personal Earnings	65,000	68,250	71,663	40,517	82,543
Interest Income	1,234	1,859	2,657	3,710	4,837
	66,234	70,109	74,320	44,227	87,380
Income & Inflation					
Gross Real Inc	66,234	70,109	74,320	44,227	87,380
Total Inc Tax	-16,214	-17,226	-17,370	-8,245	-19,877
Net Real Income	50,020	52,883	56,949	35,982	67,503
Cur Real Inc =	50,020	51,771	53,582	55,458	57,399
Purch Power Drop	0	0	0	19,476	0
At Infltn Rate of	4	4	4	4	4
Cash Flow					
Idle Cash On Hand	4,500	4,469	4,498	4,484	4,510
Norml Cash Inflow	65,000	162,150	71,663	40,517	82,543
Norml Cash Outflw	42,389	154,002	43,756	33,517	53,899
Cash Invested	22,642	8,119	27,920	6,975	28,654
Cash Balance	4,469	4,498	4,484	4,510	4,499
Net Worth					
Personal Assets	30,964	119,118	120,212	121,664	123,367
Investment Assets	39,876	37,854	68,431	79,116	112,607
Personal Liabilities	-7,985	-83,012	-79,682	-78,648	-77,517
Personal Net Worth	22,979	36,106	40,530	43,016	45,850
Investment Net Worth	39,876	37,854	68,431	79,116	112,607
Net Worth	62,855	73,961	108,961	122,132	158,456

Since their expenses will be roughly equivalent whether the Johnsons elect to either purchase a residence or remain tenants, it will be difficult for Dick to stop working entirely and stay home with their child or children. It does seem manageable, however, that even with the purchase of the residence he could stay home for the first year of the child's life and return to work thereafter. It might be possible that such a pattern could be established for each of their children, allowing Dick to stay home with the children when they are very young and then return to work as they reach the age when they would be more comfortable with a day-care situation. Another alternative would be permanent part-time employment.

These plans are based on Jane's remaining at the assistant manager level with the hotel chain. Should a promotion occur, either to manager of one of the smaller hotels or to assistant manager of one of the larger hotels in the chain, these additional responsibilities will result in an increase in her salary. Should either of these possibilities occur, a revision of Dick and Jane's plans will be essential.

Estate Planning

Neither of the Johnsons has ever made a formal estate plan nor has either executed a valid will. As a result, if either dies, most of his or her property will pass under the statutory scheme for intestate succession. Under the local law of Georgia the surviving spouse of a couple with no children will take all the property as the heir-at-law. However, if the decedent had children, the surviving spouse generally takes a child's portion, but a surviving wife takes no less than one-fifth of the estate, regardless of the number of children. This rule applies regardless of whether the child is a minor or legally an adult. If either Dick or Jane died before executing a valid will but after the birth of their first child, intestate succession could result in a minor child or children taking an interest in property as well. Needless to say, this can be problematic and should be avoided. The failure to make a will also makes it impossible to leave property to friends or even family members who are outside the statutory scheme of intestate distribution. The Johnsons' present estate plan is inadequate in that it attempts to allow beneficiary designations and settlement options to substitute for appropriate estate planning documents such as wills. In addition, it utilizes the state's estate plan, intestate distribution, rather than a plan reflecting the Johnsons' wishes. Such a plan inherently lacks the flexibility that proper estate planning documents can provide.

The Johnsons do not need a complicated estate plan at this time. Although they do not have enough assets to be concerned with federal estate taxes, each should execute a will that clearly states his or her wishes with regard to their property. This type of estate plan is very feasible in Georgia because it is an estate tax state based on the federal credit for state death taxes, and the emphasis on avoiding probate is much less important than in estate or inheritance tax states that impose these taxes only on probate property. This may simply mean that each leaves his or her property to the other, or that the bulk of property is left to the surviving spouse, but that certain items, such as family heirlooms or collectibles, are returned to a member of that particular family.

At present an estate plan in which both Dick and Jane have wills leaving the property each owns to the other would be sufficient for their needs. Each will should convey the testator's interest in his or her principal residence owned at the time of death to the surviving spouse, subject to the indebtedness secured thereby. This provision makes it clear that estate assets need not be unnecessarily depleted by paying off the entire mortgage indebtedness. Although it is recommended that the Johnsons take title to the home as joint tenants, this provision can still be included as a safeguard in the event of a different titling arrangement.

The Johnsons should make the bequests of their property to a spouse conditional on the survival of the spouse and provide that in the event the spouse fails to survive, the property will go into a trust for their living children, if any. If there are no living children and no surviving spouse, Dick and Jane may want to designate members of their families as ultimate beneficiaries under their wills.

One note of caution: a valid will is automatically revoked in Georgia by the marriage or divorce of the testator or by the birth of a child that is not contemplated by the will, so the will should state that the term *children* is intended to include after-born children, to avoid an unintended revocation when a child is born.

In addition, the Johnsons' wills should name a guardian for the child(ren). Either one of their siblings or parents on whom they can agree could be appropriate. In addition, a trustee or guardian of the property left to each child needs to be identified.

As additional life insurance is acquired, consideration should be given to having a life insurance trust own the policies and be designated as the beneficiary. This method can provide flexibility in the distribution scheme as well as professional management for the assets.

PERSONAL PLANNING: INSURANCE

Disability Income Insurance

Since it appears that both Dick and Jane must continue to work to support their present lifestyle, an analysis of the disability insurance available to both of them through their employer plans indicates that there could be a material problem even though Jane has relatively generous benefits under a long-term disability plan.

In Jane's case short-term disability does not seem to be a problem as her salary would be continued in full for the first 4 months of any disability but would drop after 4 months to 50 percent of her salary for 60 days (unless she had completed 6 years of employment, in which case her salary would be continued in full for 6 months). The long-term disability plan would then begin to pay benefits, which are equal to 60 percent of her salary reduced by her primary disability benefit under Social Security, if applicable. Under the definition of disability provided in the description of Jane's long-term disability plan, it is not necessary that she qualify for a Social Security disability benefit in order to collect from her disability insurance plan. Nonetheless, full disability benefits under Jane's plan would result in a 40 percent reduction in her gross income, which could adversely affect the family's lifestyle.

Unfortunately many disability income insurers will not provide additional coverage when existing benefits are in excess of approximately 70 percent of current salary. Jane should be aware, however, that a good disability income plan is crucial to her family, particularly in view of Dick's mother's problems with allergies, which tend to be familial, although not necessarily hereditary. If she should wish to change employment, she should carefully review both the dollar amounts and the definition of disability in her prospective employer's plan. If the plan is materially less generous than the one under which she is presently covered, she should investigate the cost of supplementing the plan by the purchase of an individual policy of disability income protection.

While Dick remains employed, his benefits, on the other hand, are extremely limited. At best if Dick were to become seriously ill and had accumulated the maximum unused sick days permitted under his plan, he would have his salary continued for only about 3 months.

It is recommended that the Johnsons look into the cost-effectiveness of personal disability income insurance for Dick, especially when they purchase a residence or start a family. The personal disability insurance should have at least a 90-day elimination period so it will not be prohibitively expensive.

Medical Insurance

As indicated, Jane has a good comprehensive major medical insurance plan through her employer. Dick, on the other hand, has a much less liberal plan. Because it is possible for Dick to be covered as a dependent under Jane's insurance plan for a cost of $65 monthly ($45 more than the amount he is already paying), it is probably appropriate that Dick withdraw from participation in his group medical insurance plan and that Dick and Jane elect to cover him under her plan, which would provide him with additional benefits such as dental insurance, which he does not have under his present plan. He would also have unlimited lifetime medical benefits that are subject to a $100 calendar-year deductible as opposed to the $200-a-year deductible that he must now satisfy. In the case of a serious injury or illness, the fact that Jane's plan contains a stop-loss limit of $2,000 for any calendar year would be very important. A change to participation under Jane's plan should certainly be implemented no later than the time the Johnsons plan to begin their family. Also, they will need dependent coverage when their first child is born.

Life Insurance

Jane's employer presently provides her with group term life insurance in the amount of $87,500 (2 1/2 times her annual salary). Dick's employer provides him with group term life insurance in a flat amount of $10,000. Jane has named her estate the beneficiary of her group term life insurance, and Dick has named Jane the beneficiary of his group term life. It may be preferable for Jane to name Dick as the beneficiary of her group life insurance. Since the Johnsons' lifestyle depends on both their earnings, the life insurance amounts they presently have appear inadequate. This will be especially true if the Johnsons go ahead with the purchase of a home and begin a family. The precise amounts of additional insurance necessary will depend on whether the Johnsons wish to replace Dick's or Jane's earnings from the income on life insurance proceeds should either die prematurely, or whether they agree that the survivor should plan to invade the principal amount of such proceeds. Perhaps the most conservative approach would be to ensure that enough life insurance protection is available so that either option is possible in the case of an untimely death of either breadwinner. In that event the total amount of death benefits necessary to replace Jane's salary, assuming an 8 percent return if the proceeds were invested, would be approximately $437,500. Of that amount Jane's employer already provides insurance of $87,500. Since the amount of insurance through Jane's group term life plan will increase as her salary increases, the additional amount of insurance necessary to assure total replacement of her salary at an 8 percent rate of earnings on the proceeds is approximately $350,000.

Dick's employer provides only $10,000 of group term insurance. Based on our facts, this amount will not increase during the term of his employment. In order to assure that Dick's salary will be replaced if the proceeds of life insurance are invested at an earning rate of 8 percent, Dick will need additional insurance in an amount of approximately $365,000.

It would be our recommendation that these amounts of insurance be applied for, obtained, and carried at least for the foreseeable future, as there are few other assets to provide income in the event of the untimely death of either spouse.

If the Johnsons had exhibited any difficulty in disciplining themselves to save toward the cash reserves of 3 to 6 months' discretionary income necessary for an emergency fund, consideration could have been given to one of the interest-sensitive whole life policies that are available. While these policies do have higher premiums, these premium levels will create cash values within the policies that are available for use as emergency funds through policy loans. If they had exhibited a present need for premium flexibility, consideration of universal life (which offers both premium flexibility and the option to withdraw part of the cash value outright without the necessity for any loan or interest implications) would also have been appropriate.

The Johnsons, however, do not appear to have these problems or needs at this time. The type of insurance that best meets their current needs appears to be available in the form of a guaranteed annual renewable convertible term product. Because of their youth the cost of this coverage would be nominal and would allow them to continue to save personally for their emergency fund and to invest for funding other personal objectives.

Of course, the insurance needs of any client should be routinely and periodically reevaluated to assure that appropriate amounts and types of insurance are being carried.

Property and Liability Insurance

The facts indicate that the Johnsons are carrying property and liability insurance on their apartment furnishings. When a residence is purchased, the lending institution will normally require that the building be insured for damage arising from fire and probably other perils. Such protection can be combined with protection against loss or damage to the contents of the house and with liability coverage by utilizing a homeowners policy. Many types of special endorsements can be obtained for such policies and may be necessary if there are significant amounts of jewelry, furs, art, or other collectibles. However, our facts do not indicate that the Johnsons need such endorsements at present. If they are needed later, they can be added to the existing policy.

The Johnsons should, however, choose a liability limit that will adequately protect them. It would be difficult to recommend a liability limit of under $100,000, and the Johnsons should consider a limit as high as $300,000 to assure that they could withstand a high jury award in the event that they were sued.

Furthermore, the Johnsons might prefer to have greater liability protection than is provided by their auto and homeowner's policies. A $1 million umbrella policy with a deductible equal to the upper limit of their existing liability coverage could offer sufficient peace of mind for its relatively small cost.

PERSONAL PLANNING: INVESTMENT

Purchasing a Home

Without question the Johnsons' most important immediate investment will be the purchase of a home. As already indicated, that purchase should provide not only personal satisfaction but also a good return on their money should they decide to sell. In addition, if they live in their principal residence for 2 out of the 5 years prior to sale, the first $500,000 of gain is excluded from income tax.

For all these reasons the purchase of a house is one of the best investments that Dick and Jane can make at this time.

Emergency Fund

The Johnsons should also be aware that most investment advisers recommend that clients maintain a relatively liquid emergency fund ranging from 3 to 6 months of disposable income (gross income less taxes). Since the Johnsons presently have few other financial assets, they should attempt to keep their emergency fund at the high end of the range (at or near 6 months' disposable income). Moreover, given the purpose of this money, it should be retained in liquid investments that provide some annual income, although safety and virtually immediate access to the money have greater priority than does income. Their money market mutual fund (MMMF) meets these criteria. However, some of the investable cash funds could be used to purchase six separate $1,000 CDs with one maturing in 30 days, one in 60 days, and so on, with the sixth CD maturing in 180 days. When the first 30-day CD matures, it can then be rolled over into a 180-day CD. The same procedure can then be followed to convert each CD to a 180-day maturity schedule. Once the initial CDs have been rolled over, a continuous 6-month period rollover can be followed. This will provide the Johnsons with $1,000 cash available monthly and without penalty for emergency purposes, in addition to the ready access of the remainder of their emergency fund in the money market mutual fund. Because of its lack of full liquidity without penalty before maturity, the yield on the CDs could be one-fourth of one percent higher than the money market mutual fund. More important, the Johnsons will establish a relationship with a bank beyond their current checking account that can provide access to other financial services the depository institution offers. This relationship could be beneficial to their total financial planning.

Investable Funds

Except for the planned purchase of a home the Johnsons have not yet developed any plans covering objectives to be satisfied through capital accumulation. An analysis of the projections in the base case shows the Johnsons will have a total of well over $140,000 of investable savings within 5 years, and establishing some plans for the eventual investing of this money is important. If they do purchase a home and have their first child in 2005, this amount will be less, yet the sooner they begin learning about and implementing a plan of investing, the more long-term financial success they will enjoy.

CLIENT CHARACTERISTICS

As a guide to their investment planning the Johnsons must first recognize their own personal and financial situation. Elements to analyze for this activity include the following:

- *Level and stability of their income.* For a young married couple who are both employed, their family income level is above the national average. Both are employed in fields for which a strong demand exists in the economy. Neither has earnings from employment that would be subject to fluctuations because of being on a commission system. Based on these considerations, the Johnsons' income position permits consideration of investing for long-term capital appreciation.

- *Family situation.* Since they have no family responsibilities other than to themselves, this opportunity to begin building for their financial future should not be overlooked. If and when any children become part of their responsibilities, a revision of any currently developed accumulation plans will be necessary.

- *Net worth.* Although net worth is modest at this time, the projections clearly indicate growth over the next few years as a result of the annual saving from their income flows. These annual increments, virtually all in the form of cash, require effective investment planning.

- *Age.* The Johnsons' age, as well as their current level of income, favors an investment strategy focusing on capital appreciation. As a general rule or guide, younger investors should position their investment assets in those media characterized by higher degrees of risk for several reasons. First, they are more optimistic about both the future and their own individual prospects than are older individuals. Second, the opportunity to recoup losses, should that happen, exists due to the longer time period remaining before withdrawal from active employment. Third, over any period of time inflation erodes the buying power of dollars invested unless the return on investments exceeds the inflation rate. These needed higher returns are associated with higher-risk investments. As long as the accumulation objective sought does not require a specific sum of money within a short period of time, as is the situation with Dick and Jane, the desirability of investments with long-term appreciation and correspondingly higher risk seems appropriate.

- *Experience.* Based on the facts of this case Dick and Jane have no investment experience. Lacking any experience in investment management and/or analysis, they must initially limit their investment activities to those media not requiring constant monitoring, care, and on-the-spot decision making.

- *Attitudes toward risk.* Dick and Jane stated that they are risk averse at this time. For this reason any recommendations for use of their investable cash flow must be relatively conservative in nature.

The Johnsons' current personal and financial situation indicates that they are young, have no financial responsibilities, have a good, stable income from employment, and are rapidly increasing their net worth. These are all factors that, when used as a prelude to making any investment recommendations, suggest investments focusing on long-term appreciation with some degree of risk. On the other hand, their lack of experience and their risk propensities suggest a more conservative approach.

RECOMMENDATIONS

The real growth in their investable income will occur 2 or 3 years from now. These next 2 or 3 years should be a time when the Johnsons obtain some experience with modest investment activities and reexamine their risk tolerances and investment objectives.

The Johnsons should embark on a relatively conservative investment strategy. Using mutual funds enables them to achieve diversification of their portfolio to minimize business and financial risks, obtain professional management, and provide the convenience of either adding to or liquidating their holdings. The liquidation aspect is important should they be unable to live with the risk of fluctuating values of the portfolio. To achieve a relatively conservative portfolio and still provide some growth potential, they could place their investable cash flow in a family of funds divided as follows:

- *50 percent into a balanced fund.* These funds spread their portfolio among bonds, common stocks, and preferred stocks. The objectives of balanced funds, in order of priority, are to preserve capital, to generate current income, and to obtain capital gains. Hence they are the most conservative of all funds that invest in common stocks. Their performance over the last 10 years suggests a compound annual return of approximately 10 percent. These funds are of two types. The first invests about 70 percent in common stocks, with the remainder in bonds. The second type reverses the allocation and has about 30 percent in common stock.

- *40 percent in an index fund.* These funds own a portfolio that replicates a broad-based market index, such as the Standard & Poor's 500. Although this type of fund has more risk than the balanced fund described above, its risk equals that of the market, and its return exceeds that of the balanced fund. The compound annual return, based on the past 10 years' data, is around 12 percent.

- *10 percent in a growth common stock fund.* This could have the greatest risk to the Johnsons since these funds are more aggressive, having a primary objective of growth, and invest in companies that continually reinvest their earnings in research and development. The stocks held in their portfolios will have minimum dividend income. The compound annual returns over the last 10 years for a typical fund, although not the most aggressive, are about 14 percent.

The experience with this modest and conservative investment plan will provide the Johnsons with the opportunity to assess their risk propensity, gain more personal knowledge of investments, and finally earn a return higher than they are currently earning on their disposable cash.

5

Planning for the Self-Employed Professional

Chapter Outline

Some professionals, such as physicians, dentists, and attorneys, earn relatively high incomes. However, because of the demands of their practices they often lack the time to inform themselves fully of the merits and problems of various financial planning techniques and are consequently somewhat unsophisticated in financial matters. As a result this type of client is often accumulating disposable income for investment or the achievement of personal objectives at a slower rate than he or she believes is desirable.

In addition, as high-income earners, professionals are likely to be on every sort of solicitation, mailing, and prospect list. Consequently professionals have been barraged with solicitations to purchase a large number of services and products, each of which has been touted as the answer to many problems. Frequently professionals have made such purchases, usually with mixed results. Because of the demands on their time that limit the opportunity to compare the advantages and disadvantages of various products or to consult with several service or product providers, the services and products professionals have purchased are likely to be poorly coordinated.

Consequently professionals may be wary about becoming involved in the financial planning process. However, once they are convinced that comprehensive financial planning can save them substantial amounts in taxes and in the cost of other services and products and can materially decrease the amount of time spent evaluating and coordinating services and products, and once they are convinced that the comprehensive financial planner is credible as a client-oriented deliverer of services and product recommendations, professionals usually engage in the planning process enthusiastically. Because professionals are already accustomed to making major decisions, they can be very satisfying clients to work with when they are presented with appropriate information about alternative solutions and asked to adopt a planner's particular recommendations. However, since the professional's time is limited, he or she should be kept adequately involved and informed throughout the planning process without being taken away from professional and personal obligations any more than is absolutely necessary.

For all these reasons planning for the professional is a highly specialized field. Many financial planning firms choose to do planning exclusively for professionals.

CASE NARRATIVE

Personal Information

Dave Anderson, aged 41, is an orthopedic surgeon. His wife, Diana, is 39. They have been married for 16 years. Diana is a registered nurse and was working as an emergency room nurse when they met. Diana enjoyed her career and continued to work until shortly before their first child, Keith, was born 10 years ago. She has not worked outside her home since that time and has no immediate plans to return to her career. She does not know whether she would like to resume nursing if she did return to work. Dave and Diana have two other children, Deidre, 9, and Melissa, 6, and have just discovered that they will have another child in about 7 months. Although they are somewhat concerned about Diana's health and the health of the child, they consider this development a happy surprise.

Dave and Diana own their home, which had an approximate fair market value of $315,000 at the end of 2001. When they purchased the house in March 1988, it cost $79,000. Of that sum they paid $16,000 in cash and financed the balance of $63,000 at 12 percent for 30 years. Property taxes on the house are $1,900 per year. Dave holds title to the house in his name alone.

They plan to take one major trip at least every third year and estimate that such travel will cost $8,000 in today's dollars. In off years family vacations are estimated to cost approximately $4,000 in today's dollars. The Andersons give about $3,000 annually to various charities, and Dave also gives $1,500 to his medical school every year for its endowment fund.

The older Anderson children have done very well in school. Although Melissa is just midway through first grade, it looks as if she will also do well. None of the children appear to have any handicaps or problems that would necessitate expensive special schooling. In fact, they are quite bright. Since the children appear gifted, the Andersons ask that you project the cost of education through the undergraduate level at a higher-quality educational institution. It is too early to tell about postgraduate or professional schools for the Anderson children, but Dave and Diana would like them to be able to pursue their education as far as they wish. Presently the children attend public schools, but there is some interest in transferring them to a private school with more rigorous academic requirements as they enter high school. At present tuition and other expenses for an appropriate private school are approximately $5,000 per year per child.

Dave and Diana do not have a luxurious lifestyle. They enjoy travel and have tastefully furnished parts of their home with antiques, most of which Diana has discovered on what she calls her "treasure hunts." They do not collect museum-quality antiques because of their attitude that it is more important for them to have a comfortable home than to have a lot of material things that have to be protected from the children and their two Shetland sheepdogs. However, they have acquired a number of very fine old pieces at nominal prices due in large part to Diana's willingness to learn about antique furniture, paintings, and other accessories. Dave and Diana do not view their household furnishings as investment vehicles, whatever their value. They enjoy living with them and are not concerned about whether a particular piece is appreciating in value. They believe their furnishings are worth approximately $50,000.

In truth, Diana is much more interested in furnishing the house than is Dave, who requires only that it be comfortable and in fact is quite content with the furnishings they acquired when they were first married. Dave is more interested in accumulating funds for investment. He is also interested in reducing income taxes to the extent that is still possible under the current federal income tax laws.

In the course of furnishing their house, Diana has acquired an appreciable amount of knowledge about antique Oriental porcelain and thinks that once the children are older, she would enjoy collecting some finer pieces more seriously and perhaps trading in them in a small way. She would also like to increase her knowledge of Oriental rugs and possibly purchase some for personal use and perhaps as an investment. She has even thought that after the children are older and need less of her time at home, she might consider opening a small shop that would specialize in Oriental rugs and antique Oriental porcelain. She had hoped that she could explore this possibility seriously within the next year or two but thinks now that she would like to stay at home full-time with the new baby for at least 2 or perhaps 3 years. However, she has not decided whether she wants to remain at home full-time as long as she did with the other children. Dave has mixed feelings about her returning to work and at this time would prefer that she remain at home with the baby at least until the child has started school. He does recognize that this will require Diana to delay any possibility of starting her own business for another 6 to 8 years.

Dave's parents are still living, and as far as he knows, they are in good health and are all right financially, although they have not accumulated a large amount of material wealth. Fred Anderson, his father, is a high-school principal and is 63 years old. Amy, his mother, 61, is a violinist who has given music lessons for many years. They were able to help Dave through undergraduate school as a result of careful saving, supplemented by Dave's obtaining a sizable scholarship.

Diana's father died when she was a teenager, and although she believes that he did not leave her mother too well provided for, she does not know for certain. While Diana was growing up, her mother implied that finances were quite limited. However, she was able to provide the funds required for Diana to go to nursing school. Diana's mother, Sarah, now 59, remarried 20 years ago. Her stepfather, Alex Smythe, now 63, is retired from the U.S. Postal Service after 30 years of service (retiring at 55 years of age) and is currently employed as the clerk of the superior court for Metropolis County. Diana's mother appears to be in good health, but her stepfather had a slight heart attack last year and later had a double heart bypass. While he seems to be recovering well, Diana is concerned about her mother's financial condition and what would become of her if something should happen to Alex. Her mother worked as a secretary after

Diana's father died, but she has been a housewife since she married Alex. Diana and Dave have discussed their concerns about Alex's health with Sarah but have not really discussed the matter of her financial future in any depth.

Diana inherited nothing from her father except a coin collection that he and she had accumulated during her childhood. She thought of it primarily in terms of sentimental value and was surprised to learn some years later that its estimated worth was approximately $5,000 when she inherited it 26 years ago. Dave became interested in the collection and has essentially taken over its management, adding to it from time to time, and he estimates that it is probably worth $20,000 today. They keep the collection in their safety deposit box at the bank.

Dave tells you that he has made some real estate investments several years ago. As an investment he purchased a single-family house in November 1990 for $57,000, financing $47,500 at 9.5 percent for 25 years. The house is rented for $550 per month and is presently worth about $120,000. Dave has been depreciating the house by the straight-line method for tax purposes over a 20-year useful life with a $10,000 salvage value. For depreciation purposes $5,000 of the purchase price was allocated to the land and the remaining $52,000 to the building.

Dave also purchased an undeveloped commercial lot in March 1990 for $100,000. He paid $20,000 down and financed the $80,000 balance at 10 percent for 20 years. He estimates that the land is worth approximately $260,000, and he has recently been approached by a buyer who is willing to pay him $270,000 if the transaction can be closed early in 2003. Dave is interested because the land does require cash flow to carry the note and taxes, and it produces no income. However, he is uncertain about whether he should sell the lot now.

Dave allocates any investable funds into securities and has benefited from the overall bull market in both stocks and bonds that has generally marked the period since 1987. Table 5-1 summarizes his purchases, sales, income, and current market values of the securities portfolio. Dave's selections followed the recommendations of an account representative from a local brokerage firm. Initially Dave acquired individual securities, but an article in a financial planning magazine describing the mutual fund features of diversification and professional management convinced him that funds would be a better approach for his personal investment plan. Dave expressed a desire to continue the investment program at the same or greater dollar level, until such time as he plans to retire.

The Andersons own two cars, both in Dave's name. Diana's car was purchased in June 2000 for $12,400; $10,000 of the purchase price was financed at 10 percent for 48 months. The value of the car is approximately $10,000. Dave's car was purchased in December 2001 for $22,000. Dave paid for the car with cash.

The Andersons have no other significant personal assets or liabilities except a $5,000 joint checking account and $20,000 in a joint savings account.

Dave and Diana had some estate planning done about 6 years ago. Their basic estate plan is described below.

Dave's will provides that an amount equal to one-half his adjusted gross estate, including the house, goes to Diana in a marital trust with a testamentary power of appointment if she survives him. The remainder of his estate after the payment of estate taxes is left in a residuary trust for the benefit of Diana, Keith, Deidre, and Melissa for Diana's life. The trustee of the trust is empowered to pay income or corpus to or for the benefit of Diana, Keith, Deidre, or Melissa as necessary for their health, support, maintenance, or education. Diana has a limited power of appointment over the principal of the trust, which can be exercised both during her life and at her death. She can appoint the principal only to Keith, Deidre, or Melissa. At Diana's death the remainder of the trust principal is to be paid equally to Keith, Deidre, and Melissa, if living. If any of them is deceased, the deceased child's portion is to go to his or her living children, per stirpes.

Diana's will leaves all her property to Dave if he survives her, otherwise equally to her living children or children of a deceased child, per stirpes. Neither will contains a provision dealing with after-born children.

The First Trust Company is named executor and trustee under Dave's will. Dave is named executor of Diana's will, with the First Trust Company named as successor if he is unable to serve. Diana is not happy with the fact that all her property would be tied up in a trust. She says she hates the idea of having to deal with a bank officer "for every little thing I need." Dave says he is only interested in having Diana and the children taken care of and in Diana's having someone to help her manage and direct the investment of the funds. He is also anxious to avoid unnecessary estate taxes. These are subjects they have discussed at various times since their last wills were drawn, and neither has changed his or her original position. Diana is also concerned that virtually all their assets are held in Dave's name.

Dave purchased a $100,000 term life insurance policy 8 years ago. Six years ago, as part of their estate planning, the insurance policy was gifted to an irrevocable insurance trust. Diana is the trustee of the trust until Dave's death, when the First Trust Company becomes the successor trustee. The dispositive provisions of the insurance trust are identical to those of the residuary trust under Dave's will. The trust document does not give the beneficiaries the right to withdraw funds gifted to the trust. The annual premiums for the years 2001 through 2005 are $279, $327, $377, $443, and $521.

Dave also carries a personal disability income policy that would provide disability income coverage after a 30-day waiting period in the event of a disabling accident or illness. If an accident causes the disability, the monthly benefits are as follows:

Date of disability through 30th day	$ 0
31st through 90th day	2,900
91st day through end of first year	5,400
First day of second year through age 60	4,900
After age 60 throughout life	4,700

TABLE 5-1
Dave Anderson's Portfolio Transactions, 1989 through 2000

Security Name	Quantity Bought	Date Bought	Total Cost	Date Sold	Sales Price	Market Value	Current Annual Income	Past Growth Rate	Current Yield
Clean Soap Inc.	250 sh[1] 250 sh[1] 500 sh	12/92 4/97 7/98	12,000 2-for-1 split 2-for-1 split	— — —	— — —	35,000	$1/sh	14.0%	2.80%
Job River Textile	20 bonds	9/94	19,800	6/94	24,000	—	—	—	—
High Fly Airlines	10 bonds	11/94	10,500	—	—	In Ch. 11 bankruptcy	zero	—	—
Nationwide Oil Co.	200 sh[1]	6/95	9,000	—	—	12,000	$2.50	5.0%	4.20%
Houseboat Finance Co.	10 bonds due 2010	1/96	10,100	—	—	12,500	9.0%	4.5%	7.20%
Deep Snow Maker Inc.	300 sh[1]	9/96	6,000	—	—	14,000	$0.10/sh	18.0%	0.20%
Burp Soda Inc.	400 sh[1] 400 sh	9/96 2000	20,000 2-for-1 split	—	—	32,000	$0.80/sh	9.0%	2.00%
Economic Fund	300 sh	11/96	3,000	—	—	1,500	$0.08/sh	-13.0%	1.60%
Wellington Mfg Corp (c)	400 sh[1] 200 sh	10/97 2001	16,000 3-for-2 split	—	—	24,000	$0.50/sh	10.0%	1.25%
Fund Mgrs Growth Fund	500 sh[1] 600 sh	8/98 7/99	19,500 24,000	—	—	21,000 25,200	$1.22/sh $1.22/sh	2.5%	2.90%
Atlantic Rim Fund	800 sh[1]	10/99	8,000	—	—	9,500	$0.57	9.0%	4.80%
Southern Fund	500 sh[1]	10/99	8,200	—	—	10,200	$0.79/sh	11.5%	3.90%
5-7 Year Bond Fund	500 sh[1]	10/99	6,000	—	—	6,200	$0.79/sh	1.6%	6.40%
Town Hall Munibonds	10 bonds due 2013	9/98	10,500	—	—	10,600	5.40%	1.0%	5.10%
State School System	15 bonds due 2013	9/98	14,900	—	—	15,150	5.25%	1.3%	5.20%
National Index Fund	900 sh[1]	11/99	27,000	—	—	44,000	$1.00/sh	20.0%	2.04%
Yum-Yum Foods	800 sh[1]	10/00	16,000	—	—	17,000	$0.70/sh	6.0%	3.29%

[1] Common stock

Assumptions
Expected growth rate for divs: 2%; expected growth rate for price of stock: same as past; no growth in either bond current yields or growth rates

If illness causes the disability, the monthly benefits are as follows:

Date of disability through 30th day	$ 0
31st through 90th day	2,900
91st day through end of first year	5,400
First day of second year through fifth year	4,900
Sixth and seventh years	2,900
Eighth year throughout life	1,400

Disability is defined under these policies as being disabled from one's own occupation for 5 years and after that being unable to perform any occupation for which one is otherwise suited by reason of education, experience, or training. The cost of the disability income coverage is $1,539 annually.

Dave has $260,000 in homeowners coverage that provides replacement-cost coverage on the family house. There is a residential rental property policy covering the rental house for 90 percent of its replacement value. Both these policies have inflation-adjustment provisions. The automobiles are new enough to warrant the collision and comprehensive coverage that is included in Dave's auto policies. The liability limits carried in these auto policies are the maximum available in the standard premium classification, and they dovetail with the Andersons' personal umbrella policy, which provides up to $1 million in protection over the homeowners and automobile policy limits.

Business Information

Dave went to medical school at Johns Hopkins University and did his internship at Johns Hopkins Hospital. He then served 2 years in the Air Force as a physician and returned to Johns Hopkins to complete his residency in orthopedic surgery. After finishing his residency, he set up his own practice in a large metropolitan area in Georgia, where he has been in practice a little over 10 years. The practice is well established and has become more profitable in recent years. Dave presently operates his practice as a sole proprietorship. He does, however, share office space with Larry Brown and Janet Cole, two other orthopedic surgeons who are also sole practitioners. They all share office overhead (rent, telephone, and the like) equally, except for direct staff costs, malpractice insurance, and some equipment, for which each physician is responsible individually. The physicians have occasionally covered each other's calls at night and on weekends, but they do not share patients or profits in any way. They sometimes refer patients to one another but have no formal professional relationship.

Dave estimates that his office equipment is worth about $45,000 and that the office furniture is worth about $20,000. Both the equipment and the furniture have been fully depreciated for tax purposes.

The total rent for the office space is $5,000 a month, and Dave's share for his office space is $2,000 a month. It is quite likely that the building in which he is located will be sold within the next 2 years. A realtor acquaintance gave Dave a casual estimate that the property (land and building) currently has a market value of $550,000 and probably would have a market value of $600,000 in 2 years. Operating expenses and property taxes, according to the realtor, would total about $10,000 annually. Dave would not like to relocate his practice because it is located conveniently near the three hospitals at which he has staff privileges. For the past 6 years his practice has provided him with net income of over $100,000 per year, and it has increased approximately 6 to 8 percent each year. Last year after his Keogh contribution his net earnings were approximately $150,000, and he anticipates that he will earn $170,000–$175,000 after the Keogh contribution this year. He feels that he devotes the maximum possible time to his practice and that the number of patients cannot increase appreciably. Dave expects that his yearly income will continue to increase but is concerned about the effect that his participation in two HMOs and a PPO will have on his income growth. He estimates that it will level off at no more than $220,000 in today's dollars. He could increase his income to a greater degree if he were willing to devote more of his time to the practice, but he feels that he is already committing so much of his time to it that his family obligations are barely being met, and he is unwilling to curtail further the time he can spend with Diana and their children. Diana would like him to spend more time with her and the children, particularly while they are growing up, and they indicate that this issue causes some friction between them. He is strongly committed to his career and must even spend some of his at-home hours trying to keep up with advances in his field.

Dave employs three full-time employees: Martha Ann Hammond, 23, his secretary-receptionist; Jeanne Smith, 22, a radiology technician; and Sally Evans, 31, a nurse. Martha Ann Hammond was hired in August 2001 and is paid $22,000 annually. Jeanne Smith was hired in November 2001 and is paid $35,000 annually. Sally Evans has been with Dave since shortly after he opened his practice and usually works with him in surgery as well as at the office. She is paid $40,000 annually.

When asked how he feels about his employees, Dave says that they are all hardworking and that they earn their salaries. He volunteers that he would not be interested in planning for employee benefits that unduly discriminate against them. When asked to clarify what he means by unduly discriminatory benefits, he says that he has no objection, for example, to providing retirement benefits to his employees at or near the current levels. In fact, he feels obligated to do so. However, he is interested in maximizing benefits for himself while minimizing costs.

In the second year of his practice Dave established a profit-sharing Keogh plan, under which participants become 100 percent vested in their plan benefits after the completion of 3 years of service. The plan now provides for immediate 100 percent vesting upon an employee's entry into the plan. However, employees are not eligible for entry into the plan until they have completed 2 years of service. Of the present members of Dave's staff only Sally Evans and Dave have vested benefits under the plan.

Dave has contributed the maximum legally available amount to the Keogh plan for the past 7 years. The Keogh account is presently invested in 10-year CDs, which pay 8 percent and were purchased in June 1999. The trustee of the account is the First Bank and Trust of Georgia. Diana is the named beneficiary of the Keogh plan.

Dave includes his three employees in his Keogh plan when they become eligible. He also provides them with medical insurance coverage with a $1 million lifetime benefit and a $100 annual deductible. Eighty percent of the first $3,000 of covered expenses is paid by the insurer and 20 percent by the employee. After $3,000 of covered expenses, the plan pays 100 percent. The costs are $200 per month for employee coverage and $275 per month for employee and dependent coverage. Dave provides medical coverage but not dependent coverage for his employees. However, he participates in the plan and carries dependent coverage despite the fact that the cost is not fully tax deductible.

In the normal course of his practice, Dave usually has $25,000 in excess funds from his practice, which he deposits in a separate money market deposit account until they are needed for quarterly tax liabilities or other expenses. In addition, he says that his accounts receivable usually average $45,000 to $55,000 and that most are covered wholly or partially by insurance, so there are rarely significant uncollected receivables.

Drs. Brown and Cole have discussed with Dave the possibility that the three of them could combine their practices and perhaps take on a younger doctor to help expand the practice. They have discussed a professional partnership or incorporating all their practices together. Dave is not too interested in this concept because he is not convinced that he would be willing to be part of a larger organization, but he is considering incorporating his own practice. He has considered incorporation in the past but has always decided it was too much trouble and expense. He is wondering whether incorporation is still as beneficial under the current tax laws. Dave does not wish to change his form of ownership unless a change would bring him significant tax or economic benefits.

When asked to rank the following standardized list of general financial objectives in order of their priority, the Andersons' response was the following:

Provide college educations for all their children	1
Take care of the family in the event of Dave's death	2
Maintain their standard of living	3
Reduce tax burden	4
Take care of self and family during a period of long-term disability	5
Invest and accumulate wealth	6
Enjoy a comfortable retirement	7
Develop an estate plan	8

Next the Andersons were individually asked to rate their responses to a standardized list of various investment vehicles from 0 to 5, with 0 representing an aversion and 5 representing a substantial preference. Their responses are shown in table 5-2.

TABLE 5-2
Investment Vehicle Preferences

Investment Vehicle	Dave	Diana
Savings account	2	3
Money market account	2	4
U.S. government bond	1	2
Corporate bond	2	3
Corporate stock (growth)	4	2
Mutual fund (growth)	4	2
Mutual fund (income)	1	3
Municipal bond	3	1
Real estate (direct ownership)	4	3
Insurance and annuities	1	2
Limited partnership units (real estate, oil & gas, cattle, equipment leasing)	3	1
Commodities, gold, collectibles	2	4*

*Diana says she would not be interested in commodities or gold, but she thinks collectibles can be very good investments.

The Andersons then each responded to a list of general personal financial concerns by rating the concerns from 0 to 5, with 5 indicating a strong concern and 0 indicating no concern. Table 5-3 shows how Dave and Diana rated their concerns.

TABLE 5-3
Andersons' Personal Financial Concerns

Area of Concern	Dave	Diana
Liquidity	2	3
Safety of principal	3	3
Capital appreciation	5	3
Current income	2	3
Inflation protection	4	4
Future income	3	4
Tax reduction/deferral	4	3

INSTRUCTIONS

Based on this information, prepare a working outline for the Andersons' financial plan. When this has been completed, it can be compared with the suggested solution that follows. After comparing your working outline with the suggested solution, turn to page 5.16 for further instructions.

WORKING OUTLINE

I. Clients' objectives
    A. For lifetime planning
        1. Fund special schools and college education for children.
        2. Accumulate enough wealth to maintain their lifestyle and to be secure at retirement.
        3. Reduce tax burden.
        4. Investigate the possibility of the sale of the commercial lot.
        5. Investigate the benefits of incorporating Dave's practice.
        6. Explore the advisability of Diana's wish to start her own business.
        7. Investigate possibility of purchasing office building.

    B. For dispositions at death
        1. Ensure that the family will have sufficient assets to maintain their lifestyle if Dave should die prematurely.
        2. Avoid unnecessary taxes at the deaths of both Dave and Diana.

II. Business planning
    A. Tax planning
        1. Present situation
        2. Choosing the appropriate business form
            a. Continuing as a sole proprietorship
            b. Forming a professional partnership
            c. S corporations
            d. C corporations
            e. Recommendations
        3. Qualified plans of deferred compensation
            a. Integration with Social Security
            b. Money-purchase pension plan
            c. Recommendation for qualified plans for Dave
        4. Buy-sell agreements to ensure that Dave's practice is marketable at death or disability

    B. Insurance planning
        1. Funding the buy-sell agreement(s)
        2. Medical, disability, and life insurance plans
            a. Medical expense insurance
            b. Disability income insurance
        3. Property and liability insurance for the business
        4. Professional liability insurance
        5. Business overhead expense disability insurance

III. Personal planning
   A. Tax planning
      1. Present situation
      2. Fund private school and/or college education for children.
         a. Gifting
            • Outright gifts
            • UGMA and UTMA gifts
         b. Income shifting
            • Sec. 2503(b) trusts
            • Sec. 2503(c) trusts
            • Family partnership
            • Caveat: parental obligations
      3. Reduce tax burden.
         a. Achieve personal objectives through income-shifting devices to reduce cost.
         b. Defer tax liability on a portion of Dave's income from the practice through the use of qualified plans.
         c. Individual retirement accounts
      4. Ensure adequate protection in the event of Dave's disability.
         a. Design buy-sell agreement to become operative in the event of Dave's disability.
         b. Personal disability income coverage
      5. Ensure a comfortable retirement.
      6. Consider various problems Diana might encounter in setting up her own business.
         a. Preliminary general planning
         b. Taking advantage of start-up losses
      7. Dispositions at death
         a. Analysis of present plans
         b. Recommendations
         c. Failure of present estate planning documents to contemplate the birth of Dave and Diana's fourth child
         d. Considerations regarding Diana
         e. Diana's dissatisfaction with leaving all assets in trust
         f. Problems with present life insurance trust

   B. Insurance planning
      1. Life insurance
         a. Ordinary whole life insurance
         b. Single-premium whole life insurance
         c. Variable life policy
         d. Universal life policy
         e. Term policy
         f. Recommendations

2. Disability insurance
3. Personal property and liability insurance

C. Investment planning
   1. Refinancing clients' home
   2. Financial status of the clients
   3. Funding the children's education
      a. Secondary school expenses
      b. College expenses
      c. Investment alternatives for education funding
         - Moderately high-risk income bond funds
         - Growth-oriented no-load mutual fund
      d. Investment media selection
         - Use of corporate bonds
         - Use of higher-risk investments
   4. Repositioning of existing assets
      a. Earned income
      b. Investment income
      c. Passive income
         - Concept of passive income
         - Special real estate rules
         - Revenue Reconciliation Act of 1993 changes
      d. Recommendations
         - The commercial lot
         - Real estate investments
         - Security portfolio
   5. Increasing net worth
      a. Collectibles (coins, porcelain)
      b. Growth-oriented no-load mutual fund
      c. Selected issues of common stock
      d. Preferred stock
      e. Corporate bonds
      f. Municipal bonds
      g. Municipal bond fund
      h. Leveraged, closed-end bond funds
      i. Junk bonds
      j. Real estate
   6. Recommendations

INSTRUCTIONS

Now prepare a financial plan for the Andersons. When you have prepared your solution, it should be compared with the suggested solution that follows.

PERSONAL FINANCIAL PLAN
FOR
DAVE AND DIANA ANDERSON
[Suggested Solution]

CLIENTS' OBJECTIVES

A. For lifetime planning
1. Fund special schools and college education for children.
2. Accumulate enough wealth to maintain their lifestyle and to be secure at retirement.
3. Reduce tax burden.
4. Investigate the possibility of the sale of the commercial lot.
5. Investigate the benefits of incorporating Dave's practice.
6. Explore the advisability of Diana's wish to start her own business.
7. Investigate possibility of purchasing office building.

B. For dispositions at death
1. Ensure that the family will have sufficient assets to maintain their lifestyle if Dave should die prematurely.
2. Avoid unnecessary taxes at the deaths of both Dave and Diana.

BASE CASE

Assumptions

1. The checking account balance is maintained at $5,000; the account is noninterest bearing.

2. The joint savings account balance of $10,000 earns 3 percent interest annually. Interest accumulates in the account.

3. The money market deposit account has an average balance of $25,000 and earns 3 percent interest annually. Interest does not accumulate in the account but is added to surplus cash.

4. Surplus cash is invested and earns 4 percent annually.

5. Dave's gross receipts and business expenses are expected to increase at 4.4 percent annually.

6. Diana inherited a coin collection from her father in 1976. The fair market value of the collection is presently $20,000 and is expected to increase annually at 6 percent.

7. The 2001 value of the personal residence ($315,000) will increase at 8 percent annually. The residence was purchased in March 1988. The original amount of the mortgage was $63,000 at an interest rate of 12 percent for a term of 30 years.

8. The 2001 value of the commercial lot ($260,000) will increase at 4 percent annually. The lot was purchased in March 1990. The original amount of the mortgage was $80,000 at an interest rate of 10 percent for a term of 20 years.

9. The 2001 value of the rental property ($120,000) will increase at 6 percent annually. The rental property was purchased in November 1990. Currently the property rents for $550 per month and has operating expenses of approximately $900 annually. All these amounts will increase at 6 percent annually.

10. Dave has office furniture valued at approximately $20,000 and office equipment valued at $45,000. No increase or decrease in value has been assumed.

11.   Dave's accounts receivable average $50,000.

12.   Property taxes on the personal residence are expected to increase at 6 percent annually.

13.   Nondeductible living expenses are expected to increase at 6 percent annually.

14.   Charitable contributions are expected to increase at 6 percent annually.

15.   Dave's Keogh plan is presently invested in 30-month CDs earning 8 percent. This earning assumption has been projected through 2004. He makes a maximum contribution to this plan in each year.

16.   Automobiles decrease in value at a rate of 15 percent annually.

17.   The expected growth rate of all dividends is 2 percent.

18.   The expected growth rate for prices of all stocks is the same as the past growth rate for each stock.

19.   No growth is expected in either bond current yields or total returns.

INCOME STATEMENT

DAVE & DIANA ANDERSON

BASE CASE	2002	2003	2004	2005	2006
Earned Income					
Business Inc-Cl	200,000	211,000	222,605	234,848	247,765
Business-Salaries	-22,500	-22,500	-22,500	-22,500	-22,500
	177,500	188,500	200,105	212,348	225,265
Interest/Dividends					
Saving/NOW Acts	300	300	300	300	300
Money Market Fund	750	750	750	750	750
Houseboat Finance	900	900	900	900	900
Clean Soap Inc	1,000	1,020	1,040	1,061	1,082
Nationwide Oil Co	500	510	520	531	541
Deep Snow Maker Inc	30	31	31	32	32
Burp Soda Inc	640	653	666	679	693
Economic Fund	24	24	25	25	26
Wellington Mfg Corp	300	306	312	318	325
FundMgrsGrowthFund	1,342	1,369	1,396	1,424	1,453
Atlantic Rim Fund	456	465	474	484	494
Southern Fund	395	403	411	419	428
5-7 Year Bond Fund	395	403	411	419	428
National Index Fund	900	918	937	956	976
Yum-Yum Foods	350	362	373	386	398
Investable Cash	1,272	3,940	6,892	10,130	13,612
	9,554	12,354	15,440	18,815	22,437
Investments					
Invest--House Loan	-3,575	-3,435	-3,282	-3,114	-2,928
Invest--House Expen	-900	-954	-1,011	-1,072	-1,136
Invest--House Rent	6,600	6,996	7,416	7,861	8,332
Invest--House Depre	-2,100	-2,100	-2,100	-2,100	-2,100
Invest--Lot Loan	-5,371	-4,962	-4,512	-4,015	-3,465
	-5,346	-4,455	-3,489	-2,440	-1,297
Adjustments					
S.E. Tax Dedctn	7,663	7,810	7,966	8,130	8,303
	7,663	7,810	7,966	8,130	8,303
	========	========	========	========	========
Adj Gross Income	174,045	188,589	204,089	220,593	238,102
Deductions					
Charitable 50%	4,500	4,770	5,056	5,360	5,681
State Tax Paid	8,246	9,075	9,908	10,850	11,802
Prop Taxes--Home	1,900	2,014	2,135	2,263	2,399
Home Mortgage	6,584	6,432	6,262	6,070	5,853
Reductn for High Inc	-1,129	-1,459	-1,815	-2,197	-1,739
Gross Deductions	20,101	20,832	21,546	22,346	23,996
Standard Deduction	7,800	8,000	8,200	8,787	9,476
Allowed Deductions	20,101	20,832	21,546	22,346	23,996
Pers Exemptions	14,750	15,250	15,750	16,000	8,800
	========	========	========	========	========
Taxable Income	139,194	152,507	166,793	182,247	205,306
	========	========	========	========	========
Fed Income Tax	47,561	51,616	56,092	62,866	69,304
	========	========	========	========	========
Fed Tax Bracket-Ord Inc	30.0%	30.0%	29.0%	29.0%	33.0%

BALANCE SHEET

DAVE & DIANA ANDERSON

BASE CASE	2002	2003	2004	2005	2006
LIQUID ASSETS					
Cash Balance	5,003	5,021	4,982	4,971	4,979
Cash Deposits					
Saving/NOW Acts	10,000	10,000	10,000	10,000	10,000
Investable Cash	64,895	136,068	215,425	301,220	393,001
Money Market Fund	25,000	25,000	25,000	25,000	25,000
	99,895	171,068	250,425	336,220	428,001
Stocks & Bonds					
Houseboat Finance	12,508	12,426	12,338	12,243	12,142
Town Hall Munibonds	10,600	10,585	10,572	10,556	10,540
State School System	15,150	15,152	15,157	15,161	15,165
Clean Soap Inc	35,000	39,900	45,486	51,854	59,114
Nationwide Oil Co	12,000	12,600	13,230	13,892	14,586
Deep Snow Maker Inc	14,000	16,520	19,494	23,002	27,143
Burp Soda Inc	32,000	34,880	38,019	41,441	45,171
Economic Fund	1,500	1,305	1,135	987	859
Wellington Mfg Corp	24,000	26,400	29,040	31,944	35,138
FundMgrsGrowthFund	46,200	47,355	48,539	49,752	50,996
Atlantic Rim Fund	9,500	10,355	11,287	12,303	13,410
Southern Fund	10,200	11,373	12,681	14,139	15,765
5-7 Year Bond Fund	6,200	6,299	6,400	6,502	6,606
National Index Fund	44,000	52,800	63,360	76,032	91,238
Yum-Yum Foods	17,000	18,020	19,101	20,247	21,462
	289,858	315,970	345,838	380,056	419,336
Liquid Assets	394,756	492,059	601,245	721,247	852,317
NONLIQUID ASSETS					
Retirement Plans					
Business-Salaries	91,168	122,761	156,882	193,733	233,532
	91,168	122,761	156,882	193,733	233,532
Investments					
Investment--House	120,000	127,200	134,832	142,922	151,497
Investment--Lot	260,000	270,400	281,216	292,465	304,163
	380,000	397,600	416,048	435,387	455,660
Personal Property					
Home	340,200	367,416	396,809	428,554	462,838
Dave's Car	18,700	15,895	13,511	11,484	9,762
Diana's Car	8,500	7,225	6,141	5,220	4,437
Furnishings--Home	30,000	30,000	30,000	30,000	30,000
Furnishings--Office	65,000	65,000	65,000	65,000	65,000
Coin Collection	21,200	22,472	23,820	25,250	26,765
Business Accts Rec	50,000	50,000	50,000	50,000	50,000
	533,600	558,008	585,282	615,508	648,801
Nonliquid Assets	1,004,768	1,078,369	1,158,211	1,244,628	1,337,994
Total Assets	1,399,524	1,570,428	1,759,456	1,965,875	2,190,311

BALANCE SHEET (cont.)

DAVE & DIANA ANDERSON

BASE CASE	2002	2003	2004	2005	2006
LIABILITIES					
Mortgage Loans					
Home Mortgage	54,208	52,864	51,350	49,644	47,721
	54,208	52,864	51,350	49,644	47,721
Notes Payable					
Diana's Car--Loan	4,223	1,478	0	0	0
	4,223	1,478	0	0	0
Investments					
Invest--House Loan	36,858	35,313	33,615	31,749	29,697
Invest--Lot Loan	51,565	47,263	42,511	37,262	31,463
	88,423	82,576	76,126	69,011	61,160
	========	========	========	========	========
Total Liabilities	146,854	136,918	127,476	118,655	108,881
	========	========	========	========	========
Net Worth	1,252,670	1,433,510	1,631,980	1,847,220	2,081,430
	========	========	========	========	========

CASH FLOW STATEMENT

DAVE & DIANA ANDERSON

BASE CASE	2002	2003	2004	2005	2006
BEGINNING OF YEAR					
Idle Cash On Hand	5,000	5,003	5,021	4,982	4,971
SOURCES OF CASH					
Cash Income					
Business Inc-CI	200,000	211,000	222,605	234,848	247,765
Interest+Dividends	9,610	9,741	9,875	10,012	10,153
	209,610	220,741	232,480	244,861	257,917
Investments					
InvestHouse - Depre	2,100	2,100	2,100	2,100	2,100
	2,100	2,100	2,100	2,100	2,100
	========	========	========	========	========
Total Cash Inflow	211,710	222,841	234,580	246,961	260,017
	========	========	========	========	========
Tot Cash Available	216,710	227,844	239,601	251,942	264,988
	========	========	========	========	========
USES OF CASH					
Fully Tax Deductible					
Business-Salaries	22,500	22,500	22,500	22,500	22,500
Home Mortgage	6,584	6,432	6,262	6,070	5,853
	29,084	28,932	28,762	28,570	28,353
Partly Deductible					
Charity Contrb-50%	4,500	4,770	5,056	5,360	5,681
	4,500	4,770	5,056	5,360	5,681
Not Tax Deductible					
Diana's Car--Loan	559	299	44	0	0
Vacations	4,000	4,240	4,494	4,764	5,050
Life Ins Prem--Dave	279	327	377	443	521
Home Ins Prem--Home	600	636	674	715	757
Ins Prem--Cars	995	1,055	1,118	1,185	1,256
Dis Ins Prem--Dave	1,539	1,539	1,539	1,539	1,539
Living Expenses	30,000	31,800	33,708	35,730	37,874
	37,972	39,896	41,955	44,376	46,998
Taxes Paid					
Fed Tax Paid	47,561	51,616	56,092	62,866	69,304
State Tax Paid	8,246	9,075	9,908	10,850	11,802
Prop Taxes--Home	1,900	2,014	2,135	2,263	2,399
	57,707	62,705	68,135	75,979	83,505

CASH FLOW STATEMENT (cont.)

DAVE & DIANA ANDERSON

BASE CASE **Purchase/Deposits**	2002	2003	2004	2005	2006
Investable Cash	63,623	67,233	72,465	75,665	78,169
	63,623	67,233	72,465	75,665	78,169
Investments					
Invest--House Loan	4,980	4,980	4,980	4,980	4,980
Invest--House Expen	900	954	1,011	1,072	1,136
Invest--Lot Loan	9,264	9,264	9,264	9,264	9,264
	15,144	15,198	15,255	15,316	15,380
Liability Liquidation					
Home Mortgage	1,192	1,344	1,514	1,706	1,923
Diana's Car--Loan	2,485	2,745	1,478	0	0
	3,677	4,089	2,992	1,706	1,923
	========	========	========	========	========
Tot Cash Outflow	211,707	222,823	234,620	246,972	260,009
	========	========	========	========	========
END OF YEAR					
Cash Balance	5,003	5,021	4,982	4,971	4,979
	========	========	========	========	========

SUPPORTING SCHEDULE

DAVE & DIANA ANDERSON

	JOINT 2002	JOINT 2003	JOINT 2004	JOINT 2005	JOINT 2006
BASE CASE					
Income					
Earned Income	177,500	188,500	200,105	212,348	225,265
Adj Gross Income	174,045	188,589	204,089	220,593	238,102
Allowed Deductions	20,101	20,832	21,546	22,346	23,996
Pers Exemptions	14,750	15,250	15,750	16,000	8,800
Taxable Income	139,194	152,507	166,793	182,247	205,306
Investments					
Ordinary Income	6,600	6,996	7,416	7,861	8,332
Depreciation	2,100	2,100	2,100	2,100	2,100
Invstmt Interest	8,946	8,397	7,794	7,129	6,393
Other Expenses	900	954	1,011	1,072	1,136
Investment Income	-5,346	-4,455	-3,489	-2,440	-1,297
Investment Interest					
Inv Int Sch E	8,946	8,397	7,794	7,129	6,393
Federal Tax Liab					
Regular Tax	32,235	35,996	38,862	43,115	48,825
Gross Fed Inc Tax	32,235	35,996	38,862	43,115	48,825
Alt Minimum Tax	0	0	1,299	3,492	3,874
AMT Credit C/Over	0	0	0	0	1,299
Disallowed	0	0	0	-1,299	-4,791
Self Employmt Tax	15,326	15,620	15,931	16,259	16,605
Fed Income Tax	47,561	51,616	56,092	62,866	69,304
Fed Tax Analysis-Ord Inc					
Indexing Factor	82	87	91	96	102
Fed Tax Bracket-Ord Inc	30.0%	30.0%	29.0%	29.0%	33.0%
$ to Next Bracket	31,606	22,743	13,007	2,253	132,744
Next Bracket	35.0%	35.0%	34.0%	34.0%	35.0%
Previous Bracket	27.0%	27.0%	26.0%	26.0%	28.0%
$ to Prev Bracket	27,144	37,507	48,793	61,197	16,006
Fed Effective Tax Rate	34.2%	33.9%	33.6%	34.5%	33.8%
Alt Minimum Tax					
Adj Gross Income	174,045	188,589	204,089	220,593	238,102
Contributions	-4,500	-4,770	-5,056	-5,360	-5,681
Home Mortgage	-6,584	-6,432	-6,262	-6,070	-5,853
Adjusted AMTI	162,961	177,387	192,771	209,163	226,568
AMT Exemptions	-45,760	-42,153	-38,307	-30,209	-25,858
AMT Taxable Inc	117,201	135,233	154,464	178,954	200,710
Gross Alt Min Tx	30,472	35,161	40,161	46,607	52,699
Fed Tax Less FTC	-32,235	-35,996	-38,862	-43,115	-48,825
Alt Minimum Tax	0	0	1,299	3,492	3,874
Other Tax Liabs					
Adj Gross Inc	174,045	188,589	204,089	220,593	238,102
GA AGI Adjstmnts	1,328	1,328	1,328	1,328	1,328
GA Adj Gross Inc	175,373	189,916	205,417	221,921	239,430
GA Standard Ded	3,000	3,000	3,000	3,000	3,000
GA Itemized Ded	20,101	20,832	21,546	22,346	23,996
GA Exemptions	13,500	13,500	14,400	14,400	14,400
GA Taxable Inc	141,772	155,584	169,471	185,175	201,034
GA Regular Tax	8,246	9,075	9,908	10,850	11,802
GA Income Tax	8,246	9,075	9,908	10,850	11,802
Georgia Tax	8,246	9,075	9,908	10,850	11,802
Tot State/Local Tx	8,246	9,075	9,908	10,850	11,802
Total Inc Tax	55,807	60,691	66,000	73,716	81,106

FINANCIAL SUMMARY

DAVE & DIANA ANDERSON

BASE CASE	2002	2003	2004	2005	2006
Gross Real Income					
Personal Earnings	200,000	211,000	222,605	234,848	247,765
Interest Income	4,550	7,218	10,170	13,408	16,890
Dividends Rcvd	6,332	6,464	6,598	6,735	6,875
InvestHouse - Depre	2,100	2,100	2,100	2,100	2,100
	212,982	226,781	241,472	257,091	273,629
Income & Inflation					
Gross Real Inc	212,982	226,781	241,472	257,091	273,629
Total Inc Tax	-55,807	-60,691	-66,000	-73,716	-81,106
Net Real Income	157,175	166,090	175,472	183,375	192,523
Cur Real Inc =	157,175	161,264	165,460	169,764	174,181
At Infltn Rate of	3	3	3	3	3
Cash Flow					
Idle Cash On Hand	5,000	5,003	5,021	4,982	4,971
Norml Cash Inflow	211,710	222,841	234,580	246,961	260,017
Norml Cash Outflw	148,084	155,590	162,155	171,307	181,840
Cash Invested	63,623	67,233	72,465	75,665	78,169
Cash Balance	5,003	5,021	4,982	4,971	4,979
Net Worth					
Personal Assets	538,603	563,029	590,263	620,478	653,781
Investment Assets	860,921	1,007,399	1,169,193	1,345,396	1,536,530
Personal Liabilities	-58,431	-54,342	-51,350	-49,644	-47,721
Investmt Liabilities	-88,423	-82,576	-76,126	-69,011	-61,160
Personal Net Worth	480,172	508,687	538,913	570,834	606,060
Investment Net Worth	772,498	924,823	1,093,067	1,276,385	1,475,370
Net Worth	1,252,670	1,433,510	1,631,980	1,847,220	2,081,430

BUSINESS PLANNING: TAXES

Present Situation

Dave has a well-established and profitable private practice as an orthopedic surgeon. The practice is conducted as a sole proprietorship, even though there is a space-sharing arrangement with two other orthopedic surgeons. The practice has produced over $100,000 in income for Dave for each of the past 6 years. Last year he earned $150,000 after his Keogh contribution, and he expects to earn at least $170,000 to $175,000 in the current year.

Dave employs three full-time employees in his practice: Martha Ann Hammond, 23, his secretary-receptionist; Jeanne Smith, 22, a radiology technician; and Sally Evans, 31, a nurse. Martha Ann Hammond was hired in August 2001 and is paid $22,000 annually. Jeanne Smith was hired in November 2001 and is paid $35,000 annually. Sally Evans is a long-time employee and is paid $40,000 annually. Dave has indicated that his employees work very hard and are well worth the salaries he pays them and that he does not want to implement employee benefits that would unduly discriminate against them, although he is interested in maximizing his own benefits.

Dave has been approached by Drs. Brown and Cole about consolidating their practices either through a professional partnership or by incorporating the three practices as one corporation.

Dave believes that bigger is not necessarily better and thinks that it would probably be a mistake to consolidate the practices. He also thinks that combining practices would greatly increase administrative problems. He has not dismissed the idea despite his reservations, but he is more interested in incorporating his own practice if he decides to incorporate at all. Prior to changing the form of his business he would like information on his options so that he can assess the changes that would be necessary in his practice under the available forms of doing business.

Dave presently provides a good medical insurance plan for each of his employees. He is also a participant in this plan, although the payments in his behalf are not tax deductible (as a business expense) for federal income tax purposes. He has set up a defined-contribution Keogh plan for himself and his employees, and he makes the maximum annual contribution to the plan. On the following pages are 5-year projections of the Andersons' tax, net worth, and cash-flow positions if they continue their present lifestyle without making any significant changes.

Choosing the Appropriate Business Form

Continuing as a Sole Proprietorship

The sole proprietorship is the most informal type of business ownership because there is such a close identity between the business and the business owner. Sole proprietorships are not separate entities for tax-reporting purposes (as are partnerships) or for tax-paying purposes (as are corporations). The owner of the sole proprietorship reports business-operating results on his or her tax return and pays taxes on the business income. There is no separate income tax form to file since all business income and losses from a proprietorship are computed on Schedule C of Form 1040 and added to or subtracted from the proprietor's gross income from other sources, if any. Bona fide business losses can be used to offset other income of the proprietor without the constraints imposed by the basis rules and passive activity loss rules for partnerships and S corporations. The taxable year of the sole proprietorship must be the same as the taxable year of the owner.

In a sole proprietorship the proprietor owns all assets and therefore has total control over the business. A proprietor can retain complete control or delegate some authority to employees on his or her own terms. There is no board of directors, and there are no partners or shareholders for the proprietor to answer to or to question his or her decisions. Some business owners enjoy the informality, flexibility, control, and freedom that the sole proprietorship affords.

Sole proprietorships are not, however, without their drawbacks. The close identity between the proprietor and the business can leave the proprietor personally vulnerable to liability for acts of employees or agents. This situation does not normally exist when business is carried on in a corporate form. There is also no opportunity to take advantage of splitting income (and thereby the income tax liability) between the sole proprietor and another taxpayer, as is the case in regular (C) corporations. In addition, there are still some restrictions with regard to qualified retirement plans that apply to self-employed persons and owner-employees that are not applicable to other employees.

Certain employee benefits that are available to shareholder-employees of C corporations free of tax cost, such as group life and medical insurance, are paid with after-tax dollars by self-employed persons.

As a physician, Dave is personally liable for his own acts of negligence or malpractice, regardless of whether he operates as a sole proprietor, a partner, or a corporation. His relationship with Drs. Brown and Cole is not of a type that could result in Dave's being held liable for their acts. Therefore with respect to personal liability exposure, incorporation would not provide him with a significant advantage over his present situation.

Forming a Professional Partnership

Like the sole proprietorship, the partnership is a non-tax-paying entity. While the partnership is a tax-reporting entity that has taxable income or losses and must file a tax return, the partnership itself is a mere conduit, and the partnership income and losses are passed through to the partners. The characterization of income or losses as capital or ordinary is made at the partnership level and is passed on to the individual partners for reporting on their individual income tax returns. The partnership can also be used to pass through tax losses (limited to the partner's basis in his or her partnership interest) to the individual partners in order to offset income from other sources.

The Internal Revenue Code defines a partnership as any business, financial operation, or venture carried on through a syndicate, group, pool, joint venture, or other unincorporated organization other than trusts, estates, or corporations (IRC Sec. 7701(a)(2)). The definition is broad and flexible, and the partnership can in fact be a very flexible form of business ownership that allows for a substantial amount of informality in business operations. A partnership is not without its potential problems, however, regarding both legal and tax issues.

One of the most troubling problems in operating a business, particularly a professional practice, in the form of a partnership is that as a legal matter all the general partners are responsible for all the debts of the partnership as well as the debts of other partners arising out of the partnership business. For a group of professionals such as physicians, this means that a malpractice suit resulting in a professional liability judgment is the responsibility of each of the partners to the full extent of the liability. If the person who made the professional error is unable to pay all the liability, each of the other partners is fully liable for the payment of the required amount. In strict legal terms each partner is "jointly and severally liable" for the total liabilities of the partnership and of the individual partners arising out of the partnership business. This can necessitate one partner's making huge payments on behalf of another partner. The amount of each partner's liability is not limited to the assets the partner has in the partnership but extends to personal assets as well. Therefore it is possible for each partner to lose everything he or she owns in satisfying the liabilities of the partnership or the malpractice judgments of the partners. Joint and several liability extends to all obligations of the partnership and is not restricted to the area of professional liability.

Partnerships, like sole proprietorships, do not offer the opportunity to split income between a business entity and an individual. Because the partnership is not a tax-paying entity, all income is taxed to the partners. If the partnership has taxable income, each partner must pay tax on his or her portion of that amount in the year in which it is recognized by the partnership regardless of whether it is actually distributed to that partner.

In addition, there are benefits available to shareholder-employees of regular (C) corporations on a tax-advantaged basis that are unavailable to partners. These benefits include group medical, disability income, and life insurance plans.

Primarily because of the increased personal liability exposure, forming a professional partnership is not recommended in this case.

S Corporations

S corporations are treated as corporations for tax purposes except that the income from S corporations is treated as if the individual shareholders had earned or received it as a dividend, regardless of whether it was actually distributed to the shareholders. It was primarily this tax attribute that made the gift of S corporation stock an effective income-shifting device. For example, income could be shifted to a child by a gift of S corporation shares without raising difficult tax issues such as reasonable compensation. Since taxable income was generally taxed to the shareholders, S corporations have always been loosely compared to partnerships despite the many differences in taxation between these two forms of business entities. In fact, until recent years S corporations were actually taxed in some ways as combinations of partnerships and regular corporations. Under current federal income tax law, the rules governing S corporation income are much closer to the rules governing partnership income than to the rules governing regular corporations. There are, however, significant differences between the formation and the eligibility requirements of an S corporation and those of a partnership.

IRC Sec. 1361 sets forth job requirements necessary to elect S corporation status. First, a corporation must be a domestic corporation that is not an ineligible corporation. Under prior law, an S corporation generally would be an ineligible corporation if it were a member of an affiliated group of corporations. Beginning in 1997, an S corporation can own 80 percent or more of the stock in a C corporation, but it cannot file a consolidated return with the C corporation affiliates. In addition, an S corporation is permitted to have a wholly owned qualified Subchapter S subsidiary (QSSS). If the QSSS election is made, all assets, items of income, deductions, and QSSS credits are treated as if they belong to the parent S corporation.

Some business entities are prohibited from electing S corporation status. These entities are referred to as ineligible corporations and include

- an insurance company subject to tax under Subchapter L of the Code
- a corporation electing the Puerto Rico and possessions tax credit under IRC Sec. 936, as amended
- a domestic international sales corporation (DISC) or former DISC

In addition, the corporation must satisfy the following four requirements:

1. The electing S corporation may have no more than a total of 75 shareholders; however, a husband and wife or their estates, each owning stock individually, are treated as one shareholder.
2. Each individual shareholder must be a citizen or resident of the United States; that is, no shareholder can be a nonresident alien.
3. Each shareholder must be an individual, an estate, or a specified type of trust. Each current beneficiary of a trust eligible to hold S stock is treated as a separate shareholder for the purpose of the 75-shareholder limit. The definition of individual shareholders does not include corporations or partnerships. However, there are basically five types of trusts that are permitted to be shareholders:

a. a grantor trust or a trust that distributes all its income to a sole beneficiary who is treated as the owner of the trust under IRC Sec. 678, provided that the grantor or owner of the trust would be an eligible shareholder

b. a trust created primarily as a voting trust, although each beneficiary of the voting trust is treated as a separate shareholder for purposes of the maximum-75-shareholder limitation

c. any trust, but only as to stock transferred to it under the terms of a will and only for up to 2 years following a deceased shareholder's death

d. a qualified Subchapter S trust (QSST), which is a trust that owns stock in one or more S corporations and distributes or is required to distribute all its current income to its sole income beneficiary, who must be an individual U.S. citizen or resident. If there is a distribution of corpus during the term of the trust, it can be made only to the income beneficiary.

e. a qualified electing small business trust (ESBT), which is created only by gifts or bequests of S corporation stock and which can have more than one beneficiary. There are tax disadvantages associated with the use of an ESBT, such as the trust being taxed on all S corporation income at a 39.6 percent rate and the lack of a distribution deduction for income distributed to its beneficiaries.

4. The corporation must have no more than one class of stock outstanding. "One class of stock" means that all shares of the corporation have identical distribution and termination rights. The Treasury regulations set forth many situations in which a second class of stock will be deemed to have been issued by the S corporation.

Any corporation meeting all the criteria listed above can elect S corporation status. The election may be made at any time during the taxable year preceding the year the election is to go into effect. For example, for a corporation with a calendar-year taxable year, the election could be made on November 1, 2002, and would become effective on January 1, 2003. The election can also be made on or before the 15th day of the third month of the year in which the election is to be effective; that is, an election made on or before March 15, 2003, would be effective as of January 1, 2003. If the corporation fails to make the election until after the 15th day of the third month of the year in which the election is intended to be effective, it will be treated as an election made for the succeeding tax year. The consent of all shareholders on the day the election is made is required. In the case of an election made on or before the 15th day of the third month of the election year, the consent of anyone who was a shareholder during the preelection portion of the year is also necessary to effect the election.

A new shareholder who wants to revoke the S election may do so if he or she owns more than 50 percent of the corporation's stock and refuses to affirmatively consent to the election within 60 days after acquiring it. If a new shareholder owning less than 50 percent of the corporation's stock becomes a shareholder while an S election is in effect, the new shareholder will be bound by the election.

Once a valid election for Subchapter S status is made, the election is in effect for the tax year for which it was made and continues in effect for all subsequent years unless it is terminated or voluntarily revoked. The election may be terminated or revoked in any of the following ways:

- Shareholders owning more than 50 percent of the stock consent to a voluntary revocation.
- The corporation fails to continue to satisfy any one of the qualification requirements (for instance, there are more than 75 shareholders or the corporation issues a second class of stock).
- More than 25 percent of the S corporation's gross receipts for 3 successive tax years is from certain types of passive income, and the corporation has accumulated earnings and profits from a period prior to the S status election when it had operated as a C corporation.

An involuntary termination of S status (such as the issuance of stock to a prohibited shareholder) is effective as of the day the disqualifying event occurs and not retroactively to the beginning of the taxable year. The IRS may waive the effect of an inadvertent termination for any period, provided the corporation corrects the event that created the termination, and the corporation and its shareholders agree to be treated as if the election had been in effect for the entire period.

A revocation of Subchapter S status can be made on or before the 15th day of the third month of the present taxable year and will be effective for that entire taxable year unless the revocation specifically requests a date in the future. In the event that a future date is specified (for example, an election to revoke on January 1, 2003, was made on November 30, 2003), the revocation will be effective on that date (January 1, 2003). If no future date of revocation is specified but the election is filed after the permissible period, the revocation is effective at the beginning of the following taxable year. Voluntary revocations result in an inability to reelect Subchapter S status for 5 years without obtaining IRS consent to the reelection. In appropriate circumstances the IRS can waive the 5-year waiting period and permit the corporation to make a new election effective for the following taxable year.

The choice of tax year for an S corporation is determined by applying the same rules that apply to partnerships and personal service corporations. A new S corporation is required to have a taxable year ending December 31 unless it can establish to the satisfaction of the IRS that it has a business purpose for choosing another taxable year. For most businesses this will be difficult to establish.

Shareholder-employees of new S corporations who own (either individually or by attribution under IRC Sec. 318) more than 2 percent of the outstanding stock of the S corporation or stock having more than 2 percent of the voting power of all the S corporation's stock are ineligible for certain tax-free benefits that are available to regular (C) corporation shareholder-employees. These benefits primarily include certain group medical, disability, and life insurance benefits (IRC Sec. 1372 applying IRC Sec. 7701(a)(2)). Recent law changes have begun to phase in these benefits for S corporation shareholders. The overall effect of these rules is to treat S corporation shareholders as if they were partners when determining the tax status of fringe benefits.

Income from an S corporation is not taxed at the corporate level. Instead it is passed through to the individual shareholders in proportion to their percentage of stock ownership. This eliminates any possibility of reducing the individual shareholder's tax liability by splitting income between the shareholder and the corporation. While the S corporation can work effectively, especially in passing through the start-up losses of a new business to offset other income of shareholders and in limiting the personal liability of shareholders, care should be taken in making a Subchapter S election or in revoking such an election once it has been made. Professionals can incorporate and elect Subchapter S status. Creating an S corporation for professionals may provide some liability protection, but it cannot shield the professional from his or her own negligence or malpractice.

C Corporations

As a general rule property can be transferred from a proprietorship or a partnership into a regular corporation (or to an S corporation) without the recognition of gain or loss on the transfer (IRC Sec. 351). The regular or C corporation is both a tax-reporting and a tax-paying entity. There are separate rates of corporate taxation, and the benefits of splitting the taxation of corporate profits between the corporation and the individual shareholders can be material, especially when the shareholders are in high tax brackets. The corporate tax rate for the first $50,000 of taxable income is 15 percent for C corporations (except for qualified personal service corporations). However, leaving excessive funds in the corporation to avoid taxation at the individual level can lead to additional tax problems such as the accumulated-earnings penalty tax, which is a punitive tax, with additional tax rates of 39.6 percent imposed on all accumulated taxable income (IRC Secs. 531–537). The accumulated-earnings tax prevents individuals from retaining funds in the corporation for purposes other than the reasonable needs of the business. However, operating businesses can maintain up to $250,000 in the corporation without subjecting themselves to the accumulated-earnings tax. Professional corporations such as a medical practice are personal service corporations and are allowed to accumulate up to $150,000 without subjecting themselves to the accumulated-earnings tax. If accumulated taxable income exceeds these amounts, the retention of earnings and profits must be to meet reasonable business needs or the corporation will be subject to the accumulated-earnings tax. This tax is imposed in addition to regular corporate tax rates. Except in unusual circumstances the accumulated-earnings tax is not a major problem in a professional corporation, since most income can be paid out in the form of salaries and tax-advantaged benefits for the shareholder-employees.

There are few intricate rules for setting up a regular corporation for tax purposes. There is no limitation on the number or type of persons or entities that can be shareholders. Any enterprise doing business in a corporate form, as defined under state law—and indeed some associations that are not technically legal corporations but possess a majority of the corporate attributes (centralized management, continuity of life, limited liability, and free transferability of interest) are treated as corporations for tax purposes. Owners of regular corporations may also be employees of the corporations and as such are entitled to reasonable salaries and certain tax-free fringe benefits.

An important nontax advantage of the corporate form, whether it is an S corporation or a regular C corporation, is the limited personal liability of the shareholders. The general rule is that in a suit or claim against the corporation a shareholder's potential liability is limited to the amount of money that he or she has invested in the corporation.

As noted earlier, the liability of a professional is not completely limited. Each professional is personally responsible for his or her own negligence regardless of whether the practice is conducted in corporate form. This risk cannot be shifted to the entity and must be insured against. Further, in Georgia one shareholder in a professional corporation may be subject to liability for the actions of another shareholder. Therefore incorporation of a medical practice does not produce a significant liability advantage in Georgia.

There is additional expense in changing the form of any business from a sole proprietorship to a corporation. These expenses will result primarily from the necessity of filing separate tax returns. There are also significant organizational expenses involved in establishing a corporation.

Limited Liability Companies

Limited liability companies (LLCs) offer many of the advantages of the corporate form of business but still allow income to pass through to the individual shareholders. A limited liability company is treated as a partnership for federal tax purposes even though it generally offers limited liability for its members.

Like corporations, limited liability companies do not offer absolute protection for members in a professional practice. As a physician, Dave cannot protect himself against malpractice claims resulting from his own negligence by forming a business entity. He can only protect himself against the malpractice claims brought against his partners. An LLC would provide Dave with protection from malpractice claims against his partners if the medical practice was allowed to operate as an LLC. Many states, however, have laws that prohibit a professional practice from operating as an LLC. Consequently an LLC would not be a viable option in this case.

Recommendations

Due to the nature of Dave's professional relationship with Drs. Brown and Cole, he should not consider forming a professional partnership with them at this time. Dave has indicated clearly that he has no wish to be part of a larger organization.

Therefore the remaining issue is whether Dave should continue to operate as a sole proprietor or incorporate his practice either as a C or as an S corporation.

As previously stated, incorporation in this case does not present significant protection from personal liability, since Dave is personally liable for his own professional acts regardless of whether he incorporates, and he has no partners for whose acts he would be liable. As long as Dave maintains adequate professional liability insurance, his personal assets should be protected. There is no compelling reason for Dave to incorporate at this time. Although the costs of incorporation are not significant, it is not appropriate to incur them without obtaining any substantial advantage. Moreover, a C corporation could present tax problems if Dave decided to liquidate the corporation, since *both* the shareholder and the C corporation are taxed on the distribution of appreciated assets in a liquidation. Dave could obtain tax-free group insurance and borrow from his qualified plan under the corporate form, but these advantages do not appear to outweigh the costs in this case.

An S corporation would not provide Dave with any significant advantages. Therefore the recommendation in this case is to continue operating as a sole proprietorship in light of an absence of any compelling reason to incorporate.

Qualified Plans of Deferred Compensation

Dave's Keogh plan is of the profit-sharing type. In a profit-sharing plan, the employer may make an annual deductible contribution of up to 25 percent of covered compensation. A separate rule (Sec. 415 limits) requires that no single employee may have more than the lesser of 25 percent of pay or $40,000 allocated to his or her account annually.

> # NOTE
>
> To avoid repetition, the technical information on defined-benefit and defined-contribution plans has been omitted from this discussion. In a complete financial plan, an analysis of qualified plan benefits would be necessary. If you are not familiar with this information, please review it before proceeding through this suggested solution.

Since Dave's plan is a Keogh plan, the maximum 25 percent deduction limit is complicated by the fact that compensation for a self-employed person is defined as his or her "earned income." Earned income is calculated after taking into account all appropriate business deductions, which include the contribution to the plan. This rule has the impact of reducing the maximum contribution for the self-employed to 20 percent of earned income by disregarding the contribution to the plan.

Also note that earned income from self-employment is also reduced by the deduction for one-half of an individual's self-employment Social Security taxes. Dave is required to pay a total of $16,327.60 in Social Security taxes. This is calculated as follows:

The OASDI tax: 12.40 percent x $84,900 (for 2002) = $10,527.60
plus
The health insurance (HI) tax: 2.9 percent x $200,000 = $5,800.

Since Dave's total Social Security taxes are $16,327.60, he can take a deduction of $8,163.80, thus reducing his maximum contribution by lowering his compensation to $191,836. Under these rules, the maximum contribution in his behalf is $38,367 ($191,836.20 x 20 percent).

However, a third rule also has to be considered, which may reduce the maximum contribution further. Under the Omnibus Reconciliation Act of 1993, the maximum amount of compensation that can be considered in determining contributions or benefits cannot exceed $200,000 (in 2002). This compensation cap is used for calculating benefits and for determining the maximum allowable deduction. For example, in Dave's nonintegrated plan he is contributing 15 percent of compensation to the plan for each employee. This means that the contribution for him is 15 percent of $200,000, or $30,000. In addition, when determining the maximum deductible contribution the limit also applies. For example, since all participants in Dave's plan are receiving 15 percent of compensation, the contribution is at the maximum deductible 15 percent limit. Note that it would be possible for Dave to have somewhat more under this rule if other participants were receiving contributions of less than 15 percent of compensation. One way to do this would be to integrate the plan with Social Security (see below).

Integration with Social Security

Dave has indicated that he is not interested in unduly discriminating against his employees with regard to benefits in the plan, although he is interested in minimizing costs. With these two considerations in mind, Dave might consider integrating his plan with Social Security. In this way, Dave can continue to make a contribution for himself in the amount of 15 percent of compensation while somewhat reducing the contribution for his employees. In the existing nonintegrated plan, contributions are allocated to participants on a pro rata basis, based on each individual's compensation. Therefore if Dave makes a contribution of 15 percent for himself, he is also making a contribution of 15 percent of compensation for each employee. With an integrated plan, Dave can make a 15 percent contribution on his behalf, while contributing only 12 percent of compensation for his employees. The integrated contribution results in significant savings, while still providing employees with an excellent retirement plan.

Mechanics of Social Security Integration. The nondiscrimination rules provide that in a profit-sharing plan, employer contributions can be allocated to participants as a level percentage of compensation. In addition, a larger portion of the employer's contribution (as a percentage of compensation) may be allocated to those employees who earn more the taxable wage base. This "disparity" is allowed in the private pension system due to the fact that employers are required to make higher contributions (as a percentage of salary) to the Social Security system for those individuals who earn less than the taxable wage base. In essence, since the Social Security system discriminates in favor of nonhighly compensated employees, the employer is allowed to make up for this in a private pension plan by discriminating in favor of the highly compensated (to the extent allowed under the rules).

In any defined-contribution plan (which includes a profit-sharing plan), the sponsor can provide a higher rate of contributions to the participant for compensation above the integration level (referred to as the excess contribution percentage) than for compensation below the integration level (the base contribution percentage). The integration level is usually the taxable wage base.

When the integration level is the taxable wage base, the difference between the two percentages (the permitted disparity) cannot exceed the lesser of the base contribution percentage or 5.7 percent. For example, a plan providing a contribution percentage of 4 percent for contributions based on compensation below the integration level could provide no more than a contribution percentage of 8 percent for contributions based on compensation above the integration level. If a plan provides 7 percent below the integration level, it could provide up to 12.7 percent above the integration level (the disparity equals 5.7 percent).

If the integration level is reduced below the taxable wage base, the 5.7 percent maximum disparity is adjusted as follows:

Integration Level	Maximum Disparity
Taxable wage base (TWB)	5.7 percent
80 percent or more of TWB	5.4
20 to 80 percent of TWB	4.3
Less than 20 percent of TWB	.7

In Dave's case, if he wants to contribute 15 percent of the $200,000 compensation cap for himself ($30,000), while reducing the contributions made on behalf of his staff, he will look to maximize the disparity allowed under the integration rules. In this case, if Dave chooses the taxable wage base as the integration level, a contribution of $30,000 is the same as an allocation of 5.7 percent of compensation in excess of $84,900 ($6,561) and 11.7 percent of total compensation ($23,439). Since each of his employees earns less than the taxable wage base, 11.7 percent will have to be contributed on behalf of each employee.

To maximize the disparity, the planner should test whether integrating at various integration levels will result in smaller contributions for the nonhighly compensated employees. In this case integrating at $67,920 (80 percent of the integration level) and at $16,980 (20 percent of the integration level) will not significantly lower the required contribution for nonhighly compensated employees.

Money-Purchase Pension Plan

Another option that Dave has is to add a second plan to supplement his profit-sharing plan. Because of the various Keogh profit-sharing limits described above, Dave is making a contribution of only $22,500 on his own behalf to the profit-sharing plan. However, under law, he can have a maximum of $40,000 allocated to his accounts under all defined-contribution plans. To make up for this difference Dave might consider increasing the profit-sharing percentage or adopting a money-purchase pension plan. With a money-purchase profit-sharing combination, the maximum deductible contribution is still 25 percent of compensation. This would allow Dave the opportunity to contribute the full $40,000.

Unlike a profit-sharing plan, a money-purchase plan must have a predetermined contribution formula. At the present time Dave is making 15 percent contributions to the profit-sharing plan. However, if at any time he wants to make a smaller contribution, he is allowed to do so. If he establishes a money-purchase pension plan, he will have less flexibility. Because of the required contributions to a money-purchase plan, if Dave establishes a money-purchase plan as a supplemental plan it should provide for the minimum contribution necessary to make up the difference between the $22,500 and the maximum of

$40,000. If Dave establishes a money-purchase pension plan, he may want to provide for an 8.75 percent contribution formula ($200,000 x 8.75 percent equals $17,500).

Recommendation for Qualified Plans for Dave

Adding this supplemental plan is an interesting solution for Dave but will require him to make annual contributions. Instead, Dave could retain complete flexibility by reserving the right to contribute up to 25 percent of compensation to the profit-sharing plan. Furthermore, if Dave restructures the profit-sharing plan to integrate it with Social Security, his employees will end up with only slightly higher contributions than they have currently under the nonintegrated profit-sharing plan. Therefore we have offered Dave two choices—either integrate the profit-sharing plan to reduce his costs and make contributions up to the 25 percent limit, or increase the contribution in his behalf while keeping the contribution level stable for his employees with the money-purchase integrated profit-sharing plan example.

Dave should seek the assistance of a pension attorney or consultant if he decides to integrate the profit-sharing plan or adopt a money-purchase pension plan. This assistance will help Dave to determine exactly how he can best meet his objectives. Also, if Dave decides to change his profit-sharing plan or add a money-purchase plan, he will incur additional expenses. Dave needs to fully understand these costs so that he can compare the cost savings of the plan redesign against the additional costs that he will incur.

Other Methods of Creating Disparity. Another plan design called *age-weighting* has emerged that could, in Dave's case, be used to create a larger disparity between the contribution made in Dave's behalf and the contributions made for other employees.

Age-weighting is a method of allocating employer contributions to a profit-sharing plan. An age-weighted allocation formula takes into consideration an individual's age and his or her compensation. Age-weighting results in larger contributions (as a percentage of compensation) for older employees. When the highly compensated employees are older than the nonhighly compensated employees, age-weighting can be even more advantageous for the highly compensated employees than integrating the plan with Social Security.

The reason that age-weighting is allowed is that the nondiscrimination rules allow a plan to demonstrate that either contributions or benefits are provided in a nondiscriminatory manner. In an age-weighted profit-sharing plan, contributions will discriminate in favor of highly compensated employees. However, benefits will not be discriminatory. Larger contributions can be justified as necessary to support the same level of benefits for older employees as for younger employees. An analogous situation is the purchase of a single-premium annuity. The price for an annuity with a specific monthly retirement benefit will increase as the age of the purchaser increases. In the same way, in an age-weighted profit-sharing plan, larger contributions can be made for older employees if the contributions result in a similar level of monthly retirement benefits for each employee.

The theory of age-weighting is simple, although the mechanics can be somewhat complex. In Dave's case, age-weighting could work since he is 8 years older than the next oldest employee. However, Dave is not a good candidate for an age-weighted profit-sharing plan since he is not interested in substantially reducing contributions for his employees.

Buy-Sell Agreements to Ensure That Dave's Practice Is Marketable at Death or Disability

One of the Andersons' most important assets is Dave's practice; in fact, it is presently their most important asset in terms of income production. However, there is no guarantee that the practice could be translated into cash within a reasonable time after his death or disability because Dave has never implemented a legally enforceable agreement for the sale of his practice. The failure to implement a legally enforceable and appropriately funded buy-sell agreement often results in significant losses upon the disposition of a closely held business.

In the event that Dave continues to live but becomes disabled, his business interest should be convertible to cash to provide him with additional monies throughout the period of his disability. The design and implementation of an appropriate buy-sell agreement is the most effective way to ensure the accomplishment of these objectives.

Because buy-sell agreements are usually funded wholly or partially with life insurance, they are particularly troublesome when the parties are of widely disparate ages or if one of the parties' health is impaired. The difference in ages or health conditions can result in the younger or healthier party being forced to personally pay nondeductible high premiums for insurance on the life of an older or impaired party.

We have no information that would indicate that such a problem might arise in this case. In the absence of these problems Dave should discuss the possibility of entering into a buy-sell agreement with either Dr. Cole or Dr. Brown or both, since they have expressed an interest in expanding their practices. Since Dave is not particularly interested in expanding his practice, it may be possible to interest one or both of the other physicians in agreeing to purchase his practice should he die or become disabled. On the other hand, it may be necessary for Dave to agree to a reciprocal purchase agreement if he wants the assurance that his practice can be quickly converted to cash. Based on the results of these negotiations, Dave can decide whether to proceed.

If Dave decides to proceed with buy-out arrangements, the provisions and funding of the agreement should be carefully considered. At a minimum the agreement(s) should provide for the other party or parties to become obligated to purchase Dave's shares if he is deceased or becomes disabled. While death is easily ascertainable, issues may arise as to when disability should trigger a buy-out.

In the event of disability, however, the definition of disability that will make the buy-sell operative must be contained within the document in order to make the document effective for this purpose.

A buy-sell agreement should not be designed to provide for the immediate buyout of a disabled party. An appropriate waiting period should be adopted to balance the client's need for disability income and the time at which the client can psychologically deal with the fact that he or she will be unable to resume professional duties.

One of the most difficult aspects of any buy-sell agreement is deciding on a valuation for the business interest. The best way to ascertain the value of a going business is to have the business appraised by an appropriate professional. In many cases, however, closely held business owners are reluctant to engage an appraiser because of the expense. In addition, even if an appraisal is made currently and a firm dollar value is entered into the buy-sell agreement, it is likely that the agreement may not become operative for many years. In that event the appraisal figure is meaningless because it is badly outdated. This does not mean, however, that the parties to the buy-sell agreement can ignore the stated dollar figure. In fact, the value of the business could have risen tenfold or fallen to half its stated value, yet if the dollar figure stated in the buy-sell agreement has not been revised, the purchasing party is obligated to pay only the original price as stated in the agreement. This can result in a significant hardship to the estate or beneficiaries of the closely held business owner if the value of the business has increased or to the purchaser if the value of the business has decreased.

It is human nature that even with a buy-sell in effect, most parties to such agreements will not meet to redetermine the value of the business on a regular basis because they are usually preoccupied with other matters. Absolute dollar values are problematic and should be avoided.

In the case of a personal service business such as Dave's professional practice, if he can be persuaded to obtain an appraisal on the current value of the business, that value can be used as the starting point for the valuation of the buy-sell agreement. Furthermore, the appraisal will almost certainly provide the criteria upon which an appropriate ongoing valuation formula for the practice can be based. A valuation formula should be included in the buy-sell agreement in lieu of a stated dollar figure if possible. The formula approach is preferable to any other since it allows the value of the business to be determined at any given point in time.

Buy-sell agreements may also be effective for establishing estate tax value if appropriately structured. In order to be binding for estate tax purposes the buy-sell agreement must (1) have a valid business purpose, (2) be binding on transfers during life and at the death of the present owner, (3) have a value that is predetermined or ascertainable according to a formula, and (4) obligate the business owner's estate to sell at the contract price at the death of the business owner. This approach is sometimes referred to as "pegging" the value and is discussed at length in Rev. Rul. 59-60 and IRC Sec. 2703.

As long as no attempt is made to transfer the business for less than its fair value, the IRS is usually bound by such an agreement. However, if any one of the four conditions set forth above is not met, the IRS is not bound by the agreement and the results can be very distressing. The purchaser could pay the estate of the deceased business owner the lower value stated in the buy-sell agreement while the IRS will include the value of the business in the estate at a much higher value. In this event there is a case, *Estate of Dickinson v. Comm'r*, 63 T.C. 771 (1975), that holds that a buy-sell agreement can validly contain a provision stating that if the Internal Revenue Service is successful in an attack on the stated valuation, the estate is no longer bound by the lower value in the buy-sell agreement.

IRC Sec. 2703 prohibits the use of any agreement for the purpose of affixing the value of a business interest unless (1) the arrangement is a bona fide business arrangement, (2) the arrangement is not a device to transfer the business interest to members of a decedent's family for less than full and adequate consideration, and (3) the arrangement is comparable to similar arrangements entered into by persons in an arm's-length transaction.

In this case a unilateral purchase agreement between one or both of Dave's professional colleagues and Dave should be explored. It is likely that Dave's colleagues will want a reciprocal buy-sell arrangement, in which case Dave will have to decide whether he is willing to rethink his decision about increasing the size of his practice. The agreement should be funded partially or wholly by insurance to the extent that it is available. A realistic value for Dave's practice should be established, preferably by an appraisal, and maintained by a formula set forth in the buy-sell agreement.

BUSINESS PLANNING: INSURANCE

Funding the Buy-Sell Agreement(s)

As already indicated, the recommendation for funding the buy-sell agreement is full or partial funding with life insurance. At this point, without further information about whether the buy-sell agreement will be a unilateral or cross-purchase agreement, specific funding recommendations for a death time buyout would be inappropriate.

The other elements that must be considered in funding the buy-sell agreement are the appropriate amount and availability of coverage if Dave's disability triggers the buy-sell.

Insurers are generally unwilling to provide coverage with lump-sum benefits for professionals who are sole practitioners. Therefore it will be necessary for Dave to discuss with Dr. Cole or Dr. Brown or both whether one or both would be willing to enter into a buy-sell agreement that would protect him in the event of his becoming disabled without the agreement being insured. If one or both of the other physicians are interested in these terms, the business valuation price according to the formula in the buy-sell agreement may be paid in installments over the shortest possible period that Dave and his attorneys can negotiate.

The crucial issues in an uninsured disability buyout are not materially different from the issues encountered in insured agreements. They include primarily the definition of disability and the waiting period before the agreement becomes operative. The parties must agree to the definition of disability, and the length of the waiting period must be set forth in unambiguous terms in the buy-sell agreement.

There is a real danger in selecting too short a waiting period for a buyout agreement as it could result in a mandatory sale of Dave's business interest because of a relatively short-term disability that lasts longer than the waiting period specified by the agreement. It would be advisable to have a waiting period of at least 24 months before triggering the buyout agreement.

Medical and Disability Insurance Plans

If Dave decides not to incorporate his practice, there does not appear to be any significant advantage to having the existing proprietorship provide additional group insurance benefits, as proprietors are not considered employees of proprietorships, and therefore contributions in their behalf are not tax deductible. Therefore no tax savings could be achieved, except for his medical coverage as discussed below.

Medical Expense Insurance

The medical insurance plan that Dave presently provides for his employees and in which he and his family participate appears to provide excellent benefits at a competitive price. The premiums paid on behalf of the employees are deductible as a business expense. However, since Dave operates as a sole proprietorship, the tax treatment of health benefits provided for himself and his family is different. In 2002 sole proprietors can deduct against gross income 70 percent of the cost of purchasing health insurance coverage for themselves and their own families. This deduction will increase to 100 percent in 2003 and thereafter. Health insurance premiums in excess of the gross income deduction are treated as medical expenses, which can be an itemized deduction to the extent that total medical expenses exceed 7.5 percent of adjusted gross income.

Disability Income Insurance

Although Dave presently has an individual disability plan, a review of the limits of its coverage makes it apparent that it is insufficient to allow him to maintain his present lifestyle. In all likelihood it will be impossible to achieve this objective solely with disability income protection, since insurers will not provide such a high ratio of coverage to total income. Generally a higher upper limit of coverage is available if an employer purchases the disability income coverage than if the employee individually purchases the coverage. In this case, however, the overall limit would be approximately $6,000 per month of benefits either through an employer plan or (as in this case) if Dave purchases the coverage individually. This results from the fact that at this high level of income, maximum benefit limits tend to merge.

Upper-limit coverage that would pay benefits if Dave is unable to perform his own occupation for a period of 5 years and thereafter unable to perform any occupation for which he is otherwise suited by reason of education can be obtained for an annual premium of $2,617 for either a corporate plan or for an individually owned policy, each with a 90-day elimination period. A 180-day elimination period would reduce the premium to $2,486, a savings of $131 annually.

Our recommendation would be that disability income coverage with a 90-day waiting period be purchased by Dave individually. Since Dave is not incorporated, coverage through a group plan would be more costly and provide no tax advantage. The 90-day elimination period is worth the approximate additional cost of $131 per year.

Property and Liability Insurance for the Business

With little information given in the case about the business assets to be covered by property and liability insurance, it is difficult to make any recommendations other than noting the necessity of having these coverages thoroughly reviewed by a professional in the field of property and liability insurance.

Professional Liability Insurance

Professional liability coverage for physicians and surgeons is often referred to as medical malpractice insurance. As a result of the significant premium increases in this type of insurance and the objections to those increases by physicians, a newer type of lower-cost policy has become popular.

The original type of coverage, known as occurrence-based coverage, protected the insured from any claims stemming from medical procedures performed while the policy was in force. This coverage would pay benefits for liability even if the incident giving rise to the liability was first discovered many years after the policy expiration date and when no further premiums were being paid. Thus the premium charged while the policy was in force had to be high enough to cover inflation and the risk associated with future claims amounts.

The newer type of policy, known as claims-made coverage, pays only for claims made during the time the policy is in force. Claims will be payable by the insurer only if the medical treatment giving rise to the claim was performed after the retroactive date specified in the policy and before the policy termination date. This type of policy necessitates continuation of coverage after the medical professional retires or otherwise discontinues practice. The extended reporting-period endorsements keep this protection in effect after the base policy terminates. Premiums must generally be paid for the first 3 years of the extended reporting-period endorsements. If the professional does not engage in any aspect of practice for the entire 3-year period, a single additional premium of less than the regular premium will extend the claims-made protection to perpetuity.

In cases where the physician changes back to an occurrence-based coverage after having a period of claims-made coverage, it will also be necessary to extend the reporting period by endorsements. Without such extension there would be a gap in coverage. The occurrence-based coverage would not cover procedures performed during the period the claims-made coverage was effective.

In terms of cost the claims-made coverage can be as low as one-quarter of the premium for occurrence-based coverage in the first year. The claims-made premiums will increase to about 85 percent of occurrence-based premiums after 5 or more years.

The potential liability for an orthopedic surgeon is quite high. In fact, there have already been single-case liability judgments in medical cases that exceeded $5 million. It is therefore suggested that professional liability coverage with policy limits of $10 million be carried. If the policy acquired is claims-made coverage, it is important to seek a retroactive date that coincides with the termination date of the most recent occurrence-based professional liability coverage. Although coverage for $1 million of liability protection is available at a cost of approximately $12,000 annually, Dave's sole proprietorship can obtain the recommended $10 million of protection on Dave and his nursing staff for about $27,000 a year. This provides 10 times the liability protection for 2.25 times the cost.

Business Overhead Expense Disability Insurance

Because of the limitations that insurers impose on the upper limits of disability income benefits, it is virtually impossible to get adequate coverage to ensure that all the usual and normal expenses of one's life are covered by insurance benefits, especially when the disabled person has continuing business overhead expenses. Business overhead expense disability coverage aims at closing this gap. In a case such as Dave's this coverage normally pays for continuing business expenses, such as office rent, utilities, nurses' salaries, postage, office equipment and supplies, and business taxes. This type of disability is usually defined as the inability to perform the duties of the insured's own occupation. Various benefit durations are available but should not exceed the effective date of the disability buyout provisions of the buy-sell agreement if Dave and Drs. Brown and/or Cole enter into such an agreement. Based on the facts of this case approximately $5,000 in monthly benefits would be the maximum available coverage, and benefits would be available for a period of 24 months. Representative annual premiums for $5,000 in monthly benefits with various elimination periods are listed below. The elimination period should be based on Dave's available cash flow. The recommendation is that a period of no less than 60 days be elected.

Elimination Period	Annual Premium
30 days	$1,025
60 days	630
90 days	385

PERSONAL PLANNING: TAXES

Present Situation

Dave and Diana have been married for 16 years. They have three children: Keith, 10, Deidre, 9, and Melissa, 6, and have just discovered that they will have another child in about 7 months. The older children are very intelligent, and the Andersons are considering sending them to a private high school with rigorous academic standards, where tuition is $5,000 per school year. Dave and Diana would also like to plan now to finance college educations for their children.

They purchased a home for $79,000 that has appreciated to its present value of $315,000. The house is furnished with some lovely antiques that Diana has acquired over the years. They own two relatively new cars.

Dave owns a single-family residential rental property and an undeveloped commercial lot. A potential buyer has made an offer for the commercial lot, and Dave is interested in a recommendation as to whether the lot should be sold. Dave has been acquiring a portfolio of stocks, bonds, and mutual fund shares.

Dave earns a substantial income from his practice as an orthopedic surgeon, and the Andersons enjoy a good life. They want to maximize their wealth accumulation, provide themselves with retirement funds sufficient to continue their lifestyle, and provide for the family if Dave should die prematurely.

Fund Private School and/or College Education for Children

Dave and Diana have asked you to prepare an estimate of projected costs for educating their children at a top-quality institution.

As discussed in the investment planning section, the cost of funding the college educations for Keith, Deidre, and Melissa would be in excess of $250,000 if the funding was accomplished with a lump sum in today's dollars, given reasonable assumptions regarding inflation and rates of return. If college education funding is done on an annual basis from the present until each child completes college, the annual funding amount would be approximately $26,000.

Since the Andersons are in a 33 percent federal tax bracket beginning in 2006 and also pay state income tax, they must earn at least $1.49 for every $1 they can accumulate for accomplishing this goal.

Obviously the best way to accumulate this sum is on a tax-advantaged basis. One of the ways this is accomplished in harmonious family situations is through the mechanism of gift giving.

Gifting

Outright Gifts. Under the current federal gift tax exclusion, a person (donor) can give any other person (donee) up to $11,000 per year per donee, gift tax free (IRC Sec. 2503(b)). That amount can be doubled if the donor's spouse agrees to join in the gift, regardless of whether the spouse actually contributes any portion of the gift (IRC Sec. 2513). This annual gift tax exclusion is often touted as an effective way for clients to shift assets to their children and take advantage of the children's lower tax brackets. However, outright gifting presents some problems. The person giving the gift (the donor) must part forever with the property that is gifted, including any earning capacity that it has. All but the wealthiest clients are reluctant to part with assets that they may need for their later years.

The Andersons could utilize outright gifting to supplement other accumulation techniques if actual college costs exceed those that are anticipated and funded for. If these "gifts" were made in the form of actual tuition payments to a qualified educational institution, the amounts would be totally exempt from federal gift taxes (IRC Sec. 2503(e)). They would, however, have to be made with after-tax dollars; therefore there are better techniques for funding the bulk of their children's educations.

UGMA and UTMA Gifts. In addition to the problems already described with outright gifting, there are problems with giving gifts to minors. The Uniform Gifts to Minors Act (UGMA) and the Uniform Transfers to Minors Act (UTMA) provide mechanisms by which a donor can give a gift to a minor without necessitating the appointment of a guardian of the minor's property. (A majority of the states have adopted the newer Uniform Transfers to Minors Act.) Instead, a custodian of the gift is designated. This custodian has full powers over the gifted property and its income on behalf of the minor child. In many cases the donor is the minor child's parent, who also functions as the custodian of the UGMA or UTMA account. Gifts under the Uniform Acts qualify under the federal gift tax provisions as present-interest gifts without the necessity of withdrawal rights or annual payments of income and as such are subject to the $11,000-per-year-per-donee gift tax exclusion (IRC Secs. 2503(b), 2503(c)).

There are some planning issues associated with UGMA and UTMA gifts:

- If the donor is the parent of the minor and also the custodian of the UGMA or UTMA account and dies while still the custodian, the total amount of the account will be included in his or her estate for federal estate tax purposes because of the control he or she can exercise over the account (IRC Sec. 2036(a)).

- The type of property that can be transferred effectively under the Uniform Acts is severely restricted in some states. The Uniform Acts are *not* uniform from state to state. When the original UGMA was being lobbied for, the most effective lobbying group consisted primarily of securities dealers attempting to facilitate gifts of stock and securities to minors. The result of this lobbying effort is that many of the UGMA statutes enacted by the various states restrict UGMA gifts to money, securities, life insurance, or annuity contracts. Other types of property, such as real estate, cannot be effectively transferred by UGMA gifts in many states. (If this is the result in the state in which a particular client is located, the UGMA transfer can be made under the UGMA statute in one of the several states that allows for transfers of almost any type of property, including real estate. This is accomplished by having the instrument specify that the transfer is being made pursuant to the Uniform Gifts to Minors Act of the more favorable state.) In states that have adopted the Uniform Transfers to Minors Act, there is more flexibility regarding the types of assets that may be transferred.

- The custodianship generally terminates when the minor reaches either age 21 or the local legal age of majority. At that time all funds in the custodial account must be distributed to the beneficiary. This gives the 18-, 19-, or 21-year-old (depending on local law) unfettered discretion over the disposition of the assets, which may result in the assets being squandered rather than being used for the purpose for which the custodianship was established.

- Income from assets in custodial accounts will be subject to the kiddie tax for minors under 14 years of age, regardless of whether the income is distributed to the minor. A custodial account, unlike a trust, is not a separate taxpayer from the minor beneficiary.

While gifts to minors under UGMA or UTMA can be utilized effectively for relatively small sums, they are generally not the technique of choice for larger sums because of the mandatory distribution at the legal age of majority, the potential kiddie tax problems, and potential federal estate tax inclusion for the donor-parent who acts as custodian.

Income Shifting

One of the most effective ways to accumulate assets for objectives such as the funding of education for children is to use a technique that splits income and family assets between highly taxed adults in the family and the children, who are taxed in lower brackets, if at all. It has long been settled under federal tax law that one cannot assign a portion of the income that one earns to another and avoid taxation (*Lucas v. Earl*, 281 U.S. 111 (1930)). It is, however, possible to assign property to another person, either irrevocably or for a statutorily required period of time, and have the income taxed to the donee or assignee. The techniques for accomplishing this are called income-shifting techniques and can result in substantial net family tax savings.

Sec. 2503(b) Trusts. A trust device that can be utilized to provide gifts to minors is the IRC Sec. 2503(b) trust, which provides certain advantages and disadvantages when compared with the Sec. 2503(c) trust, discussed later in this section. The principal advantage of the Sec. 2503(b) trust is that it need not terminate when the beneficiary attains the age of 21. A principal disadvantage is that the trust must pay the net income to the beneficiary annually or in more frequent installments. That is, it cannot accumulate income even during the minority of the beneficiary. This means that income from the trust that is paid to beneficiaries under the age of 14 will be taxed at the marginal rate of the beneficiary's parents, generally to the extent that the child's income exceeds $1,500 per year adjusted for inflation (under the kiddie tax). This substantially reduces the income shifting benefits of the 2503(b) trust.

Another disadvantage of the Sec. 2503(b) trust is that the value of the income interest and the value of the remainder interest (the property that composes the principal of the trust) are computed separately for gift tax purposes. Only the value of the income interest is eligible for the annual gift tax exclusion.

The Sec. 2503(b) trust may not allow discretionary payments to more than one beneficiary. Furthermore, there can be no postponement or delay in the payment of the net income of the trust. If there are any restrictions on distribution of trust income (for example, if the income is conditional or discretionary in any way) the annual exclusion will be unavailable.

The mandatory payment of the trust income can be a major tax and nontax disadvantage when the beneficiary is a minor. This is especially true if significant sums of money are involved, since it could necessitate the appointment of a guardian of the minor's property. This procedure is both expensive and tedious. Guardians are subject to court supervision in handling the funds of the minor and are statutorily prohibited from entering into certain investment transactions.

Because of the mandatory payment requirement and the fact that the trust beneficiaries—the Anderson children—are minors under age 14, it would not be advisable to utilize the 2503(b) trust to fund college education for the children.

Sec. 2503(c) Trusts. If a trust is structured according to the terms of IRC Sec. 2503(c), gifts to the trust qualify for the gift tax exclusion without giving the beneficiary a right to withdraw funds or without the necessity for paying the beneficiary the income at least annually. A transfer to a Sec. 2503(c) trust can be more advantageous than transfers to an UGMA custodianship because no statutory restriction on the type of property transferred is applicable in the case of 2503(c) trusts. In addition, the property can be maintained in the trust at least until the beneficiary reaches age 21, even when the age of majority under state law is less than 21. A Sec. 2503(c) trust is an irrevocable trust. Therefore the donor cannot take back the funds once they are gifted to the trust.

The Internal Revenue Code requires that both the property and the income from the property of a 2503(c) trust be available to be expended by or for the benefit of the beneficiary during the time before he or she attains the age of 21. In addition, to the extent that trust assets have not already been expended by or for the beneficiary before attaining the age of 21, the property and the income of the trust must pass to the beneficiary. If the beneficiary fails to live to the age of 21, the accumulated income and the principal must be payable to the estate of the beneficiary unless he or she can appoint it to another under a general power of appointment.

As already noted, the Internal Revenue Code requires that the principal and income of the trust must be available for distribution in the time period before the donee reaches age 21. The regulations, however, go further. Treas. Reg. Sec. 25.2503-4(b)(1) prohibits "substantial restrictions" on the trustee's power to make distributions of trust income and principal. This might prohibit any specific restrictions in the trust instrument on the distributions of income and principal for certain specified purposes, such as illness or education. As a practical matter, the trustee can make distributions or accumulate income for the purposes intended by the donor in his or her discretion as trustee.

In addition, the Sec. 2503(c) trust cannot be used for the benefit of a class of beneficiaries. Trust instruments routinely describe payments to a class of beneficiaries in substantially the following language: "All the net income from the trust is to be distributed annually or at more frequent intervals to or for the benefit of the grantor's three children, as necessary, in such amounts as the trustee in his sole discretion shall deem necessary." Although under this type of provision the terms of the trust provide that all the net income of the trust is to be distributed at least annually, the amount of the income receivable by any one of the beneficiaries remains within the discretion of the trustee and is not presently ascertainable. Accordingly the use of the annual exclusion is disallowed for transfers to such a trust. It is possible to utilize Sec. 2503(c) trusts for more than one beneficiary, however, by using either a separate trust for each beneficiary or a separate-share trust. A separate-share trust divides the trust principal into definite portions with each portion having a specified beneficiary.

As noted above, another statutory requirement of the Sec. 2503(c) trust indicates that the trust cannot exist past the date of the beneficiary's 21st birthday. The Treasury regulations, however, provide that the trust will not be disqualified provided that the donee (beneficiary) has the right to extend the term of the trust upon reaching the age of 21 (Treas. Reg. Sec. 25.2503-4(b)(2)). The right to continue the trust can apparently require that the beneficiary must affirmatively compel distribution at age 21 (Rev. Rul. 74-43, 1974-1 C.B. 285). The right to compel distribution at age 21 may exist for only a limited period of time, as long as the period of time is reasonable. Thirty to 60 days have been deemed reasonable in a number of private letter rulings (PLR 7824035; PLR 7805037). If the beneficiary fails to compel the distribution from the trust during the permissible period or otherwise affirmatively allows the trust to continue, the trust will continue until it terminates under the terms of the trust instrument.

It is often undesirable to allow the trust principal and accumulated income, if any, to pass through the estate of a minor, since a minor is not legally competent to make a will. This results in the funds passing under the intestacy laws. However, the Treasury regulations provide that if the beneficiary is given a general power of appointment over the trust principal and accumulated income and fails to exercise this power of appointment, regardless of whether he or she is competent as a minor to do so under local law, the trust continues to qualify for the annual exclusion. In fact, the trust instrument may provide that in the absence of the exercise of the power of appointment there is a gift in default of the exercise of the power. This gift-over may be made to whomever the grantor of the trust desires, including his other children. This is an especially advantageous provision, the inclusion of which should be considered in any Sec. 2503(c) trust.

The practical use of the 2503(c) trust involves several important factors. If the income is accumulated until the child reaches age 14, no kiddie tax problem emerges. The income of the trust will be taxed at the trust's marginal rate and not the marginal rate of the parents (unless the trustee distributes income to the child). The first $1,850 of trust income is taxed at a rate of 15 percent. Therefore the parents can save up to 20 percent in taxes on the income if they are in a 35 percent bracket. Even though the child must be given access to both income and principal no later than age 21, astute parents can minimize the amount of money they transfer to the trust. If the trust invests in fixed-rate-of-return investments such as bonds, a precise calculation can be made to determine how much should be contributed annually to the trust to fund a specific dollar-amount funding objective. In this way the trust fund can be fully exhausted to pay education expenses so that there is no money left in the trust when the child finishes college. The only actual risk the parents take in transferring funds in this case is that the child does not use the money for college education but instead drops out of school and uses the money for a frivolous purpose when he or she turns 21.

Table 5-4 displays the current income level and income tax rates that apply to trust (and estate) income. These figures and tax rates are based on 2002 data. The taxable income figure is indexed for inflation in subsequent years.

TABLE 5-4

If Taxable Income Is:	The Tax Is:
Not over $1,850	15% of taxable income
Over $1,850 but not over $4,400	$277.50 plus 27% of the excess over $1,850
Over $4,400 but not over $6,750	$966.00 plus 30% of the excess over $4,400
Over $6,750 but not over $9,200	$1,671.00 plus 35% of the excess over $6,750
Over $9,200	$2,528.50 plus 38.6% of the excess over $9,200

Having the first $1,850 inflation-adjusted trust income taxed at 15 percent may not seem like a substantial tax savings. However, if the trust is funded when the beneficiary is young, savings can be significant.

For example, assume the following: The trust accumulates income until the beneficiary reaches age 18; the contributions are made annually beginning at the stated age; the trust funds earn 7.5 percent annually; and the parents' marginal tax rate is 33 percent. These savings are calculated on the assumption that without the trust the same income would be taxed at the parents' rate. The calculations do not include allowances for the cost of establishing and managing the trust.

TABLE 5-5
Tax Savings from the 2503(c) Trust When Beneficiary Reaches Age 18—Assuming 7.5 Percent Return and Parents in 33 Percent Tax Bracket

Annual Gift to Trust	Age of Beneficiary When Trust Is Established		
	5	10	15
$ 1,000	$2,333	$ 823	$ 151.00
5,000	7,067	3,237	755.00
10,000	7,566	4,481	1,268.00
20,000	3,492	4,146	1,835.76

If Dave and Diana's attorney can set up a separate trust for each child, act as a trustee, and work with their CPA to file estimated and annual tax returns for the trusts (a relatively simple procedure), the tax benefits should still substantially outweigh the total costs. Typically an attorney will not charge a full fee for each separate trust if the provisions are nearly identical. Dave and Diana should be able to set up these trusts for each of their children at a total cost of $2,000 to $3,000. Annual administration and tax return preparation expenses must be paid, but these costs should be modest and substantially less than the tax savings that can be realized.

In the case of the Andersons, care should be exercised as to the amount of annual funding they will contribute in behalf of Melissa, aged 6. Based on the data in table 5-5, the tax saving is reduced if they contribute $20,000 annually instead of $10,000 due to the trust's large amount of income taxed at the 39.6 percent rate starting in the fifth year.

Despite its complexities the Sec. 2503(c) trust is the best vehicle for the Andersons to utilize as an income-shifting device. The use of this vehicle will be further discussed in the investment planning section.

Family Partnership. Family partnerships are another income-splitting device that can be valuable in allowing higher-bracket taxpayers to shift income to lower-bracket family members. In order to be effective for this purpose, however, the partnership must be a bona fide partnership and not merely an attempt to assign the income of a high-bracket taxpayer to taxpayers in a lower tax bracket. In order to test whether a family partnership can withstand an assignment-of-income attack by the IRS, the income produced by a partnership should be attributable to the capital or services, or both, contributed by the partners. These provisions are to be read in the light of their relationship to the general principle that requires, among other things, that income be taxed to the person who earns it. An impermissible assignment of income will generally not occur if (1) the income tax liability for income derived from personal services remains with the person who performed the services and (2) the income tax liability for income produced by utilizing capital remains with the owner of the capital. (Note that a shift in the ownership of the capital under this principle would result in the shifting of the income tax liability.)

For family partnerships in which "capital is a material income-producing factor," the tax status of a partner is recognized if he or she owns a capital interest in the partnership, whether such an interest was acquired by purchase or by gift (IRC Sec. 704(e)(1)). The tax status of partners in a family partnership in which capital is not a material income-producing factor is much more troublesome.

The protection of partnership status for tax purposes does not result unless the ownership of the capital interest in the partnership is bona fide. In most family situations the partnership interest will be gifted either directly or indirectly to a family member; that is, a capital interest in the partnership will either be a direct gift, or the funds necessary to purchase a capital interest will be gifted. The fact that the interest was acquired by gift does not necessarily make it suspect. There are, however, some other tests that are applied to ascertain the genuineness of the transfer. Among those tests are the following:

- a donor partner's retention of the right to control the distribution of the income of the partnership. This may indicate that the transfer is less than genuine unless the income is retained for the reasonable needs of the business with the other partners' consent. The donor partner can, however, retain the right to control and distribute partnership income without any negative implications provided that right is retained and exercised in a fiduciary capacity (Treas. Reg. Sec. 1.704-1(e)(2)).
- retention of control over the donee's disposition or liquidation of the donated interest beyond reasonable business restrictions
- retention of control over assets essential to the partnership's business (such as ownership of a crucial asset leased to the partnership) that would give the donor partner unusual power to affect the partnership's viability or business

Minors can be recognized as general partners for tax purposes without the minor's interest being held in trust (Treas. Reg. Sec. 1.704-1(e)(2)). The fact that a minor is very young, however, may result in the minor's losing his or her tax status as a partner, unless it can be demonstrated that the minor is competent to manage his or her own property and participate in the partnership activities in accordance with his or her interest in the property (Treas. Reg. Sec. 1.7041(e)(2)). The test is not based on the legal age of majority under the local law of the state but is a test of the minor's maturity and experience (Treas. Reg. Sec. 1.7041(e)(2)). Because of these limitations, minors in their individual capacity should not be made general partners. If a general partnership interest is to be transferred to a minor, the partnership interest should be conveyed to a trust for the minor's benefit.

Another option is to make minors limited partners in family partnerships. Gifts can be made of either the limited partnership interests or of money to purchase the partnership units. Limited partners by definition do not participate in the management of the partnership business. The Treasury Regulations state that in order for a limited partnership to be recognized for federal tax purposes it must be organized and conducted in accordance with the applicable state limited partnership law. The Treasury regulations further provide that the absence of services and participation in management by a donee partner in a limited partnership is immaterial (Treas. Reg. Sec. 1.704-1(e)(2)). This allows for a great deal of control to be retained by the donor general partner. That control cannot extend, however, to placing restrictions on the disposition of the partnership interest that would not be acceptable to unrelated limited partners.

The Andersons could form a family limited partnership and contribute the residential rental property to it; however, the cash flow and appreciation from this property are not sufficient to make it an effective mechanism for funding the children's educations. In addition, an interest in a limited partnership does not qualify for the special $25,000 real estate allowance under the passive-loss rules discussed in the investment planning section. For these reasons the family partnership is not the recommendation of choice.

Caveat: Parental Obligations

If an income-shifting device (such as the 2503(c) trust) is utilized, care must be taken to ensure that the resulting income is not used to satisfy the legal support obligations of the parent. If parental obligations are satisfied with these funds, the distribution is taxable to the parent despite the fact that the income-shifting device is otherwise fully effective. The extent of parental support obligations is determined under local law. In all states the parental obligation of support extends to "necessaries"—food, clothing, shelter, and the like. In some states the legislatures or the courts have extended the scope of these parental obligations to include such things as college educations and private schools when those are consistent with the family's lifestyle and are within their financial means.

In Georgia parental obligations have generally not been extended to include sending children to private schools or to college. There is a case, however, that holds that a father who enters into an agreement—incorporated into a divorce decree while a child is a minor—to send a child to college is legally obligated to provide that college education even after the child's majority.

State laws vary widely in this area. Some states make parental obligations the legal responsibility of the father only, while some states extend the duty to the mother as well. This is an area that should be thoroughly investigated prior to implementing any income-shifting device.

Reduce Tax Burden

Achieve Personal Objectives through Income-Shifting Devices to Reduce Cost

As has already been discussed, it is often advantageous to divide income among family members through the use of income-shifting devices. This allows income from certain assets to be taxed to lower-bracket family members. The use of an outright gift of a fairly nominal sum (when compared to the required accumulation amount) combined with a Sec. 2503(c) trust to fund the college education objectives of the Anderson children is such an income-shifting device. The appropriate investment techniques for educational funding will be discussed in the investment planning section.

Defer Tax Liability on a Portion of Dave's Income from the Practice through Use of Qualified Plans

Dave and Diana will be paying federal taxes in the 30 percent bracket in 2002–2003 and 29 percent in 2004–2005. Dave is contributing $22,500 a year to his Keogh plan on a tax-deductible basis. This contribution will not be taxable to Dave until it is distributed to him. Although this will mean that the Andersons forgo this amount in immediate cash flow, the net effect to the family is a cash-flow shrinkage of approximately 70 percent of this amount in 2002–2003 on an after-tax basis and 71 percent thereafter. The alternatives regarding distribution should be closely examined as Dave approaches retirement age.

Individual Retirement Accounts

Under current tax law, deductible IRA contributions are restricted to

- individuals who are not active participants in an employer-maintained retirement plan for any part of the retirement plan year ending with or within the individual's taxable year
- any other individual, as long as the individual (or married couple if a joint return is filed) has adjusted gross income below a specified limit. If the adjusted gross income exceeds this limit, the $3,000 IRA limit is reduced under a formula that eventually permits no deduction.

Under the Economic Growth and Tax Relief Reconciliation Act of 2001, the maximum contributions that can be made to individual retirement accounts are

Year	Maximum IRA Contribution
2002–2003	$3,000
2004–2005	$4,000
2006–2010	$5,000 (subject to inflation adjusted after 2006)
2011	$2,000

The *active participant* restriction applies if the individual is an active participant in a regular qualified plan, a Sec. 403(b) tax-deferred annuity plan, a simplified employee pension (SEP), or a federal, state, or local government plan, not including a Sec. 457 nonqualified deferred-compensation plan. Pursuant to the Taxpayer Relief Act of 1997, the spouse of an active participant is not "tainted" and may still be eligible to make a fully deductible IRA contribution if the spouse is not an active participant in a qualified plan or is an active participant with income below the compensation limits.

Active plan participants can make deductible IRA contributions only if their income falls within certain income limits, as shown in table 5-6:

TABLE 5-6
IRA Deduction/Compensation Limits (Taxpayer or Spouse Active Plan Participant) for 2002

Filing Status	Full IRA Deduction	Reduced IRA Deduction	No IRA Deduction
Individual/head of household	Up to $34,000	$34,000–$44,000	$44,000 or over
Married couple, joint return	Up to $54,000	$54,000–$64,000	$64,000 or over
Married, filing separately	Not available	$0–$10,000	$10,000 or over

The reduction in the IRA deduction for those affected is computed by multiplying the IRA limit ($3,000 or 100 percent of compensation) by a fraction equal to

$$\frac{\text{taxpayer's adjusted gross income in excess of full deduction limit}}{\$10,000}$$

For example, a married couple, one of whom is an active participant in a regular qualified plan, files a joint return and has an adjusted gross income of $58,000. The computation is as follows:

$$\$3,000 \quad \text{x} \quad \frac{\$58,000 - \$54,000}{\$10,000} = \$1,200$$

$3,000 – $1,200 = $1,800. This is the IRA deduction limit.

If a married couple has a "spousal IRA," the same formula is applied except that $6,000 is substituted for the $3,000 figure. Another major IRA change may soften the blow administered by the new limits just described. Individuals not permitted to make deductible IRA contributions may nevertheless make such contributions on a nondeductible basis, up to the usual $3,000/100 percent/ $6,000 limit. Nondeductible contributions (but not income on those contributions) are tax free when ultimately distributed to the individual. If nondeductible contributions to an IRA are made, any amounts withdrawn are treated as partly tax free and partly taxable under rules similar to the exclusion-ratio calculation for annuities under IRC Sec. 72.

EGTRRA 2001 allows catch-up provisions on IRAs for individuals over age 50. Since Dave and Diana are in their 40s, these provisions do not apply to them.

The Roth IRA. In addition to changing many of the rules that applied to traditional IRAs, the Taxpayer Relief Act of 1997 created a new kind of IRA, the Roth IRA. Contributions of up to $3,000 made to a Roth IRA are not deductible, but all the earnings on the IRA are tax free if the distribution from the Roth IRA occurs at least 5 years after the creation of the Roth IRA and

- the distribution is made after age 59 1/2, unless the distribution is due to the death or disability of the participant or
- the distribution is used to purchase a first home, subject to a lifetime maximum of $10,000

It is important to note that an otherwise eligible distribution will not be tax free if it is made within the 5-year period beginning with the first tax year for which a contribution was made to an individual's Roth IRA. If a nonqualifying distribution is made, the earnings in the Roth IRA that have been distributed are subject to ordinary income tax and, if appropriate, to the 10 percent early distributions penalty tax. Roth IRA contributions can be withdrawn first before earnings are withdrawn and taxed.

There are certain income restrictions for Roth IRAs. Individuals and married persons may contribute to Roth IRAs only if their income falls within certain limits. Individuals with adjusted gross income (AGI) of less than $95,000 may make a contribution of up to $3,000 to a Roth IRA. Once an individual has AGI in excess of $110,000, no contribution to a Roth IRA is permitted. A single individual's ability to contribute to a Roth IRA is phased out on a pro rata basis between AGI of $95,000 and $110,000. Married persons filing jointly may each make a $3,000 contribution to a Roth IRA if their joint AGI is less than $150,000. The ability to contribute to a Roth IRA is phased out on a pro rata basis for married couples with joint AGI between $150,000 and $160,000. Married couples filing jointly may not make a Roth IRA contribution if adjusted gross income exceeds $160,000. Under the provisions of EGTRRA 2001, the phaseout threshold for married persons will eventually equal two times the phaseout threshold for single persons.

If an individual or married person plans to make an IRA contribution and has adjusted gross income in excess of the threshold for contribution to a deductible IRA but less than the AGI ceiling for contributing to a Roth IRA, the IRA contribution should be made to a Roth IRA. In such a case, the IRA deduction will not be available whether the contribution is made to a traditional or Roth IRA; but if made to a Roth IRA, the earnings will be tax free. Individuals and married persons who have adjusted gross income in excess of the Roth IRA ceiling may still make a nondeductible contribution to a regular IRA.

The benefits, however, of making nondeductible contributions can be marginal. In Dave and Diana's case Dave's income is far in excess of both the range in which deductible contributions can be made to a traditional IRA and the range in which nondeductible contributions can be made to a Roth IRA. Since

Dave's profit-sharing plan will provide him with substantial retirement funds from deductible contributions, the establishment of an IRA is not recommended in this case.

In creating Roth IRAs, the Taxpayer Relief Act of 1997 included provisions whereby individuals could roll over existing IRAs into Roth IRAs. Upon conversion, an income tax will be due on nontaxable contributions as well as on any appreciation in value. Conversions made after 1998 will require immediate payment of all taxes due. In order to qualify for this conversion option, the adjusted gross income of a single individual or a married couple cannot exceed $100,000. Since Dave and Diana's income is far in excess of this threshold, they are not eligible for a Roth IRA conversion.

Ensure Adequate Protection in the Event of Dave's Disability

Design Buy-Sell Agreement to Become Operative in the Event of Disability

Buy-sell agreements can be designed to become operative in the event of the disability of a shareholder, but insurers generally will not provide coverage for professional sole proprietors. The buy-sell agreement for Dave's practice could be designed to become operative in the event of disability if he can get his professional colleagues to agree to an installment payout in lieu of the availability of insurance funding.

Personal Disability Income Coverage

The primary advantage of personally acquired disability income coverage is that the proceeds are received tax free. The primary disadvantage of personal disability income coverage is that the premiums for coverage are not tax deductible. In addition, there are different limitations on coverage amounts available under personal and corporate coverage plans. Generally the amounts available under personal disability coverage are lower than those available under employer disability coverage. In Dave's case the total amount available under either personal disability income coverage or employer coverage is approximately $6,000 a month, because his high income has effectively caused the coverage limits to merge. As discussed in the business planning section, Dave should obtain the maximum amount of coverage through a personally owned policy.

Ensure a Comfortable Retirement

Dave's Keogh plan is the Andersons' primary vehicle for accumulating funds for retirement. The plan balance at year end is projected at $91,168.

Contributions are projected to remain constant unless tax laws affecting Keogh plans change.

Although the plan balance is presently earning 8 percent, a more conservative rate of return should be assumed beyond the 5-year plan horizon. Dave will reach age 65 in the year 2024. If an inflation-adjusted rate of return of 4 percent is assumed for the Keogh plan (to express his retirement date plan balance in today's dollars), the plan balance in 24 years will be approximately $1,180,000.

Dave and Diana will have a number of options at that point. They could take the plan proceeds in a lump-sum distribution and systematically liquidate the principal over life expectancy. They could also choose to live on the income only. Alternatively they could use the plan balance to purchase a joint and survivor annuity with an installment refund feature. This decision, of course, will be based on their circumstances at that time.

However, it does appear that the Andersons will enjoy a comfortable retirement under the given assumptions. For example, a joint and survivor annuity with an installment refund would pay Dave and Diana approximately $12,000 per month using current rates if the funds were fully applied to the annuity. This would provide them with a before-tax income of about $144,000 per year.

The Andersons' current committed and discretionary expenses (excluding taxes and investment outlays) are approximately $66,000 per year. The retirement plan assumptions include an inflation-adjusted rate of return to express the future plan balance in today's dollars. Therefore either the annuity or an alternative payout method should provide the Andersons with sufficient funds for a comfortable retirement under the assumptions.

Assuming further that the Social Security system remains intact, the Andersons would probably receive a total monthly benefit of at least $2,100 (combined benefit) in inflation-adjusted dollars, based on the retirement benefit formulas currently in place.

As discussed in the business plan, Dave can consider the implementation of a defined-benefit plan in combination with his profit-sharing plan if he wants to provide additional security for his retirement.

Consider Various Problems Diana Might Encounter in Setting Up Her Own Business

Preliminary General Planning

Since the new baby will delay the actual start of Diana's proposed business specializing in antique Oriental porcelain and Oriental rugs, the detailed planning for that venture should be postponed until closer to the time she will be free to devote her time to such an effort. This may not be for several years, depending on a family decision about how long she should stay home with the baby. However, it is appropriate to begin doing some preliminary long-range planning in this regard.

During the interim Diana can continue developing her expertise through classes and independent study of the subject matter. After the baby is old enough to be left with babysitters or in nursery school, she might consider taking a part-time job for a few hours each week at a shop specializing in some of the items she wishes to feature in her business. This would allow her to continue developing her expertise and also to deal with some of the actual day-to-day problems that exist in such businesses.

If she finds that she is still interested in her own shop, she might consider opening it only during school hours for a few years and then expanding the shop's hours if business warrants and as her need to be home decreases. Many specialty shops have restricted hours, and their owners will see customers at other times by appointment only. The most important point is that Diana should not feel that she must delay opening her own business until she can devote 10 hours a day 6 days a week to it, as it is doubtful that she will realistically be able to do that until all her children have left home.

Taking Advantage of Start-Up Losses

When Diana does start her own business, it may not be profitable at the very beginning. It would be helpful to the Andersons' tax situation if any start-up losses could be used to offset some of Dave's income. This result can generally be accomplished by operating the business as a sole proprietorship, an LLC, or as an S corporation. While the operation of the business in any of these forms can pass through start-up losses, sole proprietorships, LLCs, and S corporations are subject to the limitations regarding deductions for hobby-type businesses under IRC Sec. 183, which should be explored prior to making a decision about the form in which to operate the business.

Dispositions at Death

Analysis of Present Plans

Dave's present will provides that an amount equal to one-half of his adjusted gross estate goes to Diana in a marital trust, with the remainder going to a residuary trust for the benefit of Diana and the children.

The problem with this arrangement is that it does not take full advantage of the applicable credit if Dave were to die in the very near future. This unnecessarily increases Diana's taxable estate should Dave predecease her.

Moreover, as Dave's estate increases, the current arrangement will result in a federal estate tax payable in Dave's estate if Dave should die first and if one-half of Dave's adjusted gross estate was more than $1 million (for 2002), the applicable credit exemption equivalent amount.

The Taxpayer Relief Act of 1997 and the Economic Growth and Reconciliation Act of 2001 provide for an increase in the amount of property that can pass to heirs estate tax free. Table 5-7 shows the progression of the applicable credit amount.

TABLE 5-7		
Year	Applicable Exclusion	Highest Rate
2001	$ 675,000	55% (plus 5% surtax)
2002	$1,000,000	50%
2003	$1,000,000	49%
2004	$1,500,000	48%
2005	$1,500,000	47%
2006	$2,000,000	46%
2007	$2,000,000	45%
2008	$2,000,000	45%
2009	$3,500,000	44%
2010	$ 0	0
2011	$1,000,000	55% (plus 5% surtax)

Recommendations

Dave's estate plan should be revised to provide that an amount equal to the unified credit equivalent should pass to a residuary credit shelter trust with provisions similar to his present residuary trust. The remaining assets should pass to Diana under the marital trust arrangement. This will avoid payment of federal estate taxes in Dave's estate if he predeceases Diana. Diana can subsequently take steps to reduce her estate and thereby reduce the total federal estate taxes ultimately payable.

At this time, Dave's plan should be revised so that he gifts $260,000 of his securities (or more if he so desires) to Diana. The purpose served by this asset transfer is to avoid having these assets included in his gross estate should Diana predecease him since he would then no longer have the benefit of a marital deduction. For the same reason Dave could consider making additional gifts of securities in the future.

To make this course of action effective, Diana's will needs immediate redrafting to include the establishment of a credit bypass trust that will use part of her applicable credit. In case Diana's securities holdings increase in value due to their appreciation or further gifts from Dave, her will should direct that her security portfolio fund the bypass trust at least up to the applicable credit exemption. Dave is to be named the income beneficiary, and their children are to be named the remainderpersons. Her will can specify that her coin collection is to pass to the children and that Dave is to hold these assets on their behalf until the youngest child attains age 21.

The following schedules illustrate the difference in results between Dave's current estate plan and the suggested revision under the current asset situation. The illustrations assume that Dave predeceases Diana but they both die in 2002.

[text continues on page 5.76]

COMPREHENSIVE ESTATE TAX REPORT

DAVE & DIANA ANDERSON
CURRENT ESTATE

Date: Dec 31, 2002 Under Present Will	DAVE Predeceasing DIANA		DIANA Predeceasing DAVE	
	DAVE's Estate	DIANA's Estate	DIANA's Estate	DAVE's Estate
Individually Held Assets	1,368,324	21,200	21,200	1,368,324
Share from Joint Assets	5,000	10,000	5,000	10,000
Life Insurance Proceeds	100,000	0	0	100,000
Assets Received from Spouse	0	562,104	0	0
Gross Estate	1,473,324	593,304	26,200	1,478,324
Own Liabilities	146,854	0	0	146,854
Administration Expenses	88,919	43,015	1,900	89,282
Adjusted Gross Estate	1,237,551	550,289	24,300	1,242,188
Marital Deduction	567,104	0	5,000	0
Taxable Estate	670,447	550,289	19,300	1,242,188
Total Taxable Amount	670,447	550,289	19,300	1,242,188
Fed Tax Before Credit	218,865	174,407	3,660	445,097
Unified Tax Credit	218,865	174,407	3,660	345,800
Net Federal Estate Tax	0	0	0	99,297
Net Federal + State Tax	0	0	0	99,297
Combined Tax		0		99,297

ESTATE ANALYSIS
ASSET DISTRIBUTION

DAVE & DIANA ANDERSON
CURRENT ESTATE

Date: Dec 31, 2002 Under Present Will	DAVE Predeceasing DIANA		DIANA Predeceasing DAVE	
	DAVE's Estate	DIANA's Estate	DIANA's Estate	DAVE's Estate
Liquid Assets	580,924	350,151	5,000	583,424
Non-liquid Assets	892,400	243,153	21,200	894,900
Total Assets	1,473,324	593,304	26,200	1,478,324
Passing to Spouse	567,104	0	5,000	0
Passing to Trust/Heirs	670,447	550,289	19,300	1,142,891
Estate Shrinkage	235,773	43,015	1,900	335,433

ESTATE ANALYSIS
LIQUIDITY SITUATION

DAVE & DIANA ANDERSON
CURRENT ESTATE

Date: Dec 31, 2002 Under Present Will	DAVE Predeceasing DIANA		DIANA Predeceasing DAVE	
	DAVE's Estate	DIANA's Estate	DIANA's Estate	DAVE's Estate
Debt	146,854	0	0	146,854
Administration Expenses	88,919	43,015	1,900	89,282
Estate Taxes	0	0	0	99,297
Charitable Contributions	0	0	0	0
Need for Liquid Capital	235,773	43,015	1,900	335,433
Liquid Capital Available	580,924	350,151	5,000	583,424
Addt'l Liquidity Needed	0	0	0	0

ESTATE ANALYSIS
MARITAL DEDUCTION

DAVE & DIANA ANDERSON
CURRENT ESTATE

Date: Dec 31, 2002 Under Present Will	DAVE Predeceasing DIANA	DIANA Predeceasing DAVE
Marital Deduction is— -Same- Your Amount Exceeds by Resulting Additional Cost	Formula Clause $0 $0	Formula Clause $0 $0
Total Family Assets	$1,499,524	$1,499,524
Joint Estate Taxes	$0 .00%	$99,297 6.62%
Total Shrinkage	$278,788 18.59%	$337,333 22.50%
Remaining for Heirs	$1,220,736 81.41%	$1,162,191 77.50%

ESTATE DISTRIBUTION FLOWCHART
(DAVE Predeceasing DIANA on Dec 31, 2002)

The ANDERSONs

Present Will DAVE

CURRENT ESTATE

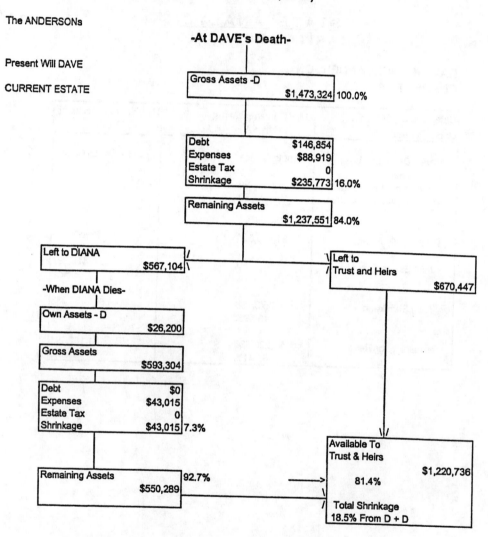

-At DAVE's Death-

Gross Assets -D		
	$1,473,324	100.0%

Debt	$146,854	
Expenses	$88,919	
Estate Tax	0	
Shrinkage	$235,773	16.0%

| Remaining Assets | | |
| | $1,237,551 | 84.0% |

| Left to DIANA | | |
| | $567,104 | |

| Left to Trust and Heirs | |
| | $670,447 |

-When DIANA Dies-

| Own Assets - D | |
| | $26,200 |

| Gross Assets | |
| | $593,304 |

Debt	$0	
Expenses	$43,015	
Estate Tax	0	
Shrinkage	$43,015	7.3%

| Remaining Assets | 92.7% |
| $550,289 | |

Available To Trust & Heirs	
81.4%	$1,220,736
Total Shrinkage 18.5% From D + D	

ESTATE DISTRIBUTION FLOWCHART
(DIANA Predeceasing DAVE on Dec 31, 2002)

The ANDERSONs

Present Will DAVE

CURRENT ESTATE

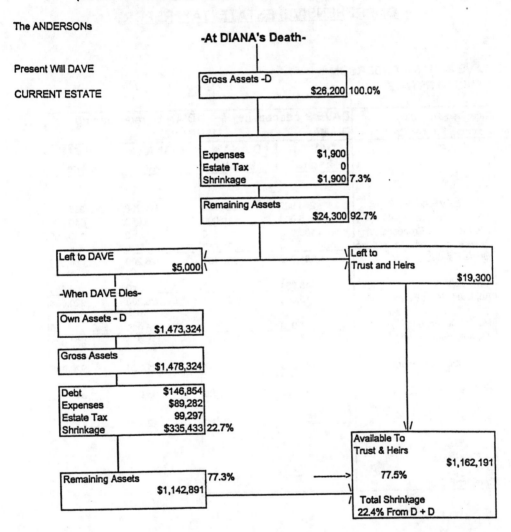

-At DIANA's Death-

Gross Assets -D		
	$26,200	100.0%

Expenses	$1,900	
Estate Tax	0	
Shrinkage	$1,900	7.3%

| Remaining Assets | | |
| | $24,300 | 92.7% |

Left to DAVE		Left to
	$5,000	Trust and Heirs
		$19,300

-When DAVE Dies-

| Own Assets - D | |
| | $1,473,324 |

| Gross Assets | |
| | $1,478,324 |

Debt	$146,854	
Expenses	$89,282	
Estate Tax	99,297	
Shrinkage	$335,433	22.7%

| Remaining Assets | | 77.3% |
| | $1,142,891 | |

Available To Trust & Heirs	
	$1,162,191
77.5%	
Total Shrinkage 22.4% From D + D	

COMPREHENSIVE ESTATE TAX REPORT

DAVE & DIANA ANDERSON
REVISED ESTATE

Date: Dec 31, 2002 Maximized Unified Credit Will	DAVE Predeceasing DIANA		DIANA Predeceasing DAVE	
	DAVE's Estate	DIANA's Estate	DIANA's Estate	DAVE's Estate
Individually Held Assets	956,902	321,200	321,200	956,902
Share from Joint Assets	5,000	10,000	5,000	10,000
Life Insurance Proceeds	100,000	0	0	100,000
Assets Received from Spouse	0	250,957	0	0
Gross Estate	1,061,902	582,157	326,200	1,066,902
Own Liabilities	146,854	0	0	146,854
Adjusted Gross Estate	915,048	582,157	326,200	920,048
Marital Deduction	427,979	0	5,000	0
Taxable Estate	487,069	582,157	321,200	920,048
Total Taxable Amount	487,069	582,157	321,200	920,048
Fed Tax Before Credit	151,403	186,198	95,008	314,619
Unified Tax Credit	151,403	186,198	95,008	314,619
Combined Tax		0		0

ESTATE ANALYSIS
ASSET DISTRIBUTION

DAVE & DIANA ANDERSON
REVISED ESTATE

Date: Dec 31, 2002 Maximized Unified Credit Will	DAVE Predeceasing DIANA		DIANA Predeceasing DAVE	
	DAVE's Estate	DIANA's Estate	DIANA's Estate	DAVE's Estate
Liquid Assets	580,924	260,957	5,000	583,424
Non-liquid Assets	480,978	321,200	321,200	483,478
Total Assets	1,061,902	582,157	326,200	1,066,902
Passing to Spouse	255,957	0	5,000	0
Passing to Trust/Heirs	659,091	582,157	321,200	920,048
Estate Shrinkage	146,854	0	0	146,854

ESTATE ANALYSIS
LIQUIDITY SITUATION

DAVE & DIANA ANDERSON
REVISED ESTATE

Date: Dec 31, 2002 Maximized Unified Credit Will	DAVE Predeceasing DIANA		DIANA Predeceasing DAVE	
	DAVE's Estate	DIANA's Estate	DIANA's Estate	DAVE's Estate
Debt	146,854	0	0	146,854
Administration Expenses	0	0	0	0
Estate Taxes	0	0	0	0
Charitable Contributions	0	0	0	0
Need for Liquid Capital	146,854	0	0	146,854
Liquid Capital Available	580,924	260,957	5,000	583,424
Addt'l Liquidity Needed	0	0	0	0

ESTATE ANALYSIS
MARITAL DEDUCTION

DAVE & DIANA ANDERSON
REVISED ESTATE

Date: Dec 31, 2002 Maximized Unified Credit Will	DAVE Predeceasing DIANA	DIANA Predeceasing DAVE
Marital Deduction is---Same- Your Amount Exceeds by Resulting Additional Cost	Formula Clause $133,555 $0	Formula Clause $0 $0
Total Family Assets	$1,499,524	$1,499,524
Joint Estate Taxes	$0 .00%	$0 .00%
Total Shrinkage	$146,854 9.79%	$146,854 9.79%
Remaining for Heirs	$1,352,670 90.21%	$1,352,670 90.21%

ESTATE DISTRIBUTION FLOWCHART
(DAVE Predeceasing DIANA on Dec 31, 2002)

The ANDERSONs

Dec 31,

REVISED ESTATE

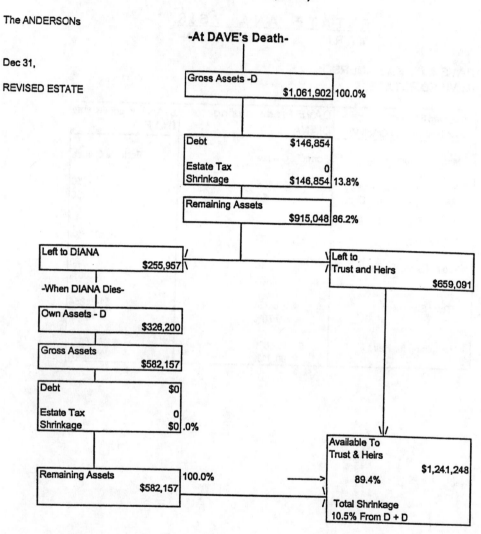

-At DAVE's Death-

Gross Assets -D	
$1,061,902	100.0%

Debt	$146,854
Estate Tax	0
Shrinkage	$146,854	13.8%

Remaining Assets	
$915,048	86.2%

Left to DIANA	
$255,957	

-When DIANA Dies-

Own Assets - D	
$326,200	

Gross Assets	
$582,157	

Debt	$0
Estate Tax	0
Shrinkage	$0	.0%

Remaining Assets	100.0%
$582,157	

Left to	
Trust and Heirs	
	$659,091

Available To	
Trust & Heirs	$1,241,248
	89.4%
Total Shrinkage	
10.5% From D + D	

ESTATE DISTRIBUTION FLOWCHART
(DIANA Predeceasing DAVE on Dec 31, 2002)

The ANDERSONs

Dec 31,

REVISED ESTATE

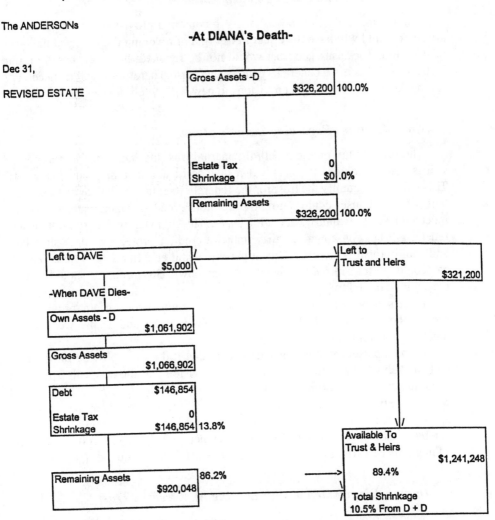

-At DIANA's Death-

| Gross Assets -D | $326,200 | 100.0% |

| Estate Tax | 0 | |
| Shrinkage | $0 | .0% |

| Remaining Assets | $326,200 | 100.0% |

| Left to DAVE | $5,000 |

| Left to Trust and Heirs | $321,200 |

-When DAVE Dies-

| Own Assets - D | $1,061,902 |

| Gross Assets | $1,066,902 |

| Debt | $146,854 |

| Estate Tax | 0 | |
| Shrinkage | $146,854 | 13.8% |

| Remaining Assets | $920,048 | 86.2% |

Available To Trust & Heirs	$1,241,248
	89.4%
Total Shrinkage 10.5% From D + D	

Failure of Present Estate Planning Documents to Contemplate the Birth of Dave and Diana's Fourth Child

The failure of the Andersons' wills to contain a provision contemplating an after-born child will have the effect in Georgia of revoking their wills at the birth of the child. The insurance trust would not be revoked; however, based on our facts, the child is not a beneficiary under that trust. Therefore it will be necessary for the Andersons to include provisions in new wills to eliminate these problems.

Considerations Regarding Diana's Status

The primary tax problem with the marital trust that Dave has in his present will is that it includes the personal residence (a non-income-producing asset). This will not disqualify the trust for the federal estate tax marital deduction. One-half of the house could currently be conveyed to Diana subject to the indebtedness as a joint owner with Dave. This transfer will not result in any federal gift tax consequences, may improve creditor protection under state law, and could probably have significant psychological benefits. In addition, Diana's car could be transferred to Diana outright now. This property should not be placed in a marital trust.

Dave's new will should also contain a simultaneous death provision to protect the federal estate tax marital deduction if he and Diana were to die together in a common disaster.

Diana's present will is adequate except that it does not provide for the new child and should be redrafted to contain a provision that the new will is made in contemplation of the birth of the new baby. Also as she acquires more assets, it would be advisable to review her estate plan with respect to (1) utilization of her applicable credit if she dies first, and (2) a provision requiring that Dave survive her by 6 months in order to inherit under her will. This provision will avoid adding unnecessarily to Dave's taxable estate if Diana should die first.

Diana's Dissatisfaction with Leaving All Assets in Trust

If the recommendations previously made are implemented, Diana would no longer have all her assets tied up in trust. There are joint checking and savings accounts, and she has been named the beneficiary of Dave's Keogh plan; consequently the funds in the account balance will go directly to her and will not pass under his will to the marital trust. The house will be held in joint ownership and she will hold title to her car. She will also have a special power of appointment over the irrevocable insurance trust, as discussed in the insurance planning section. If Diana is still concerned about the inaccessibility of the funds in the residuary and marital trusts, she can be given some additional powers in the trust instrument that will give her absolute access to some of these funds without triggering adverse estate tax consequences. A typical example of this type of power is an annual noncumulative right to withdraw the greater of 5 percent of the trust corpus or $5,000. Neither the exercise nor lapse of such a power will cause gift or estate tax problems. In fact, Diana could be the trustee or a cotrustee of the residuary trust with the bank while remaining a beneficiary without risking inclusion of the trust in her estate as long as her ability to distribute trust funds (income and corpus) to herself is limited by an ascertainable standard. The statutory language describing an appropriate ascertainable standard is that funds may be distributed for "health, education, support, or maintenance" without risking estate tax inclusion as a general power of appointment (IRC Sec. 2041(b)(1)(A)).

Problems with Present Life Insurance Trust

The present irrevocable life insurance trust does not contain a Crummey provision (that is, a provision allowing the beneficiaries of the trust to currently withdraw amounts gifted to the trust). For this reason the gifts to the trust fail to qualify as present-interest gifts and do not qualify for the gift tax annual exclusion (IRC Sec. 2503(b)). The result is that each time Dave makes a gift to the trust for the payment of the insurance premium, a taxable gift results. Although the amounts of the gifts are small, gift tax returns reflecting the total amount gifted annually should be filed. (Note that there will not actually be any federal gift tax liability since the applicable credit will be available to cover the actual imposition of any federal gift tax.)

A properly structured irrevocable insurance trust is recommended for the newly acquired insurance. The question of what to do with the present trust remains. The trust can be effectively discontinued by an immediate cessation of gifts to pay premiums; however, serious consideration should be given to maintaining this trust, even though it generates some small annual gift tax liability, at least until the new insurance is in place. It would also probably be prudent to maintain the present coverage until contestability periods under the new coverage have passed.

The dispositive provisions of the new irrevocable insurance trust can (but are not required to) be the same as the terms of the residuary trust under Dave's will. Certainly the trust should empower (but not require) the trustee to loan money to or purchase assets from either Dave's or Diana's estate.

PERSONAL PLANNING: INSURANCE

Life Insurance

Should Dave die prematurely, the Anderson family would experience a loss of cash inflow of more than $177,000 annually. While there would also be a reduction in expenses and income taxes, the family's needs after Dave's death would still run between $70,000 and $80,000 annually to maintain their present lifestyle. This amount could be partially covered by the cash flow from existing investments, which would be approximately $12,000 plus almost $4,000 of reinvested earnings on his investable cash. Assume that Dave wants to provide an $80,000 annual income to Diana and the children and that his investment assets will generate $16,000 of annual income. Dave needs to provide about $60,000 of additional annual income to maintain his family's lifestyle. The funds available from the existing Keogh plan are not adequate to make up the shortfall for a period of more than 2 years. There is an immediate need for additional insurance protection that could be reduced over a period of years in concert with the buildup of retirement fund balances and other investment assets.

Dave has a $100,000 term life insurance policy in an irrevocable life insurance trust. As discussed previously, a new irrevocable insurance trust with a Crummey provision has been recommended. If additional life insurance is applied for, owned, and paid for by the trust and the trust is the named beneficiary, the proceeds will not be included in Dave's estate for federal estate tax purposes. The trust will invest the life insurance proceeds and use the income for the benefit of Diana and the children. If the trust could earn 10 percent on this money over a long period of time, the family would have an additional income flow of $60,000. The total life insurance needed, based on a 10 percent rate of return, would be $640,000. Alternatively, should the trust earn only 8 percent on the proceeds, a total of $800,000 would be needed to generate $60,000 per year and still preserve principal. Thus Dave needs between $540,000 and $700,000 of additional insurance on his life.

This additional protection should cover the family income needs if prices remain relatively stable in the future. If there is significant inflation, however, there will be a need to increase the insurance coverage. As the children reach college age, though, the funds set aside for their education will provide much of their needed support. Also the longer Dave lives, the greater will be the accumulation of investment assets and contributions to the benefit plan that can provide income to Diana. When Diana reaches the age of eligibility for Social Security benefits, her income will also increase, so the need for insurance protection should always be periodically reviewed.

The selection of life insurance products involves choices among many available designs. Dave should consider using one of the following types of policies to provide the additional survivor protection needed.

Ordinary Whole Life Insurance

This form of insurance is based on the assumption that premiums will be paid on a level annual basis throughout the insured's lifetime. In the early years of the policy the premium exceeds the cost of protection, thereby providing the basis for cash values within the policy. The cash values of a policy depend on the size of the policy, the insured's age at the time of issue, and whether the policy is rated. Cash values are guaranteed by the contract and can be borrowed at a rate either stated therein or established by an index. In addition, the increase in cash value each year is not taxable to the policyowner. Even though the assumption is that the premium will be paid over the life of the insured, many owners convert their policies to either a reduced paid-up policy when the need for this protection decreases, such as when any children become self-supporting, or to an annuity upon retirement.

Single-Premium Whole Life Insurance

This form of insurance differs from the ordinary whole life policy in that only one premium, paid at policy inception, is made. These policies enjoy the customary life insurance advantage of tax-free internal cash value increases and income-tax-free death benefits. If owned by the insured, the proceeds would be includible in the insured's estate for estate tax purposes.

In single-premium whole life policies there is typically an initial cash value equal to the premium paid to acquire the policy. These policies also have a guaranteed minimum interest rate stated in the policy, but frequently the actual return is higher than the minimum guaranteed return. The interest rate applicable to policy loans is either equal to or a given percentage above the current rate credited to the cash value. These policies also impose a surrender charge if they are terminated within a specified period of time. They enjoy tax-deferred accumulation of especially substantial up-front cash values.

However, the current Internal Revenue Code imposes a series of rules that has altered the traditional attractiveness of single-premium whole life insurance contracts unless the policyowner plans to leave the cash values with the insurer and looks to the death benefit as the primary purpose for purchasing the contract. IRC Sec. 7702A specifies that if a contract is a modified endowment contract (MEC), any cash withdrawals, including policy loans, will be deemed to be interest earnings first and then a withdrawal of premium. Any withdrawal treated as income is obviously subject to taxation at the policyowner's marginal tax rate. In addition, a 10 percent penalty tax applies.

A modified endowment contract exists if at any time the accumulated amount of the first 7 years' premiums paid on the contract exceeds the accumulated amount of "net level premiums" that would be payable if the contract provided for paid-up future benefits after the payment of seven level annual premiums. The first year's death benefit will be deemed to apply for the purpose of computing the "net level premium" if there is no reduction in the death benefit during the first 7 years even though such a reduction might occur in a subsequent year, such as the tenth year. If a death benefit smaller than the first year's death benefit becomes the face amount during the first 7 years of the policy, then the reduced benefit is used for calculating the amount of the net level premium. Sec. 7702A defines net level premium in such a way that the 7-pay test premium varies from one insurance product to another.

A material change automatically makes a policy subject to the 7-pay premium test. If the test is failed, the policy will be characterized as a modified endowment contract. Any increase in future benefits provided under the policy is a material change, with three exceptions: (1) an increase in benefits attributable to cost-of-living adjustments (CPI or similar index related), (2) the payment of premiums to fund the lowest death benefit payable during the first 7 years, and (3) the crediting of interest and policyholder dividends to the premium paid to meet the requirements of the second exception. Special rules apply to life insurance contracts having an initial death benefit of no more than $10,000. Recent clarifications added to the federal income tax laws specify that a material change includes (1) any increase in the death benefit under the contract or (2) any increase in, or addition of, a qualified additional benefit under the contract.

These tax limitations on the use of single-premium policies have limited the benefits and flexibility previously available with such policies.

Variable Life Policy

A variable life insurance policy is also a fixed, level-premium policy for the lifetime of the insured. With variable life the insured selects the investment medium used within the policy, usually with a choice restricted to specific funds managed by the insurer. This policy differs from the ordinary whole life policy in that the face amount of the policy changes with the investment performance of the investment instrument(s) chosen by the insured. Often a minimum guaranteed floor below which the policy's face will not fall is an integral part of the policy. However, all investment risk shifts to the policyowner. Since the investment risk is transferred to the owner, no guarantees are included as to the amount of the policy's cash values. If cash values do exist within the policy, borrowing of these values is permissible. However, borrowing from the policy can result in taxation if the policy is defined as a modified endowment contract under IRC Sec. 7702A. Some policies specify a variable interest rate on the borrowing that fluctuates with changes in some previously established standard interest rate. Other policies do have fixed borrowing rates. Since these policies have a substantial surrender charge during their early years, the client should realize that a long-term commitment is being made if this policy is chosen.

In addition, the insured needs to monitor carefully the performance of the investment instrument(s) selected. If the initial choice was incorrect, or if the insured has failed to shift funds as economic conditions change, the amount of protection could fall sizably. This form of fluctuating death benefit might not be suitable to the client when the primary reason for acquiring additional insurance at this time is protection for survivors.

Universal Life Policy

A universal life insurance policy differs from the previous policies in that it has a flexible premium. Universal life is available in two forms—either a level or an increasing death benefit. In addition, a changing face amount of any life insurance death benefit payable under universal life contracts as a consequence of changes in the amount of the annual premium being paid will result in the policy's being subject to the 7-pay test at the time of the change. The insured has the option to increase, decrease, or omit the premium. However, all premiums when paid are added to the policy's cash value account, and all mortality charges are deducted from the same account. Interest is credited to this account with a minimum guarantee. Another unique characteristic of this policy, compared to the three previous policies, is that some mortality risk is shifted to the insured by the potential for increases in the mortality rate. Also a minimum interest rate on the cash value is guaranteed, and interest in excess of the guarantee depends on investment performance and insurer discretion. Any interest buildup in the policy is currently tax free. Although the cash values can be borrowed, the insured can also make withdrawals from the cash values that are not considered a loan, so interest does not have to be paid to the insurer for the withdrawals. Furthermore these withdrawn funds do not have to be repaid to the insurer. However, there may be income tax consequences of such withdrawals. As with the variable life policy, there are significant surrender charges during the early years.

Term Policy

Over the lifetime of the insured this policy has an increasing premium used solely to provide life insurance protection. Important features of this policy are its guaranteed renewability, convertibility of the policy to permanent insurance up to age 65, and no cash value buildup over the life of the insured.

Recommendations

If this protection is purchased as whole life insurance other than the single-premium form, the premium will be in the range of $15 to $23 per $1,000 of protection. The premium for a universal life policy is somewhat lower since the premium can change over the life of the policy. The single-premium policy entails an insurance premium of 30 to 35 percent of the policy's face amount. Term costs will start at about $2.25 per $1,000 of protection and reach the $20-per-$1,000 rate at or beyond age 56.

Dave's personal insurance should be applied for and owned by a properly structured irrevocable life insurance trust that should also be the beneficiary of the insurance policies. This avoids the necessity of transferring policies to the trust, which would cause the insurance proceeds to be included in Dave's estate should he die within 3 years of the transfer (IRC Sec. 2035). The insurance trust should contain provisions similar to or identical with the terms of the residuary trust under Dave's will. It should also contain a valid Crummey provision. If the terms of the insurance trust and the residuary trust are substantially identical, a provision in either or both trusts allowing the trustee to combine them can achieve savings in administrative costs. Diana can continue to function as trustee of this trust until it is funded at Dave's death, and the trust instrument should provide that the corporate trustee should then automatically take over as the successor trustee to avoid having the trust taxed in Diana's estate at her death.

The trust might contain a special power of appointment allowing Diana to make gifts of the trust principal to individuals other than herself, her creditors, her estate, and her estate's creditors. In this way the trust can purchase cash value life insurance on Dave's life, and the Andersons can have access to the inside buildup and/or side funds through Diana's special power. This power should not result in the inclusion of the insurance proceeds in either Dave's or Diana's estate. In addition, Diana has expressed concern that virtually all the Andersons' assets are in Dave's name. A special power would provide Diana with some control over the property in the irrevocable insurance trust. However, this technique is aggressive and its tax effects are uncertain. Therefore the advice of a tax attorney must be obtained before its use is seriously considered.

Dave and Diana should keep in mind that even though the investment features and tax advantages of some of the permanent forms of insurance are attractive, the primary function of insurance is to protect survivors. However, that does not prevent them from considering or even using additional permanent life insurance as part of their planning for both investment and the protection of their survivors.

Dave and Diana do have some need for temporary insurance to provide for their survivors, at least until the children are finished with college. For this purpose term insurance would provide the protection at the lowest cost. The use of term insurance will be discussed in the education funding section. However, there is a need for permanent survivorship protection extending beyond the time the children have finished their education and are self-supporting. For this purpose Dave and Diana should discuss with their life agent the possibility of using one of the forms of permanent life insurance.

A reasonable estimate of the cost of the life insurance needed at this time is about $9,500 annually. This includes the premiums for additional term insurance as recommended in the next section to assure the funds will be available for the children's college education expenses.

Disability Insurance

The maximum available levels of both disability income and disability business overhead coverage are recommended. As additional investments are made that could be relied on to produce income, these amounts should be reviewed to ensure that these coverage levels are still needed.

Personal Property and Liability Insurance

On the facts of our case the property and liability coverage carried by the Andersons is adequate, and additional protection is available through a personal liability umbrella policy. No changes appear necessary in this area.

PERSONAL PLANNING: INVESTMENT

Refinancing Clients' Home

Before the Andersons embark on any plans to achieve their financial objectives, consideration should be given to the terms and conditions of the mortgage on their home. The mortgage for the Andersons' residence was taken out when interest rates were quite high. Dave was unaware that mortgages can be paid off early and a replacement mortgage obtained that will provide substantial cash-flow savings as a result of lower market interest rates.

Because of the pooling of home mortgages to create collateralized mortgage obligation bonds, today's mortgage market conditions require that the duration of individual mortgages be standardized. With few exceptions—such as a close relationship with a lending institution that will hold, rather than sell, an individual's mortgage—the choices available to consumers are either 15- or 30-year mortgages. Because of their financial position the Andersons would not be looking at refinancing as a means of having only an additional $100 or so of disposable income to meet their expenses. In addition, they are not desirous of extending the duration of the mortgage that has about 16 years remaining, but they are interested in refinancing their home with a 15-year mortgage at the current interest rate of 7.75 percent with zero points. Dave is not interested in paying points as a means of lowering the nominal interest rate on the loan since—unlike initial financing points, which are immediately deductible—points associated with a refinancing have to be amortized over the life of the loan.

The monthly mortgage payment for the original 30-year, 12 percent mortgage is $648.03, and for the new 15-year, 7.75 percent mortgage it is $510.25, or a reduction in the monthly payment of $137.78. The new mortgage payment, with a lower interest component, will reduce the mortgage interest that the Andersons can deduct against their federal income tax. Given that their income results in their being subject to the itemized deduction phaseout for high income taxpayers, the effect of the reduced interest deductibility is not as severe as it would be for those with lower adjusted gross income.

The current mortgage, still retained by the issuing local bank, can be prepaid without penalty. The bank also is willing to refinance this mortgage and estimates that the total costs to the Andersons for refinancing will be approximately $1,000.

In light of the more than $1,600 reduction in the annual expenses for their home, it is recommended that they refinance. The full arrangements for the refinancing will be completed by March of next year.

The Andersons have four general financial objectives that may be met by proper investment planning, selection, and monitoring. They have stated these objectives in the following order of priority:

- to fund their children's education
- to reduce their tax burden

- to increase their net worth
- to enjoy retirement

The Andersons have also stated their desire to "maintain their lifestyle." This can be interpreted as a constraint on meeting the other objectives, three of which may be classified as wealth-accumulation objectives. The objective of reducing their tax burden can be met while achieving the other wealth-accumulation objectives.

There are several investment vehicles suitable in various degrees to achieving the Andersons' objectives. The planner must consider this entire array and advise the Andersons on the suitability of these vehicles and the proportion of investable funds the Andersons should place in each vehicle, keeping in mind the clients' stated preferences for particular investments. The planner must also be prepared to reposition assets within the portfolio as the clients' financial environment and preferences change.

Once the family and the business are established, the first financial objective is to provide protection to the family in case of Dave's premature death or disability. Insurance is also needed to protect the clients' assets, as previously discussed. After insurance needs have been met, any investable funds remaining must be used to best meet the clients' other needs. Therefore once properly insured, the Andersons should establish an emergency reserve fund to finance their everyday affairs, to handle unexpected contingencies, and to take advantage of favorable prices. This emergency fund could be kept in a money market fund where it earns interest and is highly liquid. Since Dave is self-employed, owns few income-producing liquid assets, and is the breadwinner for a family of five (soon to be six), an increase in their liquid financial assets to the upper 6-month limit would be appropriate. Although Dave does have $50,000 of accounts receivable from his medical practice, he will also have continuing expenses for his medical practice. Therefore it would be inappropriate to consider these accounts receivable as his emergency reserve.

Most of their surplus cash flow for 2003 should be appropriated for this purpose.

Financial Status of the Clients

The Andersons are in a strong financial position. They can maintain their current standard of living while achieving their desired objectives. Their projected cash flows, if managed prudently, are sufficient to permit the Andersons to fund their children's education, increase their net worth, and enjoy their retirement without borrowing or cutting corners.

The planner in this situation should be concerned with how best to achieve the objectives by recommending various investment vehicles that will be effective for the Andersons in accumulating wealth and reducing the tax burden.

Funding the Children's Education

The Andersons have yet to do any funding of the education expenses for their three children. At this time, accumulating money for the expected child's education would be premature. That need can be addressed after the birth of the child next year.

They have two distinct education expenses for each of their three children: those associated with tuition for secondary (high school) education and those for a 4-year college education.

Secondary School Expenses

The expenses for a 4-year private school, estimated at $4,000 per child per school year, are not considered a legal support obligation in Georgia. Therefore a Sec. 2503(c) trust, possibly in conjunction with college education funding, could be used to shift the taxation of income earned on assets set aside for this purpose. However, the Andersons expect their income to keep growing. Since the secondary school expenses are not very burdensome relative to their income, the Andersons could consider paying for these expenses from current income even if the expenses are adjusted for an 8 percent inflation rate as shown in table 5-8.

TABLE 5-8
Projected Private Secondary School Costs
(Inflated at 8 Percent per Year)

Year	Cost	
2002	$5,000	
2003	5,400	
2004	5,832	
2005	6,299	
2006	6,802	Keith
2007	7,347	Deidre
2008	7,934	
2009	8,569	
2010	9,255	Melissa
2011	9,995	
2012	10,795	
2013	11,658	
2014	12,591	
2015	13,598	
2016	14,686	Expected Baby
2017	15,861	
2018	17,130	
2019	18,500	
2020	19,980	

College Expenses

The Andersons plan to have their children attend high-quality private colleges. They estimate expenses to be $25,000 ($22,000 for tuition, $2,500 for room and board, and $500 for other expenses) in current dollars each college year for each child. An appropriate inflation adjustment needs to be applied to this current value to estimate the future annual college expenses, ascertain the lump-sum funding needed in today's dollars, and determine the amount of annual funding needed to meet this objective.

Since an 8 percent inflation rate for college expenses seems appropriate in the current environment, this rate will be used in making projections.

Because education expenses begin at a specified time and are nondeferrable, a conservative investment strategy is the most effective way to ensure adequate funding for meeting this objective. An appropriate conservative investment vehicle should yield a 7.5 percent before-tax return, on average, for their three children. The available return might be somewhat less for Keith and Deidre since their expenses start within a shorter period of time than Melissa's. However, any difference could be slight. Investment performance, however, should be monitored to verify that expected returns are being realized, and adjustments should be made if needed.

If the Andersons retain ownership of the assets used in funding this objective, their marginal tax rate of 33 percent would apply. The 7.5 percent before-tax yield converts to an after-tax yield of 4.8 percent. This after-tax yield of 4.8 percent and an 8 percent inflation rate for college expenses are used in the education funding schedules on the following pages. Summarizing the data contained in the three schedules, the Andersons' education funding needs appear as follows:

TABLE 5-9 Education Funding—4.8 Percent After-Tax Return		
	Lump-Sum Funding	Annual Funding
Keith Deidre Melissa	$ 81,129 83,764 92,148 $257,041	$ 8,930 (through 2013, $4,465 in 2014) 8,895 (through 2014, $4,448 in 2015) 8,377 (through 2017, $4,189 in 2018) $26,202

[text continues on page 5.90]

EDUCATION FUNDING SCHEDULE

Keith's Education Fund 2003–2014
School Starting Date Sept. 1, 2009
$81,129 Present Value of Education Need
4.80 Expected Rate of Return
Monthly Payments of $765 Made until School Ends

Dave and Diana Anderson
Annual Cash Flow Statement
Monthly Payments until School Ends
Invest $744 Each Month from Jan 2003 through Jun 2014

Year	Investment Needed	Education Expenses	Investment Earnings	Balance in Fund
2003	8,930	0.00	266.00	9,196
2004	8,930	0.00	775.00	18,901
2005	8,930	0.00	1,312.00	29,143
2006	8,930	0.00	1,879.00	39,953
2007	8,930	0.00	2,477.00	51,360
2008	8,930	0.00	3,109.00	63,399
2009	8,930	0.00	3,775.00	76,105
2010	8,930	13,867.00	4,260.00	75,427
2011	8,930	29,450.00	3,576.00	58,484
2012	8,930	31,894.00	2,566.00	38,087
2013	8,930	34,541.00	1,359.00	13,836
2014	4,465	18,331.00	159.00	129
	102,700	128,083.00	25,513.00	

EDUCATION FUNDING SCHEDULE

Deidre's Education Fund 2003–2014
School Starting Date Sept. 1, 2010
$83,764 Present Value of Education Need
4.80 Expected Rate of Return
Monthly Payments of $741 Made until School Ends

Dave and Diana Anderson
Annual Cash Flow Statement
Monthly Payments until School Ends
Invest $741 Each Month from Jan 2003 through Jun 2015

Year	Investment Needed	Education Expenses	Investment Earnings	Balance in Fund
2003	8,895	0.00	235.00	9,130
2004	8,895	0.00	683.00	18,708
2005	8,895	0.00	1,153.00	28,756
2006	8,895	0.00	1,646.00	39,297
2007	8,895	0.00	2,163.00	50,356
2008	8,895	0.00	2,706.00	61,957
2009	8,895	0.00	3,275.00	74,127
2010	8,895	0.00	3,872.00	86,894
2011	8,895	15,020.00	4,288.00	85,057
2012	8,895	31,898.00	3,577.00	65,631
2013	8,895	34,546.00	2,555.00	42,536
2014	8,895	37,413.00	1,347.00	15,365
2015	4,448	19,855.00	157.00	114
	111,192	138,733.00	27,656.00	

EDUCATION FUNDING SCHEDULE

Melissa's Education Fund 2003–2018
School Starting Date Sept. 1, 2013
$92,148 Present Value of Education Need
4.80 Expected Rate of Return
Monthly Payments of $698 Made until School Ends

Dave and Diana Anderson
Annual Cash Flow Statement
Monthly Payments until School Ends
Invest $698 Each Month from Jan 2003 through Jun 2018

Year	Investment Needed	Education Expenses	Investment Earnings	Balance in Fund
2003	8,377	0.00	221.00	8,598
2004	8,377	0.00	643.00	17,618
2005	8,377	0.00	1,086.00	27,081
2006	8,377	0.00	1,550.00	37,008
2007	8,377	0.00	2,037.00	47,422
2008	8,377	0.00	2,548.00	58,347
2009	8,377	0.00	3,084.00	69,808
2010	8,377	0.00	3,647.00	81,832
2011	8,377	0.00	4,237.00	94,445
2012	8,377	0.00	4,855.00	107,678
2013	8,377	0.00	5,505.00	121,560
2014	8,377	19,077.00	5,919.00	116,778
2015	8,377	40,514.00	4,896.00	89,536
2016	8,377	43,877.00	3,471.00	57,507
2017	8,377	47,519.00	1,805.00	20,170
2018	4,189	25,219.00	195.00	-665
	129,845	176,206.00	45,696.00	

At today's schedule of market interest rates, retaining the accumulated funds in the Andersons' name when the funding instrument generates taxable income would require that they contribute slightly more each year to this objective than if the funding instrument was a tax-free, public-purpose municipal bond, since currently these municipal bonds are yielding 5.6 percent. If carefully selected, the income could be exempt from state and local income taxation.

If the Andersons use the Sec. 2503(c) accumulation trust provisions as discussed in the tax planning section and establish separate trusts for each child, each trust will be taxed as a separate entity. If the trust accumulates the income, the first $1,850 of interest income the trust earns each year is subject to a 15 percent marginal tax rate regardless of the beneficiary's age. However, if the trust distributes income to a child under age 14, the kiddie tax can become a problem. After the child reaches age 14, the trust income can be distributed and will be taxed at the child's applicable tax rate at that time. At a 7.9 percent before-tax rate of return on trust assets during the accumulation period, the trust assets must exceed $82,000 before sufficient income is earned to place the trust in a higher (33 percent) income tax bracket than Dave is in. Assuming that each trust is in a 30 percent bracket, each earns an after-tax rate of 5.4 percent. This earnings rate and the 8 percent college expense inflation rate are used to develop the education funding schedules on the following pages. Summarizing the data contained in those three schedules, the Andersons' education funding needs appear as follows:

TABLE 5-10 **Education Funding—5.4 Percent After-Tax Return**		
	Lump-Sum Funding	Annual Funding
Keith Deidre Melissa	$ 76,653 78,671 85,008 $240,332	$ 8,930 (through 2013, $4,465 in 2014) 8,661 (through 2014, $4,331 in 2015) 8,096 (through 2017, $4,048 in 2018) $25,687

The interest earned by the education trusts reports after-tax trust income (7.9 percent x .72 = 5.4 percent) during some of the years that would be taxed to the trust at the 27 percent tax bracket rather than the assumed 30 percent bracket. Because of this tax difference the annual funding as indicated in table 5-10 could be more than needed to fully fund these estimated education costs. The excess is about $200 in annual funding for each trust. The Andersons must recognize this potential additional accumulation, and they should choose one of the following courses of action to handle this occurrence.

First, they could simply do nothing and allow the excess to accumulate in the trust to offset any unexpected increases in college expenses.

Second, since these are projections, the anticipated results must be carefully monitored during the accumulation period. Earning rates on fund assets or annual contributions could change and the taxation of trust income could be altered by future income tax laws. Increases or decreases in the annual funding can be made as future events unfold. Or if Dave has a particularly stellar year financially, larger contributions can be made at that time.

Third, they could reduce the annual funding by $200.

Fourth, during the years when the trusts would have taxable income in excess of $6,500, trust income could be distributed to each child whose age is at least 14. Thus there would be no kiddie tax consequence, and the child would be taxed on the income at a lower rate than the trust. Of course, the Andersons must make sure that the funds so distributed are set aside for accumulation for college costs and not frittered away on frivolous items. No decision need be made at this time to have trust income distributed in this manner, but the Andersons can keep this alternative in mind as a potential solution. Only when any of the children reach age 14 would Dave and Diana have to continue implementing this alternative, providing the children have the necessary maturity and commitment to attend college.

Last, Dave and Diana could use investments that have a higher after-tax return. However, these investments would have a higher risk and might have too much price fluctuation to justify their use to accomplish a financial objective that is not postponable.

Considering how much money will be needed to fund the children's educations, the recommendation is for the Andersons to become accustomed to these funding amounts for several years, after which they should examine the education funding for variations in investment performance or higher-than-expected inflation of education expenses. The following analysis is based on this recommendation.

[text continues on page 5.95]

EDUCATION FUNDING SCHEDULE

Keith's Education Fund 2003–2014
School Starting Date Sept. 1, 2009
$64,058 Present Value of Education Need
5.40 Expected Rate of Return
Monthly Payments of $744 Made until School Ends

Dave and Diana Anderson
Annual Cash Flow Statement
Monthly Payments until School Ends
Invest $744 Each Month from Jan 2003 through Jun 2014

Year	Investment Needed	Education Expenses	Investment Earnings	Balance in Fund
2003	8,930	0.00	266.00	9,196
2004	8,930	0.00	775.00	18,901
2005	8,930	0.00	1,312.00	29,143
2006	8,930	0.00	1,879.00	39,953
2007	8,930	0.00	2,477.00	51,360
2008	8,930	0.00	3,109.00	63,399
2009	8,930	0.00	3,775.00	76,105
2010	8,930	13,867.00	4,260.00	75,427
2011	8,930	29,450.00	3,576.00	58,484
2012	8,930	31,894.00	2,566.00	38,087
2013	8,930	34,541.00	1,359.00	13,836
2014	4,465	18,331.00	159.00	129
	102,700	128,083.00	25,513.00	

EDUCATION FUNDING SCHEDULE

Deidre's Education Fund 2003–2015
School Starting Date Sept. 1, 2010
$64,499 Present Value of Education Need
5.40 Expected Rate of Return
Monthly Payments of $722 Made until School Ends

Dave and Diana Anderson
Annual Cash Flow Statement
Monthly Payments until School Ends
Invest $722 Each Month from Jan 2003 through Jun 2015

Year	Investment Needed	Education Expenses	Investment Earnings	Balance in Fund
2003	8,661	0.00	258.00	8,919
2004	8,661	0.00	751.00	18,331
2005	8,661	0.00	1,272.00	28,264
2006	8,661	0.00	1,822.00	38,747
2007	8,661	0.00	2,402.00	49,811
2008	8,661	0.00	3,015.00	61,487
2009	8,661	0.00	3,661.00	73,809
2010	8,661	0.00	4,343.00	86,814
2011	8,661	15,020.00	4,826.00	85,281
2012	8,661	31,898.00	4,041.00	66,085
2013	8,661	34,546.00	2,901.00	43,101
2014	8,661	37,413.00	1,545.00	15,893
2015	4,331	19,855.00	189.00	558
	108,263	138,733.00	31,028.00	

EDUCATION FUNDING SCHEDULE

Melissa's Education Fund 2003–2018
School Starting Date Sept. 1, 2013
$65,840 Present Value of Education Need
5.40 Expected Rate of Return
Monthly Payments of $675 Made until School Ends

Dave and Diana Anderson
Annual Cash Flow Statement
Monthly Payments until School Ends
Invest $675 Each Month from Jan 2003 through Jun 2018

Year	Investment Needed	Education Expenses	Investment Earnings	Balance in Fund
2003	8,096	0.00	241.00	8,337
2004	8,096	0.00	702.00	17,135
2005	8,096	0.00	1,189.00	26,420
2006	8,096	0.00	1,703.00	36,219
2007	8,096	0.00	2,246.00	46,561
2008	8,096	0.00	2,818.00	57,475
2009	8,096	0.00	3,422.00	68,994
2010	8,096	0.00	4,060.00	81,150
2011	8,096	0.00	4,733.00	93,979
2012	8,096	0.00	5,443.00	107,518
2013	8,096	0.00	6,193.00	121,806
2014	8,096	19,077.00	6,683.00	117,507
2015	8,096	40,514.00	5,556.00	90,645
2016	8,096	43,877.00	3,970.00	58,833
2017	8,096	47,519.00	2,102.00	21,512
2018	4,048	25,219.00	254.00	595
	125,487	176,206.00	51,314.00	

A comparison of table 5-9 with table 5-10 shows that the Andersons will reduce the annual funding needed by $515 if they use trusts. This reduction, as well as the difference in the amount of lump-sum funding needed ($16,709), results from the difference in the assumed tax rate on trust income during the accumulation period compared with the tax rate if the Andersons retained ownership of the assets.

At the moment the Andersons do not possess sufficient assets to fully fund the education needs unless Dave were to sell the commercial lot or some of his securities. However, the commercial lot, which produces zero taxable income, could be converted into one generating income taxed at their 30 percent bracket if the funds were kept in Dave's name. If the proceeds from the sale were used to fund the trusts, each trust would soon have income in excess of $4,400 per year and would be taxed at a higher rate than 30 percent if this income was accumulated. The lump-sum funding, accomplished by using the proceeds from the sale of the commercial lot, is not the best solution. Annual funding is the recommended procedure for the Andersons.

The annual funding that is needed for each of the three separate trusts is less than the annual gift tax exclusion whether Dave makes the gift himself ($11,000) or is joined by Diana in making the gifts ($22,000) to each trust.

Consideration must also be given to the nature of Dave's profession. As a practicing physician he has liability for his professional conduct. Even though insurance is carried to protect him and his family from the consequences of malpractice, a catastrophic judgment (however unlikely) against both the business and personal assets should at least be recognized as a possibility in this planning process. Since the 2503(c) trust is an irrevocable trust, the trust assets are ultimately the property of the children and should be beyond the reach of any judgment levied against Dave. Therefore even if the tax savings from using the trusts are not large, the protection afforded by placing the assets beyond the reach of any judgment levied against Dave might be sufficient reason to justify their establishment.

The Andersons specified that the highest priority among their financial objectives is to provide college education for each of their children. Since they will be funding this objective from now until the time the last child completes college, additional assurance that the funding will be achieved should appeal to the Andersons. One effective way to obtain this assurance would be to utilize decreasing term insurance in conjunction with educational funding, with disability riders added to the policies. Thus if Dave died prematurely, the funding would be self-completing. One policy for each child's lump-sum funding need should be obtained now on Dave's life. Dave should apply for, be the owner of, and pay the premium for three decreasing term insurance policies, each equal to the amount needed to provide lump-sum funding of a child's educational fund. Each child's trust should be the beneficiary of that child's policy. The trusts should not own the policies, because such an arrangement could result in a loss of the desired income shifting. The annual premium for the three policies combined will not be over $350.

This recommended insurance in the amount of $195,000 for ensuring total funding for the children's education does not reduce the amount of life insurance that Dave needs as discussed in the insurance planning section. The assumption was made that the money Diana would have from insurance proceeds was for maintaining the current lifestyle and that the funding for college education would be treated separately.

The use of a Sec. 2503(c) accumulation trust in this situation provides significant benefits. First, since the trusts are irrevocable, the contributions are completed gifts. The trust assets ultimately belong to the children and are not included in the estates of Dave or Diana for estate tax purposes, assuming Dave is not named trustee. Second, the trust assets are beyond the reach of any professional judgments levied against Dave and beyond the reach of any of Dave's and/or Diana's personal creditors. Third, there are some income tax advantages, as described above, since much of the trust income will be taxed at a lower tax bracket than the Andersons' bracket. This income tax saving is modest for both Keith and Deidre since the accumulation time is relatively short. In Melissa's case, where the time horizon is longer, larger tax savings result.

Once a trust is created for one child, the additional costs for drafting trust instruments and for the management of additional trusts for the other two children are relatively modest. Use of a trust only for Melissa might generate future sibling animosity the Andersons want to avoid. Even though the income tax savings are modest for Keith and Deidre, should anything happen to Dave and Diana simultaneously, Melissa would be in a favored position financially unless provisions of Dave and Diana's wills considered the existence of her trust.

One additional factor to consider is the cost of establishing and maintaining these trusts. First, between $2,000 and $3,000 of expense will be incurred to have the trust instruments drafted by an attorney. If appropriate, the same attorney could also be named as trustee and be responsible for the annual income tax returns for the trust. A portion of the expenses of establishing (but not maintaining) these three trusts qualifies as a tax planning expense and therefore would be deductible by Dave and Diana in the year the trusts are established. Second, the annual expenses incurred for trust asset management and income tax preparation should be significantly less than the tax savings generated. These expenses are tax deductible by the trust, but not by Dave and Diana. Each trust would deduct its portion of the annual expense against trust income for that year. Consequently the Andersons may wish to increase their annual contributions to meet these expenses.

The expense of establishing and maintaining an UGMA custodial account is less. However, as previously discussed, income from an UGMA account would be subject to the kiddie tax until the beneficiary reaches the age of 14.

Although the Sec. 2503(c) trust, given its previously described advantages, is the best method of achieving the desired college education funding for the Andersons, clients are often uncomfortable about making irrevocable transfers. If so, alternatives do exist.

One alternative available to Dave and Diana will be to purchase Series EE bonds for the purposes of funding the children's expenses. Since recognition of the income earned on these bonds can be deferred until redemption occurs, the interest earnings will accumulate in a tax-advantaged manner. Moreover, existing federal law provides an additional incentive for parents to use EE bonds as the educational funding vehicle. The following rules must be met to qualify the interest as tax-exempt upon redemption of the bonds:

- The proceeds of the redemption must be used for qualified educational expenses such as higher education tuition.
- The total proceeds—initial acquisition cost plus accumulated interest—must not exceed the amount of incurred qualified educational expenses in the year of the redemption.
- The expenses must be made in behalf of a dependent of the taxpayer.
- The bonds must initially be acquired by the taxpayer (or spouse).
- The bond purchaser must be at least 24 years of age at the time the bond is issued.
- The bonds must have been purchased after December 31, 1989.

In March 1999 Series EE bonds guaranteed a yield of 4 percent. For taxpayers such as the Andersons, who are in the 36 percent tax bracket, this translates into a before-tax yield of 6.25 percent. If for any 6-month period 85 percent of the current U.S. Treasury 5-year interest rate exceeds 4 percent, then the higher rate will apply for the next 6-month period.

Unfortunately, as with other tax matters, the taxpayer must have income below a certain amount to obtain the full benefit of this exemption. The exemption is phased out as income exceeds the specified limit. In the case of married couples filing a joint return, such as the Andersons, the phaseout begins when the modified adjusted gross income exceeds $86,400 and ends at $116,400. These income limitations are adjusted for inflation beginning January 1, 1991, and reflect the phaseouts in effect for 2000. Because of Dave's income level the Andersons cannot benefit from this exclusion. The best they could achieve if they use Series EE bonds as the accumulation device would be the tax deferral until redemption, at which time the deferred interest will be taxable to them.

Another alternative would be for Dave and Diana to purchase municipal bonds, hold the bonds in their names, and use the interest income and sale proceeds to meet the college expenses. These bonds will earn about 5 percent tax free. This yield is similar to the after-tax income that could be earned on corporate bonds held in their name. However, since a higher after-tax yield can be obtained by using the Sec. 2503(c) trusts, the use of the municipal bonds cannot be justified unless Dave and Diana do not wish to make irrevocable gifts at this time or if they feel the cost of establishing and maintaining the trusts is excessive.

Considering all factors and particularly the placing of these funds beyond the reach of any potential lawsuits arising from Dave's medical practice, the 2503(c) trusts are the recommended education funding vehicles. Investment selections for the trusts will be discussed in the next section.

The following projections (case II) illustrate the Andersons' tax, net worth, and cash-flow positions if

- under the general insurance recommendations $9,500 of cash flow is allocated annually toward additional coverage on Dave's life beginning in 2003
- the amount of $25,687 is gifted annually to education funding trusts beginning in 2003
- the Andersons refinance their house

A new opportunity for educational funding, created by the Taxpayer Relief Act of 1997, is the Education IRA, which is not actually an IRA at all but rather a funding vehicle for a child's education. Education IRAs are available for tax years beginning after December 31, 1997. The Economic Growth and Reconciliation Act of 2001 changed the name of the Education IRA to the Coverdell Education Savings Account.

Once an Education IRA is created, contributions of up to $2,000 per year may be made on behalf of children under the age of 18. The $2,000 amount cannot be leveraged by having parents, aunts and uncles, or brothers and sisters make additional contributions since the limit is $2,000 per year *per child*. No income tax deduction is allowed for contributions to an Education IRA, but the earnings in the Education IRA are not subject to income tax if the IRA is used for qualified educational expenses of the child.

Some limitations apply to Education IRAs, however. Eligibility to contribute to an Education IRA is phased out for AGI above certain limits. Single filers with less than $95,000 in AGI may contribute the full $500. For single filers with AGI above $95,000 and less than $110,000, the amount of the allowable contribution is reduced on a pro rata basis. Single filers with AGI in excess of $110,000 are not eligible to make Education IRA contributions on behalf of any beneficiary. For married individuals, a $500 contribution may be made if joint adjusted gross income is less than $150,000. For joint AGI between $150,000 and $160,000 the allowable contribution is phased out on a pro rata basis; joint filers with AGI in excess of $160,000 are not permitted to make Education IRA contributions.

If the amounts accumulated in the Education IRA are not used for qualified educational expenses, the earnings are subject to income taxation and the 10 percent penalty tax. If the family has more than one child, and one of the children pursues education beyond high school, imposition of this tax may be avoided. Amounts held in an educational IRA for one beneficiary may be rolled over to an educational IRA of a family member of the beneficiary without tax consequences.

Because Dave and Diana's AGI exceeds the threshold that would allow them to contribute to an Education IRA, this is not a viable planning option for them. If their parents or brothers and sisters wished to create an Educational IRA for the benefit of Dave and Diana's children, assuming they fall within the income thresholds for contribution, additional funds may be able to accumulate tax free for the benefit of the children's education. The maximum contribution per child, however, would be limited to $2,000.

[text continues on page 5.109]

CASE II

New Assumptions

1. Beginning in 2003 an additional $9,500 of cash flow is allocated each year to additional life insurance on Dave.

2. Beginning in 2003 the amount of $25,687 is gifted each year to education funding trusts.

3. In March 2002 the unpaid balance of the home mortgage will be refinanced at 7.75 percent for 15 years. A one-time, nondeductible cost of $1,000 will be paid.

Continuing Assumptions

1. The checking account balance is maintained at $5,000; the account is noninterest bearing.

2. The joint savings account balance of $10,000 earns 3 percent interest annually. Interest accumulates in the account.

3. The money market deposit account has an average balance of $25,000 and earns 3 percent interest annually. Interest does not accumulate in the account but is added to surplus cash.

4. Surplus cash is invested and earns 4 percent annually.

5. Dave's gross receipts and business expenses are expected to increase at 4.4 percent annually.

6. Diana inherited a coin collection from her father in 1976. Fair market value of the collection is presently $20,000 and is expected to increase annually at 6 percent.

7. The 2001 value of the personal residence ($315,000) will increase at 8 percent annually. The residence was purchased in March 1988. The original amount of the mortgage was $63,000 at an interest rate of 12 percent for a term of 30 years.

8. The 2001 value of the commercial lot ($260,000) will increase at 4 percent annually. The lot was purchased in March 1990. The original amount of the mortgage was $80,000 at an interest rate of 10 percent for a term of 20 years.

9. The 2001 value of the rental property ($120,000) will increase at 6 percent annually. The rental property was purchased in November 1990. Currently the property rents for $550 per month and has operating expenses of approximately $900 annually. All these amounts will increase at 6 percent annually.

10. Dave has office furniture valued at approximately $20,000 and office equipment valued at $45,000. No increase or decrease in value has been assumed.

11. Dave's accounts receivable average $50,000.

12. Property taxes on the personal residence are expected to increase at 6 percent annually.

13. Nondeductible living expenses are expected to increase at 6 percent annually.

14. Charitable contributions are expected to increase at 6 percent annually.

15. Dave's Keogh plan is presently invested in 30-month CDs earning 8 percent. This earning assumption has been projected through 2004. He makes a maximum contribution to this plan in each year.

16. Automobiles decrease in value at a rate of 15 percent annually.

17. The expected growth rate of all dividends is 2 percent.

18. The expected growth rate for prices of all stocks is the same as the past growth for each stock.

19. No growth is expected in either bond current yields or total return.

INCOME STATEMENT

DAVE & DIANA ANDERSON

CASE II	2002	2003	2004	2005	2006
Earned Income					
Business Inc-CI	200,000	211,000	222,605	234,848	247,765
Business-Salaries	-22,500	-22,500	-22,500	-22,500	-22,500
	177,500	188,500	200,105	212,348	225,265
Interest/Dividends					
Saving/NOW Acts	300	300	300	300	300
Money Market Fund	750	750	750	750	750
Houseboat Finance	900	900	900	900	900
Clean Soap Inc	1,000	1,020	1,040	1,061	1,082
Nationwide Oil Co	500	510	520	531	541
Deep Snow Maker Inc	30	31	31	32	32
Burp Soda Inc	640	653	666	679	693
Economic Fund	24	24	25	25	26
Wellington Mfg Corp	300	306	312	318	325
FundMgrsGrowthFund	1,342	1,369	1,396	1,424	1,453
Atlantic Rim Fund	456	465	474	484	494
Southern Fund	395	403	411	419	428
5-7 Year Bond Fund	395	403	411	419	428
National Index Fund	900	918	937	956	976
Yum-Yum Foods	350	362	373	386	398
Investable Cash	1,272	3,255	4,822	6,646	8,681
	9,554	11,669	13,370	15,331	17,506
Investments					
Invest--House Loan	-3,575	-3,435	-3,282	-3,114	-2,928
Invest--House Expen	-900	-954	-1,011	-1,072	-1,136
Invest--House Rent	6,600	6,996	7,416	7,861	8,332
Invest--House Depre	-2,100	-2,100	-2,100	-2,100	-2,100
Invest--Lot Loan	-5,371	-4,962	-4,512	-4,015	-3,465
	-5,346	-4,455	-3,489	-2,440	-1,297
Adjustments					
S.E. Tax Dedctn	7,663	7,810	7,966	8,130	8,303
	7,663	7,810	7,966	8,130	8,303
	========	========	========	========	========
Adj Gross Income	174,045	187,904	202,019	217,109	233,171
Deductions					
Charitable 50%	4,500	4,770	5,056	5,360	5,681
State Tax Paid	8,246	9,132	9,916	10,774	11,642
Prop Taxes--Home	1,900	2,014	2,135	2,263	2,399
Original Mortgage	6,584	1,623	0	0	0
Refinanced Mortgage	0	3,095	3,989	3,820	3,639
Reductn for High Inc	-1,129	-1,439	-1,753	-2,093	-1,640
Gross Deductions	20,101	19,195	19,343	20,124	21,720
Standard Deduction	7,800	8,000	8,200	8,787	9,476
Allowed Deductions	20,101	19,195	19,343	20,124	21,720
Pers Exemptions	14,750	15,250	15,750	16,000	9,240
	========	========	========	========	========
Taxable Income	139,194	153,458	166,926	180,985	202,211
	========	========	========	========	========
Fed Income Tax	47,561	51,901	56,158	62,434	68,353
	========	========	========	========	========
Fed Tax Bracket-Ord Inc	30.0%	30.0%	29.0%	29.0%	33.0%

BALANCE SHEET

DAVE & DIANA ANDERSON

CASE II	2002	2003	2004	2005	2006
LIQUID ASSETS					
Cash Balance	5,003	5,020	4,998	4,991	4,994
Cash Deposits					
Saving/NOW Acts	10,000	10,000	10,000	10,000	10,000
Investable Cash	64,895	101,122	144,819	194,136	248,605
Money Market Fund	25,000	25,000	25,000	25,000	25,000
	99,895	136,122	179,819	229,136	283,605
Stocks & Bonds					
Houseboat Finance	12,508	12,426	12,338	12,243	12,142
Town Hall Munibonds	10,600	10,585	10,572	10,556	10,540
State School System	15,150	15,152	15,157	15,161	15,165
Clean Soap Inc	35,000	39,900	45,486	51,854	59,114
Nationwide Oil Co	12,000	12,600	13,230	13,892	14,586
Deep Snow Maker Inc	14,000	16,520	19,494	23,002	27,143
Burp Soda Inc	32,000	34,880	38,019	41,441	45,171
Economic Fund	1,500	1,305	1,135	987	859
Wellington Mfg Corp	24,000	26,400	29,040	31,944	35,138
FundMgrsGrowthFund	46,200	47,355	48,539	49,752	50,996
Atlantic Rim Fund	9,500	10,355	11,287	12,303	13,410
Southern Fund	10,200	11,373	12,681	14,139	15,765
5-7 Year Bond Fund	6,200	6,299	6,400	6,502	6,606
National Index Fund	44,000	52,800	63,360	76,032	91,238
Yum-Yum Foods	17,000	18,020	19,101	20,247	21,462
	289,858	315,970	345,838	380,056	419,336
	========	========	========	========	========
Liquid Assets	394,756	457,112	530,655	614,184	707,935
	========	========	========	========	========

NONLIQUID ASSETS

	2002	2003	2004	2005	2006
Retirement Plans					
Business-Salaries	91,168	122,761	156,882	193,733	233,532
	91,168	122,761	156,882	193,733	233,532
Investments					
Investment--House	120,000	127,200	134,832	142,922	151,497
Investment--Lot	260,000	270,400	281,216	292,465	304,163
	380,000	397,600	416,048	435,387	455,660
Personal Property					
Home	340,200	367,416	396,809	428,554	462,838
Dave's Car	18,700	15,895	13,511	11,484	9,762
Diana's Car	8,500	7,225	6,141	5,220	4,437
Furnishings--Home	30,000	30,000	30,000	30,000	30,000
Furnishings--Office	65,000	65,000	65,000	65,000	65,000

BALANCE SHEET (cont.)

DAVE & DIANA ANDERSON

CASE II	2002	2003	2004	2005	2006
Coin Collection	21,200	22,472	23,820	25,250	26,765
Business Accts Rec	50,000	50,000	50,000	50,000	50,000
	533,600	558,008	585,282	615,508	648,801
	========	========	========	========	========
Nonliquid Assets	1,004,768	1,078,369	1,158,211	1,244,628	1,337,994
	========	========	========	========	========
Total Assets	1,399,524	1,535,481	1,688,866	1,858,812	2,045,929

LIABILITIES

Mortgage Loans

	2002	2003	2004	2005	2006
Original Mortgage	54,208	0	0	0	0
Refinanced Mortgage	0	52,417	50,319	48,052	45,604
	54,208	52,417	50,319	48,052	45,604
Notes Payable					
Diana's Car--Loan	4,223	1,478	0	0	0
	4,223	1,478	0	0	0
Investments					
Invest--House Loan	36,858	35,313	33,615	31,749	29,697
Invest--Lot Loan	51,565	47,263	42,511	37,262	31,463
	88,423	82,576	76,126	69,011	61,160
	========	========	========	========	========
Total Liabilities	146,854	136,471	126,445	117,063	106,764
	========	========	========	========	========
Net Worth	1,252,670	1,399,010	1,562,421	1,741,749	1,939,165
	========	========	========	========	========

CASH FLOW STATEMENT

DAVE & DIANA ANDERSON

CASE II	2002	2003	2004	2005	2006
BEGINNING OF YEAR					
Idle Cash On Hand	5,000	5,003	5,020	4,998	4,991
SOURCES OF CASH					
Cash Income					
Business Inc-CI	200,000	211,000	222,605	234,848	247,765
Interest+Dividends	9,610	9,741	9,875	10,012	10,153
	209,610	220,741	232,480	244,861	257,917
Investments					
InvestHouse - Depre	2,100	2,100	2,100	2,100	2,100
	2,100	2,100	2,100	2,100	2,100
Liab Incurred					
Replacement Mrtgage	0	53,887	0	0	0
	0	53,887	0	0	0
	========	========	========	========	========
Total Cash Inflow	211,710	276,728	234,580	246,961	260,017
	========	========	========	========	========
Tot Cash Available	216,710	281,731	239,600	251,959	265,009
	========	========	========	========	========
USES OF CASH					
Fully Tax Deductible					
Business-Salaries	22,500	22,500	22,500	22,500	22,500
Original Mortgage	6,584	1,623	0	0	0
Refinanced Mortgage	0	3,095	3,989	3,820	3,639
	29,084	27,218	26,489	26,320	26,139
Partly Deductible					
Charity Contrb-50%	4,500	4,770	5,056	5,360	5,681
	4,500	4,770	5,056	5,360	5,681
Not Tax Deductible					
Diana's Car--Loan	559	299	44	0	0
EducationFundingTru	0	25,687	25,687	25,687	25,687
Vacations	4,000	4,240	4,494	4,764	5,050
Life Ins Prem--Dave	279	327	377	443	521
Addtl Life Ins-Dave	0	9,500	9,500	9,500	9,500
Home Ins Prem--Home	600	636	674	715	757
Ins Prem--Cars	995	1,055	1,118	1,185	1,256
Dis Ins Prem--Dave	1,539	1,539	1,539	1,539	1,539
Living Expenses	30,000	31,800	33,708	35,730	37,874
	37,972	75,083	77,142	79,563	82,185

CASH FLOW STATEMENT (cont.)

DAVE & DIANA ANDERSON

CASE II	2002	2003	2004	2005	2006
Taxes Paid					
Fed Tax Paid	47,561	51,901	56,158	62,434	68,353
State Tax Paid	8,246	9,132	9,916	10,774	11,642
Prop Taxes--Home	1,900	2,014	2,135	2,263	2,399
	57,707	63,047	68,209	75,471	82,394
Purchase/Deposits					
Investable Cash	63,623	32,972	38,875	42,671	45,788
	63,623	32,972	38,875	42,671	45,788
Investments					
Invest--House Loan	4,980	4,980	4,980	4,980	4,980
Invest--House Expen	900	954	1,011	1,072	1,136
Invest--Lot Loan	9,264	9,264	9,264	9,264	9,264
	15,144	15,198	15,255	15,316	15,380
Liability Liquidation					
Original Mortgage	1,192	54,208	0	0	0
Diana's Car--Loan	2,485	2,745	1,478	0	0
Refinanced Mortgage	0	1,470	2,098	2,267	2,448
	3,677	58,423	3,576	2,267	2,448
	========	========	========	========	========
Tot Cash Outflow	211,707	276,711	234,602	246,968	260,015
	========	========	========	========	========
END OF YEAR					
Cash Balance	5,003	5,020	4,998	4,991	4,994
	========	========	========	========	========

SUPPORTING SCHEDULE

DAVE & DIANA ANDERSON

CASE II	JOINT 2002	JOINT 2003	JOINT 2004	JOINT 2005	JOINT 2006
Income					
Earned Income	177,500	188,500	200,105	212,348	225,265
Adj Gross Income	174,045	187,904	202,019	217,109	233,171
Allowed Deductions	20,101	19,195	19,343	20,124	21,720
Pers Exemptions	14,750	15,250	15,750	16,000	9,240
Taxable Income	139,194	153,458	166,926	180,985	202,211
Investments					
Ordinary Income	6,600	6,996	7,416	7,861	8,332
Depreciation	2,100	2,100	2,100	2,100	2,100
Invstmt Interest	8,946	8,397	7,794	7,129	6,393
Other Expenses	900	954	1,011	1,072	1,136
Investment Income	-5,346	-4,455	-3,489	-2,440	-1,297
Investment Interest					
Inv Int Sch E	8,946	8,397	7,794	7,129	6,393
Federal Tax Liab					
Regular Tax	32,235	36,281	38,901	42,749	47,804
Gross Fed Inc Tax	32,235	36,281	38,901	42,749	47,804
Alt Minimum Tax	0	0	1,326	3,426	3,944
AMT Credit C/Over	0	0	0	0	1,326
Disallowed	0	0	0	-1,326	-4,753
Self Employmt Tax	15,326	15,620	15,931	16,259	16,605
Fed Income Tax	47,561	51,901	56,158	62,434	68,353
Fed Tax Analysis-Ord Inc					
Indexing Factor	82	87	91	96	102
Fed Tax Bracket-Ord Inc	30.0%	30.0%	29.0%	29.0%	33.0%
$ to Next Bracket	31,606	21,792	12,874	3,515	135,839
Next Bracket	35.0%	35.0%	34.0%	34.0%	35.0%
Previous Bracket	27.0%	27.0%	26.0%	26.0%	28.0%
$ to Prev Bracket	27,144	38,458	48,926	59,935	12,911
Fed Effective Tax Rate	34.2%	33.8%	33.6%	34.5%	33.8%
Alt Minimum Tax					
Adj Gross Income	174,045	187,904	202,019	217,109	233,171
Contributions	-4,500	-4,770	-5,056	-5,360	-5,681
Home Mortg Int	-6,584	-4,718	-3,989	-3,820	-3,639
Adjusted AMTI	162,961	178,416	192,974	207,929	223,851
AMT Exemptions	-45,760	-41,896	-38,256	-30,518	-26,537
AMT Taxable Inc	117,201	136,519	154,718	177,411	197,314
Gross Alt Min Tx	30,472	35,495	40,227	46,175	51,748
Fed Tax Less FTC	-32,235	-36,281	-38,901	-42,749	-47,804
Alt Minimum Tax	0	0	1,326	3,426	3,944
Other Tax Liabs					
Adj Gross Inc	174,045	187,904	202,019	217,109	233,171
GA AGI Adjstmnts	1,328	1,328	1,328	1,328	1,328
GA Adj Gross Inc	175,373	189,231	203,347	218,437	234,499
GA Standard Ded	3,000	3,000	3,000	3,000	3,000
GA Itemized Ded	20,101	19,195	19,343	20,124	21,720
GA Exemptions	13,500	13,500	14,400	14,400	14,400
GA Taxable Inc	141,772	156,536	169,604	183,912	198,378
GA Regular Tax	8,246	9,132	9,916	10,774	11,642
GA Income Tax	8,246	9,132	9,916	10,774	11,642
Georgia Tax	8,246	9,132	9,916	10,774	11,642
Tot State/Local Tx	8,246	9,132	9,916	10,774	11,642
Total Inc Tax	55,807	61,033	66,074	73,208	79,995

FINANCIAL SUMMARY

DAVE & DIANA ANDERSON

CASE II	2002	2003	2004	2005	2006
Gross Real Income					
Personal Earnings	200,000	211,000	222,605	234,848	247,765
Interest Income	4,550	6,533	8,100	9,924	11,959
Dividends Rcvd	6,332	6,464	6,598	6,735	6,875
InvestHouse - Depre	2,100	2,100	2,100	2,100	2,100
	212,982	226,096	239,402	253,607	268,698
Income & Inflation					
Gross Real Inc	212,982	226,096	239,402	253,607	268,698
Total Inc Tax	-55,807	-61,033	-66,074	-73,208	-79,995
Net Real Income	157,175	165,063	173,328	180,399	188,703
Cur Real Inc =	157,175	161,264	165,460	169,764	174,181
At Infltn Rate of	3	3	3	3	3
Cash Flow					
Idle Cash On Hand	5,000	5,003	5,020	4,998	4,991
Norml Cash Inflow	211,710	276,728	234,580	246,961	260,017
Norml Cash Outflw	148,084	243,739	195,727	204,297	214,227
Cash Invested	63,623	32,972	38,875	42,671	45,788
Cash Balance	5,003	5,020	4,998	4,991	4,994
Net Worth					
Personal Assets	538,603	563,028	590,280	620,499	653,795
Investment Assets	860,921	972,453	1,098,587	1,238,312	1,392,134
Personal Liabilities	-58,431	-53,895	-50,319	-48,052	-45,604
Investmt Liabilities	-88,423	-82,576	-76,126	-69,011	-61,160
Personal Net Worth	480,172	509,133	539,961	572,447	608,191
Investment Net Worth	772,498	889,877	1,022,461	1,169,301	1,330,974
Net Worth	1,252,670	1,399,010	1,562,421	1,741,749	1,939,165

Investment Alternatives for Education Funding

The next step is to assess the suitability of various investment media for meeting the objective.

INSTRUCTIONS

Background material on the various investment risks, investor profiles, the need to match the risk-return trade-off associated with the various instruments, suggestions for matching investments in the general risk category with financial objectives, and selected investments appropriate for education funding have been omitted from this chapter in order to avoid repetition. If you are not familiar with the noted material from the earlier chapters, it should be reviewed prior to proceeding through this section of the suggested solution.

In addition to the investment media previously discussed, investments that entail slightly higher degrees of risk could be considered for this client.

High-Income Bond Funds. These bond mutual funds, sometimes referred to as junk bond funds, possess a greater degree of business and interest-rate risk since they invest in a portfolio of corporate bonds at minimum or slightly below what is deemed investment-grade quality to obtain higher yields. Other than the composition of their portfolios, they do not differ from other bond funds. Since the Andersons have a relatively high income and since Dave appears willing to take some degree of risk, these could be a viable investment medium for the education funding purposes.

Growth-Oriented No-Load Mutual Fund. The Andersons could use a no-load diversified mutual fund consisting of growth-oriented blue-chip common stock. The advantages would be capital appreciation and an inflationary hedge as investment media for their children's education funds.

The no-load fund should be chosen because there is no shrinkage of productive assets as a consequence of a sales charge being deducted from the purchase price, as in a load fund. With a 6 percent sales charge found in some load funds, the investor has only 94 cents out of each dollar with which to purchase shares in the fund. With the no-load fund the full dollar of investment purchases shares in the fund. If both funds were to earn a 10 percent return on assets, for example, the return in the first year for a purchase of $10,000 would be $1,000 for the no-load fund and $940 for the load fund. Another way to express this difference is that a load fund earns $940 on a $10,000 investment (cost to the Andersons) and thus has a yield of 9.4 percent ($940/$10,000). Since studies show, on the average, little if any difference in investment performance between these two forms of funds, no-load funds should be the Andersons' choice unless extenuating circumstances favor the use of the load fund.

Numerous no-load mutual funds have instituted 12(b)(1) fees that are assessed on an annual basis against fund assets. These fees range from .25 percent to 1.25 percent. The proceeds raised by this assessment are used to pay for marketing expenses of the fund, which include advertising expenses and disguised forms of sales commissions paid to brokers. Since this is an annual fee, its compound result affects the performance of an investment in the fund. Unless there is a compelling reason, such as higher net after-tax return, to purchase a no-load with a 12(b)(1) fee, the Andersons should avoid buying no-load funds with such a fee. For an investor having the choice of either a 12(b)(1) fee of 0.75 percent annually or a front-end load of 6.5 percent and both funds earning 9 percent, if the planned holding period exceeds 8 years, the best choice is the load fund.

Mutual funds should also be attractive to this client since they provide professional management of the assets by handling the day-to-day needs for selection and timing of securities transactions. As a practicing physician, Dave may not have the time, expertise, or inclination to perform these tasks. In addition, ownership of shares in a mutual fund provides diversification of the portfolio due to the fund's ownership of securities spread over various sectors of the economy, thus reducing most of the business risk.

No-load mutual funds are purchased and redeemed at their net asset value. Immediately after dividends are declared, the net asset value of the shares falls. Consequently if the Andersons select no-load mutual funds as one of their investment choices, they should purchase shares shortly after the fund declares its periodic dividend. If shares are purchased shortly before the dividend [declaration] date, the Andersons will use after-tax savings to purchase the shares and then have taxable dividend income returned to them. In addition, the net amount of their investment working for them in the fund will be reduced by the amount of the distributed dividend.

One disadvantage of this investment vehicle is the necessity of converting the growth-oriented asset into an income-producing asset when needed for their stated objective, which would produce a taxable event. Another disadvantage of investing in a growth fund is that like any mutual fund, it cannot be expected to consistently outperform the market. Unfortunately, however, a badly managed fund can continually underperform the market.

For the education funding, the first priority of the Andersons, the trust established for each child should use relatively conservative funding instruments. However, the potential for taking some risk should not be overlooked.

Investment Media Selection

Use of Corporate Bonds. Since high-quality, investment-grade corporate bonds would, if used as the investment medium for the educational expenses, fulfill the objectives of having a fixed return during the accumulation period and a known value upon maturity, the specific amount of money will be available when needed.

Currently investment-grade bonds are providing about a 7.9 percent return. It is anticipated that this return, as an average, is sustainable during the funding period, although economic conditions could cause this expected return to change.

Each trust should acquire as many corporate bonds as possible each year using the annual contribution and any interest earnings. Idle funds (the excess of the contribution and interest earnings over the value of any bonds that can be purchased) should be placed in a money market fund until such time as sufficient funds are accumulated to make additional bond purchases.

The maturity schedules for the bonds selected for each trust should recognize the annual contribution being made as well as any interest earnings. This approach can be used to establish an appropriate maturity schedule to facilitate each trustee's portfolio management.

The above discussion was based on the assumption that the trustee acquired corporate bonds that paid their annual interest in cash each year. Obviously this cash flow, after payment of taxes along with the annual funding contribution, has to be used to acquire additional bonds. If the trustee acquired zero coupon bonds, the problem of reinvesting each year's accumulated interest would be eliminated. Although the trust would have no cash inflow from interest, the IRS would still deem the accrued interest to be income for tax purposes. However, the trust could use the annual funding contribution as the source of cash to pay the income tax, which in these trusts never exceeds the annual contribution.

Use of Higher-Risk Investments. Since Dave and Diana's cash flows are expected to be substantial over the foreseeable future, they can afford to take somewhat higher risk on the investment vehicles used to fund the education objectives.

However, it must be recognized that the total funds required for the annual education expenditure might not be available when needed if more risky investment vehicles are used. For the college years until Deidre graduates, there will be two children in college simultaneously. Despite Dave's relatively high income, shortfalls could impose a financial strain on the family. Because of this potential Dave and Diana might consider investing a portion of each year's contribution (perhaps 20 to 30 percent of the annual contribution to each trust) in the higher-risk, higher-yielding investments. Should this course of action be taken, the Andersons will need to carefully monitor the performance of the trusts, and if lower-than-anticipated investment returns occur, then either a change in their annual funding or strong recommendations to the trustee to alter the investment mix would be appropriate.

The Andersons could opt to use the higher-risk, higher-return investments. However, for illustrative purposes this discussion is based on their using corporate bonds as the investment medium.

Repositioning of Existing Assets

The Andersons' existing assets reflect Dave's strong desire to invest in individual securities and mutual funds. However, any repositioning must consider the passive-loss rules that affect the deductibility of losses from his two real estate investments, either directly or through limited partnership arrangements.

Under current federal income tax law there are three different categories of income for tax purposes: earned income, investment income, and passive income.

Earned Income

Earned income includes wages, salaries, and profits from unincorporated businesses in which the owner actively participates. Dave's income from his medical practice is considered earned income.

Investment Income

Net investment income is the excess of investment income over investment expenses. Taxpayers will need net investment income in order to deduct investment interest payments.

Until December 31, 1992, investment income was income from interest, dividends, rents, royalties, and capital gains arising from the disposition of investment assets. For tax years after 1992, as a general guideline, net capital gain from the disposition of investment property no longer qualifies as investment income that can be used to determine the deductibility of investment interest (expense). Individuals can elect to have all or a portion of capital gains treated as investment income by paying tax on the elected amount at their ordinary income tax rate rather than the more favorable maximum capital gains rate applicable to these gains.

Investment expenses include all deductible expenses other than interest that are directly connected with the production of investment income.

Individual investors can deduct investment interest expense only up to the amount of their net investment income. Any year's nondeductible investment interest can be carried forward and deducted against net investment income in future years.

Passive Income

Concept of Passive Income. A *passive activity* includes any activity that involves the conduct of any trade or business in which the taxpayer does not materially participate. Rental activity of either real or tangible personal property is defined as a passive activity for tax purposes. Individuals who engage in passive activities are not considered material participants in the business activity. However, working interests in any oil or gas property that the taxpayer holds directly or through an entity that does not limit the taxpayer's liability with respect to that interest will not be subject to the passive-loss rules.

A taxpayer will be treated as materially participating in an activity only if the taxpayer is involved in the operations of the activity on a regular, continuous, and substantial basis. Limited partnership interests are treated as an activity in which the taxpayer does not materially participate.

Generally losses generated by passive activities may not be used to offset other income such as salary, interest, dividends, and active business income. Credits from passive activities are generally limited to the tax attributable to income from passive activities. Passive-activity losses may be deducted against income from other passive activities.

The IRS has released regulations on passive-activity losses and credits, which are quite detailed and introduce many rules concerning the limitations on deductibility of losses from passive activities. Included in these regulations are definitions of what constitutes an *activity* under the passive-activity rules and what constitutes material participation in a trade or business.

Generally a rental will be considered a "rental activity" for the purpose of the passive-loss rules if the average rental period is more than 30 days. If the average rental period is 30 days or less and significant personal services are provided to the customers or if the average rental period is 7 days or less, the activity is not treated as a rental activity for passive-loss-rule purposes.

The definition of *material participation* under the Treasury regulations provides several alternative tests, including the nature of the activity and the time spent by the taxpayer in participating in the activity. A detailed explanation of these tests is beyond the scope of this text.

Taxpayers who engage in passive activities in closely held C corporations other than personal-service corporations are subject to a somewhat less restrictive rule. Passive-activity losses of such corporations are allowable as a deduction against "net active income," which includes business income but not portfolio income. Consequently taxpayers who both manage rental real estate and own passive interests in rental real estate may wish to consider the closely held C corporation as a choice of business entity. In addition, taxpayers who own tax-shelter investments and cannot deduct the losses from these investments because of the passive-activity loss limitations may consider selling their investments through a brokerage firm to C corporations that are subject to the more liberal rules.

If a taxpayer does not have enough income from passive activities to absorb all the losses from other passive activities, the losses are suspended. These suspended losses are not lost permanently. Rather, they are deferred and may be applied against income from passive activities in later years. If previously suspended losses from a particular passive activity are not used to offset future passive income, the losses are allowable in the taxable year in which the taxpayer disposes of his or her entire interest in that passive activity in a fully taxable transaction. If all gain or loss realized on the disposition is recognized in one taxable year, the current and suspended losses from that passive activity are generally allowable as a deduction against the taxpayer's income in the following order:

- income or gain from that passive activity for the taxable year (including any gain recognized on the disposition)
- net income or gain for the taxable year from all passive activities
- any other income or gain of the taxpayer from whatever source derived

Consequently taxpayers may still use losses from passive tax-shelter activities to offset income or gains from other sources but only if the taxpayer disposes of his or her entire interest in the tax-shelter activity creating the losses. There is no limitation imposed on the amount of suspended losses that will trigger a deduction in the taxable year of the disposition.

Special Real Estate Rules. To mitigate the effects of the passive-loss rules on certain individual investors who actively participate in managing real estate property, the current tax law contains one special provision. This special provision permits up to $25,000 of losses from one real estate activity to be used to offset up to $25,000 of gains from other real estate activities in which the individual *actively participates* (a concept distinct from the concept of *materially participates*). If there are no other such gains to offset a $25,000 loss, the full $25,000 is deductible against other income, provided the individual actively participated in the real estate activity and had no more than $100,000 of adjusted gross income from other sources. An individual is *not* considered to be an active participant if he or she has less than a 10 percent ownership interest in the real estate. Adjusted gross income is determined for this purpose without regard to IRA contributions and taxable Social Security benefits.

If the adjusted gross income is more than $100,000 but not more than $150,000, then for each dollar that adjusted gross income exceeds $100,000, fifty cents of the special real estate loss deduction is disallowed. For example, if adjusted gross income is $110,000, then $5,000 ($10,000 x .50) of the maximum $25,000 special real estate loss deduction is nondeductible. This $5,000 becomes a suspended loss that must be used under the general rules covering suspended losses described in the preceding section.

If the individual's adjusted gross income exceeds $150,000, then none of any real estate loss is deductible under the special provision. The deductibility of the loss is governed by the general passive-loss rules.

Revenue Reconciliation Act of 1993 Changes. Although the 1993 tax act changes do nothing with regard to the material participation requirement, a taxpayer will be able to successfully deduct losses stemming from a rental activity as long as more than 50 percent of his or her personal services have been undertaken in a trade or business involving real property. The taxpayer must, of course, materially participate. A C corporation may take advantage of this rule as long as more than one-half of the corporation's gross receipts are derived from real property business activities.

Because the Andersons' income level is so high, any losses generated by the four passive investments will become suspended passive losses and will not be available to offset any income tax liability.

Recommendations

The Commercial Lot. This lot, acquired as an investment, is vacant and is not held for the anticipation of earning rental income. Dave's sole objective in acquiring and holding the property is its appreciation in value, subsequent sale, and resulting capital gain. This property should qualify as investment property, rather than as a passive activity, since it is not rental property and Dave materially participates in the investment. Therefore the Andersons' annual interest payments should be treated as investment interest expenses deductible against their investment income.

Since the lot is investment property, the carrying costs (interest and property tax) qualify as investment expenses, so the after-tax carrying costs are reduced for the Andersons. Since their investment income is about $9,527 and their investment interest expense is $3,575 per year, the full amount of the investment interest expense is deductible.

Whether Dave should accept the offer to sell the lot depends in part on the potential taxation of the capital gain resulting from the sale as well as the tax treatment of his carrying costs. Regarding the potential capital gain, the full amount of all net capital gains is now included as income for tax purposes. Therefore the full amount of the gain will be subjected to the federal capital gains tax rate of 20 percent. Dave does not currently need the funds from selling the lot and might wish to consider retaining it to benefit from its tax-deferred appreciation.

Real Estate Investments. The rental property is subject to the special $25,000 loss allowance for real estate in which the taxpayer "actively participates." However, this property will produce a net positive income. In addition, Dave's income exceeds $150,000, thereby disqualifying him from taking the special allowance.

Security Portfolio. Dave has a sizable portfolio of stocks and bonds, some of which have been performing quite well during his holding period. An examination of the portfolio shows that Dave has largely, with but one exception, followed a buy-and-hold policy. A careful review of the portfolio is needed and should be made now.

First, an examination of his investment objectives indicates that his preferences do not include the ownership of bond funds. Since the portfolio contains this type of investment, it could be a candidate for sale with the proceeds placed into securities better matched to his objectives. Therefore, the first recommendation is to dispose of the 5–7 Year Bond Fund. Subsequent portfolio recommendations will be able to offset this long-term capital gain of $200 with long-term capital losses.

Second, Economic Fund's per share NAV has fallen sharply since the shares were acquired. Since no estimate could be made of its future performance, this investment should likewise be sold. Part of this loss of $1,500 can be used to offset the gain from the sale of 5–7 Year Bond fund.

Third, Fund Managers Growth Fund seems to not live up to its title. For a holding period of 3 years, a growth rate of 2.5 percent is relatively meager for a fund having such an objective. Also, the fund did not, at least in this year, realize large capital gains that it distributed to shareholders. The total cash flow was $1.22 per share for shares that have a NAV of $42. This nearly 3 percent return added to the NAV rise of 2.5 percent should warrant its sale. The sale results in a realized long-term capital gain of $2,700.

Fourth, the Chapter 11 bankruptcy filing of High Fly Airlines requires careful examination. It must be determined whether the existing bondholders will realize anything as a result of the financial reorganization that might prevent High Fly Airlines from emerging as an ongoing venture. If it appears that existing bondholders will realize little, this is an opportune time either to find a buyer or, if conditions are right, to write the investment off as a total long-term capital loss that would more than offset the accumulated capital gains from the first three portfolio recommendations. For any excess long-term capital loss, $3,000 could be used to reduce the Andersons' other income for this year. Unused net capital losses are carried forward and used to offset either future capital gains or offset $3,000 of other income each year until the entire amount of the loss is extinguished. For initial planning purposes, it is assumed that High Fly Airlines will not emerge from bankruptcy and that this investment is now worthless.

Fifth, the purchases of municipal bonds mesh exceptionally well with the Andersons' financial objectives and level of income. The tax-exempt income they generate, along with additional investments in municipals, will further strengthen the benefits arising from their portfolio.

The remainder of their portfolio tends to track well with their objectives. The portfolio does not spin off that much taxable income, so measures requiring the disposal of virtually all holdings at this time are not warranted. For both the Atlantic Rim and the Southern Fund Dave should consider automatically reinvesting the dividends into additional fund shares. The tax burden of their income, absent any cash inflow from them, can easily be absorbed by their cash flow. An examination should be made as to whether the corporations in which Dave has equity positions have dividend reinvestment plans. If so, Dave might consider also participating in these plans.

Based on making the sales as noted below, Dave now must place the sales proceeds into investments suited to his objectives. One possibility is to purchase additional municipal bonds that are also exempt from Georgia income taxation. Alternatively, he could acquire shares of growth common stocks or growth common stock mutual funds. A third alternative is to distribute these proceeds over the investment recommendations that will be made later in this analysis.

Portfolio Repositioning

		Selling Price	Gain Cost	(Loss)
Sale:	5-7 Bond Fund	$ 6,200	$ 6,000	$ 200
	Economic Fund	1,500	3,000	(1,500)
	Fund Managers			
	Growth Fund	46,200	43,500	2,700
	High Fly Airlines	–0–	10,000	(10,000)
	Total gain (loss)			($ 8,600)
	Loss used			$ 3,000
	Carryover loss			$ 5,600

In summary, the Andersons should not reposition any other assets at the present time. They should, however, continue to further diversify their investment assets.

Increasing Net Worth

Now that plans have been established to satisfy the Andersons' other financial objectives of funding their children's education and having an emergency reserve, they wish to invest their disposable income in such a way as to increase their net worth and maintain and improve their lifestyle. To a large extent this objective overlaps with that of reducing their tax burden. The primary concern is seeking growth while reducing the tax burden.

Collectibles (Coins, Porcelains)

One method of generating an inflation hedge while achieving growth is to invest part of one's disposable income in collectibles. Diana has already had experience in collectibles; she has a coin collection she inherited. She also has a strong interest in porcelain. Given the Andersons' age and the years until retirement, it seems appropriate to invest some portion of their disposable income in enhancing the coin collection and in porcelains. The advantages would be the growth potential of these assets, the inflationary hedge the assets might provide, the pride of ownership, and the lack of current income for tax purposes.

The disadvantages would include the illiquidity of the investment: there is an expense in terms of time and money in converting these assets to cash. A second disadvantage is the negative cash flow during the holding period: the investment has to be insured and appraised and may be warehoused. Finally, there is an opportunity cost involved.

The opportunity cost is the interest forgone on the funds invested in the porcelain or the coin collection. The Andersons are now 24 years from retirement. A commitment of $50,000 to the coin collection and the porcelains, for example, that would normally earn 8 percent in a conservative bond fund incurs an opportunity cost of $4,000 a year. This amount compounded at 8 percent per year for 24 years grows to a future value of $267,000, a significant amount. This is the result of interest forgone on funds invested in the collectibles. It may be offset somewhat by appreciation realized if the collectibles are ultimately sold.

From an income tax perspective, gains on the sale of collectibles, such as coins and porcelain, are taxed at an 28 percent capital gains rate. Collectibles are not eligible for the lower 20 percent capital gains rate.

Investing in collectibles requires a high degree of expertise on the part of the investor to avoid unknowingly purchasing counterfeits or being swayed by an improper appraisal. Another possible disadvantage is the *loss* of value that may occur from reduced demand for the collectible. Collectibles go in and out of vogue quickly. The investor must also exercise care to avoid buying at retail and later selling at wholesale, as has occurred with investments in diamonds.

If the Andersons invest in collectibles, they can potentially benefit from the inflationary hedge and capital appreciation that they desire. Despite being somewhat risky as an investment, collectibles are consistent with their risk profile. In addition, they have strong appeal to Diana. Thus the Andersons should place some of their annual investment funds into collectibles.

Growth-Oriented No-Load Mutual Fund

As stated, the Andersons are concerned with capital appreciation and obtaining an inflation hedge, both of which will be accomplished by investing in a growth-oriented mutual fund. The Andersons also seek to reduce their tax burden. That will also be achieved to some extent through a growth mutual fund in that the fund seeks capital appreciation in lieu of income. Growth in value is not taxed until the fund sells securities at a profit.

Selected Issues of Common Stock

The discussion of selected issues of common stock presented for the funding of the education objective is applicable here. However, the need for a precise dollar amount available at a specified date, such as exists with education funding needs, is not critical when considering potential investment assets to meet this objective of increasing net worth.

Since the Andersons are approximately 24 years away from retirement, if they continue to purchase selected issues of common stock for their portfolio, the stock will require some monitoring and repositioning as events and profit situations change. It appears that the Andersons do not have the time or the ability to manage a portfolio of common stocks. They could be much better off investing in a common stock mutual fund; the manager of the fund monitors, reevaluates, and repositions the fund to seek maximum growth as recommended in the previous section.

However, the "efficient markets hypothesis" suggests that a buy-and-hold strategy, applied to common stocks, will perform at least as well as a strategy of active trading. A buy-and-hold strategy of carefully selected growth-oriented blue-chip common stocks should increase a portfolio's value over time and could well provide the Andersons with their growth and inflation-protection objectives. Occasional repositioning, but not active management, might be needed. For both the selection and the periodic revision the Andersons could rely on an investment adviser.

One advantage of common stock investments is that the value of a carefully chosen portfolio has the potential of increasing faster than inflation over a long period of time. If emphasis is placed on growth securities, current income from dividends will be little, since these firms reinvest their earnings within the business rather than pay them out in the form of dividends. This would be a plus for the Andersons since they do not need additional current income at this time. The growth will, of course, be taxed at a later time, but they will have the opportunity to determine when the tax liability will occur by deciding when to sell. If the appreciated assets remain in either Dave's or Diane's portfolio at death, the stock obtains a step-up in basis that avoids any income taxation on the stock's increase in value. A distinct advantage of a buy-and-hold strategy is that transaction costs are minimal and do not erode profits as they do in an actively traded portfolio.

The Andersons should recognize the disadvantages of common stock investments. First is the presence of market risk, which could sharply reduce the value of a portfolio. If the common stock portfolio is not diversified, then a second factor, the business risk, can also produce sizable losses should one or two firms in which they own common stock fall on hard times.

Their risk attitudes appear to favor the undertaking of some risk to achieve their objectives. A portion of their annual investable funds, therefore, should be placed in growth-oriented common stocks. Each year's investment can purchase shares in two or three different companies to further the diversification of the existing portfolio. However, with the real estate currently owned and some purchasing of collectibles and growth common stock mutual funds, their total portfolio will acquire additional diversification.

Preferred Stock

Preferred stock is a unique financial instrument in that it has the legal characteristics of a stock and the financial characteristics of a bond.

As a financial instrument the preferred stock pays dividends expressed as a fixed percentage of par value, offers very little opportunity for capital growth, and does not have a maturity date. Because corporate shareholders can exclude at least 70 percent of the dividends earned on stock, preferred stocks generally have a dividend yield slightly less than that obtainable from bonds of equal risk.

Because preferred stocks are primarily an income-generating device with little possibility of capital gain, preferred stock investments are used to preserve the wealth of the investor, not to accumulate wealth. Therefore preferred stocks are not recommended for inclusion in the growth portfolio of the Andersons.

Corporate Bonds

Like preferred stock, corporate bonds are generally acquired to generate current income and to preserve wealth.

Briefly, the advantages of corporate bonds are safety if the bonds are investment quality, the certainty of receiving a known amount of income at specific dates, and the receipt of par value upon maturity of the bond. The disadvantages are the lack of an inflationary hedge, which is of special concern in inflationary times, and the lack of real growth opportunity. Also all income from the bonds is taxable.

Given their income tax bracket and the recommended use of corporate bonds as the investment medium for funding their children's education requirements, additional corporate bonds are not recommended for the Andersons.

U.S. Treasury Inflation-Indexed Bonds

In early 1997 the Treasury floated the first series of 10-year bonds that have inflation protection for the bondholder. This protection covers both the semiannual interest that bondholders will receive as well as the amount returned upon maturity. This issue yielded a base interest rate of approximately 3.45 percent. At the time of each semiannual interest payment, the base interest plus an inflation increase (less a deflation decrease), calculated by determining the change in the consumer price index (CPI) from the bond's date of issue to the date of the interest payment, is made (with an adjustment for the semiannual payment). Thus the interest payments will increase proportionately to increases in the CPI. This interest is subject to the federal income tax each year.

The process for determining the increase in the face (par) amount of the bond also employs the CPI. For each calendar year the relative increase in the index is determined and is applied to the value of the bond on January 1 of the year. For example, if the index were 100 on January 1 and 105 on December 31, a $1,000 face value bond would have an increase in its face value of 5 percent to $1,050. If the CPI went from 105 to 108 in the second year, the adjustment would be $1,050(108/105), for a new face value of $1,080. This annual increase in the face amount of the bond is considered income for tax purposes for that year. Therefore in the first year the bondholder has $50 of phantom income ($30 in the second year) that is part of his or her taxable income. For some, like the Andersons, who are in the 30 percent tax bracket starting in 2002, this is not a recommended investment to hold unless held in a tax-deferred manner. Even then, the return will match inflation, but after paying income taxes during the distribution period, the investor will not keep up with inflation. (*Note:* Since there is a guarantee that the bond will have a minimum value of $1,000 upon maturity regardless of the extent of any future deflation, should significant deflation occur, the bondholder could gain on an after-tax basis.)

Municipal Bonds

General obligation municipal bonds are the safest of all municipal bonds because the obligation to repay the investor is a legal obligation of the taxing authority. Thus the investor is guaranteed repayment out of the taxing power of the community or the state that issues the bonds. The public-purpose feature is important because if the bonds are so classified, the interest payments the Andersons receive will be exempt from both regular income taxation and the alternative minimum tax. Revenue bonds are riskier because the bondholders will be repaid from the revenue generated from whatever purpose the proceeds of the bond were used to finance. For instance, if a community issues revenue bonds to build mass transit facilities, the bondholders are to be repaid out of the revenues generated by the system. A risk element is that if the revenues are not forthcoming, the bondholders might not be repaid. Moreover, the interest earned on new revenue bonds, although exempt from ordinary income taxation, will be taxable to taxpayers who are subject to the alternative minimum tax.

Dave has acquired some municipal bonds during the past year due to the attractiveness of their tax-exempt interest income. He could consider further purchases of such bonds as a means of sheltering the income from taxation. These bonds have risks and limitations similar to those of corporate bonds.

Municipal Bond Funds

Selecting a no-load municipal bond fund is also a practical and desirable method for the Andersons to reduce their tax burden. The fund should invest in general obligation municipal bonds that are also "public-purpose" bonds to avoid potential AMT issues.

To minimize risk, the Andersons should invest in a fund in which 80 percent of the portfolio consists of general obligation bonds. The bond portfolio should contain only bonds rated AA or better. The AA rating, although not a guarantee of investment performance, is a strong indicator that default will not occur and that the investor will be repaid on time.

The advantages of a municipal bond fund include professional management, diversification, minimal record keeping, and a high degree of liquidity. Other benefits of the fund may include automatic reinvestment of income distributions, withdrawal plans, exchange privileges, and check-writing privileges.

Perhaps the most significant and best-known advantage of a municipal bond fund is that the interest earned on the fund is free of federal income tax if the fund invests in public-purpose bonds. To the extent that the fund invests in bonds issued by the state in which the Andersons live, interest on those bonds should also be free of state income tax.

The disadvantages of a municipal bond fund are the possibility of erosion of value in inflationary times, the possibility of a risk of default, and the possibility that the fund might produce an after-tax return less than that from a taxable bond fund of similar investment-quality rating.

The equivalent taxable yield of a tax-exempt investment can be computed under the following formula, assuming that the bond interest is exempt from the Georgia income tax:

$$\text{Taxable yield} = \frac{\text{tax-free yield}}{1 - t}$$

where t = marginal tax bracket of investor

Currently municipal bond funds investing in long-term obligations are paying approximately 5 percent. The taxable equivalent yield for investors such as the Andersons who will be in the 30 percent marginal tax bracket is as follows:

$$\text{Taxable yield} = \frac{5}{1 - .30}$$

$$= 7.14$$

As illustrated, a 5 percent tax-free yield is equivalent to a taxable 7.14 percent yield to an investor who is in the 30 percent tax bracket. In comparing taxable to nontaxable yields, it should be apparent that the higher the investor's tax bracket, the more desirable are tax-free municipals. As noted, the Andersons will be in the 30 percent marginal tax bracket next year and are expected to be in that bracket over the next few years.

In some instances an investor may also be able to avoid state and local income taxes when purchasing municipal bonds. In this case, the taxable yield calculation may be modified to take this into account. The same equation is used, but *t*, the investor's marginal tax rate, is substituted with the investor's combined tax rate. To calculate the investor's combined tax rate, it is first necessary to determine the effective state tax rate. The effective state tax rate takes into account the fact that state income taxes are deductible for federal income tax purposes. Failure to factor the deductibility of state income taxes into the equation would overstate the taxable yield.

Effective state tax rate = marginal state tax rate x (1– federal marginal tax rate)

The combined tax rate for use in the above equation is simply the sum of the effective state tax rate and the federal marginal tax rate.

Combined tax rate = effective state tax rate + federal marginal tax rate

The purpose of modifying the equation to use the combined tax rate is to take into account the additional yield that would have been required to pay state income taxes if the municipal bond interest was not exempt from this tax.

Disadvantages of the fund also include the possibility of a sales charge, a redemption fee, a high management fee, and interest-rate risk.

The interest-rate risk has previously been described in the discussion of corporate bonds for the children's education funding. Briefly, interest-rate risk occurs when interest rates rise, causing the present value of bonds to decline. If the bondholders sell the bonds, they can do so only at a lower price. On the other hand, if the bondholders hold the bonds until maturity, interest risk will not have created a capital loss. However, reinvestment of interest income will be at a lower rate than anticipated and cause the fully compounded return actually earned on the investment to be less than what was anticipated.

A municipal bond fund is appropriate for the Andersons' portfolio because the fund achieves one of their major objectives: tax reduction. If they invest in a fund that owns AA- or higher-rated general obligation bonds, there is a minimal level of default risk. Given the Andersons' high tax bracket, these funds should provide a satisfactory return on their investment. The Andersons could also benefit from the possibility of capital appreciation, depending on future movements in interest rates.

Leveraged, Closed-End Bond Funds

Instead of raising the full amount of capital from the sale of equity shares in the fund, some bond funds also obtain a portion of their investable funds by issuing either short-term or intermediate-term fixed-cost instruments. One form of these fixed-cost instruments is 7- to 30-day adjustable preferred stock. When the preferred matures, new preferred is issued as a replacement. Other funds raise their fixed return by arranging 30- to 90-day adjustable bank lines of credit or issue either money market notes or fixed 5-year notes. This additional capital, along with the original capital, is used to acquire a portfolio of either taxable or tax-exempt bonds, depending on the fund's stated purpose. The leverage from the borrowed funds (typically between 25 and 45 percent of total capital, although the SEC permits as much as 50 percent), if favorable, will enhance the yield to the fund's shares if a sufficient difference exists between the cost of the borrowed funds (short-term interest rate) and what can be earned on the portfolio (intermediate- and long-term interest rates). In practice these funds set a target yield they seek to achieve. Most of the taxable funds invest in high-yield corporate bonds. The tax-exempts typically invest in investment grade municipal bonds. Other than the use of leverage, these funds possess the same characteristics, advantages, and limitations of other bond funds.

Currently the taxable leveraged bond funds yield between 9 and 10 percent as compared with the tax-exempt yields of about 6 percent. The percent of this spread is close to the Andersons' expected tax bracket. The higher-yielding taxable funds could be an attractive investment opportunity to the Andersons, who should keep in mind that the interaction of the leverage and the nature of the portfolios makes them riskier than similarly invested nonleveraged funds.

Junk Bonds

Traditionally it was the default risk of either newly formed corporations or of troubled corporations or municipalities that caused the market to label certain debt instruments as junk bonds. Since these bonds receive ratings lower than investment grade, they provide relatively high rates of return to investors willing to accept the associated high risk.

In recent years a new crop of junk bonds has come to the market as a result of the numerous leveraged buyouts instigated either by existing management of publicly traded corporations or by outside interests (raiders). In either case a controlled corporation is formed for the purpose of acquiring the stock of a target corporation. Those individuals who directly own the equity interest in this controlled corporation put up a relatively small amount of the funds needed for the acquisition. The remainder of the funds for the stock tender offer is obtained through debt financing (bonds). Since these bonds represent perhaps as much as 90 percent of the capital raised by the acquiring firm, the firm is said to be highly leveraged. Despite actual profitability, if the acquired firm is unable to spin off sufficient cash flow for the servicing of the debt, default can occur. However, in this scenario the default is due to the high degree of financial leverage (debt). Regardless of whether the bond rating services rate these bonds as low or noninvestment grade, investors perceive them as high risk and thus require a high yield. An alternate scenario would involve the acquired corporation's issuing new debt and then repurchasing most of its stock from the controlled acquisition corporation. In this case the operating (acquired) corporation must have sufficient cash flow to service its own debt. When this pattern occurs, previously issued debt of the acquired corporation will be downgraded in its investment classification.

Junk bonds typically yield between 3 and 5 percent more than investment-grade bonds. Recent events have resulted in some of these bonds being sold at discounts of 35 percent or more from their face amount. This makes those bonds even more attractive provided the issuing corporations do not default. Dave could use a portion of his investable cash flow by diversifying an investment in these junk bonds through the mechanism of a mutual fund.

Real Estate

Dave currently rents the office space used for his medical practice and he indicated that the building might be sold. Since Dave has stated that direct ownership of rental real estate is his preferred investment vehicle, he might consider the purchase of the building in which his office is located.

The data in table 5-11 have been developed on the premise that the office building would be purchased at the estimated market price Dave obtained from the realtor and that rental income, operating expenses, and property taxes would all rise at an annual rate of 5 percent. Should Dave purchase the building, there would be a $16,284 operating loss in the first year. This loss would decrease by about $3,000 per year, and by the sixth year of ownership operating income should become positive. If Dave owned and managed the building personally, the losses would be passive losses for tax purposes, except for the portion attributable to Dave's own business use. These losses could be deducted against any passive income since the rental real estate currently owned will have positive income. The losses for this building would be suspended.

If Dave does purchase the building, the net cash flow picture appears attractive. Except for the first year, in which a cash flow deficit of $2,688 occurs, and the second year, in which $188 is incurred, the building's cash flow—after all operating expenses, property taxes, interest expense, and principal payments—becomes positive in the third year.

Since at this time the economics of the building appear attractive, Dave could inform either the building's owner(s) or the realtor that he might be interested in purchasing it if it is placed on the market.

Ownership of the building has other beneficial considerations for the Andersons. As stated earlier, it not only meets Dave's (and to a lesser degree, Diana's) investment vehicle preference, but it can also provide a mechanism that meets two of their general personal financial goals—capital appreciation and inflation protection. Moreover, the opportunity to employ one or more of the children in a bona fide job maintaining the building as a means of shifting some income not subject to the kiddie tax is an additional plus from the Andersons' perspective.

TABLE 5-11
Financial Analysis of Office Building

Cost-revenue analysis for office building	Year 1		Year 2		Year 3	
Projected rental income		$60,000		$63,000		$66,150
Less expenses						
Operating expenses	$4,000		4,200		4,410	
Property taxes	6,000		6,300		6,615	
Depreciation	16,000		16,000		16,000	
		26,000		26,500		27,025
Operating income		34,000		36,500		39,125
Interest expense		50,284		50,011		49,727
Income before taxes		(16,284)		(13,511)		(10,602)
Principal reduction (first year)		2,404		2,677		2,961
Total suspended losses		16,284		29,795		40,397
Cash-flow analysis for office building						
Cash revenue		60,000		63,000		66,150
Less cash outgo (operating expenses, property taxes, interest, and principal)		62,688		63,188		63,713
Net cash flow		($2,688)		($ 188)		$2,437

Other data		
Acquisition cost		
Land cost	96,000	
Building cost	504,000	
Depreciation/year	16,000	
Depreciation period	31.5	years
Interest rate	10.5	percent
Mortgage amount	480,000	
Mortgage duration	30	years
Monthly mortgage payment	4,390	

Recommendations

In 2003 the Andersons should have approximately $32,972 of additional investable cash flow for the purpose of increasing their personal net worth. As shown in the cash-flow summary in case II projections, this surplus amount increases during each of the next few years.

The Andersons' portfolio diversification was noted in the section on repositioning of assets. Future surplus cash flows provide the opportunity for the Andersons to further diversify their investments and still meet their objectives.

Dave and Diana do have some differences as to the preferred investment vehicles each would select. Dave's preferences, in addition to real estate, are for growth mutual funds, growth common stock, and municipal bonds. His investment preferences are consistent with his personal financial concerns of long-term growth, inflation protection, and tax reduction/deferral.

Diana's investment preferences, on the other hand, are for collectibles, money market funds, income-oriented mutual funds, corporate bonds, and direct ownership of real estate. However, Diana's higher-ranked personal financial concerns are for safety of principal, inflation protection, and future income. On the surface there appears to be some inconsistency between her general financial concerns and her preferences for investment vehicles. However, a closer analysis shows that two of her investment preferences, collectibles and real estate, have the potential for inflation protection and future income. Diana's other preferences, money market mutual funds, corporate bonds, and income mutual funds, are compatible with her concern for safety of principal.

Prior recommendations for the Andersons included a money market fund for their emergency reserve, corporate bonds for the education trusts, and retention of the existing real estate investments. The first two of these recommendations are consistent with Diana's preferences for safety of principal and investment vehicles. The retention of and the possible purchase of the real estate satisfy both Dave's investment preferences and his financial concerns, as well as being within Diana's range of acceptability.

To meet the objective of wealth accumulation, the Andersons can select investments carrying greater inherent risk with both increased growth and return potentials. The annual surplus cash during the planning horizon could be allocated in the following manner:

Investment Vehicle	Percent of Investable Funds	Expected Return
Growth common stock mutual funds	25	10–12%; 2% current taxable
Growth common stocks	30	10–12%; 2% current taxable
Leveraged, closed-end bond fund or high-yield bond fund	10	9–11%; taxable
Municipal bond funds	25	5.5–6%; nontaxable
Collectibles (coins and porcelain)*	10	16–19%; no current taxation
Office building	—	

*Annual allocation divided equally between coins and porcelain.

The collectibles are definitely Diana's preference. They have potential for long-term growth and do not generate taxable income until sold.

The growth common stock mutual fund and the growth common stocks are recommended to provide long-term growth and inflation protection. Since these investments provide little current income, most of their expected total return is tax deferred, fulfilling another important objective of the Andersons. The growth mutual fund offers diversification within the fund itself.

The funds invested in growth common stock, if used to purchase two or three different corporate stocks each year, will, along with the existing portfolio, further diversify the Andersons' stock holdings. In the short run having only a few common stocks does produce a somewhat risky situation for the Andersons. However, it is a relatively small portion of their total investment portfolio and would be consistent with Dave's preferences and financial concerns.

The leveraged, closed-end bond fund, despite producing taxable income, does have an attractive yield. A relatively small portion of the investable cash flow could be placed in one or two of these funds.

The municipal bond funds should be selected to produce tax-free investment income consistent with the tax-deferral/reduction objective. Also these municipal bond funds will provide safety since each holds a diversified portfolio.

The office building can provide an additional investment opportunity for some of their investable cash flow. At this time the building is not for sale, but, as stated above, Dave should monitor its availability. Should it actually be put on the market or be rumored to be coming to the market, Dave could rearrange his yearly cash investments to come up with the needed down payment. In a year or two, his cash flow will be sizable. Perhaps only a one- or 2-year hiatus in the above investment recommendations will be all that is needed to have sufficient funds for the down payment.

Overall the portfolio components selected mesh with the Andersons' preferences, concerns, and objectives. One final portfolio consideration is how the assets should be titled. The collectibles could be placed in Diana's name if this is acceptable to Dave. Consideration should also be given to titling additional investment assets in her name. If collectibles are purchased and Diana accumulates significant assets in her name, a review of her estate plan may be needed, as discussed in the estate planning section.

6

Planning for the Small Family-Owned Business and Its Owners

Chapter Outline

An important and very interesting aspect of financial planning is planning for the shareholder-employees of small family-owned businesses. These businesses usually represent both the client's largest asset and the family's primary source of income. The family in this instance may include the client, spouse, and adult children who are employed by the business, and even nonactive children or other more peripheral family members who benefit from the business either directly or indirectly. It is vital in this type of case to recognize that the business and the client typically have distinct legal and tax identities. While the needs of the business and the objectives of the client as an individual may sometimes appear to be adverse, the survival of the business and the improvement of the client's personal situation are very closely related. It is essential in these cases to seek solutions to problems and methods to achieve the client's personal objectives that will be acceptable compromises between the business and the individual and that will allow the survival and continuing vitality of the business. Naturally owners of small family businesses would not want their lifetime work placed in jeopardy or acquired by someone outside the family group.

CASE NARRATIVE

Personal Information

Lawrence (Larry) and Anne Miller are 62 and 59 respectively and live in a small town of approximately 30,000 people. They have been married 40 years and have three children. Steve, their oldest son, is 38, is married to Jennifer, and has two children, Alex, 10, and Tony, 7. Doug is 32, is divorced, and has one child, Maria, 8. Lisa is 28, is married to Tom, and has three children, Kerry, 5, Katie, 4, and Andrew, 1. The Millers have given each grandchild on his or her first birthday a gift of $1,000 under the Uniform Gifts to Minors Act. The children's parents are designated custodians of the UGMA accounts. Larry and Anne do not plan further significant gifts to their grandchildren.

The Millers started their furniture business 37 years ago with money borrowed from Anne's father. In return for the loan Anne's father owned 33 percent of the company stock until his death 12 years ago, although the indebtedness had long since been repaid. When Anne's father died, he left her 23 percent of the company stock (57.5 shares). He left Steve the remaining 10 percent of the company stock (25 shares). Because of Larry's hard work the business has grown into a profitable enterprise and has provided a good living for him and Anne and their children. Steve, the oldest son, has been involved in the business on a full-time basis since he graduated from college. He is Larry's heir apparent in the management and ownership of the business.

Larry's basis in his Millers stock is approximately $160 per share. Anne and Steve's stock, which was inherited from Anne's father, has a basis of $1,000 per share in their hands.

The younger son, Doug, also worked in Millers and in another furniture store his father owned in a town about 45 miles away. Six years ago when Larry became uneasy about dividing his time between the two stores, Doug and a business associate purchased the stock of the second store, a separate corporation. The purchase price was $230,000 for 100 percent of the stock, and it was financed with a $20,000 cash down payment and an installment note for 15 years at 10 percent interest. From the sale Larry has annual income of $27,609. This $27,609 figure is made up of the following components for tax purposes: $10,833 return of basis, $4,500 capital gain, and $12,276 of ordinary income. Doug and his business associate still own the store and seem to be doing well.

Larry and Anne's daughter, Lisa, has never been involved in the business, as she married immediately after college and her husband's career requires that they relocate frequently.

Larry says his primary concern at this point is to assure that Steve can succeed him in both the management and the ownership of the corporation. At the same time he does not wish to deprive his other children of a part of their inheritance. He does not, however, believe that leaving the business to Steve, Doug, and Lisa equally will be the most efficient way to assure the continuity of Millers, which is very important to him. In addition, the bulk of his wealth is directly or indirectly tied up in Millers and he would like to explore ways to translate this investment into a secure retirement income for himself and Anne. Larry says he is too young to retire and has no definite plans to retire at 65. However, he would like to start cutting back on his day-to-day duties in the business and give Steve some time in a more direct management position before phasing himself out of the business. He has no idea when he would like to completely give up participation in the business and sees himself as continuing to participate at some level as long as his health permits.

He does, however, wish to be free to travel more extensively and to spend more time with Anne and their grandchildren. Larry thinks he is ready to transfer effective control of the management of the corporation to Steve. Although he is still heavily involved with Millers every day, he doesn't think it necessary or fair to wait until he dies for Steve to own a controlling interest in the business.

Anne has lived in their small town all her life. In addition to 23 percent of the stock of Millers her father also left her some other assets, most of which were blue-chip securities. She continues to have a portfolio of these investments that she enjoys trading. Anne considers that she has been quite successful in managing the portfolio under the supervision and with the advice of a stockbroker with whom she has been associated for many years. Larry does not share his wife's interest in stocks and bonds; instead he has kept his excess cash in money market funds for the past 5 years.

Anne liquidated a portion of her stocks and bonds several years ago in order to buy a beach condominium in a neighboring state and financed the purchase with a 20 percent down payment and a 20-year loan at 7 3/4 percent interest. After 3 years she decided she was uncomfortable with "being in debt" and paid off the mortgage. Anne's beach condominium has potential as an income-producing property and in fact is rented for brief periods during the year, producing about $6,000 of net income annually. She prefers, however, not to treat the property as a money-making proposition because it requires her to give up too much of the flexibility she enjoys in taking the children and grandchildren to the beach for a week or a weekend whenever it is convenient for her to do so. Property taxes on the condominium were $1,000 last year and are expected to increase 6 percent annually.

The Millers are both uncomfortable with large amounts of debt and therefore have no significant liabilities. Their personal residence was purchased from Anne's grandfather 30 years ago for $25,000. It is an older home, dating back to the 1890s, and they believe it is currently worth about $400,000 in the local market. It would be expensive to replace; in fact, replacement cost would probably be in the $450,000 range. The house is completely paid for. Much of the furniture in the house was inherited from Anne's family. Larry considers that the remainder of the furniture has been gifted to her, as it has been acquired through the years. They estimate the value of the household furnishings at $100,000. Property taxes on their residence were $4,150 last year and are expected to increase at 3 percent annually. The Millers gave $3,000 to charity last year, and their nondeductible living expenses were $30,000. They expect these amounts to increase by about 6 percent annually.

Larry and Anne carry $300,000 of insurance coverage on their house under a homeowners form 3 that provides for replacement cost coverage. The personal liability coverage limit of the policy is $150,000. They also carry a personal auto policy on their automobiles with liability limits of $300,000 and physical damage coverage.

Larry has two personal life insurance policies, both of which are whole life policies. The face amount of the first policy is $83,500. It is owned by Larry with Anne as the beneficiary and has a present cash value of $19,293. The second policy has a face amount of $10,000 and a present cash value of $7,647. Larry is the owner, and his estate is the beneficiary.

Anne has only one insurance policy, the face amount of which is $10,000. There is $6,430 in accumulated dividends on deposit, making $16,430 the amount of death benefits available. The present cash value of the policy is $4,890. The insurance policy is owned by Anne and is payable to Larry as the beneficiary.

Both Larry and Anne realize that they are paying substantial income taxes, but they are not interested in any aggressive tax-planning techniques that might cause the IRS to audit them. They have never been audited and would rather pay the taxes than worry about any involvement with the IRS.

The following is a statement of net worth for Larry and Anne as of December 31 of last year.

Assets	Owner	Value
LARRY AND ANNE MILLER **Statement of Net Worth** **December 31, last year**		
Checking account	Joint	$ 3,000
Savings accounts	Anne	12,000
Money market fund	Larry	46,000
Stocks and bonds	Anne	103,000
Millers, Inc., stock	Larry	506,172
Millers, Inc., stock	Anne	173,760
Personal residence	Larry	400,000
Household furnishings	Anne	100,000
Resort home	Anne	150,000
Automobiles	Larry	16,000
Store building	Larry	530,000
Note receivable (second store)	Larry	159,000
Profit-sharing plan	Larry	65,800
Cash value (life insurance)	Larry	26,940
Cash value (life insurance)	Anne	4,890
Accumulated dividends (life insurance)	Anne	6,430
Total		$2,302,992

If Larry predeceases Anne, he would like her to be financially independent for the rest of her life. Although there is no friction between Anne and her children, she does not wish to depend on them for assistance and wishes to be able to pay for any household help or luxuries that she requires as she gets older. Larry wishes any assets remaining at Anne's death to be divided equally among his children and the share of any deceased child to be split equally among the deceased child's children.

Both Larry's parents are deceased, but Anne's mother is still living. Although she is in her late seventies, she continues to enjoy good health and a luxurious lifestyle. Anne's mother was the primary beneficiary under Anne's father's will, which left the bulk of his estate to her outright. Anne believes that she and her younger brother are the principal beneficiaries of their mother's will and that their inheritances from her could be at least $600,000 to $800,000 each.

Larry's and Anne's wills have not been updated for 16 years. Each leaves all his or her property to the other spouse, if surviving. If there is no surviving spouse, all property is left to their living children or children of a deceased child equally, per stirpes.

Business Information

Larry is proud of the business he has built and thinks he has accumulated a sufficient net worth to allow him a financially untroubled retirement. However, because so much of his accumulated wealth is tied up in Millers, he has requested advice on the implementation of some plan allowing those assets to be translated into a more liquid form so that they can provide retirement income for Anne and him. Larry also wants to be sure that his business interest is not burdensome for Anne at his death and that she can be assured of an income from his assets. At the same time he does not wish to have an estate plan or a business transition plan that will damage the continuing viability of Millers.

Larry feels that an orderly business transition of Millers to Steve during Larry's lifetime is equitable, since Steve has spent many years working for the corporation, and he should be able to have ownership or at least control of the company without waiting for Larry to die. Larry considers that the sale of the other corporation's stock to Doug has assured Doug of a secure source of income if he is willing to devote himself diligently to the business. He feels that the transition of Millers stock to Steve will achieve the same objective.

Millers is a regular (C) corporation. There are 250 shares of common stock authorized and issued. Of those shares Larry owns 167.5 shares (67 percent), Steve owns 25 shares (10 percent), and Anne owns 57.5 shares (23 percent). The corporation has never paid dividends. It uses a calendar-year accounting period and employs the specific-identification inventory accounting method. At the end of last year the net worth of the corporation was $755,480, and the book value of each of the 250 shares was $3,022, as shown on the corporate balance sheet that follows.

The corporation employs 34 people, 26 of whom are full-time. Last year salaries were $686,000, of which Larry was paid $65,000 and Steve was paid $42,500. Larry expects his and Steve's salaries to increase at about 6 percent a year. Last year the corporation had sales of approximately $2,200,000 and taxable income of $175,000.

The corporation provides a profit-sharing plan for its employees. The plan requires that if corporate pretax profits reach $200,000 a year, a 10 percent contribution will be made to the plan. If corporate profits do not reach $200,000, there is no contribution to the profit-sharing plan. Therefore the plan has been funded only sporadically.

Larry is unhappy with the performance of the plan, which he feels the employees do not view as a motivator. He comments that perhaps this situation exists because most of his employees, except for three or four rank-and-file employees, are under 40 and consequently too young to be concerned about retirement. In addition, the plan's sporadic funding does not strongly motivate employees. Larry's account balance in the profit-sharing plan is $65,800, and he is fully vested.

CORPORATE BALANCE SHEET
Millers, Inc.
12/31/01

Assets

Cash	$ 205,000
Accounts receivable	179,000
Inventory	486,000
Office equipment (net of depreciation)	20,000
Delivery vehicles (net of depreciation)	20,000
Leasehold improvements	42,000
Life insurance cash value	77,480
Total assets	$1,029,480

Liabilities and Net Worth

Current liabilities	$ 274,000
Common stock ($160 par)	40,000
Retained earnings	715,480
Total liabilities and net worth	$1,029,480

Millers provides its hourly employees with 7 days of sick leave per year and a week of vacation after a year of service. Vacation is increased to 2 weeks after 3 years of employment. Hourly employees are allowed to accumulate sick leave up to 21 days. Salaried staff are provided 2 weeks of vacation after a year of employment and 3 weeks of vacation after employment for 5 years. Sick leave for salaried employees is 10 days per year, and salaried employees may carry over unused sick leave up to a maximum of 60 days. Larry carries an excellent medical insurance plan for his employees that provides $1 million of lifetime coverage and, after a $100 deductible, provides coverage of 80 percent of the first $3,000 of covered benefits. After the $3,000 of covered benefits is reached, additional expenses are paid in full. The corporation provides employee coverage on a noncontributory basis. However, dependent coverage is available only if the employee pays the additional amount. The corporation does not provide long-term disability income benefits or life insurance benefits for employees. The corporation, however, does carry a $200,000 whole life insurance policy on Larry's life that was acquired 20 years ago. The corporation is the owner and beneficiary of this policy, which has a current cash value of $77,480.

Larry individually, and not the corporation, owns the building that houses Millers. It was built 10 years ago and has been leased to the corporation since that time. The cost to construct the building was approximately $185,000. Larry estimates its present worth at $530,000 and assumes that it will increase in value at about 4 percent per year. At present it provides net rental income of $33,000 per year.

INSTRUCTIONS

Based on this information, prepare a working outline for the Millers. When this has been completed, it can be compared with the one that follows. After comparing the working outlines, go to page 6.11 for further instructions.

WORKING OUTLINE

I. Clients' objectives

    A. Lifetime objectives
1. Assure that control of Millers goes to Steve during Larry's lifetime.
2. Enjoy a secure retirement and maintain some continuing involvement with Millers.

    B. Dispositions at death
1. Assure that Anne is well provided for and that Larry's accumulated assets are not burdensome to her at his death.
2. Divide any assets remaining at Anne's death equally among the children.
3. Achieve his other objectives without damaging Millers.

II. Business planning

    A. Tax planning
1. Present position
2. Business transition
    a. Installment sales
- General requirements
- Avoiding the limitations on the deductibility of investment interest

    b. Using an S election to facilitate the transfer of a business interest
- The tax on built-in gains
- Practical considerations in planning for an S election
- Additional principles applicable to the taxation of installment sales

    c. Redemptions
- Requirements for favorable federal income tax treatment
- Sec. 318 attribution problems
- Sec. 302(c)(2) election—the waiver approach
- Sec. 303 redemptions

    d. Recapitalizations
- General requirements
- Restrictions

    e. Private annuity
3. Shareholder-employee compensation planning
    a. Reasonable compensation for shareholder-employees

       b.   Employment contracts

       c.   Consulting contracts

    4.   Employee benefits

       a.   Qualified plans of deferred compensation

- Problems with present plans
- General requirements
- Recommendations

       b.   Nonqualified deferred compensation

- Avoiding immediate inclusion in employee's income
- Deductibility by the corporation
- Avoiding imposition of federal estate tax

B.   Insurance planning

    1.   Medical insurance plans

    2.   Disability income plans

    3.   Life insurance plans

    4.   Property and liability coverage for the business—fundamental requirements

III. Personal planning

A.   Tax planning

    1.   Present position

    2.   Assuring Larry's comfortable retirement and continuing involvement with Millers

    3.   Dispositions at death

       a.   Analysis of present plans

       b.   Possible improvements in estate plan

       c.   Concept of estate equalization

       d.   Recommendations

       e.   Life insurance placement

- General discussion
- Structuring the irrevocable life insurance trust

       f.   Deferral of estate taxes under IRC Sec. 6166

B.   Insurance planning

    1.   Personal life insurance coverage

    2.   Personal property and liability coverage

C.   Investment planning

    1.   Client profile

    2.   Investment alternatives

       a.   Certificates of deposit

       b.   Municipal bond funds

      c.   Municipal bonds
      d.   Balanced mutual funds
      e.   Convertible bonds or convertible bond funds
3. Recommendations
4. Preretirement planning
      a.   Repositioning of assets
      b.   Asset conservation
      c.   Plan distribution options
      d.   Retirement income estimation
      e.   Potentially dependent parent
      f.   Recreation/health
      g.   Personal asset acquisition
      h.   Possible new career

INSTRUCTIONS

Now prepare a financial plan for the Millers. When you have completed your financial plan, you can compare it with the suggested solution that follows.

PERSONAL FINANCIAL PLAN
FOR
LARRY AND ANNE MILLER
[Suggested Solution]

CLIENTS' OBJECTIVES

A. Lifetime objectives
1. Assure that control of Millers goes to Steve during Larry's lifetime.
2. Enjoy a secure retirement and maintain some continuing involvement with Millers.
B. Dispositions at death
1. Assure that Anne is well provided for and that Larry's accumulated assets are not burdensome to her at his death.
2. Divide any assets remaining at Anne's death equally among the children.
3. Achieve Larry's other objectives without damaging Millers.

The following pages show the 5-year income statement, balance sheet, cash flow, and summary data of the Millers' present personal situation.

BASE CASE

Assumptions

1. The checking account balance is maintained at $3,000 and is noninterest bearing.

2. The savings account earns 5 percent annually. Interest accumulates in the account.

3. Surplus cash earns 5.25 percent annually.

4. The money market funds earn 5.5 percent annually. Interest accumulates in the fund.

5. Larry's salary increases at 6 percent annually.

6. Anne's listed stocks and bonds will increase in value at 5 percent annually. Yields on these securities will average 4 percent annually.

7. Stock in Millers is based on year-end book value and will increase in value at 5 percent annually.

8. The personal residence will increase in value at 4 percent annually.

9. Property taxes on the residence last year were $4,150 and will increase at 3 percent annually.

10. The resort condominium will increase in value at 8 percent annually.

11. Property taxes on the condominium will increase at 6 percent annually.

12. Increase or decrease in the value of household furnishings is ignored.

13. The value of the commercial building will increase at 4 percent annually. Net rental income from this property increases at 6 percent annually.

14. Nondeductible living expenses and charitable contributions increase at 6 percent annually.

15. The profit-sharing plan will earn 6 percent annually.

16. The cash values of the life insurance policies will grow at 8 percent annually.

INCOME STATEMENT

LARRY & ANNE MILLER

BASE CASE	2002	2003	2004	2005	2006
Earned Income					
Salaries - Larry	68,900	73,034	77,416	82,061	86,985
	68,900	73,034	77,416	82,061	86,985
Interest/Dividends					
Notes Rec - Doug	15,508	14,296	12,958	11,479	9,845
Stocks/Bonds - Anne	4,326	4,542	4,769	5,008	5,258
Savings Acct - Anne	600	630	662	695	729
Money Market-Larry	2,530	2,669	2,816	2,971	3,134
Investable Cash	1,684	5,167	8,911	12,940	17,280
	24,648	27,304	30,116	33,093	36,246
Investments					
Rent-Commerc'l Bldg	33,000	34,980	37,079	39,304	41,662
Rent - Condo	6,000	6,000	6,000	6,000	6,000
	39,000	40,980	43,079	45,304	47,662
Net Capital Gain	4,629	5,114	5,649	6,240	6,894
	========	========	========	========	========
Adj Gross Income	137,177	146,432	156,260	166,697	177,787
Deductions					
Charitable 50%	3,000	3,180	3,371	3,573	3,787
State Tax Paid	6,759	7,272	7,818	8,397	8,996
Property Tax - Home	4,150	4,275	4,403	4,535	4,671
Property Tax -Condo	1,000	1,060	1,124	1,191	1,262
Reductn for High Inc	-127	-301	-489	-693	-609
Gross Deductions	14,782	15,486	16,226	17,003	18,108
Standard Deduction	7,600	7,800	8,000	8,526	9,292
Allowed Deductions	14,782	15,486	16,226	17,003	18,108
Pers Exemptions	5,800	5,900	6,100	6,300	5,291
	========	========	========	========	========
Taxable Income	116,595	125,047	133,934	143,394	154,388
	========	========	========	========	========
Fed Income Tax	24,995	27,247	28,824	31,286	33,216
	========	========	========	========	========
Fed Tax Bracket-Ord Inc	27.0%	30.0%	29.0%	29.0%	28.0%

BALANCE SHEET

LARRY & ANNE MILLER

BASE CASE	2002	2003	2004	2005	2006
LIQUID ASSETS					
Cash Balance	2,969	3,037	3,069	3,105	3,120
Cash Deposits					
Savings Acct - Anne	12,600	13,230	13,892	14,587	15,316
Investable Cash	65,846	136,161	212,215	293,685	381,881
Money Market-Larry	48,530	51,199	54,015	56,986	60,120
	126,976	200,590	280,122	365,258	457,317
Stocks & Bonds					
Stocks/Bonds - Anne	108,150	113,558	119,235	125,197	131,457
Miller Stock - Anne	182,448	191,570	201,149	211,206	221,767
Miller Stock -Larry	531,481	558,055	585,957	615,255	646,018
	822,079	863,183	906,342	951,659	999,242
Life Insurance					
Life Ins - Larry #1	20,836	22,503	24,304	26,248	28,348
Life Ins - Larry #2	8,259	8,919	9,633	10,404	11,236
Life Ins - Anne	5,281	5,704	6,160	6,653	7,185
	34,376	37,127	40,097	43,304	46,769
	========	========	========	========	========
Liquid Assets	986,401	1,103,937	1,229,630	1,363,326	1,506,448
	========	========	========	========	========
NONLIQUID ASSETS					
Benefit Plans					
Profit Sharing Plan	69,748	73,933	78,369	83,071	88,055
	69,748	73,933	78,369	83,071	88,055
Receivables					
Notes Rec - Doug	148,718	135,934	121,812	106,211	88,976
	148,718	135,934	121,812	106,211	88,976
Personal Property					
Home	400,000	416,000	432,640	449,946	467,943
Condo	162,000	174,960	188,957	204,073	220,399
Commercial Bldg	530,000	551,200	573,248	596,178	620,025
Automobiles	13,600	11,560	9,826	8,352	7,099
Home Furnishings	100,000	100,000	100,000	100,000	100,000
	1,205,600	1,253,720	1,304,671	1,358,549	1,415,467
	========	========	========	========	========
Nonliquid Assets	1,424,066	1,463,587	1,504,852	1,547,831	1,592,498
	========	========	========	========	========
Total Assets	2,410,467	2,567,524	2,734,482	2,911,157	3,098,946
Net Worth	2,410,467	2,567,524	2,734,482	2,911,157	3,098,946
	========	========	========	========	========

CASH FLOW STATEMENT

LARRY & ANNE MILLER

BASE CASE	2002	2003	2004	2005	2006
BEGINNING OF YEAR					
Idle Cash On Hand	3,000	2,969	3,037	3,069	3,105

SOURCES OF CASH

Cash Income

Salaries - Larry	68,900	73,034	77,416	82,061	86,985
Interest+Dividends	19,834	18,838	17,727	16,487	15,103
Rents/Royalties	39,000	40,980	43,079	45,304	47,662
	127,734	132,852	138,222	143,851	149,750

Debt Recovered

Notes Rec - Doug	11,572	12,784	14,122	15,601	17,235
	11,572	12,784	14,122	15,601	17,235
Total Cash Inflow	139,306	145,636	152,344	159,452	166,985
Tot Cash Available	142,306	148,606	155,382	162,522	170,089

USES OF CASH

Partly Deductible

Charity Contrb-50%	3,000	3,180	3,371	3,573	3,787
	3,000	3,180	3,371	3,573	3,787

Not Tax Deductible

Living Expenses	30,000	31,800	33,708	35,730	37,874
	30,000	31,800	33,708	35,730	37,874

Taxes Paid

Fed Tax Paid	24,995	27,247	28,824	31,286	33,216
State Tax Paid	6,759	7,272	7,818	8,397	8,996
FICA/Soc Sec Tax	5,271	5,587	5,922	6,175	6,246
Real Estate Tax	5,150	5,335	5,526	5,726	5,933
	42,175	45,440	48,091	51,583	54,391

Purchase/Deposits

Investable Cash	64,162	65,148	67,143	68,530	70,916
	64,162	65,148	67,143	68,530	70,916
Tot Cash Outflow	139,337	145,568	152,313	159,417	166,969

END OF YEAR

Cash Balance	2,969	3,037	3,069	3,105	3,120

SUPPORTING SCHEDULE

LARRY & ANNE MILLER

BASE CASE	JOINT 2002	JOINT 2003	JOINT 2004	JOINT 2005	JOINT 2006
Income					
Earned Income	68,900	73,034	77,416	82,061	86,985
Adj Gross Income	137,177	146,432	156,260	166,697	177,787
Allowed Deductions	14,782	15,486	16,226	17,003	18,108
Pers Exemptions	5,800	5,900	6,100	6,300	5,291
Taxable Income	116,595	125,047	133,934	143,394	154,388
Capital Gains					
Notes Rec - Doug	4,629	5,114	5,649	6,240	6,894
Net Capital Gain	4,629	5,114	5,649	6,240	6,894
LTCG Txd at Max Rt	4,629	5,114	5,649	6,240	6,894
Notes Rec - Doug	-4,629	-5,114	-5,649	-6,240	-6,894
Federal Tax Liab					
Regular Tax	25,455	27,758	29,333	31,847	33,768
Max Tax on Cap Gn	926	1,023	1,130	1,248	1,379
Gross Fed Inc Tax	24,995	27,247	28,824	31,286	33,216
Fed Income Tax	24,995	27,247	28,824	31,286	33,216
Fed Tax Analysis-Ord Inc					
Indexing Factor	77	82	87	91	96
Fed Tax Bracket-Ord Inc	27.0%	30.0%	29.0%	29.0%	28.0%
$ to Next Bracket	84	55,317	51,515	47,346	41,806
Next Bracket	30.0%	35.0%	34.0%	34.0%	33.0%
Previous Bracket	15.0%	27.0%	26.0%	26.0%	25.0%
$ to Prev Bracket	65,616	4,933	10,285	16,104	23,294
Fed Capital Gain Rate	20.0%	20.0%	20.0%	20.0%	20.0%
Fed Effective Tax Rate	21.4%	21.8%	21.5%	21.8%	21.5%
Alt Minimum Tax					
Adj Gross Income	137,177	146,432	156,260	166,697	177,787
Contributions	-3,000	-3,180	-3,371	-3,573	-3,787
Adjusted AMTI	134,177	143,252	152,889	163,124	174,000
Net Capital Gain	-4,629	-5,114	-5,649	-6,240	-6,894
AMT Exemptions	-49,000	-49,000	-49,000	-43,279	-40,724
AMT Taxable Inc	80,548	89,138	98,240	113,606	126,382
Gross Alt Min Tx	20,942	23,176	25,542	29,537	32,859
Fed Tax Less FTC	-24,995	-27,247	-28,824	-31,286	-33,216
Other Tax Liabs					
FICA/Soc Sec Tax	5,271	5,587	5,922	6,175	6,246
Adj Gross Inc	137,177	146,432	156,260	166,697	177,787
GA Adj Gross Inc	137,177	146,432	156,260	166,697	177,787
GA Standard Ded	3,000	3,000	3,000	3,000	3,000
GA Itemized Ded	14,782	15,486	16,226	17,003	18,108
GA Exemptions	5,400	5,400	5,400	5,400	5,400
GA Taxable Inc	116,995	125,547	134,634	144,294	154,279
GA Regular Tax	6,759	7,272	7,818	8,397	8,996
GA Income Tax	6,759	7,272	7,818	8,397	8,996
Georgia Tax	6,759	7,272	7,818	8,397	8,996
Tot State/Local Tx	6,759	7,272	7,818	8,397	8,996
Total Inc Tax	37,025	40,106	42,564	45,858	48,458

FINANCIAL SUMMARY

LARRY & ANNE MILLER

BASE CASE	2002	2003	2004	2005	2006
Gross Real Income					
Personal Earnings	68,900	73,034	77,416	82,061	86,985
Interest Income	20,322	22,762	25,347	28,085	30,988
Dividends Rcvd	4,326	4,542	4,769	5,008	5,258
Rent-Commerc'l Bldg	33,000	34,980	37,079	39,304	41,662
Rent - Condo	6,000	6,000	6,000	6,000	6,000
	132,548	141,318	150,611	160,457	170,893
Income & Inflation					
Gross Real Inc	132,548	141,318	150,611	160,457	170,893
Total Inc Tax	-37,025	-40,106	-42,564	-45,858	-48,458
Net Real Income	95,523	101,213	108,047	114,600	122,435
Cur Real Inc =	95,523	98,009	100,559	103,175	105,859
At Infltn Rate of	3	3	3	3	3
Cash Flow					
Idle Cash On Hand	3,000	2,969	3,037	3,069	3,105
Norml Cash Inflow	139,306	145,636	152,344	159,452	166,985
Norml Cash Outflw	75,175	80,420	85,170	90,887	96,053
Cash Invested	64,162	65,148	67,143	68,530	70,916
Cash Balance	2,969	3,037	3,069	3,105	3,120
Net Worth					
Personal Assets	1,242,946	1,293,884	1,347,837	1,404,958	1,465,356
Investment Assets	1,167,521	1,273,639	1,386,645	1,506,199	1,633,590
Personal Net Worth	1,242,946	1,293,884	1,347,837	1,404,958	1,465,356
Investment Net Worth	1,167,521	1,273,639	1,386,645	1,506,199	1,633,590
Net Worth	2,410,467	2,567,524	2,734,482	2,911,157	3,098,946

CASE II
Installment Sale of Larry's
Entire Interest in Millers to Steve

New Assumption

Steve purchases all of Larry's Millers stock on July 1, 2003, at a projected 2002 book value ($531,480) for no down payment at 9 percent interest for a term of 15 years. Larry remains active in the business for at least 4 years.

Continuing Assumptions

1. The checking account balance is maintained at $3,000 and is noninterest bearing.

2. The savings account earns 5 percent annually. Interest accumulates in the account.

3. Surplus cash earns 5.25 percent annually.

4. The money market funds earn 5.5 percent annually. Interest accumulates in the fund.

5. Larry's salary increases at 6 percent annually.

6. Anne's listed stocks and bonds will increase in value at 5 percent annually. Yields on these securities will average 4 percent annually.

7. Stock in Millers is based on year-end book value and will increase in value at 5 percent annually.

8. The personal residence will increase in value at 4 percent annually.

9. Property taxes on the residence last year were $4,150 and will increase at 3 percent annually.

10. The resort condominium will increase in value at 8 percent annually.

11. Property taxes on the condominium will increase at 6 percent annually.

12. Increase or decrease in the value of household furnishings is ignored.

13. The value of the commercial building will increase at 4 percent annually. Net rental income from this property increases at 6 percent annually.

14. Nondeductible living expenses and charitable contributions increase at 6 percent annually.

15. The profit-sharing plan will earn 6 percent annually.

16. The cash values of the life insurance policies will grow at 8 percent annually.

INCOME STATEMENT

LARRY & ANNE MILLER

CASE II	2002	2003	2004	2005	2006
Earned Income					
Salaries - Larry	68,900	73,034	77,416	82,061	86,985
	68,900	73,034	77,416	82,061	86,985
Interest/Dividends					
Notes Rec - Doug	15,508	14,296	12,958	11,479	9,845
Notes Rec - Steve	0	23,757	46,315	44,590	42,706
Stocks/Bonds - Anne	4,326	4,542	4,769	5,008	5,258
Savings Acct - Anne	600	630	662	695	729
Money Market-Larry	2,530	2,669	2,816	2,971	3,134
Investable Cash	1,684	3,071	5,938	12,412	19,220
	24,648	48,965	73,458	77,155	80,892
Investments					
Rent-Commerc'l Bldg	33,000	34,980	37,079	39,304	41,662
Rent - Condo	6,000	6,000	6,000	6,000	6,000
	39,000	40,980	43,079	45,304	47,662
Net Capital Gain	4,629	13,267	23,093	25,322	27,765
	========	========	========	========	========
Adj Gross Income	137,177	176,246	217,046	229,841	243,304
Deductions					
Charitable 50%	3,000	3,180	3,371	3,573	3,787
State Tax Paid	6,759	9,010	11,362	12,079	12,779
Property Tax - Home	4,150	4,275	4,403	4,535	4,671
Property Tax -Condo	1,000	1,060	1,124	1,191	1,262
Reductn for High Inc	-127	-1,195	-2,313	-2,587	-1,919
Gross Deductions	14,782	16,329	17,946	18,791	20,580
Standard Deduction	7,600	7,800	8,000	8,526	9,292
Allowed Deductions	14,782	16,329	17,946	18,791	20,580
Pers Exemptions	5,800	5,900	5,734	5,544	3,072
	========	========	========	========	========
Taxable Income	116,595	154,017	193,366	205,507	219,651
	========	========	========	========	========
Fed Income Tax	24,995	137,721	39,449	43,858	47,513
	========	========	========	========	========
Fed Tax Bracket-Ord Inc	27.0%	30.0%	29.0%	29.0%	33.0%

BALANCE SHEET

LARRY & ANNE MILLER

CASE II	2002	2003	2004	2005	2006
LIQUID ASSETS					
Cash Balance	2,969	3,035	2,904	2,971	2,941
Cash Deposits					
Savings Acct - Anne	12,600	13,230	13,892	14,587	15,316
Investable Cash	65,846	54,199	177,961	307,305	444,093
Money Market-Larry	48,530	51,199	54,015	56,986	60,120
	126,976	118,628	245,868	378,878	519,529
Stocks & Bonds					
Stocks/Bonds - Anne	108,150	113,558	119,235	125,197	131,457
Miller Stock - Anne	182,448	191,570	201,149	211,206	221,767
Miller Stock-Larry	531,481	0	0	0	0
	822,079	305,128	320,384	336,404	353,224
Life Insurance					
Life Ins - Larry #1	20,836	22,503	24,304	26,248	28,348
Life Ins - Larry #2	8,259	8,919	9,633	10,404	11,236
Life Ins - Anne	5,281	5,704	6,160	6,653	7,185
	34,376	37,127	40,097	43,304	46,769
	========	========	========	========	========
Liquid Assets	986,401	463,918	609,253	761,557	922,463
	========	========	========	========	========
NONLIQUID ASSETS					
Benefit Plans					
Profit Sharing Plan	69,748	73,933	78,369	83,071	88,055
	69,748	73,933	78,369	83,071	88,055
Receivables					
Notes Rec - Doug	148,718	135,934	121,812	106,211	88,976
Notes Rec - Steve	0	522,893	504,521	484,424	462,443
	148,718	658,827	626,333	590,635	551,419
Personal Property					
Home	400,000	416,000	432,640	449,946	467,943
Condo	162,000	174,960	188,957	204,073	220,399
Commercial Bldg	530,000	551,200	573,248	596,178	620,025
Automobiles	13,600	11,560	9,826	8,352	7,099
Home Furnishings	100,000	100,000	100,000	100,000	100,000
	1,205,600	1,253,720	1,304,671	1,358,549	1,415,467
	========	========	========	========	========
Nonliquid Assets	1,424,066	1,986,480	2,009,373	2,032,255	2,054,941
	========	========	========	========	========
Total Assets	2,410,467	2,450,398	2,618,626	2,793,812	2,977,404
Net Worth	2,410,467	2,450,398	2,618,626	2,793,812	2,977,404
	========	========	========	========	========

CASH FLOW STATEMENT

LARRY & ANNE MILLER

CASE II	2002	2003	2004	2005	2006
BEGINNING OF YEAR					
Idle Cash On Hand	3,000	2,969	3,035	2,904	2,971
SOURCES OF CASH					
Cash Income					
Salaries - Larry	68,900	73,034	77,416	82,061	86,985
Interest+Dividends	19,834	42,595	64,042	61,077	57,809
Rents/Royalties	39,000	40,980	43,079	45,304	47,662
	127,734	156,609	184,537	188,441	192,456
Sale/Withdrawals					
Investable Cash	0	14,718	0	0	0
	0	14,718	0	0	0
Debt Recovered					
Notes Rec - Doug	11,572	12,784	14,122	15,601	17,235
Notes Rec - Steve	0	8,587	18,372	20,097	21,981
	11,572	21,371	32,494	35,698	39,216
	========	========	========	========	========
Total Cash Inflow	139,306	192,698	217,031	224,139	231,672
	========	========	========	========	========
Tot Cash Available	142,306	195,668	220,066	227,043	234,642
	========	========	========	========	========
USES OF CASH					
Partly Deductible					
Charity Contrb-50%	3,000	3,180	3,371	3,573	3,787
	3,000	3,180	3,371	3,573	3,787
Not Tax Deductible					
Living Expenses	30,000	31,800	33,708	35,730	37,874
	30,000	31,800	33,708	35,730	37,874
Taxes Paid					
Fed Tax Paid	24,995	137,721	39,449	43,858	47,513
State Tax Paid	6,759	9,010	11,362	12,079	12,779
FICA/Soc Sec Tax	5,271	5,587	5,922	6,175	6,246
Real Estate Tax	5,150	5,335	5,526	5,726	5,933
	42,175	157,653	62,260	67,837	72,471
Purchase/Deposits					
Investable Cash	64,162	0	117,824	116,932	117,568
	64,162	0	117,824	116,932	117,568
	========	========	========	========	========
Tot Cash Outflow	139,337	192,633	217,162	224,073	231,701
	========	========	========	========	========
END OF YEAR					
Cash Balance	2,969	3,035	2,904	2,971	2,941
	========	========	========	========	========

SUPPORTING SCHEDULE

LARRY & ANNE MILLER

	JOINT	JOINT	JOINT	JOINT	JOINT
CASE II	2002	2003	2004	2005	2006
Income					
Earned Income	68,900	73,034	77,416	82,061	86,985
Adj Gross Income	137,177	176,246	217,046	229,841	243,304
Allowed Deductions	14,782	16,329	17,946	18,791	20,580
Pers Exemptions	5,800	5,900	5,734	5,544	3,072
Taxable Income	116,595	154,017	193,366	205,507	219,651
Capital Gains					
Notes Rec - Doug	4,629	5,114	5,649	6,240	6,894
Notes Rec - Steve	0	8,153	17,444	19,082	20,871
Net Capital Gain	4,629	13,267	23,093	25,322	27,765
LTCG Txd at Max Rt	4,629	13,267	23,093	25,322	27,765
Notes Rec - Doug	-4,629	-5,114	-5,649	-6,240	-6,894
Notes Rec - Steve	0	496,487	-17,444	-19,082	-20,871
Capital Gains-AMT	0	504,640	0	0	0
Federal Tax Liab					
Regular Tax	25,455	36,449	47,246	50,910	53,559
Max Tax on Cap Gn	926	2,653	4,619	5,064	5,553
Gross Fed Inc Tax	24,995	35,122	44,490	47,581	49,949
Alt Minimum Tax	0	102,599	0	0	0
Alt Min Tx Credit	0	0	5,041	3,723	2,436
AMT Credit C/Over	0	0	0	97,558	93,835
Disallowed	0	0	-97,558	-93,835	-91,398
Fed Income Tax	24,995	137,721	39,449	43,858	47,513
Fed Tax Analysis-Ord Inc					
Indexing Factor	77	82	87	91	96
Fed Tax Bracket-Ord Inc	27.0%	30.0%	29.0%	29.0%	33.0%
$ to Next Bracket	84	34,500	9,527	4,315	146,164
Next Bracket	30.0%	35.0%	34.0%	34.0%	35.0%
Previous Bracket	15.0%	27.0%	26.0%	26.0%	28.0%
$ to Prev Bracket	65,616	25,750	52,273	59,135	2,586
Fed Capital Gain Rate	20.0%	20.0%	20.0%	20.0%	20.0%
Fed Effective Tax Rate	21.4%	20.7%	20.4%	21.3%	21.6%
Alt Minimum Tax					
Adj Gross Income	137,177	176,246	217,046	229,841	243,304
Contributions	-3,000	-3,180	-3,371	-3,573	-3,787
Adjusted AMTI	134,177	173,066	213,675	226,268	239,517
Net Capital Gain	-4,629	-13,267	-23,093	-25,322	-27,765

SUPPORTING SCHEDULE (cont.)

LARRY & ANNE MILLER

	JOINT 2002	JOINT 2003	JOINT 2004	JOINT 2005	JOINT 2006
CASE II					
Capital Gains-AMT	0	504,640	0	0	0
AMT Exemptions	-49,000	0	-38,854	-32,263	-29,562
AMT Taxable Inc	80,548	664,439	151,728	168,683	182,190
Gross Alt Min Tx	20,942	137,721	39,449	43,858	47,513
Fed Tax Less FTC	-24,995	-35,122	-44,490	-47,581	-49,949
Alt Minimum Tax	0	102,599	0	0	0
Other Tax Liabs					
FICA/Soc Sec Tax	5,271	5,587	5,922	6,175	6,246
Adj Gross Inc	137,177	176,246	217,046	229,841	243,304
GA Adj Gross Inc	137,177	176,246	217,046	229,841	243,304
GA Standard Ded	3,000	3,000	3,000	3,000	3,000
GA Itemized Ded	14,782	16,329	17,946	18,791	20,580
GA Exemptions	5,400	5,400	5,400	5,400	5,400
GA Taxable Inc	116,995	154,517	193,700	205,651	217,323
GA Regular Tax	6,759	9,011	11,361	12,079	12,779
GA Income Tax	6,759	9,011	11,361	12,079	12,779
Georgia Tax	6,759	9,011	11,361	12,079	12,779
Tot State/Local Tx	6,759	9,011	11,361	12,079	12,779
Total Inc Tax	37,025	152,319	56,732	62,112	66,538

FINANCIAL SUMMARY

LARRY & ANNE MILLER

CASE II	2002	2003	2004	2005	2006
Gross Real Income					
Personal Earnings	68,900	73,034	77,416	82,061	86,985
Interest Income	20,322	44,423	68,689	72,147	75,634
Dividends Rcvd	4,326	4,542	4,769	5,008	5,258
Rent-Commerc'l Bldg	33,000	34,980	37,079	39,304	41,662
Rent - Condo	6,000	6,000	6,000	6,000	6,000
	132,548	162,979	193,953	204,519	215,539
Income & Inflation					
Gross Real Inc	132,548	162,979	193,953	204,519	215,539
Total Inc Tax	-37,025	-152,319	-56,732	-62,112	-66,538
Net Real Income	95,523	10,660	137,221	142,408	149,001
Cur Real Inc =	95,523	98,009	100,559	103,175	105,859
Purch Power Drop	0	87,348	0	0	0
At Infltn Rate of	3	3	3	3	3
Cash Flow					
Idle Cash On Hand	3,000	2,969	3,035	2,904	2,971
Norml Cash Inflow	139,306	177,980	217,031	224,139	231,672
Assets Sold	0	14,718	0	0	0
Norml Cash Outflw	75,175	192,633	99,338	107,141	114,133
Cash Invested	64,162	0	117,824	116,932	117,568
Cash Balance	2,969	3,035	2,904	2,971	2,941
Net Worth					
Personal Assets	1,242,946	1,293,882	1,347,672	1,404,824	1,465,177
Investment Assets	1,167,521	1,156,516	1,270,954	1,388,987	1,512,227
Personal Net Worth	1,242,946	1,293,882	1,347,672	1,404,824	1,465,177
Investment Net Worth	1,167,521	1,156,516	1,270,954	1,388,987	1,512,227
Net Worth	2,410,467	2,450,398	2,618,626	2,793,812	2,977,404

CASE III

Installment Sale of 101 Shares
of Millers Stock to Steve

New Assumption

Steve purchases 101 shares of Larry's Millers stock on July 1, 2003, at a projected book value ($320,483) for no down payment at 9 percent interest for a term of 15 years. Larry remains active in the business for at least 4 years.

Continuing Assumptions

1. The checking account balance is maintained at $3,000 and is noninterest bearing.

2. The savings account earns 5 percent annually. Interest accumulates in the account.

3. Surplus cash earns 5.25 percent annually.

4. The money market funds earn 5.5 percent annually. Interest accumulates in the account.

5. Larry's salary increases at 6 percent annually.

6. Anne's listed stocks and bonds will increase in value at 5 percent annually. Yields on these securities will average 4 percent annually.

7. Stock in Millers is based on year-end book value and will increase in value at 5 percent annually.

8. The personal residence will increase in value at 4 percent annually.

9. Property taxes on the residence last year were $4,150 and will increase at 3 percent annually.

10. The resort condominium will increase in value at 8 percent annually.

11. Property taxes on the condominium will increase at 6 percent annually.

12. Increase or decrease in the value of household furnishings is ignored.

13. The value of the commercial building will increase at 4 percent annually. Net rental income from this property increases at 6 percent annually.

14. Nondeductible living expenses and charitable contributions increase at 6 percent annually.

15. The profit-sharing plan will earn 6 percent annually.

16. The cash values of the life insurance policies will grow at 8 percent annually.

INCOME STATEMENT

LARRY & ANNE MILLER

CASE III	2002	2003	2004	2005	2006
Earned Income					
Salaries - Larry	68,900	73,034	77,416	82,061	86,985
	68,900	73,034	77,416	82,061	86,985
Interest/Dividends					
Notes Rec - Doug	15,508	14,296	12,958	11,479	9,845
Notes Rec - Steve	0	14,325	27,928	26,889	25,753
Stocks/Bonds - Anne	4,326	4,542	4,769	5,008	5,258
Savings Acct - Anne	600	630	662	695	729
Money Market-Larry	2,530	2,669	2,816	2,971	3,134
Investable Cash	1,684	3,863	7,073	12,629	18,480
	24,648	40,325	56,206	59,671	63,199
Investments					
Rent-Commerc'l Bldg	33,000	34,980	37,079	39,304	41,662
Rent - Condo	6,000	6,000	6,000	6,000	6,000
	39,000	40,980	43,079	45,304	47,662
Net Capital Gain	4,629	10,031	16,169	17,746	19,479
	========	========	========	========	========
Adj Gross Income	137,177	164,370	192,870	204,781	217,325
Deductions					
Charitable 50%	3,000	3,180	3,371	3,573	3,787
State Tax Paid	6,759	8,318	9,952	10,618	11,279
Property Tax - Home	4,150	4,275	4,403	4,535	4,671
Property Tax -Condo	1,000	1,060	1,124	1,191	1,262
Reductn for High Inc	-127	-839	-1,588	-1,835	-1,399
Gross Deductions	14,782	15,993	17,262	18,081	19,600
Standard Deduction	7,600	7,800	8,000	8,526	9,292
Allowed Deductions	14,782	15,993	17,262	18,081	19,600
Pers Exemptions	5,800	5,900	6,100	6,300	4,011
	========	========	========	========	========
Taxable Income	116,595	142,477	169,509	180,400	193,714
	========	========	========	========	========
Fed Income Tax	24,995	95,406	33,842	38,175	41,619
	========	========	========	========	========
Fed Tax Bracket-Ord Inc	27.0%	30.0%	29.0%	29.0%	28.0%

BALANCE SHEET

LARRY & ANNE MILLER

CASE III	2002	2003	2004	2005	2006
LIQUID ASSETS					
Cash Balance	2,969	3,023	2,941	2,997	3,030
Cash Deposits					
Savings Acct - Anne	12,600	13,230	13,892	14,587	15,316
Investable Cash	65,846	85,169	191,354	302,389	420,088
Money Market-Larry	48,530	51,199	54,015	56,986	60,120
	126,976	149,598	259,261	373,962	495,524
Stocks & Bonds					
Stocks/Bonds - Anne	108,150	113,558	119,235	125,197	131,457
Miller Stock -Larry	531,481	237,572	249,451	261,923	275,019
Miller Stock - Anne	182,448	191,570	201,149	211,206	221,767
	822,079	542,700	569,835	598,327	628,243
Life Insurance					
Life Ins - Larry #1	20,836	22,503	24,304	26,248	28,348
Life Ins - Larry #2	8,259	8,919	9,633	10,404	11,236
Life Ins - Anne	5,281	5,704	6,160	6,653	7,185
	34,376	37,127	40,097	43,304	46,769
	========	========	========	========	========
Liquid Assets	986,401	732,448	872,134	1,018,590	1,173,566
	========	========	========	========	========
NONLIQUID ASSETS					
Benefit Plans					
Profit Sharing Plan	69,748	73,933	78,369	83,071	88,055
	69,748	73,933	78,369	83,071	88,055
Receivables					
Notes Rec - Doug	148,718	135,934	121,812	106,211	88,976
Notes Rec - Steve	0	315,305	304,226	292,108	278,854
	148,718	451,239	426,038	398,319	367,830
Personal Property					
Home	400,000	416,000	432,640	449,946	467,943
Condo	162,000	174,960	188,957	204,073	220,399
Commercial Bldg	530,000	551,200	573,248	596,178	620,025
Automobiles	13,600	11,560	9,826	8,352	7,099
Home Furnishings	100,000	100,000	100,000	100,000	100,000
	1,205,600	1,253,720	1,304,671	1,358,549	1,415,467
	========	========	========	========	========
Nonliquid Assets	1,424,066	1,778,892	1,809,078	1,839,939	1,871,352
	========	========	========	========	========
Total Assets	2,410,467	2,511,340	2,681,212	2,858,529	3,044,918
Net Worth	2,410,467	2,511,340	2,681,212	2,858,529	3,044,918
	========	========	========	========	========

CASH FLOW STATEMENT

LARRY & ANNE MILLER

CASE III	2002	2003	2004	2005	2006
BEGINNING OF YEAR					
Idle Cash On Hand	3,000	2,969	3,023	2,941	2,997
SOURCES OF CASH					
Cash Income					
Salaries - Larry	68,900	73,034	77,416	82,061	86,985
Interest+Dividends	19,834	33,163	45,655	43,376	40,856
Rents/Royalties	39,000	40,980	43,079	45,304	47,662
	127,734	147,177	166,150	170,740	175,503
Debt Recovered					
Notes Rec - Doug	11,572	12,784	14,122	15,601	17,235
Notes Rec - Steve	0	5,178	11,079	12,118	13,254
	11,572	17,962	25,201	27,719	30,489
	========	========	========	========	========
Total Cash Inflow	139,306	165,139	191,351	198,459	205,992
	========	========	========	========	========
Tot Cash Available	142,306	168,109	194,374	201,400	208,988
	========	========	========	========	========
USES OF CASH					
Partly Deductible					
Charity Contrb-50%	3,000	3,180	3,371	3,573	3,787
	3,000	3,180	3,371	3,573	3,787
Not Tax Deductible					
Living Expenses	30,000	31,800	33,708	35,730	37,874
	30,000	31,800	33,708	35,730	37,874
Taxes Paid					
Fed Tax Paid	24,995	95,406	33,842	38,175	41,619
State Tax Paid	6,759	8,318	9,952	10,618	11,279
FICA/Soc Sec Tax	5,271	5,587	5,922	6,175	6,246
Real Estate Tax	5,150	5,335	5,526	5,726	5,933
	42,175	114,646	55,243	60,694	65,077
Purchase/Deposits					
Investable Cash	64,162	15,460	99,112	98,406	99,219
	64,162	15,460	99,112	98,406	99,219
	========	========	========	========	========
Tot Cash Outflow	139,337	165,086	191,433	198,404	205,958
	========	========	========	========	========
END OF YEAR					
Cash Balance	2,969	3,023	2,941	2,997	3,030
	========	========	========	========	========

SUPPORTING SCHEDULE

LARRY & ANNE MILLER

CASE III	JOINT 2002	JOINT 2003	JOINT 2004	JOINT 2005	JOINT 2006
Income					
Earned Income	68,900	73,034	77,416	82,061	86,985
Adj Gross Income	137,177	164,370	192,870	204,781	217,325
Allowed Deductions	14,782	15,993	17,262	18,081	19,600
Pers Exemptions	5,800	5,900	6,100	6,300	4,011
Taxable Income	116,595	142,477	169,509	180,400	193,714
Capital Gains					
Notes Rec - Doug	4,629	5,114	5,649	6,240	6,894
Notes Rec - Steve	0	4,917	10,520	11,506	12,585
Net Capital Gain	4,629	10,031	16,169	17,746	19,479
LTCG Txd at Max Rt	4,629	10,031	16,169	17,746	19,479
Notes Rec - Doug	-4,629	-5,114	-5,649	-6,240	-6,894
Notes Rec - Steve	0	299,382	-10,520	-11,506	-12,585
Capital Gains-AMT	0	304,299	0	0	0
Federal Tax Liab					
Regular Tax	25,455	32,987	39,650	42,579	45,000
Max Tax on Cap Gn	926	2,006	3,234	3,549	3,896
Gross Fed Inc Tax	24,995	31,984	38,194	40,982	43,221
Alt Minimum Tax	0	63,422	0	0	0
Alt Min Tx Credit	0	0	4,352	2,807	1,602
AMT Credit C/Over	0	0	0	59,070	56,263
Disallowed	0	0	-59,070	-56,263	-54,662
Fed Income Tax	24,995	95,406	33,842	38,175	41,619
Fed Tax Analysis-Ord Inc					
Indexing Factor	77	82	87	91	96
Fed Tax Bracket-Ord Inc	27.0%	30.0%	29.0%	29.0%	28.0%
$ to Next Bracket	84	42,804	26,460	21,846	15,065
Next Bracket	30.0%	35.0%	34.0%	34.0%	33.0%
Previous Bracket	15.0%	27.0%	26.0%	26.0%	25.0%
$ to Prev Bracket	65,616	17,446	35,340	41,604	50,035
Fed Capital Gain Rate	20.0%	20.0%	20.0%	20.0%	20.0%
Fed Effective Tax Rate	21.4%	21.0%	20.0%	21.2%	21.5%
Alt Minimum Tax					
Adj Gross Income	137,177	164,370	192,870	204,781	217,325
Contributions	-3,000	-3,180	-3,371	-3,573	-3,787
Adjusted AMTI	134,177	161,190	189,499	201,208	213,538
Net Capital Gain	-4,629	-10,031	-16,169	-17,746	-19,479

SUPPORTING SCHEDULE (cont.)

LARRY & ANNE MILLER

	JOINT 2002	JOINT 2003	JOINT 2004	JOINT 2005	JOINT 2006
CASE III					
Capital Gains-AMT	0	304,299	0	0	0
AMT Exemptions	-49,000	0	-43,167	-36,634	-33,985
AMT Taxable Inc	80,548	455,458	130,163	146,828	160,073
Gross Alt Min Tx	20,942	95,406	33,842	38,175	41,619
Fed Tax Less FTC	-24,995	-31,984	-38,194	-40,982	-43,221
Alt Minimum Tax	0	63,422	0	0	0
Other Tax Liabs					
FICA/Soc Sec Tax	5,271	5,587	5,922	6,175	6,246
Adj Gross Inc	137,177	164,370	192,870	204,781	217,325
GA Adj Gross Inc	137,177	164,370	192,870	204,781	217,325
GA Standard Ded	3,000	3,000	3,000	3,000	3,000
GA Itemized Ded	14,782	15,993	17,262	18,081	19,600
GA Exemptions	5,400	5,400	5,400	5,400	5,400
GA Taxable Inc	116,995	142,977	170,209	181,300	192,325
GA Regular Tax	6,759	8,318	9,952	10,618	11,279
GA Income Tax	6,759	8,318	9,952	10,618	11,279
Georgia Tax	6,759	8,318	9,952	10,618	11,279
Tot State/Local Tx	6,759	8,318	9,952	10,618	11,279
Total Inc Tax	37,025	109,311	49,716	54,968	59,144

FINANCIAL SUMMARY

LARRY & ANNE MILLER

CASE III	2002	2003	2004	2005	2006
Gross Real Income					
Personal Earnings	68,900	73,034	77,416	82,061	86,985
Interest Income	20,322	35,783	51,437	54,663	57,941
Dividends Rcvd	4,326	4,542	4,769	5,008	5,258
Rent-Commerc'l Bldg	33,000	34,980	37,079	39,304	41,662
Rent - Condo	6,000	6,000	6,000	6,000	6,000
	132,548	154,339	176,701	187,035	197,846
Income & Inflation					
Gross Real Inc	132,548	154,339	176,701	187,035	197,846
Total Inc Tax	-37,025	-109,311	-49,716	-54,968	-59,144
Net Real Income	95,523	45,028	126,985	132,067	138,702
Cur Real Inc =	95,523	98,009	100,559	103,175	105,859
Purch Power Drop	0	52,980	0	0	0
At Infltn Rate of	3	3	3	3	3
Cash Flow					
Idle Cash On Hand	3,000	2,969	3,023	2,941	2,997
Norml Cash Inflow	139,306	165,139	191,351	198,459	205,992
Norml Cash Outflw	75,175	149,626	92,321	99,998	106,739
Cash Invested	64,162	15,460	99,112	98,406	99,219
Cash Balance	2,969	3,023	2,941	2,997	3,030
Net Worth					
Personal Assets	1,242,946	1,293,870	1,347,708	1,404,850	1,465,266
Investment Assets	1,167,521	1,217,470	1,333,503	1,453,679	1,579,652
Personal Net Worth	1,242,946	1,293,870	1,347,708	1,404,850	1,465,266
Investment Net Worth	1,167,521	1,217,470	1,333,503	1,453,679	1,579,652
Net Worth	2,410,467	2,511,340	2,681,212	2,858,529	3,044,918

BUSINESS PLANNING: TAXES

Present Position

Millers is not only the largest and most important single asset that Larry and Anne have accumulated, it has also been the primary source of income to support their lifestyle and to allow them to accumulate other assets. Larry has a very strong desire to preserve the business for their oldest son, Steve, who has worked in the business for many years and who Larry thinks is capable of continuing to manage it profitably. Another corporation has already been sold to their younger son, Doug, and a business associate.

Larry has no present plan to retire completely from Millers but would like to cut back his day-to-day responsibilities there. He would like to transfer his responsibilities to Steve before planning to significantly reduce the time he spends at the store. He thinks he is ready to pass management control of the business to Steve, since he is assured that Steve will succeed in a leadership role.

Larry presently owns 167.5 (67 percent) of the corporation's 250 authorized and issued shares. Anne owns 57.5 shares (23 percent) and Steve owns 25 shares (10 percent). The book value of Larry's shares at year end was $506,172, the book value of Anne's shares was $173,760, and the book value of Steve's shares was $75,548.

Larry wishes to accomplish the transition of control to Steve while assuring that his and Anne's interest in Millers will continue to produce income that will allow them to be secure during their later years. At the same time he does not want to implement techniques that will accomplish these personal objectives while compromising the continuing viability of the business.

Business Transition

Installment Sales

General Requirements. A simple method of transferring Larry's interest in Millers to Steve is an installment sale. Generally an installment sale occurs when property is disposed of in exchange for payments, at least one of which is to be received after the close of the taxable year in which the disposition occurs (IRC Sec. 453(a)).

The seller receives sale-or-exchange federal income tax treatment to the extent of gain realized on the transaction (selling price less adjusted basis = gain realized). When the installment method of reporting is used, the gain portion is recognized and reported as a percentage of each taxable year's payment. The interest portion of the installment payment is, of course, recognized as ordinary income in the year in which it is received. Use of the installment sale method can therefore spread a large gain over a number of years, with significant income tax deferral and possible overall tax savings.

Note, however, that for installment sales of depreciable property all recapture for depreciation must be treated as ordinary income in the year of the sale, regardless of whether any payment is received in that year (IRC Sec. 453(i), 453(i)(2)). However, stock in Millers is not depreciable property.

Installment sales of stock can also provide an important income stream for retirement years, particularly in cases such as this when many of the client's assets are wrapped up in a single business entity that is essentially nonliquid. The 5-year tax, net worth, and cash-flow results of an installment sale of Larry's entire interest in Millers to Steve at book value with a 9 percent interest rate for a term of 15 years are illustrated on the previous pages.

Another important advantage of installment sales is that they take an appreciating asset out of Larry's estate and replace it with one that has a fixed value. In fact, the value of the installment proceeds can actually decrease if the proceeds are consumed prior to Larry's death.

If Larry were to sell Steve his entire interest in Millers for no down payment and monthly payments calculated at 9 percent interest for a term of 15 years, Steve's annual level payments of principal and interest would be $64,687 (in 12 monthly payments). Steve's present salary obviously would not allow him to afford such high payments. In fact, it would probably be difficult to raise Steve's salary in the near future to a level that would allow him to afford these payments and avoid an IRS challenge on the reasonableness of his compensation, particularly since Millers is a C corporation.

It would not, however, be difficult to raise Steve's salary to allow him to acquire some of Larry's stock immediately through an installment sale, especially in view of the additional duties Larry would like to see Steve undertake.

Steve could purchase 101 of Larry's 167.5 shares at a projected 2002 book value of $320,483 at 9 percent interest for a term of 15 years for annual principal and interest payments of $39,758. In the early years close to $35,000 of that amount would be interest. Since Millers is a C corporation, the interest payments would be an investment interest expense to Steve and therefore subject to the limitations on the deductibility of investment interest, discussed in the next section. If Steve purchased 101 shares, he would own 126 shares (101 + 25) and the controlling interest in the corporation.

The 5-year income statement, balance sheet, and cash-flow results to Larry and Anne of such a sale are shown on the previous pages.

Avoiding the Limitation on the Deductibility of Investment Interest. In an installment sale the purchaser's deductibility of interest payments can be a crucial issue when the purchaser's salary must be raised to make such a purchase possible. In Steve's case the inability to deduct a major portion of the interest would require a substantially greater salary increase. This would increase the likelihood of the IRS's characterizing the compensation as unreasonable and therefore nondeductible by the corporation.

Generally an individual taxpayer can deduct investment interest only up to the amount of the taxpayer's *net investment income,* which means the excess of *investment income* over investment expenses.

Investment income is income from interest, dividends, rents, and royalties. Under the facts of this case Millers pays no dividends. Thus there will be no investment income to Steve as a result of owning any stock in Millers.

Investment expenses are deductible expenses other than interest that are directly connected with the production of investment income. Steve will not be incurring investment expenses as a consequence of this transaction.

The purchase of an ownership interest in a corporation (that is, stock) has traditionally been characterized as a purchase of an asset held for investment.

The Internal Revenue Service treats interest on a debt incurred to purchase an interest in an *S corporation* or a *partnership* as interest incurred in the conduct of a trade or business and *not* as investment interest, as long as the taxpayer purchasing the interest materially participates in the business.

This means that if a taxpayer uses the installment method to purchase an interest in an S corporation or a partnership, the interest payments will be fully deductible as a business expense and not subject to the investment interest expense limitations described above.

Although Steve is not your client at this time, his ability to deduct his interest payments in connection with the purchase of Larry's stock is very important to Larry in terms of making the transaction affordable for Steve.

Millers is presently operated as a regular (C) corporation. Therefore in order to have the interest payments on Steve's obligation fully deductible as business interest payments under current IRS rules, Millers would have to make an S election. If the S election was in effect prior to the consummation of an installment sale, it is very likely that Steve could take advantage of the position taken by the IRS in Announcement 87-4 and deduct the full amount of his interest payments as a business expense. However, the other effects of making an S election in this case must be explored.

Using an S Election to Facilitate Transfer of a Business Interest

---

NOTE

To avoid repetition, background information on S corporations has been omitted. In an actual plan this information should be presented to the client for completeness. If you are not completely familiar with this material, it should be reviewed before proceeding through this suggested solution.

The Tax on "Built-in" Gains

Millers would qualify for an election to be taxed as an S corporation, since it meets the basic requirements for the election. However, qualification is not the only factor that must be considered.

First, a special income tax liability can result in the case of existing C corporations that make elections under Subchapter S. Briefly stated, this tax liability is designed to prevent taxpayers from using S elections to circumvent the corporate-level tax imposed on corporate liquidations under current federal income tax law. This tax that can result from an S election is referred to as the *built-in gains tax.*

Millers could be subject to both a corporate-level built-in gains tax and a shareholder-level tax upon the subsequent sale of any inventory that existed prior to the time of an S election that is sold within 10 years of the effective date of such election (IRC Sec. 1374(d)). The corporate-level tax in this case would be assessed at a rate of 35 percent on the amount of the inventory's untaxed gain at the time the S election became effective. The shareholder-level tax on the same gain is assessed at the marginal rate of each shareholder.

The inventory appears to be the only significant "ordinary income" type of asset that would be subject to the built-in gains tax if an S election were made in this case. Millers accounts receivable have already been "booked" for income tax purposes under the accrual method of accounting. Since the receivables have already been recognized for tax purposes, they are not subject to the built-in gains tax.

The built-in gains tax will also apply to the corporation's capital assets. Any capital assets sold by the corporation within 10 years of the S election will be subject to a 35 percent corporate-level tax (in addition to the tax on the shareholders) with respect to the amount of appreciation that was "built in" or existing at the time of the S election. However, since Larry owns the store building individually, any property or improvements the corporation owns can be taxed under these rules. If the corporation waits 10 years after an S election before selling its capital assets, the tax will not be imposed. Also any capital assets sold before an S election became effective will be taxed at the corporation's marginal rate but will not be subject to the double tax that would result if the assets were sold after an S election, provided that the proceeds are not distributed to the shareholders as a dividend.

As previously stated, sales of existing inventory *after* an S election will result in a built-in gains tax. One practical way to minimize this tax is to reduce inventory as much as possible just before the first day of the calendar year in which the S election becomes effective. If there is less inventory existing at the time an S election becomes effective, the built-in gains tax will be less of a problem.

Clearly these are sophisticated tax matters that the financial planner cannot single-handedly resolve. Larry's accountant and attorney must be consulted to determine the built-in gains tax liability that could result from an S election.

Larry's accountant would also have to examine how distributions by the corporation after an S election might be affected by the complex rules regarding previously taxed income of S corporations and the shareholders' "accumulated adjustment account" ("triple A account"). These matters are generally beyond the scope of this discussion.

It is important to note that because Millers has substantial retained earnings, dividend treatment can still be applied to certain corporate distributions even after the time of an S election because Millers would still have substantial earnings and profits accumulated during its life as a C corporation. As a result the tax rules regarding redemptions (discussed in a later section) will still apply even after an S election is made to determine whether dividend treatment would be applied to the proceeds of any proposed redemption. As discussed below, the treatment of a stock redemption as a dividend for federal income tax purposes is not a desirable result.

Practical Considerations in Planning for an S Election

Once Millers makes an S election, Larry and Steve will no longer be eligible for tax-favored fringe benefits. They will be taxed on a portion of the value of their medical coverage, for example. Most significantly the shareholders will be taxed on their proportionate shares of the corporation's taxable income, regardless of whether the income is distributed. Therefore care must be taken that Larry and Anne will receive at least enough money from Millers in the form of dividends to cover this additional tax liability.

If Steve is sold a controlling interest in Millers, he will basically have the authority to decide how much of the corporation's taxable income should be distributed to its shareholders. It is unlikely that Steve will refuse to distribute enough to allow his father to pay the additional taxes. However, the contract for the sale of Larry's stock could include a provision requiring Steve to make such distributions if Larry is concerned about the issue. This should be further explored before any agreements are signed.

It should be noted that an S election could provide Larry and Anne with additional retirement income if a substantial portion of their share of corporate taxable income is distributed to them. In addition, these distributions are derived from stock ownership and are not made in exchange for performance of services. Therefore the issue of reasonableness of compensation is generally avoided. Such distributions could be made regardless of whether Larry is working for the corporation at the time.

Treasury regulations make operating as an S corporation additionally burdensome, since compliance with certain formalities becomes more important than ever. One important example is the Treasury position dealing with the inadvertent issuance of a second class of stock. Although the latest Treasury regulations dealing with the inadvertent issuance of a second class of stock are not as strict as earlier pronouncements, this issue is still a cause for concern and needs to be borne in mind. The issuance of certain debt instruments can be viewed by the IRS as a second class of stock, which would have the effect of invalidating the S election.

The possible problems associated with an S election have been noted. However, there appears to be no substantial disadvantage to Millers if they make an S election. The principal advantage would be to allow Steve to deduct interest payments on his installment obligation incurred to acquire S corporation stock. This would make the purchase much more feasible and affordable for Steve. Another advantage would be the lower individual tax rates (as compared with corporate rates) imposed on taxable income of the corporation in excess of $75,000. Therefore, subject to the agreement of Larry's attorney and accountant, our recommendation would be for Millers to make an election to be taxed as an S corporation, effective for the 2002 tax year. The election should be made in 2002 but in no event may it be made later than March 15, 2003, in order for it to be effective for taxable year 2003. The election must be made before Larry makes an installment sale of his stock to Steve.

In addition, if Anne's stock in Millers is redeemed immediately by the corporation (as will be discussed later), it will not be necessary for Steve to purchase 101 shares from Larry in order to acquire a controlling interest in the business. After Anne's stock is redeemed, Steve need purchase only 72 shares to own more than 50 percent of the total value of the stock then outstanding. This is preferable to Steve's purchasing additional shares because it will reduce his total installment obligation. Also the gain on Anne's shares will be treated in a tax-favored manner (as will also be discussed later), since dividend treatment to Larry and Anne can be avoided for this particular redemption.

A 15-year installment sale of 72 shares will cost Steve $28,342 per year in installment payments, of which close to $25,000 will be deductible interest in the early years. Steve should be able to service this debt through either a salary increase, a distribution of the S corporation taxable income, or a combination of both.

The following are the 5-year income statements, balance sheets, and cash-flow results to Larry and Anne if Steve purchases 72 shares of Larry's stock at a 2002 book value of $228,463, payable over 15 years at an interest rate of 9 percent, and if the corporation also redeems Anne's 57.5 shares at a 2002 book value of $182,453, payable over 10 years at an interest rate of 9 percent. The projections do not show additional income from Millers as a result of an S election. Therefore the assumption is that Larry receives an annual distribution from Millers equal to his share of the tax liability arising from his stock ownership and resulting in no net cash effect.

[text continues on page 6.49]

CASE IV
Installment Sale of 72 Shares of Millers Stock to Steve
and Redemption by Millers of Anne's 57.5 Shares of Millers Stock

New Assumptions

1. Steve purchases 72 shares of Larry's Millers stock on July 1, 2003, at a projected 2002 book value ($228,463) for no down payment at 9 percent interest for a term of 15 years. Larry remains active in the business for at least 4 years.

2. Millers redeems Anne's 57.5 shares on December 1, 2003, at a projected 2002 book value ($182,453) financed by an installment note for the total amount payable over 10 years at 9 percent interest.

Continuing Assumptions

1. The checking account balance is maintained at $3,000 and is noninterest bearing.

2. The savings account earns 5 percent annually. Interest accumulates in the account.

3. Surplus cash earns 5.25 percent annually.

4. The money market funds earn 5.5 percent annually. Interest accumulates in the account.

5. Larry's salary increases at 6 percent annually.

6. Anne's listed stocks and bonds will increase in value at 5 percent annually. Yields on these securities will average 4 percent annually.

7. Stock in Millers is based on year-end book value and will increase in value at 5 percent annually.

8. The personal residence will increase in value at 4 percent annually.

9. Property taxes on the residence last year were $4,150 and will increase at 3 percent annually.

10. The resort condominium will increase in value at 8 percent annually.

11. Property taxes on the condominium will increase at 6 percent annually.

12. Increase or decrease in the value of household furnishings is ignored.

13. The value of the commercial building will increase at 4 percent annually. Net rental income from this property increases at 6 percent annually.

14. Nondeductible living expenses and charitable contributions increase at 6 percent annually.

15. The profit-sharing plan will earn 6 percent annually.

16. The cash values of the life insurance policies will grow at 8 percent annually.

INCOME STATEMENT

LARRY & ANNE MILLER

CASE IV	2002	2003	2004	2005	2006
Earned Income					
Salaries - Larry	68,900	73,034	77,416	82,061	86,985
	68,900	73,034	77,416	82,061	86,985
Interest/Dividends					
Notes Rec - Doug	15,508	14,296	12,958	11,479	9,845
Notes Rec - Steve	0	10,212	19,909	19,169	18,358
Notes Rec - Miller	1,368	15,853	14,739	13,520	12,186
Stocks/Bonds - Anne	4,326	4,542	4,769	5,008	5,258
Savings Acct - Anne	600	630	662	695	729
Money Market-Larry	2,530	2,669	2,816	2,971	3,134
Investable Cash	1,131	3,657	8,135	14,443	21,085
	25,463	51,859	63,988	67,285	70,595
Investments					
Rent-Commerc'l Bldg	33,000	34,980	37,079	39,304	41,662
Rent - Condo	6,000	6,000	6,000	6,000	6,000
	39,000	40,980	43,079	45,304	47,662
Net Capital Gain	5,275	16,757	22,050	24,179	26,516
	========	========	========	========	========
Adj Gross Income	138,638	182,630	206,533	218,828	231,758
Deductions					
Charitable 50%	3,000	3,180	3,371	3,573	3,787
State Tax Paid	6,844	9,383	10,749	11,437	12,112
Property Tax - Home	4,150	4,275	4,403	4,535	4,671
Property Tax -Condo	1,000	1,060	1,124	1,191	1,262
Reductn for High Inc	-171	-1,387	-1,997	-2,257	-1,688
Gross Deductions	14,823	16,511	17,649	18,479	20,144
Standard Deduction	7,600	7,800	8,000	8,526	9,292
Allowed Deductions	14,823	16,511	17,649	18,479	20,144
Pers Exemptions	5,800	5,900	6,100	6,048	3,499
	========	========	========	========	========
Taxable Income	118,015	160,220	182,784	194,301	208,115
	========	========	========	========	========
Fed Income Tax	48,362	80,930	36,371	40,650	44,023
	========	========	========	========	========
Fed Tax Bracket-Ord Inc	30.0%	30.0%	29.0%	29.0%	28.0%

BALANCE SHEET

LARRY & ANNE MILLER

CASE IV	2002	2003	2004	2005	2006
LIQUID ASSETS					
Cash Balance	2,908	3,066	2,933	2,997	3,034
Cash Deposits					
Savings Acct - Anne	12,600	13,230	13,892	14,587	15,316
Investable Cash	44,213	98,771	219,276	345,358	478,955
Money Market-Larry	48,530	51,199	54,015	56,986	60,120
	105,343	163,200	287,183	416,931	554,391
Stocks & Bonds					
Stocks/Bonds - Anne	108,150	113,558	119,235	125,197	131,457
Miller Stock -Larry	531,481	329,592	346,072	363,375	381,544
	639,631	443,150	465,307	488,572	513,001
Life Insurance					
Life Ins - Larry #1	20,836	22,503	24,304	26,248	28,348
Life Ins - Larry #2	8,259	8,919	9,633	10,404	11,236
Life Ins - Anne	5,281	5,704	6,160	6,653	7,185
	34,376	37,127	40,097	43,304	46,769
	========	========	========	========	========
Liquid Assets	782,258	646,542	795,520	951,804	1,117,195
	========	========	========	========	========
NONLIQUID ASSETS					
Benefit Plans					
Profit Sharing Plan	69,748	73,933	78,369	83,071	88,055
	69,748	73,933	78,369	83,071	88,055
Receivables					
Notes Rec - Doug	148,718	135,934	121,812	106,211	88,976
Notes Rec - Steve	0	224,772	216,874	208,236	198,787
Notes Rec - Miller	181,505	169,624	156,629	142,415	126,867
	330,223	530,330	495,315	456,862	414,630
Personal Property					
Home	400,000	416,000	432,640	449,946	467,943
Condo	162,000	174,960	188,957	204,073	220,399
Commercial Bldg	530,000	551,200	573,248	596,178	620,025
Automobiles	13,600	11,560	9,826	8,352	7,099
Home Furnishings	100,000	100,000	100,000	100,000	100,000
	1,205,600	1,253,720	1,304,671	1,358,549	1,415,467
	========	========	========	========	========
Nonliquid Assets	1,605,571	1,857,983	1,878,355	1,898,482	1,918,152
	========	========	========	========	========
Total Assets	2,387,829	2,504,525	2,673,875	2,850,286	3,035,347
Net Worth	2,387,829	2,504,525	2,673,875	2,850,286	3,035,347
	========	========	========	========	========

CASH FLOW STATEMENT

LARRY & ANNE MILLER

CASE IV	2002	2003	2004	2005	2006
BEGINNING OF YEAR					
Idle Cash On Hand	3,000	2,908	3,066	2,933	2,997
SOURCES OF CASH					
Cash Income					
Salaries - Larry	68,900	73,034	77,416	82,061	86,985
Interest+Dividends	21,202	44,903	52,375	49,176	45,647
Rents/Royalties	39,000	40,980	43,079	45,304	47,662
	129,102	158,917	172,870	176,540	180,294
Debt Recovered					
Notes Rec - Doug	11,572	12,784	14,122	15,601	17,235
Notes Rec - Steve	0	3,691	7,898	8,638	9,449
Notes Rec - Miller	943	11,881	12,995	14,214	15,548
	12,515	28,356	35,015	38,453	42,232
	========	========	========	========	========
Total Cash Inflow	141,617	187,273	207,885	214,993	222,526
	========	========	========	========	========
Tot Cash Available	144,617	190,181	210,951	217,927	225,522
	========	========	========	========	========
USES OF CASH					
Partly Deductible					
Charity Contrb-50%	3,000	3,180	3,371	3,573	3,787
	3,000	3,180	3,371	3,573	3,787
Not Tax Deductible					
Living Expenses	30,000	31,800	33,708	35,730	37,874
	30,000	31,800	33,708	35,730	37,874
Taxes Paid					
Fed Tax Paid	48,362	80,930	36,371	40,650	44,023
State Tax Paid	6,844	9,383	10,749	11,437	12,112
FICA/Soc Sec Tax	5,271	5,587	5,922	6,175	6,246
Real Estate Tax	5,150	5,335	5,526	5,726	5,933
	65,627	101,235	58,569	63,988	68,314
Purchase/Deposits					
Investable Cash	43,082	50,901	112,370	111,639	112,512
	43,082	50,901	112,370	111,639	112,512
	========	========	========	========	========
Tot Cash Outflow	141,709	187,116	208,018	214,930	222,488
	========	========	========	========	========
END OF YEAR					
Cash Balance	2,908	3,066	2,933	2,997	3,034
	========	========	========	========	========

SUPPORTING SCHEDULE

LARRY & ANNE MILLER

	JOINT	JOINT	JOINT	JOINT	JOINT
CASE IV	2002	2003	2004	2005	2006
Income					
Earned Income	68,900	73,034	77,416	82,061	86,985
Adj Gross Income	138,638	182,630	206,533	218,828	231,758
Allowed Deductions	14,823	16,511	17,649	18,479	20,144
Pers Exemptions	5,800	5,900	6,100	6,048	3,499
Taxable Income	118,015	160,220	182,784	194,301	208,115
Capital Gains					
Notes Rec - Doug	4,629	5,114	5,649	6,240	6,894
Notes Rec - Steve	0	3,505	7,499	8,202	8,972
Notes Rec - Miller	646	8,138	8,902	9,737	10,650
Net Capital Gain	5,275	16,757	22,050	24,179	26,516
LTCG Txd at Max Rt	5,275	16,757	22,050	24,179	26,516
Notes Rec - Doug	-4,629	-5,114	-5,649	-6,240	-6,894
Notes Rec - Steve	0	213,421	-7,499	-8,202	-8,972
Notes Rec - Miller	124,331	-8,138	-8,902	-9,737	-10,650
Capital Gains-AMT	124,977	216,926	0	0	0
Federal Tax Liab					
Regular Tax	25,881	38,310	43,649	47,100	49,752
Max Tax on Cap Gn	1,055	3,351	4,410	4,836	5,303
Gross Fed Inc Tax	25,354	36,634	41,515	44,434	46,690
Alt Minimum Tax	23,009	44,296	0	0	0
Alt Min Tx Credit	0	0	5,143	3,784	2,667
AMT Credit C/Over	0	0	23,009	62,161	58,376
Disallowed	0	-23,008	-62,161	-58,376	-55,709
Fed Income Tax	48,362	80,930	36,371	40,650	44,023
Fed Tax Analysis-Ord Inc					
Indexing Factor	77	82	87	91	96
Fed Tax Bracket-Ord Inc	30.0%	30.0%	29.0%	29.0%	28.0%
$ to Next Bracket	58,060	31,787	19,066	14,378	7,701
Next Bracket	35.0%	35.0%	34.0%	34.0%	33.0%
Previous Bracket	27.0%	27.0%	26.0%	26.0%	25.0%
$ to Prev Bracket	690	28,463	42,734	49,072	57,399
Fed Capital Gain Rate	20.0%	20.0%	20.0%	20.0%	20.0%
Fed Effective Tax Rate	20.8%	21.3%	19.9%	20.9%	21.2%

<u>S U P P O R T I N G   S C H E D U L E</u> (cont.)

LARRY & ANNE MILLER

CASE IV	JOINT 2002	JOINT 2003	JOINT 2004	JOINT 2005	JOINT 2006
Alt Minimum Tax					
Adj Gross Income	138,638	182,630	206,533	218,828	231,758
Contributions	-3,000	-3,180	-3,371	-3,573	-3,787
Adjusted AMTI	135,638	179,450	203,162	215,255	227,971
Net Capital Gain	-5,275	-16,757	-22,050	-24,179	-26,516
Capital Gains-AMT	124,977	216,926	0	0	0
AMT Exemptions	-22,665	0	-41,222	-34,731	-32,136
AMT Taxable Inc	232,675	379,619	139,890	156,346	169,318
Gross Alt Min Tx	48,362	80,930	36,371	40,650	44,023
Fed Tax Less FTC	-25,353	-36,634	-41,515	-44,434	-46,690
Alt Minimum Tax	23,009	44,296	0	0	0
Other Tax Liabs					
FICA/Soc Sec Tax	5,271	5,587	5,922	6,175	6,246
Adj Gross Inc	138,638	182,630	206,533	218,828	231,758
GA Adj Gross Inc	138,638	182,630	206,533	218,828	231,758
GA Standard Ded	3,000	3,000	3,000	3,000	3,000
GA Itemized Ded	14,823	16,511	17,649	18,479	20,144
GA Exemptions	5,400	5,400	5,400	5,400	5,400
GA Taxable Inc	118,415	160,720	183,484	194,949	206,213
GA Regular Tax	6,844	9,383	10,749	11,436	12,112
GA Income Tax	6,844	9,383	10,749	11,436	12,112
Georgia Tax	6,844	9,383	10,749	11,436	12,112
Tot State/Local Tx	6,844	9,383	10,749	11,436	12,112
Total Inc Tax	60,477	95,900	53,042	58,261	62,381

FINANCIAL SUMMARY

LARRY & ANNE MILLER

CASE IV	2002	2003	2004	2005	2006
Gross Real Income					
Personal Earnings	68,900	73,034	77,416	82,061	86,985
Interest Income	21,137	47,317	59,219	62,277	65,337
Dividends Rcvd	4,326	4,542	4,769	5,008	5,258
Rent-Commerc'l Bldg	33,000	34,980	37,079	39,304	41,662
Rent - Condo	6,000	6,000	6,000	6,000	6,000
	133,363	165,873	184,483	194,649	205,242
Income & Inflation					
Gross Real Inc	133,363	165,873	184,483	194,649	205,242
Total Inc Tax	-60,477	-95,900	-53,042	-58,261	-62,381
Net Real Income	72,886	69,973	131,441	136,389	142,861
Cur Real Inc =	72,886	74,782	76,728	78,724	80,772
Purch Power Drop	0	4,809	0	0	0
At Infltn Rate of	3	3	3	3	3
Cash Flow					
Idle Cash On Hand	3,000	2,908	3,066	2,933	2,997
Norml Cash Inflow	141,617	187,273	207,885	214,993	222,526
Norml Cash Outflw	98,627	136,215	95,648	103,291	109,976
Cash Invested	43,082	50,901	112,370	111,639	112,512
Cash Balance	2,908	3,066	2,933	2,997	3,034
Net Worth					
Personal Assets	1,242,884	1,293,912	1,347,701	1,404,850	1,465,270
Investment Assets	1,144,945	1,210,612	1,326,174	1,445,436	1,570,077
Personal Net Worth	1,242,884	1,293,912	1,347,701	1,404,850	1,465,270
Investment Net Worth	1,144,945	1,210,612	1,326,174	1,445,436	1,570,077
Net Worth	2,387,829	2,504,525	2,673,875	2,850,286	3,035,347

Additional Principles Applicable to the Taxation of Installment Sales. As a general rule installment reporting of the income from an installment sale will be allowed even though the parties to the sale are closely related persons. However, abusive tax transactions have been observed in this area. These generally involve a person selling to a close relative on an installment basis and having the purchaser (who has received a step-up in basis on the sale) dispose of the asset at little or no gain by selling it again almost immediately for cash while still paying for the original purchase over many years. To combat these abuses the Code provides that a disposition of the property that is the subject of an installment sale between related parties cannot be made by the purchaser without the seller's being treated for tax purposes as if he or she has received the balance of the purchase price (subject to some limitations) regardless of whether the price has actually been paid to the original seller (IRC Sec. 453(e)).

Since this provision is aimed at abusive situations, it does not apply in many cases. In fact, unless the property that is the subject of the installment sale consists of marketable securities, the period during which a disposition of the property will trigger adverse consequences to the related seller expires 2 years after the initial sale.

Since the stock of Millers is not a marketable security, only the 2-year rule against dispositions will apply.

Additional rules regarding the tax treatment of certain installment sales also may apply. The installment tax treatment is not permitted for sales of publicly traded property such as marketable securities. In addition, installment sales of property such as inventory and certain real estate may subject the seller to the alternative minimum tax on the full amount of gain in the year of sale. There is currently no reason for concern that the alternative minimum tax will be applied to the full amount of gain in the case of an installment sale of closely held (nonpublicly traded) stock. However, developments in the tax law should be closely monitored before entering into any installment sale, given the uncertain tax climate.

One additional potential problem associated with an installment sale is personal, not tax related. An installment purchase by a younger-generation successor of a family business means that for a very long period of time, his or her lifestyle will be curtailed by the purchase. Since Steve's ability to purchase the stock depends on substantially increasing his total income from Millers, the business must expand somewhat in order to allow him significantly more income. This means that during the period when he is raising and educating his family, available cash flow may be limited. As long as Steve and his wife have thoughtfully considered this fact and are committed to the business, there may be no further problems. It is always advisable, however, to point out these implications to the seller as well as to the purchaser.

Redemptions

Few owners of closely held businesses who spend their working life in a small business realize that as a matter of federal income tax law, it may be very difficult to transform their investment in that corporation into another type of investment that may be more appropriate for their later years without paying a heavy price in taxes. Because of the family attribution rules of IRC Sec. 318, this is especially true when several members of a family own stock in the corporation.

The problem with redemptions arises from the rule that dividends are not deductible to the corporation when distributed to corporate shareholders and are taxable to the shareholders as ordinary income. In most small wholly owned or family-owned corporations, dividends either are never paid or are paid rarely and in small, often insignificant, amounts. This is usually not troubling to the shareholders of these corporations, who are most often also employees of the corporation and who depend on salaries rather than dividends for their livelihoods.

In the absence of statutory restraints on corporate redemptions, if a shareholder of a wholly owned corporation wished to take money out of the corporation without subjecting these funds to dividend treatment (ordinary income to the recipient and nondeductible by the corporation), the shareholder could simply sell some shares back to the corporation for cash and pay the federal income tax on the gain.

An example of this type of transaction follows:

> Mickey MacDonald owns 100 percent (300 shares) of M. M. Corporation, each share of which is worth $1,000. He causes M. M. Corporation, which has earnings and profits, to redeem 10 shares of his stock for $10,000. Result: Mickey still owns 100 percent of M. M. Corporation although he now owns only 290 shares of stock.
>
> Mickey would like to treat the redemption as the sale of a capital asset and pay taxes only on the gain. Since the redemption is essentially the same as if a cash dividend had been paid to Mickey, however, the Internal Revenue Code requires the entire $10,000 to be treated as a dividend, resulting in ordinary income tax treatment.

Whether the redemption qualifies for capital-gains treatment determines whether the taxpayer will pay taxes on the entire amount of the money or other property distributed, if treated as a dividend, or only on the amount of the gain (amount distributed – basis = gain) the taxpayer realizes on the transaction, if treated as a capital gain. Furthermore, the capital-gains rate of tax for this type of asset is generally 20 percent. In terms of the example above, this principle can be illustrated as follows:

If Mickey has a basis of $400 in each of his 300 shares of stock, and if he could effect a redemption of 10 shares that would qualify for treatment as a sale or exchange, he would pay tax on only the amount of his $6,000 gain ($600 per share x 10 shares). If, however, the redemption is treated as a dividend (as it inevitably would be in our example), the entire $10,000 distribution is taxable. Note that if the distribution is treated as a dividend, Mickey's basis in the 10 shares of redeemed stock is preserved by assigning it to his remaining 290 shares.

In addition, an individual's capital losses are fully deductible against capital gains but are deductible against ordinary income only up to $3,000 in a given year. Therefore in a situation in which an individual has capital losses (such as stock sales in a down market), the losses can "shelter" capital gains fully. However, an individual's capital losses cannot "shelter" dividend income, except to the extent of $3,000 per year.

Requirements for Favorable Federal Income Tax Treatment. Particularly as they get older, the shareholders of closely held businesses may wish to take some or all of their investment out of the corporation so that their lifetime accumulation of wealth will no longer be subject to the frailties and errors of new management—-even if the new management consists of their own children.

If shareholders are willing to sell their stock either to their children or to an outsider, the problems with redemptions are avoided. A redemption is defined by the Internal Revenue Code as the acquisition by a corporation of its stock from a shareholder in exchange for money or other property (excluding stock in the corporation) (IRC Sec. 317).

The purchase of a substantial interest in a business may be difficult for a younger family member to finance without altering his or her lifestyle even if payments are made over a period of years. Therefore redemptions are usually considered in business transition plans for family businesses.

The type of redemption attempted by Mickey in the preceding example is clearly an attempt to take the earnings and profits out of the corporation without treating them as dividends. As noted above, the Code requires that a corporation's purchase of its own stock will be treated as a dividend (to the extent of the earnings and profits of the corporation) (IRC Secs. 302(d), 301(c)). This general rule will apply unless the taxpayer can meet one of the exceptions in Sec. 302(b) that will guarantee capital-gains treatment.

The exceptions include the following:

- redemptions not essentially equivalent to a dividend (IRC Sec. 302(b)(1)). This is not a precise test but basically depends on whether there is a meaningful reduction of the shareholder's interest under all the facts and circumstances of the case. For this purpose the shareholder's constructive ownership under the attribution rules of IRC Sec. 318

(discussed below) will be considered. This is a very perilous exception on which to advise a client to rely.

- substantially disproportionate redemptions. A redemption qualifies for capital-gains treatment under this exception to the general rule provided that *immediately after the redemption* (a) the redeemed shareholder's proportion of ownership of both the outstanding *voting* stock and the *common* stock of the corporation must be less than 80 percent of his or her proportionate ownership before the redemption, and (b) the redeemed shareholder must own less than 50 percent of the total voting power of all classes of stock entitled to vote (IRC Sec. 302(b)(2)).

An example of a redemption that would qualify as substantially disproportionate is the following:

> X corporation has 100 shares of one class of voting common stock outstanding. A and B each own 50 of those shares. X redeems 20 of A's 50 shares. The corporation now has 80 shares of voting common stock outstanding, of which A owns 30 and B owns 50.
>
> A's proportion of ownership before the redemption was 50 percent (50 ÷ 100). Her proportion of ownership after the redemption is 37.5 percent (30 ÷ 80). Since 50 percent x 80 percent is 40 percent, and A now owns 37.5 percent, her proportion of ownership of voting and common stock after the redemption (37.5 percent) is less than 80 percent of her proportion of ownership before the redemption (40 percent). Since A also now owns less than 50 percent of the total voting power in the corporation, both the 80 percent and 50 percent tests are met and the redemption will qualify as substantially disproportionate.

- the redemption is a complete termination of a shareholder's interest (IRC Sec. 302(b)(3))

For corporations whose stockholders are not subject to the attribution rules of IRC Sec. 318, avoiding dividend treatment through the use of these exceptions is relatively straightforward. However, when the complexities of constructive ownership through these attribution rules are present, these rules can become quite difficult. Redemptions that qualify for capital-gains treatment can become virtually impossible to achieve in family-owned corporations.

Sec. 318 Attribution Problems. For purposes of determining the ownership of a corporation before and after a redemption, the redeemed stockholder is considered to own

- all the stock he or she actually owns
- all the stock the stockholder's spouse, children, grandchildren, or parents own
- stock owned by an estate or partnership of which the stockholder is a partner or beneficiary (in proportion to his or her interest in the partnership or estate)
- stock owned by a trust of which the stockholder is a beneficiary (in proportion to his or her actuarial interest in the trust)
- stock owned by another corporation in which the stockholder also owns directly or indirectly 50 percent or more of the outstanding stock (in proportion to his or her stock ownership in the other corporation)

The family and entity attribution rules are complex, and a full discussion of them would be more extensive than necessary for this financial plan. However, some time devoted to an explanation of the family attribution rules is important to Larry and Anne's situation.

When the family attribution rules of IRC Sec. 318(a)(1) are applied to the Millers' situation, the results show that Larry owns

directly	67%
constructively (Anne's)	23
constructively (Steve's)	10
Total ownership actually and constructively	100%

If Steve buys 40 percent of the stock from Larry, the result to Larry is unchanged. He then owns 27 percent of the stock directly, *but* he still owns Anne's 23 percent and Steve's 50 percent constructively under Sec. 318. The result is that Larry's ownership for purposes of the tax treatment of a redemption under Sec. 302 is still 100 percent.

Even if Larry sold all but one share of his stock to Steve, the results are unchanged in that Larry would then own

directly	.4%
constructively (Anne's)	23.0
constructively (Steve's)	76.6
Total ownership actually and constructively	100.0%

Because Larry will always be deemed to own the stock owned by his wife and son, he will not be able to effect a lifetime redemption that will enable him both to qualify for capital-gains treatment *and* to still remain active in the business. The significance of remaining active in the business will be addressed in the next section.

Sec. 302(c)(2) Election—The Waiver Approach. The difficulties in redeeming stock in a family-owned corporation without dividend treatment could force some shareholders into very difficult tax situations. Consequently the Internal Revenue Code allows a waiver of the family attribution rules of IRC Sec. 318, thereby allowing the redemption of a shareholder such as Larry to qualify as a complete termination of his interest (IRC Sec. 302(c)(2)).

In order to waive the attribution rules, the shareholder must dispose of all of his or her stock. However, there is no requirement that all the stock must be redeemed, and combinations of sales and redemptions are not unusual. In addition, immediately after the redemption the shareholder must have no continuing interest (including an interest as an officer, director, or employee) in the corporation except that of a creditor and must agree not to acquire an interest in the corporation (except by inheritance) within 10 years from the date of the redemption. Furthermore, the employee must file an agreement with the Internal Revenue Service requiring the taxpayer to notify the IRS if an interest is acquired within the prohibited period.

Even if these conditions are met, the redemption will not qualify for capital-gains treatment if

- any portion of the stock that is being redeemed was acquired within 10 years of the date of the redemption from a person whose ownership of the stock would be attributable to the person whose stock is being redeemed, or
- if any person whose stock would be attributable to the person whose stock is being redeemed has acquired that stock within a 10-year period directly or indirectly from the person whose stock is being redeemed, unless his or her stock is also redeemed

For example, a husband cannot have given a portion of his stock to his wife and have the corporation redeem the remainder of the stock he holds under a Sec. 302(c)(2) election (to receive capital-gains tax treatment) unless the gift took place more than 10 years prior to the redemption and Sec. 302(c)(2) election. Also he could not have been the recipient of a gift of Millers stock from his wife during that 10-year period.

Since Larry wishes to continue his involvement with Millers for the foreseeable future, it is unlikely that this election out (waiver approach) would appeal to him at present. As his involvement with Millers becomes less important to him, however, this type of a redemption may become viable.

Anne, on the other hand, could take advantage of this provision immediately to have her interest in Millers redeemed. This would be beneficial to Anne because she has a basis of $1,000 per share in Millers, which could be recovered tax free when the redemption proceeds are paid. In contrast, Larry's basis in his stock is $160.

If properly structured, the redemption does not have to drain the corporation of needed cash flow and can provide Anne and Larry with a steady income stream as well as an opportunity to spread the gain over a number of years. For example, Anne's shares could be surrendered and a Sec. 302(c)(2) election could be made in return for the corporation's obligation to pay the redemption price over a period of years at an appropriate interest rate. The interest should be deductible to the corporation. The principal payments, however, are not.

In conclusion, the recommendation would be that Anne's shares be redeemed with an appropriate Sec. 302(c)(2) election and that the corporation be allowed to spread payments by an installment payout, such as the 10-year installment payout illustrated in case IV. If the income picture of Millers requires a lower payment, the term of the obligation could be lengthened, thereby lowering the annual payment. As already noted, this redemption should be coordinated with the installment sale to Steve to allow him to acquire control of the business as a result of both transactions. Larry, on the other hand, can retain his shares until he is ready to retire completely from Millers.

If he continues to be involved with Millers until his death, Larry may wish to leave his remaining shares to Steve with provisions in his will stating that Steve's portion of Larry's residuary estate should be adjusted to reflect the bequest of the stock.

Sec. 303 Redemptions. An estate liquidity problem occurs when many shareholders of family-owned businesses continue to hold stock in their corporations until their death. IRC Sec. 303 provides a method for assuring that sufficient stock can be redeemed without dividend treatment to pay estate taxes and deductible funeral and administrative expenses if certain requirements are met. Redemption proceeds in excess of the estate's funeral and administrative expenses cannot be recovered under Sec. 303. The threshold test for utilizing a Sec. 303 redemption is that the value of the stock of the corporation owned by the decedent must exceed 35 percent of his or her adjusted gross estate for federal estate tax purposes.

Capital-gains treatment is particularly important in the case of a redemption from a decedent's estate, regardless of whether the redemption is treated under Sec. 302 or Sec. 303. Since the estate has received a stepped-up basis in the redeemed stock, capital-gains treatment will generally trigger little or no income tax liability for the estate. If dividend treatment applies, the estate loses the benefit of the stepped-up basis, since the proceeds will be fully taxed (assuming the corporation has sufficient earnings and profits).

Currently, Larry's shares are valued at $286,601 and his adjusted gross estate is assumed to be $1,507,946. Therefore the 35 percent test is not satisfactorily met.

In short, if Larry were to die with his present stock holdings, his estate would not qualify for a Sec. 303 redemption. Even if Larry's estate were to qualify today for Sec. 303 treatment, the planned sale of shares in Millers to

Steve would reduce the stock ownership amount below the 35 percent threshold level.

Since Larry has indicated a strong desire not to force Steve to wait until Larry's death to take control of Millers, planning at this time for a Sec. 303 redemption would not be appropriate in any event.

Recapitalizations

General Requirements. The Internal Revenue Code provides for tax-free treatment of various corporate reorganizations (IRC Sec. 368). One type of reorganization is an "E" reorganization—a "recapitalization" (IRC Sec. 368(a)(1)(E)). The Code does not define a recapitalization and the regulations offer no definition, but they do contain some examples of transactions that would qualify as recapitalizations. The most frequently quoted general definition is from a 1942 United States Supreme Court decision that described a recapitalization as "reshuffling of a capital structure within the framework of an existing corporation" (*Helvering v. Southwest Consolidated Corp.*, 315 U.S. 194 (1942)).

In the past a common type of "reshuffling" of capital was the exchange by older shareholders of all or a part of their common stock in the corporation for preferred stock. This technique was used for some or all of the following purposes: to transfer control to younger-generation management; to assure the older shareholder of an income stream from dividends on the preferred stock; or to attempt to freeze the value of the older shareholder's interest in the corporation for estate tax purposes.

In the typical recapitalization, all the shareholders were offered an opportunity pursuant to a plan of reorganization to exchange their shares of common stock for preferred stock. Normally the older shareholders elected the exchange, while the younger shareholders chose to retain their shares of common stock.

In a recapitalization if the value of the preferred stock received is equal to the value of the common stock surrendered, the transaction is generally tax free at the time of the transfer. If the value of the preferred is less than the common surrendered, the difference in value may be treated as a taxable gift to the other shareholders. To assure equivalency of value, the preferred shares must pay a reasonable dividend, dividends must be cumulative, and the preferred stock must have liquidation preferences. The question of valuation in recapitalizations has been one of the most troublesome issues in planning to recapitalize a corporation.

Restrictions on the Use of Recapitalizations and on Other Estate-Freezing Techniques. Prior changes in the federal tax laws dealt a severe blow to recapitalizations and other techniques intended to freeze the estate tax value of an older-generation owner's interest in a family business. These changes have been codified in IRC Secs. 2701-2704, sometimes referred to as the chapter 14 estate-freeze provisions.

In essence IRC Secs. 2701-2704 are gift tax provisions that set forth rules for placing a value on a stock interest or a partnership interest transferred by gift or by sale to a family member. The prohibitions that Sec. 2701 sets forth are stringent and limit the ability of a preferred stock recapitalization to freeze the value of the estate.

Specifically Sec. 2701 provides rules for determining (a) whether the transfer of an interest in a *controlled* corporation or partnership to (or for the benefit of, such as through a trust) a *member of the family* of the transferor is a completed gift for this purpose or (b) whether the transferor has retained some interest. If the transferor has retained any interest, and the rules of Sec. 2701 are not followed, the transferor will be deemed to make a gift of his or her entire interest in the property.

Sec. 2702 deals with transfers in trust and provides for the same type of prohibition with respect to transfers of interests to a member of the family in a controlled corporation or partnership.

The enactment of the chapter 14 estate-freeze rules has made effective use of a recapitalization of a closely held corporation to shift future appreciation to family members exceedingly difficult.

Private Annuity

A private annuity is a contract for a private individual (not a commercial annuity company) to pay the purchase price for an asset over the actuarial life of the seller. If the seller does not live to his or her actuarial life expectancy, the purchaser's obligation ceases, and there is nothing remaining of the obligation to include in the deceased seller's estate. If the seller lives longer than his or her actuarially determined life expectancy, the purchaser must pay the predetermined payments for the seller's actual life.

To avoid inclusion in the seller's income in the year of the sale, the transaction must not be secured; that is, it must be a naked promise to pay.

Payments to the seller are split into several components for tax purposes. First, a portion of each payment will represent a nontaxable return of the seller's basis. Second, a portion will typically be taxed as the sale or exchange of a capital asset. The seller will pay a capital-gains tax on the portion of each payment that represents gain from the sale of the property. Third, there will be ordinary income tax on any portion in excess of the sum of the seller's return of basis and capital-gain portions. For purposes of determining gain to the seller, the sale price for the asset transferred is the present value of the total amount of all annuity payments to be made over the seller's life expectancy.

There are some drawbacks to the private annuity arrangement. For example, the purchaser cannot deduct any part of the payment, including the portion taxed as ordinary income to the seller. In contrast, under an installment sale the interest portion of the payments may be deductible subject to the limitations already discussed.

The private annuity does not meet the Millers' needs because the termination of the payment obligation at Larry's death could severely deplete Larry's estate if he died prematurely, depriving Anne of income and resulting in a windfall to Steve. Steve, on the other hand, could not afford to purchase any significant amount of his father's stock without the benefit of the interest deduction.

Shareholder-Employee Compensation Planning

Reasonable Compensation for Shareholder-Employees

The issue of unreasonable compensation is generally raised only in closely held corporations where there is a strong identity of interest between the role of employee and stockholder or where a member of the employee's family is a stockholder. The Internal Revenue Service's position is that an arm's-length transaction setting the value of personal services and effectively eliminating the unreasonable compensation issue cannot exist in most closely held corporations. The closer the identity of interest between the corporation and the employee, the more vulnerable to IRS scrutiny compensation becomes. For example, the most vulnerable situation occurs between an employee and his or her wholly owned corporation. Because of the identity of interests, the issue of unreasonable compensation is also frequently raised in family-owned corporations.

If Steve's salary, for example, was substantially raised in order to provide him with funds to buy Larry's stock, Millers might be denied a deduction for a portion of Steve's salary that the IRS deemed to be unreasonable.

However, if Millers elects Subchapter S status as previously recommended, the unreasonable compensation issue will not be a problem as long as Larry is being paid a comparable salary based on actual services rendered.

Steve and Larry will be taxed directly on their proportionate shares of corporate taxable income if Millers makes an S election. Therefore payments to Steve will not be taxable as a dividend as long as the taxable income distributed is attributable to activity of the corporation.

Employment Contracts

Employment contracts between unrelated employees and employers are often used to reduce misunderstandings about the rights and responsibilities of each party. In the case of a shareholder-employee of a closely held corporation, employment agreements are often utilized not only to clarify the duties of the shareholder-employee but also to describe compensation arrangements in an effort to support the reasonableness of compensation. The first consideration is very important for the Millers in this business transition period.

Another benefit of employment contracts is their ability to minimize shareholder dissension, which may be especially important to Larry and Steve as they work at transferring the management of the store to Steve. They should fully and thoughtfully discuss which duties are the responsibility of each, and their agreements on these issues should be included in their employment agreements.

Employment contracts can run for any period of time, but care should be taken to treat the contract as if it were being entered into between an employee and an unrelated employer, that is, as an arm's-length transaction. For this reason contract periods are usually quite short, although some contain options to renew for an additional specified period. These renewals can even be tailored to occur automatically unless the employer gives appropriate and timely notice to the employee.

For the reasons indicated, employment contracts covering corporate duties and compensation agreements should be implemented for both Larry and Steve.

Consulting Contracts

Consulting contracts are specialized forms of employment contracts. As Larry begins to reduce his daily participation in Millers, consulting contracts should be implemented to demonstrate the decrease in his duties and the new compensation arrangements. Since the primary issues that would need to be dealt with (for example, exact duties as well as amounts and methods of payment) may not be ascertainable for several years, it is only necessary to note that these contracts should be drawn at an appropriate time.

Employee Benefits

Qualified Plans of Deferred Compensation

Since Larry has noted that he is displeased with the performance of the profit-sharing plan of Millers, now would be a good time to see if the qualified plan could be improved and its performance enhanced instead of being terminated.

Problems with Present Plans. The utilization of appropriate corporate qualified plans not only reduces shareholder-employees' present tax burden, it also allows them to accumulate earnings on a tax-deferred basis within the plan.

The tax-deferred accumulation within the plan can obviously allow assets to increase at a much more rapid rate than if taxes were currently payable. Amounts deferred in qualified plans are not taxable until they are distributed to the participant. If there is a proper balance between corporate cost and present benefits to the employees, qualified plans can be good employee motivators.

The current profit-sharing plan of Millers is unnecessarily restrictive with its provision for mandatory contributions when corporate profits reach a certain level.

General Requirements. There are basically two types of qualified plans: defined-contribution plans and defined-benefit plans. Defined-benefit pension plans promise the recipient a specific benefit within statutory limits at retirement age, and the funding necessary to provide that benefit for the actuarial life of the recipient is contributed by the employer. Defined-benefit plans usually work best for funding retirement benefits for older shareholder-employees when there is only a short time left to provide significant retirement benefits. These plans can be very expensive to the funding corporation, and most have the additional disadvantage of being subject to regulation by the Pension Benefit Guaranty Corporation. Since defined-benefit plans are "pension plans" under the Internal Revenue Code, contributions to the plan are mandatory once the plan is in place.

NOTE

To avoid repetition of background material on qualified plans, that material has been omitted from this chapter. If you are not familiar with this material, it should be reviewed prior to proceeding through this section of the suggested solution.

Defined-contribution plans set a contribution level that the employer contributes to the plan. The funds are invested over the employee's working life, and the benefits available at retirement consist of the contributions that have been made to the plan, plus forfeitures that have been added to the account, plus earnings on the account assets. Defined-contribution plans are generally preferable to defined-benefit plans for younger employees because the potential benefits are greater. The defined-contribution plans that small corporations most often utilize fall into two categories: profit-sharing plans and money-purchase pension plans.

Recommendations. There is not enough information in the facts of this case to determine whether the Millers' plans would be top-heavy. Many, if not most, small plans will be subject to the top-heavy rules. However, the fact that Millers employs 34 people indicates that the plan is probably not top-heavy. The qualified retirement plan presently in place has not been perceived as performing well, and the recommendation would be to amend the plan to allow for purely discretionary contributions, which could be made regardless of whether pretax profits reach $200,000 per year. In addition, the plan must immediately comply with the eligibility and vesting requirements of the Internal Revenue Code.

An appropriate vesting schedule might be 2-to-6-year vesting, which is an acceptable vesting schedule under the current tax laws if the plan is not top-heavy. The schedule is as follows:

Years of Service	Vested Percentage
2	20%
3	40
4	60
5	80
6 or more	100

The plan will also have to meet the minimum coverage requirements. A plan cannot discriminate in coverage or in the amount of contributions made. Several safe-harbor design strategies could be recommended. Also an alternative vesting schedule would have to be included in case the plan becomes top-heavy.

An integrated money-purchase pension plan could also be instituted. Plan integration with Social Security would allow a higher rate of contributions to be applied to compensation earned over specified levels. In effect it is a permitted form of discrimination that would skew plan contributions in favor of Larry Miller.

Since Larry has expressed satisfaction with his overall net worth, assuming it can provide liquidity for his retirement, this package of qualified plans is aimed at the younger employees (primarily Steve) and will benefit them most. The plans would not, however, exclude Larry, since qualified plans cannot exclude employees from participation based on age.

Nonqualified Deferred Compensation

Another important benefit that can be available to shareholder-employees of a closely held corporation on a discriminatory basis is a nonqualified deferred-compensation arrangement. These arrangements do not have to meet the funding, employee coverage, and other requirements necessary to satisfy the qualified plan definition under IRC Sec. 401(a), as ERISA exempts from almost all its requirements an unfunded arrangement maintained "primarily for the purpose of providing deferred compensation for a select group of management or highly compensated employees." (There are a few minor requirements, however, even for nonqualified deferred-compensation plans.)

While nonqualified plans of deferred compensation may involve compensation in the form of money or other property, many are salary continuation plans of various types.

Nonqualified salary continuation plans, for example, may provide significant disability or retirement income for shareholder-employees or death benefits for the spouse or beneficiaries of shareholder-employees. They may be particularly appropriate in the case of a corporation that wishes to provide such benefits to shareholder-employees but finds a qualified plan too costly because of ERISA requirements. Alternatively these plans may be used to provide benefits to shareholder-employees in addition to those allowable under qualified plans.

There are generally three fundamental hurdles in structuring a nonqualified deferred-compensation plan. The first is structuring the arrangement so that compensation is in fact deferred, thereby escaping immediate inclusion in the shareholder-employee's income. The second is the question of whether the deferred-compensation arrangement will be deductible to the employer corporation. The third is the question of whether an attempt should be made to structure the deferred-compensation plan to escape federal estate taxation at the employee's death.

Avoiding Immediate Inclusion in the Employee's Income. Initially the deferred amount must qualify as bona fide deferred compensation to escape immediate inclusion in the employee's income. The IRS can argue for inclusion in current income under either a constructive receipt or an economic benefit theory.

The concept of constructive receipt is explained by the Treasury Regulations as follows:

> Income although not actually reduced to a taxpayer's possession is constructively received by him in the taxable year in which it is credited to his account, set apart for him or otherwise made available so that he may draw upon it at any time, or so that he could have drawn upon it during the taxable year if notice of intention to withdraw had been given. However, income is not constructively received if the taxpayer's control of its receipt is subject to substantial limitations or restrictions. (Reg. 1.451-2(a)).

The economic benefit theory provides that if compensation is readily convertible into cash, it is not bona fide deferred compensation. The economic benefit theory has not generally been extended to tax the value of an employer's unsecured contractual obligation to pay deferred compensation. However, if the contractual obligation is (1) unconditional, (2) that of a solvent employer, (3) freely assignable or transferable or immediately convertible into cash, and (4) of a type frequently transferred to banks or investors at a discount not greater than the prevailing premium for the use of money, the IRS position for immediate inclusion in income has been upheld by the courts (*Cowden v. Comm'r, Watson, Jones Co., Steen, Evans,* Rev. Rul. 68-606). It appears that the addition of a clause in the deferred-compensation agreement that prohibits the assignment, transfer, or pledging of the agreement would be sufficient protection against the inclusion of deferred compensation in present income under the economic benefit theory. It would be prudent to include such a provision.

The best guidance for avoiding immediate taxation under nonqualified deferred-compensation plans is contained in Rev. Rul. 60-31, 1960-1 C.B. 174.

This revenue ruling sets forth the IRS position that when an employee receives an unfunded promise to pay an amount in the future, deferral of the promised amount will generally be allowed provided the amount of compensation to be delivered at a future date is not set apart in any type of special fund that would be protected from the employer's creditors.

Also deferred-compensation contracts or agreements entered into prior to performance of services appear to have the best chance to withstand IRS attack (Rev. Rul. 60-31, 1960-1 C.B. 174).

Prior to the issuance of Rev. Rul. 60-31 practitioners and commentators generally believed that the one safe way to keep an amount under a deferred-compensation contract from being currently taxable was to make the payment "subject to forfeiture." Forfeiture provisions often condition payment under a deferred-compensation arrangement on the employee's agreement to (1) work for the employer for a specified number of years or until retirement; (2) render advisory or consulting services after retirement at the request of the employee; (3) refrain from disclosing customer lists, trade secrets, or other information valuable to the employer's business; or (4) refrain from engaging in a competitive business as an owner, stockholder, partner, employee, or otherwise.

Although these forfeiture provisions may no longer be necessary to avoid current income taxation after Rev. Rul. 60-31, they often offer desirable protection for the employer for other business reasons and are therefore still found in many deferred-compensation arrangements. The maintenance of forfeiture provisions may again have taken on increased importance to prevent current withholding of income tax, FICA, and other employment taxes due to recent legislation that authorizes such withholding upon the lapse of the substantial risk of forfeiture to the employee.

Well-known private rulings issued by the IRS indicate that the employer may set aside funds in a so-called *rabbi trust* (PLR 8113107) without creating problems under the constructive receipt or economic benefit doctrines. Rabbi trusts can provide additional assurance to the participants that funds will be available to pay benefits actually promised by the plan.

Rabbi trusts are trusts established by the employer in which contributions are periodically made to finance the promised benefits. The trust can be irrevocable in favor of the plan participants except that trust assets must be subject to claims of the employer's creditors. The employee-beneficiary must be prohibited from transferring or assigning any part of his or her interest in the trust assets. If these conditions are met, the funds will not be includible in the employee's income until the employee actually receives them; that is, the plan will be treated as an unfunded plan for tax purposes. The trust itself will be taxed as a grantor trust, which means that the employer will be taxed on any income the trust generates.

The deductibility of payments by the employer falls within the general rules for nonqualified arrangements discussed below.

Deductibility by the Corporation. To be deductible all compensation paid to an employee, including deferred compensation, must be reasonable and in fact paid purely for services (Treas. Reg. Sec. 1.162-7; Treas. Reg. Sec. 1.162-9). In determining reasonableness of compensation, the entire amount of compensation, present and deferred, is examined. Although the courts have enumerated factors that are important in making a determination on the issue of reasonableness, no single factor appears decisive since each situation must be considered as a whole (*Mayson Mfg. Co. v. Comm'r*).

If a deferred-compensation agreement is reasonable and is intended to provide only retirement or disability benefits to the employee, generally the corporation is entitled to a deduction for a deferred-compensation payment in the year in which the payment is made (Treas. Reg. Sec. 1.404(a)-12).

If the employer is legally obligated to pay an employee's estate or specified beneficiaries under a death-benefit-only plan, the benefits paid to the surviving spouse or beneficiary will generally be deductible by the corporation in the year paid (Treas. Reg. Sec. 1.404(a)-12).

The deductibility of a death benefit payment to a surviving spouse or beneficiary may be called into question when the survivor is a shareholder in a closely held corporation. If, in fact, the employee has been adequately compensated during his or her lifetime and the corporation will be controlled by the surviving spouse or other members of the deceased's family, extreme care should be taken to enter into an agreement with the corporation at the earliest possible date. The contract must emphasize that certain payments that will be made to a surviving spouse or other beneficiary are deferred compensation to the employee.

Avoiding the Imposition of Federal Estate Tax. In order to escape the inclusion of the benefits of a salary continuation plan in the deceased employee's estate, it must be a death-benefit-only plan. If exclusion is not a primary concern, the plan can also provide for benefits to be paid to the employee upon retirement or disability. Such a nonqualified retirement or disability agreement can provide substantial amounts of income during retirement or prolonged disability in addition to providing income to a surviving spouse after the employee's death. The tax price paid for this increased security is that the remaining value of the survivor's interest is included in the estate of the deceased employee and is subject to estate tax (IRC Sec. 2039(a)).

Even if the plan is a death-benefit-only plan, the proceeds are not automatically excluded from estate taxation. This area involves some complexity. IRC Sec. 2039(a) requires that the value of any annuity or other payment (other than from a qualified plan) receivable by a decedent as the result of a contract or agreement be included in calculating the decedent's gross estate if the decedent had the right to receive such annuity or other payment in any of the following situations:

- for life
- for a period not ascertainable without reference to the decedent's death

- for a period that does not, in fact, end before the decedent's death

An annuity or other payment is not restricted to commercial annuity payments but includes any annuity or other payment that, according to the regulations, may be equal or unequal, conditional or unconditional, periodic or sporadic, and that may be one or more payments extending over any period of time (Treas. Reg. Sec. 20.2039-1(b)(1)).

In order for the proceeds of a death-benefit-only deferred-compensation plan to be included under Sec. 2039(a), the annuity or other payment must have been "payable to the decedent"; that is, the decedent must have been receiving payments at death, or the decedent must have possessed the right to receive such payment or annuity. In other words, inclusion in the employee's estate results if the employee possessed an enforceable right to receive payments at some time in the future, regardless of whether he or she was receiving payments at the time of death (Treas. Reg. Sec. 20.2039-1 (b)(1); *Estate of Bahen*).

The inclusion of plan proceeds in an employee's estate may not be such a poor result, considering that it will generate an income stream during retirement. Furthermore, if the intended beneficiary is the employee's spouse, the proceeds may qualify for the marital deduction.

Note that even if a death-benefit-only plan is selected, other nonqualified plans (such as disability plans) will all be viewed together when determining whether the tests for includibility under Sec. 2039 are met (Reg. Sec. 20.2039-2). Benefits receivable under qualified plans of deferred compensation will not be included in determining whether the employee had the right to an annuity or other payment that meets the other criteria of Sec. 2039(a) and that would require inclusion of a death-benefit-only plan in the employee's gross estate (Rev. Rul. 76-380, 1976-2 C.B. 270).

Since Larry is concerned about providing Anne with a good income stream for her life, a death-benefit-only plan could be implemented to continue some portion of his salary to her for 5 to 7 years. Funding for this purpose could come from the insurance the corporation has on his life.

In this area care should be taken to enlist a competent attorney to draft documents to implement these plans.

BUSINESS PLANNING: INSURANCE

Medical Insurance Plans

Since the present medical insurance plan provides Millers employees with excellent benefits, no improvements appear necessary.

Disability Income Plans

As already noted, no disability income plan exists for Millers employees. It is questionable whether many of the rank-and-file employees would benefit materially from a long-term disability plan because of their modest average salaries. Most of the employees would probably have their disability benefits either eliminated or substantially reduced because of coordination with Social Security.

Disability income protection for Larry and Steve is a different matter entirely. The installment sale to Steve would provide income to Larry regardless of disability. In addition, a nonqualified deferred-compensation plan could continue Larry's salary if he became disabled before leaving Millers. As discussed in the section on nonqualified deferred compensation, a disability plan of this type would almost certainly cause inclusion of the death-benefit-only plan in Larry's estate. However, Steve should obtain the maximum amount of long-term disability income coverage that insurers are willing to underwrite. Since the S election will prevent tax-favored coverage through the corporation, Steve should obtain personal coverage. Any benefits paid are not subject to income tax. If Steve becomes disabled, he will need additional financial protection to complete the payments for the purchase of Larry's stock.

Life Insurance Plans

The group insurance coverages of Millers are characterized by an extreme dichotomy—a very comprehensive medical expense plan and an obvious lack of anything else. In reviewing an employee benefit plan it is necessary to understand the objectives of a firm in providing employee benefits. Is it primarily to meet the needs of the employees or to meet the needs of the owners? The latter tends to be particularly true for many small firms such as Millers.

If the employees' needs are of concern, the lack of a group life insurance plan is conspicuous. Most firms of this size with a relatively stable employment would provide some coverage, even if only a modest flat amount per employee, such as $5,000 or $10,000. In fact, with salespeople who are often paid on a commission basis, a flat amount of coverage may be appropriate. Salespeople could be provided with a level amount of insurance that is roughly equivalent to that provided to salaried personnel.

Millers should consider a group life insurance policy for its employees with coverage based on a multiple of salary. The multiple would depend on the corporation's ability and willingness to pay premiums. It is common for these plans to provide between one and two times salary for salaried employees.

It is important to remember that Larry and Steve would have to include the value of this coverage in their gross incomes after an S election is made because of their stock ownership.

Larry has over $1 million in separately owned assets, but only about $100,000 of this is in liquid assets. This liquidity and his present insurance coverage are currently adequate to cover the estate taxes and administrative costs at Larry's death. As long as Larry remains active in the corporation, group life insurance for him would provide additional contingency protection. Group coverage may be less expensive than individual coverage even though Larry cannot participate in a group plan on a tax-advantaged basis. The coverage could be assigned to an irrevocable life insurance trust to avoid inclusion of the proceeds in his estate. Group life coverage on Steve could help pay off the installment contract in case Steve predeceases Larry.

Although Steve is not currently a planning client, some planning for Steve is important to Larry and Anne because of the possibility that Steve could die or become disabled before the installment sale is fully paid for. If this happens, the security of Larry and Anne's retirement could be in peril because of Steve's inability to meet his obligations under the installment sale contract.

In addition, the corporation should consider a key person life insurance policy to cover Steve. Millers would be both owner and beneficiary of the policy. If Steve should die, especially after Larry has substantially withdrawn from Millers, the corporation will almost certainly have to hire someone else to replace Steve in order to keep the corporation viable. The corporation may also need to redeem Steve's shares in the corporation if he predeceases Larry. Planning for this redemption should be carefully considered and coordinated between Millers and Steve (and his family's personal objectives) to assure that Steve's estate will be able to qualify for exemption from the family attribution rules and to achieve capital-gains treatment.

The $200,000 policy owned by Millers insuring Larry can be left in place to provide funding for a salary continuation death-benefit-only plan or to fund the survivorship benefit portion to Anne of any salary continuation plan for Larry by the corporation. If necessary, Millers can always fall back on the cash value of the life insurance to help make the installment sale payments to Anne for the redemption of her stock.

Property and Liability Coverage for the Business— Fundamental Requirements

In analyzing the property and liability needs of a business, it is important to realize that the needs of businesses are much less uniform than those of individuals, and more flexibility is needed in designing their insurance coverages than in designing those of an average homeowner.

In general loss exposures of a business can be divided into four categories:

- damage to or destruction of property
- loss of possession of property
- loss of income or the imposition of extraordinary expenses
- liability for payment of damages to others

The first category is self-explanatory and includes loss or damage by fire, wind, flood, and many other perils. The second category includes loss of possessions resulting from criminal activities of others, including employee dishonesty. The third category includes such items as lost profits and additional expenses following the damage or destruction of business property. The last category includes obligations to reimburse others for legal injuries for which a business is liable.

Historically many separate policies had to be purchased to meet all a business's needs. However, in recent years package policies have been made available to most businesses so that these needs can be met with a minimum number of insurance contracts. It has also become common in situations like the one in this case (when the owner of a business also owns the real estate rented by the business) to insure the building and the business under a single package policy, with the owner of the building and the owner of the business both being named as insureds as their interests may appear.

Most of the needs of Millers (and Larry's needs for property and liability insurance on the building rented by Millers) can be met under a business owner's policy for small and medium-sized businesses. The business owner's policy is standardized and is designed for small businesses that have little need for flexibility in insurance coverages. Based on the information in the case, Millers has no unusual insurance exposures with regard to property and liability insurance and would be well suited for this contract.

The business owner's policy can now include coverage for automobiles. However, a separate workers' compensation policy will be necessary since this coverage is not included. In addition, the Millers may decide that a commercial excess-liability policy is needed to supplement the liability coverages available under the business owner's policy.

The typical business owner's policy (some variations exist among insurers) provides the following basic coverages, with the insured selecting the amount of insurance for each coverage:

- buildings. All buildings on the premises are covered on a replacement-cost basis. No coinsurance applies, but the amount of insurance must usually be equal to the full replacement cost of the property. The amount of insurance increases quarterly with inflation. Buildings can be insured on either a named-peril or an open-peril basis, with the latter providing broader protection at a slightly increased cost.

- business personal property. This is also on a replacement-cost basis without coinsurance. In addition to inventory and office equipment, it also covers tenants' improvements. There is limited coverage ($1,000) for goods away from the insured premises, such as those being delivered on the company's trucks. Additional coverage can be added if this exposure is significantly greater. Coverage also exists for the property of others in the care, custody, or control of the insured if the insured is legally liable. This coverage, for example, would cover the liability of Millers for damage to furniture that was being repaired or reupholstered for customers. One concern of a business such as Millers is to see that proper insurance is maintained on inventory that fluctuates in value. As long as the amount of insurance carried is equal to at least 100 percent of the average inventory during the 12 months prior to the loss, the amount of insurance can be increased automatically by up to 25 percent to cover peak season values.

- loss of income. Coverage for lost profits, continuing expenses, and extra expenses is provided for up to 12 months if a business suffers a loss resulting from an insured peril.
- optional property coverages. Numerous endorsements are available that provide coverage for many types of property and liability situations not adequately covered under other sections of the policy. These include employee dishonesty, plate glass, outdoor signs, earthquake, and boiler and machinery coverage.
- business liability. Coverage of up to $1 million is available for liability arising from the premises and operations. Personal injury coverage (for example, libel, slander, false arrest) is also provided.

PERSONAL PLANNING: TAXES

Present Position

Larry and Anne appear to have achieved a good deal of success in their lives both financially and personally. They have created a successful business that has provided the means for them to enjoy a comfortable lifestyle both in the past and, through proper planning, in future years. Their children are all grown and seem to have found careers in which they are content.

The primary objectives to be dealt with in Larry and Anne's personal plan are that they are able to be secure during their retirement and that Anne is well provided for as long as she lives should Larry predecease her.

Assuring Larry's Comfortable Retirement and Continuing Involvement with Millers

Most of the techniques for assuring that Larry and Anne will be guaranteed a comfortable retirement income have been discussed at length in the business plan. These techniques include (1) the installment sale of 72 shares of Millers stock to Steve for an installment obligation with a term of 15 years, (2) the redemption of Anne's Millers stock for an installment obligation with a term of 10 years, and (3) the possible later redemption of Larry's remaining Millers stock if future circumstances warrant.

Steve's installment obligation will add approximately $28,340 per year to Larry and Anne's cash flow for a 15-year period. If the corporation redeems Anne's stock with a 10-year note at 9 percent, another $28,400 will be added to the Millers' cash flow for 10 years. However, if a 10-year note places too heavy a cash drain on Millers, a longer-term obligation would still provide the Millers with substantial cash payments well into their retirement years. In addition, there will also be retirement income available from the qualified plan. Since Larry is very concerned about providing income to Anne should he predecease her, he might consider electing a term certain or a joint and survivor annuity as the method of payment for benefits from the defined-contribution plan.

Dispositions at Death

Analysis of Present Plans

The Millers' present estate plan, in which each leaves everything to a surviving spouse and then to living children or children of a deceased child, per stirpes, may have been perfectly adequate 16 years ago when it was implemented. Since the Millers have acquired a substantial amount of additional assets, however, their present plan is unnecessarily expensive in terms of estate tax liabilities. This fact remains true despite the current availability of the unlimited marital deduction, because their current wills could result in all the assets of both Larry and Anne being taxed in her estate at marginal rates of up to 50 percent (in 2002 under the changes set forth in EGTRRA 2001). Larry's unified credit is wasted. In cases like this when the surviving spouse has substantial assets (and especially considering the fact that an outright inheritance from her mother could materially increase her taxable estate), an estate plan that uses only the unlimited marital deduction is not indicated.

Although Larry has expressed his desire that any assets Anne does not consume during her lifetime be divided equally among their three children, the present estate plan contains no provision for assuring this result.

In addition, the present placement of Larry and Anne's personal insurance results in the inclusion of the proceeds in their estates for estate tax purposes.

Possible Improvements in Estate Plan

Because Anne already owns significant assets, it is not advisable to add to her taxable estate unnecessarily. This can be avoided by structuring an estate plan to make the bulk of Larry's assets available to Anne but to shield them from federal estate taxation at the time of her subsequent death. The fact that she is the potential beneficiary of a significant sum from her mother somewhat complicates the issue of the exact amount. It does not, however, alter the fact that at least an amount sufficient to allow Larry to utilize his unified credit should be left in a trust that will not be taxed again at Anne's death.

The issue of whether to utilize a marital trust or to leave the marital deduction property to Anne outright is one that should be decided between Larry and Anne.

The marital portion of the bequest can be left in a trust and can still qualify for the marital deduction provided that the trust is required to pay all the income from the trust to the wife in annual or more frequent payments. The wife may be given a general power of appointment (the power to appoint the property to herself, her estate, her creditors, creditors of her estate, and any other appointee) exercisable either during her life or by specific reference to the power in her will, or both. In other words, the wife can either be allowed to appoint property as she sees fit to herself or others during her lifetime, or she can be effectively restricted from withdrawing the principal of the marital trust until the time of her death by the use of a testamentary power alone. Alternatively a trust that pays all the income to the spouse annually or more frequently but provides for no power of appointment for the spouse qualifies for the marital deduction if the executor of the estate elects to treat the trust as qualified terminable interest property (a QTIP trust). Typically a QTIP trust will contain provisions governing the disposition of the property after the death of the surviving spouse. Many spouses, however, object to having all or most of their inheritance tied up in trusts, as they feel they must deal continuously with bank trust officers who may be less than sympathetic to their wishes.

The use of a marital trust does not seem indicated in this case, especially when considered in light of Anne's investment experience. However, if such a trust is used, there are some assets, primarily the principal residence, that should not be included in the marital trust. The management of a residence by a trustee may present practical administrative problems. For these reasons it may be advisable to convey the house as a separate item in the will, and such a bequest should be an outright bequest of all the decedent's interest to the spouse.

Concept of Estate Equalization

Some planners recommend that in addition to the utilization of the unified credit, an estate plan for clients such as the Millers should provide for the payment of some federal estate tax when the first spouse dies, instead of a complete deferral of estate tax liability to the surviving spouse's estate. This is accomplished by intentionally failing to fully use the federal estate tax marital deduction with respect to the taxable estate in excess of the applicable credit exemption equivalent ($1 million in 2002–2003) in order to achieve estate equalization. The potential benefit of estate equalization is a lower estate tax bracket applied to the portion of the estate that would otherwise be taxed in a higher estate tax bracket if the property passed to the surviving spouse under the marital deduction and thus increased the surviving spouse's estate. "Splitting" or "equalizing" the spouses' taxable estates can cause lower estate tax brackets to be utilized in each estate instead of only in the surviving spouse's estate.

This technique may be desirable for older clients and may in fact result in a tax savings if both spouses die within a relatively short time of one another.

One problem with the equalization approach is the applicability of the time-value-of-money concept. The surviving spouse and the other family members lose the use of the money paid out for the "prepaid" estate tax. If the surviving spouse lives for many years, the future value of the tax paid may be greater than the higher tax that would be payable later if the equalization approach had not been used.

Another drawback of equalization is that the surviving spouse can employ other and sometimes better planning devices, such as gifts, to reduce his or her taxable estate after the first spouse's death, which in turn will reduce the ultimate tax liability.

A third drawback is that clients generally prefer to defer taxes when possible. When both spouses are in good health, it usually does not make sense to them to "prepay" federal estate taxes.

It should also be borne in mind that there is always the danger that the surviving spouse might dispose of these inherited assets in a manner not intended by the deceased spouse.

For these reasons it is recommended that the equalization approach not be used for the Millers. The assets in excess of the applicable credit amount of the first spouse to die should pass to the surviving spouse under the marital deduction.

Recommendations

Our recommendations for Larry's estate plan would be an outright bequest of the cars and the residence to Anne, an outright bequest of a marital portion equal to the excess of Larry's taxable estate over the applicable credit exemption equivalent, and an applicable credit shelter residuary trust of which Anne is the primary beneficiary for her life. Anne could be the sole beneficiary of the residuary trust; however, it might be more prudent to allow the trustee to invade the trust for the benefit of Larry and Anne's children and grandchildren for specified purposes, such as education or catastrophic medical expenses. In some states, however, such as Pennsylvania, this provision may cause increased exposure to inheritance tax. Since Anne has assets of her own and stands to inherit substantial assets from her mother, her estate plan should take the same approach (except for the specific bequests).

Whichever form the trust takes, the trustee should be empowered to pay income and to invade the corpus of the trust as necessary for Anne's benefit. If an independent trustee is used, the trustee can be instructed to pay income and invade the corpus for her comfort and happiness.

At Anne's death the trust will terminate, and the principal remaining in the trust will be divided equally among their three children, if living. If a child has died but leaves living children, the will should be designed so that the child's portion goes to his or her living children, per stirpes. If the child leaves no living children, the assets will be shared among Larry and Anne's remaining children.

The following computer illustrations show a comparison of the Millers' present estate plans with the proposed arrangement. The illustrations assume administration and funeral expenses of 7 percent of the gross estate. It is also assumed that Larry dies in 2002 before the sale of shares in Millers is finalized, and Anne dies shortly thereafter. Assets are based on the clients' current situation and are assumed to appreciate at 5 percent annually (except for the note receivable from Doug).

[text continues on page 6.86]

COMPREHENSIVE ESTATE TAX REPORT

LARRY & ANNE MILLER
CURRENT ESTATE

Date: Dec 31, 2002 Under Present Will	LARRY Predeceasing ANNE		ANNE Predeceasing LARRY	
	LARRY's Estate	ANNE's Estate	ANNE's Estate	LARRY's Estate
Individually Held Assets	1,807,923	565,198	565,198	1,807,923
Share from Joint Assets	1,484	2,969	1,484	2,969
Life Insurance Proceeds	93,500	10,000	5,281	103,500
Assets Received from Spouse	0	1,398,394	0	493,797
Gross Estate	1,902,907	1,976,561	571,963	2,408,189
Administration Expenses	131,182	142,576	41,084	167,090
Adjusted Gross Estate	1,771,725	1,833,985	530,879	2,241,099
Marital Deduction	1,398,394	0	493,797	0
Taxable Estate	373,331	1,833,985	37,082	2,241,099
Total Taxable Amount	373,331	1,833,985	37,082	2,241,099
Fed Tax Before Credit	112,733	706,093	7,558	898,939
Unified Tax Credit	112,733	345,800	7,558	345,800
Net Federal Estate Tax	0	360,293	0	553,139
Net Federal + State Tax	0	360,293	0	553,139
Combined Tax		360,293		553,139

ESTATE ANALYSIS
ASSET DISTRIBUTION

LARRY & ANNE MILLER
CURRENT ESTATE

Date: Dec 31, 2002 Under Present Will	LARRY Predeceasing ANNE		ANNE Predeceasing LARRY	
	LARRY's Estate	**ANNE's Estate**	**ANNE's Estate**	**LARRY's Estate**
Liquid Assets	889,560	1,073,061	304,683	1,163,159
Non-liquid Assets	1,013,347	903,500	261,999	1,245,030
Total Assets	1,902,907	1,976,561	566,682	2,408,189
Passing to Spouse	1,399,879	0	495,282	0
Passing to Trust/Heirs	371,846	1,473,692	30,316	1,687,960
Estate Shrinkage	131,182	502,869	41,084	720,229

ESTATE ANALYSIS
LIQUIDITY SITUATION

LARRY & ANNE MILLER
CURRENT ESTATE

Date: Dec 31, 2002 Under Present Will	LARRY Predeceasing ANNE		ANNE Predeceasing LARRY	
	LARRY's Estate	ANNE's Estate	ANNE's Estate	LARRY's Estate
Debt	0	0	0	0
Administration Expenses	131,182	142,576	41,084	167,090
Estate Taxes	0	360,293	0	553,139
Charitable Contributions	0	0	0	0
Need for Liquid Capital	131,182	502,869	41,084	720,229
Liquid Capital Available	889,560	1,073,061	304,683	1,163,159
Addt'l Liquidity Needed	0	0	0	0

ESTATE ANALYSIS
MARITAL DEDUCTION

LARRY & ANNE MILLER
CURRENT ESTATE

Date: Dec 31, 2002 Under Present Will	LARRY Predeceasing ANNE	ANNE Predeceasing LARRY
Marital Deduction is-- Best Deduction Amount Your Amount Exceeds by Resulting Additional Cost	Overqualified $641,311 $757,083 $308,350	Overqualified $1,485 $492,312 $251,543
Total Family Assets	$2,479,590	$2,484,871
Joint Estate Taxes	$360,293 14.53%	$553,139 22.26%
Total Shrinkage	$634,051 25.57%	$761,313 30.64%
Remaining for Heirs	$1,845,539 74.43%	$1,723,558 69.36%

ESTATE DISTRIBUTION FLOWCHART
(LARRY Predeceasing ANNE on Dec 31, 2002)

The MILLERs

Present Will LARRY

CURRENT ESTATE

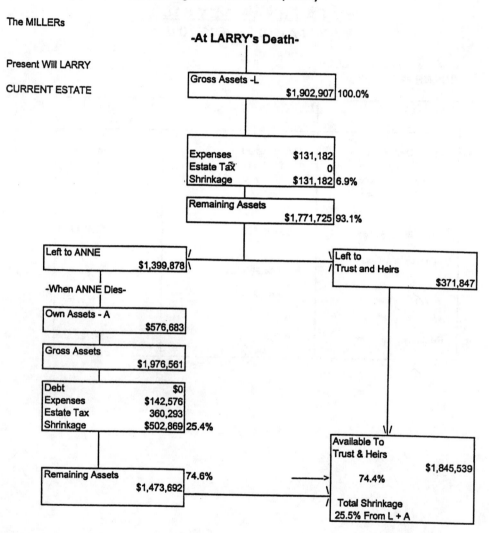

-At LARRY's Death-

Gross Assets -L		
	$1,902,907	100.0%

Expenses	$131,182	
Estate Tax	0	
Shrinkage	$131,182	6.9%

Remaining Assets		
	$1,771,725	93.1%

Left to ANNE	
	$1,399,878

Left to Trust and Heirs	
	$371,847

-When ANNE Dies-

Own Assets - A	
	$576,683

Gross Assets	
	$1,976,561

Debt	$0	
Expenses	$142,576	
Estate Tax	360,293	
Shrinkage	$502,869	25.4%

Remaining Assets	74.6%
$1,473,692	

Available To Trust & Heirs	$1,845,539
74.4%	
Total Shrinkage 25.5% From L + A	

ESTATE DISTRIBUTION FLOWCHART
(ANNE Predeceasing LARRY on Dec 31, 2002)

The MILLERs

Present Will LARRY

CURRENT ESTATE

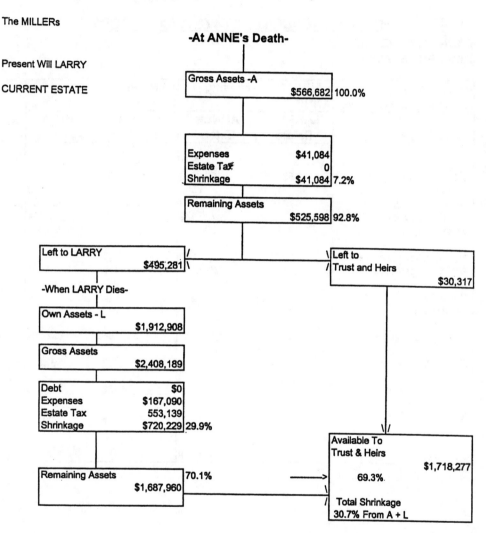

-At ANNE's Death-

Gross Assets -A		
	$566,682	100.0%

Expenses	$41,084	
Estate Tax	0	
Shrinkage	$41,084	7.2%

| Remaining Assets | | |
| | $525,598 | 92.8% |

| Left to LARRY | | | Left to Trust and Heirs |
| $495,281 | | | $30,317 |

-When LARRY Dies-

| Own Assets - L | |
| $1,912,908 | |

| Gross Assets | |
| $2,408,189 | |

Debt	$0
Expenses	$167,090
Estate Tax	553,139
Shrinkage	$720,229	29.9%

| Remaining Assets | 70.1% |
| $1,687,960 | |

Available To Trust & Heirs	$1,718,277
69.3%	
Total Shrinkage 30.7% From A + L	

COMPREHENSIVE ESTATE TAX REPORT

LARRY & ANNE MILLER
REVISED ESTATE

Date: Dec 31, 2002 Maximized Unified Credit Will	LARRY Predeceasing ANNE		ANNE Predeceasing LARRY	
	LARRY's Estate	ANNE's Estate	ANNE's Estate	LARRY's Estate
Individually Held Assets	1,827,267	593,318	593,318	1,827,267
Share from Joint Assets	1,519	3,039	1,519	3,039
Life Insurance Proceeds	93,500	10,000	5,704	103,500
Assets Received from Spouse	0	788,179	0	1,504
Gross Estate	1,922,286	1,394,536	600,541	1,935,310
Administration Expenses	132,587	100,379	43,126	132,806
Adjusted Gross Estate	1,789,699	1,294,157	557,415	1,802,504
Marital Deduction	789,699	0	1,519	0
Taxable Estate	1,000,000	1,294,157	555,896	1,802,504
Total Taxable Amount	1,000,000	1,294,157	555,896	1,802,504
Fed Tax Before Credit	345,800	467,288	176,482	691,927
Unified Tax Credit	345,800	345,800	176,482	345,800
Net Federal Estate Tax	0	121,488	0	346,127
Net Federal + State Tax	0	121,488	0	346,127
Combined Tax		121,488		346,127

ESTATE ANALYSIS
ASSET DISTRIBUTION

LARRY & ANNE MILLER
REVISED ESTATE

Date: Dec 31, 2002 Maximized Unified Credit Will	LARRY Predeceasing ANNE		ANNE Predeceasing LARRY	
	LARRY's Estate	**ANNE's Estate**	**ANNE's Estate**	**LARRY's Estate**
Liquid Assets	973,594	1,119,577	319,878	985,858
Non-liquid Assets	948,692	274,959	274,959	949,452
Total Assets	1,922,286	1,394,536	594,837	1,935,310
Passing to Spouse	789,699	0	3,024	0
Passing to Trust/Heirs	1,000,000	1,172,669	548,687	1,456,377
Estate Shrinkage	132,587	221,867	43,126	478,933

ESTATE ANALYSIS
LIQUIDITY SITUATION

LARRY & ANNE MILLER
REVISED ESTATE

Date: Dec 31, 2002 Maximized Unified Credit Will	LARRY Predeceasing ANNE		ANNE Predeceasing LARRY	
	LARRY's Estate	ANNE's Estate	ANNE's Estate	LARRY's Estate
Debt	0	0	0	0
Administration Expenses	132,587	100,379	43,126	132,806
Estate Taxes	0	121,488	0	346,127
Charitable Contributions	0	0	0	0
Need for Liquid Capital	132,587	221,867	43,126	478,933
Liquid Capital Available	973,594	1,119,577	319,878	985,858
Addt'l Liquidity Needed	0	0	0	0

ESTATE ANALYSIS
MARITAL DEDUCTION

LARRY & ANNE MILLER
REVISED ESTATE

Date: Dec 31, 2002 Maximized Unified Credit Will	**LARRY Predeceasing ANNE**	**ANNE Predeceasing LARRY**
Marital Deduction is—	Formula Clause	Overqualified
Best Deduction Amount	$637,088	$1,520
Your Amount Exceeds by	$152,611	$0
Resulting Additional Cost	$7,411	$737
Total Family Assets	$2,527,124	$2,532,828
Joint Estate Taxes	$121,488	$346,127
	4.81%	13.67%
Total Shrinkage	$354,454	$522,059
	14.03%	20.61%
Remaining for Heirs	$2,172,670	$2,010,769
	85.97%	79.39%

ESTATE DISTRIBUTION FLOWCHART
(LARRY Predeceasing ANNE on Dec 31, 2002)

The MILLERs

Dec 31,

REVISED ESTATE

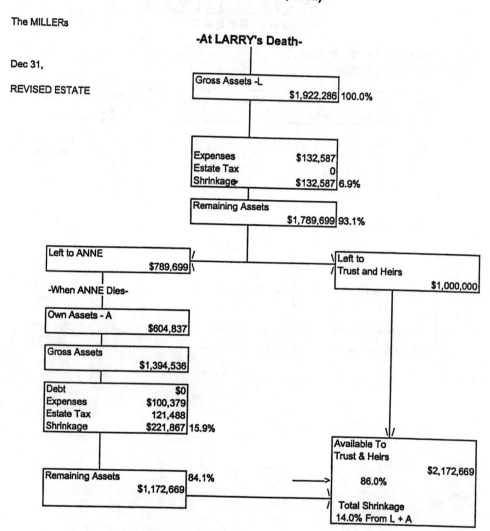

-At LARRY's Death-

Gross Assets -L		
	$1,922,286	100.0%

Expenses	$132,587	
Estate Tax	0	
Shrinkage	$132,587	6.9%

| Remaining Assets | | |
| | $1,789,699 | 93.1% |

| Left to ANNE | | | Left to Trust and Heirs | |
| $789,699 | | | | $1,000,000 |

-When ANNE Dies-

| Own Assets - A | |
| | $604,837 |

| Gross Assets | |
| | $1,394,536 |

Debt	$0	
Expenses	$100,379	
Estate Tax	121,488	
Shrinkage	$221,867	15.9%

Available To Trust & Heirs	
86.0%	$2,172,669
Total Shrinkage 14.0% From L + A	

| Remaining Assets | 84.1% |
| $1,172,669 | |

ESTATE DISTRIBUTION FLOWCHART
(ANNE Predeceasing LARRY on Dec 31, 2002)

The MILLERs

Dec 31,

REVISED ESTATE

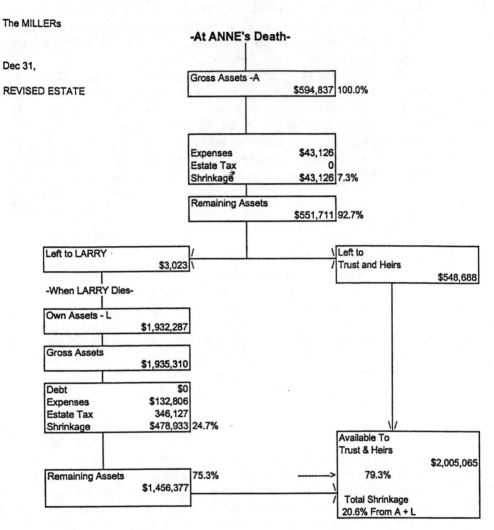

-At ANNE's Death-

| Gross Assets -A | $594,837 | 100.0% |

Expenses	$43,126
Estate Tax	0
Shrinkage	$43,126	7.3%

| Remaining Assets | $551,711 | 92.7% |

| Left to LARRY | $3,023 |

-When LARRY Dies-

| Own Assets - L | $1,932,287 |

| Gross Assets | $1,935,310 |

Debt	$0
Expenses	$132,806
Estate Tax	346,127
Shrinkage	$478,933	24.7%

| Remaining Assets | $1,456,377 | 75.3% |

| Left to Trust and Heirs | $548,688 |

| Available To Trust & Heirs | $2,005,065 |
| | 79.3% |
| Total Shrinkage 20.6% From A + L |

Life Insurance Placement

General Discussion. At present Larry has $93,500 in personal life insurance death benefits. The most significant problem with this coverage is that Larry is the owner of each of the policies, so the proceeds will be includible in his estate for estate tax purposes at his death (IRC Sec. 2042(2)) and ultimately will increase Anne's estate if Larry dies first.

The positioning of the insurance policies is very important and may become more so if Larry's estate grows, since inclusion of life insurance proceeds in his taxable estate will result in unnecessary additional estate tax liabilities. Also in order to achieve maximum economy with life insurance proceeds, each dollar should be available to meet several financial needs or contingencies should the occasion arise. These objectives can be achieved by the utilization of an irrevocable life insurance trust to own and be the beneficiary of the life insurance coverage. The terms of the trust instrument can control the distribution of the proceeds. This is a much more flexible arrangement than the use of individual beneficiary designations.

Structuring the Irrevocable Life Insurance Trust. In the usual case the terms of the irrevocable life insurance trust are tailored much like those in the residuary (nonmarital) trust under the client's will. Although this type of design is not required, we would recommend it in this case, since this would make the entire amount of the insurance proceeds available to Anne until her death.

An additional provision that is often advantageous in life insurance trusts is a provision that allows but does not require the trustee to loan money to the estate of the deceased or the deceased's spouse or to purchase assets from the estate of the deceased or the deceased's spouse. This can provide the estate with needed liquidity. However, the trust instrument cannot require loans or purchases. The Internal Revenue Service has construed loan or purchase requirements as making the proceeds available to the executor for the use of the estate and has included them in the estate tax valuation of the decedent's gross estate, defeating the purpose of the insurance trust. That purpose is to protect the insurance proceeds from estate taxation (Reg. Sec. 20.2042-1(b)(1)). When the recommended design is implemented, the insurance proceeds are protected from estate taxation in both spouses' estates. In addition, as a general rule, the proceeds of life insurance in a life insurance trust are not subject to the claims of either the insured's or the beneficiaries' creditors.

One estate tax problem remains—the fact that gifts of life insurance policies within 3 years of death will result in taxation of the proceeds of the policy in the insured decedent's estate (IRC Sec. 2035(d)(2)).

If restrictions are placed on the beneficiaries' rights to exercise immediate ownership rights on the policies or the funds to pay premiums on the policies, the gift is a gift of a future interest and the annual gift tax exclusion does not apply. The result is that an immediate gift tax liability arises. This problem can be avoided by giving the beneficiaries a withdrawal right called a *Crummey provision* (derived from the tax court case *Crummey v. Comm'r),* which gives the trust beneficiaries the right to demand the annual gifts to the trust. This withdrawal right usually lasts for only a short period of time and then lapses. The period of time must be reasonable—usually 30 to 60 days are sufficient—and notice of the withdrawal right must be given to the beneficiary. The fact that the beneficiary is a minor without an appointed guardian will not invalidate the Crummey provision. To avoid adverse federal gift tax consequences in the event of a lapse of the withdrawal right, the annual amount subject to withdrawal should not exceed $5,000.

From a legal and statutory point of view the Crummey doctrine must be viewed in light of the Code provisions dealing with the lapse of a general power of appointment. Secs. 2514(e) and 2041(b)(2) provide that the lapse of a general power of appointment (created after October 21, 1942) is a release of such power. The release of a general power of appointment is "deemed to be a transfer of property by the individual possessing such power." This concept of a release or transfer of a power, although technical and complex, is very important because it is limited to the greater of $5,000 or 5 percent of the value of the assets held by a trust. It is this "5-and-5 power" that applies to Crummey trusts. The annual contribution to the trust must never exceed the greater of $5,000 or 5 percent of the value of the assets held by a trust if the grantor wishes to avoid a lapse of a general power of appointment.

Prior to the enactment of the Economic Recovery Tax Act of 1981 (ERTA), the 5-and-5 power was not an issue for Crummey-type trusts because the gift tax annual exclusion was $3,000 per donee. Since the gift tax annual exclusion was less than the $5,000 standard amount, a problem was never created. However, ERTA increased the annual exclusion from $3,000 per donee to $10,000 per donee. Although the annual exclusion is now $11,000 per year per donee, the maximum nonlapsing withdrawal amount that may be taken as part of the Crummey power is the greater of $5,000, or 5 percent of the trust corpus.

Because the Economic Recovery Tax Act of 1981 increased the annual exclusion from $3,000 to $10,000 and there was no corresponding increase in the de minimis provisions in the Internal Revenue Code, a lapse of demand power in excess of the 5-and-5 ceiling creates a gift tax exposure. In the event that the beneficiary who possesses the withdrawal right has no other beneficial interest in the trust, the lapse in excess of the 5-and-5 power is treated as if the beneficiary had withdrawn this amount under the demand right, and recontributed the same amount back to the trust. Consequently, for tax purposes, the beneficiary will be deemed to be part grantor of the trust.

Determining whether a taxable gift has taken place will depend on the terms of the trust instrument itself. The astute estate planner, however, should be able to find a variety of ways to avoid creating a taxable lapse of a power of withdrawal.

- When the property subject to the demand power does not exceed the greater of $5,000 or 5 percent of trust assets no gift tax issue will result. Note that this does not allow the taxpayer to obtain the full amount of the annual exclusion in the form of a demand right from a trust.

- One popular technique for avoiding this potential obstacle is commonly referred to as the *hanging power*. A hanging power allows the withdrawal powers in excess of the 5-and-5 limitation to hang—that is, to continue in force from one year to the next. Therefore if a gift of $20,000, for example, is made to a trust, the demand power, if unexercised, will lapse with respect to the first $5,000, and no gift tax will be imposed on the unlapsed excess. The remaining $15,000 will be subject to the withdrawal power in the second calendar year and will lapse to the extent of the greater of $5,000 or 5 percent of the trust principal. At some time in the future the amount of withdrawal rights that hang over from year to year will be eliminated entirely because 5 percent of the trust corpus will be greater than the amount subject to the demand power.

    In Letter Ruling 8901004, the IRS took the position that hanging powers are considered invalid and will therefore be ignored for federal gift tax purposes. The ruling concerned a trust for which each beneficiary had a noncumulative right to withdraw his or her pro rata share of such property within 30 days after receiving notice that property had been added to the trust. In addition, the trust provided as follows:

    > Notwithstanding the above, if upon the termination of any power of withdrawal, the person holding the power will be deemed to have made a taxable gift for federal gift tax purposes, then such power of withdrawal will not lapse, but will continue to exist with respect to the amount that would have been a taxable gift and will terminate as soon as such termination will not result in a taxable gift.

    The IRS pointed out that

    > Here the trust provision will not be activated until after an addition to the trust has been made; notice has been given to a beneficiary and the beneficiary's right of withdrawal has lapsed. At that time, the power of withdrawal will be recharacterized as not subject to a set time limit and hence an incomplete gift, so as to avoid federal gift tax consequences of the lapse.
    >
    > Accordingly the provision is a condition subsequent and is deemed not valid as tending to discourage enforcement of federal gift tax provisions by either defeating the gift or rendering examination of the return ineffective.

The courts have chosen not to follow the IRS position. However, in the event that the courts eventually succumb to the IRS position with the result that a hanging power is ignored for federal gift tax purposes and the naming power approach proves ineffective, a powerholder will be deemed to have made a future gift to the other trust beneficiaries. The amount of the gift is the amount subject to the power over the greater of $5,000 or 5 percent of the value of trust assets.

- An additional technique to avoid the application of the federal gift tax is to grant the beneficiary a testamentary power of appointment over the trust. In the event that the appointees of the beneficiary's testamentary power are not readily ascertainable, no completed gift will be considered to have taken place since the beneficiary retains the power to change the disposition of the trust assets.
- One last approach that is sometimes employed to successfully avoid a federal gift tax is to grant each beneficiary a special power of appointment over the excess. This approach will avoid the application of Sec. 2514(b) of the Internal Revenue Code, which applies only to general powers of appointment.

If life insurance is to be placed in a Crummey trust, the policy should be applied for and owned by the trust. In this way there is no possibility of an application of the 3-year contemplation-of-death rule. Furthermore, since there is no gift of a life insurance policy to the trust, only the premiums given to the trust are subject to gift tax.

If Larry's present life insurance coverage is transferred to the trust, there will be a taxable gift in the amount of the interpolated terminal reserve of the polices. Proper structuring of the Crummey provision ensures that this amount should not exceed the annual gift tax exclusion.

There are also income tax consequences to a grantor of a trust that is empowered to use the trust income to pay premiums on policies of insurance on the life of the grantor or the grantor's spouse (IRC Sec. 677(a)(3)). In this case since no assets other than an existing life insurance policy would be transferred to the trust, as in the case of most irrevocable insurance trusts, there is little or no trust income to be taxable to the grantor.

Under the revised plan the removal of the insurance proceeds from both Larry's and Anne's estates should ultimately produce an additional federal estate tax savings of approximately $39,000.

Deferral of Estate Taxes under IRC Sec. 6166

Sec. 6166 provides that if more than 35 percent of a decedent's adjusted gross estate consists of an interest in a closely held business, the executor may elect to pay the federal estate tax attributable to such stock over a period of up to 14 years and 9 months. You will recall that Larry's estate would not qualify for a

Sec. 303 redemption after the recommended installment sale to Steve because it failed to meet the 35 percent test. For the same reason—failure to meet the 35 percent test—deferral of estate taxes under Sec. 6166 will not be available. Note that the availability of Sec. 6166 is not limited to corporations but applies to all closely held business interests as defined in IRC Sec. 6166(b). Sec. 303, on the other hand, applies specifically to redemptions of corporate stock.

PERSONAL PLANNING: INSURANCE

Personal Life Insurance Coverage

Although Larry presently has life insurance and other liquid assets that are sufficient to pay his estate taxes and administrative expenses, he should at least participate in the corporation's group insurance plan as long as he remains an employee to give him an extra margin of protection. As his investment is withdrawn from Millers and becomes more liquid, his present coverage may be sufficient.

Personal Property and Liability Coverage

From the information given in the case, two questions can be raised about the Millers' personal property and liability needs. First, the amount of insurance on the Millers' residence is inadequate to satisfy the replacement-cost provision of their homeowners policy. Under homeowners form 3, property losses are settled on a full-replacement-cost basis only if the amount of insurance carried at the time of loss is equal to 80 percent or more of the full replacement cost of the dwelling. However, loss settlements are limited to the amount of insurance carried, and an insured suffering a total loss will be fully indemnified only if insurance equal to 100 percent of the full replacement cost is carried. If the amount of insurance is less than 80 percent of the full replacement cost, the insurer's liability will be limited to the greater of (1) an amount calculated as if the policy contained an 80 percent coinsurance clause, based on the full replacement cost, or (2) the actual cash value of the damaged property. Thus the Millers will not have any losses paid in full unless they carry an amount of insurance equal to at least $360,000 or 80 percent of the dwelling's $450,000 replacement cost. (Since the actual replacement value seems to be only an estimate, an appraisal is probably in order.)

Second, no mention is made of any insurance on the condominium in another state. It can be adequately insured under a homeowners form 6, which is specifically designed to meet the needs of condominium owners. In addition to providing liability protection, it insures the real property that comprises the individual condominium unit. It is, however, up to the condominium association to insure the shell of the building. The basic form applies only to owner-occupied units, and an endorsement will be necessary since the unit is occasionally rented to others. The charge for this endorsement reflects the increased exposure resulting from tenant-occupied property. In addition, an endorsement is also needed if the real property within the unit (for example, fixtures, improvements, and alterations) is valued at more than $1,000. Finally, the basic contract provides named-peril coverage but can be endorsed to all-risks coverage as exists for real property in homeowners form 3.

PERSONAL PLANNING: INVESTMENT

Client Profile

Larry's current assets reflect his risk avoidance attitude and result in an investment program seeking stability of value and modest earnings. Their modest home and avoidance of debt also suggest that the Millers are quite conservative in their total outlook. Any recommendations for investments must recognize these views.

The projections over the next several years indicate that the Millers will have a substantial amount of cash available annually for investment purposes if the recommended solutions (the sale of 72 shares to Steve and the redemption of Anne's shares) are implemented. Larry's income from continued employment is almost sufficient to meet their cash needs. Unless the Millers drastically alter their lifestyle, most of their additional income is available for reinvestment. Any recommendations for specific investment assets should also recognize that convenience of reinvestment of income is a desirable characteristic.

Anne inherited some blue-chip stocks and bonds from her father. She has been managing the portfolio with the advice of her stockbroker, with whom she has been associated for many years. She enjoys trading the portfolio and has been successful. Since Anne enjoys successfully managing her securities, no repositioning of her portfolio is appropriate. Larry, on the other hand, keeps his cash in money market mutual funds. The following investment recommendations are directed at the cash the Millers will be receiving in the future. These recommendations should be reviewed by Anne as well as Larry.

The bulk of the Millers' investable cash will come from the sale of Millers stock owned by Larry. A portion, however, will come from the redemption of Anne's stock.

Except for Anne's inheritance the Millers should consider dividing ownership of investment assets equally between them. This is preferable to joint ownership because it will assure that both Larry and Anne will be able to make full use of the applicable credit for estate tax purposes. Jointly held assets, on the other hand, would pass under the marital deduction regardless of any estate planning documents.

Investment Alternatives

Certificates of Deposit

These are term deposits with either banks or savings and loan associations that are available with varying maturity dates and interest yields. Currently certificates of deposit (CDs) are yielding approximately 5.25 percent interest for 5-year maturities. Provided no more than $100,000 is in any one account at any one bank (or savings and loan), the account is insured by the FDIC—a desirable feature for this client's risk profile. Five-year maturities should reduce the likelihood of forced-sale problems since the Millers' annual cash flow is projected to be quite sizable. Another characteristic of CDs is that interest income can be either left to accumulate at the stipulated rate or withdrawn on a regular basis. Since the Millers will have a need for income reinvestment each year, the reinvestment feature is desirable. Furthermore, the Millers can later decide to take the current earnings on a regular basis if the return on newly issued CDs becomes higher than those already in their portfolio.

One disadvantage of CDs is that there is no growth in value other than through interest accumulations since CDs are a bank deposit. This lack of growth means CDs are subject to inflation risk. There is also a form of the interest-rate risk. Higher earnings can be realized by having investable cash in a more liquid form if interest rates rise. If interest rates do rise after any CDs are purchased, the CDs can be turned in for early redemption, the early redemption penalty paid, and the proceeds reinvested in the then-higher rate being paid on newly issued CDs. Each rollover of this type should be analyzed to determine if the higher interest rate being earned justifies paying the redemption penalty. Some banks are now issuing CDs that do not have an early redemption penalty. However, those CDs carry a lower interest rate than those with the penalty.

The Millers should plan a schedule of purchasing some CDs each year as a means of reducing a portion of the potential interest-rate risk during the period of acquisition. Also they should not have all their CDs mature in the same year. This spreading of maturity dates avoids the possibility of having to reinvest large portions of their portfolio at a particularly low point in the interest-rate cycle.

Municipal Bond Funds

This form of fund acquires a portfolio of tax-exempt bonds. The fund can pass the federal tax exemption on municipal bond income to its shareholders. Most municipal bonds issued on or before August 7, 1986, and bonds issued after that date that are deemed to be public-purpose bonds produce income that is fully exempt from federal income taxation. Bond funds that have a portfolio consisting totally of bonds issued by the states or their subdivisions in which the shareholder resides are typically free of that state's income tax. Although a state income tax exemption is a nice feature, the overriding consideration should be the quality of the bond portfolio held by the fund. For risk averters the bond fund portfolio should be high-investment grade with only a small or minor portion of the holdings having bond ratings less than AA. These funds are currently yielding approximately 5.5 percent on a tax-exempt basis, a yield that converts to an equivalent before-tax yield for clients in the 31 percent bracket of 7.9 percent (6%/1 − .31). Money market tax-exempt funds are currently yielding 4 percent after tax, which is equivalent to a 5.8 percent before-tax yield.

Since these bond funds are invested solely in debt instruments, the interest-rate risk is a cause for concern. Should interest rates rise, the fund's per-share value will fall although the interest income stream might not be affected. In addition, as with all fixed-income securities, the purchasing-power risk is an inherent characteristic and will affect the buying power of the income stream.

Municipal Bonds

Direct ownership of municipal bonds can be a desirable investment for risk-averse clients provided sufficient diversification can be achieved. Newly issued investment grade municipal bonds have a tax-exempt yield of approximately 5.5 percent (7.9 percent before tax if the owner is in the 31 percent tax bracket) for 25- to 30-year maturity dates. The disadvantages are a lack of sufficient diversification if the portfolio consists of only one or two issues and also the same disadvantages that municipal bond funds have.

Balanced Mutual Funds

These funds distribute their portfolio among the various classes of securities: bonds, common stocks, and preferred stocks. The proportion of their assets in any one security can be either at the fund manager's discretion or specified in the prospectus. These funds are generally the most conservative of any mutual fund that invests in common stock. Their investment objectives in order of priority are to preserve capital, to generate income, and to obtain capital gains if possible. During declining markets the holding of different types of securities provides protection for the investor since typically not all markets—bond, preferred stock, and common stock—fall simultaneously.

In addition to the conservative nature of balanced funds, they, like all other funds, provide diversification and professional management, and they offer automatic reinvestment of dividends, all features desirable to the Millers. These funds provide minimal growth opportunities since only a portion of their assets is invested in common stocks. But this limited potential growth can nevertheless serve as a means of offsetting some effects of inflation.

Any investor using balanced funds, or any fund for that matter, must choose between load versus no-load funds and must also time acquisitions after the date of record to avoid having a portion of the investment immediately returned as a taxable dividend or capital gain.

Convertible Bonds or Convertible Bond Funds

The unique feature of convertible bonds is the option the bondholder has to convert the bond, when desired, to common stock of the issuing corporation. Should the common stock of the issuer rise substantially in price, the holder can convert and obtain the benefit of the increased market price of the stock. The conventional wisdom is that over long periods of time, common stocks in general tend to outperform inflation. If this holds true, this form of bond provides potential inflation protection while still spinning off interest income that is greater than the dividend flow on the underlying common stocks during the years immediately following the bond's issue. However, the bond never has to be converted. At maturity the face amount is returned to the bondholders.

Like all bonds, convertibles are subject to the interest-rate risk, and unless the underlying common stock rises faster than the price level so that conversion is desirable, they are also subject to the purchasing-power risk.

Risk-averse investors could well consider purchasing convertibles, either directly or through a convertible bond fund (with the usual fund advantages and disadvantages), provided the portfolio of these bonds (individually owned or through the bond fund) is of investment-grade quality. The yield will perhaps be one-eighth of a percent less than could be earned on nonconvertible debt of the same risk. It is the potential increase in the value of the underlying common stock to offset inflation that makes this form of debt attractive, particularly to investors like the Millers. They are nearing retirement, do not wish to take undue investment risks, but will probably experience inflation during the remainder of their lives.

Recommendations

Any and all the investments described above could be appropriate for the Millers. Other investments such as growth stocks or growth stock mutual funds, for example, entail risk that does not seem appropriate for these clients.

A recommended investment plan covering the next 5 years follows:

Investment	Percent of Annual Investment Funds
5-year CDs	25%
Municipal bond fund	45
Convertible bond fund	15
Balanced mutual fund	15

For 2003 when $50,901 is available (based on the cash-flow summary in the case IV projections), the Millers could place about $12,725 (25 percent of $50,901) in CDs; $22,906 in perhaps two or three different municipal bond funds; $7,635 in one or two convertible bond funds; and $7,635 in one or two balanced mutual funds. A portfolio of this distribution matches their risk profile: safety of principal is paramount and level of income flow is secondary. These recommendations result in an investment portfolio that contains diversification, produces some tax-free income from the municipal bond funds, and also permits reinvestment of interest or dividend flows through the convenience of the CDs and mutual funds. The convertible bond fund and the balanced mutual fund provide some emphasis on growth and inflation protection. If inflation remains at current low levels, the Millers should have sufficient future income, given their modest expenditure patterns (relative to their income), to be essentially free of financial worries during their lifetime.

Preretirement Planning

At this point in their lives Anne and Larry should consider preretirement planning. They have devoted a major portion of their financial activities to the establishment and prosperity of their furniture business and are now nearing the conclusion of their peak wealth-accumulation years. Their efforts should focus on preparing the way for their actual retirement in a manner that will provide financial security during those years. Important factors for Larry and Anne to consider at this time include

- repositioning of assets
- asset conservation
- plan-distribution options
- retirement income estimation
- potentially dependent parent
- recreation/health
- acquisition of personal assets (autos, home appliances, and so on)
- possible new career

Many of these factors have received some attention in the solution as presented up to this point. Each of these factors will now be examined for the Millers.

Repositioning of Assets

The recommendation is for Larry to sell a portion of his stock in Millers through an installment sale to their son, Steve. This sale will convert a portion of his ownership in Millers to an annual cash flow that will provide income for both himself and Anne during retirement. Larry will still have 95.5 shares in Millers that are not available for repositioning due to their general nonmarketability. At some time in the future consideration could be given to a disposition of Larry's remaining shares in Millers, possibly by means of a redemption.

Anne will have her Millers stock redeemed by the corporation, thus producing a stream of income that will increase their cash flow.

An examination of the Millers' balance sheet discloses that they own few other assets that can be repositioned. Although the potential for repositioning Anne's portfolio of stock and bonds does exist, Anne enjoys managing these assets and has been successful in doing so. Any repositioning of these securities by the planner appears to be undesirable. However, this is a matter that should be explored with the client.

Another asset that might be repositioned is the store building. Again, in situations such as this the sale of the building to a third party could jeopardize much of this family's well-being. Steve would be at the mercy of an unsympathetic owner of the building and could have little option but to renew leases at the owner's terms. Although the asset is worth close to one-third of a million dollars, Larry would probably prefer to retain the ownership to protect both his installment sale, Anne's installment redemption, and Steve's livelihood from the furniture store. Larry should discuss with Steve the need for some long-term inflation protection from the rents that Steve will be paying. Perhaps the lease agreement should incorporate a form of escalator clause adjusting the rent either for some broad-based inflation measure or linked to increases in rents being paid in the town. Larry might consider doing this while he retains working control of Millers as part of his preretirement planning.

The beach condo Anne owns provides her with the satisfaction of being able to use it as she and the family desire. With approaching retirement promising to bring Anne and Larry more leisure time, it does not seem prudent to convert the condo into either a more full-time, rental real estate property or to sell it and use the proceeds to acquire additional income-producing securities. Under the current situation since the property is free of any debt, the modest rental income earned more than covers the annual cash drain for taxes and insurance. Continued ownership should enhance their retirement leisure time. Fortunately the Millers' financial position is such that the opportunity cost (forgone interest earnings) of the money invested in the condo does not affect their ability to meet their financial goals. Of course, the potential does exist for a subsequent sale should the need arise.

The remaining assets do not appear suited for repositioning. Perhaps the return being earned on Anne's accumulated life insurance dividends could be examined to determine whether a higher return could be obtained on the funds if placed elsewhere. The remaining assets, such as the checking and savings accounts, money market fund, automobiles, and life insurance cash values, need not be considered for repositioning at this time.

Asset Conservation

Asset conservation has two elements. The first is to create a relatively risk-free portfolio. The second is to keep the bulk of the assets available for the clients' use should the need arise.

As is the case with many owners of small businesses, most of the Millers' wealth accumulation is in their family business, so these ventures typically involve high risk. Through the mechanisms of the installment sale to Steve and the installment payout of Anne's stock redemption, the Millers will begin to move some of their wealth out of the family business. However, their retirement income flow will depend on the ability of the furniture store to produce income to meet these obligations. Also Larry will continue to own some shares in Millers.

Only two of their existing assets—the store building and Anne's stock and bond portfolio—exhibit high-risk characteristics. The store building probably has alternative uses and in that sense is less risky than a special-purpose building would be. The composition of Anne's portfolio is not specifically stated, and perhaps a somewhat less risky mix of stocks and bonds could provide additional asset conservation.

The recommendations presented earlier for the Millers to employ for their investable cash flow during the next several years are relatively conservative in nature and are consistent with an asset-conservation objective.

Maintaining their accumulated assets for their use is the method recommended for the Millers (that is, the installment sale) in transferring ownership in Millers. In addition, their recommended estate plans provide the maximum protection to the surviving spouse. Thus their assets are being managed in a manner that will provide them with the desired economic benefits.

Plan Distribution Options

Larry presently has almost $70,000 in the profit-sharing plan of Millers. He plans to continue his employment for several years before withdrawing from any active involvement in the business. Even if no further contributions are made for his benefit, and assuming the plan earns about 8 percent annually over the next several years, Larry should have at least $90,000 of plan assets available for income-producing purposes. Since retirement is not imminent, there is no immediate need for Larry and Anne to choose between a lump-sum distribution and installment distribution or a joint and survivor annuity. Given their expected cash flows during the next few years, the Millers should continue deferring the removal of plan assets as long as is feasible without incurring penalties in order to obtain the maximum benefit of tax deferral.

Retirement Income Estimation

Table 6-1 projects the amount of cash inflow Larry and Anne will have during the first 5 years of their retirement under the assumption that Larry retires from Millers in 2007.

During the first 5 years of retirement the Millers' cash outflows will rise less than the increase in their cash inflows from sources presently available to them.

TABLE 6-1
Retirement Cash Inflow/Cash Expense Estimation

	2007	2008	2009	2010	2011
Cash Inflow					
Installment sale (Doug)	$ 27,080	$ 27,080	$ 27,080	$ 27,080	$ 27,080
Installment sale (Steve)	27,800	27,800	27,800	27,800	27,800
302 redemption	27,734	27,734	27,734	27,734	27,734
Social Security	17,484	18,009	18,549	19,105	19,678
Pension plan	10,500	10,500	10,500	10,500	10,500
Building rental	44,000	46,640	49,438	52,405	55,549
Anne's portfolio	5,466	5,739	6,026	6,328	6,644
Investment portfolio (reinvested cash flow [12/31/03])	27,388	27,388	27,388	27,388	27,388
Interest on retirement savings	0	3,687	7,393	11,112	14,842
Total cash inflow	$187,452	$194,577	$201,908	$209,452	$217,216
Cash Outflow					
Expenses	47,000	49,820	52,809	55,978	59,336
Federal and state income taxes	69,000	72,000	75,000	78,000	81,000
Vacation/travel	10,000	11,000	12,100	13,310	14,641
Total cash outflow	$126,000	$132,820	$139,909	$147,288	$154,977
Net cash inflow (annual cash savings)	$ 61,452	$ 61,757	$ 61,999	$ 62,164	$ 62,238
Accumulated net savings during retirement	$ 61,452	$123,209	$185,208	$247,372	$309,610

The effect of this is shown on the net cash inflow line in table 6-1. Based on this data the Millers will be able to save a rather sizable sum each year, which, if invested in bonds yielding a 6 percent return, will result in a year-to-year increase in their income. The Millers should be financially secure during their years of retirement.

One important point to consider is that the annual cash inflow from the proposed redemption of Anne's stock in Millers will cease with the payment in 2012 (if a 10-year installment term is in fact implemented), so their income will be reduced beginning in 2013. The payments from Doug for the purchase of the second store will end in 2011. The combined effect of these two events is to reduce their annual saving by the after-tax cash inflow from these two installment transactions.

The following assumptions were made with respect to the cash inflow and outflow of the Millers:

- The installment payments from Doug will cease at the end of 2011.
- The installment sale to Steve of some of Larry's stock will be completed in 2003 and will provide an annual cash inflow of (approximately) $27,800 for 15 years.
- The stock redemption by Millers of Anne's shares will be completed in 2003 and will provide a cash inflow of (approximately) $27,734 for 10 years.
- Social Security benefits will commence in 2007, with Larry receiving the stated benefit and Anne obtaining the 50 percent spousal benefit. It is assumed that Social Security benefits will grow at a rate of 3 percent each year.
- Larry will have about $90,000 in the profit-sharing pension at the end of 2006. This amount could be higher if Millers alters its plan or increases its profitability. The $90,000 could purchase a joint and survivor annuity of $10,500 per year (at current rates) for Larry and Anne (although the Millers might opt to take a lump-sum distribution or an installment payout at that time).
- The rental income from the store building is $33,000 annually and is anticipated to increase at a rate of 6 percent each year. It will be about $44,000 in 2007.
- The reinvested cash flow the Millers will have at the end of the planning period, 2006, will be $521,679. A 5.25 percent return will be earned after retirement.
- Anne's portfolio will continue to increase in value at a 5 percent annual rate. The yield on these securities will average 4 percent annually.
- It is assumed that Millers will be converted to S corporation status. Since Larry will retain 95.5 shares, a portion of the firm's net profits must be included in his income. It is assumed that Larry will receive distributions equal in amount to his income tax liability arising from his pro rata share of Millers' taxable income. These figures have not been entered into the table.
- Anne currently receives about $6,000 in rental income from the condo. Since this is a relatively small portion of the Millers' expected income and might well be reduced if they use the condo to a greater degree when in retirement, it is excluded from these projections.

- Their committed, discretionary, and property tax expenses are expected to be about $47,000 in 2007. Inflation will cause these to increase at an annual rate of 6 percent.
- Both federal and state income tax rates are assumed to remain at their current rates.
- Vacation/travel expenses will increase 10 percent each year.
- Any excess cash flow after January 1, 2007, will be accumulated. The yield is assumed to be 5.25 percent.

Potentially Dependent Parent

Anne's mother, the sole surviving parent of Anne and Larry, appears to be financially independent and in good health at this time. Unless serious medical problems or long-term nursing care deplete her assets, it is unlikely that the Millers will be called upon to provide financial support. Therefore they need not include any expenditure planning for the benefit of Anne's mother in their retirement plans. However, they might have to consider the possibility of providing some personal time to care for her should she experience a deterioration in health.

Recreation/Health

At this time both the Millers expect to travel and to use their condo to a greater degree when Larry either spends less time with Millers or fully retires. Fortunately the Millers enjoy good health, so these factors do not create any unique planning considerations at this time.

Personal Asset Acquisition

Since Larry is in the furniture business, it can be assumed that furniture for the home is not needed now or at retirement. The Millers might wish to consider the purchase of a new car when Larry retires completely if their travel plans include lengthy car trips. Other than the car, it does not appear they have any unfulfilled wishes in this category.

Possible New Career

Larry has not indicated any interest in possibly embarking on a different career upon retirement. His expressed desire to travel and to spend more time with Anne and their grandchildren is the extent of his expected use of his retirement time.

7

Planning for the Officer of a Large Organization

Chapter Outline

In addition to the group of self-employed persons and small business owners, managers and officers of large organizations are rapidly becoming clients of professional financial planners. These clients often have a comprehensive set of benefits from their employment, but they also have many of the same priorities and concerns that can benefit from a financial planner's expertise. With increasing awareness of the availability of comprehensive, well-trained financial planners, some large organizations offer personal financial counseling as an executive benefit. In other cases the relationship with the financial adviser is developed as an outgrowth of some single-purpose planning provided by an insurance agent, a securities broker, a CPA, or a lawyer.

In contrast to the young couple with only the potential to accumulate substantial assets, these clients, typically between 45 and 60 years of age, have reached or are nearing the peak of their careers. Hence a portfolio of investment assets is commonly present. In addition, the prospect of further significant accumulation exists, since children's education expenses are actually or almost completely paid. These clients can focus on the adequacy of their retirement planning. Although included in the upper ranks of their employer's management team, these clients lack the requisite clout to install benefit programs suited to their specific situation, and any desirable changes in employment-related benefits may be beyond their power or influence. Thus individual plans, although lacking some of the tax advantages found in corporate plans, provide the means to meet the clients' financial objectives.

Today medical advances and increased longevity enhance the likelihood that clients in this age bracket should consider their potential need for long-term care outside their home for themselves and their spouse. Also some of these clients may need to provide financial assistance to care for a parent or to provide resources for the care of a disabled child over a long period. Once again, personal planning and funding techniques may provide the only adequate basis for a satisfactory course of action that will meet the objective.

CASE NARRATIVE

Personal Information

Edgar (Ed) and Amy Martinson are 54 and 45 respectively and reside in a suburb of Atlanta, Georgia. They have been married 24 years and have two children. Beatrice (Bea) is 22, single, and has been employed in the international division of a large bank since graduating from college 2 years ago. Their son, Scott, is 16 and attends high school.

Shortly after Amy and Ed were married they had simple, reciprocal wills drafted in which each left all of his or her respective estate properties to the surviving spouse. No revisions have been made to these wills.

Ed joined Inc, Inc., 20 years ago as an assistant to the plant superintendent. He has progressed to his current position of vice president of manufacturing, which became effective on December 1 of last year. Details of Ed's employment and benefits are described in the section titled "Employment Information."

Amy began a career in retailing as a buyer for a large department store but interrupted her career at their daughter's birth. When Scott entered kindergarten, she returned to her former employer. When their son was injured 7 years ago, Amy resigned to care for him and presently has no plans to continue her career.

Ed, Amy, and Bea all enjoy excellent health, but Scott has serious health problems. Seven years ago he fell from a tree, severely injuring his leg and hip. After a long hospital stay and months of rehabilitation therapy he appeared to be fully recovered. However, about 3 years ago Scott began to experience pain and stiffness in the hip joint and eventually was unable to move about. Although he had a hip replacement at that time, it only slightly alleviated the pain and did little to improve his mobility. Ed's health insurance under Inc's plan has covered most of the medical expenses resulting from the accident, but the Martinsons are uncertain about Scott's future medical costs. In addition to paying the deductible and other out-of-pocket medical expenses, Amy took several specialized courses at their expense at the local hospital so she could give Scott some care that would otherwise have required hospitalization or semiskilled nursing experience.

As a result of this serious health problem Scott has become rather frail physically. Although he continues to attend school, he lacks a positive attitude toward education. Since his grades reflect this attitude, the Martinsons doubt that he will continue any education beyond high school. They worry that this lack of education beyond the high school level, combined with his physical condition, will make it impossible for him to support himself adequately.

By the time Bea started college, the Martinsons had accumulated about $25,000 for her educational expenses. These funds, plus some of their annual income, were sufficient to cover Bea's college expenses. Ed's mother, who was very fond of Bea, died when Bea was 4. Her will established a testamentary trust for Bea's benefit with Grass Roots Bank as the trustee. The terms of the trust permit each year's trust income to be paid out annually if Bea notifies the trustee, but Bea has not yet exercised her option to withdraw any trust income. The corpus and accumulated income, if any, can be invaded to fund an elaborate wedding or a down payment on a home. When Bea is 35, any funds remaining must be distributed to her. Trust assets have a current market value of $70,000.

Since Bea's prospective financial concerns appear to be largely taken care of, the Martinsons want to focus their attention on providing for Scott. Currently they have about $26,000 set aside for him. These funds are invested in conservative common stocks, and although Ed and Amy are the owners, the stocks are held in street name in a separate account maintained with a large brokerage firm. The stocks are increasing in value at a rate of 6 percent a year and are paying a dividend of 3 percent a year. All dividend income is automatically invested in the issuers' dividend reinvestment plans. Until Ed retires and perhaps for a few years thereafter, the Martinsons anticipate that they can provide for Scott's needs from their current income. However, by the time

Ed retires they would like to have some provision in place for a lifelong stream of income to supplement Scott's impaired earning capacity and to cover his continuing medical expenses. At today's prices the Martinsons' target is to provide Scott with an annual supplemental income of $3,000, adjusted for inflation. Ed planned to retire by age 62 but is now unsure whether this will be feasible in light of their objective to provide long-term support for Scott.

A further concern of Ed's is Amy's life expectancy. Not only is she a bit younger than he, but her family history indicates it is likely that she will have a longer-than-normal life expectancy. Although he doesn't need to make any decisions now about distributions from the corporate defined-benefit, noncontributory pension plan and the contributory 401(k) plan, Ed and Amy believe these decisions must be considered in conjunction with some retirement planning necessary to supplement the retirement benefits available from both Inc and Social Security.

Both of Amy's parents are in their 70s, and three of her four grandparents are still hale and hearty folk. Although some of Amy's elderly relatives may need support, Amy and Ed are not concerned about accumulating any funds for this contingency because fortunately Amy's father was very successful financially and is able to afford the support necessary at this time. He has been open with Amy about his finances and, barring unforeseen financial reverses, expects to provide economic assistance for Amy's grandparents as well as provide for his and his spouse's support. Amy has a brother, Bob, aged 48, who is a physician in a different state.

Ed's family does not include such long-lived ancestors. Both his parents died in their early 70s. Except for an unmarried brother, Jack, who is 10 years younger than he, Ed has no living relatives other than his spouse and children.

In 1997, expecting that Ed would rise to the executive ranks of Inc, the Martinsons sold their home for $200,000 and purchased a newly built $350,000 home in an exclusive suburb. Their adjusted basis in the old home was $58,000. The Martinsons made a down payment of $225,000 and financed the remainder of the acquisition cost with a 25-year mortgage at a fixed interest rate of 8.5 percent. The estimated fair market value of their home is $375,000.

When Ed and Amy were married 24 year ago, Ed purchased a $50,000 whole life policy with an annual premium of $1,120. He is the owner and Amy is the primary beneficiary. He has since named Bea and Scott as the contingent beneficiaries, per stirpes. This policy has a current cash value of $18,100. Amy converted her group term life insurance into a $5,000 whole life policy 21 years ago, naming Ed as the primary beneficiary. The children are the contingent beneficiaries, per stirpes. The policy has a $120 annual premium and a cash value of $1,800. Ed has two $25,000 policies with combined premiums of $1,215 and a total cash value of $16,325. Each of these policies was purchased when a child was born. Each child is the named primary beneficiary on a policy, and Amy is the contingent beneficiary for both policies.

Over the years the Martinsons have invested their excess income in several different instruments. First, during the years when the IRA window permitting fully tax-deductible contributions of up to $2,000 annually without an income limitation was open for participants in qualified pension plans, Ed funded an IRA and a spousal IRA at the local savings and loan when their finances permitted. CDs were used as the investment instrument. The blended current return based on differing maturity dates of the CDs is 8.1 percent. When the contributions ceased being tax deductible, Ed discontinued adding money to the IRA. Overall he put $9,800 into his IRA, which now has an accumulated value of $22,800. The spousal IRA for Amy, with $1,250 invested, has an accumulated value of $2,400. Its current return is about the same as Ed's.

They maintain a regular joint checking account that currently has a $12,000 balance. They also have a money market deposit account at the same bank. The account typically has a target average balance of about $25,000 and currently earns 4.75 percent. Their monthly mortgage payment and other large bills are paid by drafts drawn on this account. If the deposit account becomes too large, the excess is divided between investments in a balanced mutual fund and a growth mutual fund. In both funds all dividends and capital gains have been reinvested. Their basis is $45,000 in the balanced fund, which now has a current value of $84,000. The investment in the growth fund is worth $120,000 and has a basis of $57,000. The estimated annual return on these funds has averaged 9.5 percent and 13 percent respectively over the last 5 years.

The taxable portion of the total return from the balanced fund averages 4.3 percent and from the growth fund it is 1.5 percent. The remainder of each fund's return is unrealized capital gains on the portfolio and increases in the net asset value of their shares.

Amy has furnished their new home with $30,000 worth of additional purchases, which were partially financed over 2 years. Furnishings and other personal property they own increase the value of the contents to about $75,000.

Ed's auto was purchased in December of last year and is being financed with 42 monthly payments of $440. Currently the vehicle is worth about $20,000. Amy's station wagon is fully paid for and has a value of $12,000.

Until the additional problems with Scott began to drain some of their potential savings, Ed and Amy anticipated having Scott's education fully funded before he entered college. They then expected to establish a side fund for their retirement. Their target was and still is to have an additional $5,000 of annual income beginning at the expected retirement date. This additional income, they thought, would enable Ed to retire at age 62, the earliest date permitted under Inc's pension plan. They felt the side fund was needed because of the difference in their ages and Amy's potential long life.

Employment Information

Ed's job requires him to spend about 30 percent of his time on visits to Inc's facilities in North America and Europe. Inc plans to commence building at least one manufacturing operation in an Asian country during the next 2 years.

Whenever Ed is traveling on company business, he is covered by accidental death insurance that is double his annual base salary. This is in addition to other employment-related life insurance described below.

In his new position Ed's salary is $100,000 per year, and he is now eligible for Inc's executive bonus plan that over the past several years has distributed an annual bonus equal to 10 percent of each participating executive's salary. The total bonus distributed by the plan is directly related to corporate profits. The percentage of corporate profits distributed by the bonus plan has remained constant over the past several years. Each plan participant's potential share of next year's profits is determined by Inc's board at its December meeting. Inc uses the calendar year for financial statement and income tax purposes.

Coverage for 100 percent of lost salary for short-term disability (maximum of 6 months) is provided under a nonfunded sick-pay plan. Salary lost due to a disability's preventing a return to employment status after a period of 6 months is replaced at 75 percent, including Social Security disability benefits, for the duration of the disability or until normal retirement age, whichever comes first. For Ed this would amount to almost $6,250 a month. Inc will continue to credit years of employment for pension plan coverage and make both the employer and the employee contributions to the 401(k) plan. In addition, coverage will be continued under the company's insured medical plan at no cost to the disabled employee. If Ed should become disabled, the Martinsons stated that they want to have the equivalent of Ed's current salary of almost $8,750 a month. Therefore they have a shortfall of $2,000 a month.

Inc's qualified noncontributory defined-benefit pension plan will provide a maximum retirement income of 1.5 percent of the average of an employee's highest 5 years of income times the number of years of service, with the maximum number of years of service for the purpose of the plan being 25 years. The pension benefit is not offset by retirement income provided under Social Security. The value of the future pension benefit, reduced to present value, is approximately $190,000.

Six years ago Inc instituted a voluntary-participation, salary reduction type 401(k) plan for its employees. About 85 percent of Inc's employees participate in the plan. For employee contributions up to 5 percent of salary, Inc will contribute 50 percent of the employee's contribution during the first 5 years of service and 75 percent until 10 years of service are achieved. At that point Inc will match the employee's contribution. The plan permits lump-sum withdrawals upon retirement or severance from the employer. The 401(k) plan is self-directed; plan participants may choose the investment instruments and may shift invested funds within a limited set of alternatives. Investment options include Inc's common stock, which is traded on a national exchange; a no-load family of mutual funds that includes a money market, a U.S. government bond, a corporate bond, a balanced, a growth, and an international fund as its "family"; and Series EE U.S. government savings bonds. Ed has participated in the plan since its inception and divides both his and Inc's contributions equally between the U.S. government bond fund and Inc's stock. At the end of last year Ed's account in the bond fund was $50,000, and Inc's stock had a market value of $74,000. He anticipates contributing 5 percent of salary each year until retirement.

As a result of Ed's promotion last December he became a participant in Inc's nonqualified deferred-compensation plan. Assuming that Ed remains with Inc until normal retirement age (65), the plan will provide a benefit of $1,500 per month for a period of 10 years provided Ed does not engage in activities deemed to be in direct competition with Inc. Should Ed die before the end of the 10-year period, the plan will continue the payments to Amy for the unpaid period of time. If Amy fails to live until the end of the 10-year period, the remaining payments will be made to her estate. Although Inc is placing funds into a separate account earmarked to fund the deferred-compensation obligation, these funds are part of Inc's assets and are available to its creditors.

Inc provides noncontributory group term life insurance in the amount of 1.5 times annual base salary for all employees. Ed has named Amy as the primary beneficiary of the policy and Bea and Scott, per stirpes, as the contingent beneficiaries. Upon retirement the insurance protection decreases to $10,000 and then declines over the next 5 years to a face amount of $5,000.

Inc's comprehensive medical insurance plan provides $500,000 of lifetime coverage for each family member. Each year after a $250 per-person deductible, the insurance provides coverage for 80 percent of the first $5,000 of each year's covered benefits for the family. After the $5,000 of covered benefits is incurred in any one year, additional medical expenses are paid in full. The plan is noncontributory for employee coverage, but dependent coverage is available only if the employee contributes $20 monthly to the cost of coverage. Scott is covered under the plan until graduation from high school, and coverage would be continued if he were a full-time, post-high-school student until age 23. When Scott's qualification as a student for participation in the health plan ends, the COBRA rules permit coverage to extend for 36 months as long as the premium is properly paid.

When an employee retires at normal retirement age (65), Inc pays the full cost of medical insurance to supplement Medicare for both the employee and the employee's spouse. If the joint and survivor option is selected under Inc's pension plan, Inc will continue to pay the supplemental premium for the surviving spouse. If the retired or deceased employee's spouse is not eligible for Medicare, then Inc provides a group supplemental plan that will pay 80 percent of the surviving spouse's medical expenses in excess of a spouse's basic Blue Cross/Blue Shield plan until such time as the spouse is eligible for Medicare. Before Medicare coverage is available, the spouse pays the premium for the basic insurance, and Inc pays for the supplemental insurance. When Medicare coverage becomes available, the spouse is provided the Medicare supplemental insurance as described above.

Because of the Financial Accounting Standards Board requirement that the present value of retirees' medical expenses must be reported in a company's annual financial report and because of the rapid inflation of medical costs, Inc is currently studying the possibility of (1) discontinuing its payments for the supplemental medical insurance, (2) having the retired employee pay for the coverage under a group plan, or (3) having the employee make contributions during his or her employment years toward the retirement medical insurance. If either of the first two options were implemented, Inc would make some improvements in its pension plan to partially compensate for the loss of the full payment of the supplemental medical insurance. Whatever changes are made will affect only future retirees, such as Ed.

The Martinsons' property tax assessment is $70,000 for the land and $310,000 for home improvements, although they anticipate that the property would sell for no more than $375,000. They carry an HO-3 homeowners policy that insures the dwelling for $300,000, which is the amount they anticipate it would cost to replace the structure. The contents are insured for one-half the limit on the dwelling. The policy provides $500,000 of liability coverage and what they believe is adequate additional living expense coverage should a loss occur that precludes living in their home. Although the homeowners policy would provide some coverage, the Martinsons have opted to insure Amy's jewelry and furs for scheduled values on a separate policy.

The automobiles are covered under one policy that has a liability limit of $500,000 and medical expense coverage of $10,000. In addition, the policy includes uninsured motorists, towing, collision, and other-than-collision coverages (comprehensive). The latter coverages have $500 deductibles.

To further protect themselves, the Martinsons carry a $1 million umbrella policy that requires liability insurance for both the home and the automobile in the amount of $500,000.

TABLE 7-1
Inventory of Assets

Assets	Cost or Basis	Fair Market Value	Current Return %	Current Return $	Form of Ownership[1]	Available for Liquidity	Collateralized	Location
Checking account	$12,000	10,000	—	—	JT	Yes	No	Bank
Money market deposit account	25,000	25,000	4.75	1,188	JT	Yes	No	Bank
Residence	183,000	375,000	—	—	JT	No	Yes	—
Life ins. cash value	18,100	18,100	—	—	S(H)	Yes	No	Safe-deposit box
Life ins. cash value	1,800	1,800	—	—	S(W)	Yes	No	Safe-deposit box
Life ins. cash value	16,325	16,325	—	—	S(H)	Yes	No	Safe-deposit box
IRA	9,800	22,800	8.1	1,720	S(H)	No	No	Safe-deposit box
IRA	1,250	2,400	8.1	180	S(W)	No	No	Safe-deposit box
Balanced fund	45,000	84,000	4.3	3,612	S(H)	Yes	No	Mutual fund
Growth fund	57,000	120,000	1.5	1,800	S(H)	Yes	No	Mutual fund
401(k) bond fund	—	50,000	6.5	3,250	S(H)	No	No	Mutual fund
401(k) stock	—	74,000	2.0	1,480	S(H)	No	No	Mutual fund
Group term life	—	142,500[2]	—	—	S(H)	Yes	No	Employer
Nonqualified deferred compensation	—	52,000[2]	—	—	S(H)	No	No	Employer
Vested pension benefit	—	190,000[2]	—	—	S(H)	Yes	No	Employer
Common stock	60,000	104,000	3.0	3,120	JT	Yes	No	Safe-deposit box
Household furnishings	75,000	75,000	—	—	S(H)	No	No	—
Auto	28,000	20,000	—	—	S(H)	Yes	Yes	—
Auto	20,000	12,000	—	—	S(W)	No	No	—

[1] JT = joint tenants with right of survivorship; S = single ownership; H = husband; W = wife
[2] Value of plan benefits

INSTRUCTIONS

Based on this information, prepare a working outline for the Martinsons' financial plan. When this has been completed, it can be compared with the suggested solution that follows. After comparing the two working outlines, turn to page 7.12 for further instructions.

WORKING OUTLINE

I. Client's objectives

   A. For lifetime planning
1. Accumulate sufficient wealth to assure that current lifestyle continues following retirement.
2. Address the retirement planning issues stemming from Amy's family history of longevity and Amy's likelihood of surviving Ed by many years.
3. Accumulate a fund that will assure an adequate stream of income to Scott for purposes of maintenance and medical costs
4. Provide current medical insurance coverage for Scott both while he is covered by Inc's plan and after he is no longer covered by the plan.
5. Assess current insurance coverage and restructure such coverages optimally.

   B. For disposition at death
1. Provide for Amy since she is likely to outlive Ed.
2. Construct the estate plan so that Scott's disability is adequately addressed should Ed and/or Amy predecease him.
3. Plan eventual inheritances in some equitable manner to allow Bea to receive an equal benefit and an equal amount of estate property.
4. Ensure that the entire family will have sufficient assets to maintain their lifestyle if Ed should die prematurely.
5. Provide for estate liquidity at death.
6. Avoid unnecessary taxes at the death of either Ed or Amy.

II. Personal planning

   A. Tax planning
1. Present situation
2. Treatment of distributions from nonqualified deferred-compensation plan
3. Creation of fund for Scott
    a. Outright gifts
    b. 2503(b) trust
    c. 2503(c) trust
    d. UGMA gifts
4. Dispositions at death
    a. Revision of estate plan
    b. Analysis of present situation

    c.   Imposition of the excise tax

    d.   Modification of present plan to consider concept of "equity of inheritance"

    e.   Considerations stemming from Amy's family's history of longevity

    f.   Use of irrevocable life insurance trust

B. Accumulation planning

C. Insurance planning

    1.   Long-term care protection for Scott

    2.   Long-term care protection for Amy

    3.   Current life insurance coverage and recommendations

    4.   Insurance to fund income supplements for retirement and for Scott

    5.   Equalization of benefit for Bea

    6.   Additional income for Amy should Ed die first

    7.   Review of accidental death and dismemberment coverage

    8.   Review of disability insurance

    9.   Review of medical coverages for Ed and Amy

  10.   Evaluation of existing personal property and liability coverage

  11.   Summary of insurance needs

D. Investment planning

    1.   Refinancing the home

    2.   Evaluation of portfolio with regard to objectives

    3.   Recommended portfolio

    4.   Additional considerations

        a.   Maximizing use of Inc's 401(k) plan

        b.   Family of funds

        c.   Ownership considerations

INSTRUCTIONS

Now prepare a financial plan for the Martinsons. When you have prepared your solution, you can compare it with the suggested solution that follows.

PERSONAL FINANCIAL PLAN
FOR
EDGAR AND AMY MARTINSON
[Suggested Solution]

CLIENTS' OBJECTIVES

A. For lifetime planning
1. Accumulate sufficient wealth to assure that current lifestyle continues following retirement.
2. Address the retirement planning issues stemming from Amy's family history of longevity and Amy's likelihood of surviving Ed by many years.
3. Accumulate a fund that will assure an adequate stream of income to Scott for purposes of maintenance and medical costs.
4. Provide current medical insurance coverage for Scott both while he is covered by Inc's plan and after he is no longer covered by the plan.
5. Assess current insurance coverage and restructure such coverages optimally.

B. For disposition at death
1. Provide for Amy since she is likely to outlive Ed.
2. Construct the estate plan so that Scott's disability is adequately addressed should Ed and/or Amy predecease him.
3. Plan eventual inheritances in some equitable manner to allow Bea to receive an equal benefit and an equal amount of estate property.
4. Ensure that the entire family will have sufficient assets to maintain their lifestyle if Ed should die prematurely.
5. Provide for estate liquidity at death.
6. Avoid unnecessary taxes at the death of either Ed or Amy.

BASE CASE

Assumptions

1. The checking account balance is maintained at $12,000; the account is noninterest bearing.

2. Ed's salary is increased at 5 percent annually.

3. The money market deposit account earns 4.75 percent annually.

4. Investable cash is invested and earns 5 percent annually.

5. Expenditures for food, clothing and cleaning, utilities, phone, vacations, and charitable contributions will increase annually at 3 percent.

6. Expenditures for transportation will increase 4 percent annually.

7. Expenditures for entertainment will increase 5 percent annually.

8. Expenditures for medical insurance and other medical expenses will increase at 6 percent annually.

9. Decreases in the value of furniture have been ignored.

10. Automobiles decrease in value at a rate of 15 percent annually.

11. The value of the home will increase at one percent annually.

12. The common stock portfolio will increase at 9 percent annually.

13. Dividends from the common stock portfolio are currently $3,120, will increase 4 percent annually, and are reinvested in the portfolio.

14. IRAs will earn 8.1 percent annually over the next 4 years.

INCOME STATEMENT

EDGAR & AMY MARTINSON

BASE CASE	2002	2003	2004	2005	2006
Earned Income					
Compensation-CI	100,000	105,000	110,250	115,763	121,551
Company Bonus	10,000	10,500	11,025	11,576	12,155
401(k)-Ed's contr	-4,750	-4,987	-5,237	-5,499	-5,774
	105,250	110,513	116,038	121,840	127,932
Interest/Dividends					
Money Market Fund	1,188	1,188	1,188	1,188	1,188
Stock Portfolio	850	884	919	956	994
Investable Cash	662	2,068	3,660	5,541	7,758
Growth Mutual Funds	3,345	3,834	4,394	5,035	5,771
Balnced Mutual Fund	3,545	3,898	4,285	4,712	5,181
	9,590	11,871	14,446	17,433	20,892
	========	========	========	========	========
Adj Gross Income	114,840	122,384	130,485	139,273	148,824
Deductions					
Charitable 50%	2,000	2,060	2,122	2,185	2,251
State Tax Paid	4,783	5,212	5,656	6,157	6,703
Property Tax--Home	3,000	3,090	3,183	3,278	3,377
Home Mortgage	12,893	12,713	12,511	12,286	12,038
Gross Deductions	22,676	23,075	23,472	23,906	24,369
Standard Deduction	7,600	7,850	8,100	8,787	9,568
Allowed Deductions	22,676	23,075	23,472	23,906	24,369
Pers Exemptions	8,700	9,000	9,300	9,600	10,050
	========	========	========	========	========
Taxable Income	83,464	90,309	97,713	105,766	114,406
	========	========	========	========	========
Fed Income Tax	16,325	17,975	19,294	20,748	23,279
	========	========	========	========	========
Fed Tax Bracket-Ord Inc	27.0%	27.0%	26.0%	26.0%	25.0%

BALANCE SHEET

EDGAR & AMY MARTINSON

BASE CASE	2002	2003	2004	2005	2006
LIQUID ASSETS					
Cash Balance	11,975	12,004	12,014	12,015	12,018
Cash Deposits					
Investable Cash	27,121	57,658	92,408	134,769	183,305
IRA (CD's) - Ed	24,323	26,293	28,423	30,725	33,214
IRA (CD's) - Amy	25,944	28,045	30,317	32,773	35,428
Money Market Fund	25,000	25,000	25,000	25,000	25,000
	102,388	136,996	176,148	223,267	276,947
Stocks & Bonds					
Stock Portfolio	109,000	118,810	129,503	141,158	153,862
Growth Mutual Funds	137,530	157,620	180,645	207,034	237,278
Balnced Mutual Fund	92,360	101,551	111,658	122,770	134,989
	338,889	377,982	421,806	470,963	526,129
Life Insurance					
LifeInsCashValu-Ed	34,425	34,425	34,425	34,425	34,425
LifeInsCashValu-Amy	1,800	1,800	1,800	1,800	1,800
	36,225	36,225	36,225	36,225	36,225
	========	========	========	========	========
Liquid Assets	489,477	563,207	646,194	742,469	851,318
	========	========	========	========	========
NONLIQUID ASSETS					
Retirement Plans					
401(k) Plan	134,540	145,976	158,384	171,847	186,454
401(k)-Ed's contr	4,750	9,738	14,975	20,474	26,248
401(k)-Emplyr contr	4,750	9,738	14,975	20,474	26,248
Vested Pension	149,625	157,106	164,961	173,209	181,869
	293,665	322,558	353,295	386,004	420,819
Personal Property					
Home	378,750	382,538	386,363	390,227	394,129
Ed's car	17,000	14,450	12,283	10,440	8,874
Amy's car	10,200	8,670	7,370	6,264	5,324
Home Furnishings	75,000	75,000	75,000	75,000	75,000
	480,950	480,658	481,015	481,931	483,327
	========	========	========	========	========
Nonliquid Assets	774,615	803,216	834,310	867,935	904,147
	========	========	========	========	========
Total Assets	1,264,092	1,366,423	1,480,504	1,610,404	1,755,465

BALANCE SHEET (cont.)

EDGAR & AMY MARTINSON

BASE CASE LIABILITIES	2002	2003	2004	2005	2006
Mortgage Loans					
Home Mortgage	118,505	116,733	114,759	112,560	110,113
	118,505	116,733	114,759	112,560	110,113
Notes Payable					
Ed's Car Loan	11,429	6,998	2,151	0	0
	11,429	6,998	2,151	0	0
	========	========	========	========	========
Total Liabilities	129,934	123,731	116,910	112,560	110,113
	========	========	========	========	========
Net Worth	1,134,158	1,242,692	1,363,594	1,497,844	1,645,352
	========	========	========	========	========

CASH FLOW STATEMENT

EDGAR & AMY MARTINSON

BASE CASE	2002	2003	2004	2005	2006
BEGINNING OF YEAR					
Idle Cash On Hand	12,000	11,975	12,004	12,014	12,015
SOURCES OF CASH					
Cash Income					
Compensation-Cl	100,000	105,000	110,250	115,763	121,551
Company Bonus	10,000	10,500	11,025	11,576	12,155
Interest+Dividends	2,038	2,072	2,107	2,144	2,182
	112,038	117,572	123,382	129,483	135,888
	========	========	========	========	========
Total Cash Inflow	112,038	117,572	123,382	129,483	135,888
	========	========	========	========	========
Tot Cash Available	124,038	129,547	135,387	141,497	147,903
	========	========	========	========	========
USES OF CASH					
Fully Tax Deductible					
401(k)-Ed's contr	4,750	4,988	5,237	5,499	5,774
Home Mortgage	12,893	12,713	12,511	12,286	12,038
	17,643	17,701	17,748	17,785	17,812
Partly Deductible					
Med Ins Premium	240	254	270	286	303
Other Medical Expen	2,800	2,968	3,146	3,335	3,535
Charity Contrb-50%	2,000	2,060	2,122	2,185	2,251
	5,040	5,282	5,538	5,806	6,089
Not Tax Deductible					
Ed's Car Loan	1,228	849	433	49	0
Food	8,000	8,240	8,487	8,742	9,004
Clothing	3,000	3,090	3,183	3,278	3,377
Entertainment	2,000	2,100	2,205	2,315	2,431
Vacations	3,000	3,090	3,183	3,278	3,377
Transportation	1,000	1,040	1,082	1,125	1,170
Home Insurance Prem	500	510	520	531	541
Prop/Liab Ins Prem	100	102	104	106	108
Auto Insurance Prem	1,000	1,040	1,082	1,125	1,170
Ed's Life Ins Prems	2,335	2,335	2,335	2,335	2,335
Amy's Life Ins Prem	125	125	125	125	125
Home Improvements	1,000	1,030	1,061	1,093	1,126
Utility/Phone	2,000	2,060	2,122	2,185	2,251
Personal Care Items	1,300	1,339	1,379	1,421	1,463
	26,588	26,950	27,300	27,708	28,477

CASH FLOW STATEMENT (cont.)

EDGAR & AMY MARTINSON

BASE CASE	2002	2003	2004	2005	2006
Taxes Paid					
Fed Tax Paid	16,325	17,975	19,294	20,748	23,279
State Tax Paid	4,783	5,212	5,656	6,157	6,703
FICA/Soc Sec Tax	6,580	6,660	6,743	6,831	6,924
Property Tax—Home	3,000	3,090	3,183	3,278	3,377
	30,688	32,937	34,876	37,014	40,283
Purchase/Deposits					
Investable Cash	26,460	28,469	31,090	36,820	40,778
	26,460	28,469	31,090	36,820	40,778
Liability Liquidation					
Home Mortgage	1,592	1,772	1,974	2,199	2,447
Ed's Car Loan	4,052	4,431	4,847	2,151	0
	5,644	6,203	6,821	4,350	2,447
	========	========	========	========	========
Tot Cash Outflow	112,063	117,542	123,372	129,483	135,885
	========	========	========	========	========
END OF YEAR					
Cash Balance	11,975	12,004	12,014	12,015	12,018
	========	========	========	========	========

SUPPORTING SCHEDULE

EDGAR & AMY MARTINSON

BASE CASE	JOINT 2002	JOINT 2003	JOINT 2004	JOINT 2005	JOINT 2006
Income					
Earned Income	105,250	110,513	116,038	121,840	127,932
Adj Gross Income	114,840	122,384	130,485	139,273	148,824
Allowed Deductions	22,676	23,075	23,472	23,906	24,369
Pers Exemptions	8,700	9,000	9,300	9,600	10,050
Taxable Income	83,464	90,309	97,713	105,766	114,406
Federal Tax Liab					
Regular Tax	16,328	17,980	19,298	20,169	21,042
Gross Fed Inc Tax	16,325	17,975	19,294	20,169	21,042
Alt Minimum Tax	0	0	0	579	2,237
Disallowed	0	0	0	0	-579
Fed Income Tax	16,325	17,975	19,294	20,748	23,279
Fed Tax Analysis-Ord Inc					
Indexing Factor	79	85	92	98	105
Fed Tax Bracket-Ord Inc	27.0%	27.0%	26.0%	26.0%	25.0%
$ to Next Bracket	29,586	26,691	23,387	19,584	15,344
Next Bracket	30.0%	30.0%	29.0%	29.0%	28.0%
Previous Bracket	15.0%	15.0%	15.0%	15.0%	15.0%
$ to Prev Bracket	36,714	41,909	47,613	49,966	54,379
Fed Effective Tax Rate	19.6%	19.9%	19.8%	19.6%	20.4%
Alt Minimum Tax					
Adj Gross Income	114,840	122,384	130,485	139,273	148,824
Contributions	-2,000	-2,060	-2,122	-2,185	-2,251
Home Mortgage	-12,893	-12,713	-12,511	-12,286	-12,038
Adjusted AMTI	99,947	107,611	115,852	124,802	134,535
AMT Exemptions	-49,000	-49,000	-49,000	-45,000	-45,000
AMT Taxable Inc	50,947	58,611	66,852	79,802	89,535
Gross Alt Min Tx	13,246	15,239	17,381	20,748	23,279
Fed Tax Less FTC	-16,325	-17,975	-19,294	-20,169	-21,042
Alt Minimum Tax	0	0	0	579	2,237
Other Tax Liabs					
FICA/Soc Sec Tax	6,580	6,660	6,743	6,831	6,924
Adj Gross Inc	114,840	122,384	130,485	139,273	148,824
GA Adj Gross Inc	114,840	122,384	130,485	139,273	148,824
GA Standard Ded	3,000	3,000	3,000	3,000	3,000
GA Itemized Ded	22,676	23,075	23,472	23,906	24,369
GA Exemptions	8,100	8,100	8,400	8,400	8,400
GA Taxable Inc	84,064	91,209	98,613	106,966	116,056
GA Regular Tax	4,783	5,212	5,656	6,157	6,703
GA Income Tax	4,783	5,212	5,656	6,157	6,703
Georgia Tax	4,783	5,212	5,656	6,157	6,703
Tot State/Local Tx	4,783	5,212	5,656	6,157	6,703
Total Inc Tax	27,688	29,847	31,693	33,736	36,906

FINANCIAL SUMMARY

EDGAR & AMY MARTINSON

BASE CASE	2002	2003	2004	2005	2006
Gross Real Income					
Personal Earnings	110,000	115,500	121,275	127,339	133,706
Interest Income	1,850	3,256	4,848	6,729	8,946
Dividends Rcvd	7,740	8,615	9,598	10,704	11,946
	119,590	127,371	135,721	144,771	154,598
Income & Inflation					
Gross Real Inc	119,590	127,371	135,721	144,771	154,598
Total Inc Tax	-27,688	-29,847	-31,693	-33,736	-36,906
Net Real Income	91,902	97,524	104,028	111,035	117,692
Cur Real Inc =	91,902	95,118	98,447	101,893	105,459
At Infltn Rate of	4	4	4	4	4
Cash Flow					
Idle Cash On Hand	12,000	11,975	12,004	12,014	12,015
Norml Cash Inflow	112,038	117,572	123,382	129,483	135,888
Norml Cash Outflw	85,603	89,073	92,282	92,663	95,107
Cash Invested	26,460	28,469	31,090	36,820	40,778
Cash Balance	11,975	12,004	12,014	12,015	12,018
Net Worth					
Personal Assets	529,150	528,887	529,254	530,170	531,570
Investment Assets	734,942	837,536	951,249	1,080,234	1,223,895
Personal Liabilities	-129,934	-123,731	-116,910	-112,560	-110,113
Personal Net Worth	399,216	405,156	412,344	417,610	421,457
Investment Net Worth	734,942	837,536	951,249	1,080,234	1,223,895
Net Worth	1,134,158	1,242,692	1,363,594	1,497,844	1,645,352

PERSONAL PLANNING: TAXES

Present Situation

There are 10 separate issues stemming from the Martinsons' current situation that need to be addressed within the framework of tax planning. Each of the following current situations contains some financial and/or tax considerations that will affect their ability to achieve their objectives:

- the corporate defined-benefit noncontributory pension plan
- the contributory 401(k) plan
- the tax implications of the residential real estate purchase
- the $50,000 whole life insurance policy
- the individual retirement account (IRA)
- taxability of money market account income
- the reinvestment of income and capital gains in the mutual funds
- the current salary of $100,000
- the nonqualified deferred-compensation plan
- the group term life insurance

The Corporate Defined-Benefit Noncontributory Pension Plan

Ed's employer, Inc, established a qualified noncontributory defined-benefit pension plan that provides a maximum retirement income benefit of 1.5 percent of the average of an employee's highest 5 years of income times the number of years of service, with the maximum number of years of service for the purpose of the plan being 25 years. The plan benefit is not offset by retirement income provided under Social Security.

The Contributory 401(k) Plan

Inc also established a voluntary participation salary-reduction-type 401(k) plan for its employees 6 years ago. At this time almost 85 percent of Inc's employees participate in the plan. For employee contributions up to 5 percent of salary, Inc will contribute 2.5 percent of salary during the first 5 years of service and 3.75 percent until 10 years of service are achieved. After that time Inc will match the employee's 5 percent contribution. The plan further stipulates that employee contributions in excess of 5 percent are permitted but that no increased contribution on the part of Inc shall be made. The 401(k) plan does permit lump-sum withdrawals upon retirement or severance from the employer. Further features of the plan are that it is self-directed so that plan participants may choose the investment instruments and may shift invested funds within a limited set of alternatives.

Tax Implications of the Residential Real Estate Purchase

When the Martinsons sold their house for $200,000 in 1997 (under pre-1998 tax law), they paid $350,000 for their newly built house, which today has a fair market value of $375,000. The Martinsons' basis in the first house was $58,000. Since a new principal residence was purchased within a 2-year period following the sale of the prior principal residence, the Martinsons' gain on the sale was not recognized for purposes of federal income taxation. However, the original basis in the prior principal residence was carried over. Therefore if the Martinsons were to sell their new home today for $375,000, the cost basis to be used for purposes of determining the capital gain after the Section 121 exclusion available beginning in 1998 would be $58,000 plus any additional after-tax funds added to the purchase price.

The $50,000 Whole Life Insurance Policy

When Ed and Amy were married, Ed purchased a $50,000 whole life policy. He is the owner of the policy, and Amy is the primary beneficiary.

Under federal estate tax law if an insured has any "incidents of ownership" in a life insurance policy at the date of death, the face amount of the policy will have to be included in the insured's gross estate for federal estate tax purposes. Since Ed is the policyowner, if he dies today the face amount of the life insurance policy, $50,000, will be included in his gross estate.

The Individual Retirement Account (IRA)

The Martinsons have continuously invested their excess income in several different instruments. During the years that the individual retirement account (IRA) provisions under IRC Sec. 408 permitted fully tax-deductible contributions of up to $2,000 annually for everyone, including those who were also participating in other qualified plans without limitation, Ed funded a personal IRA at the local savings and loan. Although Ed can no longer make deductible contributions to an IRA, the funds that were previously contributed to the plan will continue to generate interest income on a tax-deferred basis until distributions are taken from the plan. (Because Ed is a participant in a corporate pension plan and because his adjusted gross income exceeds the allowable amount, he is prevented under current tax law from making deductible contributions to an individual retirement account.) Ed could consider the possibility of making a contribution to a Roth IRA, since the Martinsons' adjusted gross income is less than $150,000. Contributions to a Roth IRA will not be tax deductible, but future withdrawals will be tax free if the Martinsons comply with the new Roth IRA requirement.

Taxability of Money Market Account Income

The Martinsons jointly own a money market deposit account at the local savings and loan. The account typically has an average balance of about $25,000. Since these funds are not invested in tax-exempt vehicles, the interest income generated by the money market deposit account is currently taxable as ordinary income.

The Reinvestment of Income and Capital Gains in the Mutual Funds

The Martinsons monitor the money market account and if the balance grows too large, the excess is divided between investments in a balanced mutual fund and a growth mutual fund. In both these funds, all dividends and capital gains are being reinvested. With regard to federal income taxation, the capital gains and dividend reinvestments will have to be recognized currently as part of the Martinsons' gross income.

The Current Salary of $100,000

Currently Ed's salary is $100,000 per year. This amount is taxable as ordinary income and will translate into a sizable federal income tax liability each year. Unfortunately, there is little that can be done when a taxpayer/client is an employee of a large corporation and does not have the power or influence to determine the internal salary/benefit structure.

The Nonqualified Deferred-Compensation Plan

When Ed was promoted last year, he became a participant in Inc's nonqualified deferred-compensation plan. During the years that Ed will work at Inc, the firm will earmark funds in a separate account to fulfill the deferred-compensation obligation. It should be remembered, however, that these funds are part of Inc's assets and are available to its creditors and not to Ed. At this time, Ed does not have to recognize any current income on these assets.

The Group Term Life Insurance Plan

Inc provides noncontributory group term life insurance in the amount of 1.5 times annual base salary for all employees. IRC Sec. 79 permits the cost of the first $50,000 worth of coverage on an insured-employee to be free of federal income tax. Furthermore, the cost of the additional coverage will be taxable to the insured-employee on a tax-favored basis because of the IRS-approved rate-of-insurance tables.

Treatment of Distributions from the Nonqualified Deferred-Compensation Plan

Nonqualified deferred compensation is an extremely popular employee benefit for executives such as Ed Martinson. The highlights of nonqualified deferred-compensation plans are

- Nonqualified deferred compensation is an employee benefit that allows an employee to defer income taxation of compensation that is earned currently and would therefore be subject to current taxation.
- A properly structured plan will pay the former employee income over a period of years following retirement. The fact that it is *nonqualified* will permit the employer to escape the strict nondiscrimination, reporting, and disclosure requirements that ERISA imposes on qualified plans.
- The employee who participates in the plan enters into an agreement with his or her employer providing that specific payments are to be made to the employee or beneficiaries named by the employee in the event of death, disability, or retirement. Because certain standards must exist in the employer-employee relationship before federal income tax may be effectively deferred, the agreement must contain a clause establishing a contingency that can cause the employee to forfeit rights to future payments.

There are several federal income tax consequences of nonqualified deferred compensation that must be considered. It is helpful to separately analyze the federal tax implications affecting the employer and those affecting the employee.

The Employer

- Usually the employer funds the nonqualified deferred-compensation plan with life insurance acquired on the life of the employee. The employer pays the premiums, but premiums are not deductible for federal income tax purposes.
- To fund the retirement obligation, the employer frequently uses one of the settlement options available under the terms of the life insurance policy. A part of each installment payment the employer receives will be taxable income under the annuity rules. Sometimes, however, the employer will choose to surrender the policy and receive a lump-sum payment. In this case the amount that exceeds the employer's cost will be taxed as ordinary income.
- Any death proceeds the employer receives at the employee's death are free of federal income tax.

- The employer will generate a federal income tax deduction when the benefits are paid either to the employee or to the employee's family after the employee's death.

The Employee

- While employed, the plan participant is not required to include in gross income the portion of compensation that is deferred under the deferred-compensation plan.
- Any benefit the employee or the employee's named beneficiaries receive will be taxed as ordinary income when received.

There are also federal estate tax implications stemming from participation in a nonqualified deferred-compensation plan. The present value of the future benefits of a nonqualified deferred-compensation benefit payable to an employee or an employee's named beneficiary will be includible in the employee's gross estate for federal estate tax purposes. Estate inclusion is required because the employee had a present right to receive a future income stream under the deferred-compensation plan.

Creation of a Fund for Scott

Because of Scott's medical situation, the Martinsons should begin to fund a separate account for Scott's benefit. Several approaches may be considered including

- outright gifts
- 2503(b) trusts
- 2503(c) trusts
- UGMA gifts

Each of these vehicles will be explored separately.

Outright Gifts

IRC Sec. 2503(b) allows a donor to exclude the first $11,000 of value from gift tax if a gift of a present interest is made. If the donor of the gifted property is married, the spouse can split the gift, doubling the amount of the allowable annual exclusion to $22,000. This annual exclusion applies to each donee of the gifted property and applies per calendar year. Since Scott will need funds for the balance of his life, it would be a prudent planning step for Ed and Amy to begin a continuous and concerted gifting effort. However, making outright gifts to Scott would not be wise under these facts since no control could be imposed on Scott's spending.

The Sec. 2503(b) Trust

Given Amy and Ed's objective to provide Scott with a lifetime supplemental income, they should consider lifetime or testamentary transfers of assets into a trust so that Scott will have the supplemental income available to him. It is advisable for Ed and Amy to begin to transfer assets now to a trust for Scott's benefit in order to avoid gift or estate taxation on the posttransfer appreciation.

Ed and Amy could make inter vivos asset transfers to a trust. IRC Sec. 2503(b) provides that $11,000 ($22,000 for a married couple) worth of property may be transferred free of federal gift taxation as long as the gift is a completed gift and as long as it is a "gift of a present interest." Because this annual exclusion is such a valuable technique, it is prudent to make use of it on a regular basis.

The Sec. 2503(b) trust permits the donor to apply the annual exclusion to property transferred into the trust. The trust *requires* income to be distributed at least annually to (or for the use of) the minor beneficiary. The trust agreement identifies the income beneficiary. The minor beneficiary receives the trust's principal whenever the trust agreement specifies. A distribution of principal does not have to be made by age 21; corpus may be held for as long as the beneficiary lives—or for any shorter period of time. As a practical matter the principal can actually bypass the income beneficiary and go directly to other individuals whom the grantor—or even the named beneficiary—has specified. The trust instrument itself can also control the pattern of asset distribution in the event that the minor dies prior to receiving the corpus of the trust. It is not necessary that trust assets be paid to the minor's estate or appointees.

Many feel that the mandatory payment of income to (or in behalf of) the beneficiary will become burdensome—especially while the beneficiary is still a minor. Income distributions could be deposited in a custodial account and used for the minor's benefit or left to accumulate in a custodial account until the minor attains majority—at which time any amounts remaining would be turned over to the beneficiary. Ed and Amy should create a 2503(b) trust at this time for Scott's benefit. The primary advantage of using the Sec. 2503(b) trust is that principal need not be distributed when the minor reaches age 21. Since Scott is 16, the adverse consequences of the kiddie tax are not a consideration.

The Sec. 2503(c) Trust

Unlike a Sec. 2503(b) trust, a Sec. 2503(c) trust requires that income and principal be distributed when the beneficiary attains age 21 but does not require the trustee to distribute income on an annual basis.

Gifts to a Sec. 2503(c) trust qualify for the gift tax annual exclusion if the following requirements are met:

- income and principal must be expended by or on behalf of the beneficiary

- to the extent that it is not so expended, income and principal must pass to the beneficiary at age 21 or
- if the beneficiary dies prior to that time, income and principal will go to the beneficiary's estate or to appointees under a general power of appointment

One of the primary advantages of the Sec. 2503(c) trust is the significant degree of flexibility that can be built into the arrangement. Income that has been accumulated, in addition to any principal in the trust, can be paid to the donee when he or she attains age 21. Given the facts presented here, however, Ed and Amy will probably want the trust to continue to age 25, 30, or even longer. It is possible to provide continued management of the trust assets and at the same time avoid forfeiting the annual exclusion by giving the donee, at age 21, a right for a limited period to require immediate distribution by giving written notice to the trustee. If the beneficiary fails to give written notice, the trust can continue automatically for whatever period the donor specified when he or she created the arrangement. This is a technique that Ed and Amy will want to consider.

To summarize, Ed and Amy anticipate that because of their son's unfortunate medical situation, he will need financial assistance throughout his life. Rather than having assets pass through Ed and/or Amy's estate and having federal estate tax imposed at what will be a higher tax liability (particularly if the assets appreciate in value), the assets can be gifted into either a Sec. 2503(b) or 2503(c) trust. The annual exclusion will be available in both types of trusts. To the extent that the value of the property transferred into the trust exceeds the annual exclusion amount, a gift tax will be payable, but the applicable credit will eliminate the need to actually pay any gift tax. As a practical matter it is more prudent to pay federal transfer tax on assets valued at today's lower values than to have appreciating assets pass through an estate, triggering a higher federal transfer tax.

Uniform Gifts to Minors Act

The Uniform Gifts to Minors Act (and Uniform Transfers to Minors Act) provide an alternative to the Sec. 2503(c) trust. The UGMA (and UTMA) is frequently used for smaller gifts because of its simplicity and because it offers the benefits of management, income and estate shifting, and the investment characteristics of a trust with few or none of the start-up costs associated with the use of trusts.

The Uniform Gifts to Minors Act and Uniform Transfers to Minors Act have been adopted in every state. The acts allow lifetime gifts of securities, money, a life insurance or annuity policy, or other property (which differs on a state-by-state basis) to an individual who is a minor on the date of the gift.

Because Scott is 16 and already in high school, he will attain majority in a few short years and have ready access to the accumulated funds. Therefore the use of the UGMA approach is not recommended in this case.

Dispositions at Death

So far our analysis has focused primarily on lifetime planning concerns. These issues should be addressed as soon as possible. Another integral component of the comprehensive financial planning process is estate planning.

Revision of Estate Plan

The Martinsons have wills they have not updated since they were married, and these wills no longer address their estate planning needs. At this time revision is needed to reflect their changed personal and financial situation. Because of the unlimited federal estate tax marital deduction, many tax advisers encourage the full use of the unlimited marital deduction of the estate by the first spouse to die. This approach will assure a deferral (but not a total forgiveness) of federal estate taxation at the first death. Of course, the tax will subsequently be imposed at the death of the second spouse. However, when the first spouse dies, the applicable credit should be used in combination with the federal estate tax marital deduction in estates where the combined assets of the husband and wife are greater than the amount of a single applicable credit exemption equivalent, which is $1 million in 2002.

The most important objective within the estate planning framework is not only to plan the estate of the first spouse to die but also to anticipate the planning needs at the surviving spouse's subsequent death. In any situation in which the unlimited federal estate tax marital deduction is utilized (as it is here because of the Martinsons' use of their respective "simple wills" that leave all estate assets to the surviving spouse), the applicable credit of the first spouse to die is wasted. The result is that the entire value of marital deduction assets will end up being taxed in the estate of the surviving spouse.

The Martinsons' revised wills should direct the integration of the applicable credit exemption equivalent with the marital deduction amount. Use of a credit shelter trust prevents overqualification of the marital deduction as illustrated under the current scenario. This revision ensures that the unified credit will not be "wasted."

An alternative approach would be an estate plan in which assets equal in value to the applicable credit equivalent can be directed by an appropriate will to a trust that provides the surviving spouse with access to the funds without requiring inclusion of the trust's assets in the surviving spouse's gross estate. The surviving spouse's access may be totally unrestricted, or it may be restricted if that is the Martinsons' wish.

Assuming Ed predeceases Amy, a portion of his estate assets should be placed into a testamentary trust for the benefit of Scott. Of course, a sufficient amount of assets would need to pass for the benefit of Amy in order to qualify for the estate tax marital deduction.

Analysis of Present Situation

Under the federal estate tax laws all property a decedent owns at the date of death is included in the gross estate. The larger the taxable estate, the larger the estate tax liability. Therefore the starting point is determining the size of the gross estate. Once this has been accomplished, we can then make recommendations to reduce the amount of the projected federal estate tax liability.

The current ownership of the life insurance policies poses a problem because Ed possesses incidents of ownership over the policies. Under IRC Sec. 2042(2) the face amount of these policies will be required to be included in Ed's gross estate for federal estate tax purposes.

Concept of "Equity of Inheritance"

Ed and Amy are caring and fair parents who love both their children. They do not show favoritism to either one of them. However, Scott's accident and subsequent medical problems have made it difficult to reconcile their philosophy of equity with the fact that Scott will need more financial aid than Bea.

One vexing issue that Ed and Amy have discussed is the favorable treatment that Bea has already received. First, they paid her college education expenses, and her degree has enabled her to begin a promising career with the potential for a high income. In addition, Bea was the sole recipient of Ed's mother's largesse (Scott was not born at the time of her demise) and now has a nice nest egg of her own. Because of these two considerations, Ed and Amy believe that their objective to fund a program designed to provide a lifetime income for Scott tends to equalize the financial benefits bestowed on both children. This view of equity may also involve unequal distributions from their estates.

Should the funding for Scott result in any inequitable treatment for Bea, Ed and Amy could acquire some life insurance on their lives at a later date, naming Bea as the beneficiary.

Considerations Stemming from Amy's Family History of Longevity

Because of their age difference the chances are quite good that Amy will outlive Ed by many years. An integral part of the planning process for the Martinsons involves initiating steps to resolve the problems stemming from this factor. It is clear that supplemental coverage will be necessary to add to the retirement benefits available from Inc and from Social Security.

The Use of the Irrevocable Life Insurance Trust

Prior discussion indicated that the face amount of certain life insurance policies will be included in Ed's gross estate for federal estate tax purposes at the date of his death. Specifically the $50,000 whole life policy will be included in Ed's gross estate because he will own the policy on his life at the time of his death and because IRC Sec. 2042(2) requires inclusion of the policy proceeds of any life insurance policy owned by the decedent-insured at the date of death. For the same reason the two $25,000 policies will also be included in his estate. Removal of the life insurance from Ed's gross estate is an easy yet effective step in the right direction.

IRC Sec. 2042 addresses the issue of includibility of life insurance proceeds in the insured's gross estate. IRC Sec. 2042(1) provides that the face amount of the policy will be included in the insured's gross estate if the estate is named as the beneficiary of the life insurance policy. Nothing in the facts indicates that this is the case here. IRC Sec. 2042(2) provides that to the extent that the decedent-insured possesses any incidents of ownership in the policy, the proceeds will likewise be included in the insured's gross estate. Incidents of ownership not only include situations in which the insured is named as the owner but also include the right on the part of the insured to borrow against the policy, change the beneficiary, pledge the policy against a loan, and so on. If Ed has any incident of ownership in a policy, he must relinquish ownership of the policy to remove the policy proceeds from his gross estate.

Ed could transfer the three whole life insurance policies that he currently owns to Amy, which would clearly remove all policy proceeds from Ed's gross estate (provided he lives for 3 more years) since he would no longer possess any incidents of ownership over the policy. However, cross-ownership of life insurance policies between spouses is not the best approach since the transferee-spouse could predecease the transferor. Furthermore, since divorce is so prevalent in this country, cross-spousal ownership is often unwise.

The preferable approach would be to use an irrevocable life insurance trust (ILIT). Ed could create an ILIT and transfer the three life insurance policies that he currently owns to the trust. Amy and the two children would be named as beneficiaries of the trust. Upon Amy's death, her share of the trust assets would be distributed to the children in equal shares, per stirpes. Because of Scott's medical situation his portion of the policy proceeds should remain in trust for the balance of his life with the named trustee directed to apply income (and principal if necessary) for Scott's benefit. Upon Scott's death, the trust is to terminate, with the trust assets to be distributed to Scott's heirs, if any; if none; to Bea if living; if Bea has predeceased Scott, to her heirs, if any; if none, to a named charity, Ed's college. Bea's portion could be distributed to her outright. The beneficiary of the whole life policies would be the ILIT.

IRC Sec. 2035 provides that if a decedent-insured transfers a life insurance policy and fails to live 3 years following this transfer, the policy proceeds still must be included as part of the insured's gross estate. Therefore Ed should be advised that if he fails to live 3 years following the creation of the irrevocable life insurance trust and the transfer of the policy into the trust, the policy proceeds will still be included in Ed's gross estate for federal estate tax purposes.

PERSONAL PLANNING: WEALTH ACCUMULATION

Amy and Ed desire to accumulate additional funds to ensure an adequate income during their retirement. Until Scott's accident and subsequent medical expenses they anticipated that between Scott's graduation from high school and Ed's retirement they would be able to concentrate their assets on this objective: the accumulation of sufficient funds to provide an additional $5,000 annual income (in current prices) during their retirement. Considering Scott's failure to recover fully from the accident, they feel they have an obligation to provide a source of income for him for life, apart from sources they might develop for themselves. Their goal is $3,000 per year in current prices. They estimate that prices will rise an average of 4 percent per year over the entire planning period; therefore the 4 percent inflation rate will apply before and after retirement.

Ed is now 54, and both Amy and he wonder how meeting these two accumulation goals will affect their cash flow. In addition, they are concerned about the impact of these accumulation goals on the possibility of Ed's retiring at age 62 in 8 years. Their target annual income for the income supplements, allowing for 4 percent inflation, is $6,842 for their supplement at age 62 and $7,696 at age 65. For Scott's funding, the target annual income is $4,105 if Ed retires at age 62 and $4,618 at age 65. They have indicated that the retirement supplement should provide an annual income stream for 40 years and that the funds available for Scott should provide him an income stream for 50 years. In both cases they prefer to begin with an age 62 retirement, but Ed does not want to reduce the payout time if his retirement is delayed.

Table 7-2 shows the estimated accumulation and annual funding needed for retirement at age 62 and age 65. A 4 percent rate of inflation is assumed for both the preretirement and postretirement periods. Also a 6 percent after-tax rate of return is used for both periods. The funds will be liquidated over the 40-year period as stated above.

TABLE 7-2
Funding for Retirement Income Supplement

Ed's Age	Target Annual Income	Lump Sum at Target Age	Annual Funding	
			Level	Rising at 5 Percent Each Year
62	$6,842	$193,378	$16,381	$14,016
65	7,696	217,514	13,705	11,437

Table 7-3 shows the estimated accumulation and annual funding needed to achieve their goal of having funds set aside for Scott's benefit. Again the assumptions are made that Ed retires at age 62 and at age 65. The after-tax earnings assumption is 6 percent, the inflation assumption is 3.5 percent, and the payout period for liquidating the accumulation is 50 years.

			Annual Funding	
Ed's Age	Target Annual Income	Lump Sum at Target Age	Level	Rising at 5 Percent Each Year
62	$4,105	$133,632	$13,337	$10,831
65	4,618	150,332	9,472	7,547

TABLE 7-3
Funding for Scott's Income Supplement

The Martinsons have $22,000 set aside for Scott's education and doubt that these funds will be used for that purpose. If these funds were integrated into their funding plans, the $22,000 would grow to $35,064 during the next 8 years and to $41,762 during the next 11 years. Using these accumulated educational funds as part of the accumulated funds for Scott's benefit will reduce their annual contributions to those shown in table 7-4.

TABLE 7-4
Annual Funding for Scott's Income Supplement Using the
Accumulated Educational Funds

			Annual Funding	
Ed's Age	Target Annual Income	Lump Sum at Target Age (in Addition to $22,000 Already Accumulated)	Level	Rising at 5 Percent Each Year
62	$4,105	$ 98,568	$9,395	$7,989
65	4,618	108,569	6,841	5,449

Table 7-5 consolidates the annual funding needed for these twin objectives, assuming the $22,000 education fund set aside for Scott is used as part of his target amount.

TABLE 7-5 **Total Annual Funding**		
	To Age 62 (8-Year Funding)	
	Level	Rising
Amy and Ed Scott Total	$16,381 9,395 $25,776	$14,016 7,989 $22,005
	To Age 65 (11-Year Funding)	
	Level	Rising
Amy and Ed Scott Total	$13,705 6,841 $20,546	$11,437 5,449 $16,886

Table 7-6 consolidates the information developed for the annual funding (both level and at a 5 percent rising amount) with the amount of their cash flow as shown in the base case over years 2003–2006.

If the Martinsons were to fund these objectives with either a level contribution or an annual contribution that increases by 5 percent each year over an 8-year period, their annual cash flow would be sufficient to meet the amount needed.

TABLE 7-6 **Comparison of Annual Cash Flow and Needed Annual Funding**					
		Annual Funding Increasing		Level Funding	
Year	Investable Cash Flow (Base Case)	8-Year	11-Year	8-Year	11-Year
2003	$28,469	$22,005	$16,886	$25,776	$20,546
2004	31,090	23,105	17,709	25,776	20,546
2005	36,820	24,161	18,594	25,776	20,546
2006	40,778	24,473	19,524	25,776	20,546

The Martinsons also have the following objectives that require use of their cash flow:

- long-term care protection for Scott
- long-term care protection for Amy
- life insurance protection against reduction in income should Ed die first and the pension benefit be reduced
- life insurance protection against estate shrinkage due to loss of the marital deduction

Until the annual costs of these other dimensions of their financial planning are determined, the final recommendation for these two accumulation objectives will be postponed.

PERSONAL PLANNING: INSURANCE

Long-Term Care Protection for Scott

Scott's medical condition is probably the most critical component of the Martinsons' overall financial plan. Since it is likely that Scott will require some form of long-term care protection, the Martinsons must take steps to be sure that this virtually certain development is appropriately addressed as part of the financial planning process.

Scott could be considered uninsurable because of the preexisting medical condition. Therefore the Martinsons must be prepared to provide funding for long-term care for Scott's benefit without the assistance of long-term care coverage.

Long-Term Care Protection for Amy

With Amy's family history of longevity, the Martinsons should acquire long-term care protection for her. The situation is different from Scott's, and the Martinsons will have no problem acquiring this coverage on Amy, as she is in excellent health.

Because approximately 30 million people over the age of 65 face a significant risk of requiring nursing home services sometime during their remaining years, the insurance industry has made long-term care policies available. The Martinsons should seriously consider acquiring one on Amy as soon as possible.

Long-term care policies contain many differing provisions, and they also differ from one insurance company to another. There are many insurance companies offering long-term care coverage, and the specific range of coverage goes from very limited protection to total and complete protection. The

Martinsons need to address the following issues before the appropriate policy can be selected:

- preexisting conditions
- elimination periods
- exclusions
- premium structure
- underwriting
- benefit provisions
- renewability
- inflation protection
- long-term care added to an existing life insurance policy

Preexisting Conditions

Long-term care insurance policies often contain preexisting-condition provisions. For an established time after the policy has been issued benefit payments are excluded for causes stemming from conditions that existed—and for which the insured has previously received medical advice and treatment—within a specified period of time before the policy was issued. Of course, the rationale behind a preexisting condition clause in a long-term care policy is to prevent adverse selection against the insurance company issuing the policy.

The National Association of Insurance Commissioners (NAIC) model contract provides that the preexisting-condition provisions should not exclude benefits for more than 6 months after policy issue and that specific exclusions should not be predicated on conditions that initially showed up more than 6 months prior to the date the policy was issued. Although most of the long-term care policies available today have incorporated and accepted the NAIC model concerning the 6-month standard, some states still permit long-term care policies to adopt a longer preexisting-condition provision. Some insurance companies will require a preexisting-condition provision of longer than 6 months for long-term care policies being issued to persons under the age of 65.

Since Amy is in good health, the preexisting-condition issue will not be a problem for the Martinsons.

Elimination Period

All long-term care policies contain a provision for an elimination or waiting period. The elimination period may be thought of as a form of deductible that establishes the specific time at which the benefits will begin. In essence the elimination or waiting period is the amount of time that will elapse following the point when an insured can satisfy benefit eligibility but when no benefit will be paid. For example, if a long-term care policy contains a 120-day elimination period, the insured would have to be in the care-giving facility for 120 days before the policy benefits would be payable. There would be 120 days of long-term care with no benefits paid, but on the 121st day the benefits would begin and payment would occur 30 days later.

The length of the elimination period affects the premium. The longer the elimination period under the terms of the policy, the lower the premium.

The actual length of elimination periods in long-term care policies can vary dramatically. It is possible for the Martinsons to acquire a long-term care policy with no elimination period (which would be very expensive), with an elimination period of 2 years (with a much lower premium), or with some time period in between. Since this decision involving the elimination period will directly affect costs, it will have to be considered very carefully in light of the their total financial resources available to meet the costs incurred during the elimination period.

Exclusions

All insurance policies that provide any form of health care coverage contain provisions dealing with exclusions. Although the actual exclusions in long-term care insurance policies are usually not very extensive, it is possible that a single exclusion might eliminate benefit payments for a cause for which other carriers could conceivably provide full coverage. Consequently the Martinsons must "shop" very carefully when choosing the appropriate coverage for Amy's long-term care.

Premiums

How the Martinsons pay for the long-term care coverage is of paramount importance. Although the immediate acquisition of this insurance is vital, the premiums can be relatively expensive, so care will have to be devoted to selecting the most cost-effective package. Most long-term care policies have level premiums for the balance of the insured's life, although some insurance carriers structure costs of long-term care products as increasing premiums. In this type of situation premiums will increase on an annual basis or at 2-, 3-, or 5-year intervals with level steps between adjustment points.

Regardless of whether the long-term care premium is level or increasing, the amount of the premium will be determined by the age of the insured at the time the policy is issued. Historically premium increases are significant only after age 40, and they become very steep after age 65. Waiting until age 70 to purchase this coverage could mean a tenfold increase in premium compared to a purchase at age 45.

One last point on the subject of premiums is that insurance carriers will not guarantee premium levels because the concept of long-term care coverage is a new one, and to date there are very few statistics on experience available to carriers. Long-term care policies are presently "guaranteed renewable," which means that the carrier can increase premium rates for all policyowners (for an entire class of policies) but only on the basis of claims experience rather than on the basis of changes in an insured's age or health. This arrangement is due to the fact that, since long-term care policies are so new, there is limited experience data, so all insurance companies could have computed premium levels at too low a figure. If so, in the future the industry might be forced to increase premium levels for existing policies as well as for newly issued products.

Some representative premiums are as follows:

Female Aged 45

| | Yearly Premium | |
| | No Inflation | Inflation |
$110/Day Benefit	Protection	Protection
3-year benefit period, 20-day waiting period	$247	$413
6-year benefit period, 20-day waiting period	294	491
Lifetime benefit period, 20-day waiting period	N/A	594

Underwriting Principles

The underwriting process has always been a complex aspect of any insurance company's internal operation. Because long-term care policies deal with the health of the insured and because these types of policies are sometimes issued through the older ages, a series of specialized underwriting principles is often necessary. Most carriers that currently market long-term care products have adopted a single classification approach for purposes of underwriting, which means that the insurance carrier will either accept or reject the application for the insurance coverage. However, a few of the carriers that are more involved in the marketing of long-term care products have begun rating policies. As long-term care products continue to grow in popularity and use, it is likely that additional underwriting classifications will be developed.

Benefits

When the Martinsons choose the right long-term care policy for Amy, they will need to be concerned primarily with benefits. Issues to be concerned about are the maximum duration of the benefits provided, the types and levels of care for which benefits will be provided, prerequisites for benefit eligibility, and the actual level of benefits payable.

With respect to duration the Martinsons will consider the fact that some long-term care policies provide unlimited benefit periods that would allow the insured to enjoy coverage for any length of stay required in a nursing home. The Martinsons will also learn, however, that some long-term care policies specify a maximum benefit duration such as 3 years or 5 years. Some policies will provide coverage for as short a period as one year. The Martinsons will need to select the appropriate coverage realizing, of course, that the longer the benefit period is, the more comprehensive the policy's level of protection will be.

With respect to the benefit payable, most long-term care policies will set forth the benefit as a specified dollar amount per day of benefit eligibility. The Martinsons must be especially cautious to select an adequate benefit level to provide the necessary protection for Amy.

Inflation Protection

Almost all long-term care policies contain some form of inflation protection or offer an inflation rider. This protection will come in the form of either an automatic increase in the benefit each year on a formula basis linked to a measure of inflation or a guarantee that the insured will have the opportunity to purchase additional increments of coverage at certain specified, preestablished intervals. Which approach is used is not too critical. The important thing is that the Martinsons must be sure to have some form of inflation protection.

Renewability

From the perspective of renewability there are two different types of long-term care policies currently available in the marketplace. Some insurance carriers market a long-term care product that is *conditionally renewable*. This type of policy sets forth specified, preestablished conditions that authorize the carrier either to refuse to renew the policy or to cancel the in-force protection. The Martinsons should be sure to avoid this type of policy. The other, referred to as *guaranteed renewable*, provides that the insured will be able to maintain the coverage in force as long as the premiums are paid when they come due. The insurance carrier that has issued the long-term care policy will be unable to refuse to renew the insurance protection or otherwise terminate the coverage for any reason whatsoever other than for nonpayment of premiums. Although this is the type of coverage that the Martinsons should select, it is somewhat more costly.

Benefit Period

Studies have shown that the average stay in a full-service care facility is less than 3 years. Many carriers are currently offering policies that provide coverage at the customer's preference, for any number of years from one to 6 inclusive or for life. Since the average stay in a full-service care facility is less than 3 years, it is tempting for clients to select a 3-year benefit period. In Amy's case purchasing a policy with a $110-per-day benefit, a 3-year benefit, a 20-day elimination period, and inflation protection represents an approximate annual savings of $181 per year when compared to a similar policy with a lifetime benefit—$594 versus $413. However, the major purpose of insurance is to protect against the worst-case financial scenario, not the average case. Thus Amy should select lifetime coverage, especially because of her family history of higher-than-average longevity.

Medicaid Spend-Down Strategy

Some planners have advised clients to select a short benefit period as part of a so-called "spend-down" strategy to maximize benefits available from Medicaid. This Medicaid benefit would be automatically processed if the care facility were Medicare approved. (Medicaid cannot reimburse a facility for services provided unless it is Medicare approved.)

One of Medicaid's programs provides financial assistance for individuals who need long-term care and whose income and nonexempt assets fall below state-specified levels. For individuals whose income or assets are above these levels, this spend-down strategy circumvents the restrictions so that the government, rather than the clients, will foot the bill for long-term care.

The spend-down approach usually involves the client's gifting enough assets to his or her adult children to reduce the individual's nonexempt assets below the state's threshold level. Assets exempt under federal guidelines include a primary residence if the spouse or a minor or disabled child still lives there, household effects, an automobile, and a prepaid burial contract. Each state has its own rules regarding other exemptions such as life insurance and securities.

Since Social Security payments and pension income are included in the maximum income threshold and cannot be gifted, it is critical to verify whether these income flows will preclude the client from qualifying for Medicaid.

Gifts must be irrevocable with no strings attached, and the client must refrain from filing for Medicaid coverage until at least 36 months after gifting the assets. If the client files before 36 months pass, Medicaid will deny benefits under its look-back provision according to the following formula:

$$\begin{array}{c} \text{Number of months} \\ \text{ineligible for} \\ \text{Medicaid benefits} \end{array} = \frac{\begin{array}{c}\text{total value of all assets}\\\text{transferred during look - back period}\end{array}}{\begin{array}{c}\text{average monthly cost of}\\\text{private nursing home}\end{array}}$$

Example: An incapacitated client applies for admission to a high-quality, Medicare-approved care facility. He retains assets until admitted in case the facility questions the ability to pay the monthly bill. The client then gifts assets to his adult children. The client retains an amount of nonexempt assets sufficient to make 36 months of care facility payments plus just enough additional nonexempt assets to stay below the Medicaid asset threshold. Thirty-six months after gifting the money, the client applies for Medicaid to pay for his care in the facility. Since the care facility is Medicare-approved, it must accept Medicaid's compensation as payment in full and cannot evict the client even though the payment may be below market rates.

If the spend-down strategy is designed in advance of the client's incapacity, he can purchase long-term care insurance with a benefit period equal to or slightly greater than the Medicaid look-back period. Thus, instead of paying out-of-pocket for 36 months while in the facility, the client receives insurance benefits.

Problems associated with the spend-down approach are numerous. First, many clients oppose the strategy on moral or ethical grounds. Second, many clients are unwilling to give up control of their assets. Third, the strategy does not lend itself well to the typical husband-wife planning situation since the spouse's income and assets are included to determine Medicaid eligibility. Even if the couple's income qualifies, the nonincapacitated spouse must give up assets without benefit of Medicaid compensation for his or her living expenses. Fourth, care facility operators are aware of this strategy and recognize the devastating effect that below-market compensation from Medicaid can have on their financial viability. Many high-quality facilities simply choose not to seek approval or seek to give up approval. Fifth, the facility could fail for reasons that are independent of Medicare, forcing the client to enter an approved facility that is much less comfortable. Sixth, the client may recover his or her health and no longer qualify for long-term care. Having transferred almost everything to the children, the client must then rely on the children's largesse, assuming that the children haven't spent everything.

In Amy and Ed's case, even if they were comfortable with the ethics, complexity, and viability of the Medicaid spend-down strategy, their current situation does not match the optimal conditions for that approach. One alternative is simply to do nothing now, anticipating use of the strategy later when their situation changes. For example, if Ed dies first and Amy subsequently requires long-term care, she can initiate the strategy at that time.

Unfortunately, if Medicaid rules change in the future, making the spend-down strategy impossible, any financial planning that anticipates using the strategy could be disastrous. A future need for extended long-term care could consume the entire estate, even if Amy owns a long-term care policy with a 3-year benefit period. Although she may be able to purchase additional coverage later, it is possible that she will become uninsurable or that policies available in the market in the future will not meet her needs.

A more efficient approach for the Martinsons to insulate themselves from potential financial disaster resulting from long-term care is to purchase a long-term care insurance policy with a lifetime benefit period. The additional expense relative to a 3-year benefit is relatively small, and owning such a policy eliminates the need for a strategy that may prove counterproductive.

Long-Term Care Added to Existing Life Insurance Coverage

So far we have looked at long-term care policies that are issued for a specific, one-dimensional purpose. There are some insurance carriers that have combined life insurance coverage with long-term care protection. This is accomplished administratively by adding a rider to the existing life insurance policy.

This rider accelerates the payment of a previously established portion of the death benefit to the insured when the insured becomes critically ill, requires custodial care, and is not expected to recover. In this situation a percentage of the face amount will be paid each year for a specified number of years.

Until the passage of the Health Insurance Portability and Accountability Act of 1996, life insurance proceeds when distributed in this manner to the insured have been treated as ordinary income for federal income tax purposes. This act provides that accelerated death benefits received by an individual from the insurer may be excluded from gross income if certain requirements are met. The act distinguishes two categories of individuals who can meet these requirements in whole or in part:

- The first is a terminally ill individual. This individual has obtained certification from a physician that death is reasonably expected to occur within 24 months of the date of certification. For this individual, the accelerated death benefits would be excluded from his or her gross income.
- The second is a chronically ill individual. This individual has been certified within the preceding 12-month period by a licensed health care practitioner as being unable to perform at least two activities of daily living for at least 90 days, certified as having a similar level of disability or requiring substantial supervision because of severe cognitive impairment. This individual can exclude accelerated death benefits from income if the benefit payment is for the actual costs of incurred qualified long-term care not compensated by insurance or otherwise. This rule applies for lump-sum accelerated death benefits that are received by the individual. However, if the accelerated death benefits are determined by a per diem, rather than a lump-sum, method, then the entire amount received from the insurer would be excludible from gross income regardless of the actual costs incurred by the individual.

In the Martinsons' situation, adding the rider that obtains accelerated death benefits to an existing life insurance policy is not appropriate for two reasons. First, when a separate long-term care policy is used, the annual premium qualifies as a potential medical deduction subject to the 7.5 percent-of-adjusted-gross-income rule. Second, at this time there is not sufficient life insurance coverage on Amy's life to make this a feasible rider to an existing policy.

Current Life Insurance Coverage: Comparison of Present Status with Estimated Needs and Recommendations for Coverage and Form of Ownership

The case narrative explains Ed and Amy's current life insurance situation. Ed is the insured on a $50,000 whole life insurance policy with an annual premium of $1,120. He is the owner of the policy, and he named Amy as the primary beneficiary. He subsequently named his two children—Bea and Scott—as the contingent beneficiaries, per stirpes.

Amy converted her group term life insurance to a $5,000 whole life policy with a $5,000 face value and named Ed as the primary beneficiary. For this policy it is recommended that the children be named as primary beneficiaries and that a charity be named as successor beneficiary. The two children have been named as contingent beneficiaries, per stirpes. Ed is also the owner and the insured on two $25,000 policies that have a combined premium of $1,215 and a total cash value of $16,325. Each of these $25,000 policies was acquired when a Martinson child was born. Each child is the named primary beneficiary on one policy, and Amy is the contingent beneficiary for both policies.

The financial services professional must determine whether the current coverage is adequate. Our starting point will be to compute the approximate "cost of dying." Expenditures such as costs of administration, paying off debts, federal estate tax, and state inheritance tax (if any) need to be considered. Next the amount of available liquid assets will be ascertained. Finally a decision about the adequacy of the current life insurance coverage can then be reached.

From the data presented in the case, Ed and Amy's gross estates are $941,800 and $262,900 respectively, determined as follows:

	Ed's Gross Estate	Amy's Gross Estate
Checking account	$ 6,000	$ 6,000
Money market deposit account	12,500	12,500
Residence	187,500	187,500
Life insurance—whole life	50,000	
Life insurance	25,000	
Life insurance	25,000	
Life insurance		5,000
IRA	22,200	
IRA		2,400
Balanced fund	84,000	
Growth fund	120,000	
401(k) bond fund	50,000	
401(k) stock fund	74,000	

Group term life insurance	157,500	
Nonqualified deferred compensation	52,000	
Vested pension benefit	190,000	
Common stock	104,000	
Household furnishings	37,500	37,500
Auto	20,000	
Auto		12,000
Miscellaneous	600	
Gross estate	$1,217,800	$262,900

The case narrative states that Ed and Amy have simple, reciprocal wills. This type of will leaves all of the deceased's respective estate properties to the surviving spouse.

Based on the data above, Ed's gross estate is $941,800, and his total costs at the date of death will be as follows:

<u>At Ed's death:</u>

	Ed's Estate Computations	Ed's Estate Shrinkage
Gross estate	$1,217,800	
Less costs of administration (8 percent)	97,424	$ 97,424
Less mortgage	120,097	
Adjusted gross estate	1,000,279	
Less federal estate tax marital deduction	1,000,279	
Taxable estate	–0–	
Federal estate tax	–0–	
Less unified credit	N/A	
Federal estate tax owed	–0–	–0–
State inheritance tax	–0–	–0–
Total estate shrinkage at Ed's death		$ 97,424

<u>At Amy's subsequent death:</u>

	Amy's Estate Computations	Amy's Estate Shrinkage
Gross estate*	$1,263,179	
Less costs of administration (8 percent)	101,054	$101,054
Adjusted gross estate	1,162,125	
Less federal estate tax marital deduction		–0–

*Assumes no increase in value of assets in her name

Taxable estate	1,162,125	
Federal estate tax	412,271	
Less unified credit	345,800	
Federal estate tax owed	66,471	66,471
State inheritance tax	–0–	–0–
Total estate shrinkage at Amy's death		$167,525
Total shrinkage at both deaths		$264,949

In a simple will arrangement, all estate property passes to the surviving spouse. Therefore, all of Ed's property passes to Amy. This means that although the full federal estate tax marital deduction is available for use by Ed's estate at his (the first) death, too much estate property passes to Amy and is taxed without the benefit of a marital deduction at her subsequent death. A marital deduction that integrates the benefits of the applicable credit with the marital deduction concept would be more prudent.

If the marital deduction trust approach is adopted, the computations are as follows:

At Ed's death:

	Ed's Estate Computations	Ed's Estate Shrinkage
Gross estate	$1,217,800	
Less costs of administration (8 percent)	97,424	$ 97,424
Less mortgage	120,097	
Adjusted gross estate	1,000,279	
Less federal estate tax marital deduction	279	
Taxable estate	1,000,000	
Federal estate tax	345,800	
Less unified credit	345,800	
Federal estate tax owed	–0–	–0–
State inheritance tax	–0–	–0–
Total estate shrinkage at Ed's death		$ 97,424

At Amy's subsequent death:

	Amy's Estate Computations	Amy's Estate Shrinkage
Gross estate	$263,179	

Less costs of administration		
(8 percent)	21,054	$ 21,054
Adjusted gross estate	242,125	
Less federal estate tax		
marital deduction	–0–	
Taxable estate	242,125	
Federal estate tax	68,280	
Less unified credit	68,280	
Federal estate tax owed	–0–	–0–
State inheritance tax	–0–	–0–
Total estate shrinkage at Amy's death		21,054
Total estate shrinkage at both deaths		$118,478

There are sufficient liquid assets available at the time of Ed's death (including the present value of the future benefit of the vested pension). Therefore from an estate liquidity perspective there is no need for additional life insurance.

However, there are several reasons why additional life insurance coverage on Ed's life may be necessary:

- to fund Scott's income supplement
- to fund retirement income supplements for Amy
- to provide funds to pay estate obligations at Ed's and Amy's deaths
- to supplement loss of income when Ed dies
- to equalize Bea's inheritance, if needed

Insurance to Fund Income Supplements for Ed and Amy's Retirement and for Scott

To achieve Ed's desire to retire at age 62, the Martinsons will need to accumulate approximately $200,000 ($193,378 from table 7-2, page 7.32). An additional $100,000 ($98,568 from table 7-4 on page 7.33) for Scott's benefit must also be accumulated. This combined amount of $300,000 will be in jeopardy if Ed dies before funding is completed. If an after-tax rate of return of 6 percent can be earned, then the present value of the $300,000 is about $190,000. This is the amount of life insurance needed on Ed's life. Since this insurance need is temporary, term insurance would be appropriate. Level term would have the Martinsons paying an annual premium for more insurance than they need for this purpose. The additional premium needed to pay for the level term is a relatively small cost that the Martinsons should be able to afford. This insurance will cost approximately $800 per year.

Because of the cost saving in having only one policy in the amount of $190,000 rather than two separate policies, a single policy should be purchased. The Martinsons' interests will be best served if Ed does not have any incidents of ownership in this policy because at his death the face amount of the policy will be included in his estate. An irrevocable life insurance trust containing a Crummey provision can be established that will apply for and own the policy. Ed will contribute sufficient money each year to pay the premium, and at his death the trust will use the proceeds to complete the funding for Scott and Amy.

Equalization of Benefit for Bea

Scott's unfortunate medical condition means that more of Ed and Amy's estate assets will probably pass to him so that after his parents' deaths he will be assured of being adequately cared for. Bea may have mixed feelings about this situation. Surely she understands that she is more fortunate than her brother and does not actually fault her parents for leaving more assets to Scott than to her. After all, Bea is healthy, self-sufficient, and better able to take care of herself. Despite Bea's understanding attitude about the situation, at some times she might feel that an inequity has transpired.

Ed and Amy are good parents as well as perceptive individuals. They know that a form of inequity would take place if Scott received more of the estate assets. To prevent any perceived inequity of treatment, the use of life insurance is recommended. Ed should acquire a life insurance policy on his own life with a face amount equal to the excess value of assets that will ultimately pass to Scott. In order to avoid inclusion of the policy proceeds in Ed's gross estate for federal estate tax purposes, Bea could be named as owner of the policy. More significantly, however, Bea should also be named as the primary beneficiary of the policy. At Ed's death Bea will receive policy proceeds in an amount that will eliminate what would otherwise be an inequity between her and her brother regarding the receipt of valuable estate assets.

Since the Martinsons want to treat both children in an equitable manner, they feel that some specific assets should become available to Bea to balance the funds being accumulated for Scott's benefit. The total accumulation for Scott will be about $122,000. Since the Martinsons spent about $60,000 for Bea's education, an additional $60,000 would be a reasonable amount to give Bea to achieve their desire for equalization.

A $60,000 whole life insurance policy on Ed's life should be acquired for this purpose. An interest-sensitive insurance product would place too much risk on the Martinsons, given their age. As with the previous insurance recommendation, the same life insurance trust would be the appropriate vehicle. The premium would then be a gift of a present interest for federal gift tax purposes, and the proceeds, *if* the trust applied for and owned the policy, would not be included in Ed's estate.

This insurance need, as well as the insurance need described in the next section, should be purchased as one policy. The trustee can be directed to distribute $60,000 of the total proceeds to Bea.

Additional Income for Amy Should Ed Die First

Should Ed predecease Amy, there will be a reduction in the amount of the Social Security benefits payable to her. Indeed, there may be a period of years when her age prevents her from receiving a surviving spouse's benefit, and this gap must be provided for. In addition, if Ed and Amy choose a joint and 50 percent survivor pension, there will be a sizable setback due to the age difference. This is part of the reason why the Martinsons want to set up the fund that will provide them with the additional $5,000 income each year. Also if Ed dies first, Amy will have a reduction in the benefit from Inc's pension plan, so some additional provision for the Social Security and pension reductions should be part of their overall financial plan.

If Amy was old enough to receive Social Security benefits as Ed's surviving spouse, there would be a reduction (loss of spousal benefit) in these benefits of approximately $400 per month ($4,800 per year). Ed's pension, based on $105,000 as his estimated 5-year average salary under the plan, would be $37,500 before applying the plan's setback for both early retirement at age 62 and the age differential. The combined effect of these setbacks reduces the pension by $12,000 to $25,500 yearly. At Ed's death this amount would be further reduced by 50 percent. It is this subsequent reduction for which the Martinsons must make some provision.

Although the Social Security benefit will decline, it is not necessary for the Martinsons to replace this income for Amy except for the few years during which she might not qualify for the benefit if she is under age 60. A fund of about $50,000 should be adequate. For the pension reduction the replacement need is $12,500 annually. If this annual total reduction of $17,300 for the Social Security gap and pension-reduced benefits is capitalized at 7.2 percent, then $240,000 of income-producing assets will be needed to provide the income replacement for Amy. Since the Martinsons' excess cash flow will be used to fund the supplemental income streams for their retirement and for Scott's need, they will also need insurance to fund Amy's need for income replacement.

However, there is an existing $50,000 of insurance on Ed's life, which can be used to reduce the amount of insurance protection needed for meeting Amy's need. Therefore an additional $190,000 ($240,000 − $50,000) of insurance is needed to achieve the necessary target. Ed should be the insured, and the life insurance trust should apply for and own the policy. The annual cost for one participating whole life policy in the amount of $250,000 ($190,000 + $60,000) is $8,800.

Review of Accidental Death and Dismemberment Coverage

Ed has an accidental death and dismemberment policy as an employee benefit from Inc. The policy carries a death benefit of double Ed's annual base salary. This coverage is in addition to other employment-related life insurance. Because Ed travels frequently on business, such a benefit is a good one and is adequate. There seems to be no need for Ed to have any additional accidental death coverage on an individual basis. To the extent that Ed does decide to acquire more coverage, whole life or universal life would be more appropriate than additional accidental death coverage.

Review of Disability Insurance

The case narrative indicates that Ed receives short-term disability benefits as part of his benefits package from Inc. Specifically coverage for 100 percent of lost salary for short-term disability (maximum of 6 months) is provided under a nonfunded wage contribution plan. Salary lost due to a disability that is serious enough to prevent a return to work after a 6-month period is replaced at 75 percent (including Social Security disability benefits) for the duration of the disability or until normal retirement age, whichever comes first. In the event of disability Inc will continue to credit years of service for purposes of coverage in the qualified pension plan and will make both the employer and the employee contributions to the 401(k) plan. Also the facts indicate that coverage will be continued under Inc's medical insurance plan at no charge to the disabled employee.

The issue is whether the employer-sponsored disability benefit is ample or whether Ed should purchase additional coverage on an individual basis. As stated earlier, Ed estimates a need of an additional $2,000 per month if he becomes disabled. It is therefore clear that the current employer-provided disability package is inadequate. One strong recommendation in the insurance planning portion of the financial plan is for Ed to purchase individual disability insurance coverage that pays $2,000 a month until age 65 and has an annual cost of $1,220. Having the insurance until age 65 protects Ed should he not retire at age 62 as planned.

Review of Medical Coverage for Both Ed and Amy

Under the current arrangement Ed is covered by Inc's comprehensive medical insurance plan. Such coverage provides $500,000 of lifetime coverage for each family member. Each year after a $250 per-person deductible the insurance provides coverage for 80 percent of the first $5,000 of covered benefits for the family. After $5,000 of covered benefits is reached, additional covered medical expenses are paid in full under the terms of the policy.

The plan is noncontributory for employee coverage. Dependent coverage is available only if the employee will contribute to the cost of the coverage, for which the employee will pay $20 monthly. When an employee retires at normal retirement age (65), Inc pays the full cost of the Medicare supplemental insurance for both the employee and the employee's spouse. Inc is currently studying the possibility of (1) discontinuing its payments for the supplemental Medicare insurance, (2) having the retired employee pay the coverage under a group plan, or (3) having the employee make contributions during his or her employment years toward the retirement medical insurance. Ed would be affected as a future retiree and may need to review expected postretirement medical coverage should Inc change its existing plan.

Summary of Insurance Needs

Table 7-7 summarizes the Martinsons' insurance needs, for which the yearly costs total $11,414.

TABLE 7-7 **Recommended Insurance for the Martinsons**		
Purpose	Policy Type	Cost Per Year
Disability income protection for Ed	Disability income	$1,220
Income supplements for Scott and the Martinsons	Yearly renewable term	800
Income supplement for Amy when Ed dies	Whole life	8,800
Long-term care for Amy	Long-term care	594

Recommendations for the Martinsons

Table 7-8 combines data for the Martinsons' cash flow and the dollar amount for funding their supplemental income needs (table 7-6) and the cost of the recommended insurance (table 7-7).

TABLE 7-8 **Martinsons' Projected Cash Inflows and Outflows to Meet Objectives**				
		Cash Outflow		
Year	Investable Cash Inflow (Base Case)	8-Year Increasing Annual Funding	Projected Insurance Costs	Cash Inflow Minus Cash Outflow
2003	$28,469	$22,005	$11,414	($4,950)
2004	31,090	23,105	11,414	(3,429)
2005	36,820	24,161	11,414	1,218
2006	40,778	24,473	11,414	4,891

Comparison of their cash inflow and cash outflow over the 4-year period shows that the Martinsons currently have sufficient cash to provide the supplemental income funding and acquire their needed insurance. For 2003 and 2004, they could consider reducing their idle cash at the start of the year with the intention of replacing the funds using their excess cash inflow for 2005 and 2006.

In family situations where the financial success depends on the earnings of one family member—in this case Ed—adequate life and disability income insurance to provide the future income stream of the surviving family members normally takes precedence over competing uses for scarce dollars. For the Martinsons, then, the recommendation is that they acquire the following insurance in the amounts previously stated in the insurance section:

- whole life insurance on Ed for the purpose of protecting Amy in case he should die before her
- level term life insurance on Ed to assure completion of the accumulation funding for their retirement years and for Scott
- disability income insurance to provide income equal to what would have been earned until age 65

The long-term care insurance covering Amy could be deferred for several years without significantly increasing the current annual premium. The amount of this premium is included in the insurance cost column of table 7-7, and it is assumed that the coverage will be purchased at this time.

One point to note with this recommended insurance package is that Ed is slightly overprotected with the level term insurance used to fund the income supplements. Should Ed die, these excess insurance proceeds can be channeled to provide additions to the income stream being provided for Amy.

These recommendations specify that the remainder of their cash flows be channeled into investment assets as outlined in the investment section. In addition, if Ed's income from Inc increases more than anticipated over the 4-year planning horizon, then every effort should be made to add this income to the after-tax fund. Their net cash flow will become positive in 2005.

Although Ed expressed a desire to retire early, he did not make a firm commitment to retiring at age 62. Subsequent evaluations of the progress toward goal achievement might reveal that age 62 is feasible or perhaps that retirement at age 63 would best serve their aggregate goal achievement if sufficient funds have not been accumulated.

PERSONAL PLANNING: INVESTMENT

Refinancing the Home

Because of the decline in mortgage rates, the Martinsons should consider refinancing their home to lower the current monthly payment of $1,207.11, of which $1,080 is interest. When questioned, they reveal that they prefer a fixed-rate mortgage since they want to avoid the risk associated with mortgages that have an adjustable rate. They are willing to finance the existing $120,097 balance of their loan. However, they do not want to remove any of their equity in their home by refinancing more than the unpaid balance.

Because of a trend in standardization in the secondary mortgage market, most lenders offer fixed-rate mortgages with only 15- and 30-year maturities. A review of local rates has revealed that a 15-year mortgage at a rate of 7.25 percent with three points is available for a monthly principal-plus-interest payment of $1,096.32.

If the Martinsons choose a 30-year mortgage, the rate rises to 7.5 percent with three points, but the payment drops to $839.74, of which $750.61 is interest. Of course, this means that they have to make payments for 9 years longer than the current mortgage requires.

An alternative approach involves obtaining a 30-year mortgage and then making payments using a 21-year amortization schedule to match the current loan. This appeals to many clients since they often prefer not to extend the payment period beyond their original obligation. This calculation results in a planned payment of $947.76, but the required payment remains at $839.74.

The Martinsons' home mortgage interest is tax deductible. The interest payment in the 49th (current) month of the existing loan is $1,080.88. The after-tax mortgage payment for the 27 percent tax bracket is $915.27, calculated as follows: $1,207.11 − ($1,080.88 x 0.27). (Note that if mortgage interest is deductible at the state and/or local level, those marginal rates should be added to the federal marginal rate for this calculation.) Of course, interest on the mortgage declines every month, so the after-tax cost rises every month. At the time of the last mortgage payment, the after-tax cost will be within $5 of the mortgage payment. For the 30/21 year approach, the initial monthly after-tax cash outflow is $745.10, calculated as follows: $947.76 − ($750.61 x 0.27).

Both the 15-year mortgage and the 30-year mortgage require an immediate payment of three discount points to the lender ($3,602.92). Under current regulations, this is deductible but must be amortized over the life of the loan. (The original loan had no discount points.) Each of the proposed loans will also require other fees, including legal expenses, appraisal fees, and title insurance, totaling $2,850, which are not deductible.

The Martinsons should evaluate the proposed refinancing carefully. First, they must decide if the changes in cash flows caused by the new loan are affordable since discount points plus other fees total $6,452.92. Fortunately, the Martinsons have the ability and willingness to commit the funds. Second, they should analyze the proposals in greater detail, including the use of discounted cash-flow techniques.

An intuitively appealing comparison of the old loan to a new loan is the break-even point in months. This approach, which does not consider the time value of money, divides the initial outflow associated with the new loan by the change in the monthly after-tax cash flow. Assume the 30/21 year mortgage is the approach favored by the Martinsons:

$$\text{break-even in months} = \frac{\text{discount points plus other fees}}{\text{monthly tax}}$$

current after-tax payment − new after-tax payment + savings from amortization of points

$$= \frac{\$3,602.92 + \$2,850}{\$904.46 - \$737.59 + [(\$3,602.92/360 \times 0.27)]}$$

$$= \frac{\$6,452.92}{\$164.17}$$

$$= 39 \text{ months}$$

Based on the foregoing, it will be 39 months before the monthly savings of the new loan total the costs associated with obtaining that loan. (It should be noted that the break-even would have been shorter if payments were made on a 30-year amortization, but the Martinsons' monthly payments would continue for 9 additional years.) If the Martinsons plan to move within that period, refinancing would not make sense.

Another approach to analyzing the proposed refinancing is to use the concept of time value of money. Two methods that consider the time value of money are the net present value approach and the after-tax internal rate of return approach. Each is theoretically sound, but the after-tax internal rate of return approach is more understandable. Both methods reach the same conclusion but the after-tax internal rate of return is easier to explain and will be used to analyze the refinancing.

Calculating the internal rate of return is a job for specialized computer software or a custom spreadsheet package. Again, there are outflows and inflows, although we handle them differently. For the existing loan the inflow is simply the current balance of the loan, and the outflows are the monthly after-tax mortgage payments. (Recall that the after-tax mortgage payment rises over the life of the loan due to the reduction in interest.) The annual rate that discounts the future outflows back to the present to equal the inflows is the after-tax internal rate of return.

For the new loan the process is more complicated. The inflow consists of the current balance of the loan reduced by any points and fees that are required. Outflows for the new loan are the after-tax monthly payments on the loan reduced by the monthly tax savings from the allocation of discount points on the new loan. However, since the Martinsons would be paying a 30-year mortgage over 21 years, they would have received only 70 percent (21/30) of the tax savings due to them from the allocation of discount points. Thus we reduce the last monthly cash outflow by an amount equal to the discount points times 30 percent times a projected tax rate of 27 percent (assumed to equal their current rate).

Our calculations reveal that the after-tax rate on the old loan is 8.06 percent, while the after-tax rate on the new loan is 6.14 percent. This implies that the new loan, even when we consider points and fees, is the better option.

Since the Martinsons have no intention of moving from their house, refinancing makes sense. They can obtain the funds necessary for refinancing, and the break-even point is only 39 months. A 30-year mortgage gives the flexibility of a much lower monthly house payment, and using a 21-year amortization period makes the time frames of both loans identical. Most important, the after-tax financing rate over the intended holding period is better for the new mortgage than for the old mortgage.

The new mortgage will be in place so that the first payment will be in January 2003.

Evaluation of Portfolio with Regard to Objectives

The investment instruments that a client will use depend on the following variables:

- the client's risk profile
- the relative importance of the objective
- the possibility of postponing the date when the funds are needed
- the purpose for which the income from the accumulated assets or the assets themselves will be used

In light of the Martinsons' current situation, the first of these variables would suggest that relatively conservative investment instruments should be their choice. Their existing portfolio of common stocks and mutual funds is not overly aggressive and implies that the Martinsons are not high-risk takers. Some of their investment is in Inc common, which could be doubly risky if Inc's fortunes decline, since both Ed's position and the value of the stock could be affected. Also their ages, especially Ed's, would indicate that their portfolio should not be incurring higher and higher risk each year as Ed approaches his retirement date.

The portfolio should slowly be restructured to move away from investments stressing capital appreciation, thus reducing its overall risk and increasing its income stream.

The Martinsons consider their two accumulation objectives, their retirement supplement and the income supplement for Scott, extremely important. Therefore placing any of these future savings funds into high-risk instruments could jeopardize their situation. (The extra retirement supplement, outside of the qualified and nonqualified pension plans, also helps to accomplish Ed's vital objective of providing for Amy.) When the funds accumulated are for achieving highly rated objective(s), appropriate investments typically include only those having a relatively low risk of loss.

Although Ed has expressed a desire to retire at age 62 if the needed funds can be accumulated within the next 8 years, the retirement date can be postponed until he reaches 65 and perhaps beyond if he is not considered an executive or employee in a high policy-making position as specified in the federal Age Discrimination in Employment Act. The fact that the date by which the funds will be needed can be deferred would make the use of investments with a somewhat higher risk/return profile appropriate.

The objective that these accumulations will seek to meet is an income stream over a long period. Once the long-term income stream begins, inflation starts to erode the dollar's buying power. Although the accumulation amounts and target sums specified in table 7-5 are adjusted for 4 percent inflation during the accumulation and payout periods, inflation can exceed that rate, making the buying power of the income stream diminish for both the Martinsons and their son. One way to offset this effect would be to place part of the funds in investments that would tend to provide after-tax returns in excess of the anticipated 4 percent inflation rate. The remainder of the funds would use relatively low-risk investment instruments.

A second aspect of this long-term income flow is the erratic behavior of investment returns. Some financial experts suggest that the direction of interest rates over the next several years will be downward. If this should transpire and if the Martinsons are planning to use only conservative, fixed-income instruments, the likelihood of achieving the estimated 6 percent after-tax return used in developing tables 7-2 to 7-6 might not be realized. However, periods of declining interest rates during the past 20 years have been associated with a generally buoyant and rising stock market.

Recommended Portfolio

Since both accumulation objectives are similar except for the income recipients, the same portfolio design can be appropriate for both. Based on the previous discussion of these objectives, the funds set aside for each portfolio could be allocated as follows:

U.S. government 5-year notes	25 percent
No-load corporate bond fund	25 percent
No-load balanced fund	30 percent
Individual common stock investments (such as Inc or conservative, defensive stocks)	20 percent

The government notes should not have more than a 5-year duration at this time due to the uncertainty of the direction of long-term interest rates. Currently they are lower than during the past few years, and they continue to move downward. If this direction should change, the Martinsons could end up in the unfortunate position of owning low-yield investments for their long-term purpose if they purchased 25- or 30-year bonds at this time. The government bonds do provide safety and a base of stability for their portfolio.

For the various mutual funds that comprise a sizable portion of the proposed portfolio, no-load funds are recommended, assuming that the returns are comparable. The amount of funding shown in tables 7-1 to 7-5 is the gross amount that must be invested at the assumed, blended, after-tax return of 6 percent. If load funds are used, the net amount the Martinsons will have working for them will be less. Thus a higher return would be needed from the load fund, for an equivalent risk, to achieve their targets.

Like the government notes, the bond fund provides stability but with a slightly higher rate of return. The balanced fund, with its slightly increased risk, provides some degree of potential growth due to this type of fund's being partially invested in common stock. Usually a balanced fund has safety of principal and current income as its primary investment objectives, which blends with the Martinsons' situation.

The last two categories, a growth stock fund and direct ownership of common stocks, provide the somewhat higher-risk section of the portfolio and over the long term should also offer somewhat higher returns that can compensate for unexpected variations in interest rates or inflation.

INSTRUCTIONS

To avoid repetition of background material on the various investment risks, investor profiles, the need to match the risk-return trade-off associated with the investment instruments, suggestions for matching investments in the general risk category with financial objectives, and selected investments appropriate for accumulation funding, that material has been omitted from this chapter. If you are not familiar with the noted material from the previous chapters, it should be reviewed before proceeding through this section of the suggested solution.

Additional Considerations

Maximizing the Use of Inc's 401(k) Plan

Ed participates in Inc's 401(k) plan by contributing 5 percent of salary, a contribution of approximately $5,000 this year. Although the Internal Revenue Code permits a maximum employee contribution of $11,000 (in 2002) each year subject to a possible lower limit because of rules in other sections of the Code, Ed has been unable to verify that Inc permits contributions in excess of 5 percent of salary. If the plan permits additional contributions, Ed should further reduce his salary by making larger, tax-deferred contributions that Inc does not match through the plan. Sufficient cash flow in excess of his additional insurance premiums permits him to take advantage of this feature, if permissible, in the 401(k) plan and still have after-tax cash flow available to make individual investments outside the qualified plan.

Several of the investment choices in Inc's plan are consistent with the recommendations made earlier regarding the composition of the Martinsons' portfolio for this accumulation objective. Allocating a portion of their 401(k) contribution to the corporate bond or balanced mutual fund and then investing the remaining cash flow in other investment instruments as recommended previously will meet their objective.

Taking advantage of the favorable tax treatment currently afforded 401(k) plans will reduce the underfunding of the supplemental income streams that they plan to fund.

Family of Funds

Many sponsors of mutual funds offer a variety of funds referred to as a *family of funds.* The reasons for doing this are twofold. First, investors who might want to allocate their portfolio in funds with different objectives and risk/return characteristics can do so without seeking a competing firm's product. Second, many investors prefer to switch their holdings, essentially those practicing market timing, as economic conditions have changed or are expected to change.

Most authorities recommend that investors using common stocks or stock-invested mutual funds within a portfolio have a minimum planning horizon of 3 to 5 years for these securities. They also advise not allowing short-run market fluctuations to influence investment choices or decisions to buy or sell. But should fundamental conditions in the economic or securities spheres change, then portfolio restructuring can be desirable. For the convenience of making changes within their portfolio and not for the purpose of short-term trading, the Martinsons could consider selecting such a family of funds.

Ownership Considerations

Retirement Income Supplement. The age disparity between Ed and Amy plus Amy's family history suggests she will outlive him. In addition, she currently owns few assets. For these two reasons the best recommendation for the Martinsons to follow would be to title the assets being acquired in Amy's name. The advantages of this course of action would be as follows:

- No gift tax would be incurred because of the unlimited deduction for gifts between spouses.
- Should Amy predecease Ed, she would have assets that could be shielded from estate taxation by using the $1 million applicable credit amount (for 2002). To continue Ed's retirement income supplement for which these funds were accumulated, she could set up a testamentary trust that would give Ed the trust income for life and at his death have the corpus pass equally to the children, per stirpes.

One disadvantage of this ownership structure is that should Ed predecease Amy, his assets that pass to her could create estate tax liabilities and shrinkage before the net estate passes to the children. It is recommended that Ed's estate be structured so that most of his income-producing assets are placed in a bypass trust for Amy's benefit. Thus the total estate assets passing to Amy would not create major estate tax liabilities at her subsequent death.

Scott's Income Supplement. Using a trust for this objective would give the Martinsons the assurance that the funds they set aside would be used solely for Scott's benefit and that prudent supervision of trust assets and their disposition would take place over a long period.

The funding for this objective will continue past the time that Scott reaches age 21. Since the 2503(b) trust requires the annual distribution of trust income, funds could not be accumulated over the next few years that would provide a portion of the necessary long-term income flow to Scott. Therefore a 2503(c) trust would meet the Martinsons' needs because it would have two desirable features. First, the trust can accumulate income. Second, gifts made to the trust qualify for the annual gift tax exclusion. A disadvantage is that the trust corpus must be distributed when Scott attains age 21. At that time, 5 years from now, the Martinsons will not have completed the funding for this purpose. In addition, the corpus, when Scott receives it, could be dissipated rather quickly.

To use the 2503(c) trust in this situation, the instrument should contain a Crummey provision that will allow Scott to withdraw trust income for a period of 20 consecutive days each year. With this clause in the document the life of the trust will extend beyond the time that Scott reaches age 21. In addition, whether the Martinsons fund the trust over the next 8 or 11 years (or some intermediate time), their annual contributions will continue to qualify for the annual gift tax exclusion because Scott has this withdrawal power.

Of course, if he makes any withdrawals, the total amount needed at the end of the funding period will not be available for his long-term income supplement. Ed and Amy hope they will be able to convince him of the need for restraint during the funding period. They will also need to stress the importance of his withdrawing only the amount of the annual income after the funding is completed each year so the desired income stream will not be jeopardized.

Since the possibility exists that Scott might not live as long as the 50 years for which the trust income stream is designed to provide the supplemental income, one or more corpus beneficiaries should be named. Since Ed has indicated that providing for Amy is his primary objective, Amy should be the corpus beneficiary if she survives Scott. Should Amy predecease Scott, Bea and her issue, per stirpes, would become the corpus beneficiaries. If Bea also predeceases Scott and leaves no issue, the corpus could be given to a qualified charity, such as Ed's college.

Finally, although Ed can retire anytime between age 62 and age 65 or perhaps later, he may not prefer this course of action. Indeed, instead of staying with Inc until the normal retirement age, 65, he has expressed a preference to leave at 62. Depending on the Martinsons' ability to achieve the necessary accumulation, based on their available cash flow and the direction of interest rates, Ed might be able to meet his targeted retirement age of 62.

After refinancing their residence and acquiring the recommended insurance, the Martinsons' cash flow for the two accumulation objectives (supplementary retirement income for Ed and Amy and lifetime income stream for Scott) are shown in table 7-9. For the next year the available cash is not sufficient to meet their funding needs as brought forward from table 7-8. A shortfall will exist for 3 years, after which time catch-up funding becomes feasible as their available cash flow improves.

TABLE 7-9
Martinsons' Cash Inflow and Outflow to Meet Funding Objectives after Acquiring Insurance and Refinancing Their Residence

Year	Investable Cash Flow (Case II)	8-Year Increasing Annual Funding	Cash Inflow Minus Cash Outflow
2003	$20,438	$22,005	($1,567)
2004	23,194	23,105	(89)
2005	29,002	24,161	4,841
2006	33,028	24,473	8,555

CASE II
Acquisition of Additional Insurance
and Refinancing of the Residence

New Assumptions

1. Beginning in 2003, $11,414 will be spent on the additional insurance.

2. The investable cash flow for the years 2003–2006 inclusive will be allocated for the accumulation objectives and will earn a before-tax return of 8.35 percent.

3. The residence will be refinanced for a period of 30 years with a fixed interest rate of 7.5 percent with 3 points being paid.

Continuing Assumptions

1. The checking account balance is maintained at $12,000; the account is noninterest bearing.

2. Ed's salary is increased at 5 percent annually.

3. The money market deposit account earns 4.75 percent annually.

4. Investable cash is invested and earns 5 percent annually.

5. Expenditures for food, clothing and cleaning, utilities, phone, vacations, and charitable contributions will increase annually at 3 percent.

6. Expenditures for transportation will increase 4 percent annually.

7. Expenditures for entertainment will increase 5 percent annually.

8. Expenditures for medical insurance and other medical expenses will increase at 6 percent annually.

9. Decreases in the value of furniture have been ignored.

10. Automobiles decrease in value at a rate of 15 percent annually.

11. The value of the home will increase at one percent annually.

12. The common stock portfolio will increase at 9 percent annually.

13. Dividends from the common stock portfolio are currently $3,120, will increase 4 percent annually, and are reinvested in the portfolio.

14. IRAs will earn 8.1 percent annually over the next 4 years.

INCOME STATEMENT

EDGAR & AMY MARTINSON

CASE II	2002	2003	2004	2005	2006
Earned Income					
Compensation-CI	100,000	105,000	110,250	115,763	121,551
Company Bonus	10,000	10,500	11,025	11,576	12,155
401(k)-Ed's contr	-4,750	-4,987	-5,237	-5,499	-5,774
	105,250	110,513	116,038	121,840	127,932
Interest/Dividends					
Money Market Fund	1,188	1,188	1,188	1,188	1,188
Stock Portfolio	827	877	929	985	1,044
Investable Cash	971	2,876	4,938	7,530	10,748
Growth Mutual Funds	1,115	1,278	1,465	1,678	1,924
Balnced Mutual Fund	1,182	1,299	1,428	1,571	1,727
	5,283	7,518	9,948	12,952	16,631
	========	========	========	========	========
Adj Gross Income	110,533	118,030	125,986	134,792	144,563
Deductions					
Charitable 50%	2,000	2,060	2,122	2,185	2,251
State Tax Paid	4,782	5,197	5,629	6,127	6,679
Property Tax--Home	3,000	3,090	3,183	3,278	3,377
Home Mortgage	8,617	8,497	8,366	8,227	8,076
Amortization-Points	0	120	120	120	120
Gross Deductions	18,399	18,964	19,420	19,937	20,503
Standard Deduction	7,600	7,850	8,100	8,787	9,568
Allowed Deductions	18,399	18,964	19,420	19,937	20,503
Pers Exemptions	8,700	9,000	9,300	9,600	10,050
	========	========	========	========	========
Taxable Income	83,434	90,066	97,267	105,255	114,010
	========	========	========	========	========
Fed Income Tax	16,317	17,910	19,178	20,608	23,170
	========	========	========	========	========
Fed Tax Bracket-Ord Inc	27.0%	27.0%	26.0%	26.0%	25.0%

BALANCE SHEET

EDGAR & AMY MARTINSON

CASE II	2002	2003	2004	2005	2006
LIQUID ASSETS					
Cash Balance	9,963	9,995	10,013	10,054	10,078
Cash Deposits					
Investable Cash	24,228	47,542	75,674	112,206	155,982
IRA (CD's) - Ed	22,917	24,773	26,780	28,949	31,294
IRA (CD's) - Amy	2,378	2,571	2,779	3,004	3,247
Money Market Fund	25,000	25,000	25,000	25,000	25,000
	74,523	99,886	130,233	169,159	215,523
Stocks & Bonds					
Stock Portfolio	28,340	30,891	33,671	36,701	40,004
Growth Mutual Funds	45,843	52,540	60,215	69,011	79,093
Balnced Mutual Fund	30,787	33,850	37,219	40,923	44,996
	104,970	117,281	131,105	146,636	164,093
Life Insurance					
LifeInsCashValu-Ed	34,425	34,425	34,425	34,425	34,425
LifeInsCashValu-Amy	1,800	1,800	1,800	1,800	1,800
	36,225	36,225	36,225	36,225	36,225
	========	========	========	========	========
Liquid Assets	225,681	263,387	307,577	362,074	425,919
	========	========	========	========	========
NONLIQUID ASSETS					
Retirement Plans					
401(k) Plan	67,270	72,988	79,192	85,923	93,226
401(k)-Ed's contr	4,750	9,738	14,975	20,474	26,248
401(k)-Emplyr contr	4,750	9,738	14,975	20,474	26,248
Vested Pension	149,625	157,106	164,961	173,209	181,869
	226,395	249,570	274,103	300,080	327,591
Investments					
Points Paid	0	3,480	3,360	3,240	3,120
	0	3,480	3,360	3,240	3,120
Personal Property					
Home	346,430	349,894	353,393	356,927	360,496
Ed's car	17,000	14,450	12,283	10,440	8,874
Amy's car	10,200	8,670	7,370	6,264	5,324
Home Furnishings	75,000	75,000	75,000	75,000	75,000
	448,630	448,014	448,045	448,631	449,695
	========	========	========	========	========
Nonliquid Assets	675,025	701,064	725,508	751,951	780,406
	========	========	========	========	========
Total Assets	900,706	964,451	1,033,085	1,114,025	1,206,325

BALANCE SHEET (cont.)

EDGAR & AMY MARTINSON

CASE II	2002	2003	2004	2005	2006
LIABILITIES					
Mortgage Loans					
Home Mortgage	117,973	116,237	114,370	112,364	110,207
	117,973	116,237	114,370	112,364	110,207
Notes Payable					
Ed's Car Loan	11,429	6,998	2,151	0	0
	11,429	6,998	2,151	0	0
Total Liabilities	129,402	123,235	116,521	112,364	110,207
Net Worth	771,304	841,216	916,564	1,001,661	1,096,118

CASH FLOW STATEMENT

EDGAR & AMY MARTINSON

CASE II	2002	2003	2004	2005	2006
BEGINNING OF YEAR					
Idle Cash On Hand	10,000	9,963	9,995	10,013	10,054
SOURCES OF CASH					
Cash Income					
Compensation-CI	100,000	105,000	110,250	115,763	121,551
Company Bonus	10,000	10,500	11,025	11,576	12,155
Interest+Dividends	2,015	2,065	2,117	2,173	2,232
	112,015	117,565	123,392	129,512	135,938
	========	========	========	========	========
Total Cash Inflow	112,015	117,565	123,392	129,512	135,938
	========	========	========	========	========
Tot Cash Available	122,015	127,527	133,387	139,525	145,992
	========	========	========	========	========
USES OF CASH					
Fully Tax Deductible					
401(k)-Ed's contr	4,750	4,988	5,237	5,499	5,774
Home Mortgage	8,617	8,497	8,366	8,227	8,076
	13,367	13,485	13,603	13,726	13,850
Partly Deductible					
Med Ins Premium	240	254	270	286	303
Other Medical Expen	2,800	2,968	3,146	3,335	3,535
Charity Contrb-50%	2,000	2,060	2,122	2,185	2,251
	5,040	5,282	5,538	5,806	6,089
Not Tax Deductible					
Ed's Car Loan	1,228	849	433	49	0
Food	8,000	8,240	8,487	8,742	9,004
Clothing	3,000	3,090	3,183	3,278	3,377
Entertainment	2,000	2,100	2,205	2,315	2,431
Vacations	3,000	3,090	3,183	3,278	3,377
Transportation	1,000	1,040	1,082	1,125	1,170
Home Insurance Prem	500	510	520	531	541
Prop/Liab Ins Prem	100	102	104	106	108
Auto Insurance Prem	1,000	1,040	1,082	1,125	1,170
Ed's Life Ins Prems	2,335	2,335	2,335	2,335	2,335
Amy's Life Ins Prem	125	125	125	125	125
Additionl Insurance	0	11,414	11,414	11,414	11,414
Home Improvements	1,000	1,030	1,061	1,093	1,126
Home Refinance Cost	2,850	0	0	0	0
Utility/Phone	3,000	3,000	3,000	3,000	3,000
Personal Care Items	1,300	1,339	1,379	1,421	1,463

CASH FLOW STATEMENT (cont.)

EDGAR & AMY MARTINSON

CASE II	2002	2003	2004	2005	2006
Points Paid	3,603	0	0	0	0
	34,041	39,304	39,592	39,936	40,640
Taxes Paid					
Fed Tax Paid	16,317	17,910	19,178	20,608	23,170
State Tax Paid	4,782	5,197	5,629	6,127	6,679
FICA/Soc Sec Tax	6,580	6,660	6,743	6,831	6,924
Property Tax--Home	3,000	3,090	3,183	3,278	3,377
	30,679	32,857	34,733	36,844	40,150
Purchase/Deposits					
Investable Cash	23,257	20,438	23,194	29,002	33,028
	23,257	20,438	23,194	29,002	33,028
Liability Liquidation					
Home Mortgage	1,616	1,736	1,867	2,006	2,157
Ed's Car Loan	4,052	4,431	4,847	2,151	0
	5,668	6,167	6,714	4,157	2,157
	========	========	========	========	========
Tot Cash Outflow	112,052	117,533	123,374	129,471	135,913
	========	========	========	========	========
END OF YEAR					
Cash Balance	9,963	9,995	10,013	10,054	10,078
	========	========	========	========	========

SUPPORTING SCHEDULE

EDGAR & AMY MARTINSON

CASE II	JOINT 2002	JOINT 2003	JOINT 2004	JOINT 2005	JOINT 2006
Income					
Earned Income	105,250	110,513	116,038	121,840	127,932
Adj Gross Income	110,533	118,030	125,986	134,792	144,563
Allowed Deductions	18,399	18,964	19,420	19,937	20,503
Pers Exemptions	8,700	9,000	9,300	9,600	10,050
Taxable Income	83,434	90,066	97,267	105,255	114,010
Federal Tax Liab					
Regular Tax	16,315	17,912	19,181	20,036	20,943
Gross Fed Inc Tax	16,317	17,910	19,178	20,036	20,943
Alt Minimum Tax	0	0	0	572	2,227
Disallowed	0	0	0	0	-572
Fed Income Tax	16,317	17,910	19,178	20,608	23,170
Fed Tax Analysis-Ord Inc					
Indexing Factor	79	85	92	98	105
Fed Tax Bracket-Ord Inc	27.0%	27.0%	26.0%	26.0%	25.0%
$ to Next Bracket	29,616	26,934	23,833	20,095	15,740
Next Bracket	30.0%	30.0%	29.0%	29.0%	28.0%
Previous Bracket	15.0%	15.0%	15.0%	15.0%	15.0%
$ to Prev Bracket	36,684	41,666	47,167	49,455	53,983
Fed Effective Tax Rate	19.6%	19.9%	19.7%	19.6%	20.3%
Alt Minimum Tax					
Adj Gross Income	110,533	118,030	125,986	134,792	144,563
Contributions	-2,000	-2,060	-2,122	-2,185	-2,251
Home Mortgage	-8,617	-8,497	-8,366	-8,227	-8,076
Amortization-Points	0	-120	-120	-120	-120
Adjusted AMTI	99,916	107,353	115,378	124,260	134,116
AMT Exemptions	-49,000	-49,000	-49,000	-45,000	-45,000
AMT Taxable Inc	50,916	58,353	66,378	79,260	89,116
Gross Alt Min Tx	13,238	15,172	17,258	20,608	23,170
Fed Tax Less FTC	-16,317	-17,910	-19,178	-20,036	-20,943
Alt Minimum Tax	0	0	0	572	2,227
Other Tax Liabs					
FICA/Soc Sec Tax	6,580	6,660	6,743	6,831	6,924
Adj Gross Inc	110,533	118,030	125,986	134,792	144,563
GA Adj Gross Inc	110,533	118,030	125,986	134,792	144,563
GA Standard Ded	3,000	3,000	3,000	3,000	3,000
GA Itemized Ded	18,399	18,964	19,420	19,937	20,503
GA Exemptions	8,100	8,100	8,400	8,400	8,400
GA Taxable Inc	84,034	90,966	98,167	106,455	115,660
GA Regular Tax	4,782	5,197	5,630	6,127	6,679
GA Income Tax	4,782	5,197	5,630	6,127	6,679
Georgia Tax	4,782	5,197	5,630	6,127	6,679
Tot State/Local Tx	4,782	5,197	5,630	6,127	6,679
Total Inc Tax	27,679	29,767	31,551	33,566	36,773

FINANCIAL SUMMARY

EDGAR & AMY MARTINSON

CASE II	2002	2003	2004	2005	2006
Gross Real Income					
Personal Earnings	110,000	115,500	121,275	127,339	133,706
Interest Income	2,159	4,064	6,126	8,718	11,936
Dividends Rcvd	3,124	3,454	3,822	4,234	4,695
	115,283	123,018	131,223	140,291	150,336
Income & Inflation					
Gross Real Inc	115,283	123,018	131,223	140,291	150,336
Total Inc Tax	-27,679	-29,767	-31,551	-33,566	-36,773
Net Real Income	87,603	93,251	99,672	106,725	113,563
Cur Real Inc =	87,603	90,670	93,843	97,127	100,527
At Infltn Rate of	4	4	4	4	4
Cash Flow					
Idle Cash On Hand	10,000	9,963	9,995	10,013	10,054
Norml Cash Inflow	112,015	117,565	123,392	129,512	135,938
Norml Cash Outflw	88,795	97,095	100,180	100,469	102,885
Cash Invested	23,257	20,438	23,194	29,002	33,028
Cash Balance	9,963	9,995	10,013	10,054	10,078
Net Worth					
Personal Assets	494,818	494,234	494,284	494,910	495,998
Investment Assets	405,888	470,217	538,801	619,115	710,327
Personal Liabilities	-129,402	-123,235	-116,521	-112,364	-110,207
Personal Net Worth	365,416	370,999	377,763	382,546	385,791
Investment Net Worth	405,888	470,217	538,801	619,115	710,327
Net Worth	771,304	841,216	916,564	1,001,661	1,096,118

8

Planning for a Surviving Spouse

Chapter Outline

Frequently a financial services professional needs to counsel the soon-to-be- or already-widowed spouse. In the event that such a client is affluent, many complex, sophisticated, and challenging issues require the financial planner's expertise. Are there unusual federal income tax and estate tax issues to consider for the first time now that the client will soon be widowed? Are the current insurance policies still appropriate, or must the insurance program be adjusted in accordance with the change in personal status? Is the existing investment picture still viable in light of the new situation? These are but a few of the issues for which the client requires professional advice.

Clearly the financial planner should allow the client time to adjust to a changed personal situation, but in some cases immediate action must be taken to deal with the impending death of a spouse and to marshall resources to provide for long-term financial needs arising from changes in health or marital status. Widowed status, either actual or impending, means many changes in tax, estate, insurance, and investment planning that require the client to take appropriate steps in these areas in a timely fashion. One factor that may be helpful in motivating the client to act is that the spouse's impending or actual death triggers planning regarding federal estate tax, state inheritance tax, insurance, and investments. Clients may feel that this situation is a learning experience and that failure to consider and develop effective plans harms the family's or the survivors' financial future. The financial planner may find clients in such a situation to be very cooperative.

Often the planner has been only recently sought out, not having previously advised the client. A debilitating illness, a comment of a friend or confidant, or the client's own recognition of the need for advice can lead to using a planner's service.

CASE NARRATIVE

Present Situation

Curtis Kelley, aged 67, and Constance Kelley, aged 60, live in western Pennsylvania in the city in which they were born and in which Constance attended high school and college. She met her husband, Curt, while in her senior year at college. Curt, now a chemist for a local concern, was a graduate student and teaching assistant in the chemistry department when they met. They have been married for 36 years. The Kelleys have four children—Pat, aged 34; Peggy, 32; Margie, 29; and Glenn, 26. Three of the four children reside in western Pennsylvania. None are married at this time, although Peggy and Margie are both divorced and each has three children. Margie's three children— Jennifer, aged 7; Scott, 4; and Adam, 2—all live with their mother in Erie. Peggy's three children—Kimberly, 6; Rachel, 4; and Heather, 18 months—all live with their mother in Corona, California.

A year ago, Curt contracted a rare liver disorder. He has been totally disabled for 3 months now and has been declared terminally ill by his team of physicians. He is covered by his employer's short-term disability plan and is receiving payments each month. Medical reports indicate that Curt has approximately 12 weeks to live.

Curt has been employed by Galaxy Pharmaceuticals, Inc., a large international drug company, for 31 years. At the time of Curt's disability, he was senior vice president in charge of research and development and was earning an annual salary of $229,000. Curt has participated in the firm's qualified profit-sharing plan every year since its inception and has accumulated $694,940 in the plan.

Employee Benefit Package

Since Galaxy provides a 26-week salary continuation (short-term disability) plan for Curt, the Kelleys' income has not yet been reduced. The benefit coincidentally will terminate near the doctor's approximation of Curt's date of death. Should Curt live beyond that date, company-paid long-term disability income insurance benefits will begin, since the elimination period—the contractually specified period of disability that must pass before benefits begin—matches the salary continuation plan's benefit period.

Curt also owns an individual disability policy with the following provisions: "own-occupation" coverage, lifetime benefits, and a 180-day elimination period. Own-occupation coverage requires that the insurer pay the full benefit if the disability renders the individual incapable of performing his own occupation even though he or she may be able to earn a substantial living in another occupation.

Current Residence

The Kelleys' current residence was acquired 7 years ago at a cost of $375,000. They used the proceeds from the sale of their former primary residence and a mortgage of $100,000 to purchase this property. They have $225,000 of rolled-over, untaxed capital gains from previously owned primary residences. Like other homes they owned, this property and its furnishings are jointly owned.

Jewelry and Automobiles

Since Connie enjoys wearing fine jewelry, Curt has used occasions such as holidays and birthdays to give her additional pins, rings, and earrings set with precious or semiprecious stones. The jewelry was recently appraised at $50,000 and is insured as scheduled property. Curt and Connie each own an automobile, valued at $25,000 and $10,000 respectively.

Individual Life Policies

The individual life insurance policies on Curt's life, of which he is the owner, have cash values as follows: $18,000 in cash value for a $100,000 universal policy and $56,400 in cash value for a $150,000 whole life policy. Curt has paid all the premiums on these two policies and there are no outstanding loans against the cash values. The group term policy, fully paid for by Galaxy, is two and one-half times his salary, or $572,000. Connie is the primary beneficiary of all the policies, and their four children, per stirpes, are the contingent beneficiaries.

Other Assets

During their lifetime, the Kelleys have acquired a significant amount of other assets. Curt's salary rose somewhat steadily until he was promoted to vice president. Initially the Kelleys used savings to acquire a base of secure assets consisting of U.S. Treasury bonds, corporate bonds, Series EE bonds, and money market funds.

Investment History

Since their main income flow was stable, the Kelleys decided to take above-average investment risks for a major portion of their holdings and began to place funds directly into individual securities with the potential for capital appreciation. Most of these investments were made during the last decade, when Curt's income increased sharply as a consequence of his promotion. Curt believed that through his knowledge of the drug industry he could select drug company common stocks, in addition to Galaxy's, with the potential for above-average growth. To this end an aggressive portfolio consisting primarily of drug company stocks has been accumulated. To decrease their dependence on this industry, the Kelleys have added an aggressive growth fund and an international fund, again with the intention of capturing above-average returns. Several years ago Connie used the inheritance she received to purchase a utility fund and an index fund that were recommended by her then son-in-law. These were acquired with the objectives of current income (utility fund) and average stock market risk (index fund).

Need for Estate Planning

Recently Connie attended a meeting of the local chapter of the American Association of University Women, of which she is an active member, on the need for appropriate estate planning as a means of marshaling and conserving personal assets. Given Curt's serious medical problem, they wonder if their wills, executed many years ago, properly serve their current needs. Both wills leave the deceased's assets to the surviving spouse, if living, and if the spouse is not living, the assets are distributed to their children, per stirpes. The meeting Connie attended suggested, as a first step, they prepare a list of assets and then a separate asset list for each spouse. After preparing tables 8-1 and 8-2, the Kelleys realized that some planning might be needed.

Life Insurance Portfolio

Connie has no life insurance but is in excellent health. She now sees how useful the coverage on her husband will be and wants to acquire some insurance on her life, if appropriate in her situation.

Charitable Giving

Curt and Constance both hope to make charitable gifts. Curt wishes to make a generous contribution to his alma mater but is not sure whether the gift should be made prior to his death or afterward. Connie's interest is in assisting organizations that care for abused children, and she would like to make some charitable gifts during her lifetime as well as at the time of her death.

Qualified Plan Guidance

The Kelleys need guidance on how to make best use of the profit-sharing plan assets. When Curt was in good health, they were willing to take investment risk. Since his illness, Connie has become more concerned about the risks of their portfolio.

Final Planning

The Kelleys know that Curt has only a short time to live, and they want to be sure that their financial planning is up-to-date and proper before Curt's death. They know that they have some serious problems and they have retained the services of a financial planner to review their financial affairs on an integrated basis. Curt is primarily concerned with providing for all of his heirs. In addition, Constance wants to be very sure that at Curt's death and at her subsequent death, the proper financial planning will have been undertaken so that the children and grandchildren can receive as much of the family assets as possible per stirpes, free of federal estate tax, state inheritance tax, and other burdens.

They also realize that, despite the medical prognosis, Curt might live for some time beyond the estimated 12 weeks.

TABLE 8-1
Inventory of Assets

	Cost or Basis	Fair Market Value	Current Return %	Current Return $	Form of Ownership[1]	Available for Liquidity	Collateralized	Location
Checking accounts	$ 70,000	$ 70,000	3.1	$2,325	JT	Yes	No	First National
Money market funds	75,000	75,000	5.0	1,000	JT	Yes	No	First National
Certificates of deposit	20,000	20,000	6.0		JT	Yes	No	First National
Series EE bonds	15,000	50,000		3,000[2]	S(H)	Yes	No	Safe-deposit box
Life insurance cash value		74,400			S(H)	?	No	Insurance company
Treasury bonds	110,000	125,000	7.2	9,000	S(H)	Yes	No	Safe-deposit box
Corporate bonds	85,000	100,000	7.3	7,300	JT	Yes	No	Safe-deposit box
Aggressive Growth Mutual Fund	65,000	125,000	1.5	1,875	S(H)	Yes	No	Safe-deposit box
International Fund	110,000	150,000	1.2	1,800	JT	Yes	No	Safe-deposit box
Galaxy Pharmaceutical Co. stock, 10,000 shares	200,000	500,000	1.5	7,500	JT	Yes	No	Safe-deposit box
Acme Drug Co. stock, 2,000 shares	40,000	70,000	1.8	1,260	JT	Yes	No	Safe-deposit box
Zenith Drug Co. stock, 3,000 shares	30,000	40,000	2.0	800	JT	Yes	No	Safe-deposit box
Utility Fund	125,000	150,000	5.0	7,500	S(W)	Yes	No	Safe-deposit box
Index Fund	150,000	200,000	2.5	5,000	S(W)	Yes	No	Safe-deposit box
Qualified retirement plan	0	694,940	—	—	S(H)	?	No	Galaxy
Residence	150,000	400,000	—	—	JT	No	$76,230	At home
Furnishings	125,000	125,000	—	—	JT	No	No	At home
Jewelry/furs	50,000	50,000	—	—	S(W)	No	No	At home
Autos Curt	38,000	25,000	—	—	S(H)	Maybe	No	Garage
Connie	20,000	10,000	—	—	S(W)	No	No	Garage

[1] JT = joint tenants with right of survivorship; S = single ownership; H = husband; W = wife.
[2] Interest deferred until redemption

TABLE 8-2
Assets Owned by Each Spouse

Asset	Curt	Connie
Checking account	$ 35,000	$ 35,000
MMMF	37,500	37,500
CDs	10,000	10,000
Series EE bonds	50,000	——
Treasury bonds	125,000	——
Corporate bonds	50,000	50,000
Aggressive Growth Fund	125,000	——
International Fund	75,000	75,000
Galaxy Pharmaceutical	250,000	250,000
Acme Drug	35,000	35,000
Life insurance	822,000	——
Zenith Drug	20,000	20,000
Retirement plan	694,940	——
Residence	200,000	200,000
Household furnishings	62,500	62,500
Jewelry/furs	——	50,000
Automobiles	25,000	10,000
Utility Fund	——	150,000
Index Fund	——	200,000
Total	$2,616,940	$1,185,000

INSTRUCTIONS

Prepare a working outline for the Kelleys. Check your outline with the one that follows. Then prepare a financial plan for the Kelleys. When you have prepared your solution, you can compare it with the suggested solution that follows.

WORKING OUTLINE

I.   Clients' Objectives

    A. Lifetime objectives
        1. Devise a proper estate plan prior to Curt's death.
        2. Reduce federal income tax liability.
        3. Maintain comfortable lifestyle for Connie.
        4. Make appropriate decisions concerning distribution of husband's qualified plan proceeds.
        5. Settle Curt's estate promptly.
        6. Make charitable contributions to organizations that care for abused children.

    B. Dispositions at death
        1. Minimize estate shrinkage.
        2. Provide generously and equitably for Constance's children and grandchildren.
        3. Make charitable contributions for maximum benefit to the charitable organization and for maximum federal tax benefit.
        4. Minimize the effect of the generation-skipping transfer tax.

II. Personal Planning

    A. Tax planning
        1. Unlimited marital deduction and unified credit
        2. Generation-skipping transfer tax (GSTT)
        3. Charitable giving
            a. Inter vivos and testamentary gifts
            b. Split-interest arrangements (IRC Sec. 170(f)(2)(A))
               • Charitable remainder annuity trust
               • Charitable remainder unitrust
               • Pooled-income fund
        4. Present situation
            a. Inadequacy of will and estate plan
            b. Estate tax liability at Connie's subsequent death
            c. The life insurance
                • Use of trust with sprinkle provision
               • Generation-skipping transfer tax (GSTT) implications
               • Charitable gift of insurance policy
               • Election to annuitize the policy proceeds
               • Lump-sum distribution with proceeds invested
               • Accelerated benefits and viatical settlements

    d.   The Series EE bonds

    e.   The qualified retirement plan

    f.   The family residence

- Sale of the residence while both spouses are alive, the property held as joint tenants with right of survivorship
- Sale of the residence when only one spouse is alive, the property having been held as joint tenants with right of survivorship
- Other factors influencing the decision to sell

    g.   Aggressive growth mutual fund

    h.   The Treasury bonds

    i.   The securities and bank accounts held as joint tenants with right of survivorship

  5. Connie's income needs

B. Initial planning for Connie's income flow and adjustments to Curt's estate plan

  1. Connie's financial status following Curt's death, having received only all jointly owned property

    a.   Portfolio revision

C. Further planning of Connie's finances

  1. Decisions and the reasons for them

    a.   Qualified pension plan

    b.   Aggressive growth mutual fund

    c.   Social Security

    d.   Curt's car

D. Effects on Connie's finances

  1. Connie's gross income

    a.   The pension lump-sum distribution

    b.   Curt's car

E. Further planning decisions and reasoning

  1. GSTT/credit shelter

  2. Qualifying Terminable Interest Property Trust (QTIP)

  3. The life insurance and life insurance trust

  4. The Series EE bonds

  5. The Treasury bonds

F. Effect of these changes on Curt's and Connie's estates

  1. Curt's estate size

  2. Estate tax reduction techniques

  3. Connie's will

    4.   Connie's financial status

    5.   Revised estate costs

G. Combined effect of all decisions on Connie's financial situation

    1.   Income

    2.   Possible changes in portfolio

    3.   Connie's expressed interest for life insurance

    4.   Connie's checking account balance

PERSONAL FINANCIAL PLAN
FOR
CURTIS AND CONSTANCE KELLEY
[Suggested Solution]

CLIENTS' OBJECTIVES

A. Lifetime objectives
1. Devise a proper estate plan prior to Curt's death.
2. Reduce federal income tax liability.
3. Maintain comfortable lifestyle for Connie.
4. Make appropriate decisions concerning distribution of husband's qualified plan proceeds.
5. Settle Curt's estate promptly.
6. Make charitable contributions to organizations that care for abused children.

B. Dispositions at death
1. Minimize estate shrinkage.
2. Provide generously and equitably for Connie's children and grandchildren.
3. Make charitable contributions for maximum benefit to the charitable organizations and for the maximum federal tax benefit.
4. Minimize the effect of the generation-skipping transfer tax.

BASE CASE

Assumptions

1. The checking account balance is maintained at $70,000; the account is noninterest bearing.

2. Curt's salary is increased at 5 percent annually, assuming that Curt lives and continues to be employed for the next 5 years.

3. The money market deposit account earns 3.1 percent annually.

4. Investable cash is invested and earns 5 percent annually.

5. Expenditures for food, clothing and cleaning, utilities, phone, vacations, and charitable contributions will increase annually at 3 percent.

6. Expenditures for transportation will increase 4 percent annually.

7. Expenditures for entertainment will increase 5 percent annually.

8. Expenditures for medical insurance and other medical expenses will increase at 6 percent annually.

9. Decreases in the value of furniture have been ignored.

10. Automobiles decrease in value at a rate of 15 percent annually.

11. The value of the home will increase at one percent annually.

12. The various securities will increase at rates shown in table 8-3.

13. Income from the securities portfolio equals $44,360 and will grow at rates shown in table 8-3 on the following page.

TABLE 8-3
Expected Growth Rate in Dividends and Market Value for Securities Owned by the Kelleys

Security	Dividend Growth Rate %	Market Price Growth Rate %
Aggressive Growth Fund	5.0	10.2
International Fund	3.0	7.0
Galaxy Pharmaceutical	2.0	9.0
Acme Drug	3.0	6.5
Zenith Drug	1.5	9.0
Utility Fund	3.0	3.0
Index Fund	2.5	9.0

INCOME STATEMENT

CURTIS & CONSTANCE KELLEY

BASE CASE	2002	2003	2004	2005	2006
Earned Income					
Salary - Curt	229,000	240,450	252,473	265,096	278,351
	229,000	240,450	252,473	265,096	278,351
Interest/Dividends					
Money Market Fund	2,325	2,325	2,325	2,325	2,325
Corporate Bonds	7,300	7,300	7,300	7,300	7,300
U S Treasury Bonds	9,000	9,000	9,000	9,000	9,000
Galaxy Pharmceutcal	7,500	7,650	7,803	7,959	8,118
Acme Drug Company	1,260	1,298	1,337	1,377	1,418
Zenith Drug Company	800	812	824	837	849
Aggrssve Grwth Fund	1,875	1,969	2,067	2,171	2,279
International Fund	1,800	1,854	1,910	1,967	2,026
Utility Fund	7,500	7,725	7,957	8,195	8,441
Index Fund	5,000	5,150	5,305	5,464	5,628
CDs	1,000	1,050	1,103	1,158	1,216
Overall Investmnt	2,873	8,845	15,345	22,413	30,080
	48,233	54,978	62,275	70,165	78,680
	========	========	========	========	========
Adj Gross Income	277,233	295,428	314,747	335,261	357,031
Deductions					
Charitable 50%	2,000	2,060	2,122	2,185	2,251
State Tax Paid	7,511	8,020	8,561	9,135	9,745
Home - Property Tax	3,500	3,640	3,786	3,937	4,095
Home Mortgage	7,173	6,695	6,174	5,601	4,976
Reductn for High Inc	-4,225	-4,664	-5,134	-5,637	-4,118
Gross Deductions	15,959	15,751	15,508	15,221	16,949
Standard Deduction	7,800	8,000	8,200	8,787	9,476
Allowed Deductions	15,959	15,751	15,508	15,221	16,949
Pers Exemptions	2,360	1,830	1,260	512	2,200
	========	========	========	========	========
Taxable Income	258,914	277,847	297,979	319,528	337,882
	========	========	========	========	========
Fed Income Tax	72,556	78,728	82,815	89,678	94,445
	========	========	========	========	========
Fed Tax Bracket-Ord Inc	35.0%	35.0%	34.0%	34.0%	33.0%

BALANCE SHEET

CURTIS & CONSTANCE KELLEY

BASE CASE	2002	2003	2004	2005	2006
LIQUID ASSETS					
Cash Balance	69,949	70,045	70,105	70,169	70,357
Cash Deposits					
Overall Investmnt	117,807	244,827	384,335	534,588	698,689
CDs	21,000	22,050	23,153	24,311	25,527
Money Market Fund	75,000	75,000	75,000	75,000	75,000
	213,807	341,877	482,488	633,899	799,216
Stocks & Bonds					
U S Treasury Bonds	125,000	125,000	125,000	125,000	125,000
Series EE Bonds	50,000	53,000	56,180	59,551	63,124
Corporate Bonds	100,000	100,000	100,000	100,000	100,000
Galaxy Pharmceutcal	540,000	583,200	629,856	680,244	734,664
Acme Drug Company	74,550	79,396	84,556	90,053	95,906
Zenith Drug Company	43,600	47,524	51,801	56,463	61,545
Aggrssve Grwth Fund	137,750	151,801	167,284	184,347	203,151
International Fund	160,500	171,735	183,756	196,619	210,383
Utility Fund	154,500	159,135	163,909	168,826	173,891
Index Fund	218,000	237,620	259,006	282,316	307,725
	1,603,900	1,708,410	1,821,349	1,943,421	2,075,388
Life Insurance					
UnivLifePrem - Curt	18,000	19,080	20,225	21,438	22,725
WhlLifePrem - Curt	56,400	58,656	61,002	63,442	65,980
	74,400	77,736	81,227	84,881	88,705
	========	========	========	========	========
Liquid Assets	1,962,056	2,198,068	2,455,169	2,732,369	3,033,666
	========	========	========	========	========
NONLIQUID ASSETS					
Retirement Plans					
VestedPensionBeneft	694,940	789,489	893,549	1,007,978	1,133,710
	694,940	789,489	893,549	1,007,978	1,133,710
Personal Property					
Home	404,000	408,040	412,120	416,242	420,404
Car - Curt	25,000	21,250	18,063	15,353	13,050
Car - Connie	10,000	8,500	7,225	6,141	5,220
Home Furnishings	125,000	125,000	125,000	125,000	125,000
Jewelry & Furs	50,000	50,000	50,000	50,000	50,000
	614,000	612,790	612,408	612,736	613,674
	========	========	========	========	========
Nonliquid Assets	1,308,940	1,402,279	1,505,957	1,620,715	1,747,384
	========	========	========	========	========
Total Assets	3,270,996	3,600,347	3,961,126	4,353,084	4,781,050

BALANCE SHEET (cont.)

CURTIS & CONSTANCE KELLEY

BASE CASE	2002	2003	2004	2005	2006
LIABILITIES					
Mortgage Loans					
Home Mortgage	76,327	70,802	64,756	58,137	50,893
	76,327	70,802	64,756	58,137	50,893
	========	========	========	========	========
Total Liabilities	76,327	70,802	64,756	58,137	50,893
	========	========	========	========	========
Net Worth	3,194,669	3,529,545	3,896,370	4,294,947	4,730,157
	========	========	========	========	========

CASH FLOW STATEMENT

CURTIS & CONSTANCE KELLEY

BASE CASE	2002	2003	2004	2005	2006
BEGINNING OF YEAR					
Idle Cash On Hand	70,000	69,949	70,045	70,105	70,169

SOURCES OF CASH

Cash Income

	2002	2003	2004	2005	2006
Salary - Curt	229,000	240,450	252,473	265,096	278,351
Interest+Dividends	44,360	45,083	45,827	46,594	47,384
	273,360	285,533	298,299	311,690	325,735
	========	========	========	========	========
Total Cash Inflow	273,360	285,533	298,299	311,690	325,735
	========	========	========	========	========
Tot Cash Available	343,360	355,481	368,344	381,795	395,904
	========	========	========	========	========

USES OF CASH

Fully Tax Deductible

	2002	2003	2004	2005	2006
Home Mortgage	7,173	6,695	6,174	5,601	4,976
	7,173	6,695	6,174	5,601	4,976

Partly Deductible

	2002	2003	2004	2005	2006
Medical Ins Premium	500	530	562	596	631
Charity Contrb-50%	2,000	2,060	2,122	2,185	2,251
	2,500	2,590	2,684	2,781	2,882

Not Tax Deductible

	2002	2003	2004	2005	2006
Food	8,000	8,240	8,487	8,742	9,004
Clothing	7,000	7,350	7,718	8,103	8,509
Entertainment	6,000	6,300	6,615	6,946	7,293
Vacations	8,000	8,240	8,487	8,742	9,004
Transportation	1,000	1,040	1,082	1,125	1,170
Home - Ins Premium	700	714	728	743	758
Auto - Ins Premium	1,200	1,248	1,298	1,350	1,404
Jewlry&Furs-InsPrem	1,000	1,020	1,040	1,061	1,082
Disability Ins-Curt	1,500	1,560	1,622	1,687	1,755
UmbrellaPolicy Prem	185	191	196	202	208
UnivLifePrem - Curt	2,200	2,200	2,200	2,200	2,200
WhlLifePrem - Curt	2,100	2,100	2,100	2,100	2,100
Home - Repair/Maint	3,000	3,090	3,183	3,278	3,377
Utility/Phone	4,000	4,120	4,244	4,371	4,502
Other Persnl Expnse	6,000	6,180	6,365	6,556	6,753
	51,885	53,593	55,365	57,206	59,118

CASH FLOW STATEMENT (cont.)

CURTIS & CONSTANCE KELLEY

BASE CASE	2002	2003	2004	2005	2006
Taxes Paid					
Fed Tax Paid	72,556	78,728	82,815	89,678	94,445
State Tax Paid	7,511	8,020	8,561	9,135	9,745
FICA/Soc Sec Tax	8,305	8,471	8,646	8,829	9,021
Home - Property Tax	3,500	3,640	3,786	3,937	4,095
	91,872	98,859	103,807	111,579	117,306
Purchase/Deposits					
Overall Investmnt	114,934	118,175	124,163	127,840	134,021
	114,934	118,175	124,163	127,840	134,021
Liability Liquidation					
Home Mortgage	5,047	5,525	6,046	6,619	7,244
	5,047	5,525	6,046	6,619	7,244
	========	========	========	========	========
Tot Cash Outflow	273,411	285,437	298,240	311,626	325,547
	========	========	========	========	========
END OF YEAR					
Cash Balance	69,949	70,045	70,105	70,169	70,357
	========	========	========	========	========

SUPPORTING SCHEDULE

CURTIS & CONSTANCE KELLEY

	JOINT	JOINT	JOINT	JOINT	JOINT
BASE CASE	2002	2003	2004	2005	2006
Income					
Earned Income	229,000	240,450	252,473	265,096	278,351
Adj Gross Income	277,233	295,428	314,747	335,261	357,031
Allowed Deductions	15,959	15,751	15,508	15,221	16,949
Pers Exemptions	2,360	1,830	1,260	512	2,200
Taxable Income	258,914	277,847	297,979	319,528	337,882
Federal Tax Liab					
Regular Tax	72,556	78,728	82,815	89,678	92,575
Gross Fed Inc Tax	72,556	78,728	82,815	89,678	92,575
Alt Minimum Tax	0	0	0	0	1,870
Fed Income Tax	72,556	78,728	82,815	89,678	94,445
Fed Tax Analysis-Ord Inc					
Indexing Factor	82	87	91	96	102
Fed Tax Bracket-Ord Inc	35.0%	35.0%	34.0%	34.0%	33.0%
$ to Next Bracket	46,136	35,153	23,171	9,972	168
Next Bracket	38.6%	38.6%	37.6%	37.6%	35.0%
Previous Bracket	30.0%	30.0%	29.0%	29.0%	28.0%
$ to Prev Bracket	88,114	102,597	118,179	135,028	148,582
Fed Effective Tax Rate	28.0%	28.3%	27.8%	28.1%	28.0%
Alt Minimum Tax					
Adj Gross Income	277,233	295,428	314,747	335,261	357,031
Contributions	-2,000	-2,060	-2,122	-2,185	-2,251
Home Mortgage	-7,173	-6,695	-6,174	-5,601	-4,976
Adjusted AMTI	268,060	286,673	306,451	327,475	349,804
AMT Exemptions	-19,485	-14,832	-9,887	-631	0
AMT Taxable Inc	248,575	271,841	296,564	326,844	349,804
Gross Alt Min Tx	66,101	72,615	79,538	88,016	94,445
Fed Tax Less FTC	-72,556	-78,728	-82,815	-89,678	-92,575
Alt Minimum Tax	0	0	0	0	1,870
Other Tax Liabs					
FICA/Soc Sec Tax	8,305	8,471	8,646	8,829	9,021
PA Taxable Inc	268,233	286,428	305,747	326,261	348,031
PA Regular Tax	7,511	8,020	8,561	9,135	9,745
PA Income Tax	7,511	8,020	8,561	9,135	9,745
Pennsylvania Tax	7,511	8,020	8,561	9,135	9,745
Tot State/Local Tx	7,511	8,020	8,561	9,135	9,745
Total Inc Tax	88,372	95,219	100,022	107,642	113,211

FINANCIAL SUMMARY

CURTIS & CONSTANCE KELLEY

BASE CASE	2002	2003	2004	2005	2006
Gross Real Income					
Personal Earnings	229,000	240,450	252,473	265,096	278,351
Interest Income	22,498	28,520	35,073	42,196	49,921
Dividends Rcvd	25,735	26,458	27,202	27,969	28,759
	277,233	295,428	314,747	335,261	357,031
Income & Inflation					
Gross Real Inc	277,233	295,428	314,747	335,261	357,031
Total Inc Tax	-88,372	-95,219	-100,022	-107,642	-113,211
Net Real Income	188,861	200,209	214,726	227,620	243,820
Cur Real Inc =	188,861	193,774	198,816	203,988	209,295
At Infltn Rate of	3	3	3	3	3
Cash Flow					
Idle Cash On Hand	70,000	69,949	70,045	70,105	70,169
Norml Cash Inflow	273,360	285,533	298,299	311,690	325,735
Norml Cash Outflw	158,477	167,262	174,077	183,786	191,526
Cash Invested	114,934	118,175	124,163	127,840	134,021
Cash Balance	69,949	70,045	70,105	70,169	70,357
Net Worth					
Personal Assets	758,349	760,571	763,740	767,786	772,736
Investment Assets	2,512,647	2,839,776	3,197,386	3,585,298	4,008,314
Personal Liabilities	-76,327	-70,802	-64,756	-58,137	-50,893
Personal Net Worth	682,022	689,769	698,984	709,649	721,843
Investment Net Worth	2,512,647	2,839,776	3,197,386	3,585,298	4,008,314
Net Worth	3,194,669	3,529,545	3,896,370	4,294,947	4,730,157

PERSONAL PLANNING: TAXES

Unlimited Marital Deduction and Unified Credit

The estate of every married individual may take advantage of the federal estate tax marital deduction as long as the surviving spouse is a U.S. citizen and a resident. Internal Revenue Code Sec. 2056 provides that as long as an estate owner is married at the date of death and a nonterminable interest in estate property passes from the decedent to the surviving spouse at death, the estate property will pass free of any federal estate tax liability. However, special rules apply for the marital deduction if the surviving spouse does not meet the U.S. citizenship or residency requirements.

In addition, every individual or his or her estate is entitled to take advantage of the unified credit for taxable gifts during lifetime or through bequests at death. If taxable gifts are made during life, the applicable credit must be used. (However, gifts between spouses are not considered taxable gifts, and there is no need to use any of the applicable credit when making these gifts, although special rules apply as they do for at-death transfers.) Whatever applicable credit is left will be used at death. The applicable credit amount in 2002 is $345,800, which translates into an equivalent amount of $1 million of estate assets (which will increase gradually to $3.9 million by 2009). If the applicable credit is not used, it is wasted, as it cannot be carried forward in any manner or transferred to another individual.

For a married client a properly drafted will should integrate the applicable credit with the federal estate tax marital deduction. Since a taxable estate in 2002 of $1 million triggers no federal estate tax liability, this is the minimum taxable estate that should be created from the spouse's assets upon his or her death. In general, any overage should pass to the spouse in a manner that qualifies for the marital deduction. However, in certain cases effective estate planning dictates that the taxable estate exceed the applicable credit amount.

If estate property is jointly titled between husband and wife, the ultimate disposition of such property will be unaffected by will provisions, as this property will pass from the decedent to the surviving spouse by operation of law. This property would qualify for the marital deduction.

If an estate owner's will is improperly drafted or does not effectively operate to pass estate property from a decedent to the surviving spouse, the unfortunate result may be that too many assets qualify for the federal estate tax marital deduction, leaving insufficient assets in the estate to make use of the applicable credit. For example, if all of an estate owner's property is titled jointly with his or her spouse, it will pass by operation of law at the first death. Nothing remains to make use of the $1 million exclusion, and the will provisions are ineffective. Even if the will had been structured to integrate the applicable credit amount with the federal estate tax marital deduction, it would be inoperative and the applicable credit would be wasted.

Generation-Skipping Transfer Tax (GSTT)

Not long ago federal transfer taxes consisted of only the federal estate tax and the federal gift tax. Now there is an additional transfer tax to consider—the generation-skipping transfer tax (GSTT). The GSTT may be assessed whenever property is transferred to a skip person. A skip person is defined as a lineal descendant more than one generation below the grantor or a nonlineal person aged 37 1/2 years younger than the grantor. Transfers to skip persons can take three forms.

The first type of generation-skipping transfer is a taxable distribution of either income or principal from a trust to a person two or more generations below the transferor's generation who is not otherwise subject to an estate or gift tax.

> *Example:* Renee Roland, the wealthy real estate developer, created a testamentary trust under the terms of which $6 million in cash is held in trust for the benefit of Renee's three great-grandchildren. Under the terms of the trust, when each child attains age 18 years, a proportionate amount of income shall be distributed to such child. This is an example of a taxable distribution.

The second form of generation-skipping transfer is a taxable termination, which occurs if there is a termination of an existing arrangement by reason of death, lapse of time, or release of a power, or if the property interest held in trust passes to a skip beneficiary. Internal Revenue Code Sec. 2612(a)(2) provides that, upon the termination of an interest in property that is held by a trust, if a specific portion of the trust assets is distributed to skip beneficiaries who are lineal descendants of the holder of such interest, this termination is considered a taxable termination with respect to that portion of the trust property.

> *Example:* Renee Roland, the wealthy real estate developer, created a testamentary trust under the terms of which $6 million in cash is held in trust for the benefit of Renee's three great-grandchildren. Under the terms of the trust, when the youngest of the three great-grandchildren attains age 35, the corpus and accumulated income thereon are to be distributed. This triggers a termination of the trust and is an example of a taxable termination.

The final type of transfer that is subject to the generation-skipping transfer tax is the direct skip. Outright transfers of property that skip a generation trigger the application of the generation-skipping transfer tax. Direct skips may take place either during lifetime as gifts or at death by virtue of law or will.

Regardless of whether assets are transferred to grandchildren outright or through trust arrangements, the GSTT is imposed on all generation-skipping transfers unless an exemption can be found in the Internal Revenue Code. Specifically, the law provides that every individual or the individual's estate is permitted to make aggregate transfers of up to $1,090,000 (as indexed for inflation in 2002), either during lifetime or at death, that will be wholly exempt from imposition of the generation-skipping transfer tax. Pursuant to the Taxpayer Relief Act of 1997, the $1 million exemption amount will be indexed for inflation beginning in 1998. The Economic Growth and Tax Relief and Reconciliation Act (EGTRRA) of 2001 ties the GSTT lifetime exemption to the applicable credit amount once the applicable credit amount exceeds the GSTT lifetime exemption as indexed by the Taxpayer Relief Act of 1997. Under current law the generation-skipping transfer tax does not apply to direct-skip annual exclusion gifts of $11,000 ($22,000) that are not made through trusts, or to payments made on behalf of an individual directly to an educational institution or medical provider. Some restrictions apply to annual exclusion type generation-skipping transfers in trust.

Charitable Giving

Inter Vivos and Testamentary Gifts

Individuals may make charitable contributions in several ways. Gifts may be made during the donor's lifetime (inter vivos charitable gifts), or they may be made after the donor's death (testamentary charitable gifts). Gifts may be made outright or through a trust. If a donor uses a trust, the charitable beneficiary may receive some benefit at once, or there may be a split-interest arrangement, with both a charitable and a noncharitable beneficiary.

When assets are transferred to a trust with a qualifying charitable organization named as the sole and immediate beneficiary, a federal income tax deduction is triggered. Sometimes the donor wants both charitable and noncharitable beneficiaries to enjoy the property. If a charity receives a portion of estate property directly, either as a gift or as an immediate beneficiary of a trust, the federal estate tax deduction is equal to the fair market value of the property on the date of death (or on the alternate valuation date). But if there are noncharitable beneficiaries before the property passes to the charitable organization, the allowable tax deduction depends on the nature of the trust arrangement.

Split-Interest Arrangements

Situations in which both charitable and noncharitable beneficiaries are to receive benefits from the trust are referred to as *split-interest arrangements*. The various split-interest vehicles considered here are (1) the charitable remainder annuity trust, (2) the charitable remainder unitrust, (3) the charitable lead trust, and (4) the pooled-income fund.

A charitable remainder annuity trust (CRAT) provides either the taxpayer (if still living) or other noncharitable trust beneficiaries with a lifetime income interest in the property transferred to the trust, with the charitable organization receiving the remainder interest. Since an estate can create a CRT, for example, with a university, on a testamentary basis, the estate would receive a federal estate tax charitable deduction determined by reference to the life expectancy of the noncharitable beneficiaries. The amount of the federal estate tax charitable deduction is limited to the actuarial value of the remainder interest deemed passing to the university. The trust beneficiaries (usually family members) receive the right to the income from the property for the rest of their lives (or for a term of specified years), and at their deaths (or upon the expiration of the term), the remainder interest will pass to the university. The charitable remainder annuity trust must provide for an annual payout of a "sum certain" that is not less than 5 percent or more than 50 percent of the initial net fair market value of the trust property. This amount may be expressed as a specified dollar amount or as a percentage or fraction of the initial fair market value of the trust assets. The amount of each payment is fixed initially; thus the annual payouts are the same.

A charitable remainder unitrust (CRUT) is similar to a charitable remainder trust, and must provide for a payout each year of a fixed percentage of at least 5 percent but not more than 50 percent of the annually determined net fair market value of its assets. Therefore, the amount of the annual payment from a CRUT will be different each year depending on the value of the trust principal.

The charitable lead trust (CLT) is the opposite of the charitable remainder trust. When property is transferred by a donor to a charitable lead trust, the charitable recipient enjoys the income from the property for a term of years, with the noncharitable beneficiary or beneficiaries receiving the remainder interest in the property thereafter.

A pooled-income fund is operated directly by the charitable organization and is made up of assets donated by multiple contributors and commingled into one fund. A donor retains the right either to receive a share of the fund's income for life or to select one or more individuals living at the time the contribution is made to receive the income.

The Code [Sec. 170(f)(2)(A)] provides that gifts of a remainder interest in a trust are deductible for tax purposes only if the trust is a charitable remainder annuity trust, a charitable remainder unitrust, or a pooled-income fund. A charitable income trust arrangement does not qualify as a charitable deduction for estate tax purposes. Treasury Department tables must be consulted to ascertain the actual amount of the deduction available. These tables, derived from actuarial data, incorporate the life expectancy of the noncharitable beneficiaries. The value of the gift in this type of arrangement is its fair market value on the date of the transfer. This is the basis of the gift. No other value is used.

Present Situation

Inadequacy of Will and Estate Plan

Everyone should be certain that the estate planning process is current and tailored to his or her individual needs, especially when death is imminent. Unfortunately, Curt is terminally ill, and to make matters even worse, the current estate plan is ill-conceived and essentially nonresponsive to the family's needs.

As shown in table 8-2 Curt's gross estate would be $2,616,940 should he die today. Because his current will is a "simple will," all of his assets will pass to Constance at his death. As a practical matter, many of Curt's assets are jointly titled with his wife, and upon his death these assets will pass automatically to her by operation of law. In conjunction with the beneficiary status for the life insurance policies and the simple will approach for the remainder of the assets, the entire estate passes to Connie outright and results in an overqualification of the federal estate tax marital deduction.

At Curt's Death	Computations	Actual Expenses Incurred
Gross estate	$2,616,940	
Less: Debts[1]	(76,327)	76,327
Less: Costs of administration[2]	(196,271)	196,271
Adjusted gross estate	$2,344,342	
Federal estate tax marital deduction[3]	2,344,342	
Taxable estate	–0–	
Federal estate tax owed	–0–	
Less unified credit[4]	N/A	–0–
State inheritance tax	–0–	–0–
Total costs at first death		$ 272,598
Amount of estate passing to Connie	$2,344,342	
At Connie's Subsequent Death		
Gross estate[5]	$3,529,342	
Less: Debts	–0–	–0–
Less: Costs of administration[2]	(264,701)	264,701
Adjusted gross estate	$3,264,641	
Federal estate tax marital deduction[6]	–0–	
Taxable estate	3,264,641	
Federal estate tax	1,408,121	
Less unified credit (2002–2003)	(345,800)	
Less state inheritance tax credit	(159,274)	159,274
Federal estate tax owed	$ 903,047	903,047
Total costs at second death		$1,327,022
Total combined costs at both deaths		$1,599,620

Notes

[1] Curt's estate will pay off the mortgage on the residence.

[2] The costs are assumed to be 7.5 percent of the gross estate.

[3] Pursuant to current simple wills, the entire estate passes from Curt to Connie.

[4] There is no federal estate tax liability because of the application of the unlimited federal estate tax marital deduction; thus the unified credit is wasted.

[5] This figure represents $2,344,342 passing from Curt's estate to Connie *plus* $1,185,000, which is the sum of Connie's share of the jointly titled property and her separate property. It is assumed there is no appreciation in the value of the assets in her estate.

[6] There is no federal estate tax marital deduction available, as Connie is assumed to be unmarried at the time of her death.

Estate Tax Liability at Connie's Subsequent Death

Under the current wills and property ownership structure, there is no federal estate tax liability at the time of Curt's death, since all his property ownership interests pass to his surviving spouse in a manner that qualifies for the marital deduction. This results in additional assets being owned by Connie and, when added to her own assets, creates a sizable estate. At her death the estate will not have the benefit of the marital deduction. Since her gross estate exceeds $3 million, a portion of the estate assets will be subject to the 50 percent tax rate. Even if her will makes use of the applicable credit, the result is a very sizable shrinkage of the estate. Effective estate planning while Curt is alive will reduce some of this shrinkage and also enable the Kelleys to achieve some of their goals.

At this point there should be an examination of the problems in the estate plan and of how Curt's assets, both separate and joint, can be most effectively used for the family's benefit. However, before reaching any decision concerning the use or disposition of these assets, the amounts and sources of income that Connie will require after Curt's death must be determined. Once this is determined plans and provisions maximizing the benefits from Curt's estate can be developed so that Connie's income needs are met.

The Life Insurance

The largest single amount that will pass to Connie from Curt is the $822,000 of death benefits from his life insurance. The Kelleys should explore the possibility of removing these policy proceeds from Curt's gross estate. Under current law if a life insurance policy is given away, the policy proceeds will be included in the donor's estate if the gift was made within 3 years of death. Since Curt is expected to live for only a short time, the opportunity to transfer ownership of any of the policies and thereby remove the proceeds from his estate does not really exist. In other circumstances a trust could be established and policies given to the trust. If the donor survives at least 3 years after the date of transfer, the proceeds are removed from the estate. Little chance exists that this course of action would succeed in Curt's case because of his medical prognosis.

Use of Trust with Sprinkle Provision. Even if the proceeds of these policies that are in a trust are included in his taxable estate, Curt could specify Connie and the grandchildren as the trust's income beneficiaries. The trustee could be granted a "sprinkle provision" that would permit the use of the trustee's discretion as to what percentage of trust income each beneficiary would receive each year. The trust instrument could also grant the trustee the power to accumulate income while Connie could receive discretionary annual distributions, a valuable planning technique if integrated with the children's tax status. Curt might desire to have the income accumulated until each grandchild attains majority. The grandchildren would be the corpus beneficiaries of the trust when Connie dies or when the youngest grandchild-beneficiary of the trust attains majority, whichever occurs last. Using the trust in this manner enables Curt to provide for both Connie and the grandchildren.

Generation-Skipping Transfer Tax Implications. If a trust is used, the generation-skipping transfer tax (GSTT) rules will apply. Until now Curt has not used any of his $1,090,000 (2002 value) exemption. The allocation of this exemption to lifetime gifts is very useful, since the exemption only needs to shelter the value of the contribution at the time of the gift on a dollar-for-dollar basis. Gifts of appreciating property are well suited for lifetime gifts used to take advantage of the GSTT lifetime exemption. Any amounts placed in trust will not qualify for the marital deduction, since Connie does not have the power to appoint the trust corpus to herself or her estate. However, Curt's $1 million estate tax exemption would offset all of the $822,000 proceeds. If this is the only portion of his estate subject to the applicable estate and gift taxes, the tax paid by his estate would be at a lower rate than if the proceeds were taxed in Connie's estate at a later date.

Charitable Gift of the Insurance Policy. Since Curt is interested in making charitable gifts, one or more of the policy ownership interests could be gifted to a qualified charity while Curt is still alive. If the whole life policy were given, the amount gifted for income tax purposes is the amount of its terminal reserve. Should Curt die before the end of 3 years, the policy proceeds would be brought back and included in his estate. However, the proceeds would then qualify for a charitable deduction in his estate; thus the Kelleys would receive both a current income tax deduction and an estate tax deduction for the gift of an insurance policy. Whether one or more of the policies can be used in this manner depends on Connie's income needs and the Kelleys' other objectives.

Election to Annuitize Proceeds. Taking a different approach, since Connie is the named beneficiary of these policies, no change in beneficiary need be made and she could elect to annuitize the entire proceeds. Table 8-4 shows an example of the cost to purchase $10 of monthly income with different annuity options and the resulting total annual income that Connie would receive if she took this course of action after Curt's death.

TABLE 8-4
Annual Income from Different Life Insurance Annuity Options from Insurance Proceeds of $822,500 for a Female Aged 60

Annuity Option	Cost per $10 Monthly Income	Annual Income
Pure life annuity	$1,344	$73,437
10-year certain	$1,373	$71,886
Full refund	$1,402	$70,399

Lump-Sum Distribution with Proceeds Invested. Connie could take the lump sum and invest the proceeds in long-term government or corporate bonds with staggered maturities and earn an average return of 7.5 percent. This action would provide her with an annual income, without annuitizing the proceeds, of $61,687.

Accelerated Benefits and Viatical Settlements. Another life insurance option especially relevant for the Kelleys (because of Curt's terminal illness) concerns accelerated benefits. Many policies and policy riders available in today's market offer a lump-sum benefit when the insured is diagnosed with both a terminal illness and a life expectancy of 12 months or less. The accelerated benefit is paid in lieu of part or all of the policy's current death benefit and usually reflects discounting for the time value of money. Some contracts provide a benefit when the insured has a qualifying disease or experiences a specific event, such as a heart attack, even if the prognosis does not indicate a shortened life expectancy.

Typically, accelerated benefits are used to offset increased expenses or lost income associated with the medical condition, but the actual use is unrestricted. Definitions and requirements for obtaining accelerated benefits differ significantly among policies. The policyowner, who is often neither the insured nor the beneficiary, has the right to decide whether to seek accelerated benefits and how to use them.

The taxation of accelerated benefits has been a critical concern due to the activities of both life insurers and viatical settlement companies. However, effective January 1, 1997, IRC Sec. 101 has been modified. Legislation enacted in 1996 specifies that proceeds received prior to death are exempt from federal income taxation if two conditions are met. The first condition is that the insured's medical prognosis projects death within 24 months of the date of payment. The second condition is that the benefit can be reduced only by an amount consistent with a life expectancy of 24 months or less. The language of the regulations indicates that there will be no subsequent income tax liability even if the insured lives more than 24 months as long as the first condition was satisfied at the time of payment.

An option available to the terminally ill whose life insurance policies do not offer accelerated benefits is a *viatical settlement.* This relatively new concept involves a third party (the viatical settlement provider) that makes a lump-sum payment to the policyowner (viator) in exchange for ownership or absolute assignment of the policy. The payment is the discounted value of the current death benefit and reflects the provider's target rate of return and its perception of the insured's life expectancy. However, because of the inherent riskiness of projecting individual life expectancies, and the relatively small number of competitors, viatification often results in substantial discounts from policy death benefits. The interest rate used in these situations must be reasonable.

The National Association of Insurance Commissioners has adopted the Viatical Settlements Model Act, and many states currently regulate viatical settlements.

Because of rapid changes in regulation and in product markets, financial advisers must be diligent in keeping track of the implications of both accelerated benefits and viatical settlements.

For the Kelleys, even if the policies had accelerated benefits features, there would be no compelling reason to exercise them since there is no immediate need for cash and Curt's life expectancy is so short. Likewise, a viatical settlement is unnecessary.

The Series EE Bonds

This separate property of Curt's provides a unique planning opportunity for the Kelleys. Since Curt deferred any recognition of interest on these bonds, at his death, when the bonds are redeemed, this deferred interest must be included for income tax purposes. In addition, their total accumulated value must be included in his gross estate. If Curt specifies that these bonds are left to charity through his will, the accumulated interest would not be part of either his estate or the Kelleys' income for income tax purposes. The same income and estate tax deductions explained for the lifetime gift of a life insurance policy would apply to a similar gift of the EE bonds.

Since Curt owns the Series EE bonds as separate property, another course available is to convert them to Series HH bonds that have a maturity date 20 years from the date of conversion and from which the owner receives semiannual interest. The tax-deferred, accumulated interest on the EE bonds is rolled into the face amount of the HH bonds, with no income tax due on this deferred EE bond interest until the HH bonds are redeemed. If these EE bonds are converted into HH bonds as Curt's separate property, the bonds could be redeemed after his death and the EE bonds' deferred interest would then be taxable. Also the bonds could be reissued at Curt's death as a distribution to Connie, with no current income tax consequence. The bonds would retain their original maturity date, and the deferred interest would be taxable upon redemption at maturity.

Alternatively, while still alive Curt could have the HH bonds issued to them as joint tenants with right of survivor, thereby making a gift to Connie, and at his death Connie could have the bonds titled in her name, as survivor, and the deferred interest would not have to be recognized as taxable income until redemption at maturity.

The Qualified Retirement Plan

Curt participates in a defined-contribution retirement plan at work. Curt, being on disability, can elect to take early retirement.

If no change in Curt's status is made and he should die while on long-term disability, then the Qualified Preretirement Survivor Annuity (QPSA) provisions would come into play; that is, Connie would receive the survivor's portion of a joint and 50 percent survivor annuity. A check with Galaxy determined that Connie's annual QPSA benefit would be $40,312, since the joint and 50 percent survivor benefit would have been $80,624 annually. A better course of action would be for Curt to retire immediately and elect a joint and 100 percent survivor annuity, which under Galaxy's plan would produce a total annual benefit of $71,309.77 for as long as both or either of the Kelleys lived.

Another possibility is lump-sum distribution from the plan of Curt's benefit of $694,940. Curt would qualify for the 10-year averaging since his birth date predates January 1, 1936. But because of the use of the pre-1986 tax rates and the amount that Curt has in the plan, 10-year averaging would result in an income tax of $232,939 on the distribution.

In addition to the lump-sum distribution made directly to Curt, another option is a trustee-to-trustee lump-sum distribution to an IRA that Curt creates for this purpose, naming himself and Connie as the IRA's beneficiaries. By making the trustee-to-trustee distribution, the 20 percent income tax withholding is avoided. If Curt dies without having begun taking periodic withdrawals from the IRA, mandatory withdrawals can be based on Connie's age rather than his. She need not begin withdrawing from this IRA for more than a decade.

The Family Residence

At some point, the family residence will probably be sold, either while Curt or Connie or both are alive or by the estate of the last to die. The tax consequences of such a sale are somewhat different in each of these situations.

Sale of the Residence While Both Spouses Are Alive, the Property Held as Joint Tenants with Right of Survivorship. A taxpayer can exclude from income taxation the gain from the sale of a primary residence. Gain can be excluded once every 2 years, provided the taxpayer used the residence as a principal residence for 2 out of the last 5 years. Married individuals filing jointly may exclude up to $500,000 of the gain, and single taxpayers can exclude $250,000. Based on the facts in this case, the Kelleys have a basis of $150,000 in the home that they jointly own. Should they decide to sell the home while Curt is alive and realize the estimated value of $400,000 net of selling expenses, they will have a gain of $250,000 ($400,000 − $150,000 basis), which is excluded from their taxable income.

Sale of the Residence When Only One Spouse Is Alive, the Property Having Been Held as Joint Tenants with Right of Survivorship. When property is held as joint tenants with right of survivorship, each spouse is assumed to own one-half of the property and to have contributed one-half of its basis. At the death of the first spouse, the surviving spouse obtains ownership of the jointly held property. However, the ownership interest of the deceased spouse receives a step-up in basis for which no income tax is levied on the capital gain. Should Curt Kelley die before their primary residence is sold, Connie will obtain full ownership of Curt's interest. Curt's interest has a basis of $75,000 ($150,000 ÷ 2), but his estate's basis would be $200,000 ($400,000 ÷ 2). By operation of law (the property having been held as joint tenants with right of survivorship) the property will become Connie's, and she will pick up the stepped-up basis of $200,000 to add to her $75,000 for a total basis of $275,000. As Curt's spouse, Connie can receive his $200,000 stepped-up basis estate tax free (through the unlimited marital deduction). If Connie then sells the property for a net realized price of $400,000, she has a $125,000 ($400,000 − [$75,000 + $200,000]) realized capital gain. Connie can exclude the full amount of the gain, and no capital gain tax would be paid on the residence's appreciation in value.

From a financial and tax perspective there is no difference whether the residence is sold during Curt's lifetime or after his death. However, other factors should be considered. Living in the home could contribute to making Curt's remaining life more comfortable. Furthermore, the activities associated with the sale and moving to a new residence are substantial and could be detrimental to Curt's physical condition.

Other Factors Influencing the Decision to Sell. Widowed clients often are reluctant to sell the family home and move to a new and different physical environment. Indeed, this action is stressful under the best of circumstances. When moving to a new house or location occurs along with the upcoming or recent death of a spouse (which is, according to psychologists, a person's most stressful event), the cumulative effect of the stress can affect the survivor's ability to cope. Consequently many advisers recommend that a surviving spouse not make a hasty decision to sell the family residence immediately but rather to wait, perhaps a year or more if personal factors and finances permit, before offering the property for sale. On the other hand, some widowed individuals are anxious to leave the residence to hasten their transition to a new phase of life.

Additional personal factors influence this decision, including the desire to remain in the family residence to provide a base for other family members to consider home, preference, enjoyment, the ability or financial wherewithal to manage the necessary upkeep and maintenance needs of the property, and—on the other hand—a fear of making an incorrect choice of a new residence, particularly without the benefit of the spouse's input in the decision. In situations such as the Kelleys', the planner must be aware that factors other than solely financial ones are highly important to the client and may well be the deciding factor(s) in whether to sell or keep the property.

One further matter about the residence concerns property on which there is a debt and that is held as joint tenants with right of survivorship. In this situation, the full amount of the unpaid mortgage can be deducted as a debt in the estate of the first to die, namely Curt. This was the procedure followed in determining the amount of Curt's estate. Connie thus can inherit the residence free of any mortgage payments, which reduces the amount of annual income she will need during widowhood. However, she will not have any income tax deduction for any interest that would have been paid during those years.

After giving due consideration to both tax and other factors involved in a sale, it appears that the sale of the Kelleys' residence is not an appropriate course of action at this point.

Aggressive Growth Mutual Fund

The total return earned on this mutual fund has been more than satisfactory during the time it has been held in the Kelleys' portfolio. However, most of the return has been in the form of appreciation in the value of the fund shares, not in the form of current dividends. While Curt was employed, his salary provided them with a very comfortable standard of living, and the current return on their investment (dividends) was of little importance. When this separate asset of Curt's passes to either his estate or Connie, then it might be a candidate for sale, with the proceeds used to acquire securities (stocks or bonds) that will produce a higher annual stream of income to augment Connie's income.

The Treasury Bonds

Other than his automobile, Curt's only remaining separate property is the Treasury bonds. These will receive a step-up in basis upon his death, and under the terms of his current will they pass to Connie in a qualifying manner. They are liquid and could be used to pay some of the expenses, debts, and state inheritance taxes of the estate.

An earlier discussion of using the Series EE bonds for a charitable contribution described the income and estate tax consequences of lifetime gifts. These Treasury bonds could also be used for charitable contributions with somewhat similar tax consequences.

The Securities and Bank Accounts Held as Joint Tenants with Right of Survivorship

Curt's share of these assets will automatically pass to Connie because of the form of ownership. Some consideration could be given to changing the ownership to separate property for some of these assets so that there would be sufficient liquidity should a decision be made to fund a trust with the life insurance proceeds. Separate property could also be used either to make charitable contributions (with tax considerations as described for life insurance, EE bonds, or Treasury bonds) or to provide for the grandchildren.

Connie's Income Needs

Now that some of the alternative ways Curt's property can be used to provide for Connie have been examined, the next phase of the planning for the Kelleys is to determine the amount of income she will need after Curt's death. Then choices must be made as to how best to achieve this and other goals.

The Kelleys' current income from their portfolio is shown in table 8-5. This excludes the deferred interest on the Series EE bonds. Adding Curt's salary of $229,000 to their $45,360 of portfolio income, they have a total income of $274,360.

TABLE 8-5
Curt and Connie's Portfolio Income

Income Source	Ownership		
	Jointly Titled	Curt	Connie
Money market fund	$ 2,325		
CDs	1,000		
EE bonds		No current	
Treasury bonds		$9,000	
Corporate bonds	7,300		
Aggressive Growth Fund		1,875	
International Fund	1,800		
Galaxy Pharmaceuticals	7,500		
Acme Drug	1,260		
Zenith Drug	800		
Utility Fund			$ 7,500
Index Fund			5,000
Income Totals	$21,985	$10,875	$12,500

Unfortunately no precise formula exists for ascertaining the exact amount of income Connie should have or would need to maintain the same lifestyle she currently enjoys. However, the Kelleys' assets can provide ample income for her needs, both currently and for the rest of her life. The question is how best to use the assets. Examination of some of the Kelleys' personal finance and income tax records, discussions with the Kelleys, and consideration of Connie's expected lifestyle point to a targeted annual income of $105,000, in current dollars, as sufficient for providing Connie with a lifestyle similar to the one she has been recently enjoying with Curt. This income should also permit Connie to purchase any major assets such as a car when needed and to give meaningful sums on an annual basis to either charities, children, or grandchildren as she desires.

Estimates were made of her itemized deductions (charitable contributions, property and state income taxes, etc.) and expected federal income taxes. With about $7,000 of itemized deductions, income taxes would be about $28,000, leaving Connie with an income in excess of $85,000 after state and federal taxes. Since the mortgage on the home can be treated as a debt of Curt's estate, Connie's income will be free of any mortgage payments, which on their 15-year, 9 percent $100,000 mortgage are nearly $12,200 a year.

In addition, the deployment of the assets that will provide this level of income now must be such that the income will rise to offset the effects of long-term inflation without regularly liquidating securities to make up shortfalls.

Several courses of action exist that emphasize maximizing the use of Curt's assets to provide Connie with this income as well as providing for the other objectives. These plans begin with a base income this year of $35,164 of dividends and interest from securities she owns in her own name and the full value of those owned jointly with Curt. The dividend income from some of these stocks is rather low. This income flow could be increased by repositioning some of these investments, either now or at some time in the future. The two major assets in Curt's estate, the life insurance proceeds and the qualified retirement plan distribution, can provide more than the additional income needed by Connie—$69,836 ($105,000 − $35,164)—either as an annuity or, if lump-sum distributions are taken, from the investment income. Annuitizing either the life insurance proceeds or the lump-sum distribution from the pension plan will achieve the target.

A major decision that clients such as the Kelleys face is whether to annuitize the principal over an expected lifetime or to retain the principal and use the return earned on the principal as the source of their income. Choosing between these two alternatives is not easy, particularly since the annuity decision tends to be final whereas taking the lump sum keeps open the option to acquire an annuity later. Of course, the lump-sum approach results in the individual, rather than the insurance company, bearing the investment risk.

Despite the fact that a life annuity would provide an income that cannot be outlived, many clients who have a large accumulation of assets are reluctant to use up those assets. They want to distribute the accumulated assets to their children and grandchildren and to make capital contributions to charities. They are aware that if their income needs should exceed the annual cash flow, some of the assets could be liquidated. The Kelleys, and particularly Connie, know that annuitizing the life insurance proceeds, even with a full refund option, would provide her with sufficient additional income to meet her current target of $105,000. However, their decision is to include the annuitization of the insurance proceeds in their plans designed to provide income for Connie.

Since Curt is permitted to take both early retirement and a lump-sum distribution under the terms of Galaxy's pension plan, a trustee-to-trustee rollover IRA could be established for Curt with Connie as the beneficiary. This would allow Connie to receive less than the QPSA benefit from Galaxy's plan. When Curt dies, Connie could commence distributions from the IRA that probably would be sufficient to enable her to receive the annual targeted income. This, however, is not consistent with their preferences.

However, any course of action requires early retirement and, obviously, a cessation of income to the Kelleys from Galaxy's disability plan. If the medical prognosis proves to be correct, the Kelleys could use some of their existing assets as income sources until Curt dies. For the relatively short period, this would not use up very much of their assets. Should Curt retire, the Kelleys would be covered by Galaxy's fully paid health plan for retirees, which has the same benefits as for Galaxy's employees until a retiree or the spouse is eligible for Medicare. As each becomes eligible for Medicare, the retiree or spouse would be part of the Medicare supplemental health insurance plan provided by Galaxy.

Social Security benefits can be an additional source of income, both to the Kelleys at this time and for Connie after Curt's death. Curt's income has exceeded the Social Security base for a sufficient number of years so that his PIA at age 65 will be the maximum benefit. If Connie were to take the widow's benefit at age 60, the maximum benefit would be reduced to about 71 percent.

Based on the above analysis and preferences of the Kelleys, a course of action must be developed that will do the following:

- provide Connie with the desired income
- use some of Curt's estate to provide for grandchildren
- make a sizable charitable contribution

The following set of assumptions shows the effect of all jointly owned property passing to Connie as well as the effect of the expected growth of Connie's portfolio on her annual income after Curt dies.

[text continues on page 8.42]

CASE II
Connie's Portfolio Income Beginning in 2002

New Assumptions

1. Curt dies on December 31, 2002.

2. All jointly owned property passes to Connie.

3. Income from the portfolio owned by Connie will grow at rates shown in table 8-3.

Continuing Assumptions

1. The checking account balance is maintained at $70,000; the account is noninterest bearing.

2. The money market deposit account earns 3.1 percent annually.

3. Investable cash is invested and earns 5 percent annually.

4. Expenditures for food, clothing and cleaning, utilities, phone, vacations, and charitable contributions will increase annually at 3 percent.

5. Expenditures for transportation will increase 4 percent annually.

6. Expenditures for entertainment will increase 5 percent annually.

7. Expenditures for medical insurance and other medical expenses will increase at 6 percent annually.

8. Decreases in the value of furniture have been ignored.

9. Automobiles decrease in value at a rate of 15 percent annually.

10. The value of the home will increase at one percent annually.

Deleted Assumptions

1. Income from the portfolio equals $44,360 and will grow at rates shown in table 8-3.

2. Curt's salary is increased at 5 percent annually.

INCOME STATEMENT

CONSTANCE KELLEY

CASE II	2003	2004	2005	2006	2007
Interest/Dividends					
Money Market Fund	2,325	2,325	2,325	2,325	2,325
Corporate Bonds	7,300	7,300	7,300	7,300	7,300
Galaxy Pharmceutcal	7,650	7,803	7,959	8,118	8,281
Acme Drug Company	1,298	1,337	1,377	1,418	1,461
Zenith Drug Company	812	824	837	849	862
International Fund	1,854	1,910	1,967	2,026	2,087
Utility Fund	7,725	7,957	8,195	8,441	8,695
Index Fund	5,150	5,305	5,464	5,628	5,796
CDs	1,050	1,103	1,158	1,216	1,276
	35,164	35,863	36,582	37,321	38,082
	========	========	========	========	========
Adj Gross Income	35,164	35,863	36,582	37,321	38,082
Deductions					
Charitable 50%	2,060	2,122	2,185	2,251	2,319
State Tax Paid	985	1,004	1,024	1,045	1,066
Home - Property Tax	3,640	3,786	3,937	4,095	4,258
Gross Deductions	6,685	6,912	7,146	7,391	7,643
Standard Deduction	4,650	4,800	4,900	5,050	5,150
Allowed Deductions	6,685	6,912	7,146	7,391	7,643
Pers Exemptions	2,950	3,050	3,150	3,200	3,300
	========	========	========	========	========
Taxable Income	25,529	25,901	26,286	26,731	27,139
	========	========	========	========	========
Fed Income Tax	3,529	3,585	3,643	3,710	3,771
	========	========	========	========	========
Fed Tax Bracket-Ord Inc	15.0%	15.0%	15.0%	15.0%	15.0%

BALANCE SHEET

CONSTANCE KELLEY

CASE II LIQUID ASSETS	2003	2004	2005	2006	2007
Cash Balance	56,947	42,907	27,835	11,676	-5,612
Cash Deposits					
CDs	22,050	23,153	24,311	25,527	26,803
Money Market Fund	75,000	75,000	75,000	75,000	75,000
	97,050	98,153	99,311	100,527	101,803
Stocks & Bonds					
Corporate Bonds	100,000	100,000	100,000	100,000	100,000
Galaxy Pharmceutcal	583,200	629,856	680,245	734,664	793,437
Acme Drug Company	79,396	84,556	90,053	95,906	102,140
Zenith Drug Company	47,524	51,801	56,463	61,545	67,084
International Fund	171,735	183,756	196,619	210,383	225,110
Utility Fund	159,135	163,909	168,826	173,891	179,108
Index Fund	237,620	259,006	282,316	307,725	335,420
	1,378,610	1,472,885	1,574,522	1,684,114	1,802,299
	========	========	========	========	========
Liquid Assets	1,532,607	1,613,945	1,701,668	1,796,317	1,898,490
	========	========	========	========	========

NONLIQUID ASSETS

Personal Property					
Home	408,040	412,120	416,242	420,404	424,608
Car - Connie	8,500	7,225	6,141	5,220	4,437
Home Furnishings	125,000	125,000	125,000	125,000	125,000
Jewelry & Furs	50,000	50,000	50,000	50,000	50,000
	591,540	594,345	597,383	600,624	604,045
	========	========	========	========	========
Nonliquid Assets	591,540	594,345	597,383	600,624	604,045
	========	========	========	========	========
Total Assets	2,124,147	2,208,290	2,299,051	2,396,941	2,502,535
Net Worth	2,124,147	2,208,290	2,299,051	2,396,941	2,502,535
	========	========	========	========	========

CASH FLOW STATEMENT

CONSTANCE KELLEY

	2003	2004	2005	2006	2007
CASE II					
BEGINNING OF YEAR					
Idle Cash On Hand	70,000	56,947	42,907	27,835	11,676
SOURCES OF CASH					
Cash Income					
Interest+Dividends	34,114	34,760	35,424	36,105	36,806
	34,114	34,760	35,424	36,105	36,806
Total Cash Inflow	34,114	34,760	35,424	36,105	36,806
Tot Cash Available	104,114	91,707	78,331	63,941	48,482
USES OF CASH					
Partly Deductible					
Medical Ins Premium	530	562	596	631	669
Charity Contrb-50%	2,060	2,122	2,185	2,251	2,319
	2,590	2,684	2,781	2,882	2,988
Not Tax Deductible					
Food	5,000	5,150	5,305	5,464	5,628
Clothing	5,000	5,250	5,513	5,788	6,078
Entertainment	6,000	6,300	6,615	6,946	7,293
Vacations	5,000	5,150	5,305	5,464	5,628
Transportation	1,040	1,082	1,125	1,170	1,217
Home - Ins Premium	714	728	743	758	773
Auto - Ins Premium	1,248	1,298	1,350	1,404	1,460
Jewlry&Furs-InsPrem	1,020	1,040	1,061	1,082	1,104
UmbrellaPolicy Prem	191	197	203	209	215
Home - Repair/Maint	3,090	3,183	3,278	3,377	3,478
Utility/Phone	4,120	4,244	4,371	4,502	4,637
Other Persnl Expnse	4,000	4,120	4,244	4,371	4,502
	36,423	37,741	39,111	40,533	42,011
Taxes Paid					
Fed Tax Paid	3,529	3,585	3,643	3,710	3,771
State Tax Paid	985	1,004	1,024	1,045	1,066
Home - Property Tax	3,640	3,786	3,937	4,095	4,258
	8,154	8,375	8,604	8,849	9,095
Tot Cash Outflow	47,167	48,800	50,495	52,265	54,094
END OF YEAR					
Cash Balance	56,947	42,907	27,835	11,676	-5,612

SUPPORTING SCHEDULE

CONSTANCE KELLEY

CASE II	SINGLE 2003	SINGLE 2004	SINGLE 2005	SINGLE 2006	SINGLE 2007
Income					
Adj Gross Income	35,164	35,863	36,582	37,321	38,082
Allowed Deductions	6,685	6,912	7,146	7,391	7,643
Pers Exemptions	2,950	3,050	3,150	3,200	3,300
Taxable Income	25,529	25,901	26,286	26,731	27,139
Federal Tax Liab					
Regular Tax	3,529	3,589	3,641	3,709	3,769
Gross Fed Inc Tax	3,529	3,585	3,643	3,710	3,771
Fed Income Tax	3,529	3,585	3,643	3,710	3,771
Fed Tax Analysis-Ord Inc					
Indexing Factor	82	87	91	96	102
Fed Tax Bracket-Ord Inc	15.0%	15.0%	15.0%	15.0%	15.0%
$ to Next Bracket	2,571	2,899	3,264	3,619	4,011
Next Bracket	27.0%	26.0%	26.0%	25.0%	25.0%
Previous Bracket	10.0%	10.0%	10.0%	10.0%	10.0%
$ to Prev Bracket	19,529	19,901	20,286	20,731	21,139
Fed Effective Tax Rate	13.8%	13.8%	13.9%	13.9%	13.9%
Alt Minimum Tax					
Adj Gross Income	35,164	35,863	36,582	37,321	38,082
Contributions	-2,060	-2,122	-2,185	-2,251	-2,319
Adjusted AMTI	33,104	33,741	34,397	35,070	35,763
AMT Exemptions	-35,750	-35,750	-33,750	-33,750	-33,750
AMT Taxable Inc	0	0	647	1,320	2,013
Gross Alt Min Tx	0	0	168	343	523
Fed Tax Less FTC	-3,529	-3,585	-3,643	-3,710	-3,771
Other Tax Liabs					
PA Taxable Inc	35,164	35,863	36,582	37,321	38,082
PA Regular Tax	985	1,004	1,024	1,045	1,066
PA Income Tax	985	1,004	1,024	1,045	1,066
Pennsylvania Tax	985	1,004	1,024	1,045	1,066
Tot State/Local Tx	985	1,004	1,024	1,045	1,066
Total Inc Tax	4,514	4,589	4,667	4,755	4,837

FINANCIAL SUMMARY

CONSTANCE KELLEY

CASE II	2003	2004	2005	2006	2007
Gross Real Income					
Interest Income	10,675	10,728	10,783	10,841	10,901
Dividends Rcvd	24,489	25,135	25,799	26,480	27,181
	35,164	35,863	36,582	37,321	38,082
Income & Inflation					
Gross Real Inc	35,164	35,863	36,582	37,321	38,082
Total Inc Tax	-4,514	-4,589	-4,667	-4,755	-4,837
Net Real Income	30,650	31,274	31,915	32,567	33,245
Cur Real Inc =	30,650	31,447	32,265	33,105	33,966
Purch Power Drop	0	173	350	538	721
At Infltn Rate of	3	3	3	3	3
Cash Flow					
Idle Cash On Hand	70,000	56,947	42,907	27,835	11,676
Norml Cash Inflow	34,114	34,760	35,424	36,105	36,806
Norml Cash Outflw	47,167	48,800	50,495	52,265	54,094
Cash Balance	56,947	42,907	27,835	11,676	-5,612
Net Worth					
Personal Assets	648,487	637,252	625,218	612,300	598,433
Investment Assets	1,475,660	1,571,038	1,673,833	1,784,641	1,904,102
Personal Net Worth	648,487	637,252	625,218	612,300	598,433
Investment Net Worth	1,475,660	1,571,038	1,673,833	1,784,641	1,904,102
Net Worth	2,124,147	2,208,290	2,299,051	2,396,941	2,502,535

INITIAL PLANNING FOR CONNIE'S INCOME FLOW AND ADJUSTMENTS TO CURT'S ESTATE PLAN

Connie's Financial Status Following Curt's Death, Having Received Only All Jointly Owned Property

Case II presents a preliminary picture of Connie's finances under the assumption that only the jointly owned property passes to her. Although the income statement reveals that Connie's income will be considerably short of their desired goal of $105,000, this statement provides little insight into the effect of her receiving only the jointly held property. Both the balance sheet and the cash-flow statement provide greater information about her financial affairs.

Analysis of Connie's Cash Flow

The cash-flow statement provides the analysis of what will happen to Connie's financial status over the next few years. First, she will experience a negative cash flow each year, with the result that her ending cash balance, which started at $70,000 at the beginning of January 2003, will be exhausted by 2007. Given that their plans were for her to have an income of about $105,000 after Curt's death, this result is not unexpected even though some reductions in her cash expenses have occurred. The result of this decline in Connie's cash balance appears as the first item on her balance sheet. Obviously she would not be in a negative financial situation, since some assets could be sold. But a year-to-year practice of selling assets to meet cash needs would not be consistent with the Kelleys' objective of not using up principal.

A second observation from the balance sheet is that the interest earned on the CDs accumulates at the bank, with no cash received by Connie despite the fact that this income creates an annual cash drain for the amount of the income tax due on the earnings. The amount is small, but if the bank permits, this income can be converted into quarterly payments to Connie.

Third, Connie holds more than $1,300,000 of financial assets (bank deposits, stocks, and bonds) and yet has an income stream from these assets of only $35,164 (2.7 percent), since most of these assets are in stocks whose primary characteristic is long-term growth with little current income. This was an appropriate investment focus as long as Curt was employed. Now a revision of the portfolio's strategy could enhance Connie's financial well-being.

Portfolio Revision

An investment objective that focuses more heavily on producing current income could be pursued. This would entail shifting a portion of the common stocks from their emphasis on the pharmaceutical industry to either stocks that provide higher annual income, bonds, or some combination thereof. The particular securities that could be used for this restructuring are Curt's former ownership interests in the jointly owned stocks. After his death these will receive a step-up in basis and can be sold with little or no capital gain. The sale of one-half of the pharmaceutical stocks and the international fund would provide more than $400,000 of cash that can be repositioned so that this portion of the portfolio would earn between 3 and 6 percent more than it does currently, depending on the particular assets acquired.

Consequences of this restructuring are, first, that the portfolio will experience a lower growth rate and might not provide sufficient inflation protection for Connie's future income needs. Second, no consideration has yet been made as to the asset ownership and income flows available from two of Curt's major assets—the life insurance proceeds and the pension plan. Until the effects of any decisions concerning these two assets are examined in light of Connie's financial situation, it is somewhat premature to consider any portfolio revision solely for the purpose of enhancing current income.

There is a need for some portfolio revision for meeting other investment objectives, such as a reduction of investment concentration in one specific industry. The same securities that were identified for sale to produce income, as well as some of Connie's holdings in the pharmaceutical stocks, can constitute some of those to be reinvested in securities that provide greater diversification and hence less risk to the portfolio. Stock and bond mutual funds are alternatives that would provide diversification and increase her current cash flow. She would also benefit from professional management. After the consequences of the decisions concerning Curt's remaining assets have been determined, then recommendations as to the portfolio restructuring can be made.

Lastly, the balance sheet shows the residence as an asset of Connie's. As was discussed earlier, the prudent course of action from a tax standpoint is to retain the property and benefit from the step-up in basis. Following Curt's death the property could be sold and the proceeds used to acquire either a portfolio of securities (should Connie move to an apartment) or a less expensive residence that is less costly to operate. The remaining proceeds would then be available for investment. Whether this course of action is needed for cash-flow purposes, as with the portfolio restructuring, depends on the remaining cash flows available to her.

At this point the assumptions and resulting financial statements for Connie should be examined to determine the effects of some of the Kelleys' remaining decisions regarding Connie's income needs and their other objectives.

FURTHER PLANNING OF CONNIE'S FINANCES

Based on the information contained in the financial statements of Case II, the Kelleys have made several decisions as to the treatment of the assets that would be included in Curt's estate.

Decisions

Qualified Retirement Plan

Curt arranges to take early retirement and elects a joint and 100 percent survivor annuity, which under Galaxy's plan would produce a total benefit of $71,309.77 for as long as both or either of the Kelleys live.

Aggressive Growth Mutual Fund

The shares in the Aggressive Growth Mutual Fund will be distributed to Connie from Curt's estate. This provides further inflation protection, if needed, and also slightly increases her income.

Social Security

Connie will begin receiving Social Security payments as a surviving spouse as soon as possible after Curt's death. Since Curt experienced such a sudden decline in his health, the Kelleys feel that life is precarious and that a similar misfortune could befall Connie. If so, she might never receive any retirement benefits from Social Security. In addition, the marginal amount of income that is forgone by taking early benefits does not seem important to someone with Connie's financial wherewithal, and, if really needed, it could be made up from other sources.

Curt's Car

Curt's car is much more luxurious than Connie's and they prefer that she obtain that as a distribution from the estate and then dispose of hers. They questioned their children, none of whom expressed any interest in her car. If she finds that using his car affects her emotionally, she will use the proceeds from the sale of her car, the trade-in value of Curt's, and any cash needed to acquire a replacement without the emotional ties.

EFFECTS ON CONNIE'S FINANCES

Connie's Gross Income

With these changes implemented into the Kelleys' plans, as shown in Case III, we find that Connie's adjusted gross income for tax purposes, as shown on the income statement, will rise by $83,613 for 2003. This increase comes from the following sources:

- $71,310 of interest income from the bond portfolio
- $8,925 of taxable Social Security benefits
- $1,969 of dividend income from the Aggressive Growth Mutual Fund
- $1,409 earnings on dividends and interest income

[text continues on page 8.53]

CASE III
Addition of Pension Plan Income, Social Security Benefits, and Aggressive Growth Mutual Fund Dividends to Connie's Projected Income

New Assumptions

1. Curt takes early retirement and elects to receive a joint and 100 percent survivor annuity of $71,310 per year.

2. The Aggressive Growth Mutual Fund will pass to Connie as part of her distribution from Curt's estate.

3. Social Security benefits in the amount of $10,500 annually will begin in January 2003 and will have an annual inflation increase of 2.8 percent.

4. Connie will sell her car, receive Curt's from his estate, and reduce her automobile insurance by 50 percent.

Continuing Assumptions

1. Curt dies on December 31, 2002.

2. All jointly owned property passes to Connie.

3. Income from the portfolio owned by Connie will grow at rates shown in table 8-3.

4. The checking account balance is maintained at $70,000; the account is noninterest bearing.

5. The money market deposit account earns 3.1 percent annually.

6. Investable cash is invested and earns 5 percent annually.

7. Expenditures for food, clothing and cleaning, utilities, phone, vacations, and charitable contributions will increase annually at 3 percent.

8. Expenditures for transportation will increase 4 percent annually.

9. Expenditures for entertainment will increase 5 percent annually.

10. Expenditures for medical insurance and other medical expenses will increase at 6 percent annually.

11.   Decreases in the value of furniture have been ignored.

12.   Automobiles decrease in value at a rate of 15 percent annually.

13.   The value of the home will increase at one percent annually.

Deleted Assumptions

1.   Income from the portfolio equals $44,360 and will grow at rates shown in table 8-3.

2.   Curt's salary is increased at 5 percent annually.

INCOME STATEMENT

CONSTANCE KELLEY

CASE III	2003	2004	2005	2006	2007
Interest/Dividends					
Money Market Fund	2,325	2,325	2,325	2,325	2,325
Corporate Bonds	7,300	7,300	7,300	7,300	7,300
Galaxy Pharmceutcal	7,650	7,803	7,959	8,118	8,281
Acme Drug Company	1,298	1,337	1,377	1,418	1,461
Zenith Drug Company	812	824	837	849	862
Aggrssve Grwth Fund	1,969	2,067	2,171	2,279	2,393
International Fund	1,854	1,910	1,967	2,026	2,087
Utility Fund	7,725	7,957	8,195	8,441	8,695
Index Fund	5,150	5,305	5,464	5,628	5,796
CDs	1,050	1,103	1,158	1,216	1,276
Overall Investmnt	1,409	4,031	6,486	9,014	11,617
	38,542	41,961	45,238	48,615	52,092
Other					
Txbl Social Sec	8,925	9,175	9,432	9,696	9,967
J&S Retirement Ben	71,310	71,310	71,310	71,310	71,310
	80,235	80,485	80,742	81,006	81,277
	========	========	========	========	========
Adj Gross Income	118,777	122,446	125,980	129,621	133,370
Deductions					
Charitable 50%	2,060	2,122	2,185	2,251	2,319
State Tax Paid	3,076	3,172	3,263	3,358	3,455
Home - Property Tax	3,640	3,786	3,937	4,095	4,258
Gross Deductions	8,776	9,080	9,385	9,704	10,032
Standard Deduction	4,650	4,800	4,900	5,050	5,150
Allowed Deductions	8,776	9,080	9,385	9,704	10,032
Pers Exemptions	2,950	3,050	3,150	3,200	3,300
	========	========	========	========	========
Taxable Income	107,051	110,317	113,445	116,717	120,037
	========	========	========	========	========
Fed Income Tax	26,400	26,428	27,198	27,139	27,932
	========	========	========	========	========
Fed Tax Bracket-Ord Inc	30.0%	29.0%	29.0%	28.0%	28.0%

BALANCE SHEET

CONSTANCE KELLEY

CASE III	2003	2004	2005	2006	2007
LIQUID ASSETS					
Cash Balance	70,047	70,060	70,079	70,095	70,114
Cash Deposits					
Overall Investmnt	57,750	107,537	158,391	211,185	265,105
CDs	22,050	23,153	24,311	25,527	26,803
Money Market Fund	75,000	75,000	75,000	75,000	75,000
	154,800	205,690	257,702	311,712	366,908
Stocks & Bonds					
Corporate Bonds	100,000	100,000	100,000	100,000	100,000
Galaxy Pharmceutcal	583,200	629,856	680,244	734,664	793,437
Acme Drug Company	79,396	84,556	90,053	95,906	102,140
Zenith Drug Company	47,524	51,801	56,463	61,545	67,084
Aggrssve Grwth Fund	151,801	167,284	184,347	203,151	223,872
International Fund	171,735	183,756	196,619	210,383	225,110
Utility Fund	159,135	163,909	168,826	173,891	179,108
Index Fund	237,620	259,006	282,316	307,725	335,420
	1,530,410	1,640,169	1,758,870	1,887,264	2,026,170
	========	========	========	========	========
Liquid Assets	1,755,257	1,915,920	2,086,650	2,269,071	2,463,192
	========	========	========	========	========

NONLIQUID ASSETS

Personal Property	2003	2004	2005	2006	2007
Home	408,040	412,120	416,242	420,404	424,608
Car - Curt	21,250	18,063	15,353	13,050	11,093
Home Furnishings	125,000	125,000	125,000	125,000	125,000
Jewelry & Furs	50,000	50,000	50,000	50,000	50,000
	604,290	605,183	606,595	608,454	610,701
	========	========	========	========	========
Nonliquid Assets	604,290	605,183	606,595	608,454	610,701
	========	========	========	========	========
Total Assets	2,359,547	2,521,103	2,693,245	2,877,525	3,073,893
Net Worth	2,359,547	2,521,103	2,693,245	2,877,525	3,073,893
	========	========	========	========	========

CASH FLOW STATEMENT

CONSTANCE KELLEY

CASE III	2003	2004	2005	2006	2007
BEGINNING OF YEAR					
Idle Cash On Hand	70,000	70,047	70,060	70,079	70,095
SOURCES OF CASH					
Cash Income					
Soc Security Inc	10,500	10,794	11,096	11,407	11,726
Interest+Dividends	36,083	36,827	37,594	38,385	39,199
J&S Retirement Ben	71,310	71,310	71,310	71,310	71,310
	117,893	118,931	120,001	121,102	122,236
Sale/Withdrawals					
Car - Connie	10,000	0	0	0	0
	10,000	0	0	0	0
	========	========	========	========	========
Total Cash Inflow	127,893	118,931	120,001	121,102	122,236
	========	========	========	========	========
Tot Cash Available	197,893	188,978	190,061	191,181	192,331
	========	========	========	========	========
USES OF CASH					
Partly Deductible					
Medical Ins Premium	530	562	596	631	669
Charity Contrb-50%	2,060	2,122	2,185	2,251	2,319
	2,590	2,684	2,781	2,882	2,988
Not Tax Deductible					
Food	5,000	5,150	5,305	5,464	5,628
Clothing	5,000	5,250	5,513	5,788	6,078
Entertainment	6,000	6,300	6,615	6,946	7,293
Vacations	5,000	5,150	5,305	5,464	5,628
Transportation	1,040	1,082	1,125	1,170	1,217
Home - Ins Premium	714	728	743	758	773
Auto - Ins Premium	624	649	675	702	730
Jewlry&Furs-InsPrem	1,020	1,040	1,061	1,082	1,104
UmbrellaPolicy Prem	191	197	203	209	215
Home - Repair/Maint	3,090	3,183	3,278	3,377	3,478
Utility/Phone	4,120	4,244	4,371	4,502	4,637
Other Persnl Expnse	4,000	4,120	4,244	4,371	4,502
	35,799	37,092	38,436	39,831	41,281
Taxes Paid					
Fed Tax Paid	26,400	26,428	27,198	27,139	27,932
State Tax Paid	3,076	3,172	3,263	3,358	3,455
Home - Property Tax	3,640	3,786	3,937	4,095	4,258
	33,116	33,386	34,398	34,592	35,645

CASH FLOW STATEMENT (cont.)

CONSTANCE KELLEY

CASE III	2003	2004	2005	2006	2007
Purchase/Deposits					
Overall Investmnt	56,341	45,756	44,368	43,780	42,303
	56,341	45,756	44,368	43,780	42,303
	========	========	========	========	========
Tot Cash Outflow	127,846	118,918	119,982	121,085	122,217
	========	========	========	========	========
END OF YEAR					
Cash Balance	70,047	70,060	70,079	70,095	70,114
	========	========	========	========	========

SUPPORTING SCHEDULE

CONSTANCE KELLEY

CASE III	SINGLE 2003	SINGLE 2004	SINGLE 2005	SINGLE 2006	SINGLE 2007
Income					
Adj Gross Income	118,777	122,446	125,980	129,621	133,370
Allowed Deductions	8,776	9,080	9,385	9,704	10,032
Pers Exemptions	2,950	3,050	3,150	3,200	3,300
Taxable Income	107,051	110,317	113,445	116,717	120,037
Federal Tax Liab					
Regular Tax	26,400	26,428	27,198	27,139	27,932
Gross Fed Inc Tax	26,400	26,428	27,198	27,139	27,932
Fed Income Tax	26,400	26,428	27,198	27,139	27,932
Fed Tax Analysis-Ord Inc					
Indexing Factor	82	87	91	96	102
Fed Tax Bracket-Ord Inc	30.0%	29.0%	29.0%	28.0%	28.0%
$ to Next Bracket	35,049	35,483	36,155	36,783	37,413
Next Bracket	35.0%	34.0%	34.0%	33.0%	33.0%
Previous Bracket	27.0%	26.0%	26.0%	25.0%	25.0%
$ to Prev Bracket	38,951	40,467	41,745	43,167	44,587
Fed Effective Tax Rate	24.7%	24.0%	24.0%	23.3%	23.3%
Alt Minimum Tax					
Adj Gross Income	118,777	122,446	125,980	129,621	133,370
Contributions	-2,060	-2,122	-2,185	-2,251	-2,319
Adjusted AMTI	116,717	120,324	123,795	127,370	131,051
AMT Exemptions	-34,696	-33,794	-30,926	-30,033	-29,112
AMT Taxable Inc	82,021	86,530	92,869	97,337	101,938
Gross Alt Min Tx	21,326	22,498	24,146	25,308	26,504
Fed Tax Less FTC	-26,400	-26,428	-27,198	-27,139	-27,932
Other Tax Liabs					
PA Taxable Inc	109,852	113,271	116,548	119,925	123,402
PA Regular Tax	3,076	3,172	3,263	3,358	3,455
PA Income Tax	3,076	3,172	3,263	3,358	3,455
Pennsylvania Tax	3,076	3,172	3,263	3,358	3,455
Tot State/Local Tx	3,076	3,172	3,263	3,358	3,455
Total Inc Tax	29,476	29,600	30,461	30,497	31,387

FINANCIAL SUMMARY

CONSTANCE KELLEY

CASE III	2003	2004	2005	2006	2007
Gross Real Income					
Interest Income	12,084	14,759	17,269	19,855	22,518
Dividends Rcvd	26,458	27,202	27,969	28,760	29,574
J&S Retirement Ben	71,310	71,310	71,310	71,310	71,310
Soc Security Inc	10,500	10,794	11,096	11,407	11,726
	120,352	124,065	127,645	131,332	135,129
Income & Inflation					
Gross Real Inc	120,352	124,065	127,645	131,332	135,129
Total Inc Tax	-29,476	-29,600	-30,461	-30,497	-31,387
Net Real Income	90,876	94,465	97,184	100,834	103,742
Cur Real Inc =	90,876	93,240	95,666	98,155	100,709
At Infltn Rate of	3	3	3	3	3
Cash Flow					
Idle Cash On Hand	70,000	70,047	70,060	70,079	70,095
Norml Cash Inflow	127,893	118,931	120,001	121,102	122,236
Norml Cash Outflw	71,505	73,162	75,614	77,305	79,914
Cash Invested	56,341	45,756	44,368	43,780	42,303
Cash Balance	70,047	70,060	70,079	70,095	70,114
Net Worth					
Personal Assets	674,337	675,243	676,673	678,549	680,815
Investment Assets	1,685,210	1,845,859	2,016,572	2,198,976	2,393,078
Personal Net Worth	674,337	675,243	676,673	678,549	680,815
Investment Net Worth	1,685,210	1,845,859	2,016,572	2,198,976	2,393,078
Net Worth	2,359,547	2,521,103	2,693,245	2,877,525	3,073,893

Connie's gross cash flow will increase by a total of $86,238, comprised of the increases just listed above plus the 15 percent of Social Security, or $1,575, that is not subject to income taxation and the $1,050 interest on the CD that has been recognized as income but not received in cash. The effect is to improve her cash flow by this amount and her total adjusted gross income by $82,560 ($83,613 – $1,050). This increase, plus her dividend and interest income, results in Connie's having $120,352 ($118,777 taxable plus $1,575 tax exempt) of annual available income, a figure above their $105,000 target. At this point no portfolio restructuring is recommended, since decisions must yet be made with respect to the life insurance proceeds.

Further analysis of the cash-flow statement in case III shows that in 2003 Connie will have an excess of cash inflow over cash outflow of approximately $56,341, although this amount will decline somewhat during the next 4 years. As stated in the earlier discussion concerning her income needs, her targeted income following Curt's death was to be sufficient not only to maintain her current lifestyle but also to enable her to make charitable gifts and provide any needed assistance to children and grandchildren. Although this goal appears to be satisfied with the existing income level, because of uncertainties, the Kelleys want to overprovide for Connie, which will result in larger annual cash-flow surpluses that can be used for these gift-giving purposes.

FURTHER PLANNING DECISIONS AND REASONING

At this point, Connie's income falls above the target but not by a large amount. In addition, no decisions have been made as to the use of the life insurance proceeds, nor has any thought been given to Curt's objectives of providing for the grandchildren and making substantial charitable contributions.

GSTT/Credit Shelter

Earlier in the case it was observed that the current estate plan of the Kelleys—the use of simple wills that pass all of Curt's estate assets to Connie (and all of Connie's estate assets to Curt)—forgoes valuable federal estate tax-sheltering opportunities. The proper way to structure the Kelleys' wills is to assure the optimal use of the federal estate tax marital deduction. To take maximum advantage of this marital deduction and in turn to reduce estate tax liability, a credit-shelter bypass trust should be created under the terms of the will.

This bypass trust should empower the trustee to accumulate income or to sprinkle income among income beneficiaries in accordance with the trustee's discretion. At Connie's death, the trust will terminate and the trust corpus will be distributed to the Kelley grandchildren, assuming the youngest grandchild has attained majority. The Kelley children would not be named beneficiaries of

Curt's credit-shelter trust, as they would be provided for under the terms and provisions of Connie's revised will.

When the Kelley grandchildren receive the trust corpus from Curt's credit-shelter bypass trust, a generation-skipping transfer will be deemed to have taken place under the GST tax rules. In essence, when the trust terminates and the trust corpus is distributed to the Kelley grandchildren, a taxable termination under Sec. 2612(a)(2) will occur. This section of the Code provides that upon the termination of an interest in property held in trust, if a specified portion of the trust assets is distributed to skip persons who are lineal descendants of the holder of such interest, such termination constitutes a taxable termination with respect to such portion of the trust property. Therefore, when Curt's credit-shelter trust terminates and the corpus passes to the Kelley grandchildren, a generation-skipping transfer will take place. However, the exemption created by Sec. 2631 makes this an academic point only. Under this section of the Code, every individual is permitted to make aggregate transfers of up to $1,090,000 (in 2002) that will be exempted from the imposition of the generation-skipping transfer tax. Unless accumulated income, plus any growth in value of trust assets when added to the trust corpus, exceeds $1,090,000, the GSTT will not apply if appropriate elections are made to exempt the assets from the GSTT.

Qualifying Terminable Interest Property Trust (QTIP)

When structuring the credit-shelter bypass trust arrangement, one must consider whether a QTIP trust should be employed. In non-QTIP trust situations, the surviving spouse can leave to anyone the property that passed from the decedent to the surviving spouse. Sometimes the first spouse to die is reluctant to allow his or her estate property to pass in such a fashion. Often the reluctance is based on a fear that this estate property will ultimately pass to an individual or class of individuals who, in the view of the first spouse to die, is undeserving of such property (for example, new spouse, children from a different marriage, etc.). In these cases a QTIP trust should be used. With this device, the first spouse to die may direct where the estate property will ultimately end up at the death of the surviving spouse. Considering the facts and circumstances of the Kelley case, there is no logical reason to employ a QTIP arrangement. There is no fear on Curt's part that his estate assets will ultimately pass to undeserving recipients.

However, the wills do need to be rewritten. Focusing first on Curt's, his will should establish a credit-shelter bypass trust. Given the facts as shown earlier, the estate settlement costs for Curt's estate will be somewhat more than $272,598. As will be shown later in an estate plan that takes into consideration all the changes, this figure can be reduced. However, the planned use of $822,500 of life insurance proceeds, $125,000 of Treasury bonds, and $50,000 of Series EE bonds of Curt's property has yet to be determined. Indeed, the life insurance proceeds plus the Treasury bonds exceed the amount needed to fully fund the credit bypass trust and pay all estate settlement costs. This leaves the Series EE bonds available for charitable giving. Curt's will should specify the alternatives as developed below, as well as those that have been developed earlier in this case (such as the distribution of the automobile and the aggressive stock growth mutual fund shares to Connie).

The Life Insurance and Life Insurance Trust

A life insurance trust could be established to own the policies, and if Curt were to live for 3 years, this would effectively remove them from his estate. However, the facts of the case indicate that he is not expected to survive that long. The costs associated with establishing the trust, the implications of the trust's beneficiaries' receiving gifts of a future interest, and bringing back the policies into the estate for estate tax purposes all combine to preclude the use of the life insurance trust, at least according to what the Kelleys wish. They do not want to pursue this course of action and prefer to have the proceeds pass directly to Curt's estate by changing the beneficiary designation from Connie to his estate. The proceeds will be used to fund a credit bypass trust in an amount at least equal to $1 million. It is anticipated that the trust corpus will be invested in a portfolio comprised equally of corporate bonds and common stocks. This portfolio should have a total return of about 10 percent annually and a cash income of about 3.3 percent. Under the terms of the trust described below, Connie will have additional income of about $16,500 in 2003 and that will increase 2 percent yearly. It is assumed that the stocks will increase in value at about 8 or 9 percent annually.

Connie is to receive one-half of the trust income. The remainder can be either accumulated or distributed under a sprinkling power to either Connie or the grandchildren. The grandchildren will be the remainder beneficiaries of the trust, which will not be terminated during Connie's lifetime. If she dies prematurely, the trust will be terminated when the youngest grandchild-beneficiary attains age 21.

The Series EE Bonds

Curt has expressed a desire to make charitable contributions from his assets. He could use the $50,000 of Series EE bonds for this purpose.

The Treasury Bonds

This asset is needed in Curt's estate, along with some of the proceeds of the life insurance, to provide the cash to pay the various estate administrative costs, debts, and taxes.

EFFECT OF THESE CHANGES ON BOTH ESTATES

Curt's Estate Size

At this point, the estates of Connie and Curt should be reviewed, with particular emphasis on Curt's estate.

Curt's gross estate will be reduced in the amount of $50,000 as a result of the gift ($50,000 in EE bonds) made by Curt to the charity. Under current law there is no requirement that any of this $50,000 be brought back into Curt's gross estate.

Estate Tax Reduction Techniques

The result is that the estate will have some federal estate tax liability in addition to the state inheritance tax. There are several possible ways for the Kelleys to reduce the estate taxes further and also meet Curt's desire to make charitable contributions. The first method is to sell some of the Treasury bonds and make a charitable gift of about $40,000 while he is still alive, which would enable the Kelleys to obtain the income tax deduction for the amount of the gift as well as removing that amount from his estate. The second method is to instruct the trustee to use any estate assets remaining after deducting all debts, administration costs, state inheritance taxes, marital deduction, and the $1 million funding of the bypass trust for a qualifying charitable gift. A third method is to specify an amount, such as $40,000, to be given as a charitable gift from the estate. Use of any of the above methods would reduce the federal tax to a relatively inconsequential amount.

The Kelleys' choice was to have the estate make the charitable contribution of $40,000, and any estate assets remaining in the estate are to be placed in the bypass trust.

At Curt's Death	Computations	Actual Expenses Incurred
Gross estate[1]	$2,566,940	
Less: Debts[2]	(76,327)	76,327
Less: Costs of administration[3]	(192,521)	192,521
Adjusted gross estate	$2,298,092	
Less: Marital deduction[4]	(1,258,092)	
Less: Charitable deduction	(40,000)	
Taxable estate	1,000,000	
Federal estate tax	345,800	
Less: Unified credit	(345,800)	
State inheritance tax	–0–	
Federal estate tax owed	–0–	–0–
State inheritance tax	–0–	–0–
Total costs at first death		$ 268,848

At Connie's Subsequent Death		
Gross estate[5]	$1,748,152	
Less: Costs of administration[3]	(131,111)	131,111
Adjusted gross estate	$1,617,041	
Federal estate tax marital deduction[6]	–0–	
Taxable estate	1,617,041	
Federal estate tax	667,468	
Less: Unified credit	(345, 800)	
State inheritance tax credit	(64,340)	
Federal estate tax owed	257,328	257,328
State inheritance tax		64,340
Total costs at second death		$ 452,779
Total combined costs at both deaths		$ 721,627

Notes

[1] Gross estate of $2,616,940 reduced by $50,000 (EE bonds).

[2] Curt's estate will pay off remaining mortgage on residence.

[3] Assumed to be 7.5 percent of gross estate

[4] The value of the property passing to Connie plus the value of the joint and 100 percent survivor annuity ($694,940)

[5] This figure represents $563,152 passing from Curt's estate to Connie (not including the annuity, which will expire at Connie's death) plus $1,185,000, which is the sum of Connie's share of the jointly titled property and her separate property.

[6] There is no federal estate tax marital deduction available, as Connie is assumed to be unmarried at date of death.

Connie's Will

With the upcoming change in Connie's marital status, a new will becomes essential. Since Curt has provided some funds for the grandchildren by virtue of the terms of the bypass trust, it now behooves Connie to make her children equal beneficiaries, per stirpes, of her estate. The will could also direct that contributions be made to specified charities. These changes should enhance fulfillment of the goals the Kelleys have established.

Connie's Financial Status

Now that decisions concerning the use of the life insurance proceeds to further their objectives have been made a part of Curt's estate planning, an examination of Connie's estimated financial situation, including the trust income, is the last area of this case to review.

Revised Estate Costs

The effect of the changes that have been implemented is to reduce the total costs of Curt's and Connie's estates from $1,599,620 to $721,627. The combined estate cost reduction of almost $877,993 was achieved without sacrificing the Kelleys' goals. Most of the reduction came from using the credit-equivalent bypass trust and annuitizing the pension benefit.

[text continues on page 8.67]

CASE IV
Addition of Bypass Trust Earnings to Connie's Projected Income

New Assumption

1.   Connie will receive one-half of the income earned by the bypass trust. This is assumed to be $16,500 for 2003 and is expected to grow at 2 percent a year.

Continuing Assumptions

1.   Curt takes early retirement and elects to receive a joint and 100 percent survivor annuity of $71,310 per year.

2.   The Aggressive Growth Mutual Fund will pass to Connie as part of her distribution from Curt's estate.

3.   Social Security benefits, in the amount of $10,500 annually, will begin in January 2003 and will have an annual inflation increase of 2.8 percent.

4.   Connie will sell her car, receive Curt's from his estate, and reduce her automobile insurance by 50 percent.

5.   Curt dies on December 31, 2002.

6.   All jointly owned property passes to Connie.

7.   Income from the portfolio owned by Connie will grow at rates shown in table 8-3.

8.   The checking account balance is maintained at $70,000; the account is noninterest bearing.

9.   The money market deposit account earns 3.1 percent annually.

10.   Investable cash is invested and earns 5 percent annually.

11.   Expenditures for food, clothing and cleaning, utilities, phone, vacations, and charitable contributions will increase annually at 3 percent.

12.   Expenditures for transportation will increase 4 percent annually.

13.   Expenditures for entertainment will increase 5 percent annually.

14. Expenditures for medical insurance and other medical expenses will increase 6 percent annually.

15. Decreases in the value of furniture have been ignored.

16. The automobile decreases in value at a rate of 15 percent annually.

17. The value of the home will increase at one percent annually.

Deleted Assumptions

1. Income from the portfolio equals $44,360 and will grow at rates shown in table 8-3.

2. Curt's salary is increased at 5 percent annually.

INCOME STATEMENT

CONSTANCE KELLEY

CASE IV	2003	2004	2005	2006	2007
Interest/Dividends					
Money Market Fund	2,325	2,325	2,325	2,325	2,325
Corporate Bonds	7,300	7,300	7,300	7,300	7,300
Galaxy Pharmceutcal	7,650	7,803	7,959	8,118	8,281
Acme Drug Company	1,298	1,337	1,377	1,418	1,461
Zenith Drug Company	812	824	837	849	862
Aggrssve Grwth Fund	1,969	2,067	2,171	2,279	2,393
International Fund	1,854	1,910	1,967	2,026	2,087
Utility Fund	7,725	7,957	8,195	8,441	8,695
Index Fund	5,150	5,305	5,464	5,628	5,796
CDs	1,050	1,103	1,158	1,216	1,276
Overall Investmnt	1,687	4,885	7,951	11,125	14,414
	38,820	42,815	46,703	50,726	54,889
Other					
Txbl Social Sec	8,925	9,175	9,432	9,696	9,967
J&S Retirement Ben	71,310	71,310	71,310	71,310	71,310
By-Pass Trust Incom	16,500	16,830	17,167	17,510	17,860
	96,735	97,315	97,908	98,516	99,138
	========	========	========	========	========
Adj Gross Income	135,555	140,130	144,612	149,242	154,027
Deductions					
Charitable 50%	2,060	2,122	2,185	2,251	2,319
State Tax Paid	3,546	3,667	3,785	3,907	4,034
Home - Property Tax	3,640	3,786	3,937	4,095	4,258
Reductn for High Inc	0	-5	-30	-38	-58
Gross Deductions	9,246	9,569	9,877	10,215	10,554
Standard Deduction	4,650	4,800	4,900	5,050	5,150
Allowed Deductions	9,246	9,569	9,877	10,215	10,554
Pers Exemptions	2,950	2,989	3,087	3,157	3,212
	========	========	========	========	========
Taxable Income	123,359	127,572	131,648	135,870	140,261
	========	========	========	========	========
Fed Income Tax	31,293	31,432	32,476	32,502	33,595
	========	========	========	========	========
Fed Tax Bracket-Ord Inc	30.0%	29.0%	29.0%	28.0%	28.0%

BALANCE SHEET

CONSTANCE KELLEY

CASE IV	2003	2004	2005	2006	2007
LIQUID ASSETS					
Cash Balance	70,056	70,055	70,070	70,112	70,124
Cash Deposits					
Overall Investmnt	69,156	131,143	194,831	261,309	329,651
CDs	22,050	23,153	24,311	25,527	26,803
Money Market Fund	75,000	75,000	75,000	75,000	75,000
	166,206	229,296	294,142	361,836	431,454
Stocks & Bonds					
Corporate Bonds	100,000	100,000	100,000	100,000	100,000
Galaxy Pharmceutcal	583,200	629,856	680,244	734,664	793,437
Acme Drug Company	79,396	84,556	90,053	95,906	102,140
Zenith Drug Company	47,524	51,801	56,463	61,545	67,084
Aggrssve Grwth Fund	151,801	167,284	184,347	203,151	223,872
International Fund	171,735	183,756	196,619	210,383	225,110
Utility Fund	159,135	163,909	168,826	173,891	179,108
Index Fund	237,620	259,006	282,316	307,725	335,420
	1,530,410	1,640,169	1,758,870	1,887,264	2,026,170
	========	========	========	========	========
Liquid Assets	1,766,673	1,939,520	2,123,081	2,319,212	2,527,748
	========	========	========	========	========
NONLIQUID ASSETS					
Personal Property					
Home	408,040	412,120	416,242	420,404	424,608
Car - Curt	21,250	18,063	15,353	13,050	11,093
Home Furnishings	125,000	125,000	125,000	125,000	125,000
Jewelry & Furs	50,000	50,000	50,000	50,000	50,000
	604,290	605,183	606,595	608,454	610,701
	========	========	========	========	========
Nonliquid Assets	604,290	605,183	606,595	608,454	610,701
	========	========	========	========	========
Total Assets	2,370,963	2,544,703	2,729,676	2,927,666	3,138,449
Net Worth	2,370,963	2,544,703	2,729,676	2,927,666	3,138,449
	========	========	========	========	========

CASH FLOW STATEMENT

CONSTANCE KELLEY

CASE IV	2003	2004	2005	2006	2007
BEGINNING OF YEAR					
Idle Cash On Hand	70,000	70,056	70,055	70,070	70,112

SOURCES OF CASH

	2003	2004	2005	2006	2007
Cash Income					
Soc Security Inc	10,500	10,794	11,096	11,407	11,726
Interest+Dividends	36,083	36,827	37,594	38,385	39,199
Other Income-Csh	87,810	88,140	88,477	88,820	89,170
	134,393	135,761	137,167	138,612	140,096
Sale/Withdrawals					
Car - Connie	10,000	0	0	0	0
	10,000	0	0	0	0
	========	========	========	========	========
Total Cash Inflow	144,393	135,761	137,167	138,612	140,096
	========	========	========	========	========
Tot Cash Available	214,393	205,818	207,222	208,682	210,207
	========	========	========	========	========

USES OF CASH

	2003	2004	2005	2006	2007
Partly Deductible					
Medical Ins Premium	530	562	596	631	669
Charity Contrb-50%	2,060	2,122	2,185	2,251	2,319
	2,590	2,684	2,781	2,882	2,988
Not Tax Deductible					
Food	5,000	5,150	5,305	5,464	5,628
Clothing	5,000	5,250	5,513	5,788	6,078
Entertainment	6,000	6,300	6,615	6,946	7,293
Vacations	5,000	5,150	5,305	5,464	5,628
Transportation	1,040	1,082	1,125	1,170	1,217
Home - Ins Premium	714	728	743	758	773
Auto - Ins Premium	624	649	675	702	730
Jewlry&Furs-InsPrem	1,020	1,040	1,061	1,082	1,104
UmbrellaPolicy Prem	191	197	203	209	215
Home - Repair/Maint	3,090	3,183	3,278	3,377	3,478
Utility/Phone	4,120	4,244	4,371	4,502	4,637
Other Persnl Expnse	4,000	4,120	4,244	4,371	4,502
	35,799	37,092	38,436	39,831	41,281
Taxes Paid					
Fed Tax Paid	31,293	31,432	32,476	32,502	33,595
State Tax Paid	3,546	3,667	3,785	3,907	4,034
Home - Property Tax	3,640	3,786	3,937	4,095	4,258
	38,479	38,885	40,198	40,504	41,887

CASH FLOW STATEMENT (cont.)

CONSTANCE KELLEY

CASE IV **Purchase/Deposits**	2003	2004	2005	2006	2007
Overall Investmnt	67,469	57,102	55,737	55,353	53,928
	67,469	57,102	55,737	55,353	53,928
	========	========	========	========	========
Tot Cash Outflow	144,337	135,763	137,152	138,570	140,084
	========	========	========	========	========
END OF YEAR Cash Balance	70,056	70,055	70,070	70,112	70,124
	========	========	========	========	========

SUPPORTING SCHEDULE

CONSTANCE KELLEY

CASE IV	SINGLE 2003	SINGLE 2004	SINGLE 2005	SINGLE 2006	SINGLE 2007
Income					
Adj Gross Income	135,555	140,130	144,612	149,242	154,027
Allowed Deductions	9,246	9,569	9,877	10,215	10,554
Pers Exemptions	2,950	2,989	3,087	3,157	3,212
Taxable Income	123,359	127,572	131,648	135,870	140,261
Federal Tax Liab					
Regular Tax	31,293	31,432	32,476	32,502	33,595
Gross Fed Inc Tax	31,293	31,432	32,476	32,502	33,595
Fed Income Tax	31,293	31,432	32,476	32,502	33,595
Fed Tax Analysis-Ord Inc					
Indexing Factor	82	87	91	96	102
Fed Tax Bracket-Ord Inc	30.0%	29.0%	29.0%	28.0%	28.0%
$ to Next Bracket	18,741	18,228	17,952	17,630	17,189
Next Bracket	35.0%	34.0%	34.0%	33.0%	33.0%
Previous Bracket	27.0%	26.0%	26.0%	25.0%	25.0%
$ to Prev Bracket	55,259	57,722	59,948	62,320	64,811
Fed Effective Tax Rate	25.4%	24.6%	24.7%	23.9%	24.0%
Alt Minimum Tax					
Adj Gross Income	135,555	140,130	144,612	149,242	154,027
Contributions	-2,060	-2,122	-2,185	-2,251	-2,319
Adjusted AMTI	133,495	138,008	142,427	146,991	151,708
AMT Exemptions	-30,501	-29,373	-26,268	-25,127	-23,948
AMT Taxable Inc	102,994	108,635	116,159	121,863	127,760
Gross Alt Min Tx	26,778	28,245	30,201	31,684	33,218
Fed Tax Less FTC	-31,293	-31,432	-32,476	-32,502	-33,595
Other Tax Liabs					
PA Taxable Inc	126,630	130,955	135,180	139,546	144,059
PA Regular Tax	3,546	3,667	3,785	3,907	4,034
PA Income Tax	3,546	3,667	3,785	3,907	4,034
Pennsylvania Tax	3,546	3,667	3,785	3,907	4,034
Tot State/Local Tx	3,546	3,667	3,785	3,907	4,034
Total Inc Tax	34,839	35,099	36,261	36,409	37,629

FINANCIAL SUMMARY

CONSTANCE KELLEY

CASE IV	2003	2004	2005	2006	2007
Gross Real Income					
Interest Income	12,362	15,613	18,734	21,966	25,315
Dividends Rcvd	26,458	27,202	27,969	28,760	29,574
J&S Retirement Ben	71,310	71,310	71,310	71,310	71,310
By-Pass Trust Incom	16,500	16,830	17,167	17,510	17,860
Soc Security Inc	10,500	10,794	11,096	11,407	11,726
	137,130	141,749	146,276	150,953	155,786
Income & Inflation					
Gross Real Inc	137,130	141,749	146,276	150,953	155,786
Total Inc Tax	-34,839	-35,099	-36,261	-36,409	-37,629
Net Real Income	102,291	106,650	110,015	114,544	118,157
Cur Real Inc =	102,291	104,953	107,683	110,485	113,359
At Infltn Rate of	3	3	3	3	3
Cash Flow					
Idle Cash On Hand	70,000	70,056	70,055	70,070	70,112
Norml Cash Inflow	144,393	135,761	137,167	138,612	140,096
Norml Cash Outflw	76,868	78,661	81,415	83,217	86,156
Cash Invested	67,469	57,102	55,737	55,353	53,928
Cash Balance	70,056	70,055	70,070	70,112	70,124
Net Worth					
Personal Assets	674,346	675,238	676,665	678,566	680,824
Investment Assets	1,696,616	1,869,465	2,053,012	2,249,100	2,457,624
Personal Net Worth	674,346	675,238	676,665	678,566	680,824
Investment Net Worth	1,696,616	1,869,465	2,053,012	2,249,100	2,457,624
Net Worth	2,370,963	2,544,703	2,729,676	2,927,666	3,138,449

COMBINED EFFECT OF ALL DECISIONS ON CONNIE'S FINANCIAL SITUATION

Income

As shown on the income statement in Case IV, Connie's income is well over their target. This income statement follows the definition of income as used for income tax purposes. In 2003 Connie will receive Social Security benefits of $10,500. Given her level of income, 85 percent of these benefits will be taxable and will appear on the income statement. The remainder, $1,575, will be exempt from income taxation.

Examination of the cash-flow statement indicates that in 2003 she will have an excess cash inflow of $67,469. If Connie desires to use more than that amount for charitable and family gifts, then some portfolio repositioning is desirable. Alternatively, if the situation is satisfactory, then little can be gained by such moves and it would be best to continue holding low-dividend-paying stocks.

Possible Changes in Portfolio

Now that the income has reached the targeted level, one possible recommendation is for Connie to shift some of the portfolio from its dependence on the pharmaceutical industry. Curt suggests she consider disposing of most of the pharmaceutical stocks, as he will not be around to assess the future success of the corporations. For emotional reasons she could find it difficult to dispose of the full investment in Galaxy. However, at least half could be sold, using the specific identification method so that Curt's stock interest is sold. Unless Galaxy's stock rises in value from the date of the estate valuation, no capital gain would result. The full position in the Acme and Zenith stocks could be disposed of with a small amount of realized capital gains. The proceeds could be invested in several mutual funds, such as a growth and income fund, a balanced fund, and an additional investment in an index fund.

Connie's Expressed Interest for Life Insurance

The case situation shows there is no life insurance on Connie's life. After observing how the insurance increased Curt's estate, will provide income for her, and will benefit their grandchildren, she expressed an interest in acquiring some coverage on her life. Based on the revised estate analysis and her balance sheet shown in Case IV, Connie will have a large estate that will continue to grow over the years. Since she will not have the benefit of an unlimited marital deduction, the estate that she will be able to pass to her children will shrink as a result of the taxes due upon her death.

Since Connie has made their four children the beneficiaries of her will, some provision to reduce some of the impact of the estate taxes now becomes paramount. One way to accomplish this is for Connie to establish a life insurance trust that will apply for and own the policies on her life.

NOTE

To avoid repetition of background material on life insurance trusts, that material has been omitted from this chapter. If you are not familiar with the noted material from previous chapters, it should be reviewed prior to proceeding through this section of the suggested solution.

The recommendation is that the trust acquire a $1 million whole life policy, rather than a universal policy, on Connie's life since she prefers the guarantees of this type of policy. In today's market, for a nonsmoker in good health, such a policy can be obtained for about a $25,000 annual premium. This size premium is feasible for Connie, given the excess cash inflow she is expected to have during the next few years.

Little reason exists for any delay in acquiring the insurance policy. As a matter of fact, the policy could be acquired before Curt dies. Its acquisition will limit Connie's ability to make charitable and family gifts from her income, but if making such gifts is really important, she could further reposition her portfolio to provide increased income for these purposes.

Connie's Checking Account Balance

One last recommended change is to consider reducing the amount of the idle cash balance being maintained in the checking account. By shifting $40,000 into a money market account (2.9 percent current rate) or a short-term bond fund (4.5 percent current rate), Connie could increase her annual income by a minimum of $1,160 or $1,852. Connie has agreed that she would be comfortable with $30,000 in her checking account.

NOTE

This solution to the Kelleys' case is not meant to be the only way to achieve this family's objectives. Many other decisions concerning the use of the life insurance proceeds, accrued pension benefit, and the securities could have been made that would have been equally effective.

What this case shows is that some last-minute, before-death planning can be effective, that sequential choices can be analyzed to show their effect in achieving objectives, and that using the personal financial statements can aid in planning and decision making.

Planning for the Successful Closely Held Corporation and Its Owners

Chapter Outline

The successful closely held business may be a corporation wholly owned by one or two families, or it may have a small number of shareholders who are unrelated to the majority shareholders but who are key employees in the business. In the first and second generation of management the general trend seems to be that all stockholders are active in the business. The problems of closely held businesses that have both shareholders who are active in the business and shareholders who are inactive are entirely different from the problems of businesses whose shareholders are all employees, since the objectives of active shareholders and those of inactive shareholders are inherently different. Our concentration in this case will be on the typical second-generation closely held business with active shareholders.

Many of the problems of closely held businesses are the same regardless of the size of the business; that is, they differ in scope but not in type. On the other hand, the solutions to some of these problems may be relatively simpler for the larger, more successful businesses because they generally have more cash flow, more assets, and more types of assets, all of which can make more options available to them. This case attempts to highlight the difference in terms of options and choice of techniques that the size and type of a business can make.

In addition, this book has emphasized the importance of comprehensive financial planning in terms of serving the client's best interests in an organized and cohesive fashion. Many financial planners and financial planning firms are so committed to this concept that as a general rule they refrain from doing more limited planning. Sometimes, however, special clients—perhaps those who have already had a comprehensive plan done for themselves and their families—will need additional advice in a particular area, such as tax planning for business transition. In this case assume that comprehensive personal planning such as that for educating children and for dispositions at death was done for Judy Templeton 7 years ago when her father, John, was much more active in the business. Assume further that John Templeton was not interested in comprehensive financial planning at that time. Now that circumstances have changed, Judy seeks advice on a business tax plan addressing the particular issue of her father's withdrawal from the business.

Although the focus of this case is on business planning for Templeton Contractors, Inc., a major change in the personal affairs of one of the business owners necessitates some revision of her personal plans. These will be addressed subsequent to and separate from the business plan.

CASE NARRATIVE

John Templeton, Sr., and Allen Lewis, an unrelated party, started a contracting partnership 28 years ago as equal partners. When they incorporated the business 7 years later, they became equal shareholders in Templeton and Lewis Contractors, Inc. The corporation issued 4,400 shares of $10 par voting common stock to each partner in return for his partnership interest.

Judy Templeton Blake entered the business 20 years ago at the age of 25. At that time she held a B.S., in civil engineering and had four years experience with International Contractors Corporation. She devoted herself to learning the business from the bottom up with the idea of eventually taking over its management. Judy, an only child, is now 45.

When Allen Lewis retired 15 years ago at age 72, he sold his stock in the corporation to Judy since no member of his family was interested in becoming involved in the business. At the time of the sale the corporation was changed to Templeton Contractors. Judy purchased the stock for $590,000 under the following terms: $50,000 down and an installment note for 25 years at 7 percent. Although Allen Lewis died last year, Judy continues to make annual payments to his estate. Judy has been president of the corporation for 3 years and is now seeking advice on behalf of herself and the corporation.

John is now 65 and his stock in Templeton Contractors makes up approximately 80 percent of his total assets. He and his wife, Lottie, depend on his income from the corporation to support a fairly lavish lifestyle. John is currently earning approximately $200,000 annually in salary and bonuses. His stock had a book value of $2,931,000 at the end of 2002. (See the balance sheet on page 9.5.)

John has been decreasing his involvement in the daily operations of the corporation for about 7 years but remains the chairman of the board of directors. However, the time he spends in the business on a daily basis is now limited to no more than 2 days a week. During the period that Judy has been the president of the company, it has grown appreciably under her leadership. Until the death of Judy's husband, Randy, 5 months ago, the board of directors consisted of John, Lottie, Judy, and Randy. Needing a director to replace Randy, Templeton Contractors selected Gale Browning, who is the executive vice-president of International Contractors. Judy had worked for him during her time with that organization. The corporation presently has 40 permanent nonunion employees and a nonunion payroll of $2,500,000 annually.

John has become quite concerned that so much of his wealth is tied up in Templeton Contractors. He would like to remove himself even further from corporate operations but does not want to forgo his salary unless another way can be found to fund his lifestyle. Judy is concerned that she could not really justify as reasonable compensation the present salary and bonuses paid to her father if the corporation were to be audited by the IRS.

John has offered to sell his shares to Judy, but Judy still has 10 years during which she is obligated to pay for the shares she has already purchased from Allen Lewis. She does not feel that she can undertake another such obligation, at least until her three daughters and her son are educated and established in careers of their own. As a matter of fact, Judy doesn't really want to incur this heavy obligation when it is likely that all or a majority of the shares will come to her at the death of her parents. At the same time she does not want to put her parents in a position that would require their giving up a lifestyle that they enjoy and for which they have worked very hard.

John has also suggested that he would be willing to have the corporation redeem all or a portion of his stock. Judy would be willing to consider a modest partial redemption but feels that the corporation cannot afford a complete redemption of John's stock, even with an extended payout period.

Another concern of Judy's is her father's federal estate tax problems. Since John's estate is still appreciating through its investment in Templeton stock and is so illiquid, Judy is concerned that the corporation will be called on to redeem at least enough of her father's stock to pay estate taxes and funeral and administrative expenses at his death. She states that her father is uninsurable and says she would feel morally obligated to attempt this type of a redemption, despite the fact that there are no buy-sell agreements that would legally obligate her to do so.

Judy's children are still relatively young: Claudia is 20, LeAnne is 17, Lauren is 15, and Toby is 12. Only the oldest, Claudia, has expressed any interest in the business as a career. Currently she is a civil engineering major at the state university. Although Judy wishes to preserve the opportunity for all her children to participate if they choose, she does recognize that she must prepare for the continuity of the business if her children discover other careers that they find more fulfilling. Judy is also determined that two unrelated key employees, Ron Harrell and Greg Manion, be allowed to begin to participate in the ownership of the company. She has discussed with John the possibility of selling Ron and Greg at least some portion of John's shares. However, since they are both in their late thirties with families, their financial capacity to undertake an obligation to purchase shares from John would be severely limited. Their salaries and bonuses from Templeton Contractors were approximately $85,000 each last year, and they have no other significant source of funds.

Judy's current compensation is $200,000 annually, which last year was comprised of a base salary of $100,000 and an end-of-the-year bonus of $100,000. John's base compensation is also set at $100,000 annually. Equal bonuses are usually paid to John and to Judy, and much smaller bonuses are paid to Ron, Greg, and no more than five other employees. Because there is no set bonus plan, bonuses are determined at the end of each year by the board of directors and are usually based on overall corporate profits.

Judy has accumulated approximately $600,000 in assets outside the corporation, the majority of which are growth oriented and consequently produce little current income. She feels that she is paying too much in federal income taxes and wonders if there are better ways to use the corporation and its assets to personally take advantage of tax benefits to accumulate assets other than value in her Templeton stock.

The primary business of Templeton Contractors in recent years has been heavy construction work for the federal government, which serves to insulate them to some degree from the generally cyclical nature of the construction industry. Judy believes that the nature and quality of work Templeton Contractors performs for the federal government will not be affected by the current downsizing in Washington. Last year the corporation had taxable income of $680,000. The corporation offers all its full-time employees good medical insurance coverage and nominal amounts of group term life insurance. Disability income coverage is provided for only Judy, Ron, Greg, and five other management employees. The corporation operates on a percentage-of-completion method of accounting for tax accounting purposes.

Templeton Contractors has never provided its employees with qualified deferred-compensation plans, primarily because John thought they were too much trouble and that employees weren't concerned about them. Judy, however, is interested in this employee benefit but does not want to involve the corporation in anything that would constitute an uncontrollable drain on its cash flow. The corporation's 2002 balance sheet follows.

TEMPLETON CONTRACTORS
12/31/02

Assets

Cash	$1,043,000
Accounts receivable	4,600,000
Building (net of depreciation)	475,000
Property and equipment (net of depreciation)	1,532,000
Total assets	$7,650,000

Liabilities and Capital

Current liabilities	$1,788,000
Common stock	88,000
Retained earnings	5,774,000
Total liabilities and capital	$7,650,000

INSTRUCTIONS

Based on these facts, prepare a working outline or a business tax plan for Templeton Contractors. When you have completed the outline, compare it with the suggested solution that follows.

WORKING OUTLINE

I. Client's objectives

    A. Explore methods that would allow John to withdraw enough of his investment in Templeton Contractors stock to continue funding his lifestyle after retirement.

    B. Assure continuity of management when Judy retires regardless of whether her children participate in the business.

    C. Explore some tax-advantaged ways to allow the corporation or its assets to provide Judy with some personal tax benefits.

    D. Provide Ron Harrell and Greg Manion with some of the stock in the corporation.

    E. Provide a mechanism that will provide John's estate with sufficient liquidity to assure that a corporate redemption for federal estate taxes will not be necessary.

II. Business tax planning

    A. Present position

    B. Assuring business transition and continuity
       1. Redemptions
          a. Requirements for sale-or-exchange treatment
          b. Sec. 318 attribution problems
          c. Sec. 302(c)(2) election—the waiver approach
          d. Sec. 303 redemptions
       2. Qualified plans of deferred compensation
          a. Benefits of use
          b. Utilizing a special type of qualified plan (ESOP) for business transition and continuity
       3. Installment sales
          a. General requirements
          b. Avoiding the limitations on deductibility of investment interest
       4. Nonqualified stock bonus plan
       5. Buy-sell agreements

    C. Reasonable compensation considerations

INSTRUCTIONS

Now prepare a business tax plan for Templeton Contractors. When you have completed your solution, it should be compared with the suggested solution that follows.

BUSINESS TAX PLAN
FOR
TEMPLETON CONTRACTORS
[Suggested Solution]

CLIENT'S OBJECTIVES

A. Explore methods that would allow John to withdraw enough of his investment in Templeton Contractors stock to continue funding his lifestyle after retirement.

B. Assure continuity of management when Judy retires regardless of whether her children participate in the business.

C. Explore some tax-advantaged ways to allow the corporation or its assets to provide Judy with some personal tax benefits.

D. Provide Ron Harrell and Greg Manion with some of the stock in the corporation.

E. Provide a mechanism that will provide John's estate with sufficient liquidity to assure that a corporate redemption for federal estate taxes will not be necessary.

BUSINESS PLANNING: TAXES

Present Position

Although the Templetons have been very successful in their business, the bulk of the wealth of two generations is now tied up in Templeton Contractors. Both Judy and John are uneasy about having this situation continue and would like to explore some methods to alleviate it in John's case and to prevent it from recurring when Judy reaches retirement.

In addition, Judy wishes to assure that her two key management people will continue at Templeton Contractors and would like to do so by allowing them to own some stock in the corporation.

Judy would also like to explore using the corporation or its assets more efficiently for personal tax benefits.

Assuring Business Transition and Continuity

Redemptions

Many owners of closely held businesses fail to realize that after spending their working lives in a business, it may be very difficult to transform their investment in that corporation into another type of investment that may be more appropriate for their later years without paying a heavy price in taxes.

One problem with the corporate form of organization arises from the fact that dividends paid to corporate stockholders are not deductible by the corporation and are taxable to the shareholders as ordinary income. In many, if not most, wholly owned or family-owned corporations, dividends are either never paid or are paid rarely and in small, often insignificant, amounts. This is usually not troubling to the shareholders of these corporations, who are most often also employees of the corporation and who depend on salaries rather than dividends for their livelihood.

In the absence of the statutory restraints on a corporate redemption of its stock, any time a shareholder of a wholly owned and closely held corporation wished to take money out of the corporation without receiving dividend treatment, the shareholder could simply sell some shares back to the corporation for cash and pay tax on the gain.

There is now a maximum tax rate of 20 percent for most long-term capital gains. Since capital gains are part of a taxpayer's adjusted gross income (AGI), however, the recognition of these gains can lead to a loss of some of the personal exemptions and deductions allowable against AGI. The net result is an effective tax rate in excess of 20 percent in some cases. Nevertheless, capital-gain treatment still provides two significant advantages over ordinary income treatment in a redemption. First, it allows the shareholder to recover his or her basis in the redeemed stock tax free. Second, capital gains can be fully offset by capital losses, while ordinary income can be offset by capital losses only to the extent of $3,000 per year.

An example of a dividend-type redemption follows:

> Shareholder T owns 100 percent (500 shares) of ABC corporation, which has earnings and profits. Each share is worth $1,000. He causes ABC corporation to redeem 30 shares of his stock for $30,000. Result: T still owns 100 percent of ABC corporation although he now owns only 470 shares of stock.

> T would like to treat the redemption as the sale of a capital asset and receive capital-gain treatment. The Internal Revenue Code provides that the redemption is essentially the same as if a cash dividend had been paid to T and that the entire $30,000 will be treated as ordinary income.

Requirements for Sale-or-Exchange Treatment. The Internal Revenue Code defines a redemption as the corporation's acquisition of its stock from a shareholder in exchange for property (excluding stock in the corporation) (IRC Sec. 317). For this purpose property is defined to include money.

As stated above, whether the redemption qualifies as a sale or exchange of a capital asset determines whether the taxpayer pays federal income tax on the entire amount of the money or other property distributed (if treated as a dividend) or only on the amount of the gain (amount distributed – basis = gain) the taxpayer realizes on the transaction. Using the example above, this principle can be illustrated as follows: If T has a basis of $300 in each of his 500 shares of stock and he can effect a redemption of 30 shares at $1,000 a share that will qualify for treatment as a sale or exchange, he will pay tax on only the amount of his $21,000 gain [$30,000 – (30 x $300)]. T's basis in his stock is returned tax free before gain subject to tax is determined. If, however, the redemption is treated as a dividend (as it would be in our example), the entire $30,000 distribution is taxable. T's basis in the 30 shares of redeemed stock is then preserved by allocating it to his remaining 470 shares.

Shareholders of closely held businesses, particularly as they get older, like John, may wish to take some or all of their investment out of the corporation so that their lifetime accumulation of wealth will no longer be subject to the frailties and errors of new management—even if the new management consists of their own children. In John's case, a redemption will enable him to replace the salary on which he came to depend so that he can withdraw from the business.

If the shareholder is willing and able to sell his or her stock either to the children or to an outsider, the tax problem of dividend treatment triggered by a redemption is avoided.

Since the direct purchase of a substantial interest in a business may be difficult for younger family members or key employees to finance without altering their lifestyle, family businesses often consider redemptions in their business transition plans.

The Internal Revenue Code treats the shareholder's entire family as an economic unit for this purpose through the attribution rules of IRC Sec. 318. As a result, in situations when one family owns all or a large majority of shares and when it is especially desirable to use a corporate redemption, it may be very difficult to qualify such redemptions for capital-gain treatment.

The type of redemption that has been discussed in the preceding example is clearly an attempt to take the earnings and profits out of the corporation without treating them as dividends. As such, this is a transaction that should be taxed as a dividend. Therefore, to prevent such abuses the Internal Revenue Code requires that, as a general rule, a corporation's purchase of its own stock will be treated as a dividend (to the extent of the earnings and profits of the corporation) (IRC Secs. 302(d), 302(c)). This general rule applies unless the taxpayer can meet one of the exceptions in Sec. 302(b) that will result in capital-gain treatment.

The exceptions include

- redemptions not essentially equivalent to a dividend (IRC Sec. 302(b)(1)). This is not a precise test, and the result under the test depends on whether there is a meaningful reduction of the shareholder's interest under all the facts and circumstances of the case. For this purpose the shareholder's constructive ownership under IRC Sec. 318 (discussed below) will be considered. Since the test is imprecise, it is unreliable for planning purposes.
- substantially disproportionate redemptions. A redemption qualifies for capital-gain treatment under this exception provided that *immediately after the redemption* (a) the redeemed shareholder's proportion of ownership of both the outstanding *voting* stock and the *common* stock of the corporation is less than 80 percent of his or her proportionate ownership before the redemption, and (b) the redeemed shareholder owns less than 50 percent of the total voting power of all classes of stock entitled to vote (IRC Sec. 302(b)(2)).

An example of a redemption that would qualify as substantially disproportionate is the following:

> X Corporation has 100 shares of one class of voting common stock outstanding. Unrelated persons A and B each own 50 of those shares. The corporation redeems 20 of A's 50 shares. The corporation now has 80 shares of voting common stock outstanding, of which A owns 30 and B owns 50.
>
> A's proportion of ownership before the redemption was 50 percent (50 ÷ 100). Her proportion of ownership after the redemption is 37.5 percent (30 ÷ 80). Eighty percent of A's prior 50 percent ownership equals 40 percent. Since A now owns 37.5 percent, her percentage of ownership of voting and common stock after the redemption (37.5 percent) is less than

80 percent of her ownership percentage before the redemption (40 percent). Since A also now owns less than 50 percent of the total voting power in the corporation, both the 80 percent and 50 percent tests are met, and the redemption will qualify as substantially disproportionate.

- a redemption that is a complete termination of a shareholder's interest (IRC Sec. 302(b)(3))

For corporations whose stockholders are not subject to the attribution rules of IRC Sec. 318, these exceptions are relatively straightforward. However, when they are combined with the complexities of constructive ownership through the attribution rules, tax-advantaged redemptions can become quite difficult. Redemptions that qualify for capital-gain treatment can become virtually impossible to achieve in family-owned corporations.

Sec. 318 Attribution Problems. For purposes of determining the ownership of a corporation before and after a redemption, the redeemed stockholder is considered to own

- all the stock he or she actually owns
- all the stock owned by the stockholder's spouse, children, grand-children, or parents
- stock owned by an estate or partnership of which the stockholder is a partner or beneficiary (in proportion to his or her interest in the partnership or estate)
- stock owned by a trust except an ESOP trust of which the stockholder is a beneficiary (in proportion to his or her actuarial interest in the trust)
- stock owned by another corporation in which the redeemed stockholder also owns directly or indirectly 50 percent or more of the outstanding stock
- stock on which an option to acquire is owned

A discussion of the complexities of the family and entity attribution rules is beyond the scope of this text. However, a simple example of the application of the family attribution rules to John and Judy's situation can illustrate some of the difficulties.

When the family attribution rules of IRC Sec. 318(a)(1) are applied to the Templetons' situation, the results show that John owns

Directly	50 percent of stock
+ <u>Constructively (Judy's)</u>	+ <u>50 percent of stock</u>
Total ownership actually and constructively	100 percent of stock

The result is the same for Judy who owns

Directly	50 percent of stock
+ <u>Constructively (John's)</u>	+ <u>50 percent of stock</u>
Total ownership actually and constructively	100 percent of stock

Because John will always be deemed to own the stock his daughter owns, he will not be able to effect a lifetime redemption that will qualify for capital-gain treatment and still remain active in the business.

Sec. 302(c)(2) Election—The Waiver Approach. Because redeeming shares in family-owned corporations could force some shareholders into very difficult tax situations even though they are making no improper attempt to withdraw the corporation's earnings and profits, the Internal Revenue Code provides an exception that can be used to waive the family attribution rules of IRC Sec. 318 and allow the redemption to qualify as a complete termination of his interest (IRC Sec. 302(c)(2)).

In order to waive the family attribution rules, the shareholder must dispose of his entire interest in the corporation. There is no requirement, however, that all the stock must be redeemed, and combinations of sales and redemptions are not unusual. In addition, immediately after the redemption the shareholder must have no continuing interest (including an interest as an officer, director, or employee) in the corporation except that of a creditor and must agree not to acquire an interest in the corporation (except by inheritance) within 10 years from the date of the redemption. Furthermore, the employee must file an agreement with the Internal Revenue Service agreeing to notify the IRS if an interest is acquired within the prohibited period.

Even if these conditions are met, the redemption will not qualify for capital-gain treatment if either (1) any portion of the stock that is being redeemed was acquired within 10 years of the date of the redemption from a person whose ownership of the stock would be attributable to the person whose stock is being redeemed, or (2) any person whose stock would be attributable to the person whose stock is being redeemed has acquired that stock within a 10-year period directly or indirectly from the person whose stock is being redeemed, unless his or her stock is also redeemed. For example, a father cannot have given a portion of his stock to his son or daughter and have the corporation redeem the remainder of the stock he holds under Sec. 302(c)(2) and receive capital-gain treatment unless the gift took place more than 10 years prior to the redemption, or unless the son's or daughter's stock is also redeemed.

Since John seems content to terminate his employment at Templeton Contractors, a waiver of the family attribution rules would provide him a means to redeem all his stock and receive capital-gain tax treatment. It would require, however, that the corporation pay him in excess of 2.9 million nondeductible dollars. This is a tremendous cash drain on the corporation even if it is undertaken on an installment basis, and it could jeopardize the company's continued viability. This is especially true since contractors are required to maintain certain amounts of liquid and near-liquid assets to obtain bonding, without which they generally cannot operate.

If an installment payout is elected, the corporation would also experience an additional cash drain from paying interest on the obligation, although the interest payment would be deductible.

Our conclusion is that a redemption would not be a suitable technique for transferring John's stock into a more liquid investment.

Sec. 303 Redemptions. Many shareholders of family-owned businesses do continue to hold stock in their corporations until death, with the result that their estates are very illiquid. The rules for redemptions are not materially eased at death. However, to avoid hardship in these cases, IRC Sec. 303 provides a method for assuring that sufficient stock can be redeemed and treated as a sale or exchange of a capital asset to pay estate taxes and deductible funeral and administrative expenses if certain prerequisites are met. The value of the corporation's stock owned by the decedent must exceed 35 percent of the decedent's adjusted gross estate to qualify for a 303 redemption.

A second requirement is that the Sec. 303 redemption is available only if the person receiving proceeds of the distribution has an obligation to pay estate taxes and deductible funeral and administrative expenses. For example, in a typical will with a marital and a residuary trust, the marital trust will bear none of the expenses of administration or estate taxes. Therefore, stock to be redeemed under Sec. 303 should not be used to fund this marital trust. Instead the Sec. 303 redemption would be available to the residuary trust, which would be liable for administration expenses and estate taxes.

Most assets in a decedent's estate receive a stepped-up basis equal to their fair market value at the date of the decedent's death (IRC Sec. 1014). Therefore there is usually little or no income tax liability resulting from a Sec. 303 redemption. The sales price is usually equal to the value of the stock at the time of the shareholder's death, allowing the estate to receive the proceeds income tax free. This makes capital-gain treatment particularly important when stock is redeemed from a decedent's estate.

If John were to die with his present stock holdings, his estate would qualify for a Sec. 303 redemption. However, since Judy has indicated a strong preference not to utilize this option unless she is forced to do so, other methods for providing liquidity to meet estate settlement costs must be explored.

Qualified Plans of Deferred Compensation

Benefits of Use. Rather surprisingly, the facts indicate that Templeton Contractors has never implemented a qualified deferred-compensation plan. Many entrepreneurs are apprehensive about qualified plans because they perceive that these plans subject the corporation to more unwanted governmental interference. However, when a corporation has significant taxable income and is not using a qualified plan, it is losing a valuable tax benefit.

NOTE

To avoid repetition of background material on qualified plans, that material has been omitted from this chapter. If you are not familiar with the material from prior chapters, it should be reviewed before proceeding through this section of the suggested solution.

Utilizing a Special Type of Qualified Plan (ESOP) for Business Transition and Continuity; ESOP Described. An employee stock ownership plan (ESOP) is either a qualified stock bonus plan or money-purchase pension plan that requires plan assets to be invested primarily in qualifying employer securities (IRC Sec. 4975(e)(7)). As a qualified plan it is subject to the requirements described in the materials referred to above. Most important, these rules require that the plan

- satisfy minimum coverage requirements
- meet minimum vesting requirements
- allocate contributions to participants using a method that does not discriminate in favor of the highly compensated employees
- meet special minimum contribution and vesting requirements when the plan is top-heavy
- does not exceed allocations to a participant of the lesser of 25 percent of compensation or $40,000 each year, counting all contributions and forfeitures allocated to a participant

The corporation can make annual tax-deductible contributions to an ESOP in cash or corporate stock. Under the stock bonus type of ESOP the maximum deductible contribution is 25 percent of covered compensation, and under the money-purchase type the maximum contribution is 25 percent of covered payroll. If an employer maintains more than one plan, the contributions in all plans are generally subject to the 25 percent limit. However, a special rule allows for greater deductions in leveraged ESOPs. The employer may find the stock bonus type more appealing, since the plan can be designed to provide for discretionary contributions instead of fixed contributions as required in a money-purchase pension plan.

As with contributions to other types of qualified plans, ESOP contributions are not taxable to employees until they (or their beneficiaries) receive the benefits they have accumulated at retirement, disability, termination, or death. Earnings on amounts invested in a qualified plan are also not taxed until they are distributed.

In these ways an ESOP is subject to the same requirements as any other stock bonus plan or money-purchase plan. However, an ESOP is subject to some additional qualification requirements. These are summarized briefly below:

- The plan has to invest primarily in the employer's securities.
- The plan can invest only in "qualifying employer securities," which for the closely held company means stock containing both the greatest voting power of any class of stock and the greatest dividend rights of any class of stock.
- Voting rights have to be passed through to the participant in a publicly traded company. In a closely held company the voting rights pass-through applies only to major issues such as sales of the firm's assets, liquidations, or mergers and consolidation.
- Distributions generally must be available in the form of stock. However, employers whose charter or bylaws restrict ownership of substantially all outstanding employer securities to employees or a qualified plan may distribute cash only.
- Distributions do not have to be distributed in the form of cash. However, in a closely held company the participant must have the right to sell the stock back to the company within the 60-day period after any stock is distributed, as well as during a 60-day period in the following year. This right is referred to as a "put option." If the put option is exercised, the company can repurchase the stock over a 5-year period. At the end of the 5-year period the participant has received a total distribution from the plan.
- Stock has to be valued at fair market value. A nonpublicly traded company must establish an acceptable procedure for appraising and determining the fair market value of stock. The determination must be made at least annually, and the appraiser has to be independent.
- An ESOP cannot be integrated with Social Security benefits.
- To protect the value of a participant's plan benefit, an ESOP must allow participants who are at least age 55 and have completed 10 or more years of participation the right to direct the trustee to diversify the investment of a portion of their accounts. The plan must offer three (nonstock) investment options. In the first year that the right applies, the

participant must have the right to diversify a minimum of 25 percent of his or her account. In each following year, the amount subject to the diversification requirement increases by 5 percent until the participant has the right to diversify 50 percent of the account after 5 years.

- Special rules apply to the timing of distributions from an ESOP. If an ESOP allows participants the option to receive a single-sum payment at the time of distribution, these special rules have no impact. However, if the plan wants to delay the timing of the distribution or limit the forms of the distribution by excluding a single-sum option, special rules applicable only to ESOPs will apply. The law requires that a distribution must begin within one year after the plan year in which an individual separates from service due to retirement, death, or disability and within 5 years if the individual terminates employment for any other reason. The plan must allow the participant to elect a payout period that does not exceed 5 years, unless the individual has an account that exceeds $500,000.

Although ESOPs are subject to additional qualification requirements, they are also eligible for special treatment. In the right situation an ESOP has significant advantages over other qualified plans. These advantages are summarized below:

- The corporation can make tax-deductible cash contributions that are used to purchase stock, either from the company or from another shareholder, creating a "market" for such stock.
- The corporation can also contribute its securities and receive a deduction for the fair market value of the contributions, resulting in an income tax benefit without a corresponding cash-flow drain.
- An ESOP can borrow money to purchase securities, allowing the plan to purchase large blocks of stock at one time. This type of ESOP, referred to as a "leveraged ESOP," has additional advantages. A company can raise capital by selling stock to the plan and retire the debt on a pretax basis by making tax-deductible contributions to the plan. A special rule allows an additional deduction for the amount of dividend payments paid on plan stock that are used to retire the loan. Until August 1996, a bank or other financial institution lending money to an ESOP could exclude from taxable income one-half of the interest received on the loan when the ESOP owned more than 50 percent of the value of all stock and several other requirements were met. The Small Business Job Protection Act of 1996 eliminated this favorable tax benefit.

    A leveraged ESOP can either borrow money from a "disqualified person" (a party related to the company or plan), or the company may guarantee the loan payments when the loan is made by the ESOP from an unrelated bank or other financial institution. Such loans or guarantees are allowed as long as the loan is set at a reasonable interest rate. The ESOP can use the stock purchased with the proceeds of a loan only as collateral. The stock held as collateral is placed in a separate suspense account. As the loan is repaid, shares are released from the suspense account and allocated to participants.

- In limited circumstances a shareholder may sell stock to the corporation and defer paying income tax on the gain due to the stock sale. To qualify, during the period 3 months before the sale until 12 months after the sale the shareholder must use the entire proceeds from the sale to purchase "qualified replacement property." The stock sold must have been held by the seller for one year prior to the sale. Additionally, the ESOP has to own at least 30 percent of the total value of outstanding employer securities after the sale. Qualified replacement property that may be purchased includes debt securities or stock of another domestic corporation that does not have passive investment income in excess of 25 percent of its gross receipts and that uses at least 50 percent of its assets for the active conduct of a trade or business. Also the selling shareholder (and family members) and any other person owning more than 25 percent of any class of the employer securities generally will not be able to participate in the ESOP if this option is exercised. An exception to this rule provides that lineal descendants (children and grandchildren) may participate in the plan if no more than 5 percent of the stock is allocated to the accounts of all such descendants during the 10-year period following the sale.

- In a closely held corporation where the owners are concerned about who holds corporate stock, the plan may contain a provision known as a "right of first refusal" in favor of the employer and/or the ESOP. Such provision would require that a participant who has received stock and wishes to sell it give the employer and/or the plan the first opportunity to buy the stock at the greater of the fair market price or the price offered by the buyer.

- The maximum annual allocation limit (the lesser of 25 percent of compensation or $210,000) applies to the amount of contribution made by the employer and not to the value of stock as it is allocated to a participant's stock or to dividends paid on such stock.

- Generally an employer is not allowed a tax deduction for dividends paid to shareholders. However, a deduction is allowed on dividends paid on stock held by the ESOP if the ESOP either pays the dividends currently to participants or if the dividends are used to repay a leveraged loan.

- In a leveraged ESOP the company can deduct contributions of up to 25 percent of covered compensation that is used to repay the principal of an ESOP loan. An additional deduction may be taken on contributions used to repay loan interest.

- Employer stock distributed as part of a lump-sum distribution is eligible for special tax deferral. The taxation of the appreciation in value from the time of purchase by the plan until the distribution may be deferred until the stock is actually sold by the participant.

Using an ESOP to Transfer John's Ownership Interest. John's stock in Templeton Contractors can be sold to the ESOP by one of several methods. The first and simplest is a series of periodic cash sales to the ESOP. On an annual basis the company can make a contribution to the plan, which can be used to purchase a portion of John's stock (see figure 9-1). This approach will give John a stream of income during retirement, and John will be taxed only on the purchase price of each sale, less his basis in the stock sold.

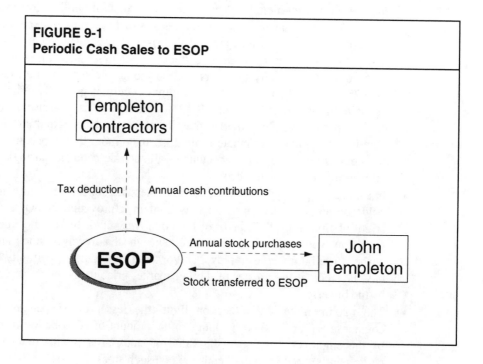

FIGURE 9-1
Periodic Cash Sales to ESOP

As an alternative, the ESOP can purchase all of John's stock at one time by financing the purchase (see figure 9-2). John can finance the transaction himself by agreeing to receive periodic installment payments. With this approach, John delivers all his stock to the plan. The company makes periodic contributions that are used to make promised installment payments to John. In order for John to have some protection, the stock can be held as collateral and kept in a separate suspense account. As the installment payments are made, a portion of the stock is released from the suspense account and allocated to plan participants.

Each installment payment that John receives contains three components: basis, capital gain, and interest. The capital gain (sale price less John's basis in the stock) will be prorated and recognized (taxed) over the years in which payments are received. The amount that represents interest payments will be recognized as ordinary income in the year received.

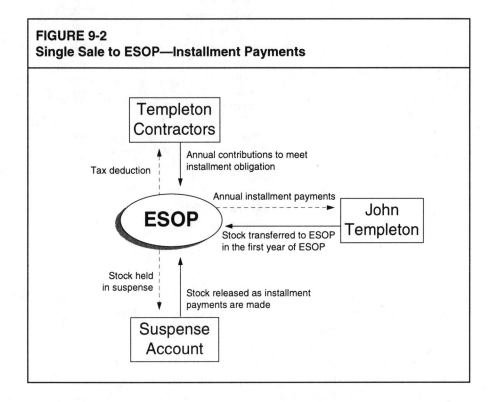

FIGURE 9-2
Single Sale to ESOP—Installment Payments

Another way in which the ESOP can purchase John's stock in one step is to borrow from a bank, repaying the loan with annual contributions to the plan (see figure 9-3). With a bank loan, the bank generally requires that the stock be held in suspense as described above. In addition, the bank generally also requires that the company guarantee the repayment of the note. With this approach, John receives the entire purchase price at one time. Such amount, less his basis in the stock, will be taxable at the time of receipt.

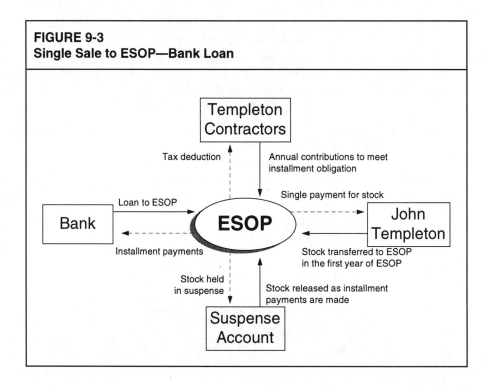

FIGURE 9-3
Single Sale to ESOP—Bank Loan

Creating a Market for All or Part of a Shareholder's Stock. Using an ESOP in any of these three methods solves the problem of transforming John's valuable equity interest in the company into retirement income without burdening Judy with large personal payments or selling the stock to an unrelated third party. With the periodic sale approach, John loses some control because he does not have a contract for the purchase of the entire value of his stock. He cannot be certain that the ESOP will continue or that the company will continue to have the cash to make contributions to the plan. However, the company is still within family control, and presumably this will not be an issue. With the periodic sale approach, stock can be purchased during John's life, and if John dies prior to selling his entire ownership interest, sales can continue from his heirs, providing cash to pay estate taxes and to meet John's heirs' income needs.

Price. The plan must pay John the fair market price of his shares. This can be determined by an independent third-party appraisal. Since an appraisal must be done annually for valuing the stock held in the ESOP, one single appraisal will generally be needed each year. Note that the purchase price established may undergo scrutiny by the Department of Labor (DOL), since the stock is being purchased from a "prohibited party." The sale should occur as close to the date of valuation as possible, and if stock is purchased over a period of years, the value will have to be determined at the time of each sale. Therefore in a periodic sale, John will be subject to price uncertainty. The projected valuation of company stock is certainly a relevant consideration in determining whether a single purchase or periodic purchases will be more advantageous. In contrast, in an installment sale or a sale financed with a bank loan, the purchase price for all of John's stock is based on the current fair market price.

Stock Redemption. A sale to the ESOP can generally avoid the previously discussed complicated redemption problems associated with a direct sale back to the corporation. A sale to the ESOP should be taxed as a sale or exchange of a capital asset.

However, under limited circumstances, the IRS has indicated that a sale of stock to an ESOP will be treated as a redemption for tax purposes (Rev. Proc. 87-22, 1987-20 I.R.B. 11). As specified in that ruling, dividend treatment will *not* result if the stockholder and his or her ancestors and descendants do not hold more than 20 percent of the beneficial interest in the ESOP after the stock is sold to the company and if none of the stock sold to the plan is subsequently sold to the company. The IRS will determine the tax implication of such sales in accordance with procedures set forth in the ruling.

In John's case the 20 percent beneficial interest rule is an issue that requires careful analysis. As discussed above, in normal circumstances Judy would be allowed to participate in the plan and would probably like to participate to the fullest extent possible. Apparently, under Rev. Proc. 87-22 the 20 percent beneficial interest rule is tested after the completion of the sale. Therefore the plan needs to be designed accordingly to ensure compliance with the rule. In this case, it may be prudent for Judy to hire an attorney to request a ruling that the sale will not be deemed a redemption. The problem becomes somewhat more complex if John sells all of his stock at one time or a portion periodically over several years to the plan. In the periodic sale situation, the issue will have to be considered each time a sale is made.

Deferring Taxes on Proceeds from the Sale of John's Stock. It may be possible for John to defer taxation on the sale of his stock to the ESOP as long as after the sale the ESOP owns at least 30 percent of Templeton's shares outstanding. However, if John wants to take advantage of the deferral, his daughter Judy (and any of Judy's children) will either have to forgo participation in the plan entirely or participate to a very limited extent. (All of John's descendants cannot collectively have allocated to their account more than 5 percent of the stock purchased by the plan from John during the 10-year period following the sale.) If John does not try to take advantage of the tax deferral, under normal circumstances Judy would be allowed to participate fully in the plan (subject to the 20 percent limitations discussed above) and would ultimately be the beneficiary of a substantial portion of John's shares through the ESOP. Because of this conflict, the better solution may be for John to sell the stock over a period of time (using either the periodic sale or installment sale method), resulting in a deferral of taxation. Since John needs periodic retirement income, such periodic sales will defer taxation until the time of each payment.

Assuring Continuity of Management Control. It is impossible to ascertain at this time which, if any, of Judy's children will eventually enter the business and be able to succeed her in corporate leadership or whether that leadership will eventually go to unrelated key management personnel. Naturally it is important to Judy that she continue to maintain control of the corporation until successors can be ascertained and she is ready to retire. With an ESOP Judy will still have almost the same control as if she owned all the stock directly. If the transaction is leveraged, some of the shares will be held in a suspense account, which can be voted by the trustee. The law allows Judy to be the trustee as long as the decisions that she makes as trustee are made "solely in the interests of the plan participants and beneficiaries." For the shares that are allocated to accounts of participants, the trustee can also vote on most issues. Only major issues, such as mergers or acquisitions or the sale of the company's assets, will require a voting pass-through to participants.

In an ESOP stock generally has to be distributed at the time of retirement or termination of employment. However, if Judy were willing to amend the company's bylaws to specify that only the plan or company employees can own stock, the plan could distribute cash instead. As an alternative, the plan could be designed to include a right of first refusal so that if participants wanted to sell their shares to outsiders, the company would have the right to purchase the stock instead. Assuming that there will continue to be no outside market for the stock, most participants are going to elect to cash in their shares at the time of distribution.

Estate Planning. The ESOP can also be helpful in transferring Judy's ownership interest to her children upon her death. At this point it is unclear which of her children will participate in the business. Typically, if all the children of a deceased business owner are not active in the business, family friction can result. Those children who are active get direct benefits from the corporation in the form of salaries and fringe benefits, while children who are inactive can benefit from their stock ownership only if dividends are paid. Dividends, of course, are not tax deductible and deplete the company's net worth and working capital, a fact that frequently distresses the active children. This conflict of interest can lead to enormous dissension and can even result in litigation or an eventual sale of the business to outside interests.

Having an ESOP in place provides an excellent method of dealing with this problem. If some of Judy's children decide not to be involved in the business, there would be a market for stock they inherit. The ESOP can purchase their stock, and the proceeds can be invested to give them a return that does not depend on the corporation.

Preferred Method of Stock Purchase. Of the three proposed transactions, purchasing John's entire interest in the company with a bank loan to the ESOP is the least preferable. A bank loan may not be feasible because of the cyclical nature of the construction business. A bank might not be convinced that the company will be able to make annual contributions in amounts sufficient to meet the loan payments. Also, if John were to receive the entire purchase price for the stock at one time, he would have to pay income taxes on the payment. As discussed above, John would not be able to defer income tax by purchasing "qualified replacement property" without severely limiting Judy's ability to participate in the ESOP. Also, since John needs a source of annual income, he might not be able to purchase replacement securities (whether he takes advantage of the tax deferral or not) that generate enough dividend income to support his income needs.

Either the installment sale or the periodic payments method will work well. The key issues will be the current price of the stock and current "reasonable interest rate." As described above, the installment method will give John more security since his entire interest will be purchased at a fixed price. The price paid in an installment purchase will be the current fair market price plus interest payments (which must be based on a reasonable interest rate) on the unpaid balance. The real question will be whether the current fair market value and current interest rates will produce an income stream necessary to meet John's income needs. If the answer is yes, the installment method is probably the best approach. The installment method also fixes the value of John's ownership interest. If the value of the business rises, the increase will not be included in John's estate and will not be subject to estate taxes. Note, however, that the installment method is tantamount to a loan, and the ESOP will be treated as a leveraged ESOP and will be subject to "special scrutiny" by the DOL.

If the installment method does not generate sufficient income, then periodic sales to the ESOP is the preferable approach as long as the value of the company is expected to rise. The increasing value will support larger payments to John during his retirement. Also, the periodic sales approach is somewhat simpler since the ESOP will not be considered a leveraged ESOP.

Conclusion. An ESOP has many advantages for Templeton Contractors. For Templeton, as well as for other closely held businesses whose older shareholders have accumulated the bulk of their wealth in the business and cannot redeem less than their total interest and escape dividend treatment on the money received, an ESOP can be invaluable.

However, an ESOP does not come without its costs. The plan will have significant setup costs and ongoing administrative expenses, including the annual appraisal. These costs should be fully understood before embarking on this course of action. Also, an ESOP cannot be easily unwound, and the transactions may result in scrutiny by the DOL and IRS. Before any corporation actually implements an ESOP, it should arrange for a thorough independent feasibility study that includes such things as a liquidity analysis for funding and projections for participants' account balances after 10 years. There should also be an appraisal to ascertain the fair market value of the company's stock since the value of the stock will allow the corporation to determine the number of shares it can contribute to the plan on a tax deductible basis. Like any other complex business plan, the success of an ESOP will depend on how carefully it is planned and implemented.

Installment Sales

General Requirements. A simple method of transferring some of John's stock to Ron and Greg is the use of an installment sale. An installment sale occurs when property is disposed of for payments, at least one of which is to be received after the close of the taxable year in which the disposition occurs (IRC Sec. 453(a)). The exceptions to the general rule—that is, the persons and types of property dispositions for which installment reporting is inapplicable—are not pertinent to this case (IRC Sec. 453(b)).

Interest payments made pursuant to an installment sale may be subject to the investment interest expense limitations of IRC Sec. 163, which will be discussed below as they apply to this case.

The seller receives capital-gain treatment to the extent of gain realized on the transaction (selling price less basis = gain realized). However, when the installment method of reporting is used, the capital-gain portion is recognized and reported as a percentage of each taxable year's payment. The interest portion of the installment payment is, of course, recognized as ordinary income in the year in which it is received. Use of the installment sale method can therefore spread a large gain over a number of years, with potentially significant income tax savings.

An installment sale also takes appreciating assets (Templeton stock) out of John's estate and replaces them with an asset that has a fixed value.

Avoiding the Limitations on Deductibility of Investment Interest. Generally an individual taxpayer can deduct investment interest only up to an amount of the taxpayer's net investment income (IRC Sec. 163(d)(1)).

Templeton Contractors is a C corporation. Interest payments on an installment obligation incurred by individuals in the acquisition of the stock of a C corporation are not treated as business-incurred interest and are therefore subject to the limitations on investment interest expenses. Therefore Ron and Greg will not be able to deduct interest payments in excess of their net investment income.

NOTE

To avoid repetition of background material on the investment income and investment interest expense, that material has been omitted from this chapter. If you are not familiar with the noted material, it should be reviewed prior to proceeding through this section of the suggested solution.

One additional potential problem of an installment sale such as has been proposed here should be noted, even though it is a purely personal one and not in any way tax related. The undertaking of such a purchase by a younger-generation successor of a closely held business means that for a very long period of time the purchaser's lifestyle may be curtailed, so that during the period when the family is being raised and educated, available cash flow may be limited. As long as the purchaser and spouse have thoughtfully considered this fact and are committed to the business, there may be no further problems. It is always advisable, however, to point out this potential problem to a client.

Nonqualified Stock Bonus Plan

An installment sale would not be a tax-favored method for Ron and Greg to acquire stock in Templeton Contractors. However, another alternative, a nonqualified stock bonus plan, would achieve this objective.

The stock bonus plan is a nonqualified plan of deferred compensation intended to benefit only "officers, shareholders, and other highly compensated individuals." Such a plan is specifically exempt from virtually all the rigorous regulations of ERISA. It is intended to be totally discriminatory in favor of a highly compensated group—generally shareholders and top management. The only type of governmental regulation that a nonqualified plan must comply with is that it must constitute "reasonable compensation" to the employee-participant.

Ron and Greg could participate in the plan as part of their compensation arrangement. A predetermined dollar amount of Templeton Contractors stock could be bonused to each of them annually. If it is desirable to keep the bonus amount level despite inflation, the amount of the stock bonus can be adjusted upward each year. This method assures that Ron and Greg will always receive the predetermined dollar amount of stock measured in today's dollars. This is a basic stock bonus plan and is not conditioned on performance.

If an incentive stock bonus plan is desired, the amount of stock awarded to Ron and Greg would depend on their performance based on established criteria. Either the basic stock bonus or the incentive-based plan can be used alone, or both can be used together.

For example, if both plans were implemented, Ron and Greg could each become eligible to receive an incentive stock bonus for achieving profitability in excess of a predetermined level in their areas of responsibility. The incentive plan could even require that to receive an incentive bonus, both the profit center for which the employee has responsibility and the corporation must achieve a certain level of profitability. This method balances the need to reward individual performance with the need to promote overall corporate cooperation among management personnel.

The bonused stock can vest in the employees at any time chosen by the corporation since nonqualified plans are not required to adhere to any specific vesting schedule. Care should be taken, however, that the vesting schedule chosen is not so lengthy that the employee is unable to view it as a substantial motivating influence. A reasonable vesting schedule for this purpose might be serial vesting over 5 to 7 years after the date on which the stock is bonused. If a 5-year vesting plan is adopted, this type of vesting results in a recipient's being fully vested in stock received in the first year at the end of the fifth year.

In addition to the regular vesting schedule, the bonus plan could provide for complete vesting when an employee reaches retirement age, or if the employee becomes permanently disabled or dies prior to normal retirement.

Since the stock that is bonused to an employee under the plan is compensation, it is subject to federal income taxation the same as any other portion of salary. There is an option, however, regarding the time the fair market value of the stock is taken into the employee's income for income tax purposes.

IRC Sec. 83(a) allows the delay of reporting income until the earlier of the time that the property can be transferred by the recipient or the time that the property is no longer subject to a substantial risk of forfeiture. In a plan such as the one discussed, the fair market value of the stock would be included in the employee-recipient's income when the stock is vested, and the corporation would receive a tax deduction at that time. Since the value of the stock at the time it vests in the employee is impossible to ascertain in advance, this leaves the employee responsible for a tax liability that cannot be predetermined.

Another option for both the corporation and the employee is available under IRC Sec. 83(b). This option requires that the employee affirmatively elect to include the current fair market value of any stock bonus received during his or her taxable year in income for that year. This election must be filed with the Internal Revenue Service and is irrevocable as a general rule. The use of the Sec. 83(b) election allows the employee and the corporation to project the tax liability with much more precision and to plan for it effectively. The use of the Sec. 83(b) election has an additional advantage: it allows the corporation to take a tax deduction for the full value of the stock bonus in the year in which it is taken into income by the employee, regardless of whether it is fully vested.

Once an employee has affirmatively elected to take the value of a stock bonus plan into current income and has paid the associated tax liability, the stock will not give rise to taxation again until it is sold. At the time of a sale the increase in value since the stock was bonused is taxed as capital gains. The portion of the stock's value at time of sale that does not exceed the value when bonused will be received tax free as a return of basis.

If it appears that the tax liability associated with a stock bonus of this type may be difficult for an employee to pay without a change in lifestyle, the corporation can combine a stock bonus with a cash bonus sufficient to pay the employee's tax liability. Because both the stock and cash portions of the bonus are deductible despite the fact that the stock portion requires no cash expenditure, the corporation's after-tax cash-flow position is barely affected by this type of plan. Such a combination plan would seem to be a good one for Templeton Contractors.

If the combination plan is implemented, the bonus plan should require that the employee elect the IRC Sec. 83(b) option to take the amount of the combined stock and cash bonus into income in the year it is received.

If the employee does not remain with the corporation until all the stock vests, the unvested portion is forfeited. In that event the employee is entitled to a capital loss for the amount paid, if any, less any amount received upon forfeiture. The amount taken into income for income tax purposes is not considered to be an amount paid. If employees have been bonused cash in an amount to meet the additional tax liabilities attributable to the stock bonus, they are not harmed, in the event of forfeiture, when they are not allowed to take a tax deduction for the forfeited stock.

The corporation must include the deduction attributable to the forfeited stock in income in the year of the forfeiture.

Buy-Sell Agreements

Buy-sell agreements are usually of two basic types:

- redemption agreements in which the corporation and the shareholder enter into an agreement containing the provision that the corporation will redeem the shareholder's stock upon death or disability
- cross-purchase agreements that are agreements between and among the shareholders that in the event of death or disability, the remaining shareholders will purchase the deceased or disabled shareholder's interest

The effective use of redemption agreements may be difficult when family members are involved in a closely held corporation, because the family attribution rules of IRC Sec. 318 can produce adverse tax effects. Mandatory redemption agreements can also require enormous nondeductible corporate expenditures. Also if a C corporation receives proceeds of life insurance to fund a redemption agreement, it may be subject to income tax of up to 10 percent on those proceeds under the corporate alternative minimum tax.

Cross-purchase agreements are problematic when there are wide differences in shareholders' ages or if there is a shareholder whose health is impaired, because the agreement is usually funded wholly or partially with life insurance. The difference in ages or health conditions can result in the younger or healthier shareholders being forced to pay high nondeductible insurance premiums for insurance on the life of the older or impaired shareholder. These problems would be particularly applicable in the case of Templeton Contractors as it appears that it may be impossible and will certainly be extremely expensive to insure John.

Since an ESOP has been recommended for Templeton Contractors, many of the objectives that are normally accomplished by buy-sell agreements can be accomplished more efficiently through the ESOP. It has already been noted that the employees who are ESOP participants should be required to give the ESOP (or the corporation) the right of first refusal to acquire their stock when they leave Templeton Contractors to prevent Templeton stock from remaining in the hands of outsiders.

In addition, either a contract or a stock restriction should require that other minority shareholders, such as Ron and Greg and other key management personnel who may own stock outside the ESOP, offer their stock to the ESOP or the corporation at the time they terminate their employment with Templeton Contractors.

A majority shareholder such as Judy would be able to impose a stock-transfer restriction that requires that any of her children who inherit her stock and who are not directly involved in the business offer their stock to the ESOP (or the corporation) before offering it for sale to a third party.

Reasonable Compensation Considerations

Salaries are one method available to transfer funds from a corporation to shareholder-employees without subjecting them to double taxation—once at the corporate level and again at the individual level when it is received by the shareholder-employee. To avoid this double taxation the salary paid must be reasonable in amount and must be paid for personal services actually rendered (IRC Sec. 162 (a)(1)). If the salary meets this test, it is deductible by the corporation as an ordinary and necessary trade or business expense and is taxed only once—to the shareholder-employee.

As already indicated, the principal way in which salaries can lose their tax-favored status is a determination by the Internal Revenue Service that some amount of the salary is "unreasonable compensation." In making such a determination, the IRS is taking the position that the "unreasonable" portion is not salary at all, but a distribution of the corporation's earnings and profits—a dividend. If the IRS makes such a determination, the deduction to the corporation is disallowed because dividends are not deductible.

The issue of unreasonable compensation is generally raised only in closely held corporations where there is a strong identity of interest between the role of employee and that of stockholder or where a member of the employee's family is a stockholder. The Internal Revenue Service's position appears to be that an arm's-length transaction setting the value of personal services and effectively eliminating the unreasonable compensation issue cannot exist in most closely held corporations. Obviously the closer the identity of interest between the corporation and the employee, the more vulnerable to IRS scrutiny compensation becomes; for example, the most vulnerable situation occurs between an employee and the employee's wholly owned corporation. Because of the identity of interests the issue of unreasonable compensation is also frequently raised in family-owned corporations.

Effective planning in this area is very difficult, as there are no specific guidelines that have been uniformly applied. Even careful planning cannot assure that the IRS will not challenge a shareholder-employee's compensation. However, careful planning can diminish the chances of the IRS's being successful in a disallowance.

The appropriate test is to determine whether the compensation is reasonable under all the facts and circumstances of the particular case. That is, each case will be considered separately based on its particular facts, and this may explain to some extent why the court cases in this area are decidedly less than definitive.

This somewhat confusing state of affairs does not mean, however, that no guidelines exist for setting shareholder-employee compensation arrangements that can withstand IRS scrutiny. The following points are critical and should always be kept in mind when negotiating compensation arrangements:

- All compensation, present or deferred, will be considered together to determine whether the total is reasonable.
- The compensation must be for services actually performed.
- Technically the appropriate time for measuring the reasonableness of a compensation arrangement is the time the arrangement was entered into, not at some later point when circumstances may have changed so dramatically that compensation payments exceed the expectations of all the parties. Although IRS audit agents often ignore this rule, it is a decided advantage to the taxpayer in litigation if the compensation plan was set long before the IRS challenge arose.

Corporations that are subject to severe fluctuations in business, such as contractors, may wish to utilize a bonus formula in addition to base salaries. Contingent compensation, such as bonuses, is not unreasonable in itself. Bonuses can actually provide incentives for both shareholder-employees and other employees to increase corporate profitability and can also build in flexibility to let total compensation adjust to any cyclical nature of the business. It would be appropriate in the case of Templeton Contractors to authorize a base salary and a bonus formula that would allow the board of directors to grant bonuses to the shareholder-employees and others based on established criteria, such as performance of various profit centers.

As a practical matter compensation arrangements should always be set in advance. It is unwise to wait until the close of the corporate year to determine bonuses or other contingent amounts. An advance determination of compensation should set out all compensation (base salaries, bonus formulas, deferred compensation, automatic cost-of-living adjustments, and any other payments). If a bonus is to be used, there are three principal guidelines that are very important: (1) the formula for computing the bonus should be predetermined, (2) the formula should never be based on the percentage of shares held or net profits, and (3) bonuses should not be restricted to shareholder-employees.

Corporate minutes and employment contracts can and should be used to document compensation arrangements and the reasons for establishing them at a particular level. Some helpful factors that should be included in employment contracts, corporate minutes, or both are the following:

- The employee's compensation is at or near the amount the employee earned in prior years, or if the compensation is adjusted materially, the reasons for the adjustment are fully documented.
- Compensation was set taking into consideration the employee's education, experience, skill, knowledge, standing in the industry, and other special qualifying attributes.
- Compensation was set taking into consideration responsibilities assigned to the employee.
- The employee's outside activities, if any, are not expected to interfere with the performance of the duties enumerated in the employment contract, and such outside activities, if any, are reflected in the compensation arrangements.
- The compensation arrangement reflects the standard compensation level in the trade or business.

Let's use John's situation to illustrate the effect of unreasonable compensation. John owns 50 percent of the stock of Templeton Contractors, a regular (C) corporation. He is an employee of the corporation but devotes substantially less than his full time to its business. The corporation paid him salary and bonuses of $200,000 last year.

Assume that on audit the IRS seeks to disallow $100,000 of John's total compensation as unreasonable compensation. If the IRS is successful in the disallowance, the corporate deduction for the unreasonable amount is lost, and an additional $34,000 tax (assuming a 34 percent corporate tax rate) is due at the corporate level. It should be noted, however, that regardless of the outcome of the audit at the corporate level, the individual income tax result is the same-ordinary income taxable at the individual level.

Corporate Tax Results of IRS Disallowance
of $100,000 of John's Compensation as Unreasonable

Corporation pays	$200,000
Corporation deducts	100,000
Additional corporate taxable income	$100,000
34 percent corporate rate	x .34
Additional tax	$ 34,000

Based on the information given in regard to John's compensation, Judy's concern about a potential disallowance as unreasonable compensation appears warranted, particularly on the grounds that the compensation does not constitute payment for personal services actually rendered. John's withdrawal from the company will eliminate this problem after the period for auditing prior years' tax returns has expired.

There are, however, other problems with the way Templeton Contractors determines compensation, particularly bonuses. It is advisable for Templeton to keep paying bonuses, since they can provide incentives for shareholder-employees and other employees to increase corporate profitability, as well as to build in flexibility that allows total compensation to adjust to any cyclical nature of the business. However, the corporation should set base salaries and authorize bonuses that could be granted by either the president or the board of directors, based on a predetermined formula or on established criteria, such as the performance of various profit centers. A formula for bonuses should never be based on the percentage of shares held or net profits. Such an approach appears to be a disguised method of paying dividends to shareholders. This approach to bonuses appears to be a problem with Templeton Contractors' current method of determining bonuses.

If Templeton Contractors elected to be taxed as an S corporation, the problems of unreasonable compensation would be eliminated, since the corporation's income would be taxed directly to its shareholders. Templeton Contractors had approximately $680,000 in taxable income last year. If an S election were in effect, the corporation's taxable income would be taxed at the maximum individual rate (38.6 percent) rather than the appropriate 34 percent corporate rate.

Despite the fact that The Small Business Job Protection Act (SBJPA) of 1996 permits S corporations to establish an employee stock ownership plan (ESOP) effective for tax years beginning after December 31, 1997, it is recommended that Templeton Contractors remain as a C corporation. SBJPA prohibits S corporations from taking advantage of three special rules that apply to C corporations that implement ESOP. The absence of each of these special rules significantly reduces the attractiveness of an ESOP for Templeton Contractors.

The first of these, and the most onerous from John's standpoint, is that he would no longer have a tax-free rollover benefit from selling his stock in

Templeton to the ESOP. This tax-free rollover provision applies only to the sale of qualified C corporation stock from an owner to the ESOP. Therefore John would be subject to capital gains taxation on the proceeds that exceed his adjusted basis.

The second rule that makes an ESOP less attractive to an S corporation than it is to a C corporation is that the S corporation is not able to take advantage of the income tax deduction for dividends paid to ESOP participants.

The third and last issue is that Templeton Contractors would be limited to a 25 percent (of compensation) deduction for payments made to an ESOP that is repaying loans undertaken for the acquisition of the corporation's stock.

The burden of the capital gain arising from the sale of John's stock is sufficient to reject conversion to S corporation status at this time. When the second and third rules are added, an S corporation cannot be recommended.

In addition to the disadvantages of using the ESOP, Templeton Contractors could be subject to a significant income tax liability with respect to its "built-in gains" as a result of an S election. Therefore, based on all the facts currently available, an election to be taxed as an S corporation is not appropriate at this time.

PLANNING FOR JUDY'S CHANGED CIRCUMSTANCES

When Judy left International Contractors to work with her father at Templeton Contractors 20 years ago, Judy and her husband, Randy, relocated to be near her new work. Randy found a position as a research biologist (his college major) convenient to their new location. After several years, Randy's employer decided to move the research facilities to a distant site. Although offered a position at the new location, Randy rejected the transfer. Randy had long harbored a desire to teach biology at the high-school level. They agreed this would be desirable since he would have summers off and other vacations simultaneous with their children's vacations. Randy returned to college, took sufficient education courses to qualify for teaching biology and related science courses, and obtained a position at the local high school. He had been there 8 years prior to the onset of his terminal illness.

Judy Templeton Blake, aged 45, was widowed 5 months ago when Randy died after several years of illness. Medical expenses of $75,000 in addition to insurance coverage were incurred on his behalf during that time. Randy insisted that his individual assets be used to pay the uninsured portion of these expenses.

Randy and Judy owned their home, bank accounts, and automobiles in joint tenancy with right of survivorship. Randy's shares of these assets had a value of $325,000 at the time of his death.

In addition, Randy's separate property, after paying his medical, funeral, and estimated estate settlement costs, is $350,000, largely invested in blue chip common stocks with a small amount in a stock index mutual fund.

Randy's will specified that his entire estate would pass to Judy. The will contained a simultaneous death clause that placed his estate assets into trust for the benefit of their children, with trust income and assets to be divided equally among the four children. Said trust would terminate when the youngest child attained age 21. Income was to be distributed to each child annually. The will also specified that should Judy disclaim, then his estate assets that would pass by will are to be placed in trust in the same manner as if simultaneous death occurred.

Judy's estate plans as specified in her existing will parallel those of her husband. However, she now is concerned that the children are of different ages and the younger ones will require greater resources for their care and education should anything happen to her. She has yet to revise her will or include provisions for the children.

Many years ago, Randy and Judy discussed possible remarriage of the survivor should either be widowed. Both agreed that life should go on. In no case did this imply that their marriage was in jeopardy or falling apart. Rather, they felt that their marriage added much to their lives and that the sharing of life with another is part of a full lifestyle. Now that Judy is alone, she ponders what her life will be, beyond Templeton Contractors. Particularly she desires to be assured that the children receive the assets from her estate if she remarries. At this time she has no romantic attachments.

JUDY TEMPLETON'S BALANCE SHEET*
12/31/2001

Assets

Cash and short-term securities	$ 150,000
Growth stock portfolio	550,000
Templeton Contractors stock (at book value)	2,930,000
Life insurance cash value	45,000
Residence	200,000
Total assets	$3,875,000

Liabilities

Utility and credit card current liabilities	$ 7,000
Present value of remaining payments to estate of Allan Lewis	151,710
Total liabilities	158,710
Equity	3,716,290
Total liabilities and equity	$ 3,875,000

*Does not include assets in Randy's estate

INSTRUCTIONS

Based on these facts, prepare a working outline for Judy Templeton Blake. When you have completed the outline, compare it with the suggested solution that follows.

At this time, it is not necessary to be concerned with Judy's interest in Templeton Contractors, Inc. Discussions are under way with respect to including Judy, as a seller of stock to the ESOP, to sell some of her interest to key employees and to pass some ownership to her daughter if her interest in entering the business continues.

WORKING OUTLINE
[Suggested Solution]

I.   Client's Objectives

    A.   Explore how Randy's will can be used for Judy's estate tax planning.

    B.   Provide Judy with guidance to provide equitable financial treatment for each of her children.

    C.   Familiarize Judy with information as to how a prenuptial contract can be used in her situation.

II.   Personal Planning

    A.   Randy's Will
       1.   Present situation
       2.   Jointly owned versus separate property
       3.   Consequences of Randy's will
       4.   Qualified disclaimer
       5.   Trust for children

    B.   Judy's assets
       1.   Present situation
       2.   Guardian needs
       3.   Trusts for children
          a.   age differences
          b.   fairness

C. Remarriage—Prenuptial agreement
   1. Concern for children's well-being
   2. Equalizing trust(s) for the children

INSTRUCTIONS

Now prepare a personal financial plan for Judy Templeton Blake. After you have prepared your solution, compare it with the suggested solution that follows.

PERSONAL FINANCIAL PLAN
FOR
JUDY TEMPLETON BLAKE
[Suggested Solution]

CLIENT'S OBJECTIVES

I.   Client's objectives

    A.   Explore how Randy's will can be used for Judy's estate tax planning.

    B.   Provide Judy with guidance to provide equitable financial treatment for each of her children.

    C.   Familiarize Judy with information as to prenuptial contracts and how one can be used in her situation.

II. Personal planning

    A.   Randy's will
        1.   Present situation
        2.   Jointly owned versus separate property
        3.   Consequences of Randy's will
        4.   Qualified disclaimer
        5.   Trust for children

    B.   Judy's assets
        1.   Present situation
        2.   Guardian needs
        3.   Trusts for children
            a.   Age differences
            b.   Fairness

    C.   Remarriage—Prenuptial agreement
        1.   Concern for children's well-being
        2.   Equalizing trust(s) for the children

PERSONAL PLANNING: TAXES

Randy's Will

Present Situation

Randy's will specifies that all of his assets, regardless of how they are owned, will pass to Judy, if living, upon his death. Since she is still alive, the simultaneous death clause contained in the will does not apply. Further, his will does not require the beneficiary to survive for a specified period of time, although this is not a problem in this situation.

Randy's will does contain a clause that permits Judy to sign a qualified disclaimer of her right to take against the will. As of this date, Judy has not done so, although she has heard this tactic could be a valuable planning tool for her needs. Should she do so, Randy's will stipulates that a testamentary trust for the equal benefit of their four children should be established and that the trust corpus is to be distributed when the youngest child attains age 21. Under this arrangement the older children will receive income from the trust long after they have reached age 21.

Jointly Owned versus Separate Property. Property in the deceased's estate passes either by operation of law (contract) or by operation of will. In the case of Randy's estate, the jointly owned property with right of survivorship passes by operation of law; that is, the will does not direct who the owner of the property will be. Judy will receive the jointly owned assets, valued at $325,000.

Separate property, on the other hand, can be disposed of by will. A limitation is that a surviving spouse is entitled by law to a specified percentage of a deceased spouse's assets. Randy's will specifies that, in addition to the jointly held property, all of his separate property will pass to Judy. These assets, with their step up in basis that occurred at Randy's death, currently are valued at $350,000.

Consequences of Randy's Will. The full value of Randy's estate, $675,000, will be added to the almost $4 million of assets owned by Judy. If she remains unmarried, no unlimited spousal exemption is available to shield some or all of her assets from being subject to the federal and state estate taxes at her death. The assets passing to Judy would be subject to the federal estate tax rate of approximately 53 percent if she died today. The portion of Randy's assets that pass by operation of law cannot be altered by any action by Judy, and thus her assets as shown on her balance sheet will rise by $325,000.

As to the additional $350,000 of Randy's estate assets, Judy could make annual gifts of $10,000 to each of her four children for a period of 9 years and thereby remove Randy's separate assets from her estate without reducing her existing assets.

Qualified Disclaimer. The possibility may arise that a beneficiary does not wish to accept either a bequest under the decedent's will or an intestate share of the estate that he or she is entitled to receive. A reason may be that the beneficiary's own estate is substantial. The beneficiary may not want to further burden his or her own estate with additional estate taxes. Alternatively, it may be a way of releasing an inheritance so that it will go to other beneficiaries in greater need than himself or herself. If a beneficiary does not wish to accept an inheritance, it is possible to refuse this legacy by making a qualified disclaimer. If the requirements of a qualified disclaimer are met, the property will be treated as if it had never passed to the individual. There are four requirements under the Internal Revenue Code to qualify a disclaimer for federal estate tax or gift tax purposes:

- There must be an unqualified refusal by the beneficiary to accept the bequest or the gift.
- This refusal must be written and received by the donor, the donor's legal representative, or the legal titleholder of the property within 9 months of the decedent's death or 9 months from the date of the gift or, if later, within 9 months after the beneficiary becomes 21 years of age.
- The beneficiary must not have accepted the interest or any of its benefits.
- The interest must then pass to someone other than the person making the disclaimer or to the spouse of the decedent without the beneficiary's direction.

The law provides that a disclaimer complying with the requirements of the federal tax statute is considered to qualify for federal estate and gift tax purposes, regardless of qualification under the local law. The law provides some uniformity in the application of the federal disclaimer statute, although state law may still hold the disclaimer ineffective to pass title directly to the later beneficiary without gift tax considerations.

Judy can elect to make a qualified disclaimer against Randy's separate assets. By doing so, she is able to have those assets out of her estate and have the income from them and the eventual corpus pass to the children. The value of the assets, $350,000, is less than the dollar equivalent of the unified credit and will not be subject to federal estate taxation.

Trust for Children. Since Judy will execute a qualified disclaimer for Randy's separate property, the disclaimer clause becomes operative, and his will creates a testamentary trust with their children as income and corpus beneficiaries. The terms are that the income as earned and the corpus when divided are distributed equally among the beneficiaries.

The wording of the will implies that one trust would be established. Considering the amount of the money currently available for funding and the costs for the establishment and administration of four trusts, a single trust is fine.

Judy's Assets

Judy's balance sheet shows that, even without the jointly held property that will pass to her when Randy's estate is distributed, she has nearly $4 million of assets, with only the remaining payments for the purchase of her interest in Templeton Contractors as a significant liability. However, more than three quarters of her wealth is the ownership interest in Templeton Contractors. As stated earlier, discussions are under way to develop plans for this ownership interest.

Beyond her interest in Templeton Contractors, Judy's main objectives are the following:

- to manage her personal affairs
- to manage Templeton Contractors during this transition period of her father's departure
- to provide guidance for her children and implement a will that is fair to each of them

Judy is quite certain she can meet the first two of her objectives but must have assistance in planning for her children's needs.

Concern for the Children's Well-Being

A widowed or single parent must provide for the guidance of minor children in a manner that both reflects his or her desires and considers what is most appropriate for them. Otherwise state laws or the courts make the determination. From the view that the child(ren)'s interests are paramount, responsibility can be divided into two parts:

- guardian(s) for the child(ren)
- guardians for the child(ren)'s assets

Guardian for the Children. The parent may name a guardian for any minor children in a will. Unless there is good reason to override this choice, the court usually honors the parent's selection and appoints that person as the testamentary guardian in the event of the parent's death. Since the youngest child is aged 12, Judy has some concern since whoever is so named will be expected to continue in this role for some years. Fortunately none of the children are young enough to require constant care and monitoring. The oldest is 20 and the youngest is 12. According to the facts of the case, Judy has no siblings who could fulfill this role. We have no facts regarding Randy's family or whether any of his relatives would be an appropriate guardian. Judy must examine her options.

In this type of situation, the most likely thought is to name one's parents as joint guardians of the children. From the facts of the case, Judy's parents' health does not appear to be a concern, but their expectations of retiring and enjoying the fruits of their lifelong labor would be curtailed. One favorable factor is that one of Judy's daughters is interested in being associated with the Templeton Contractors upon her college graduation. John, as guardian, might welcome the opportunity to nurture this interest.

Another frequently chosen testamentary guardian is an older sibling. However, Claudia is only 20 and a college student. To burden her with the added responsibility of her siblings could severely interfere with her education.

Unless there is a close friend of Judy's or a relative of Randy's who willingly will undertake the guardianship role, one avenue Judy could pursue would be to have her parents be the guardians until Claudia completes her college education, at which time she will become the guardian. This could be the solution that meets Judy's needs.

A related aspect of the guardianship is where the children will reside. Until Claudia assumes the guardianship, residence should be with Judy's parents, providing their home is adequate for several additional people. If not, they could move into Judy's home, with the cost of maintaining that residence being borne by her estate. Then when Claudia becomes the guardian, the home is there for their use. This tactic would provide the greatest continuity in her children's lives. Should her parents' residence be appropriate, Judy's home could be leased and then be available for Claudia's and the children's later use.

All of these issues should be fully discussed with Judy's parents, children, and legal counsel before implementation. But then no delay should occur before the decisions are incorporated in her will.

In case Judy is unable to provide for the children due to accident, illness, or other cause, then many of the decisions reached that would apply should she die could also be implemented. Since her parents are healthy, Judy feels she can defer any specific planning for this contingency.

Guardian for the Property. An estate of the size and complexity of Judy's (given the ownership interest in Templeton Contractors) requires careful husbanding of the assets. In addition, prudent advice is that a person (or institution) different from the one having guardianship of the person(s) be named for this purpose. Thus a semblance of checks and balances is created in that the property guardian is responsible for disbursing funds that are to be used for the purpose of providing for the child(ren) as beneficiaries and as such should require relevant documentation. Further, the skills needed for personal guardianship differ from those for financial guardianship. There is the possibility of some conflict between the two guardians, but this could be a small price to bear for the oversight provided.

Judy must give serious consideration as to who will be the financial guardian. For the testamentary trust, this function most likely will be served by the institution or individual(s) named as trustee(s). The same selection could suffice should she suffer any lifetime incapacitation.

Equalizing Trust(s) for the Children. The age spread of Judy's children is 8 years, with the youngest being 12 and the oldest 20 and partway through a collegiate education. Therefore these children have different financial needs. At age 20, Claudia has benefited from her parents' largesse during her teen years but still requires assistance with her education. Toby, aged 12, requires financial assistance through the teen years and for college. The remaining two children, aged 17 and 15, also require more assistance than Claudia.

An equal distribution of the income and corpus as established by Randy's will fails to achieve Judy's objective. Fortunately trust instruments can specify the distribution requirements of the grantor (testator). Therefore, Judy can state that trust income and/or assets are to be expended for the care, comfort, and educational needs of her children and that upon completion of college, no further benefits will flow to the graduate until such time as the trust corpus is distributed. A complex trust could accumulate unused income for years in which insufficient income is earned. A cutoff age could be stated for each child so that benefits from the trust would end whether or not college was completed, so as to prevent educational malingering. The trustee could be granted specific judgmental authority to extend benefits beyond the cutoff date should circumstances so dictate.

A specific distribution time for the trust, stated in terms of an event such as Toby's graduation from college or his attaining a certain age, could be used. At distribution, accumulated income and trust assets could then be distributed to each child on a per stirpes basis. In this manner, each child would have received approximately the same from the parents and their estates, although there are timing and delay factors that prevent absolute equality.

Possible Remarriage

Although Judy has no immediate plans for remarriage, she is most desirous of having the resources accumulated during her marriage with Randy and subsequently, up to remarriage, to benefit the four children, as described in the preceding section. One widely used technique is the premarital agreement.

Premarital Agreement. A premarital agreement, sometimes referred to as a prenuptial agreement or antenuptial agreement, is a legal contract entered into by prospective spouses before marriage that defines the disposition of and use of assets before, during, and after a marriage. Since the 1970s, the use of premarital agreements has been on the rise, especially among individuals who are marrying later in life or who are entering a second marriage.

A premarital agreement is like any other contract. In order for there to be a valid contract, the elements of offer, acceptance, and consideration must be present. Offer and acceptance are inherent in the negotiations that lead to the execution of the agreement. Under the Uniform Premarital Agreement Act (UPAA), the act of marriage itself is sufficient consideration. There is no need for money or other property to change hands to meet the requirement of consideration. In order to be valid, however, the agreement must be in writing. Much time will pass between the execution of the agreement and the time when it may have to be enforced, so requiring the agreement to be in writing is the only way to be sure what the arrangement between the parties is.

In a premarital agreement the parties can agree to anything they desire, although a court will typically enforce only the financial provisions. Under the UPAA the parties may deal with any property rights, including rights and obligations in any property, the right to manage and dispose of the property, the disposition of property in the event of divorce, the modification or elimination of spousal support, the making of a will, trust, or other arrangement to carry out the terms of the contract, and the ownership and disposition of life insurance proceeds. Typical provisions in premarital agreements include allocating the ownership of separate property owned before marriage and the income stream from employment; the right to income and principal from gifts, trusts, and inheritances; the right to the earnings from intellectual property and professional licenses; alimony; and the allocation of pension assets in the event of divorce (although this involves a complex application of both the Internal Revenue Code, the Employee Retirement Income Security Act (ERISA), and the Retirement Equity Act (REA)). Premarital agreements are commonly used to protect a business interest from the grasp of a future spouse and are almost always advisable when one party to the marriage has a family business or closely held business interest.

The key to the enforceability of a premarital agreement is that it must be fair on its face and in its application. Courts are hesitant to enforce agreements that disadvantage one of the marital partners. For a premarital agreement to be fair, it must be executed voluntarily and under contract law and must not be unconscionable. An unconscionable contract is one that shocks the conscience of the court to such an extent that the court will refuse to enforce the contract. Unconscionability often results from nondisclosure. In the past, courts have found the following situations to be unconscionable:

- There was no reasonable disclosure of the property and financial obligations of the parties.
- There was no waiver of the right to disclose the property and financial obligations of the parties.
- A party had no adequate knowledge of the property or financial obligations of the other party (for example, assets were hidden).

To ensure that the agreement meets these requirements, each party to the agreement should be represented by independent counsel. An agreement that is not deemed to be fair will not be enforced, defeating the purpose of the agreement.

If at some future time Judy contemplates remarriage, then she should retain legal counsel and have this form of contract developed.

Bibliography and Recommended In-depth Readings

Beam, Burton T., Jr., and McFadden, John J. *Employee Benefits*. 6th ed. Chicago: Dearborn Financial Publishing, Inc., 2001.

Canan, Michael J. *Qualified Retirement and Other Employee Benefit Plans* (West's Handbook Series). St. Paul: West Publishing Co., 2002.

Graves, Edward E., ed. *McGill's Life Insurance*. 4th ed. Bryn Mawr: The American College, 2002.

Lehmann, Michael B. *The Business One Irwin Guide to Using The Wall Street Journal*. 4th ed. Homewood, Illinois: Business One Irwin, 1993.

Tacchino, Kenn Beam, and Littell, David A. *Planning for Retirement Needs*. 5th ed. Bryn Mawr: The American College, 2002.

McFadden, John J., ed. *Financial Planning—The New Century: The American College's Guide to the State of the Art for Financial Services Professionals*. Bryn Mawr: The American College, 2001.

Stephens, Richard B.; Maxfield, Guy B.; Lind, Stephen A.; and Calfee, Dennis A. *Federal Estate and Gift Taxation*. 6th ed. Boston: Warren Gorham & Lamont, Inc., 2001 (with supplements).

Tax Management United States Income Series. Tax Management, Inc., a division of The Bureau of National Affairs, Inc. Washington, D.C.

Tax Management Estate, Gifts and Trust Series. Tax Management, Inc., a division of The Bureau of National Affairs, Inc. Washington, D.C.

The statute and the regulations thereunder are available as the Complete Internal Revenue Code of 1986 (as amended), the Income Tax Regulations (as amended), and the Estate and Gift Tax Regulations (as amended) from various legal publishers, such as Prentice-Hall, Inc., Commerce Clearing House, Inc., and others.

Index